People of the Circle,
People of the Four Directions

People
of the Circle,
People of the
Four Directions

Scott McCarthy

Blue Dolphin Publishing

Published by Blue Dolphin Publishing, Inc.
P.O. Box 8, Nevada City, CA 95959
Orders: 1-800-643-0765
Web: www.bluedolphinpublishing.com

ISBN: 1-57733-013-7 soft cover

Library of Congress Cataloging-in-Publication Data

McCarthy, Scott.
    People of the circle, people of the four directions / Scott McCarthy.
        p.   cm.
    Includes bibliographical references.
    ISBN 1-57733-013-7 (pbk. : alk. paper)
    1. Indians—Rites and ceremonies. 2. Indians of North
America—Rites and ceremonies. 3. Circle—Religious aspects.
4. Orientation (Religion) 5. Four (The number)—Religious
aspects.   I. Title.
E59.R38M33 1999
299'.7—dc21   99-43461
                                                            CIP

Cover design: Lito Castro

Printed in the United States of America

10   9   8   7   6   5   4   3   2

DEDICATION

To the First Nations of North and South America
and to all People of good will everywhere:
That these People might live!

And in a special way to my father, John (1914–1998),
whose multicultural experiences and travels
allowed me to grow and come to some of the knowledge
that is contained in this work.

TABLE OF CONTENTS

PREFACE

As a priest, as a spiritual leader, I am very interested in affirming people as they draw closer to God and helping them to live their lives in harmony because of teachings that have been of great help to others of my faith tradition down through the ages. Though I follow the ways of Christianity, I have learned through experiences with family and friends, to be open to the ways of God in every culture, even though they may not be the ways of my own familial, cultural, or religious ancestors.

My own life journey has come to be expressed in both the Catholic Way and what I will call the Indian Way. Born in London, England, of Scottish and Irish parents, I took in, like a sponge, the goodness that my family faith had to offer and went on to become a priest. I have lived in Canada and California and have had a chance to visit a part of South America and the Caribbean. I have had many opportunities to travel throughout North America and Europe as well. I have spent time speaking with Native People coming from many places in the Americas. All along the way I have been exposed in very direct, almost miraculous ways, to Native American spirituality, and I have taken it in and made it a part of my own spiritual life without rejecting what I already had received. My own sense of being a Catholic priest has been enriched.

I have had the privilege of being present at or participating in a good number of Native ceremonies over the years. As a student of liturgy (worship) and as a priest, I was always intrigued by the externals of the ceremonies. More often than not, in certain ways they related to the worship forms that I had been raised with as a child. For example, for thousands of times in my life I have "made the sign of the cross" of Jesus over myself as is the Catholic custom throughout the world. With the right hand I would touch four parts of my upper body: the forehead ("In the name of the Father . . ."), the area near the navel ("and of the Son . . ."), and both shoulders ("and of the Holy Spirit"). Though there are slight additions or variations to this simple yet sacred action depending upon the culture, it is essentially the same movement and words, whether voiced or prayed silently. Until a few decades ago every Catholic altar was set facing the east to symbolize both the rising of the sun and the expected direction of the appearance for Christ at his second coming. The art in the church building often depicted circles: golden halos or nimbuses over saints' heads or simply a circle (often with an equilateral triangle within it representing the Holy Trinity) to speak of the oneness of God. I also remember as a child being gathered occasionally in a circle with many others outdoors to make a "living rosary," each child taking turns to offer one of the prayers of this particular time-honored devotion. It was also lots of fun. The foregoing are just a few ancient non-Native practices that seem to me to be illustrative of how the directions (in this case "east" for church altar orientation), the circle (meaning the unity of God), and doing something four times (four times touching the torso in signing the cross) were utilized in my own spiritual heritage.

Such examples of my own spiritual formation are mentioned here simply to indicate how I have built on the spiritual traditions that I myself have graciously received from my family and the larger Catholic faith community. This lifelong experience has enabled me to recognize the crossing points of Native as well as other world spiritual traditions. I know that anyone can do the same. It is simply a matter of being open to the larger spiritual picture of what happens when people pray.

I live in northern California, an interesting and quite vibrant kind of place that is home to representatives, to a greater or lesser degree, of just about every culture and nationality known, including the indigenous People of the continent. Though each representative of a particular culture has a certain point of reference, most of us seek some kind of understanding of the other and others. We know from experience that we are often quite ethnocentric or biased or even racist in our points of view regarding other human beings. Nevertheless, intercultural contacts are great occasions for changes of opinion and personal and societal growth.

It is inevitable that cultures will come into contact with each other; it has probably always been this way everywhere in the world. Over the last five hundred years or so, many cultures have not only met, but often collided, with each other, especially in that vast tract of territory, now much subdivided, that we call the Americas.

I know that many, many mistakes were made in the past in regards to cultural contact on this continent; but I also recognize that good has come from such contact and will continue to grow as more time passes. What has happened, for better or worse, is our heritage. What we together make of the past is up to the present and future generations. I believe cultures can affirm one another, especially in regard to spiritual insights.

Though primarily offering an exposure to documented examples of indigenous spiritual ways, this book also seeks to open up to a larger audience discussion between those from differing cultures who seek a fuller understanding of indigenous spiritual thought and practice and the Native People of North and South America themselves who may or may not be on a similar quest.

A kind of unofficial dialogue has already been going on for at least five hundred years. Certain things have been worked out to the satisfaction of some, but the dialogue needs to go further. Some folks are only now entering into the dialogue and perhaps could use some basic background information that could be gleaned from the material contained within this book. No one is sure exactly where a dialogue will lead us, but we can be sure that the journey together will benefit not only this generation, but also the seventh generation from now . . . and beyond. Spiritual growth for all concerned will undoubtedly be part of the first fruits of the harvest of true and open dialogue.

The following thematic approaches to Native spirituality offer possibilities for study and reflection and practice concerning this larger spiritual view. Such times may lead to that enlightened moment of "Ah-hah!"—the moment when a connection is permanently made, understanding follows, and spiritual growth occurs, at least on one level of human life.

This book offers a kind of survey of various ways of "praying and doing" with the cardinal directions, with circles, and with the number 4. Some of the observers quoted speak casually of the events described, others are highly technical in detail. All are from written accounts or explanations by those who were interested at the time. Some writers may have been inaccurate in their recording of an event or even way off in explaining a ceremony, but they are offered here so that we might consider the rich heritage that is expressed by means of these special ritual or ceremonial actions. I do not expect the reader to agree with all the quoted material from the various authors. I simply present parts of the writings of a great variety of people: scholars, ethnologists, writers, teachers, indeed the People themselves. Some are reflections of the People as they share with other Natives and non-Natives their own traditions, spiritual and other.

Nor do I expect the reader to agree with my writing and comments on the quoted materials. My desire is to present a plethora of examples that one might read, reflect upon and draw some conclusions. In fact, perhaps like the reader, I personally do not agree with certain portions of the quoted materials because of the writers' prejudicial, biased, or uniquely slanted viewpoints, early or recent, but I include these materials because they shed a certain amount of helpful light on the subjects discussed. I have even included a few examples of "both ways," Native and Christian, coming together.

The lifeways and ceremonies described and commented on in this book are many and varied. They partially embody the life of the People throughout the centuries. I consider that ceremonies are always built on previous ones; the times and the needs may have changed but the People always adapted. Both architectural methods or other daily ways of doing things were necessarily built on the experiences of the previous generations. If changes were ever to be made, they were usually well thought out and then, and only then, tried. Doing something haphazardly does not seem to be a tradition among the People. It has probably always been this way.

All life is one; there is an interconnectedness with everything. Though the traditional explanations may vary as to why, both Native and Christian heritages would attest to this. (The) Creator is the reason. Without a sense of (the) Creator's presence it would be difficult for many human beings to comprehend life. The People inherently knew this as they lived with one another and with all the created life forms around them. They know this today.

The following pages may help to open us up to the ways of the Spirit. Perhaps we can learn together for, I believe, our future must necessarily be together.

ACKNOWLEDGMENTS

THE GREAT SPIRIT OF GOD: Who has guided me to develop a heart open to experiences that are multi-cultural and multi-spiritual in dimension, especially as I celebrate life as a priest in the Diocese of Monterey.

My Family: my parents, John and Margaret, and my brother Tony for encouragement.

Irvin and Sara Sings Good Stewart, my adopted Crow parents, and all my Crow friends at Pryor and Crow Agency, Montana, Pete Chiefchild, Preston and Tom Onion, Bert and Cornelia Plainbull, John and Veline Plainfeather, Rocky Bulltail (r.i.p.), Turk Plainbull and family, and many other Apsáalooke (Crows).

Norman and Angeline Whiteman and family of Billings, Montana and other Crows who took time to give insights to my many questions about Native spirituality.

Ron and Toni Bird (Blackfeet) and family who have shared with me their hospitality and helped me to open up my experience to the ways of their People.

Robert Mucaro Borrero (Taíno), Sonny Carlson (Cheyenne), Antonio Ajanel Chiti (Quiché Maya), Stan (Makah) and Jeannie (Apache) Corpuz, Rev. Collins Jordan (Lakota), Rev. Joan LaLiberty (Métis), Blaine Lucero (Navajo, r.i.p.), Juan Mancias (Kickapoo), Tom and Orlando Nakai (Navajo), Tom "Little Bear" Nason (Esselen), Tek Diego Itzep Pasá (Quiché Maya), Mary Riotutar and Family (Chippewa/Cree), Leon Stiffarm (Gros Ventre), Bernice Torres (Pomo, r.i.p.), and other friends of the Crow, Blackfeet, Sioux, Cheyenne, Arapaho, and California Tribes who have helped me to understand some of their ways.

Numerous individuals, whose original heritage is "south of the border," who have helped me to see the actuality and further possibility of bringing together different cultural and spiritual ways: Genaro

Arista, Rufino Calderón, George, Robert and Ernie Carmona, Carlos Cervantes, Santos Cortez, Julio De La Cruz, Frankie G. Delgado, Joe Dominguez, Alfredo Escandón, Manuel Gaitan, Joe Garcia, Patrick Leonard, George Lizaola, Aaron, Alvaro, Juan, Luis and Lupe Lopez, Jorge Martinez, Omar Mercado, Martin Muñoz, Gabe Ortero, George Rios, Hector Rodriguez, Jesús, George and Nui Rocha, Nena Sanchez, Matt Perez, Justin Salinas, Loretta Salinas, Tony Vega, Ricardo Yniguez.

Justus Casale, Paul Kay, Fathers Randolph Graczyk O.F.M. Cap., and Charlie Robinson, O.F.M. Cap., John and Dan Shubeck, Andrew Lilles, David Hertel, Paul Peralta, Art and Sara Jensen, Robert Bray for celebration, support, and dialogue.

Mike Curran (Navajo), José Ortiz (Taíno), and Jim McPharlin for research and encouragement.

The Tekakwitha Conference for setting the scene for me to meet in friendship and spirituality many Native People of North America.

Toni Hunt, my invaluable secretary, for typing, organization, and editing.

John Grinnell for research assistance and proofreading.

Colleen Bonfiglio, Carol Chealander, Cynthia Kerr, Robert Loranger, Mamie Nubin, Joe Ortman, Beth Rosenblum, Don Underwood for their technical assistance.

For photography: I was very pleased that so many people wanted to share a part of themselves through photographic materials. Some submitted photos that they themselves had taken or had in their possession simply because for them such images spoke so well of what they wanted to share. Others wanted to be part of the images themselves so that they could illustrate or give a sense of what the written materials were referring to. Still others are professional photographers who had a desire to make some of their work available as it pertained to the writings.

I am most grateful to Sean Sprague of Mendocino, California, Holger Thoss of New York City, New York, and Ken Cook of Ken's Photography in Salinas, California.

Likewise, I am most grateful to: Isabel Alexander, Albert Alvarez, Genaro Arista, Ronell Bird, Roberto Mucaro Borrero of the United Confederation of Taíno People, Manuel Botello, José Gregorio Cortez Cadales, Carmona Family, Justus Casale, Rene Cibanacan (Nación Taína), Nathan and Joseph Cordero, Santos Cortez, Jesse De la Cruz,

Julio De la Cruz, Mike Curran, Frankie G. Delgado, José Diaz, Tek Itzep Pasá Diego and Family, Hilary Frederic (Cacique Chief of Dominica), Manuel Gaitan, Ricky Gaitan, Marco A. Garnica, Nanci Guzman, Sharman Haverly, Robert and Espy Hernandez and family, Art and Sara Jensen, Paul Kay, Mary Ann Kline, Ruben and Jaime Lemus and Grupo Ixcálli, John Kalani Kaleo III, Brian Krilanovich, George Lizaola, Eliza Llensa, Alvaro Lopez, Juan Lopez, Jorge Martinez, Omar Mercado, Dennis and Claudia Meza, Ramiro Millán, Ramón Nenadich, Santiago Obispo, Maria Onion, Joe Ortman, Adelina Alva Padilla, Elizabeth and Gerald Petkus, José Luís Piaroa, Bartell Plainbull, Jolene Miranda Plainbull, Turk Plainbull, John Plainfeather, Luis and Esdras Ramos Santana, George Rios, Rayola Running Crane, Hugo Ruiz, Justin Salinas, Efren Serrano, José Serrano, r.i.p., Irvin and Sara Sings Good Stewart, Diane Stein, Moisés, Moy, Ria and Zane Suarez, Jeremy Teck, Rita Uribe and Friends, Epi Ventura, Josh and Noelia Verwolf, Robert Virgin, Judy Whiteman, Junior and Carol Whiteman.

For Artwork: David Hohmann, Patricia Kay Shubeck, Jacqueline Graham PVBM, and the anonymous artist who many years ago did some watercolors of Native People in the Monterey area of California.

Those who financially supported this book project: Wilmot Nicholson and his daughter Kathy Nicholson Hull, Margaret McCarthy, Walt deFaria, and Robert Bray.

Parishioners of Our Lady of Refuge (Castroville, California) and Our Lady of Mount Carmel (Carmel Valley, California) for their openness, patience, and encouragement.

The Native Peoples living within the Diocese of Monterey, California.

Friends, past and present, who have helped me to learn.

AHÓO	PILA MAYA
GRACIAS	THANKS

Irvin and Sara Sings Good Stuart, adopted Crow parents of author

Introduction

INTRODUCTION

Picture in your mind, if you will, the following scenarios:

- A Spanish soldier or Franciscan friar and an Aztec merchant sometime shortly after the invasion of Mexico.
  As they "size up" each other, what are the religious symbols that each wears to express a particular spirituality?

- A French immigrant in the 16th century living in what is now Quebec and a Mohawk trade goods with each other.
  What prayer ways preceded their act of trading? How did each of them offer prayer in the morning or in the daytime before they began to barter?

- In 1640 a "courier de bois," a runner of the woods, and a Huron are hunting together somewhere in Ontario.
  How did they show respect and thanks for the taking of the animals? Like the Huron, did the courier de bois offer thanksgiving immediately after the kill or later on when the venison was cooked and served?

- An English Puritan recently arrived in Connecticut and a member of the Pequot Tribe exchange angry words about who the land belongs to.
  How do the concepts of ownership of the land and what is on it differ? What were the similarities and differences in the ways that the Puritans and the Pequots usually prayed?

- A Dutch trader on Long Island in New York and a member of the Shinnecock Tribe share a time of pipe smoking and a meal before trading.
  What is each one thinking about during the period of smoking and the meal together?

- A Métis of French and Native ancestry hunts buffalo in Manitoba with Crees in 1867.
  In which ways are both the Crees and the Métis similar as they pray before and after the hunt and in which ways are they different now that cultural and religious contact has happened for some time?

- A mid-nineteenth century settler living in Wyoming greets some Cheyenne visitors at his homestead.
  What might be the content of their individual prayers later that night: Prayers for understanding? Prayers for protection? Or what?

- A gold-seeking prospector in the California Sierra in the 1860s sees a member of Ishi's family. They were among the last remnants of the Yahi People.
  Do both recognize each other as human beings coming from the same Creator, or are both already biased against each other because of hearsay or bad experiences or prejudice?

- In 1997 Brazilian gold panners *(garimpeiros)*, woodcutters, and heavy machinery operators encounter Yanomami leaders who are enraged about the destruction of the rain forest that is their ancient home.
  Both the Brazilian invaders and the Yanomami come from cultures that pray. Do their prayer traditions have anything in common at this moment?

- Modern day tourists passing through the Black Hills area, visit Bear Butte State Park (a huge mountain rising above the plains that was, and is, an ancient place of worship for several tribes) and are surprised to see and hear Sioux and Cheyenne vision questers praying and singing as they are sequestered among the bushes, trees, and rocky mountain ledges.
  Some are praying, others are simply enjoying the outdoors. Do they share any aspects of spirituality in common?

- A contemporary pow wow gathering in California at which both Indian and non-Indian onlookers see an eagle feather pick-up ceremony.
  For the one who is non-Indian, is an eagle feather merely a pretty "thing" that might be picked up and replaced on a headdress,

*and is it something sacred that symbolizes a whole world of
meaning to the other person who is Indian?*

We all share the earth and the solar system together; we drink
from the same water and breathe the same air, and our bodies go back
to the same earth. And all human beings have in common something
that, depending on what aspect of it is being referred to, goes by
various kinds of names. Some use the word "creation," others "the
material world," "the cosmos," "the universe" or "planet earth," but
there are many, many other words and descriptions for it as well. There
is much in us that is the same, but we do have some differing
perspectives on life and how we might relate to it spiritually.

To many people throughout the continents of North and South
America, both those who are indigenous and those who trace their
heritage to later arrivals, preserving these differences is crucial.

Among the many ways of preserving and celebrating one's culture
is to pray, both individually and communally. The communal way of
praying allows us to connect, not only with (the) Creator and the gifts
of (the) Creator, but also with our past. The spiritual heritage of the
culture, or sub-culture, often is the context for prayer—communication with the Highest Power, Creator—a capacity of all human beings.

How a People believes is demonstrated in the ceremonies. Those
who lead ceremonies are, I believe, crucial for the passing on of the
spiritual aspects of their culture. How they celebrate the sacred ways
affirms for others all that is important in their ancient system of belief.
They are life givers for the Spirit among their People. Much preparation
is always a requisite. Some spiritual leaders are quite flexible in
adapting certain aspects of a ceremony to a particular situation; others
are rigid about it. There is always a danger of "playing with" what has
been given in trust from the past and not using it properly.

While the "melting pot" theory never really did work and will
probably never work, and cultural isolation from one another works
only for a time, perhaps there are special ways to maintain one's
cultural dignity and also share in the good things of other cultures. I
am sure that this has happened quite successfully in the past in
various places and at different times on these lands.

One of the special gifts that each culture can share with another is
its unique spirituality. However, it must be kept in mind that some
aspects of spirituality are for everyone, while some are for certain

people and must be celebrated in appropriate ways. Another person's spirituality should never be grasped at by someone else. This kind of religious arrogance and theft bears no good fruit. People must be always rooted in their own culture before they take on aspects of other cultures, even religious or spiritual aspects.

With these concerns in mind, the ceremonies and lifeways that make up the body of this book are presented to encourage a sharing and understanding between cultures. It is also important to keep in mind the historical and physical context of these cultures. Let me begin with a summary of Native spirituality and the history of its interaction with Christianity, followed by a few words about the People themselves from a cultural perspective.

Indigenous Spiritual Offerings

Indian spirituality always seeks to express the unity of everything; other world religions also try to do the same. Each one has its own history, its own heroes and heroines, and its own means of offering prayer. But since we are all humans, we often make mistakes as we commune with (the) Creator and the creation (which includes ourselves). Often egotism and ethnocentrism or religious or cultural phobias get in the way of our efforts towards greater unity.

The desire for balance and harmony are hallmarks of indigenous religion before, during, and after contact with those who came to these shores. Power was, and is, gained from connections with the sources of all life as they come from (the) Creator through Mother Earth. Among Native Peoples of this continent it has always been understood that human beings are created, not to be apart from the rest of nature, nor above it (nor even, because of modern technology, to be alienated from it), but to be in a harmonious relationship with all else that exists: the fellow creatures who swim, fly, crawl, walk, or are invisible to our eyes, yet nevertheless, are very much a part of our shared planetary home.

As this book indicates, there is great variety and depth to indigenous spirituality; there also exists great variety and depth in other religious traditions. Though these abound in the particulars, many of the Peoples are essentially in agreement that there is a Creator (who goes by various names and whose self-expression is manifold) and a creation, usually called Grandmother Earth or Mother Earth. The earth, like everything else, is known to be a living being who supports other life forms: plants, animals, people, etc. Some of the life forms are visible to us and many others remain invisible, unless the microscope happens to give us a glimpse of them. Other manifestations of power that are allowed for by the Creator are often understood as being involved with the four quadrants of the world. From these quadrants, which are north, south, east and west, gifts come to us; our prayers also may go "out" to each direction, just as they go "up" to the Creator and "down" to Mother Earth. The circle also demonstrates unity, while the pattern of fourness opens up the possibilities of balance and togetherness of all things. At the risk of over-simplifying, we might still say that all of this describes a unity at every level and in every direction of that which we call Life.

Catholic Spiritual Offerings

Most of the early immigrants who came to the Americas in the 16th and 17th centuries were Catholics; they came from Spain, Portugal, or France, and many practiced a kind of Catholicism that was ancient but more medieval in style. Much of it was unaffected by the church reforms initiated by the Protestant Reformation. It is interesting nowadays to see this heritage in so many devotional practices that are popular among the indigenous Peoples who were recipients of the 16th-century Spanish or Portuguese versions of Catholicism. For example, many indigenous Latin Americans name their children after saints who are remembered annually on the church calendar. Some of these obscure Latin saints' names are often unknown to those who follow the Catholic ways coming from other parts of Europe which were so strongly affected by the Protestant Reformation (including a revision of the church calendar regarding particular saints' feast days and balancing of some peculiar, often misleading, devotional practices).

Early Church Efforts

In the 17th century French Jesuits shared their experience of the Catholic way with Hurons and Iroquois of Ontario and New York, Montagnais of Quebec, Abenakis and Micmacs, Illinois and Ottawas,

Foxes, Miamis, and Ojibway, Bayagoulas of Louisiana, Natchez of Mississippi, and many other Peoples. Jesuit Father Jacques Marquette (1636-1675) reached the Mississippi River from Wisconsin and travelled down it. He participated in many pipe ceremonies as he prayed with the Peoples. Considering their European background and the times, these missionaries went beyond many of their contemporaries in that they adapted their understanding of Christianity to the ancient pre-Contact ceremonial ways of the People whenever possible. Perhaps they were among the first to acculturate themselves in this way. Father Eusebio Francisco Kino is well known for the way that he shared the Catholic Way with the Pima People of the American Southwest.

Even today the Jesuit presence on certain reservations in the United States is significant, as is the holy work of the Franciscans in California and the Southwest, and the Capuchins in the West and Midwest.

Spanish Jesuits served among those who lived in the American Southwest, Mexico, and in other parts of the New World. Bartolomé de Las Casas (1474-1566) became an advocate for the Peoples throughout those parts of the Americas that were under Spanish domination. He spoke out constantly about their mistreatment and used every means at his disposal to alleviate the evils of colonialism. People like Father Louis Hennepin, who was the first missionary to share his faith in the Mississippi region, and the controversial Father Junipero Serra who lived among the Peoples in Mexico and California, are well known in the history books of the United States.

Spanish Franciscans have also labored around Florida and the Southeastern and Southwestern parts of the United States as well as in other areas in the Americas. As they shared their message and life, the military often was not too far from them, and many times the Peoples became confused and angered and felt taken advantage of. Much ignorance and opportunism on the part of many of the Spaniards decimated a good many of the People. Some of what happened can never be made up for. Sadly, the history books do not tell us of the many genuine and lasting friendships that must have taken place between Natives and Franciscans over the centuries. However, their positive contributions are still felt; their original work is being carried on but in newer ways and with greater understanding and sensitivity to the original ways of the People.

Developing Church Efforts

In the last century much Catholic outreach to the Rocky Mountain West was initiated and coordinated by a Jesuit priest from Belgium named Pierre-Jean DeSmet (1801-1873). During his own lifetime he ministered to Potawatomis, Sioux, Blackfeet, Salish, Coeur d'Alene, Pend Oreille, Colville, Kootenai, Kalispels, and to many of the Peoples between the Mississippi and the Rockies. He is still remembered with fondness by many of the People. Prior to his arrival Catholic Iroquois shared their faith with the People on the western side of the Rocky Mountains, especially by hymns and prayers and discussions.

The work of the sisters through the Americas must not be neglected. Various orders of nuns shared the lives of the Peoples from the beginning. Special mention must be made of the Sisters of Providence, the Ursuline Sisters, and the Sisters of Charity who have already spent many years with the Peoples of Montana and the West since the last century. The work of Mother Katherine Drexel (1858-1955) who founded the Sisters of the Blessed Sacrament is well known throughout the United States.

Contemporary Church Efforts

Prior to the 1960s much research and study was done by Native People and Church leaders throughout the Americas concerning their heritage of ways and procedures. Some could easily look back on a history of excellent mutual cooperation; others saw large gaps in the fabric of what had happened over the years. The Catholic (and Protestant) world paused to consider its accomplishments and future directions. The Vatican Council II (1963-1965) was instrumental in setting the tone for a newer, and yet much more ancient, way of doing things around the world. Its impact has also been felt throughout much of Indian Country throughout the Americas. Wider understanding has been achieved in the dialogue; there seems to be a greater sense of hope and respect for native ways in relation to the larger Church.

> Even in the liturgy, the Church has no wish to impose a rigid uniformity in matters which do not involve the faith or the good of the whole community. Rather, she respects and fosters the spiritual adornments and gifts of the various races and Peoples. Anything in their way of life that is not indissolubly bound up with superstition and error she

studies with sympathy and, if possible, preserves intact. Sometimes, in fact, she admits such things into the liturgy itself, as long as they harmonize with its true and authentic spirit (Section 37).

Documents of Vatican II, Walter Abbott, 1966, p. 51

It seems that a Mohawk woman named Kateri Tekakwitha (1656-1680) is calling the North American Catholic Peoples together into greater unity on many levels. It is hoped that she will soon be officially recognized as a saint as she is already that among the Peoples. The Tekakwitha Conference annually brings together thousands of Native People and clergy and sisters and brothers to share both Indian culture and faith. It is a good thing; thousands have found that both Ways can come together in harmony and balance. The Tekakwitha Conference describes itself as "a growing unity within Native Catholic Communities. . . ." Regular regional and local gatherings bind the Peoples together, no matter what their tribal affiliation or blood mix. Most Catholic Native ministry is somehow connected with this unifying body across Canada and the United States. The Tekakwitha Conference promotes all native ceremonial ways and sees the spiritual value of the circle and the four directions and the sacred use of 4.

Outside Grouard, Alberta, Canada, the Kisemanito Center provides a spiritual setting for holy moments on holy ground for the Peoples who are both Native and Catholic, and there are many other holy places frequented by the People. Both Canada and the United States and the other countries of the Americas have traditional places where both Ways have been respected and celebrated for many years.

Protestant Spiritual Offerings

In their desire to fulfill the "great commission" *("Go out into the whole world; proclaim the gospel to all creation"* Mark 16:15, and *"Go, therefore, make disciples of all nations; baptize them in the name of the Father, and of the Son, and of the Holy Spirit, and teach them to observe all the commands I gave you"* Matthew 28:19-20), Protestant churches have tried to share their understanding of the Gospel with the indigenous Peoples of this continent. Like the Catholics, their success depended mostly on the degree of good example that they set over a period of time in any of the places where the missionaries went. Often there was squabbling among the denominations or mutual mistrust between Catholic and Protestant missionaries. Very often government or military interference negated their energies. The Peoples saw this and were often confused.

Sometimes the government intervened and divided up the reservations among the churches; the personnel who were sent to the Peoples often brought with them prejudiced points of view as to how the Peoples should behave in an encroaching White world, but not all carried this attitude, or if they did for a time, it quite often changed as they lived among the People. But it has been hard for the Peoples to forget those who came and misrepresented even their own spiritual ways.

- Puritans, though they did not stress missionary work, nevertheless did have some influence on the "Praying Indians" among the Wampanoags and Pequots and other tribes near the settlements.

- Congregationalists shared their ways with many of the New England tribes: Myron Eels, a congregational minister, spent 33 years among the Twanas, Klallams, Makahs, Quinaults, and other tribes in Washington State during the latter part of the 1800s.

- Prior to the American Revolution, in 1735 the Moravians went to Winston-Salem, Massachusetts, and later developed missions in Pennsylvania among the Susquehannocks and the Delawares.

- Pennsylvania Quakers, not as rigid as the Puritans, were quite accepting of Indian Ways and gently shared their own with them. Later Quakers worked with tribes on the southern plains.

- Lutherans sent Jacob Schmidt and Carl Krebs and others to the Wyoming area to work among the Crows, Cheyennes, and Arapahos (1858-1866). Nowadays their efforts are directed to urban Indian ministries.

- In 1787 *A Mohawk Book of Common Prayer* was published and distributed among the People by Church of England members. Their descendents, Episcopalians, have a long record of working with the Sioux in Minnesota and North and South Dakota. In fact the Native Episcopalians outnumber their White counterparts in South Dakota. They boast several bishops and numerous Native clergy. Their presence is also strongly felt among the Navajo in the Southwest. The Anglican Church of Canada also has many Native clergy and lay leaders.

- Mennonites sent representatives to the Southern Cheyenne in Oklahoma in 1891 and later on to the Northern Cheyenne in Montana, especially around Busby and Lame Deer. Many Native hymns and spiritual songs may be attributed to their influence.

- Methodists and Presbyterians sent missionaries to the Northwest at various times, Marcus and Narcissa Whitman and Henry Spalding being among the first. Sometimes the missionaries paid more attention to the politics of the time rather than to their pastoral work. Some missions flourished, while others died out. Most of the major denominations have developed ministry for and with Native Americans.

Sometimes it was difficult for the missionaries to adapt to Indian ways, other than translating the Bible and prayers and hymns into Native languages. But some were able to adapt rather well because they were either unafraid to experiment or the People showed them how. Perhaps some of the congregations that are most active today can trace their heritage to such open-minded missionaries. On many reservations and in many cities, the Native language hymns that are sung are shared by People who obviously appear to be "ecumenical" by nature.

In my opinion, other than a change to a Native language for Bible, prayers, songs, and preaching, fundamentalist (or evangelical) missionaries have not really been able to maintain and celebrate "Indianness" among the People. They fear that many of the old ways are superstitious. Perhaps this example from a fundamentalist Christian Indian publication might illustrate what I mean:

QUESTION: *"I've been confused about my Christian faith. There has been a lot of talk in our community about Christians using sweetgrass and getting involved in sweat lodge ceremonies. Can you tell me what place all of this has in the Christian faith?"*

THAT IS THE QUESTION. NOW . . . LET THE COUNCIL SPEAK

ANSWERS

The ceremony of the sweat lodge, sweetgrass and the drumming and singing that go along with it, do not belong to Christianity. The people who believe and practice this do not claim to be born again Christians. . . . They believe that God gave the North American Indian his own religion which includes the above.

Beliefs are not necessarily in written form, but they are taught by word of mouth and practice. I do not think that the deity of Jesus Christ is taken seriously by most people who follow the traditional way. Certainly the Scriptures have no place of authority in their faith and practice of worship. . . . (BILL JACKSON)

My dear friend, Christ transforms lives and cultures. . . . If part of our culture is against the Bible, then we have to follow what the Bible says.

We must see what the different ceremonies mean. Then we should ask ourselves if they take away from the work of Jesus on the cross. Let us look at the sweetgrass ceremony.

My understanding is that the smoke, when spread over a person, purifies him and he is cleansed. Then he can come before the Great Spirit. If we look at the Bible, it tells us that the blood of Jesus cleanses and purifies us (1 John 1:7; 3:3; Hebrews 9:14). Now according to the Bible, I am made pure by the blood of Jesus and my faith in Him. I cannot be made pure by sweetgrass smoke. Therefore, I should not take part in any sweetgrass ceremony.

Concerning the sweat lodge, you have to see what happens in this ceremony. Then you need to go to the Bible and see if you can take part in it. My understanding is that these ceremonies are different in many places. Generally, a spiritual leader prays and asks for the spirits to give them advice and direction. I know one man who used to go to sweat lodges. The spirit talking there did not like Jesus.

As a believer, we are not to have anything to do with spirits that reject Jesus and who say that Jesus did not come in the flesh (1 John 4). So use that as a guide to see if you should go to a sweat lodge or not. . . . (NOBLE COPPAWAY)

As a citizen of the Kingdom of God, we should learn that God does not accept our former religious belief . . . we put away those practices that are understood by Indian people as so-called Indian religion.

Indian Christians who now trust in Christ for forgiveness of sins, and everlasting life, no longer need sweetgrass and the sweat lodge. If certain people believe that they must have symbols of Indian religion, then they are saying that faith in Christ is not enough. (WILBERT ROBERTSON)

"Council Speak," *Indian Life Magazine,* Bill Jackson et al.,
May-June 1990, p. 20

Many other folks who follow Jesus, both Native and non-Native, would definitely disagree with the above. But as time goes by, and as more people enter into the dialogue, things will probably change for the better all around.

Contemporary Search for Spirituality

Numerous contemporary Westerners who are voluntarily or involuntarily dispossessed or bereft of ancient sacred ways seek an understanding of native spiritual practices. In the last twenty years or so there has developed a kind of transpersonal movement that many people call "The New Age Movement." Its roots may be in the turbulent 60s when many sought to go outside of their culture to find religious fulfillment. Some turned East and sought after gurus and babas and koans, while others read books about Native Americans and tried to emulate their ways. It appears to be a kind of neo-gnosticism. Many of its adherents are sincere. They are most interested in "teachings" and feel free, for one reason or another, to drop the spiritual traditions of their ancestors in order to feast on tidbits that come from quite diverse spiritual and cultural traditions. Meditation techniques and alternative music recordings offer a way of going beyond the ordinary, everyday experience of life; books on a variety of spiritual subjects, especially Native American stories and ceremonies, are popular. Often the writers are non-Indian or claim some native ancestry or purport to have been trained in some shamanistic practices by a medicine man or woman who is never actually available for an interview. Their books are found alongside scholarly works, usually in the "Native American" section. They make for interesting reading, but their truth is often difficult to get at. Many such people have, I believe, a great yearning for the sacred, as well as a similar wish for the material benefits of today's modern technology.

Sometimes the symbols are misunderstood or reinterpreted by the new-agers who are using them. The ubiquitous "dream catchers," recently sold in stores around the United States, and wild bird feathers hanging from rear view mirrors and beaded or feather earrings manifest a contemporary interest in Indian Ways. It might be too soon to judge the deeper reasons for the popularity of these things. Often there is a hastiness to use or adapt particular ceremonies without permission from anyone, not to mention the elders of the People. Often such ceremonies and rituals become a parody of the real thing, and it sometimes happens that people are "paid" for their ministrations in ways that are just not acceptable to Native People. Many of the People are angered by these recent events; only a few, if any, condone the goings on. Perhaps the non-Native "shamans" might better look into their own cultures' spiritual roots, understand them well, and then, and only then, attempt to share in ceremonies that are led by Natives or by individuals properly delegated by them. It would seem that many new-agers have never really entered into the dialogue; such spiritual seekers usually take what they want and move on. Nevertheless, their presence in the dialogue would be beneficial to all concerned.

A Native/Christian Spiritual Synthesis?

Most human beings around the world have a tendency to take what is good and reject what is bad. Since first-contact over five hundred years ago, this process has made sense, especially in regard to things that have to do with the sacred. Reactions to the way of Christ, especially as it has been presented by missionaries and early settlers, have been many and varied. I think that friendship was the binding factor over and over again. If genuine friendships were made, then the goodness of the spirituality concerned was able to come through and be gratefully received. Whenever things were forced, especially those things that dealt with the sacred ways and symbols of God, then there was much less acceptance. Friendship was always the key. In my own experience it is the same today.

In Mexico and much of Latin America, depending on the influences of the newcomers and the reception of the local People, often a kind of syncretism occurred. Local custom would usually prevail, even though the introduced Catholic Way was originally patterned in an hispanic style. The People made their own what they themselves considered to be important. The signs and the symbols that they had originally known often came to have added meanings. It was not always an easy transition, but it appears, for all practical purposes, to be still going on.

In some cases, the People stayed aloof from the Catholic Way and continued following their ancient Way. Others used the symbols of both Ways and integrated the ancient learning with the newer learning. Many see being Indian and being a follower of Christ as not mutually exclusive. This is not so everywhere. The traditional path, which is sometimes merged with the Christian Way, is alive and well and needs to be respected and nurtured wherever it is found in North or South America. The dialogue must continue for the benefit of everyone.

It is interesting to note that on the Crow Reservation in Montana it is not unusual for individuals to go to church on Sunday, receive holy communion, and later on in the afternoon go to the sweat lodge to pray. Those who are proud to call themselves Catholic also participate in the Sundance and all the other traditional ceremonies of the Tribe. Some Crows follow only the traditional way, while others, to mixed degrees, participate in various denominational worship and activities. The response is also mixed, depending on the individuals' choice and pattern of faith. Only a few, I believe, have difficulty with the ancient cedar smudging prayer or with the sweat lodge as they follow the Way of Jesus. On the nearby Cheyenne Reservation many Native Catholics recognize a synthesis in the teepee shaped contemporary chapel of the St. Labre Indian School at Ashland. This "church teepee" is seen as a special sign of the dwelling place of God with its cross rising up to the sky. For Christians, Native or other, the cross is part of the great Circle of Life. The cross of Jesus (expressing the ultimate release of a completed life) preludes the Resurrection—his and our birth to life everlasting.

Nowadays, and for quite a few years, many Protestants have worked with Catholics and the People on the reserves and reservations and in urban settings. Church ministry with Native Christians is necessarily and most respectfully an ecumenical endeavor. For many years I have been invited to participate in Native-led ecumenical cooperative efforts. In May of 1998, I was part of a conference in Denver, Colorado, whose theme was "The Circle of Life in a Square Church: A Search for a New Vision, Renewed Community, and Justice for Native America." It was truly a sign of hope because those who are both Native and Christian of many church backgrounds met honestly with those who follow only Native traditional spiritual ways.

Over the years various kinds of spiritual movements have existed among the Peoples, often as a reaction to non-Indian pressures. Sometimes elements of the Christian Way were consciously or unconsciously blended with the ancient Indian Way, depending upon the time and place and the need.

- 1680: The Pueblo prophet Popé called the People to resist the unnecessary pressures of the missionaries.

- 1763: The Delaware Prophet influenced Pontiac (an Ottawa) to unite an army of Potawatomis, Hurons, Ottawas, Ojibwas, and Mississaugas against the British.

- 1799: Handsome Lake founded the Longhouse Religion among the Iroquois and reformed some of the ancient ceremonies.

- 1811: Tenskwatawa ("The Open Door"), also called the Prophet, (a Shawnee) and his brother Tecumseh united Kickapoos, Potawatamis, Creeks, Cherokees, and others against American invaders on the traditional lands.

- 1832: White Cloud, the Winnebago Prophet, influenced Black Hawk (a Sauk) to gather a portion of the Sauk and Fox (Sac and Mesquakie) Tribes to defend their traditional lands.

- 1850: Smohalla (a Wanapum) began the Dreamer Cult which used flags, drums, and various Christian and traditional prayer forms to energize the Peoples' prayers.

- 1882: John Slocum (a Squaxin) started the Shaker Church which helped many of the Peoples in the Northwest of the United States. Some still follow this tradition.

- 1888: Wovoka (a Paiute) asked for Ghost Dances among the Tribes to help bring them together in preparation for future apocalyptic events.

- 1900: Quanah Parker (a Comanche/White) followed the Peyote Road and helped to restore the spirit to many of the Peoples. He composed many spiritual songs.

- 1918: The Native American Church became officially chartered as an official denomination. Some branches use the cross symbol and the Bible and Jesus songs in the ceremonies along with the use of Peyote.

As they proselytized one another, the adherents of some of these movements unified the Tribes. They helped the People in their times of need, if only for a short time. But, like any movement, they only serve a purpose for a certain length of time depending on the needs of those who share in the movement. Some movements have died out, while others continue to serve the Peoples' needs.

Nowadays

Choices are always before us. When it comes to spiritual contacts between Native People and those of other heritages, especially at times when a ceremony might occur, individuals choose to react in different ways. Some stay away from Christianity and its symbols and only celebrate in the Traditional way. Others will do both Ways, but separately and at different times. While still others at times will celebrate both together. It really depends on the individual and his or her interpretation of what should be done.

Today the People experience a mixed heritage: openness, frustration, healing, anger, understanding, disappointment.... But I am hopeful when I experience things like an Aztec dance of the four directions being celebrated during a special blessing Mass celebrated for a Latina girl's fifteenth year of life *(Quinceañera)*. Or when a priest or bishop is invited to offer a prayer for the Peoples at the pow wow grand entry. Here both traditional prayers and Christian prayers go together toward (the) Creator: and I believe that they are well received.

The dialogue still goes on.

CULTURAL AREAS

People generally are able to celebrate their faith and spirituality in a variety of contexts. Just as we belong to the earth, so do we belong to (the) Creator. We find ourselves living in several dimensions, or realities, at the same time. We celebrate the present as we move towards our future, mindful of the heritage of the past, and we do so within a particular spatial environment. That environment differs as we move from one place to another.

The usual place where we reside most often has the greatest effect on us. We feel attached to our environment, and we become quite familiar with both the positive and negative effects of what the place has to offer throughout the seasons. We might love the golden leaves of Fall, but we also dread the oncoming cold and snow. We might enjoy excitement in a large city like Los Angeles or New York or Toronto, but then again, we also become disenchanted because of the problems of so many concentrated people and buildings, muggings, traffic congestion, and twenty-four-hour noise. Although we often temporarily overcome the less desirable aspects of our physical milieu, they are always there before us.

From ancient times the Native Peoples of the Americas have lived in and with habitats that were indeed many and varied. They always recognized and appreciated the diverse gifts that each region provided, blessing both Creator and Mother Earth for what they received. They adapted well to their environments. As generations passed, the People living in a specific area could be recognized and known by the way that they lived with the local terrain. Language and dialect, art and handiwork, song and dance, housing and games—all these and many others expressed their relationship with what was around them.

Some lived a nomadic life; others, more settled, built lasting dwellings and planted a variety of crops. However, many of the People

MAPS OF THE CULTURAL AREAS

did some of both. They shared and traded and enjoyed hearing about what was going on nearby and far away just as anyone does today.

The geology, the fauna and flora, and the weather patterns of their habitat became known to the Peoples, and they found marvelously ingenious ways of, not only surviving, but also benefitting from everything that surrounded them. Rocks, trees, and animals became tools and shelter material, weapons, clothing, and art. Manufactured items of practicality and great beauty became part of the heritage of each People's culture.

The physical environment and its climate always has some control over those who live within it. We must always work with the materials available to sustain our lives. Sometimes the terrain and weather are harsh, but often they are conducive to leisure and a more relaxed life. We do what we can with what is at our disposal. For many of the People, the saying has been most often true: bloom where you are planted.

Ethnologists and those who try to learn of the ways of Native Peoples have for various reasons grouped them into "cultural areas" because of their similarity in habitat, language, or customs. We know that scholarly or bureaucratic (or even racist) classifications of human beings have often caused pain and misunderstanding for many of us, especially due to erroneous conclusions drawn from the available, and often scanty, data. Still, I believe that there is also a benign way of considering one another in regard to our cultural ways.

The cultural areas mentioned in this book roughly follow the classifications that have been offered by many scholars of note over the past decades of this and the last century. They are not put forth here in any definitive way, but rather as a means of illustrating some of the remarkable ways that the People have lived and worked with a great variety of natural environments and developed generational lifeways that are there for us to become familiar with even now.

In reality, there are myriads of examples of how the Native People have lived with the land and developed cultures that endure even to our own day. Perhaps it would be helpful to first speak of some of the more specific areas of culture that are found north of that rather arbitrary modern boundary, the Rio Grande River, which divides Mexico from the United States.

The four directions themselves will be our guide on this societal survey. Many centuries after the People had developed wonderful and sustainable ways of life on the Eastern shores of the United States and Canada, travelers and visitors were able to remark on their lifeways. Sometimes these foreigners understood the transcultural connections and entered into the life of the People. Many times they gave them short shrift and limited themselves to their own particular kind of ethnocentrism. More often than not a welcome was offered by the Native People, but it seems that it was seldom well received by most newcomers and journeyers from across the oceans. It should be noted that due to voluntary and forced migrations, over the centuries (but especially in the last 500 years) the People found that they had to adapt to a variety of terrains and climates. Their spirit and ingenuity not only made them survivors, but also helped them to become versatile members of the highly technological society of today.

Woodlands Cultures

A large section of eastern Canada and the United States, which includes the Great Lakes (Huron, Ontario, Michigan, Erie, Superior) region, the Ohio River Valley, the maritime provinces and states, Labrador, Quebec, and Ontario, was and is home to many Peoples who hunted its game, camped and fished its rivers and lakes, and cultivated corn, beans, and squash ("the three sisters"), tobacco, and many other plants. Some, like the Iroquois (Ho-dé-no-sau-nee), founded leagues of mutual cooperation and protection that endure to this day, though some have suffered greatly through war, governmental interference, and forced relocation. Some leagues were short-lived because of the overwhelming influences of rival tribes or European political contrivances, like playing one People against another. They were close to the soil and knew how to utilize the trees to construct worthy birch and elm bark canoes that were light enough to carry but strong enough to transport provisions and game. They gleaned sap from the abundant maple trees to make syrup, and they knew the multiple uses of pine pitch to waterproof both canoes and household containers. These were the People of wampum (woven beaded message strings) made of purple or black or white quahog shell beads that symbolized war or peace, a marriage invitation, or an uplifting message of condolence to someone recently bereaved. Many houses were constructed of wood and bark and built in a rectangular shape that allowed for several families to live together; others were rounded, or even "wigwam" shaped, each style serving well the needs of the People using it. Their art was wonderfully expressed in bird or porcupine quillwork and in a tremendous array of pottery, carving, and hand-weaving.

Some of the tribes whose ancestors loved to wander the mountains, forests, the eastern seashores, the lakes and rivers are the Mikmak (Mi'Qmaq), the Abenaki (Wapanahki), the Pequot (Paquatauog), the Delaware (Lenni Lenape, Unami Lenape), the Nanticoke (Nentego), the Passamaquoddy (Peskedemakddi), the Chickahominy (K'chick-aham-min-nough), the Miami (Twaat-waa, Twightwees), the Illinois (Iliniwek), the Sac (Asa-ki-waki) and Fox (Meskwahki-haki), the Chippewa/Ojibwa (Anishnabeg, Anicinabek, Anishnaubag), the Menomini (O-maeh-no-min-u-wk, O-maeh-no-min-ni-wsk), the Winnebago (HoChunk, Hochangara, Hocak Wyijaci), the Potawatomi (Potawatamink, Potawaganink), the Ottawa (Ota-wa, Adawa), the Huron (Wyendot, Ouendat), the Munsee-Mahican (Min-asin-ink + Muhneakunnuk), the Naskapi (Nenenot), and the Algonquin (Elakomkwik).

Southeast Cultures

The Peoples of the Southeastern part of the United States, an area edged by the Atlantic Ocean and the Gulf of Mexico, reaped the goodness of Mother Earth as they fished, farmed, and hunted in the forests and plains. They are the ones whose ancestors built great ceremonial places of worship. The remains of these temples are still visible today, as are the great earthen mounds, which were often used for burials and sometimes put into use for civic affairs.

Some of the People formed alliances with one another (like the Creek Confederacy) that formed long lasting networks of special relationships which held the Peoples together for many generations. They had their *talwa*, or capital town, in a place where everyone could come together to celebrate ceremonial and political unity. Some towns were considered "war" towns and their special color was red; others were "peace" towns and displayed white as the symbol of concord and peace. They became places of refuge for criminals and even enemies. The Peoples of the Southeast loved to play lacrosse, the "little brother of war," as it was often called. Sometimes white towns played red towns; at other times allies, or even former enemies, played together.

Much adrenaline would flow, and perhaps lots of blood, as this was and is a rough game requiring great strength and good strategy. It is the official game of Canada, and though now it is played by modern rules, it would probably still be recognized by the ancient People to be essentially the same game that got whole villages and towns involved in a variety of ways for several days at a time. It was a good alternative to war and allowed for aggressions be expressed in dexterity and teamwork rather than in battle.

The People gave thanks for the special gifts of the seasons, each according to their own tradition. Among the Creeks the *Boskita* (called "Busk" by the Euro-Americans) lasted eight days and was dedicated to the Master of Breath, the One Above, (the) Creator. The Southeastern-ers well understood the importance of both sacred fire and corn among the People. For these and all other gifts they gave thanks, much as we do today when we consider all the gifts that are at our disposal. Many private and communal ceremonies filled out the year. For example, the Cherokee round of ceremonies included several important rituals of thanksgiving. Here is a summary of them:

First New Moon of Spring, which included ritual burning of dried tobacco flowers and a deer's tongue, feasting, and the lighting of the sacred fire, the burning embers of which were distributed to all the households.

Green Corn Ceremony, an August celebration at which seven ears of corn from the fields of each clan were brought to the spiritual leader. Kernels from the corn were then burned in the sacred fire along with a deer's tongue and tobacco. Meals made from new corn were shared by all except by the chief and his seven counsellors, who for another week had to subsist on corn from an earlier harvest.

Ripe Corn Ceremony: This enjoyable four-day harvest festival called for men dancing in a single file around a central tree in the square ground with green boughs in their hands while the chief's right-hand man did a special dance on a platform held up by the shoulders of other men. A feast with the women followed.

Great New Moon: This October festival recalled the Cherokee understanding of the beginning of Creation. There was a good amount of feasting. When the moon appeared, the People lined up at the river and waited until dawn, at which time they submerged themselves seven times. With a crystal they divined if they would live past spring;

if the signs were negative, they made the appropriate decisions to affect their fate positively.

Reconciliation Ceremonies: Through ritual drinking and dancing the People blessed relations between two persons of either the same or opposite sex. Those in deep friendship came to share in the symbolic union of (the) Creator with the People. It was a time of reconciliation and purification as well as renewal of commitment, and it affected everyone in the community.

Bounding Bush: This four-night symbolic sacrifice ceremony included feasting, special couples' dances, and dropping tobacco or pine needles into a special box while circling the fire. These were then sacrificially assigned to the flames.

Uku Dance: Every seven years this special thanksgiving ceremony was held, replacing the Great New Moon Ceremony. The principal chief was its leader. He was disrobed, bathed by his seven counsellors, given bright yellow garments, carried on a counsellor's back with music and fanning to a special seat in the square ground. His people danced all night in the temple while he and the seven counsellors kept silent vigil. The next morning, after being placed in a sacred circle, he began to dance while the officials imitated his dance steps. Then he was placed at his throne to preside in silence until sunset while the people feasted. He was then returned to his home. Similar rituals were offered for the following three days. Afterwards he officially regained his governing and spiritual responsibilities with the people.

Each tribe had its own particular ceremonies set to take place throughout the year. The recipe of sacred herbs might have varied among the People, the dance steps, the melodies and words of the songs might have been a bit different, and the decorative clothing might have had unique personal, family, clan, or tribal significance, but there was some similarity and recognizable regularity in the sacred ceremonies of the Peoples of the Southeast. The rituals always included seeds, tree branches, herbs, feathers, rocks and crystals, flowers, bones, and many other natural items which expressed their solidarity with Mother Earth. Many of the details of these ceremonies are lost to us nowadays, nevertheless some are still celebrated in a modified form.

Though some are extinct or have been amalgamated with other Peoples, some tribes of note within this cultural area are the Lumbees (Croatans, Lumber River People), the Catawba (Esaw), the Calusa

(Calloosas), the Timucua (Utina), the Apalachee (Apalachi), the Mikasuki (Miccosukee), the Seminole (Ikaniuksalgi, Sim-a-no-le, Isti-sima-note), the Choctaws (Oklafolaya + Ahepatokla + Oklahannali), the Houma (Huma), the Biloxi (Taneks Haya), the Natchez (Natches), the Chickasaw, the Shawnee (Sa-wanwa), the Alabama (Alabamu), Coushatta (Koasati), and the Yuchi (Tsoyaha Yuchi) Peoples.

Southwest Cultures

The majestic Southwest covers a vast domain of striking beauty. This territory generally includes a good portion of Arizona, New Mexico, Texas, and Utah. Some of the People also have relatives in the northern parts of Mexico. Much of it is desert and mountain. The temperatures vary from tremendous heat in the summertime to extreme cold in the winter. Some of the People moved about this arid land and travelled great distances; others built adobe dwellings and were more settled, depending greatly upon corn and squash and beans. They developed excellent irrigation techniques and were able to produce fine crops without needlessly wasting the precious water supplies. The Peoples of this region are well known for their weaving, basketry, ceramics, turquoise and silver jewelry, and intricate ceremonials. Their spirituality kept them in touch with the cycle of rain and drought and their prayers always acknowledged the source of all life, (the) Creator. They petitioned beings in the spirit world to bring the much needed rains at the appropriate times.

The enduring Peoples of the southwestern part of the United States spoke several languages and many dialects, and they developed their own area-appropriate words, rituals, and symbols for celebrating their spiritual and environmental realities. Their trading abilities extended the influence of their culture far beyond their own lands as they communicated with Peoples farther away. This was true for all the Peoples across the Americas, no matter how limited in size was the territory or how bounded it was by the physical nature of a mountain, a river, an ocean, or a desert.

Today we are able to enjoy the friendship and share in the heritage of such Southwestern Peoples as the Indéh (Apache), the Diné (Navajo), the Hopi (Hópi), the Tohono O'odham (Papago), the Quechan (Xam Kwatcan), the Pima (A'a'tam, O'odham, Akimel O'odham), the Yavapai (Enyaéva Pai), the Walapai (Epa), the Havasupai (Akbasupai), the Cahuilla (Kawia), the Chemehuevi (Tántáwats), the Maricopa (Pipatsje), the Tonkawa (Tonkaweya), and the Pueblos (Adobe Town Peoples).

California Cultures

California is a place of great contrasts. It has its share of expansive desert areas (like Death Valley), breathtaking coastlines unparalleled in the world, valleys with the most fertile of soil, mountains covered with redwoods, cedars, and pines, and foothills teeming with many kinds of oaks. I myself give thanks daily for the variety of terrain and animal and bird habitat that is nearby.

Most of the People hunted the ever-present game animals and gathered nearby food from the trees, the land, or the ocean. Acorns were transformed into a staple bread and delicious soup. Many were skilled boat-makers, and some ventured far from shore in great carved canoes to hunt for whales and other large water creatures. It is interesting to note that there were well over 100 languages and dialects at the time of first contact with Europeans. Many are not spoken now, but there is a language restoration and renewal movement going on among many of the Tribes.

Their origin stories were diverse and very interesting for all to hear, both young and old. Coyote, the trickster, was often present as the hero/anti-hero. Some of the People built great roundhouses for meetings and dancing, as well as partially underground sweat lodges. Even their architecture expressed their desire to be close to Mother Earth. Depending upon the terrain and their yearly round of activities, the various Peoples made temporary shelters of bark or grass or ramada-like structures to get relief from the heat of the sun. The eagle, condor, hawk, woodpecker, and hummingbird were special birds for the People and their feathers adorned their ritual clothing and basketry. Some even attached eagle or condor feathers to their netted men's dance skirts and capes. In some areas the bear and the mountain lion signified special blessings for the People.

As a single ethnological cultural area, California has an amazing gathering of cultures. Though they may be differentiated by language groups, terrain, or specific customs, it is difficult and incorrect to lump the Peoples together just because they are found within the geographical defines of a particular modern political state. The eastern part of California is still home to the Monos (Nümü), the Tubatulabals (Pahkanapüi, Phkanapil), the Maidu/Konkow (Maidüm) and the Yokuts. The Wintun (Wintoo) inhabited some of the central area. The south was claimed by the Tipai (Tipai), Ipai (Ipai), the Kumeyaay (Kamia), the Cupeños (Kupa-ngakitom) and the Cahuillas (Ivil-uwenetem), and the Mojave (Hamakhava, Makháv). The western shores of the state are populated by descendents of the Gabrieleño (Kumi-vit), the Chumash (Michumash), the Esselen (Ecselens), the Ohlone (Oholone), the Miwok (Miwu-k), and the Pomo (Paum). In the north resided the Shasta (Sustí-ka), the Hupa (Natinook-wa, Noti-nook-na), the Yurok (Yuruk, Olekwo'l, Alikwa), the Karuk (Karúk, Arar), the Achomawi (Pit River People), and the Modoc (Ma-klaks, Móatokni).

Northwest Cultures

Many of us are familiar with the great carved cedar totem poles of the Northwest Peoples. Their territory roughly includes the coastal areas from Oregon in the south to Alaska in the north. Though not particularly known for agriculture, they nevertheless knew how to reap the harvests from the sea, rivers, and forests. These are the People of the salmon, the ones who have shown us their spiritual ways by means of woodcarving and woodworking. They are the People of the potlatch giveaway feast and of beautifully danced ceremonies. Many were known for their blanket and bag weavings. They are the ones who ventured great distances on the ocean waves to bring in the mighty whales and to be in contact with other coastal tribes. Raven, wolf, salmon, bear, and many other totemic animal-people figure greatly in the spirituality of their daily life.

The whole Northwest cultural area is permanently saturated with the memory and presence of Peoples like the Nooksak Salish (Nook-sak), the Wanapum (Wanapam, Sokulk), the Cowichan (Hue-la-muh), the Cowlitz (Cow-e-lis-kee), the Klikitat (Qwulah-hwai-pum), the Tolowa (Xes), the Tillamook (Nekelim), the Siletz (Sailetc, Sai-letc-ic-me-tunne), the Clatsop (La'k-elak), the Chinook (Tsinuk), the Makah (Q-idicca-atx), the Nootka (Nu-tka, Nuu-chah-nulth), the Kwakiutl (Kw'agul, Kwa-kwa-ka'wakw, Kwakwala), the Lillooet (Stlatliumh), the Bella Bella (Heiltsuk), the Bella Coola (Nuxalk), the Haida (Ha-te), the Tsimshian ('cmsyan, Ocmayan) and the Tlingit (Li-ngit), to name a few.

Great Basin Cultures

What is called the Great Basin Culture area is a somewhat arid territory of great beauty typified by a lot of desert, many snow-capped mountains, and abundant pine and cedar trees, sage, and mesquite. Rabbits, deer, antelope, elk, and eagles figured prominently in the stories of the Peoples, as did coyote. Some of them wove baskets, rabbit-skin blankets, and fishing weirs; others harvested piñon nuts and reaped the produce of hundreds of desert and mountain plants. They were and are great surveyors of the land and have always felt close to it. Nowadays their fight is still for the land; others would like to make it a dumping ground for nuclear waste or a site for military maneuvers. The struggle goes on for them in this area of quiet beauty.

For countless centuries the People have been in this desert country and know it well. They have also exerted much influence on those around them. For example, a Paiute visionary named Wovoka (Jack Wilson) shared his apparitions and their significance with his own People and many others. In a short time this Ghost (Spirit) Dance Movement travelled very far indeed and affected a good many of the tribes from California to South Dakota and even Canada, much to the fear and consternation of the military and settlers. Each tribe adapted the teachings to its own needs. Some still continue to celebrate versions of the Ghost Dance in our own time.

The Peoples of the Great Basin include the Shoshone (Shoshoni, Shoshoko, So-so-goi), the Ute (Yuuttaa, Noo-chee, Nu-cl)), the Paiute (Paiyuhts), the Bannock (Ni-mi), the Gosiute, and the Washoe (Wasiw).

Plateau Cultures

Many of the People lived in an environment that was essentially bordered on the east by the Rocky Mountains, on the south by parts of Idaho, on the west by the Cascade mountains in Oregon, and on the north by the Fraser River in British Columbia. These Peoples also had tribal relatives in areas very distant from the Plateau complex. Many had come to the Plateau area because of hunting or trading or even pressure from other tribes or settler expansion. Salmon fishing was all important and many ceremonies surrounded both fishing and feasting. Storytelling by the elders abounded with narratives about salmon and the other animals and how the People should relate prayerfully and respectfully to one another and to all life forms. They sought after camas and other edible roots. Some wove various kinds of bags of twisted hemp.

Their homes often were tipis or tipi-like structures of rush mats; usually their winter houses were partially subterranean. Like many of the People in other areas, they were avid horsemen and horsewomen and to this day their Cayuse and Appaloosa breeds of horses are bargained for and traded. The People here blended some of the cultural methods and styles of both the Plains and the Northwest coast, making them uniquely their own. Some of the People are the Coeur d'Alene (Skitswish), the Nez Perce (Nimipiu, Nimipuu), the Cayuse (Waletpu), the Walla Walla (Walula), the Umatilla (Ewmitilly), the Yakima (Waptai'lmin, Waptailim, Ya-ki-má), the Spokan (Senoxami'naex), the Wenatchee (.s.npeskwu'zux), the Klamath (Eukshikai Makloks), the Thompson River People (Nlaka'pamux, Ntlakyapamuk), the Shuswap (Suxwapmux), Okanagan (Isonkuaili), and the Kootenai (Kutonaga, Sán'ka).

Plains Cultures

The Plains regions of Canada and the United States (much of Alberta, Saskatchewan, Manitoba, Montana, Idaho, Wyoming, North and South Dakota, Colorado, Utah, and Texas) is one vast undulating grassy ocean laced with rivers and bounded by the Rocky Mountains. The plow and the surveyor's work have caused this part of Mother Earth to be divided and subdivided countless times in the last 150 years to make room for cattle and crops of corn and wheat as well as to provide areas for townships. Here buffalo, antelope, elk, and deer were abundant and always at the disposal of the People who greatly appreciated these four-footed gifts of (the) Creator. Many of the People of the prairies were nomadic, constantly following the movements of the larger animals like the elk and buffalo, as they did the seasons.

Some, like the Mandans (Numakaki, Nu-eta), Arikaras (Tannish, Sáhnis), and Hidatsas (Hidátsa + Awaxawi + Awatixa), grew corn and tobacco while others, like the Crow (Apsáalooke), tended sacred tobacco plants even as they moved about within their traditional lands. Others, like the Pawnee (Skiri, Chahiksichahiks), lived in dome-like earth lodges, but the majority of Plains People lived in tipis of buffalo skins. Some other significant tribes are the Kiowa (Ga-i-gwa), the Wichita (Kirkitish), the Missouri (Niutachi), the Blackfoot (Siksika), the Peigan (Apikuni), the Blood (Kainai), the Caddo (Hasinaï), the Osage (Ni-u-kon-ska, Wazhazhe), the Arapaho (Hinanae-ina), the Cheyenne (Tse-tsehese-stahase), the Sioux, the Gros Ventre (Aaninena), the Ute (Nunt'z), the Comanche (Néme-ne), the Cree (Nahiawuk, Ne-i-yah-wahk), and the Sarcee (Tsotli'na).

Arctic Cultures

In the imagination of a good many outsiders, the Arctic appears to be one great expanse of snow and ice, the land of caribous and bears and seals, walruses and whales. But it is much more than that. It is the great homeland of the Inuit (Yupik of Alaska + Inyupik of Canada and Greenland) and Aleut (Unungun, Unangan) Peoples who have adapted well to the harsh climate. The Aleuts have traditionally lived on the Alaskan Aleutian Islands, while the Inuit are found from Alaska to Greenland. But, like many of the People, they often live in towns and metropolises across North America. Their languages are similar. It is said that the Aleuts developed some rather sophisticated medical and anatomical knowledge that helped them survive their difficult environment. They discovered ingenious ways to make warm, waterproof clothing from the skins or intestines of some of their land's fellow inhabitants: the seals and birds. The walrus gave them meat for the sled dogs and the outer covering for their boats (*umiaks* and *kayaks*). The caribou was and is especially important to the Inuit (Eskimos) of the inland areas. They used blocks of snow to make shelters (*igloos*) for themselves and were thus protected from the cold and piercing winds. Many northern Cree (Eeyouch) continue to hunt in the subarctic James Bay area; others, like the Beaver (Duneza) and the Slavey (Acha'ottine) Peoples, live in the various reaches of the western subarctic region.

Caribbean Cultures

Contemporary Native Peoples of the Caribbean cultural area include those whose ancestors inhabited the present day island countries of Puerto Rico, Dominican Republic, Haiti, Cuba, Dominica, Jamaica, and Trinidad, as well as the coastal sections of Panama, Costa Rica, Nicaragua, Honduras, Guatemala, and Belize. It is thought that those on the mainland between the Andes mountains and Mesoamerica gradually reached the Caribbean Islands and settled there. These were the ancestors of the Caribs, the Ciboneys, the Taínos, the Ciguayos, and the Arawaks. Some of the coastal mainland People are the Cuna and the Guaynii of Panama, the Miskito of Nicaragua, the Jicaque of Honduras, and the Mayas of Belize. The Bahamas were inhabited by the Lucayans. Many were farmers, hunters, and fisherman. They religiously held the sun and moon in high esteem and called (the) Creator Yocahú. Their chiefs, or *caciques,* presided over groups of large villages. They developed fine pottery and basketry. An important dietary staple was manioc (a yam-like tuber), but they also grew corn, peanuts, pineapples, tobacco, and cotton. They fished in the ocean and the rivers and hunted sea turtles, birds, and iguanas. The Island Peoples were good at making fine seafaring dugout boats from ceiba (silk cotton) trees. Nowadays many of the islands exhibit the remains of special courts *(bateys)* where a socio-religious ball game was played with a rubber ball and from 20 to 30 players. To this day, the Island of Dominica has a territory for the Carib People who are governed by their own *cacique* (chief).

Puerto Rico, called Borikén by its ancient and contemporary Taíno People, just recently played host to a unique all-nations gathering. In March of 1998, recognizing both the painful abuses and contemporary destruction of Mother Earth (Nature), and knowing that they have not forgotten their unique position as guardians and stewards of Mother Earth in this hemisphere, the People sent delegates to "The Native Gathering of the Americas: For Natural, Cultural and Ecological Planetary Diversity (El Encuentro Indígena de las Américas: Por la Diversidad Natural, Cultural y Ecologica Planetaria)."

At the University of Puerto Rico on the native Taino island of Borikén (Puerto Rico), they met one another as distinct tribal groups, both those living in a highly technological society and those who only recently have come to experience the ravages of intrusions into their traditional lands. All the visiting delegates continuously felt the Taíno hospitality throughout the island.

Almost from the start of this encounter, everyone recognized a common cosmovision that would help them to travel through the existing labyrinth of problems with various traditional and contemporary approaches for resolution. But above all, they knew that immediately they must mobilize their own People and inspire other indigenous Peoples near them to do something that will strongly encourage the protection of Mother Earth, especially in this hemisphere. They know full well that through both ceremony and social action they must embody their spirituality for the benefit, not only of themselves and the dominant societies around them, but for the very life of our Mother Earth. No matter what the odds may seem to be, this developing indigenous network shows all the signs of success as the People continue to recognize in themselves that they must do this for, as the Lakota say, *Mitakuye oyasin* (all my relations), every living being on Mother Earth.

We will probably never really know the depth of pain caused by the slave trade in the Americas, beginning in the Caribbean. The mixing of People's from the New World, Africa, and the Old World still continues to take place, but perhaps under different conditions. It is less violent, conceivably, and the coming together is more by individual choice. It always leads to beautiful looking children, but not always to greater understanding and appreciation of another's race and culture. It is a reality that must seriously be considered as we enter the next millennium together.

Mesoamerican Cultures

It seems that the controversial border between the United States and Mexico exists only for those who are students of political realities. For many People of Mesoamerica it is simply a recently created fence that has many breaks in it. For millennia it did not exist at all. The People passed back and forth on migratory or trading expeditions, much the same as they do today. Today's countries of Mexico, Guatemala, Belize, Honduras, El Salvador, Nicaragua, and Panama are home to millions of people whose ancestors developed writing systems, calendars, and highly developed ceremonial edifices and cities. They are also found throughout North America. In pre-European contact times they exerted trade and religious influences on the Peoples of the Southwestern and Southeastern cultural areas of the United States. Their territories were made up of pristine beaches, deserts, mountains, fertile valleys, and thick tropical rainforests.

There were those who, like the Toltecs, Aztecs, and Mayas, established militaristic and dynastic empires and who traded with or subjugated many of the Peoples living at great distances from the urban centers of their conquerors. Prior to Europeans coming upon their lands and bringing with them the Spanish language, many diverse tongues were spoken throughout Middle America. A good number of the People survive to this day with their languages intact, though modified for today's contemporary demands. There are some for whom Spanish is still very much a foreign language, though many are bilingual (Native language plus Spanish) or even trilingual (Native language plus Spanish and English). A good portion of the People have blended Christian spirituality with that of their ancestors and do so proudly, much to the amazement of some North Americans. Over a period of centuries each country's government desired to unite their inhabitants with a common sense of destiny though education and common language (Spanish). As a result, many of the People have forgotten their tribal ways and see themselves as Mexican or Guatemalan, etc., more so than as indigenous People of a particular tribe. But their diet gives them away! Corn, beans, squash, nopales, cilantro, chile: these are all part of the ancient native diet and are today the cultural foods of Aztlán (the mythical origin place of Aztecs, situated somewhere to the north of the Gulf of California, that is so symbolic for Chicanos and other Latinos of today) and other places of Mesoamerica.

Today many of the Peoples still live within their traditional homelands. They are often identified by the languages or dialects that they speak. Some of the Peoples in Mexico are the Pápago (Todono o'odham), the Pimas (A'a'tam, O'odham), the Yaquis (Yoemem), the Seris (Comcáac), the Guarijíos, the Tarahumaras (Rarámuri, Ralámari), the Kikapués (Kiikáapoa), the Mayos (Yoremem), the Tepehuanes (O'dami), the Huastecos, the Otomíes (Ñahñu or Ñaños), the Pames, the Chichimecas, the Coras, the Huicholes (Wixarika), the Tarascos (Purépechas), the Mazahuas, the Nahuas, the Totonacas, the Popolucas, the Amuzgos, the Zapotecas, the Triques (Triquis), the Chatinos, the Huaves, the Mixes, the Chontales, the Mayas, the Zoques, the Tzotziles, the Lacandones (Hach Winik), the Mixtecos, the Tzeltales. Much needs to be written about these diverse Peoples of Mexico, as well as those who ancestry is also mestizo, mixed.

The famous Ruta Maya (Mayan Route), which spans several modern-day Central American countries, allowed many of the Peoples to be in contact with each other through conquest or commerce. Some have relatives living in two or more countries. Guatemala also has many Mayan People, though their dialects and customs differ. Honduras claims many descendents of the Lencas, Miskitos, Pipils, the Sumos, and the Ulvas; El Salvador is home to the Chortí, the Pocomán, and the Cacaopera; Nicaragua receives its name from the Nicaraos; Costa Rica is the country of the Boruca and the Talamanca, while Panama is the traditional territory of the Cuna and the Guaymi. The People's customs, dress, fiestas, handicrafts, dances, and traditions speak to us of the rich and varied cultural mosaic of Mesoamerica.

South American Cultures

South America is one vast piece of the world puzzle, having a great variety of temperatures and climes, not to mention hundreds of unique species of plants, trees, animals and birds, and languages, both indigenous and imported. Much of it has only been seen by the Native People themselves. Only in recent times have others, whether they are missionaries, explorers, visitors, or settlers, come to experience such a wealth of Mother Earth's bounty. However, it is becoming more common knowledge that the land itself is in great danger from misuse and improper and inappropriate development. The land is the basis for all the forms of wildlife, as well as the original Peoples. Wisdom, prudence, and respect are needed now more than ever in regard to the future of South America. Long before the countries and their boundaries were declared, it was home to the People. In their own lifetimes some travelled great distances, others only a few square miles. But what they needed for their survival and enjoyment was always nearby. There are several important language groups for the multitude of tribes.

The eastern part of what is now Brazil contains the great tropical forests and savannas of the Mato Grosso. Here dwell the Ge-speaking People. They generally prefer trails to canoes as they hunt peccaries and birds, along with sloths and anteaters. Others in a large territory called Amazonia subsist on fish, turtles, shellfish, birds, rodents, peccaries, and tapirs. The primary rivers, the Amazon and the Orinoco, and their countless tributaries influence greatly how the Peoples live. Many are the little gardens outside the villages where the tuber-rooted cassava (manioc) is grown along with sweet potatoes, corn, yams, squash, taro, arrowroot, beans, and peanuts. Bananas and plantains are also harvested.

As it is anywhere in the world, human beings both individually and communally necessarily react to the needs of life: food, shelter, sexual intimacy, etc. Those who hunt or farm (or drive to work) must make tools. These are life's important conveniences and they must be used well, whether they are bows and arrows, blow guns, spears, slingshots, axes, hoes, plows, machetes, guns, or motorized vehicles. This region is no exception. For the generations to go on, the Peoples needed to adapt quickly and successfully to their environments. Even now, as modern technology and people of other languages and cultures enter traditional tribal territories, the People see, judge, and act. They learn to adapt even though they would much rather prefer to be left alone. The People of the east Brazilian section of South America include the Tupinambá, the Camacán, the Botocudo, the Kaingáng, the Kaiapó, the Bororo, the Shavante, the Karajá, the Timbira, the Sherenti, the Acroa, and many more.

Throughout Amazonia and many other places of South America, the hammock is all-important as a bed that is safe from snakes and other creatures. It can also be used to secure gourds, weapons, and household necessities. Many hours with family and friends are whiled away in the interior of the tropical rainforests, just as they are in the backyards and gardens throughout North America. The hammock is for the People a symbol of safety and conviviality. We who live in other parts of the world have our own methods of safety and friendly social exchange: the locked door and living room chairs.

Though some of the People are quickly being introduced to the benefits of technology, they really would like to be left alone to plan and live out their own destiny. But it is painfully difficult. Daily their habitat becomes more and more forcefully invaded by those who would replace the tropical forests with cattle ranchlands. Many South American cities are over-populated by the "have-nots" who seek a new life as they follow "progress" to the Amazonian interior. It is a crucial time for all concerned. Not only do the native People need national and international advocacy, but also the mixed blood Peoples and immigrants need both understanding and education so that they do not continue to wreak havoc on the land and People as did their forebears just a few decades ago. Too much is at stake.

Some of the inhabitants of the Amazonian interior are the Guajajara, Txicao, Txukahamai, Waura, Bakairí, Sirionó, Amahuaca, Jivaro, Auca, Cofán, Yagua, Tucanoan, Cubeo, Yanomamo, Piaróa, Waiwai, Tirió, Yanomami, Sanuma (Sanema), Hiwi (Guajibo), Ye'kwana (Yekuana), Curripaco, Baré, Baniwa (Baniva), Tsatse (Piapoco), Puinave, Warekena, Hoti, Yabarana, E'ñapa (Panare), and many more tribes and tribelets besides.

Many have called the Gran Chaco area "green hell" because of the mosquitoes, mites, snakes, the heat and the aridity, and the swamps during the rainy season flooding. More or less located in the middle section of South America, this great hunting ground, which covers the north part of Argentina, Paraguay, and Bolivia, has an abundance of animals and bird life for subsistence. With temperatures well over 100 degrees Fahrenheit, many immigrants have found it a difficult climate as they accepted the challenges of the savannas, forests, and bushy lowlands. Nowadays many of the People work in lumber camps, with sugar cane, and also in the cotton fields. In ancient times the *bola* (a weapon made up of two or more heavy balls secured to the end of one or more strong cords and hurled in such a way that it entangles the legs of the animals) was used for hunting, along with spears and bows and arrows. Wild game included deer, rabbits, rheas, partridges, and other birds, not to mention armadillos. Prayer, under the guidance of a shaman, usually preceded hunting. The Lengua, the Maca, the Toba, the Abipón, the Mocovi, the Mataco, the Chulupí, the Tapieté, the Chamacoco, the Tonocoté, and the Guarayo are representatives of this large territory.

The southern Andean highlands and the coast down to Tierra del Fuego at the bottom of Patagonia were well gleaned by the pre-Colombian hunters and gatherers. The natives of this mountainous region close to the ocean made bark canoes and temporary shelters which were often made with earth sods. Sea lions were their food, as well as the llama-like small guanaco. Much of their world came to an end as they themselves were hunted, in many cases, to extinction. European-introduced diseases also took their toll as they still do throughout the Americas.

But here the Mapuche People, who fought off Inca interference, also heroically resisted colonization by Spain. Nowadays they must keep Chilean government bureaucracies at a distance. Other Peoples to the south had a more difficult existence as they searched the nearby shores for fish and shellfish. They ate seals and sea otters along with cormorants, ducks, geese, and guanacos. Eels were part of their diet as were many roots and plants. Today their descendents are Mestizos and are very much a part of the contemporary world.

Other Peoples of the grasslands, like the North American prairie tribes, became horse people very quickly. The dwellers of the pampas had a more recent experience akin to that of their United States and Canadian sisters and brothers. Immigrants just kept coming into their lands and they needed to resist them. Mixed blood gauchos nowadays still maintain a lot of the earlier cultural ways of the pampas Peoples as they use bolla and lasso and knife to support themselves in a ranching tradition.

Many of those of this southern section, who find themselves living within the modern countries of Uruguay, Argentina, Chile, Bolivia, Peru, and Ecuador, carry the bloodlines of the Charrúa, the Querandí, the Chehehet, the Puelche, the Tehuelche (Gununa'kena and Aonikenk), the Mecharnuekenk, the Selk'nam (Ona), the Haush (Mannekenk), the Yamana (Yahgan), the Alakaluf (Halakwulup, Kawéskor), the Chonos, the Picunche, the Huarpe, the Guaraní, and descendents of the Incas. These are simply a few of the Peoples that might be mentioned here.

Over countless centuries the Peoples of the Andes Mountains became highly developed in many areas of human life. They were great farmers and could subsist on difficult rocky land that even today is a challenge for the modern farmer who has lots of machinery available. They cultivated different kinds of potatoes and squashes, beans and chiles, corn, peanuts, and avocados. They knew well how to terrace and irrigate their lofty fields. With stone they built both roads and great edifices. They were goldsmiths of renown and weavers of the most beautiful textiles. A deeply spiritual People, they understood the movements of the stars and planets and saw the handiwork of (the) Creator in everything. They discerned the power of their medicines and how to make them from the local and distant herbs, roots, and tubers. They even performed delicate brain surgery with much success. Healing by prayer and other methods was an everyday occurrence. Much of their business life, especially the textile industry, and travel depended on local species of animals: guanacos, llamas, vicuñas, and alpacas. News would travel very quickly because of a well devised system of mountain runners and signal givers. The Incas pursued military conquests and had put together a vast mountainous empire, extending their own cultural influences throughout the lands on the western side of South America. The Europeans were quite amazed at what they saw when they arrived.

The all-consuming European desire for gold and silver caused the penetration and colonization of not only the Andes but many parts of what came to be called the New World. They were firm believers in the myth of the Gilded One (El Dorado): The Native leader who prior to diving into a sacred lake had his whole body covered with gold dust. As it left his body and descended to the bottom of the lake, it became a sacrifice for the ancestral gods. The Spaniards wanted some, if not all, of this gold, and other things besides. Not only would the plants and trees and minerals be affected by the "change of ownership," but the Peoples as well. Their lifestyles changed drastically as they now had to come face to face with those who not only lived near them, but would want to take over the land for their own purposes. This age-old story is still true today throughout the Americas: those with the money or the power, the influence or the technology, always try to call the shots.

Some of the Peoples of the Andes and contiguous areas are the Charca, the Diaguita, the Atacama, the Lipe, the Lupaca, the Camaná, Urú, the Rucana, the Chincha, the Huanca, the Huacho, the Huayla, the Tumbes, the Manta, the Salasaca, the Chachapoya, the Conchuco, the Quechua, Canelos Quichua. Of course, these are only a few of the Tribes within the countries of northern Chile, Argentina, and Ecuador. There are many, many more besides the ones given here.

For about five hundred years now, the "Raza de Bronce" (The Bronze People), those of Native and European blood and heritage, has been among us. And not only that. In more recent times the People have beautiful children who carry the blood and heritage of those who come from many other places in the world. We live in a time of great change. Our societies are in tremendous flux. Nevertheless, I believe that the wisdom of all our backgrounds and cultures and spiritualities will help us to live in harmony as the ages pass. (The) Creator will watch over us.

NOTE: To emphasize the Four Directions, the Circle, and the Number Four in the quoted material that follows, pertinent words and phrases have been highlighted in ***bold italic***.

Four Directions

FOUR DIRECTIONS

The aires, *or the directions of the compass, have their own lore in Celtic traditions: not unusual in a people living on the Western seaboard of Europe to whom the sea, its tides, currents and winds, were of such importance. Each of the directions has its own wind, each having a distinctive color.*

It is interesting to listen to modern fishermen on any part of the Celtic seaboard describing the weather: they frequently speak of a black wind and preserve their own lore about the table of dawn.

The Celtic Tradition, Caitlín Matthews

My first thematic division concerns the four directions as sacred geometry. Other world cultures also acknowledge north, east, south, and west directionality. As has already been said, until more recent times the main altar in a Catholic church usually faced east—a reference to the rising sun and its symbolic meaning for the resurrection and return of Christ (*"The coming of the Son of Man will be like lightning striking in the east and flashing far into the west."* Matthew 245:27). Four directions were important for certain considerations, but probably not as important symbolically or ceremonially as they were for Native Peoples of the Americas. Much data is still to be sought to fully bear this out, and it will probably take a long time as many accounts of the last 500 years have yet to be translated from the Portuguese, Spanish, or other Native languages. Further knowledge may need to come from other witnessed contemporary ceremonies or folkways as well. But I do believe that there is enough accumulated information to assess the general situation which seems to indicate that directionality was usually taken into special account by the many Peoples found up and down the longitudes of the Americas.

In considering the many cultural areas, I place before the reader selected tribal activities ranging from special rituals to dances, songs, customs, and building techniques. They are grouped in this manner so that one may consider the tribal entity and the basic culture with which they identify, or with which others say they identify. As one considers an account of a ceremony or activity, it might be helpful to ponder my brief commentary about that particular subject in relation to the theme at hand, the Four Directions. A similar process will be helpful as we consider the ensuing themes of the Circle and the Number 4.

Let us take a look at how the Four Directions of north, south, east, and west have been understood among some of the Peoples. I will first briefly outline them.

Our journey of discovery begins in the eastern and southeastern parts of North America where, among other concerns, we come to learn how the directions are included in the origin stories of the Unami Lenape and Iroquois. Other tribes, like the Menomini and the Ojibway, are also remembered in regard to their cosmology and pipe ceremonies. We can almost visualize the drawing plans and seating arrangements for the ceremonial houses of the Munsee Mahicans and the Delawares. The Naskapis tell us of the importance of the winds that come from four places in the world, while we hear Ojibway relating about the directional guardian spirits of the universe.

The pipe ceremonies of the Natchez and Creeks are described for us. The Cherokee, well-known for their knowledge of herbs, inform us about how to purify ourselves with a sacred herbal emetic drink and celebrate the ritual colors of "four corners of the world." Two tribes, originally from the southeast but later removed to Texas, the Alabamas and the Coushattas, offer a beautiful song to these sacred directions.

The inhabitants of the Southwest, having a different environment and history, nevertheless possess many wonderful directional rituals and songs. Some of the Pueblo tribes share with us poetry and prayer as we are made privy to some of the ancient desert symbolism which governs tribal identity as well as the setting up of altar-shrines. We learn something of the Navajo healing and house blessing prayers. We can almost visualize the celebrated Geronimo praying at his birthplace, and we become witnesses to a teenager's puberty ceremony as well as observe the People giving homage for the gifts of the animal world, especially the deer nation (Yaquis).

Though the many California Native Peoples experienced tremendous diversity in their section of Mother Earth, nevertheless, whether they celebrate their origin stories, pray at the time of approaching death or for healing, work with symbolic colors, hunt and fish, care for the land, heal, mourn the dead, or even make a fire, they more often than not are cognizant of the importance of north, east, south, and west in their daily lives.

The Washoe of the Great Basin cultural area inform us of the meaning of putting up the first four poles of a tipi and understanding dreams, while from the Plateau Peoples we come to understand the connection between prayer and the seasons and winds that originate in each of the directions. Enlightened with regard to time-honored symbolism, we almost find ourselves ready to enter a Nez Perce hand-game competition.

Not only do some of the Plains People teach us about ceremonies regarding the pipe and the sweatlodge, the sundance, the ghost dance, the blessing of a child, playing games, how to orient one's own self properly, or what it is like to go on a vision quest, they also offer us prayers for healing or gathering power from (the) Creator through nature.

The Mesoamerican experience of the four directions is rich in imagery and theology. Each day the ancient Aztecs and Mayas recounted the activities of the gods and goddesses, especially those who guarded the four directions. They danced their beliefs as their descendents still do today. They sought out and came to understand a relationship between time and the spatial directions.

The Peoples of the Caribbean, like their present day children, the Arawaks, the Taínos, and the Caribs, named colors for the directions. Often those in South America looked to the directions as they contemplated procedures for running an empire (Incas) or making proper dance attire (Kaiapó) or considering the winds (Onas) or ceremonially adopting another human being (Amahuaca).

Nowadays, many of us have opportunities to learn firsthand of the People's prayer ways. This is good.

Praying to the Four Directions

WOODLANDS CULTURAL AREA

FOUR DIRECTIONAL SPIRITUAL BEINGS
UNAMI LENAPE

But as the Great Spirit, who is known to their descendants as "Gicelamu-Kaong," was supposed to be permanently settled in this highest realm of inert enjoyment, it was necessary to assume that any duties of a practical order for the benefit of mankind in which the Spirit might be concerned, would be delegated to less preoccupied and stationary personages. . . .

A Manitto, or manito may be taken to have meant the mysterious power of life. As the white man assumed it, the word may have at times indicated either a good or a bad spirit, and by inference a god or a devil. The form of the term is probably Algonkian, for it appeared in the Massachusetts tongue as "Manitto" with the meaning "he is a god," and Roger Williams records the shortened form of "Manit" as "god.". . .

The early colonists, whose ministers, like Megapolensis, assumed that the Indian was limited in his belief to a single "Manitto," could have made little or no enquiry into the form of character of their belief; and had no appreciation of the extent or nature of their deep-seated religious system.

The "Manitto" which he described as their only object of worship, comprised, according to the description of their descendants, *four spiritual beings*, each of which had control of a fourth part of the terrestrial system, *north, south, east,* and *west,* directing the winds and rains from each direction and acting as the helpers or delegates of the Great Spirit. The earth itself was regarded as the Mother of the race, providing as it did, the site of their homes, the food grown upon its bosom, and the wild forest which afforded cover for the coveted game.

These and other lesser spirits, even such as were believed to make animals and plants their habitation, controlled the minds and largely directed the doings of the Lenape.

Indian Life of Long Ago in the City of New York,
Reginald Pelham Bolton, 1972, pp. 22-23

The ancient inhabitants of what is now New York City celebrated the directions as they prayed.

—————————————— + ——————————————

MIGRATION STORY
LENAPE

After the rushing water (had subsided) the Lenape of the turtle were close together, in hollow houses, living together there.

It freezes where they abode, it snows where they abode, it storms where they abode, it is cold where they abode.

At this *northern* place they speak favorably of mild, cool [lands], with many deer and buffaloes.

As they journeyed, some being strong, some rich, they separated into house-builders and hunters:

The strongest, the most united, the purest, were the hunters.

The hunters showed themselves at the *north,* at the *east,* at the *south,* at the *west.*

In that ancient country, in that northern country, in that turtle country, the best of the Lenape were the Turtle men.

All the cabin fires of that land were disquieted, and all said to their priest, "Let us go."

To the Snake land to the *east* they went forth, going away, earnestly grieving.

Split asunder, weak, trembling, their land burned, they went, torn and broken, to the Snake Island.

Those from the *North* being free, without care, went forth from the land of snow, in different directions.

The fathers of the Bald Eagle and the White Wolf remain along the sea, rich in fish and mussels.

Floating up the streams in their canoes, our fathers were rich, they were in the light, when they were at those islands.

Head Beaver and Big Bird said, "Let us go to Snake Island," they said.

All say they will go along to destroy all the land.

Those of the *north* agreed,
Those of the *east* agreed.
Over the water, the frozen sea,
They went to enjoy it.

On the wonderful slippery water,
On the stone-hard water all went,
On the great Tidal Sea, the mussel-bearing sea.

Ten thousand at night,
All in one night,
To the Snake Island, to the *east,* at night,
They walk and walk, all of them.

The men from the *north,* the *east,* the *south,*
The Eagle clan, the Beaver clan, the Wolf clan,
The best men, the rich men, the head men,
Those with wives, those with daughters, those with dogs.

They all come, they tarry at the land of the spruce pines;
Those from the *west* come with hesitation,
Esteeming highly their old home at the Turtle land.

Where Is the Eagle?, William Coffer, 1981, pp. 142-144

This story comes from the Walum Olum, the "painted record" of this People. It tells of their migrations by means of pictographs, story-telling, and song. It seems also to give clan associations, each with a different directional identification.

———————————— + ————————————

DIRECTIONAL SEATING IN CEREMONIAL HOUSE
DELAWARE

The Delaware Indians—who lived along the river of that name before being displaced to Oklahoma—tell of a time long ago when their ancestors grew careless and neglected their time-honored observances. Before long, a great earthquake struck their homeland and shook the ground so terribly that even the animals began to pray. Full of remorse, the Delaware gathered in council to consider what they could do to placate their angry creator. Several men rose to relate an identical vision. Each imparted the same message: "First of all, there must be a house built."

Thus was established the institution of the Delaware Big House, the heart of every community, where countless generations would gather dutifully to praise their maker. Its design obeyed the plan dictated by the Creator in the vision—a long house with a gabled roof and two firepits set beneath smoke holes on either side of a tall center post. The Creator also decreed that the center post be carved with two identical faces "just like mine, painted half black and half red, as mine is, and I will put my power in them." The carved image . . . also appears on the 10 wall posts. Each of the masks represented 1 of the 12 levels that made up the universe.

The center post of the Big House became the focal point of a rite of thanksgiving that lasted 12 days. To the Delaware, this sacred post represented the World Tree that ascended to heaven from soil deposited on the back of a great turtle to form the earth. Among the three societies that convened in the Big House for the annual rite, the Wolf Clan generally played host and sat at the *north* end. Two other societies, the Turkey and Turtle clans, sat at the *south* and *west* side, respectively. Periodically, worshipers would rise to sing and dance, circling the center post and firepits. As the days passed, the celebrants could feel themselves drawing closer to the Creator. Then, on the twelfth night, they put on their finery and symbolically entered heaven. The morning after, they returned to earth, prayed a thanksgiving, and again took up their daily tasks, but they remained ever mindful of the Creator's solemn warning: "Never give up the Big House."

American Indians: The Spirit World, Henry Woodhead (Ed.), 1992, p. 164

The Delaware (Lenape) Big House religion was still practiced until 1924, not in the ancient tribal lands on the east coast, but in and around Copan, Oklahoma. The four directions were carefully considered before the work began on the building, and they were also expressed in the architecture itself.

———————— + ————————

FOUR DIRECTIONAL ROOTS OF UNIFYING TREE
IROQUOIS

Many winters ago our wise ancestors predicted that a great monster with white eyes
would come from the east and consume the land

They advised their children to plant a tree
with four roots
to the *north*
to the *south*
to the *east* and to the *west*

and collecting under its shade
to dwell together in unity
and harmony

The Magic World: American Indian Songs and Poems, William Brandon, 1971, p. 104

This prophetic utterance by O-NO-SA about one hundred and fifty years ago, and slightly revised from the 1851 edition of Lewis Henry Morgan's League of the Ho-Dé-No-Sau-Nee or Iroquois, *seems to be coming true more and more. The revitalization of Native spiritual life has the four directions as one of its bases. There is security in being rooted with the ancient ways of understanding, even in our contemporary situation.*

A prayer to Creator while facing west, surrounded by living trees and grounded on Mother Earth

———————— + ————————

POEM
ONEIDA

Let us survive
Inside a sacred space.
Look at the Earth.
She feels us. She feeds us.

Look to the *West*.
Look to the *North*.
Look to the *East*.
Look to the *South*.

*Turtleshell
Rattle*

Look at the Sky.
He feeds us. He heals us.
Inside a sacred space
Let us survive.

Star Quilt, Roberta Hill Whiteman, 1984

*This contemporary poem captures in just a few words a basic concept
in Native spirituality: the terreniel, terrestrial, and directional sacred
encompassing of human beings.*

———————————— + ————————————

PIPE CEREMONY
MENOMINI

One of the earliest ethnologists, Walter J. Hoffman, obtained
considerable data on another Algonkian speaking culture, the Menomini of Wisconsin in the 1880s. He presents a general but detailed
account of the smoking of the Sacred Pipe:

> When several Menomini are sitting together for social purposes,
> smoking is individual, and no offer of a pipe by one to another is made,
> unless the other desires a whiff, or may perhaps be with his own pipe.
> When sitting in council and having in hand the consideration of tribal
> affairs or deliberations relative to important social secrets, or when
> participating in ritualistic ceremonials, the smoker who fills the pipe
> hands it to his right-hand neighbor to light. The latter individual takes a

few whiffs at intervals, inhaling each mouthful, after which the pipe is passed back to the owner at the left, who then takes several whiffs, when he passes it to the next person to his left. In this manner the pipe continues on its way around the circle, always to the left, until the bowl of tobacco is exhausted. He who concludes the smoking knocks out the ashes and hands the pipe to its owner.

During the passage of the pipe silence is maintained, and if any conversation becomes necessary, it is conducted only in a whisper.

At various intervals of ceremonial smokes, especially during the smoking preliminary to prayers and chants, puffs of smoke are directed toward the *four cardinal points* as well as toward the abode of the wind gods, or the zenith—the abode of Kisha'Ma'nido—and towards the earth. . . .

The true Indian pipe stem usually terminates in a cylindrical mouth-piece an inch or more in length and from one-fourth to one-third of an inch in diameter. When smoking, an Indian does not put this part into his mouth . . . but he will press between the lips, and as the stem enters the mouth the outer and dry portion of the lips follow, so that the stem does not become moist. In sucking the stem and gaining a mouthful of smoke, the lips are slightly parted at either side or towards the corner of the mouth and air inhaled so as to mix with and pass down the throat into and filling the lungs.

Offering Smoke: The Sacred Pipe and Native American Religion,
Jordan Paper, 1988, pp. 28-29

Over one hundred years ago the Menomini People still used the pipe in deliberations and during decision-making times. Perhaps the pipe-smoking times are less in number, but, nonetheless, they are still a part of their contemporary life, especially their ceremonial life.

———————————— + ————————————

DIRECTIONAL ORIENTENTATION
IN CEREMONIAL HOUSE
MUNSEE-MAHICAN

. . . the symbolism of the Munsee-Mahican ceremony:

The Munsee-Mahican Big House is a sky projection upon earth, specifically the constellation Ursa Major projected upon the floor of the Big

House sanctuary. The interior furnishings of the sanctuary and the stations formally occupied by the ceremonial officials correspond to the position of the stars forming the constellation. The acts and movements of the ritual performers parallel the movements of Ursa Major as the events of the annual life cycle of the earth bear sacrificed in the ceremony is conceived as a fragment of the celestial bear, and everything done during the ritual is a transcendental reference to him.

The ceremony was held in the Big House, Xwate'k'an, a rectangular wooden building (fifty by thirty feet) with its long axis running *east to west*. The structure represented the universe: its bare floor the earth, its four walls the *four directions*, its ceiling, the sky spaces thought to consist of twelve layers atop which the Supreme being resides. The center pole, a tree trunk, symbolized the world tree *(axis mundi)*. There were an *east* door and a *west* door. Halfway between the doors and the center pole were two fires; there were two smoke holes in the roof above them. A carved wooden mask above each door faced the center pole; the one on the *east* side was white; the one on the *west* side was red. Two more masks, suspended on the center pole, faced *east and west*. The one on the *east* side was red; the one on the *west* side was white. Thus two red masks faced *east,* two white masks faced *west,* indicating the colors of the two directions and the inherent dualism in the universe (earth-sky, life-death, male-female). This concept was also expressed in the arrangement of participants: Women were located in the *eastern* half of the structure, men in the *western* half.

The skin of the sacrificed bear was tied around the center pole beneath the red and white face masks, thus ceremonially unifying both opposites on the world tree.

The Wolves of Heaven: Cheyenne Shamanism, Ceremonies, and Prehistoric Origins, Karl Schlesier, 1987, pp. 176-177

Architecture tells something about how a People orders its world or lives within the world. Like Solomon of biblical times who built the temple according to divine plans, so, too, other Native Peoples of the Americas have built their homes and holy gathering places according to what they have been told from above.

———————————— + ————————————

FOUR DIRECTIONAL WINDS
NASKAPI

Among the supernatural forces at times mentioned as personified beings are a group of poetical concepts: *wábanu*, "day sky"; *wabanicú*, "east wind"; *tci wétenicu'*, "north wind"; *tci wétenec*, "little north [west] wind"; also *nekabehéncu; cawenecú*, "south wind"; *nemict-cúwets*, "thunder"; *wutéiátek*, "heart of tree" [sap]; *tamwini bég*, "deepest part of the sea"; *tcícegwets*, "skies, clouds, days." The wind names may be rendered as "man of the east," "man of the north," and so on. The preceding are all given in the Mistassini dialect.

The winds, next in rank of power below the Creator, are preeminent as spirits of the four quarters—forces controlling the universe; the life and growth of man and of animal and plant life. An explanatory myth (Mistassini) satisfies our quest for the origin belief of this condition of nature.

Origin of the Four Earth Winds

There was a hunter long ago when the world was being formed who dreamed that he would meet with good luck if he killed a lynx and ate the whole of it. The next time he went out he caught a lynx and ate it all. His dream had told him that his good luck would be to kill something big. So when he went out to find what was promised him he suddenly came upon something truly big but not what he expected. It was indeed a *wi'ndigo*! But by the help of the spirits which came to his aid he finally killed the *wi'ndigo*. And there it lay dead on the ground while all the people came to look at the creature. They formed in a half-circle around the body of the *wi'ndigo* standing facing the *east*, some on the ***north*** side, some on the ***west*** and some on the *south*, but none on the east side. They were waiting for the ***Man of the East***, the ***Man of the North***, the ***Man of the West*** and the ***Man of the South*** to come and take their shares as was done when they lived on earth among the creatures.

While they were standing thus waiting, the ***Man of the East*** [East Wind], the most feared of all, came walking from the *east*. He came within the circle of the people and started to take his share. He cut off the head of the *wi'ndigo*, then his right arm and leg and finally his heart. That was more than his share for it should have been divided among the four spirits equally. That is why he is called the Stingy One. He takes everything without regard for others, so when the east wind blows ever after he takes all the game and fish away from the people. When the *Man of the East* had taken nearly all the best part of the *wi'ndigo,* the *Man of the North* came for his share. He too is hard and cruel and he took more than his [quarter] share, the other leg and arm. Then the *Man of the West* came for his share and he took the rest of the meat from the body of the *wi'ndigo.* Last of all came *Man of the South*. He is the most gentle and mild and so all he got was the back bone for his share. [Since then the four spirits of the winds and the four quarters have acted in the same way as they did then and are known by these characters.]

The Lake St. John and Mistassini hunters declare it to be the truth that when the east wind blows there is no use to go hunting or fishing because they will get nothing in their nets and no animals can be found in their traps nor to be shot.

Naskapi: The Savage Hunters of the Labrador Peninsula,
Frank Speck, 1977, pp. 56, 59

Among the Naskapi People the winds are important. They have a special knowledge of the winds, and without it life would indeed be difficult in their part of the world. In this section we hear about how the four winds came to exist. Even in our own time we need to know much more about the winds and the havoc that they can wreak if we do not understand them, as well as the gifts that they can bring us if we are ready for them.

———————————— + ————————————

FOUR DIRECTIONS MILITARY TECHNIQUE
ABENAKI, MICMAC, PENOBSCOT, IROQUOIS, ETC.

Major Robert Rodgers (1731-1795) was very familiar with 18th-century Eastern Woodland Native Peoples. Many of his wilderness fighting techniques stemmed from his intimate knowledge of warfare with Indians that were friendly to the British and against Indians allied with the French.

The Abenaki Indians were native to Vermont and were extremely loyal to the French. The Mohawk members of the Iroquois Federation were incensed that they were losing hunting and trading routes to the Abenaki and their French allies.

One fighting technique which is used by the Elite Army Rangers today called "disperse" is when a small unit narrowly misses making contact with a large enemy unit.

The patrol leader quickly raises his hand with palm extended and pushes in *each of the four cardinal directions* in order to disperse and hide his group.

> Interview with Michael P. Curran, a former member of
> the U.S. Army 101st Airborne, January 21, 1997

Though many years have passed from the time of "Roger's Rangers," still many of the earlier fighting techniques have become part of the training for today's army. It is interesting to note how the four directions were originally honored, perhaps for their gift of protection of the warriors. This spiritual dimension has, for all practical purposes, dropped out, but this military survival technique is nevertheless a good one.

+

MANIDOS OF THE FOUR DIRECTIONS
OF THE UNIVERSE
OJIBWAY

Since the Great Spirit seemed so far away, and so little active in the universe, the Indians naturally made their supplications to the lesser *manidos,* those who concerned themselves more directly with human affairs. Some of the Parry Islanders postulate *four* "deputy" *manidos* who rule the *four quarters* of the universe through an indefinite number of minor agencies. The old Ottawa Indian, Jim Nanibush, named them thus: the ruler of the *east, Wabenokkwe,* "wabeno woman" or the moon, sister of the sun over whom she has charge; the ruler of the *south, Shauwanigizik,* "southern sky"; the ruler of the *west, Nanibush,* and the ruler of the *north, Giyuedin,* "wind blows home" (because the winds have their home in the *north). . . .*

Yet not all the Indians subscribe to this doctrine of "deputy" *manidos* at the *four cardinal points,* coequal, and all drawing their power directly from the Great Spirit. Some hold that there are innumerable *manidos* independent of one another, though endowed by the Great Spirit with varying powers . . . they may admit the existence of "deputy" *manidos,* but attach to the notion little or no significance. If the doctrine developed in the first place merely as a generalization from certain rituals, as seems quite probable, it would naturally have little interest except for the few speculative individuals who look beyond those rituals. At all events, the ordinary Indian who blows smoke to the *four quarters* and asks for help does not address his prayer to any specific "deputy" *manidos* in those quarters, but to the general hosts of *manidos,* without considering their number or their powers.

> *The Ojibwa Indians of Parry Island: Their Social and Religious Life,*
> Diamond Jenness, 1935, pp. 30-32

Here is a band of Canadian Ojibwas from the Georgian Bay area who were interviewed about 1929. The four directions figure into their understanding of things, but there are some differences in perception of both the number and strength of the manidos.

———————————— + ————————————

FOUR DIRECTIONAL INCORPOREAL BEINGS
OJIBWAY

Kitche Manitou created *four* incorporeal beings: *Zhawano (South), Keewatin (North), Waubun (Morning or East),* and *Ningo-bianong (Evening or West).* He assigned each one to a quarter of the world and to a portion of time. To each he gave a power over life to be exercised with wisdom. Legend relates that these beings lived in harmony.

With the coming of plant and animal beings and the Anishnabeg, the guardian beings tested one another in battle.

> *Ojibway Heritage,* Basil Johnston, 1990, pp. 27-28

The Creator, Kitche Manitou, is uniquely manifested through the four directions. Perhaps the latter-day testing accounts for the struggle between good and evil that we experience daily.

———————————— + ————————————

PIPE CEREMONY
OJIBWAY

From the fire, the Oshkaubaewis (Keeper of the Pipe), would light the sacred pipe. An elder of the Midewewin would then take the pipe from the keeper, and hold it reverently as he made an invocation.

"Great Mystery! Look upon our thoughts and upon our ritual. We ask you to look with favour upon our ceremony and upon our deeds. We need your guidance and your favour so that we may do what is good."

"Mother Earth! We honour you as we honour our mothers. We thank you for all the benefits that you have bestowed upon us. You have given us plants for food and medicine. You have given us beauty to behold. You are the first of mothers. You are mother to all mankind."

And, on behalf of the Anishnabeg, the elder would make his petitions.

PETITION TO THE NORTH

To you, muses, who dwell and abide to the *north*: this day we ask you to grant us good dreams. Come this night and every night. Come into our homes and into our minds and fill us with the yearning for good. Show us the good that we may follow and observe it.

Banish evil dreams from our sleep and from our lives. Let neither deceit nor remorse, neither selfishness nor ill will towards our brothers, disturb our sleep.

Guard us at night when we are helpless. Come like the *north* winds; dispel the evil. Watch over us, blanket our spirits as the snow covers the earth. And do not abandon us until we are awake and restored.

PETITION TO THE WEST

To you, muses, who dwell and abide to the *west*: bestow upon us goodwill. Show us the path so that we do not stumble or stray. Inspire us with goodwill so that we may achieve. Teach us to seek after kindness, courage, cheerfulness, wisdom, patience, and fairness. And give us the wisdom to know right from wrong.

Let me not think ill of my brothers or my sisters. Let me not doubt our forefather' teachings, or despise the animals of the forest, or forget the poor, or scorn our ceremonies, or envy my brothers and sisters, or distrust my vision, or cower when in danger.

Let us seek goodwill. Help us honour the Great Mystery, our forefathers, our parents, and our dead. Inspire us when we are in doubt and in sorrow; lend us strength when we are in danger and when we falter. Temper our anger and envy. Endow us with forbearance. And guide us in abiding by our visions.

PETITION TO THE SOUTH

We were given speech by the Great Spirit to foster goodwill among ourselves, and to commune with the spirits. It has both a practical and a spiritual end. It is a sacred act.

But we have too often given hurt by angry words, or misled our brothers and sisters by hasty words. When giving council, we have offered the benefit of our experience and knowledge either too soon or too late to do good. By habit, we either talk too much or too little. And we have often paid heed to untruths about our neighbors, and then carried them abroad.

If we utter words as if they are nothing more than sound, our thoughts will be regarded as shallow and worthless . . . and so will we. And if we are careless of the truth we must, in the end, lose the trust of our brothers and sisters.

In order to inspire trust we must attend to our elders, who have urged us to listen and to talk—but to be as gentle in our speech as the balm of the *south* wind.

PETITION TO THE EAST

When we wake at dawn we are refreshed and ready to direct our hands and our feet to our labour. But we also remember that among us are brothers and sisters who cannot look forward to the new day with the same spirit as ourselves. With us dwell a blind man, a lame woman, several orphans, a widow, a mute, and a woman seeking dream.

Our patron! With our hearts, our arrows, and our medicines, we will make the day as light as we can for our brothers and sisters. We will lead the blind man, we will bear the lame woman, we will shelter the orphans, we will comfort the widow, we will speak for the mute, and we will guide the woman seeking dream.

Make game abundant, corn plentiful, and medicines strong for them and for us.

Ojibway Ceremonies, Basil Johnston, 1990, pp. 109-111

This prayer, part of a pipe ceremony, and perhaps interpreted in dominant society language, nevertheless reveals the Ojibway way of relating to the four directions.

A young Onondaga prays to the four directions

SOUTHEAST CULTURAL AREA

Praying in the direction of the setting sun during springtime

PIPE CEREMONY
NATCHEZ

Albert Pickett, quoting Charlevoix, who was among the Natchez at approximately the same time, writes of the grand chief at sunrise:

> A pipe, which was never used but upon this occasion, was then handed to him, from which he puffed smoke, *first toward the sun* and then toward the other *three quarters* of the world.
>
> *Offering Smoke: The Sacred Pipe and Native American Religion*,
> Jordan Paper, 1988, p. 21

The ubiquitous pipe ceremony is here mentioned by some early nineteenth century travellers among the Southeastern Peoples. The four directions are obviously regarded in this sunrise ceremony .

———————————— + ————————————

PIPE CEREMONY
CREEK

William Bartram described a Creek council meeting of 1789. During the meeting he observed the pipe lit by the miko [chief], who then blew smoke first towards the *east* and then towards the *other three cardinal directions*; the pipe was then passed to the principal leaders and warriors and back to the *miko,* while all the others were taking black drink and smoking tobacco.

Offering Smoke: The Sacred Pipe and Native American Religion,
Jordan Paper, 1988, p. 21

The pipe was prayed with in the four directions. After this ceremony the black drink emetic would have been taken with ceremonial movements of a four-fold pattern. All would then have been both prepared and purified for the ensuing deliberations.

—————————— + ——————————

HERB GATHERING RITUAL
CHEROKEE

. . . when hunting ginseng, the herbalist addressed the mountain on which he stood as the "Great Man," assuring him that he was only going to take a small piece of his flesh. He then pulled up the plant, root and all, and dropped a red or white bead, whichever was appropriate, into the hole. Then he covered it up. He collected bark from the *east* side of the tree, and roots and branches were likewise taken from the *eastern* side, the reason being that they had absorbed the greatest potency from the rays of the sun.

The Southeastern Indians, Charles Hudson, 1976, p. 342

For many People the eastern side of things is very important because it indicates a powerful beginning energy that is related to the rising of the sun, an important source of power or "medicine."

—————————— + ——————————

FOUR DIRECTIONAL COLOR SYMBOLISM
CHEROKEE

The red spirits invoked always lived in the *east,* and everything pertaining to them was the same color.

Black was always typical of death . . . and . . . the soul of the enemy is continually beaten about by black war clubs and enveloped in a black fog. In conjuring to destroy an enemy, the priest used black beads and invoked the black spirits which always lived in the *west*—bidding them to tear out the man's soul, carry it to the *west,* and put it into the black coffin deep in the black mud, with a black serpent coiled above it.

Blue was emblematic of failure, disappointment, or unsatisfied desire. To say "They shall never become blue" expressed the belief that they would never fail in anything they undertook. In love charms, the lover figuratively covered himself with red and prayed that his rival would become entirely blue and walk in a blue path. The formulistic expression, "He is entirely blue," approximates the meaning of the common English phrase, "He feels blue." The blue spirits lived in the *north*.

White denoted peace and happiness. In ceremonial addresses, as at the Green Corn Dance and ball play, the people symbolically partook of white food and, after the dance or the game, returned along the white trail to their white houses. In love charms, the man, to induce the woman to cast her lot with his, boasted, "I am a white man," implying that all was happiness where he was. White beads had the same meaning in bead conjuring, and was the color of the stone pipe anciently used in ratifying peace treaties. The white spirits lived in the *south*.

So then, in setting forth the colors of the cardinal directions, red was *east,* black was *west,* blue was *north* and white was *south*.

The Cherokee People: The Story of the Cherokees from Earliest Origins to Contemporary Times, Thomas Mails, 1992, p. 101

Color symbolism is a helpful way of describing spiritual realities. It also guided the People in their ceremonial activities, much the same way that the liturgical colors help many Christians to celebrate the holy mysteries of the church year.

———————————— + ————————————

ORIGIN OF THE FOUR DIRECTIONS
CHEROKEE

Older Cherokees said the Creator—supposed in this case to mean a *Ye ho waah* who supervised the affairs of the universe and whose abode was the center of the sky immediately overhead—in the beginning directed certain lines from a center place to points upon the earth that white men called *"north, south, east,* and *west."* To each of these points the Creator sent newly created beings of different colors: in the *north* was placed the blue man; in the *west,* the area called, "the region of the setting sun," the black man was placed and named *Ewe kah waisk hee,* "the fearless"; to the *south* was sent the white man, the man of purity and peace; but the first and most important of all was the red man, and he was placed in the *east* and signified the sun.

These four lines, or directions, were in their spirit form existing on high as the vice-regents, or agents, of the Supreme Beings and the mediators between them and creation, of which the sun, or "red man," was the first created. To these four beings power was given over the world. To each of them, Cherokee supplications were to be addressed in a regular succession. Whatever was addressed to the black man would forthwith be attended to, and for all that related to goodness, the white man was to be invoked. But over the four directions the Creator reigned supreme, enthroned above in the center of the place where those four lines met. His eye at once beheld them and mankind. He knew everything that anyone in this world could do or think, and he knew what was best for each created thing. To him, after first invoking in order the men of the *east,* the *north,* the *west,* and the *south,* must be offered the final and most fervent of mankind's prayers.

> *The Cherokee People: The Story of the Cherokees from Earliest Origins to Contemporary Times*, Thomas Mails, 1992, pp. 157-158

The four cardinal directions have their origin in the Creator, according to the Cherokees. They are cared for by various "men" who mediated the powers that have their origin in God.

+

EMETIC MEDICINE
CHEROKEE

The emetic medicine can be taken shortly after noon or anytime during the afternoon. Members fast before receiving it, and a meal follows its

Ancient composite design of woodpeckers and wind at the center

taking. Usually, four lines are formed to the *west* of the pot—two of men and two of women. The medicine pot itself is positioned just *north* of the fire and *west* of the cooking area. A medicine man dips out the liquid with cans. Some members only drink it, while others drink part of it and use the rest to bathe their hands, face, and chests. Some people fill small vials with it and take these home for private use later on. It is a rule that a person always faces *east* while he drinks the medicine.

Willie Jumper, who formerly was the head medicine man at Sugar Mountain . . . gave us a list of the ingredients used in the medicine along with some instructions for the proper preparation and use of it.

They use a small, red root of Cherokee huckleberry, which some call snakeroot, which is not the real huckleberry the white know of, and add flint weed—a wood medicine that is a red willow wood. This red medicine is the basis for any of the medicines that the medicine men use—most will have red root in them. Also used are pine and cedar leaves. The root, weed, and leaves are placed in a pot of water and boiled. The brew is set aside to cool, and the medicine men start working on it. They blow on it through a cane tube, then insert the tube into the liquid and make bubbles. When they have done this four times, it is ready to drink—which means it is pure medicine. Only one piece of cane is used. The medicine men share it.

When you drink the medicine, it makes you throw up and cleans out your insides. It purifies you, and a teaspoonful assures good health. You must drink it while it is warm. If you drink more than a teaspoon you will throw up after two or three minutes. If you are not in good health, the medicine will lie on your stomach and bother you. If you are in good health it won't bother you. And if you can stand a full drink without throwing up you know that your health is very good.

The Cherokee People: The Story of the Cherokees from Earliest Origins to Contemporary Times, Thomas Mails, 1992, p. 314

The Peoples of the southeast used emetics to prepare themselves for ceremonies. It was a way of purifying themselves "from the inside out." Directional orientation and standing in four lines define the correct ritual posture, while four times bubbling the liquid assures that it is properly prepared.

——————————— + ———————————

FOUR DIRECTIONS SONG
ALABAMA-COUSHATTA

In most performances or ceremonies, participants will dedicate the area in which the dancing and singing will take place before any performances begin, usually starting with the acknowledgement of the *four directions*. This song does not accompany a dance, *per se,* but is a typical way to create the appropriately respectful attitude that is considered the foundations for a gathering or event.

DANCE INSTRUCTIONS

This song to the *Four Directions* is a musical offering honoring the *four directions: East*—in which the sun rises; *South*—from which the light comes; *West*—where the sun sets; and *North*—from which the cold comes. (Tribes also associate specific times of life, colors, types of power or healing as coming from each direction; however each tribe does not necessarily duplicate the interpretation of the others.) The song is sung very freely with the dotted-eighth/ sixteenth rhythm being quite ambivalent (as in jazz) and a gliding "portamento" between notes on the syllable "yo." During the last section of the song, the singer faces each direction with the right hand

lifted, palm upwards, as if in suppli- cation. The direction is changed dur- ing the rest following each fermata.

Moving Within the Circle: Contemporary Native American Music and Dance, Bryan Burton, 1993, pp. 48-49

This blessing prayer ensures that the area for performance and ceremony is sacralized for the duration of the events.

EARTH MOTHER EARTH NAVEL MIDDLE PLACE
TEWA

Among the Tewa the "earth mother earth navel middle place" was the sacred center of the village and was thought to be the center of centers or navel of navels around which there were, in the *four cardinal directions,* associated colors, mountains, springs, and so on.

Santiago's Sword: Chatino Peasant Religion and Economics,
James Greenberg, 1981, p. 32

In earlier times it was perhaps not so difficult to be a bit "ethnocentric" due to difficulties in communications and modes of travel. But there always existed recognition of the value of other Peoples in the near and distant surrounding parts of the cosmos.

———————————— + ————————————

DIRECTIONAL PRAYER POEM
ACOMA

now that i have lighted my smoke
i am motioning to the *east*
i am walking in thought that direction
i am listening for your voices
i am occurring in my mind this instance that i am here
now that i have breathed inwards
i am seeing the mountains *east*

i am travelling to that place of birth
i am aware of your voices
i am thinking of your relationship with me
   this time in the morning that we are together
now that i have breathed outwards
i am letting you take my breath
i am moving for your sake
i am hearing the voices of your children
i am not myself but yourself now
   at this time your spirit has captured mine
now that i am taking breath in again
i have arrived back from that place of birth
i have travelled fast and surely
i have heard what you wanted me to hear
i have become whole and strong with yourself

 this morning i am living with your breath.

"Smoking My Prayers," Simon Ortiz, *Literature of the American Indian*,
Thomas Sanders (Ed.), 1976, p. 242
Originally published in *South Dakota Review*

Time and place and the beginning and renewal of life is celebrated in this poem of Simon Ortiz called "Smoking My Prayers." Tobacco smoke and the experienced beauties of God's awakening creation are celebrated with an acknowledgement of a particular direction, the East.

———————————— + ————————————

DIRECTIONAL POEM
SAN JUAN PUEBLO

Kachina
dolls

I was directed by my grandfather
To the *East,*
   so I might have the power of the bear;
To the *South,*
   so I might have the courage of the eagle;
To the *West,*
   so I might have the wisdom of the owl;
To the *North,*
   so I might have the craftiness of the fox;

To the Earth,
   so I might receive her fruit;
To the Sky,
   so I might lead a life of innocence.

"Direction," Alonzo Lopez, *Literature of the American Indian*,
Thomas Sanders (Ed.), 1976, p. 235
Originally published in *South Dakota Review*

*This short contemporary poem by Alonzo Lopez called "Direction"
condenses a rich heritage of belief and spirituality. Plants and animals
are the outward signs of the holiness that is desired.*

––––––––––––––––– + –––––––––––––––––

TRIBAL DIRECTIONAL COMPONENTS
ZUNI

When Coronado discoverd Zuni, there were seven towns, "the
Seven Cities of Cibola." Today, there is one town, with seven "wards"
which are the geographically separated towns of old ... there were
nineteen clans. Each of these clans belonged to one of the seven
divisions (towns, wards), and each of the divisions mytho-symboli-
cally represented one of the seven directions: **north, south, east,
west,** the upper world, the underworld, and the midmost. The
midmost, thus verbalized as a direction, actually was a center, a
synthesis of the other six directions; it pervaded all the others, was
their union, their "spirit of the whole."

In order to build up the significance of the above, some paragraphs
of Cushing's must be quoted:

By this arrangement of the world [and of Zuni society] into great quarters,
or rather, as the Zunis conceive it, into several worlds corresponding to the
four quarters and the zenith and the nadir, and by this grouping of the
towns, or later the wards (so to call them) in the town, according to such
mythical division of the world, and finally the grouping of the (clan) totems
in turn within the divisions thus made, not only the ceremonial life of the
people, but all their governmental arrangements as well, are completely
systematized. Something akin to written statutes results from this and
similar related arrangements, for each region is given its appropriate color
and number, according to its relation to one of the regions I have named or
to others of those regions. Thus the **north** is designated as yellow by the

Zunis, because the light at morning and evening in winter time is yellow, as also is the auroral light. The *west* is known as the blue world, not only because of the blue or gray twilight at evening, but also because westward from Zuniland lies the blue Pacific. The *south* is designated as red, it being the region of summer and of fire, which is red; while for an obvious reason the *east* is designated white (like the dawn light); while the upper region is many-colored, like the sunlight on the clouds, and the lower region black, like the caves and deep springs of the world. Finally, the midmost . . . is colored all of these colors, because, being representative of this (which is the central world and of which Zuni in turn is the very middle or navel), it contains all the other quarters or regions, or it is at least divisible into them. . . .

No ceremonial is ever performed and no council ever held in which there is the least doubt as to the position which a member of a given clan shall occupy in it, for according to the season in which the ceremonial is held, or according to the reason for which a council is convened, one or another of the clan groups of one or another of the regions will take precedence for the time; the natural sequence being, however, first the *north,* second the *west,* third the *south,* fourth the *east,* fifth the upper and sixth the lower; but first, as well as last, the middle (midmost). . . .

American Indian Ceremonial Dances, John Collier, 1972, pp. 175, 177

What a beautiful way to understand oneself and one's People! Each section of the tribe lives out the gifts and responsibilities of the four directions as well as the zenith and nadir. Color and season are experienced in all the tribal activities. The dominant cultures of North America, indeed, many cultures, have a lot to learn from this kind of understanding.

———————————— + ————————————

ALTAR SYMBOLISMS
HOPI

The Two Horn Society's symbol of two horns designates knowl-edge of, and remembered experiences in, the three previous worlds as well as in this present Fourth World. Their Six Directions altar represents the First World at the time of Creation, with colored sands spread for the four primary directions: yellow for the *West,* blue for the *South,* red for the *East,* and white for the *North.* An ear of dark mixed corn is laid for the Above, and an ear of sweet corn for the Below. The wooden backdrop of the altar is painted with the corresponding colors of the successive four worlds, and there are symbols of the primary elements: fire, earth, water, and air represented by eagle down.

The Book of the Hopi, Frank Waters, 1963, p. 170

No People really wants to forget what God has done for them. The Hopi altar "brings it all together" in sign and memory. It is a participation in the unity of past and present through signs and symbols that are well understood by the People.

——————————————— + ———————————————

SONG OF THE DAWN
NAVAJO

I am walking among them, I am walking among them;

Towards the place under the *East,* I am walking among them;
The dawn people surround me, I am walking;
The white corn surrounds me, I am walking;
Sahanahray Bekay Hozhon surrounds me, I am walking
I, I am Sahanahray Bekay Hozhon, I am walking;
Before me, it is beautiful, I am walking;
Behind me, it is beautiful, I am walking;

I am walking among them, I am walking among them;

Towards the place under the *South,* I am walking among them;
The sun people surround me, I am walking;
The blue corn surrounds me, I am walking;
Sahanahray Bekay Hozhon surrounds me, I am walking;
I, I am Sahanahray Bekay Hozhon, I am walking;
Behind me, it is beautiful, I am walking;
Before me, it is beautiful, I am walking;

I am walking among them, I am walking among them.

Towards the place under the *West,* I am walking among them;
The people of the yellow afterglow surround me, I am walking;

The yellow corn surrounds me, I am walking;
Sahanahray Bekay Hozhon surrounds me, I am walking;
I, I am Sahanahray Bekay Hozhon, I am walking;
Before me, it is beautiful, I am walking;
Behind me, it is beautiful, I am walking;

I am walking among them, I am walking among them;

Towards the place under the *North*, I am walking among them;
The people of the *North* surround me, I am walking;
All sorts of corn surrounds me, I am walking;
Sahanahray Bekay Hozhon surrounds me, I am walking;
I, I am Sahanahray Bekay Hozhon, I am walking;
Behind me, it is beautiful, I am walking;
Before me, it is beautiful, I am walking;

I am walking among them, I am walking among them.

"Last Song of the Dawn," *Texts of the Navajo Creation Chants*
(sound recording), Mary Wheelwright (Transl.), 1950, p. 27

*In this "Last Song of the Dawn" we are able to notice the movement
towards each direction: east, south, west, north. It is as if a kaleido-
scope of beauty is before us. And the movement takes into account the
progression of the sun as well as the varieties of life-giving corn that
grow in great abundance. It is truly a song of praise that also teaches.*

---------------------------------- + ----------------------------------

HOGAN SYMBOLISM
NAVAJO

The Blessingway, the Navajo tale of creation, relates how a deity
named Talking God made a home for First Man and First Woman.
Taking as his model a promontory in New Mexico that the Navajo
called the "Heart of the Earth" (known today as Gobernador Knob),
Talking God built a rounded peak, supported by poles made of white
shell, turquoise, abalone, and obsidian. Covered with sunbeams and
rainbows, this was the first hogan, or "home place" in the Navajo
language.

The earthly incarnations of this mythical shelter include a number of circular, single-roomed structures made of different materials and built in accordance with a variety of plans. The forked-pole hogan however, is believed to be the oldest and truest to the fabled form. Its entryway faces *east,* toward the blessing rays of the rising sun. Three forked, interlocking support poles, which have been planted to the *north, west,* and *south,* provide the basic framework of the building. In a symbolic link to the first hogan, small chips of shell, turquoise, and abalone are frequently placed underneath the posts. The frame is filled in with shorter timbers, chinked with narrow strips of wood and bark, and then coated with either mud or earth.

Tradition divides the small interior . . . —rarely more than 12 feet in diameter—into male and female sectors, with men keeping their belongings on the *south* side, and women confining such items as dishes and food to the *north* side. Movement within the hogan is ritually prescribed: People must make their way around the ceremonial hearth in a sunwise, or clockwise, direction, mimicking the course of the sun as it arcs from *east* to *west* across the southern sky.

American Indiants: The Spirit World,
Henry Woodhead (Ed.), 1992, p. 161

Perhaps it is not so unusual to "canonize" a particular tribal lifeway or custom. When People have felt connected to both cosmos and Creator for eons, it is understandable that they would want to live out the pattern of existence given by the Creator. In following closely a way of life given from above, every detail is important, even the building of a home that was designed in heaven.

———————————— + ————————————

BUILDING A HOME
NAVAJO

The shape of the hooghan is important and can be traced in the actual construction procedures. . . . The first step in building is to make a shallow roundish dug-out in the ground representing Mother Earth lying on her back, slightly curved. (Her head is pointing to the *east,* her feet are in the *west.*) In the center of the dug-out a small wooden box is constructed in which four wooden poles, pointing to the four cardinal directions, are placed. In Navajo mythology the four original Navajo clans started out from the center of the earth and moved towards each cardinal direction. The poles symbolically stand for these initial clans:

east = Its Leaf Clan
south = Bitter Water Clan
west = Close to Water Clan
north = Mud Clan

In the practice of building the hooghan, these poles serve as a sort of compass. The one pointing to the *north* should be made of a tree withered by lightning. After finishing the walls of the hooghan, they are removed.

Once the four cardinal directions are identified, upstanding poles are introduced into the soil. Sometimes they are eight in number, sometimes twelve. For technical reasons the building of a large and/or a round hooghan requires many upstanding poles. In my opinion, the marked preference for more or less roundish structures goes back to the belief that sharp-angled spaces or objects and even pointing actions are too direct and thus hinder the free movement of the roaming forces. (For example, arrowheads and plants with thorns are considered to offer protection against the negative use of forces, such as witchcraft. They stop these forces in their tracks, so to speak.)

Between these upstanding logs, planks are attached horizontally. The eventual gaps between them are filled up with clay. Only one opening is left in this wall. It is situated on the *east side* of the hooghan. When the hooghan is used, be it as a homestead or for ceremonial purposes, this doorway should be closed off only with a piece of cloth, in order to allow for the necessary communication with the forces of the outside world. (When the hooghan is used as a living place this rule is not followed, as the winters on the reservation are hard and in springtime there are many sandstorms.) On top of the upstanding logs a whirling roof made of wood is constructed with a smoke-hole in the centre. This wooden construction is covered with clay on the outside. The roof represents Father Sky, who lies on top of Mother Earth. The smoke hole represents the opening in the sky which permits the future access to a new world. I suppose it is acceptable to state that the smoke hole represents the zenith of the Navajo-world. The fire-place which is built perpendicularly to it represents the nadir.

"Navajo Hooghan and Navajo Cosmos," *The Canadian Journal of Native Studies*, Ingrid Van Dooren, 1987, pp. 262-263

To build a house in any culture is a large enterprise. Nowadays most people are concerned with the finances and location of their home. But here we have a different priority: to situate a family dwelling on a particular part of Mother Earth while giving honor to the four directions.

———————————— + ————————————

DIRECTIONAL PRAYER ACTION
APACHE

Geronimo was born sometime around 1823, near where the Middle Fork of the Gila joins the West Fork, not far from the Gila cliff dwellings in Southwestern New Mexico. As an infant, he bathed in the hot springs that made the Middle Fork such an appealing campsite for the Bedonkohe, just as it had been for the Mogollon who had built the cliff dwellings six centuries before them. The towering canyon walls, of ruddy andesite and conglomerate, sheltered Geronimo's people; huge sycamores and cottonwoods stood along side the stream whose thread ran clear and sweet through the year.

Like all Apaches, Geronimo attached a special significance to his birthplace: whenever in his wanderings he came again to the Middle Fork, he would roll on the ground to the *four directions.*

Once They Moved Like the Wind: Cochise, Geronimo, and the Apache Wars, David Roberts, 1994, pp. 104-105

Geronimo never forgot his tribal ways even as he honored the beginning of his earthly life. He seeks a blessing from the Creator as he signs forth the four-directions meaning with his own body.

———————— + ————————

Navajo woven four directions cross

BLESSING PRAYER
APACHE

Big Blue Mountain God,
You of the blue clouds
There! Standing before me
With life!
Great Blue Mountain God.

Big Yellow Mountain God in the *south*,
You of the yellow clouds
Holy Mountain God
Standing toward me with life.

Big Mountain God in the *west*
You of the white brightness
Holy Mountain God
I am happy over your words,
You are happy over my words.

Big Black Mountain God in the *north*
You of the black clouds
The way of the *North,* Big Black Mountain God
Holy Mountain God
I am happy over your words,
You are happy over my words.
Now it is good!

Chiricahua and Mescalero Apache Texts,
Harry Hoijer, 1938, p. 203

This Apache song celebrates the directions and the person's responsibility for each direction. Life is being offered and celebrated. Happiness is the mood that is both experienced and prayed for. A good God blesses the People.

———————— + ————————

Apache Gan dancer

ORIGINAL FEUD
YUMA

Long ago there was a time when Earth was a woman and Sky was a man. One day a drop of water fell from Sky and landed on Woman and she conceived twins. They came to being by emerging through a volcano.

At this time Earth and Sky were close together and the twins' first task was to raise the heavens and set the *cardinal points*. They next established the land and water and created all the inhabitants. One brother taught the newly created men all the good things, and the other brother taught the humans jealousy and war which brought about the division of mankind. This also brought on a feud between the two brothers, and the evil one in his rage caused a rain which lasted for many days. It eventually covered the earth with water and destroyed the world.

The good brother gathered up his people when the flood came and carried them in his arms until the water receded. They were then placed back on earth and became the grandparents of all humans.

Where Is the Eagle?, William Coffer, 1981, pp. 90-91

Because the cardinal directions are so important in a variety of ways for the People, it is not surprising for the tribes to speak of them at the outset of creation.

Carved eagle katchinas

SOUTHWEST/MESOAMERICA CULTURAL AREA

Temple Pyramid of the Sun at Teotihuacán near Mexico City, Mexico

PASCOLA DANCING
YAQUI

Pascola dancers are found among many Indian groups in northern Mexico and in Arizona. The Yaqui, Mayo, Tarahumara, Warihio, Pima Bajo, Seri and Papago Indians have pascola dancers, though some groups do not use masks. It is not known how long Yaqui Indians have had masked dancers. But by the early 1600s, when Jesuit missionaries entered the Yaqui River Valley of Sonora, Mexico, they observed this masked ritual clown, known today as a pascola. . . .

The 400 mile distance between the Tucson Basin and the Yaqui River Valley has not had much effect on the ceremonial life of the Yaqui Indians. There is very little difference, if any at all, between traditional pascola masks made in Sonora and those made in Tucson today or, for that matter, fifty years ago. . . .

Probably more than any other fiesta participant, the pascola brings Yaqui art and culture together in a beautiful and exciting way. This masked and costumed figure plays a prominent role in all Yaqui fiestas and ceremonies including Lent, Easter, saint days, weddings and death anniversaries. The pascola is always a male and his role is carried out by dancing, clowning and storytelling. Even though he is often the center of attention at a ceremony, his role is purely secular. While the pascolas dance for Jesus and the saints, they are not part of a church group.

A fiesta is not possible unless at least one pascola and his accompanying musicians are available to open and close the fiesta. In fact, a fiesta does not begin until the pascolas are led into the dance ramada by their moro (manager) and the oldest pascola gives a speech reminding the Yaquis of their heritage.

The pascolas do most of their dancing and performing away from the church, in a dance ramada that measures roughly twenty by twenty feet, has a dirt floor and is made of assorted building materials. The pascolas and deer dancer, if one is participating, and their accompanying musicians and managers use one-half of the ramada. The other half is reserved for the women's altar group, a church group, to prepare an altar and sing and pray throughout the fiesta.

The pascolas usually begin their participation in the fiesta shortly after sunset by taking turns dancing to the music of the harpists and violinist, who sit on a bench in the far end of the ramada. Before dancing, each pascola makes the sign of the cross with his feet in the dirt floor in the *four directions*.

"Yaqui Pascola Masks from the Tucson Area," Thomas Kolaz, *American Indian Art Magazine*, Winter 1985, p. 31

Here is an example of the putting together of two spiritualities: Christianity (the sign of the cross) and Indigenous America (the four directions). The present day Yaquis see them as complementary.

Grupo Ixcalli, Aztec dancers from Salinas, California

Two Esselen brothers pray with sage burning in abalone shells

CALIFORNIA CULTURAL AREA

CREATION OF EARTH AND MOON
LUISEÑO

In the beginning, everything was empty; Empty Quietness was the only being. Then came a whitish greyness and, from this, two whitish objects which were eggs. They lay there three days and then were made alive and recognized each other. From them came two beings which were Father Sky and Mother Earth. They conversed with each other in a very strange language which no one on earth could understand today.

"I am stretched," said Mother Earth. "I am extended. I shake, I resound, and I am earthquake."

Father Sky answered, "I am night. I am the arch of the heavens. I rise, I kill, I sever life."

These two married in the darkness and gave birth to children, who came in pairs. These were all sacred things used in ceremonies. Even the food which the people eat and the tools they use were born in this way and were once people. For instance, the sacred mortar in which the Jimsonweed root was ground for the boys' ceremony was the oldest child of all. Other children were the strings of shell money and the dancing stick with the crystal at the end; also the eagle and the bear, the palm tree, the cottonwood, and the acorns. The sun came forth at the same time and because he was so hot, his brothers and sisters sent him into the sky.

When all things had been born, the Earth Mother lay quiet with her feet to the **north** and her head to the **south** as she is today. The people wandered all over the earth and settled. One of them was a great hero called Wiyot who was wise and taught the people their games and art. Wiyot had a daughter, the frog, who became very angry with him. She was a woman and she knew magic, so she made him ill. Wiyot was ill for a long time and the people, one by one, tried to help him. During this time he sang death songs which are now sung at the mourning anniversary. As each month came, he described it and sang, "Shall I die this month?" The people carried him all over the country trying to make him better, but at last he died and became the moon. The people burned his body just as they have burned their dead ever since.

The people always hold a ceremony for the new moon. It is a form of greeting Wiyot and is thought to keep him strong and give them all health and good fortune.

Where Is the Eagle?, William Coffer, 1981, pp. 227-228

This People from the Mission San Luis Rey area of southern California anthropomorphized the earth and sky as they made sense of cosmic phenomena, the "stuff" of our existense. Mother Earth is understood as stretching from north to south. This posture is complemented by the east-west activity of the sun.

———————————— ✛ ————————————

NEAR DEATH PRAYER
LUISEÑO

At the time of death,
When I found there was to be death,
I was very much surprised.
All was failing.
My home,
I was sad to leave it.

I have been looking far,
Sending my spirit *north, south, east,* and *west,*
Trying to escape from death,

*Stone grinding bowls for acorns
in Esselen tribal territory,
Carmel Valley, California*

But could find nothing,
No way of escape.

"The Religion of the Luiseño Indians of Southern California,"
*University of California Publications in American Archaeology and
Ethnology*, Constance Goddard DuBois, 1908, p. 110

*This prayer, "Song of the Spirit" by José Albaños, captures the man's
desire to remain on earth (illustrated by the mention of the directions)
even through the inevitability of death is close.*

———————————— + ————————————

DEATH SONG
CUPEÑO

From the *east* they cried
From the *east* they cried
From the *east* they cried
They suffered, their faces
Having painted, their faces
Having painted, they cried from the *east*.

From the *southeast* they cried
From the *southeast* they cried
From the *southeast* they cried
They suffered, their faces
Having painted, their faces
Having painted, they cried from the *southeast*.

To the *south* they cried
To the *south* they cried
To the *south* they cried
They suffered, their faces
Having painted, their faces
Having painted, they cried to the *south*.

From the *southwest*, they cried
From the *southwest*, they cried

*One of the many ancient oak trees that once
were so prevalent and a source of the
People's food*

From the *southwest,* they cried
They suffered, their faces
Having painted, their faces
Having painted, they cried from the *southwest.*

From the *west,* they cried
From the *west,* they cried
From the *west,* they cried
They suffered, their faces
Having painted, their faces
Having painted, they cried from the *west.*

From the *northwest,* they cried
From the *northwest,* they cried
From the *northwest,* they cried
They suffered, their faces
Having painted, their faces
Having painted, they cried from the *northwest.*

To the *north,* they cried
To the *north,* they cried
To the *north,* they cried
They suffered, their faces
Having painted, their faces
Having painted, they cried to the *north.*

> *Mulu-Wetam: The First People; Cupeño Oral History and Language,*
> Jane Hill & Rosinda Nolasquez, 1973, p. 81a

This "Death Song VI" is most expressive of both the cardinal and inter-cardinal directions and was very personal to the singer. It was a special way of preparing for the inevitable.

---- + ----

DIRECTIONAL COLOR SYMBOLISM
DIEGUEÑO

The Diegueño are the only tribe in California as yet known to possess a system of color-direction symbolism. This is: *East,* white;

South, green-blue; *West,* black; *North,* red. It is interesting that there is little if any idea of a circuit of the directions as fixed sequence of the colors, as in the Southwest. The Diegueño thinks of two pairs of directions, each with its balance of colors, white-black or red-blue. . . .

Handbook of Indians of California, Alfred Louis Kroeber, 1977, p. 717

Here is another way of regarding the four directions: opposite directions complement each other and so do their colors.

———————————— + ————————————

SHAMANIC DISPLAY OF POWER
GABRIELEÑO

Shamans deliberately cultivated a public image of superiority and power to inspire respect and obedience, and this enabled them to serve as important instruments of social control. Not only could the shaman's power be used to ward off enemies, but it could also enforce adherence to the laws and precepts of *Chengiichngech.* To this end shamans engaged in elaborate shows of magical power and extravagant displays of ritual paraphernalia.

José de los Santos Juncos told another story about the shaman Ramon Valencia in which the hechicero hosted a fiesta that was attended by many guests including Ventureño and Cahuilla Indians. This fiesta may have taken place during the mid-1800s as the Cahuilla chief Juan Antonio is mentioned as being in attendance; Juan Antonio first became a leader of the Cahuilla during the early 1840s. During the fiesta, Valencia was buried alive and then rose from his grave. After Valencia was buried

an old Indian stayed outside & had a fire [at the] side of the pit. . . . The old man waved [a] fire brand in *4 directions* and as he did so he gave the cry— this same kind of cry with falling scale & slapping hand over mouth. . . . At this first cry [the] earth trembled some. At [the] second waving & cry it trembled more. At [the] third waving & cry it rocked & [the] people asked one another if they had ever seen anything like that. At [the] second cry V. had started to rise from [the] earth—at [the] 3rd he came out.

The First Angelinos: The Gabrielino Indians of Los Angeles,
William McCawley, 1996, pp. 99-100

Perhaps this particular ceremony had an extra meaning for the Native People connected with the California Mission of Saint Gabriel, as they would have also been familiar with the teaching of the resurrection of Jesus Christ. Whether influenced by Christianity or not, it must have been a spectacular ceremony to witness. Chengiichngech is the Gabrieleño name for Creator.

---------------- + ----------------

FOUR DIRECTIONS ORIGINS
MOJAVE

First direction names taught—

He said again: "Now we are here in this house: all will know and hear it. Now when I mean here," and he pointed his hand to the ***north***, "all say: *'Amai-hayame'.*" But they did not do so: they kept their hands against their bodies; they wanted another name; they did not like that word. Then he said: "And there is *Amai-hakyeme;* all say that!" And he pointed ***south***. But again all sat still: they did not want to call it that. He said again: "Well, there is another: there is the way the night goes. I do not know where its end is, but when we follow the darkness that is called *Amai-hayime.*" He said that, but none of the Mohave said a word: they sat with their hands against the body. Then Mastamho said once more: "You see the dark coming. I do not know where it comes from: I did not make it. But where darkness comes from, I call that *Amai-hayike.*" Again they sat still and did not point.

Final direction names taught—

Then Mastamho said once more: "I have named all the directions but you have not answered. Well, there are other names. Listen: I call this (the ***north***) *Mathak.* Can you say that?" Then all said, "Yes," and stood up, and pointed ***north***, and said, *"Mathak."* He said again: "This (to the ***south***) I call *Kaveik.* Can you say it?" Then all said, "Yes," and pointed and called the name and clapped their hands and laughed. He said again: " I told you that the night went in that direction. I gave it a name, but you did not say it. There is another way to call it: *Inyohavek.* All of you say that!" Then they all said: "Yes, we can say that. We can call it *Inyohavek,*" and all pointed as he directed them. He said again: "Where the dark comes from, you did not call that as I told you to. There is another way to call it: *Anyak.* " Then all said: *"Anyak,"* and pointed *east* and clapped their hands and laughed. Then Mastamho said: "That is all."

"Seven Mohave Myths," *University of California Publications, Anthropological Records*, A.L. Kroeber, 1948, p. 60

For the Mojave, the four directions are so important that they merit a second vocabulary to speak of them properly.

———————————— + ————————————

CELESTIAL ORDER IN CEREMONIES
CHUMASH

Dualism is a fundamental concept affecting all aspects of Chumash speculation about the cosmos. This is evident in the values the Chumash associate with the **world directions**. Kitsepawit makes this *very clear* in his explanation that the **northern sky** was important because it was 'fixed' (by the world axis), while the **south** was unbounded. The **north** was the male force maintaining order, and the **southern** sky was the female force relatively free of restrictions, and thus capable of greater creativity—for both good and evil. Native ceremonies honored this cosmological order by having male dancers go to the **north side** of a dance arena while the women stood in the **south**. The women represented the stars in this disordered part of the heavens, whose celestial bodies were continuously in contact with the middle and lower worlds as they dropped below the earth's horizon.

A Circle Within the Abyss: Chumash Metaphysics,
John Anderson, 1994, pp. 10-11

"As above, so also below," goes a popular saying. For many People it is another way of expressing the relatedness of all that exists and how that harmony and unity can be celebrated in dance and ceremony.

———————————— + ————————————

Miwok flute

HEALING CEREMONY BLESSING
CHUMASH

The next morning I arose early, made my coffee, and then I went to Chicherero's camp. I found the man still in bed. "We have here the remedy at hand," I said. Chicherero got up and spoke about building a fire. "No," said I, "dress now and put on heavy socks and underwear, and see what your fate is going to be." The man did so. Then I began to empty the sea water from the bottles into a bucket in front of the tent where the sick man was. I wouldn't allow the man to come out at all. "We are going to try a remedy of the Indians," I said. "You will see how the Indians get the blessing when it is in the name of the Indian god."

I stood facing toward the pail and facing *east*. I spread my arms for the first word, second word, and for each of the three a sounds. I said:

Minimol ka minawan
North and *South*
A A A

The a sounds were breathy, long, and each with a crescendo diminuendo. Then facing *north*, I continued:

'Atapli'ish ka 'alkulul
East and *west*
A A A

This blessing was in the Ventura Chumash language. In the version of Santa Cruz Island, they say the order of *north* and *south* reversed, since they are of the water. They also add u sounds, which the Ventura people do not do. The blessing in Santa Cruz Island Chumash is thus:

Minawan hywan mili'imol
South and *north*
A A A U U U
Lapli'ish hywan lale
East and *west*
A A A U U U

I have seen the old Indians perform this blessing.

I then put some of the water into a tomato can and went inside the tent, saying, "I forgot you were a Catholic." So I made a motion in the air with my right hand and said: "In nomine patris filii et spiritus sancti amen."

Breath of the Sun, Fernando Librado, 1979, pp. 66-67

This healing prayer combines the facing of the four directions with a certain sung formula. Opposite directions are twinned. The Catholic "sign of the cross" pattern is also significant.

—————————————— + ——————————————

HEALING CEREMONY
CHUMASH

. . . an actual curing ceremony. The sick man was named Juan Moinal, a captain of a village at Tejon. He had been bewitched and became ill, so word was sent out to find an Indian doctor. Soon one arrived, named *'Alwutr* "El Cuervo" (the crow), and probably a Kitanemuk Indian, dragging a blanket upon the ground as he ran through a crowd of people in the village, yelling, "Open up! Clear the way." When *'Alwutr* reached the body of Captain Juan, he said *hahahahahaha,* and then began to sprinkle the sick man with water, all over. Then the doctor put around his neck a small band which had the head of some kind of animal on it, and began talking to the Sun. The sickness was cast out and Captain Juan revived. *'Alwutr* then told the chief that if another attack were to come, it would take all the medicines that he had to cure him, but that the ultimate service that *'Alwutr* could do was to come and serve. *Shapaqay,* another doctor close by, said then that he could see that another attack of the sickness would come.

In the late afternoon another attack did occur, and this time *'Alwutr* was very tired. He ordered the people to stir the fire and place Captain Juan near it. *Shapaqay* returned and said that the sickness was very bad. Singers and dancers were present and took their places.

Shapaqay watched as the old man waved his hand-held feathers over the body of the sick man, who was choking and dying. Then suddenly *'Alwutr* straightened up and shouted out prayers to the **cardinal points,** and Captain Juan was cured.

Chumash Healing: Changing Health and Medical Practices in an American Indian Society, Philip Walker & Travis Hudson, 1993, p. 69

The Chumash of central California had many healing practices. This one demonstates that the ritual became most effective when the one leading the ceremony shouted out prayers to the four directions.

——————————— + ———————————

HEALING PRAYERS
CHUMASH

The Chumash considered sea water a powerful medicine and administered it for a variety of ailments. It was consecrated by prayers to each of the *cardinal directions* before its use. The mainland Chumash chanted their prayers with arms extended, in this fashion.

Minimol ka minawan

A A A (said when facing *east*)

Atapliish ka'alkulul

East and **West**

A A A (said when facing *north*)

The island Chumash used the same basic form; however, they reversed the *cardinal directions,* since they were "of the water," and they added sounds as follows:

Minawan hywan miliimol

South and **North**

A A A U U U (said when facing *east?*)

East and **West**

A A A U U U (said when facing *north?*)

Fresh water from a sacred spring or shrine also was used for healing. One shrine, located near Ventura, was called "Deer Urine," and the water from it was called "Tears of the Sun." When someone became ill, the head of the family might visit a shrine with an offering of beads and seeds, and place pieces of broken *pespibata* made from the native tobacco plant at points around the spring representing the *four cardinal directions*. Standing on the *north* side of the shrine and facing *south*, he spoke to the sun concerning the "Tears of the Sun":

Look at me! Dear God, here I stand in the middle of the earth—look at me well! What I am about to do is take away water—the urine of a doe—so that a creature of yours might quench his thirst. We know there is no other who holds us with such tenderness—only you. Look upon one who is cold and let him warm himself. Winter comes and rains fall, the rains cease and the earth warms. What is called grass is born, and all that your creatures eat, including the bear. Lastly, I now say: He who wishes to realize the dreams of his mind must leave his native land. There is no other—only you, the Sun, who illumines here at the middle of the earth. Difficult times come, and he who draws apart of his own volition approaches the poorest of mankind and says to him: Take courage! Do not reject me! I am your kin. Thus he speaks in his repentance. He who has the strongest of spirit says that there is no other—only you. So speaks the generous person.

Then the speaker addressed the *four directions*, saying:
Ha (4 times)
'U (3 times)

The water would then be collected, taken back to the village, and given to the sick man to drink.

Chumash Healing: Changing Health and Medical Practices in an American Indian Society, Philip Walker & Travis Hudson, 1993, pp. 71-72

The melody of these prayers is probably lost in time. But the four directions were addressed in a classic way. Nothing was hurried. Islanders adapted this order of the prayer to their own reality, but there were enough similarities to recognize it as a ritual prayer of the same People.

———————————— + ————————————

TAKING POSSESSION OF A TERRITORY RITUAL
COSTANOAN

On June 3, 1770, Pentecost Sunday, on the shore of the Port of Monterey, there being assembled Commander Don Gaspár de Portolá with his officers, subalterns, soldiers and the rest of the expedition, Don Juan Perez, captain of the packetboat *San Antonio* with his sub-captain, Don Miguel de Pino, the whole crew and the rest of the sea expedition, and the Rev. Fr. Lector and Presidente of all the Missions, Fr. Junipero Serra, and Fr. Juan Crespi, an arbor (enramada) having been erected on the very spot by the side of the little ravine, and near the live-oak where in the year 1602 the Rev. Carmelite Fathers, who had come with the expedition of Comandante Don Sebastian Vizcaíno, had celebrated the holy sacrifice of the Mass, an altar was arranged, the bells were suspended, and the celebration began with the loud ringing of the bells.

The Fr. Presidente named, vested in alb and stole, all kneeling, implored the assistance of the Holy Ghost (whose coming upon the small assembly of the apostles and disciples of the Lord, the Universal Church celebrated that day) and intoned with all possible solemnity the hymn of the day, the *Veni Creator Spiritus.* Thereupon he blessed water and with it the great cross, which had been constructed, and which all helped to raise and place in position, and then venerated. He then sprinkled the whole surroundings and the shore with holy water. . . . Thereupon High Mass commenced at the altar. . . .

When this first function of the Church was concluded, the commander proceeded to take formal possession of the land in the name of our King, Don Carlos III (God protect him) by raising anew the royal standard, which had already been unfurled after the erection of the holy cross. To this were added the customary ceremonies of pulling up some grass, throwing stones and earth to the *four winds,* and drawing up a record of all that had taken place. From this day began the Divine Worship, and the famous Port of Monterey came under the dominion and government of our King. Thereupon all the gentlemen together with the Fathers dined on the shore of the port, as did all the men of the sea and land expeditions, repeated volleys of the cannon and muskets in the meantime accompanying the various functions of the celebration.

Mission San Carlos Borromeo, Zephyrin Englehardt, 1973, pp. 24-25

Though the foregoing appears to be a Spanish ceremony of formally "taking possession" of a territory, it may very well be a ritual witnessed by the local indigenous People of Monterey. They most probably did not "take part" in it; yet, significantly, it is possibly the first time that a four-directions ceremony was simultaneously experienced by both Spaniards and Natives in this part of the world.

———————— + ————————

Chumash medicine woman during a break at a tribal healing ceremony

RAIN SONG
TACHE-YOKUTS

Then they began a song that sounded familiar. It was the Rain Song! The door opened in the cabin and an old woman was led out. They seated her on a chair near the fire.

The medicine man stood before her and, chanting magic words, removed the feather top of his headdress and held it over her head.

"What is he doing?" said someone near me.

"He is trying to cure her," was the answer.

"Kee-tee hen-na o-nook-o my yah wah" ('Round and 'round, rain-rock, over my head)

So the song went. It was a powerful song. To her it recalled memories of childhood, when her grandparents still lived, before the coming of the white settlers. They knew no teacher then but Nature, and no gods but the Ancient Ones. The Ancient Ones had lived in the land before the Indians came and they had made the journey to Tipknits Pahn, the Yokuts' Land of the Dead. There they had turned themselves into animals and birds. These were the spirits who guided the Indians

"Hyo wah-ha mee—nee o-nook-o my yah wah" (Toward the *west*) (rain-rock, over my head)

The medicine man blew on the woman's face with his lips held tightly together so the blowing made a loud sound. He waved his headdress and feathers over her head and before her breast, half talking, half singing. The words were not of the Tache language. The meaning was known only to the medicine man himself.

"Ye hay-hay lo ho wah!"

Josie held the woman's hands up toward the fire and in them were placed the feather swatch and the feather hat. Over her head the medicine man stretched his arms and, pleading to his power in his strongest voice, he appealed to the spirits to heal her.

The singing provided the background as the strong voice of the medicine man continued to call to the spirits. The old woman trembled with excitement and her face was wet with tears.

"Toe-ka lee-na way ten-y hen-na h'yo"

So went the Rain Song. The clicking sticks urged the song forward and above all could be heard the cry of the dancer.

"Toe-ka lee-na way ten-y hen-na h'yo"
And then . . . the healing rite ended.

The Tache-Yokuts, Indians of the San Joaquin Valley: Their Lives,
Songs and Stories, Margorie Cummins, 1978, pp. 96-98

As the dancer faces west, the direction of Tipknits Pahn, which is the
Land of the Dead, healing power is beckoned forth.

———————————— + ————————————

CONTROLLED BURN RITUAL
WUKCHUMNI YOKUTS

How did they know where to burn? Indian people would go out walking in the forest and they knew that an area just didn't look right, or they could tell because it didn't produce enough of the materials or foods and they knew that a fire would be beneficial. There were mangled groves of trees, areas that were overgrown, areas that had too many pine needles. The people knew that if there were too many pine needles collecting in an area it would hurt the trees when they'd burn. The fire has to be a gentle fire—it can't be a type of fire that's going to be real destructive. But at the same time, the fire has to be such that it is going to do some good. . . .

They knew exactly when it was time. We would consult with the spiritual people, the tribal elders, and usually they did most of the burning in the fall, right after the harvest of the acorns. And of course a lot of other things were also harvested at that time to prepare for the winter. And then we'd have our fall ceremonies, almost when Thanksgiving is celebrated now, maybe the latter part of October, the first part of November.

. . . They never did it in the summertime because it was too hot. Fires were hard to control then. They'd burn when there wasn't a whole lot of wind. Moisture in the air was important—it wasn't going to be a fire that was going to rage out of control and be real hot. . . .

The people would gather plant materials, shrubs, herbs, make offerings of tobacco and make a little pile. One in the *north*, one in the *south*, one in the *east*, and one in the *west*, and then they would stand in the middle and say prayers and do this ceremony to help clean the land. In the prayer the people would always talk to the animals and all the plants to tell them what they were doing. It's just our way of respecting them. Like asking permission because it was their land before it was our land.

When they burned they wanted it to spread in *four directions*. It's ceremony—that is all part of their religious belief. They didn't just go out there with a road flare and set fire like I've seen done with controlled burns. We, Indian people, we talk to the fire. We've learned through religious teachings that fire lives inside of us also. That would be the electrons that course through your body. Fire was thought of in a very reverent manner. It wasn't taken lightly at all.

"That Place Needs a Good Fire," *News from Native California*,
Kat Anderson & Hector Franco, Spring 1993, p. 19

This interview with Hector Franco concerning the traditional use of fire as a forest management tool is enlightening. The positioning of four little piles of plant materials and tobacco, one for each direction, tells us of the People's recognition of not only the directions, but also the various living things that will be caught up in the fire. When the four little piles were lit, and the fires spread out, it was a way of sending out their requests for future foods and materials for survival. After the fire, new gifts would come from the four directions as the foliage grew and increased.

———————————— + ————————————

DIRECTIONAL EARTH ROPES
KONKOW

The Konkow practiced the ritualistic Kuksu cult and believed in the number four, which was a sacred number among the cult. The Konkow oriented themselves to the *four directions* from which the supportive ropes of the earth were stretched: **north, south, east** and **west**.

Handbook of North American Indians, Vol. 8 (California),
Robert Heizer, 1978, p. 383

Here, instead of the trees that are characteristic of the Mesoamerican explanation of the directions, we have four ropes which stretch out the earth in the important directions.

———————————— + ————————————

ORIGIN STORY
MAIDU

From First Man and First Woman sprang a great family—a People. And in those early days, every phase of life was as World Maker had planned. No one worked, no one sickened, no one died. Age was erased by soaking in a magic lake.

And food was everywhere. Women, setting out their baskets in the night beneath the acorn tree, would in the morning find their baskets full—baskets full of fruit, baskets full of warm acorn mush, full of steaming acorn bread wrapped in wild grape leaves, full of curled acorn disks soaked in hot sweet juices.

Thus all was provided for in those good and early times.

But there is another story, long and tearful, telling of deeds of Coyote, how he showed these early people Evil, showed to them their shady side, the earthen side of man. It is a tale that the old storytellers claim has no end, for life still goes on.

But Coyote was the one the people blamed. Coyote was the one they heard and saw, who always seemed to want more than he deserved or needed. It was he they saw lie and cheat to get what others had. And though Coyote showed them through his actions how everything was lost to him each time he tried it, no one understood the lesson. No one did the thing the opposite way.

Coyote was the one they blamed. Yet it was each person by himself who really wanted more than others. Instead of running, the people one by one tried this evil, and when they tried it, all seemed ruined.

From that time on the life of mankind was marked with troubles, work, sickness, tears and death. From that time on each person by himself has been divided, one side laughing with Coyote, the other side running from Coyote.

In this way too, the people were divided, divided into tribes, each speaking differently from their neighbors. And First Man, receiving instruction in the night from World Maker, in turn counseled his people on all things he had learned.

First Man gave the tribes their laws and legends, taught them how to hunt and cook and willow weave, when to have their festivals and dances. Then he sent his people out in *all directions. Northward* went the warriors, singers to the *west,* flute players traveled *eastward* and dancers to the *south.*

And as the tribes left one by one, First Man told the women more about the acorn—how, of all life created, it had been first, meant for Mankind and endless food for life to come.

He showed them how the acorn should be gathered, how the shells were taken from them, how to pound the acorn into powder, how to sift them, how to take the bitter from them. He showed the women how to bake them deep in coals, how to boil them in willow baskets, how to make the water biscuit.

So the people spread away in *all directions* with a knowledge of the acorn, World Maker's gift to Man, always there to feed these people until he came again, until all the world would be made over.

Ooti: A Maidu Legacy, Richard Simpson, 1977, pp. 34-35

This origin story seems similar to the one in the Book of Genesis known so well by those raised in Western societies. And yet, no matter how the People behave, down through each generation, the Creator maintains for them a special gift for their sustenance: acorn (ooti). In this story the directions are identified with particular vocations, or callings, that were anciently known to the People and respected by them.

———————————— + ————————————

DIRECTIONAL RECOGNITION
MAIDU

Directions were pointed out, or in speech were referred to, as sunrise and sunset for *east* and *west* respectively. Directions were commonly given with respect to features of the local geography: in the direction of such and such a village or toward a named river, spring, or mountain which was conspicuous or generally known. We must remember that the territories of the local tribes were small and that the terrain was intimately known. . . . Maidu recognized directions as we know them, but . . . the *northeast* or mountain Maidu had five: *west, northwest* (the direction of Lassen Peak), *north, east,* and *south*.

Indians of Lassen, Paul Schulz, 1980, p. 140

Because of its great height and importance spiritually to the People, Lassen Peak was regarded as the fifth important direction.

———————————— + ————————————

RE-PEOPLING THE EARTH
PATWIN

Once there was a man who fell in love with two sisters and wanted them both for his wives. The old man was very ugly and the women, who were magpies, laughed at him when he proposed. He became very angry and cursed the women and went away to the far *north* country. He was so angry that he set the world on fire and rowed out to sea in a tule boat and was never seen again.

The fire, however, was burning fiercely and ate its way *southward*, consuming everything in its path. It burned people, animals, trees, rocks, water, and even the ground itself. Old Coyote saw the fire and smoke of the fire from his home away to the *south* and ran as fast as he could to put it out. He took with him two little boys, whom he put in a sack, and ran like the wind to the *north*. He ran so hard that, by the time he got to the fire, he was exhausted and dropped the sack which held the two boys.

Coyote finally mustered up enough strength to chew up some Indian sugar which he spat on the fire and put it out. Now there was no more danger from fire and Coyote was very thirsty but there was no water. He chewed some more Indian sugar, dug a hole in the bottom of the creek, and put the chewed sugar in it. This turned to water and filled all the streams so earth had water again.

Coyote next turned his attention to the two little boys who were sad because they were the only people on earth. Building a sweat lodge, Coyote split a number of little sticks and laid them out in a particular pattern over night. The next morning these sticks had all turned to people who were company for the boys. Coyote sent them out to the various areas of the world and, in this way, the earth was repeopled.

Where Is the Eagle?, William Coffer, 1981, pp. 236-237

As in ancient times, we live with the danger of wild fires wreaking havoc in the forest, in the grasslands, or in other areas where we still choose to build our homes. This People also knew what it was like to be victims of conflagration. The hasty journey of Coyote from south to north allows us to sense the speed of a fire's destructive movement.

———————————— + ————————————

EARTHLY LIFE CLOSURE SONG
WINTU

Oh Olelbes, look down on me.
I wash my face in water, for you,
Seeking to remain in health
I am advancing in old age; I am not capable of anything anymore.
You whose nature it is to be eaten,
You dwell high in the *west,* on the mountains,
   high in the *east,* high in the *north,* high in the *south;*
You, salmon, you go about in the water.
Yet I cannot kill you and bring you home.
Neither can I go *east* down the slope to fetch you, salmon.
When a man is so advanced in age, he is not in full vigor.
If you are rock, look at me; I am advancing in old age.
If you are tree, look at me; I am advancing in old age.
If you are water, look at me; I am advancing in old age.
Acorns, I can never dip you up and fetch you home again.
My legs are advancing in weakness.
Sugar pine, you sit there; I can never climb you.
In my *northward* arm, in my *southward* arm,
   I am advancing in weakness.
You who are wood, you wood,
   I cannot carry you home on my shoulder.
For I am falling back into my cradle.
This is what my ancestors told me yesterday,
   they who have gone, long ago.
May my children fare likewise!

"Some Indian Texts Dealing with the Supernatural,"
Review of Religion, Dorothy Demetracopolou Lee, 1941, p. 407

In this Wintu prayer one can see that each direction is considered to be filled with life. Each being is asked to witness the sadness of one who soon will no longer be able to experience the goodness of the flora and fauna, who will miss the rocks and rivers, and who will be unable to walk in any direction.

———————— + ————————

THE BODY AND DIRECTIONALITY
WINTU

The Wintu use of right and left, as compared with ours, shows . . . the difference in orientation. . . . To the Wintu, the terms left and right refer to the inextricable parts of the body, and are very rarely used. . . . When the Wintu goes up the river, the hills are to the *west,* the river to the *east*; and a mosquito bites him on the *west* arm. When he returns, the hills are still to the *west,* but when he scrataches his mosquito bite, he scratches his *east* arm. The geography has remained unchanged, and the self has had to be reoriented in relation to it.

> "Notes on the Conception of the Self Among the Wintu Indians,"
> *Journal of Abnormal and Social Psychology*,
> Dorothy Demetracopolou Lee, 1950, p. 543

It is interesting to see how all Native People understand their position to the rest of the universe. Rather than considering themselves "above it," they cheerfully recognize their relationship to everyone and every-thing else. The directions can be used to express this.

———————————— + ————————————

LINGUISTIC DESCRIPTION OF DIRECTIONALITY
WINTU

They went to the *east* side of the house, they went around to the *east* side, and after that they went up the hill to the *north,* following him running. They went northward at a running pace over the flat, wishing to see the man who had gone down the hill northward. And the man was not there but there lay his tracks going forward. And they ran, they went at a running pace, they went rapidly. And at the *South*-slope-climb, when they came in full view of the *north,* they looked north-ward but they did not see him.

> "Notes on the Conception of the Self Among the Wintu Indians,"
> *Journal of Abnormal and Social Psychology*, Dorothy Demetracopolou Lee,
> 1950, p. 543

This passage gives an understanding of directional movement in regard to a love pursuit of a young man by two women. A horse, a hill, a flat piece of land, some tracks, and the directions themselves are the principle items mentioned. This is a simple, and yet linguistically complex, way of speaking about where one is in relationship to the four directions.

———————————— + ————————————

MOURNING CEREMONY
MIWOK

Get up! Get up! Get up! Get up! Get up!
Wake up! Wake up! Wake up!
People get up on the *south* side,
East side, east side, east side, east side,
North side, north side, north side,
Lower side, lower side, lower side!
You folks come here!
Visitors are coming, visitors are coming.
Strike out together!
Hunt deer, squirrels!
And you women, strike out, gather wild onions, wild potatoes!
Gather all you can! Gather all you can!
Pound acorns, pound acorns, pound acorns!
Cook, cook!
Make some bread, make some bread!
So we can eat, so we can eat, so we can eat.
Put it up, and put it up, and put it up!
Make acorn soup so that the people will eat it!
There are many coming.
Come here, come here, come here, come here!
You have to be dry and hungry.
Be for a while.
Got nothing here.
People get up, people around get up.
Wake!
Wake up so you can cook!
Visitors are here now and all hungry.
Get ready so we can feed them!
Gather up, gather up, and bring it all in, so we can give it to them!

Go ahead and eat!
That's all we have.
Don't talk about starvation, because we never have much!
Eat acorns!
There is nothing to it.
Eat and eat!
Eat! Eat! Eat! Eat!
So that we can get ready to cry.
Everybody get up! Everybody get up!
All here, very sad occasion.
All cry! All cry!
Last time for you to be sad.

"Central Miwok Ceremonies," *University of California
Publications, Anthropological Records,* Edward Gifford,1955, p. 263

*The chief's calling of the People from the four directions is significant.
It requests that they activate themselves from the four directions to
prepare for visitors and to "charge up" their energies during this time
of grief and mourning in order to prepare for another outlook on life.*

———————————— + ————————————

MOURNING CEREMONY
MIWOK

. . . the old chief arose, carrying a long staff in his right hand,
entered the inner space, and began a slow march around the fire,
taking very short trotting steps and uttering a prolonged sad cry in
musical cadence, in which the others joined. The words most often
repeated were, "Ha-ha-ha-yah, ha-ha-ha-yah," pronounced simultaneously and in perfect time by all. Some of the women mourners—the
number varied from four to seven—now arose and followed the old
chief in single file. They were soon joined by three mourning chiefs,
and the procession continued to circle from left to right around the fire
for an hour and a half with slight intervals, the old head chief always
in the lead.

During the entire ceremony the Indians not engaged in the mourning chant occupied the outer space, sitting or reclining in little groups
on the carpet of pine needles that covered the hard ground. . . .

Save the dull light from the fire, the smoke-blackened interior was absolutely dark, forming an appropriate background for the solemn rite. . . . The flickering fire disclosed at intervals the forms of the people reclining in the outer circle and cast a dim and lurid light on the band of mourners as they continually circled round it. All was silence save the steady rhythmic chant of the marchers and an occasional muffled sob from the obscurity of the outer space.

At one time the march stopped and the mourners faced the *west* and cried; then they faced the *north* and cried, meanwhile wailing and swaying their bodies to and fro. At another time three women from the outer circle stepped forward and each took hold of one of the women marchers and led her to one of the four inner or central posts where they immediately sat down cross-legged in facing couples—one couple at the foot of each of three of the posts. They then grasped each other by the elbows or shoulders and swayed their bodies backward and forward, sometimes stopping to caress each other on the face and neck, but still sobbing and crying.

While this was going on the others continued the march. Sometimes the leader halted and seemed to utter commands, whereupon the marchers faced about, changed the words of the cry, and gesticulated in a different manner. At times the head chief looked down at the ground, with his arms and the palms of his hands extended toward a spot on the earth floor, around which he moved in a semicircle, addressing it as if speaking to a dead person or to a grave. Sometimes all of the women simultaneously extended their arms forward and slightly upward with open hands, as if in supplication, sobbing and wailing as they did so. One of the mourners, a woman with hair clipped short and face blackened in memory of the recent death of her husband, did not join the marchers but throughout the ceremony remained sitting on the *west* side of the outer circle with her face to the wall, uttering continually a peculiarly sad and at the same time plaintive musical lament, in slow rhythmical cadence. It was a beautiful strain, full of pathos and melody. She was very much in earnest and was so exhausted by the excitement and effort that, when the march was over, she fell on her side and remained motionless in that position for more than an hour.

When the march was over, the mourners retired to the outer circle, and So-pi-ye, the old blind chief from Murphys, delivered a solemn oration. His voice was remarkably loud, deep, and clear. Another chief, who sat on the ground at his side, joined in from time to time. . . .

SECOND NIGHT

On the second night, October 10, the proceedings began shortly after dark and lasted about two hours, when the old head chief fell from exhaustion and the affair came to an abrupt end.

The character of the performance differed materially from that of the first night. In the beginning, the head chief faced the *south*, standing with his staff in his right hand. He then turned and faced the *north*, speaking and exhorting. Then a woman on the *east* side of the outer circle began sobbing. Then two women on the *south* side stepped out and sat on the ground with their arms around one another, sobbing and crying. The head chief remained standing on the *south* side of the inner space, facing in; he then turned and faced out, continuing his exhortations. After this he moved to the *east* and kneeled by the side of So-pi-ye, the blind chief, who was sitting on the ground with his legs crossed. Immediately two other chiefs took places facing each other, squatting close together on the ground, and both couples moaned and cried. At the same time the women in the outer circle were wailing and sobbing. The chiefs who were squatting on the ground facing each other rested their hands on each other's arms and shoulders. The four chiefs then changed places and partners, everybody crying, after which three of the chiefs arose and began a slow dancing march back and forth from the *west* side of the inner space, singing, "Ha-ha-ha-ha, ha-ha-ha-ha." While this was going on the women mourners were squatting on the ground in facing couples, crying and sobbing as before.

The old head chief, leaning on his staff, next approached one of the couples to the *south* and seemed to address them personally, while another chief continued the dance alone, moving slowly around the fire. Then the wife of one of the chiefs went to So-pi-ye and sat down facing him; they placed their hands on each other's arms and shoulders. There were now three chiefs standing near the fire. Then another old woman danced once around the fire alone, slowly swaying her body and arms, and sat down facing one of the chiefs who was a mourner, so that there were two couples kneeling or squatting on the ground, each consisting of a chief and an old woman. At this time the old head chief was slowly moving around the fire with one of the subordinate chiefs. The march stopped and the head chief kneeled by an elderly woman mourner and placed his hands on her head and she hers on his shoulders, both kneeling and weeping. The local chief danced slowly around the fire alone, bending his body and pointing to the ground in various directions with his wand. He then squatted on the ground, and an old woman put one hand on his heart and reached over with the other and patted him on the back.

The three chiefs and three old women exchanged partners and continued to sway their bodies and mourn as before. Then the local chief arose and went to the fire, and three of the chiefs took places on the *south* side, facing outward. Another old man squatted by one of the old women as before, and the local chief danced slowly around the fire, facing first to the right, then to the left, motioning with his wand. He then sat cross-legged on the ground by the side of a visiting chief who was one of the mourners. This left the head chief the only man standing. He continued to face the *south,* speaking and gesticulating. Two women knelt by the visiting chief, who knelt down and placed a hand on the shoulder of each, and all three remained kneeling. The old head chief continued to exhort, still facing the *south,* but showed signs of great fatigue. Then the wife of a local chief approached the fire, stood close to it, and, swaying her body back and forth, pointed across it. Another woman began the slow dancing march around the fire alone. A young mother, not a mourner, went to a woman at the fire, led her away, and they sat down together, facing each other, sobbing and rubbing one another with their hands.

The local chief now faced the fire and exhorted. He was soon joined by two other chiefs and the three stood in a row, while one of the women continued the march alone, swaying her body and arms and sobbing. She was soon joined by another woman and the local chief took his place at the head; a third woman followed at the rear. The head chief beat time and moved slowly back and forth on the *east* side of the fire. He then, in spite of his obvious exhaustion, led the dancing march and was followed by two other chiefs, after which he again faced *south* and continued to exhort, in different directions but continuing to move slowly around the fire. The old chief again led the march, then halted and called out; the others also halted and swayed their bodies and arms.

The old chief now moved alone to the *north* side of the inner space and exhorted, his voice becoming feebler and feebler. The others faced him, standing on the *south* side. A few minutes later seven persons were marching around the fire, when the head chief stopped them by putting his hands on the old women and men. Again he led off, and the marchers were joined by others, until there were in all eleven persons marching around the fire, the largest number at one time during the ceremony. The head chief then stopped and sang out, "Hi-ha-ho-ho," and everyone stood still. He then faced the *west,* and the women continued the march alone, soon joined however by two of the other chiefs, while the old head chief continued to exhort from the *north* side. The dancers fell away until only three were left. By this time the old head chief's strength was gone and he fell to the ground exhausted. He was carried to his place at the foot of the *south-west* post by a local chief and an old woman, and it was a long time before we were sure whether he would live or die. This put a stop to the proceedings.

At intervals throughout the ceremony of the second night, as on the first, the woman mourner with the cropped hair and blackened face, who sat on the *east* side of the outer circle with her back to the others, remained in her position and continued to wail, keeping up her peculiarly pathetic musical lament.

THE MO-LAH-GUM-SIP

The ceremony of the second night, so abruptly ended, recommenced before daylight the following morning, when the final act, known as the Mo-lah-gum-sip, or "wash," was performed.

Since the old head chief was too ill to take part, his place was taken by a local chief, Pedro, who at half-past five addressed the mourners in the roundhouse. He finished sometime before daylight, after which there was an interval of silence. Shortly before sunrise, some of the women brought out a large basket, set it on the ground near a small fire about forty feet north of the entrance to the ceremonial house, filled it with water and heated the water in the usual way by means of hot stones which previously had been put into the fire. When the water was hot, the chief ("eph") from the neighboring village at West Point and an old woman who had been designated for the place, each holding a cloth in the right hand, took positions facing one another, one on each side of the basket (called choo-soo-ah').

Then there was a stir inside the ceremonial house, and a local chief led out three of the women mourners and brought them to the basket. As each in turn leaned over it she was seized by one of the washers, who immediately proceeded to wash her face vigorously with the cloth, which was frequently dipped in the hot water. After the women's faces had been washed, their wrists and hands were treated in the same way, but were held outside so that the water would drip away from, not into, the basket. When these three had been washed, a chief and an old woman led out two old men chiefs, also mourners, and they were washed in the same way as the others. Then two more mourners, both old women, were led out and washed. After this one of the local chiefs went to a place in the chaparral, at some little distance, where a middle-aged couple were sleeping, grasped the woman by the hand, and led her all the way back to the choo-soo-ah', or hot-water basket, where she was treated as the others had been before.

This completed the ceremony of the Mo-lah-gum'-sip or "wash," and was the last act of the Yum'-meh or mourning ceremony. It also ended the period of mourning for those who had been washed, thus freeing them from the restrictions imposed upon them during its continuance. . . .

The sun now rose above the mountains in the *east,* and the feeble old head chief got up slowly from his place at the foot of the *southwest* post and with his staff walked out to an open place on the *west* side of the ceremonial house, where he stood in silence for a long time, *facing the sun.*

After this, breakfast was served, consisting of coffee, acorn mush, and biscuit. . . .

Studies of California Indians, C. Hart Merriam, 1955, pp. 52-56

This detailed description of a Mourning Ceremony, the Cry of the Miwok, mentions both the cardinal and the intercardinal directions. A lot of planning must have been called for to provide maximum grief support and to ensure that the ceremony was carried out in the traditional way.

———————————— + ————————————

NAMES OF PEOPLE
LIVING IN DIFFERENT DIRECTIONS
MIWOK

The only general names applied to people by the Miwok were terms formed upon the names of the *cardinal points*. Examples of such names are: *ta'muleko,* northerners, from *ta'man* or *tama'lin,* **north**; *hi'sostoko,* easterners, from *hi'sum,* **east**; *tcu'metoko,* southerners, from *tcu'mete,* **south**; and *olowitoko,* westerners, from *olo'win,* **west**. This ending, which is equivalent to "people of," takes the following forms: *oko, ok, k.* That these names have no tribal signification is clearly shown by the fact that each is applied not to any particular people but to all people, no matter now near or remote, living in the given direction to which the names refers. These names, and also the terms applied to the *cardinal points*, vary according to the laws of phonetic change in passing from one dialect to another. There are also certain different endings used by different individuals speaking the same dialect. For example: the people living to the **south** are called *tcumetoko, tcu'metok,* and *tcumte'ya,* those to the **east** are called *hi'sotoko* and *hisu'wit.* In the last term ending *-wit* is really a directive with the signification of towards.

"The Geography and Dialects of the Miwok Indians," *University of California Publications in American Archaeology and Ethnography,*Samuel Alfred Barrett, 1908, p. 341

S.A. Barrett, who did ethnographical research among the Miwok in the first decade of our century, noted their geography and dialects and drew some conclusions concerning directionality.

———————— + ————————

RECOGNITION OF TWO DIRECTIONS
SHASTA

The Shasta recognized only two cardinal directions, "daylight side" *(East)* and "dark side" *(West)*. They believed that after death a soul first travelled *east* up into the sky and then *east* to *west*

*Miwok Cocoon and
Feather Rattle*

along the Milky Way, finally arriving at the house of Mocking Bird, who migrated up the Klamath in the Spring and down in Autumn.

Handbook of North American Indians, Vol. 8 (California),
Robert Heizer, 1978, p. 220

The California tribes seem to be quite unique in contrast to those of other continental cultural areas. The sun's movements and the sunrise and sunset directions figured more fully into their own lifestyle and storytelling. The riverine movement of Mocking Bird perhaps accounts for the other two directions.

---------------------- + ----------------------

PROTECTION RITUAL
PIT RIVER

Afterwards I took Jack down to my little ranch in the mountains south of Monterey. We had to go fifty miles by horse-stage, then fifteen miles more by trail over the ridges. When we were on top of the highest ridge the sun was dipping into the ocean, and we stopped to eat some sandwiches and make a little coffee. But before he ate, Jack chewed a piece and spat some to the *east,* and to the *north,* and to the *south,* and to the *west.* "See, Doc, I am doing that because I am in a new country. Them people you don't see, them coyotes and foxes and all kinds of *dinihowis* and *damaagomes* that live around here, they don't know me, because I am a stranger. They might hurt me. So I am telling them: I am all right, I don't mean no harm to you people, see, I am feeding you; and you people don't hurt me neither, because I am a stranger but I want to be friends with you. That's the way to do, Doc, that's the good way.

"Indians in Overalls," *The Hudson Review,*
Jaime deAngulo, Autumn 1950, p. 376

The author, a somewhat unorthodox anthropologist, offers us a special memory of Jack Folsom of the Pit River People whose traditional homeland was in the northeastern section of California. In this vignette he is visiting territory several hundred miles to the south on the Big Sur coast, and feels the need to recognize the four directions in an abbreviated kind of ritual.

---------------------- + ----------------------

CONTEMPORARY POEM
PIT RIVER

You don't know me, but I took your rejected
and made them welcome.
    I took your sick and made them well.
    I took your weak and made them strong.
Together we went to the center of the Universe:
    back to the womb of Mother Earth, and were reborn.
You don't know me, but I took our uneducated
and made them learn.
    I took them to the classrooms,
    I took them to the courtrooms.
Together we studied the laws of man and
the laws of nature and gained knowledge.

You don't know me, but I took your dejected
and gave them happiness.
    I took your hopeless and gave them hope,
    I took your aimless and gave them purpose.
Together we discovered each others' worth,
and now we have value.
You don't know me, but I took your beaten and
taught them when, how, and who to fight.
You don't know me, I brought the wisest
elders and the strongest warriors from
the four directions to guide and to teach.

And now, like shining stars in an unlit
world, my new family travels, trying to light
your path.

My name is D-Q U.

"D-Q U, " Beverly LeBeau, 1985

This poem, written by a student at D-Q U (Deganowideh-Quetzalcoatl University), an accredited college for indigenous People that is near Davis, in northern California, offers a contemporary understanding of the four directions. The poet, a loving grandmother, nurtured her

*children in her tribal ways and was a strong proponent of education,
both Native based and larger-culture based.*

———————————— + ————————————

WEATHER PRAYER
HUPA

yi-tsin te-nal-dit-do-te
West it will draw back,

yi-de kuñ te-nal-dit-do-te
north too it will draw back,

yi-duk kuñ te-nal-dit-do-te
east too it will draw back,

yi-nuk- te-nal-dit-do-te
south it will draw back.

nais-xun-te
There will be sunshine.

na-nu-wiñ-hwoñ-te
It will be good weather

niñ-nis-an meuk
the world over.

na-xo-wiL-tun-te
It will be wet.

nal-hwin-te
Will melt away

nin-xos-tin-ne-en
frost used to be.

na-win-tau
It will settle down.

tce-na-xon-neL-tiñ
I brought it down.

TRANSLATION: *West* it [a present source of bad weather] will draw
back, *north* too it will draw back, *east* too it will draw back, *south* it
will draw back. There will be sunshine. It will be good weather in the
world. It will be wet. The frost that used to be will melt. It will settle
down. I brought it down.

"Hupa Texts," *University of California Publications in American
Archaeology and Ethnology,* Pliny Earle Goddard,1904, pp. 273-274

*Pliny Goddard, working at the beginning of this century,
published this "Formula of the Rain-Rock Medicine,"
which called to mind sources of power of rain
rocks and allowed for the recitation of a prayer
that would bring on good weather.*

*Ohlone
Musical Clapper*

———————————— + ————————————

RIVERINE DIRECTIONAL MEANINGS
KARUK

Little has been recorded concerning Karok views of the universe. . . . However, many myths describe how the ways and features of the world were ordained . . . before their transformation—for example, the use of salmon and acorns. In fact, the Karoks seem mainly interested in their immediate surroundings. The Klamath River, running between Klamath Lakes and the sea is the basis for their terms of spatial orientation: Karúk 'up-river'; Yúruk 'down-river'; Máruk 'away from the river, uphill'; and Sáruk 'toward the river, downhill' are the *four cardinal points.*

Handbook of North Americans Indians, Vol. 8 (California),
Robert Heizer, 1978, p. 188

The points of spiritual reference may not be exactly north and south and east and west, as was common among many Peoples; with this northern California tribe they are simply four riverine directions that approximate the four directions.

———————————— + ————————————

IMPORTANT DIRECTION PLACES
KARUK

And Coyote jumped up. And he said, "My country!" And he kicked earth out towards the river. And he kicked it out from *tishánnik* (a village-site at present day Camp Creek, below Orleans). He kicked it out from *káttiphirak* (a village-site across-stream from Camp Creek). He kicked it out from *túuyvuk* (a village-site at Ullathorne Creek, below Camp Creek). Coyote was so happy, when he came back to his country. That's why he kicked it out.

"The Karuk Language," *University of California Publications in Linguistics,* William Bright, 1957, p. 169

For these northern California Indians the directions were never just four generic and endless lines; rather, they were closely identified with specific places that were well known to the People.

———————————— + ————————————

FIRST SALMON CEREMONY
KARUK

The Karuk held the annual First Salmon Ceremony only at Ameekyaaraam during Ikrivkihan (The Sixth Moon), which occurred in late March or early April, commencing it ten days before the dark of the moon. It lasted for ten days, followed by ten days of retreat. This ceremony, also called *iduramva,* meaning "people run away and hide," seems to have been the Karuk's only harvest festival. It meant that the season for fishing had come; the people could once again collect salmon and steelhead, their main sustenance.

Eating fresh fish prior to this ceremony was strictly forbidden. . . .

On the first day only, the medicine man walked uphill with an elk-horn chisel and stone maul to cut a madrone pole. He then carried the young tree back down on his left shoulder to a pepperwood tree near the sweathouse and left it there to rot.

On the ninth day, an assistant medicine man and a young virgin, the wood-gatherer, entered the ceremony. The virgin crossed the river on a ferry from Asanaamkarak to Ameekyaaraam.

At about four the next morning, on the day commencing the dark of the waning moon, a group of men would shout "Iduramva!" (Go and hide!) ten times, first at the sweathouse and then at other places. At this time, people left for the day so they would not see the sacred fire or its smoke.

Two men then ferried the virgin back to Asanaamkarak where she chopped up a dead madrone for firewood and carried it and its chips back to the sacred fire site at the river's edge. One of the men ferried her again to Ameekyaaraam. There, she entered the sacred dwelling house and busied herself so she would not peek at the fire.

The medicine man and his assistant now crossed the river to Asanaamkarak. The assistant paddled while the medicine man sat quietly. Before embarking he puffed his pipe twice on the Ameekya-araam side, blowing smoke to *all directions* while praying. On the Asanaamkarak side, he repeated the smoking ritual once.

After arriving at the fire site, the assistant leveled a place for the fire. The medicine man used a willow-root drill and cedar-bark tinder to start a flame. The assistant tended it with the madrone wood that the virgin had cut. Both avoided looking at the ascending smoke. They then proceeded to cook the first salmon. When the salmon was half-baked, the assistant ate it until he vomited, for the half-cooked flesh made him sick. This brought him good luck. The two men then built an altar with rocks, and, after bathing, returned to Ikriripan, staying in the structure for ten more days.

Upon their return to Ameekyaaraam, men sang songs, while someone went to the edge of the nearby bluff and shouted to the people. "Come home!" The virgin went to bathe in the creek. . . . The people returned from the hills by evening.

Five days after the ceremony of eating the first salmon, the virgin wood-gatherer emerged from the sacred living house where she had been in retreat. She gathered two river cobbles, heated them, and boiled salmon with them. The water was tossed into the river along with the small stones in the cooking basket that had been used to cook acorn soup for the priests. After this was done, the people could prepare salmon in the usual manner.

Karuk: The Upriver People, Maureen Bell, 1991, p. 101-104

Though the Karuk are a mountain and river-bound People, they nonetheless have some regard for the four directions; the pipe ceremony attests to this. But their main daily and ceremonial reference points have a lot to do with being "upriver" or "downriver."

———————————— + ————————————

FIREMAKING SYMBOLISM
YUROK

When the Indians go camping far back into the mountains . . . they always insist on making the first campfire when a camping place is selected. In building the fire, the first stick of wood they lay down points directly **north** and **south**; on the **north** end of this stick of wood they place another stick some eight or twelve inches back from the **north** end, placing this branch **east** and **west,** thus making a cross. When the cross is made they proceed to kindle the fire, and during the whole time they are offering up a prayer to God in a low tone of voice. This prayer is earnestly offered up to the Almighty, asking Him to protect them from the Indian devils and wild animals while they are in the wilds and to keep them from accidents. After the first worship has been offered up, anyone can build the campfire as long as they camp in the same place, and the Indians do not repeat this form of worship until they move away to a different camping place.

To the American Indian, Lucy Thompson, 1916, p. 98

Even the campfire becomes a holy, living center of light and unity and an occasion for prayer for protection.

———————— + ————————

JUMP DANCE
YUROK

Now the Master takes his place in the *southeast corner* of the lodge, sitting . . . and in his hand he holds his staff, or rod, which is the stalk of the walth-pay. This staff is the stalk which grows from the herb or root that God made woman from in the first creation, and the staff is so old that it is black with age. The next one in authority sits in the *northeast corner* of the lodge, while the third one sits in the *northwest corner* of the lodge. The lodge sits *north* and *south*; the entrance is at the *south* end, **the** *west* side being left dark.

Now all . . . inside of the lodge . . . give the whole night to chanting and praying to God, to please the Creator, to give them health, wealth and to watch over them, keeping them safe from disease. They keep this up until five o'clock in the morning, and then they all go down to the house where the dance is to be held, and this house is called Ah-pure-way. They build a small fire and place some roots on it. . . .

To the American Indian, Lucy Thompson, 1916, p. 114-116

The Jump Dance or most sacred festival lodge dance (Wah-neck-wel-la-gaw) of the Yuroks shares similarities with their neighbors' dances. Here, both the cardinal and intercardinal directions are referred to. I have been present at the Hupa version of the dance and was much touched by its unique mystical qualities.

———————— + ————————

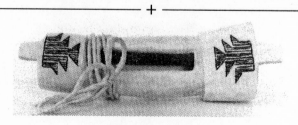

Karuk elkhorn purse

ORIGIN STORY
INTERTRIBAL

In the beginning there was no land, no light, only darkness and the vast waters of Outer Ocean where Earth-Maker and Great-Grandfather were afloat in their canoe. Earth-Maker cast a long line into the water and brought up from the bottom of the ocean a pat of earth no larger than his hand. He placed it on the surface of the sea where it drifted on the waves. Then he stretched his arms, fingers open, toward the piece of drifting earth and it grew and spread and thickened until it became the World.

Earth-Maker and Great-Grandfather beached their canoe on the shore of the new-made world and walked from end to end, for it was flat and empty. As they walked they thought and thought of all they must do before people could live there. While they thought and spoke together, they reached their arms, fingers extended to the *North*, the *East,* the *South,* the *West,* to the Above and to the Below. In this way they caused mountains and hills and valleys to form where there had been only flatness, and creeks and rivers to flow and cut through the land to the sea. They called Sun and Moon to come to light the World.

They planted the seeds of acorn oaks, of fruit trees, of berry bushes and grasses, which sprouted and sent roots deep into the ground.

They put deer and elk and bear and small four-footers to live in the hills and open valleys; low-flying birds in the trees and brush; high-flying birds to go back and forth between the earth and the Sky World; and salmon and eels and the lesser fish to swim up rivers and into creeks.

When the world was finished and complete, Earth-Maker took soft clay and formed the figure of a man and of a woman, then many men and women, which he dried in the sun and into which he breathed life: they were the First People.

He gave homes to them, some in a fold of the hills, others by the sea. To each he said, "Here is your home and the home of the children who will be born to you. Your land reaches from here to here." So saying he indicated a place upstream and one downstream, to show the boundaries beyond which the land belonged to someone else.

Then Earth-Maker and Great-Grandfather taught the First People to hunt and fish, to make fire, to build houses and to fashion tools.

They taught them also the tongue which each should speak, its songs and ritual words; the taboos to be observed for each age and each special event in a man's and a woman's life and all the rules of customary belief that go to make the Way.

When Earth-Maker and Great-Grandfather saw that the First People had learned and understood all these matters, their task was finished. Sadly, because they loved the world they had made, they said farewell and went underground forever. Since that time, since the beginning, the descendants of those First People, even to us here in this house, continue to live in the place where the Ancestors lived, to speak the old tongue, to keep the taboos, and in all matters to follow the Way.

Almost Ancestors: The First Californians,
Theodora Kroeber & Robert Heizer, 1968, p. 62

This is a unique narrative of creation in that the creation is given definite form from the arms and fingers of Earth-Maker and Great-Grandfather. The four directions and above and below were there at the beginning as the hills and valleys and the rivers and creeks and sea were given shape as the flatness underwent a metamorphosis.

Creator's sun shines forth, bringing a new day for the People

GREAT BASIN CULTURAL AREA

A Shoshone woman prays with sage, tabacco, and a hawk feather

PEYOTE TIPI POLE SYMBOLISM
WASHOE

But you can't do this just any old way. It's got to be the right Way. In this Tipi things is set up just right. It is the Way we learned from them old Indians . . . the Way Medicine showed us. Inside there you got to keep your mind straight so you can help. Everything in there is there for a reason . . . everything got a meaning. Nobody knows all the reasons for everything. We is learning all the time.

This Tipi got a meaning. It's what them old Indians live in to keep warm and dry. It's got four big poles go up first. That is for the different people in the world. They is tied together at the top because that means they is all One . . . someday they all going to meet at the top. I heard this from Members in other tribes too. That's what the Medicine shows you. Them poles is *the four corners of the world . . . North, South, East, West.* The Tipi always faces *East.* That is the main direction for us. But each direction got its own meaning. All them other little poles got some meaning too, but I ain't learned about that yet. The canvas we put on there, it means deerskin or buffalo skin or some kind of animal Indians understand from long time ago. We can't deal with them good animals like we used to . . . so we got to use this canvas.

Straight with the Medicine: Narratives of Washoe Followers of the Tipi Way, Warren L. D'Azevedo, 1978, p. 5

Though the Washoes were not originally teepee dwellers, many have come to be followers of the Peyote Way of the Native American Church. Those who promoted this new "pan-Indian" spirituality, many years back, had their origins on the Plains where teepees were common. The fact that the Washoes practice this kind of spirituality illustrates native proselytism among the various tribes.

———————————— + ————————————

SHAMAN'S POWER DREAM
WASHOE

In 1902, at the age of seventeen, Henry experienced his power dream, the event which marked him with certainity as shamanic material and which conferred certain abilities upon him. He described it to me as follows:

> I was sleeping in the school dormitory. I had a dream. I saw a buck in the **west**. It was a horned buck. It looked **east**. A voice said to me: "Don't kill my babies anymore." I woke up, and it was raining outside, and I had a nosebleed in bed.

Henry interpreted the dream in the following way. The conjunction of buck and rain suggested that he could control the weather, since the buck was the "boss of the rain." The buck was standing in the **west**, but looking **east**. The Washo believed that the souls of those who have been evil turn **east**. The buck looking **east** was interpreted as a warning against developing certain potentialities which could become evil. The voice in the dream and that of a snake warning against the indiscriminate taking of life; previously Henry had killed wildlife, insects, and snakes without much concern. The rain, as he awakened, indicated that his major spirit power would be water. Awakening with a nosebleed placed the stamp of legitimacy upon the whole experience, since the Washo believed that this kind of physical reaction is necessary if the dream is to confer power. The fact that his spirit power was to be water was unusual, since most Washo shamans had animate rather than inanimate objects as their spirit helpers. Thus, while water baby was a fairly common spirit helper, water was not. In addition, weather control was highly unusual among the Washo, being more prevalent among both the Northern Paiute and the Shoshone.

"The Development of a Washo Shaman," Don Handelman,
Native Californians: A Theoretical Retrospective, Lowell Bean & Thomas
Blackburn (Eds.),1976, pp. 385-386

The relationship of the directions to one another is an important aspect of the people's spirituality and, we might say, theology; because of Creator's handiwork all is alive: both the animate and the inanimate.

A Shoshone woman with her sacred items for prayer

PLATEAU CULTURAL AREA

A young man recognizes the importance of directionality for his life

CONTEMPORARY DIRECTIONAL PRAYER
KLAMATH

Grandfather,
Great Spirit,
We ask you to help us today
As people come before us and tell us
What they are trying to do for the people.
We are here to help people,
Grandfather.
We ask you to give us the knowledge to do this.
Open our ears, Grandfather,
So that we can hear what is said.
We ask you for that power.
We pray for all the people that are on the streets,
Grandfather,
And that are having a hard time.
Help them.
Help the people that are in the hospitals
And that are locked up in the prisons.
Give them the power and the strength to carry on.
Then we ask you for the powers
from the *four directions* to guide us. Amen.

The First Oregonians: An Illustrated Collection of Essays on Traditional Lifeways, Federal-Indian Relations, and the State's Native People Today, Carolyn Buan & Richard Lewis (Eds.), 1991, p. 68

This prayer offered by Clayton Schultz at the opening of a Commission on Indian Services meeting in the 1980s expresses the directional powers' ability to effect healing. It is an ancient but contemporary prayer.

───────────── + ─────────────

PRAYER FOR THE DIRECTIONAL WINDS
SAHAPTIN LANGUAGE GROUPS

The sun (an) is Father; water (cuus), the first sacred food. It is drunk as a sacrament to begin and end each *eaasani* feast. The winds are each named. The prevailing **westerly wind** is *huli,* which may also be used to refer to wind in general. Myths recount epic battles between the frigid **North wind** (atya) and the Chinook wind (winaaway), a strong **southerly flow** of air that can thaw the frozen land in hours and provide relief from the midwinter chill. Hot dry **east winds** (txawna) in spring can burn the precious roots, cutting the harvest short. Winds are powers to be reckoned with. Steep temperature gradients in winter and spring between coast and plateau send air rushing through the Columbia Gorge and the lower passes to sweep across the dusty central plain. Indians here may burn the wood of the pallid evening primrose (kaluz-mi acas, "blueback salmon's eyes"; Oenothera pallida)—the blooms of which freckle the sandy slopes at low elevations at the end of spring—as a prayer to halt the forceful play of the winds.

Nch'i-wana, "The Big River": Mid-Columbia Indians and Their Land,
Eugene Hunn with James Selam & Family, 1990, p. 91

For a lot of the Peoples who lived along or near the Columbia River that runs between Washington and Oregon, the winds were important because they caused drastic temperature changes which affected the life forms wherever they blew. The Peoples today still respect the winds and know them to be four in number, each with spiritual properties. They can be communicated with through the burning of a certain kind of pallid evening primrose.

───────────── + ─────────────

HAND GAME PREPARATIONAL SYMBOLISM
NEZ PERCE

The mat should be laid *east* and *west,* the logs or board put on the *north* and *south* edges and the counting sticks placed in two piles of fifteen each on the ends of the mat. The players sit on the ground, a row on each side of the mat to the *north* and *south*. Lots are drawn to decide which side shall have the bead "in hand." The Leader and the singers must always stand behind the row of players who have the bead "in hand." The opposite side must have the drumstick and beat on the log or board in time with the singers.

When the players are seated in two rows, one on each side of the mat, the Leader hands the bead to a player on the side that has drawn the right to have the bead "in hand," and then takes his place beside the singers, who stand behind that row, and starts the . . . song. All in that row join in the singing. . . .

Indian Games and Dances with Native Songs,
Alice C. Fletcher, 1994, p. 81

The hand-game, a game of guessing, concerns the secretive passing of a stick, a bead, or other items from one member of a team to another. Someone on the opposite team must guess who has it. Spatial orientation is important, as is singing and drumming and rhythmic movements of the hands.

———————————— + ————————————

ORIGINS OF THE SEASONS
YAKIMA

Many years ago when the world was first made, there were five brothers and a sister living in the warm *southland*. There was an abundance of sunshine and just enough warm, gentle rain to make everything grow well. The brothers, who were hunters, never failed to bring home plenty of meat for the family. While they hunted, the sister remained at home. She mended their clothes and made new garments from the hides of the animals the brothers brought home. She was always nicely dressed in buckskin that was ornamented with elk's teeth and beads of bone.

At the same time, in the cold *northland,* lived five brothers and their sister. Their home was just the opposite of the *southern family* for they lived in the land of ice and snow. These brothers were also hunters, but they were not very successful and many times they went hungry. One time when there was no game and they were about to starve, the *northern brothers* sent their sister to the home of the *southern brothers* to ask for some food.

She started out with her brothers following her. They had large icicles in their hands which they used as spears. As she approached, the southern brothers told their sister to dress in her finest buckskin and go to welcome her.

When she was ready, the *southern girl* walked out to meet the *girl from the north.* The girl from the south smiled and the air was warmed. The icicles which the northern boys planned to use as weapons melted and fell to the ground. The northern girl ran back and told her brothers what happened. They were very angry and said to each other, "Let's challenge the southern brothers to wrestle with us."

They sent their challenge and the *southern* brothers accepted. When it was almost autumn, the two families met halfway between their homes. The sisters each took along five buckets filled with water; the northern girl had cold water and the southern girl had warm. They planned to throw the contents at the feet of the wrestlers.

When everything was ready, the oldest brother from the *north* began wrestling with the oldest brother from the south. They were evenly matched and no one seemed able to get an advantage. Suddenly, the girl from the north threw one of her buckets of ice and water at the feet of her brother. This made him fight harder and he started to overcome his rival. Then the southern sister threw her warm water at the feet of the wrestlers. The ice melted and immediately the southern man beat the man from the north and killed him.

At once, the next oldest brother from the *north* attacked the victor. In a fierce fight he overcame the southern brother who soon lay on the ground dead. One by one, the brothers from each tribe wrestled with a brother from the other tribe. After a while only the youngest in each family was left alive.

These two wrestled for five days and neither was able to defeat the other. On the sixth day the boy from the *South* weakened and was almost beaten, but somehow rallied. They both agreed to stop and rest for a while, and the southern boy went to his home and stayed there five moons.

At the end of that time, he traveled *north* and met the northern boy where they had fought before. This time the northern boy was soundly defeated and driven far back into the cold land. For about six moons the southern brother had possession of the land of the northern family. At the end of six moons, the northern boy returned, and they wrestled for a whole moon. This time the southern boy was defeated and driven home.

Even today, the two boys continue to wrestle for mastery of the land. When the *southern* boy defeats the *northern* one, we have summer. When the northern wrestler defeats the southern one, we have winter. Two battles are waged every year. Just before spring, the southern boy conquers the northern boy; in the autumn, the northern boy conquers the southern boy. Each rules the land for a few months.

Where Is the Eagle?, William Coffer, 1981, pp. 205-206

This People recognizes the importance of direction, even in this origin story. It is somewhat similar to a Patagonian story of a wrestling match between the winds that come from the four directions.

Praying with sweetgrass braid and buffalo

RESPECT FOR PRIMAL ELEMENTS OF CREATION
KIOWA

Throughout the centuries the Kiowas witnessed floods and volcanic eruptions, and they marveled at the power of *Dom-oye-alm-daw-k'hee* as the Recreator of the Earth. They felt the force of the *four winds* and respected the Earth-maker's mysterious spirit power, *Daw-k'hee.* Amidst these wonders, they prayed to the spirit god reflected through the sun, *Pahy-ghya-daw-kee.* The Kiowas accepted creation as good and they lived as free people in the natural order.

Kiowa Voices: Ceremonial Dance, Ritual and Song,
Maurice Boyd, 1981, p. 5

Most people enjoy the feeling of a breeze blowing upon the face and body. It is a good feeling. When it is particularly strong, the wind can do damage and one must be ready. The four winds speak of a power beyond the individual, a power that must be respected and properly lived with.

———————————— + ————————————

FEATHER DANCE
KIOWA

The dance ritual followed the instructions originally given to the Kiowas by the apostle Sitting Bull. First the priest lighted a pipe and blew smoke *heavenward* as an offering to the sun; next, he repeated the gesture *to the earth* and then *to the lodge fire.* After smoking to the *east, south, north,* and *west* in succession, he solemnly offered a prayer for the welfare of the tribe, for help, and for the coming of the messiah. All stood while they prayed, extending their hands with palms down as they implored the messiah to come. Since the crow was the sacred bird of the Ghost Dance, the Crow Signal Song always ended the ceremonies.

The ten dance leaders, holding sacred feathers as the sign of leadership, prayed while sprinkling a sacred powder upon the dance ground. The sacred number for the dance was ten, and the ten leaders of the ceremony formed ten dance groups. Everyone held a sacred feather, which had been painted on a special day as revealed in a vision.

The body of each dancer was painted with a pattern seen in a vision. The multicolored designs included symbols for the sun, moon, stars, crosses, and crows, among others. The dancer's face was spotted blue with a red and yellow line in the center of his forehead.

To begin the dance the ten leaders entered the dance circle followed by their groups of dancers, all wearing blankets. The participants joined hands, intertwining their fingers and facing inward toward the cedar pole in the center while softly singing their first song. With the next song, their voices grew in volume as they moved about the circle in a clockwise fashion, *east* to *west*. The halting dance step was performed by slowly dragging one foot after the other, barely lifting either from the ground.

The Feather Dance songs were constantly repeated to produce a hypnotic effect. As the leaders waved their wands, emotions grew. A leader often waved his sacred feather before a single ecstatic dancer so that the dancer's eyes were forced to look directly into the sun, thereby enhancing the hypnotic effect. At this point the dancer sometimes rushed into the open clearing and ran in circles, or stood rigid with arms extended, or spun like a whirling top before falling into a trance, apparently unconscious. This part of the Feather Dance was called the frenzy, *guan a'kalk-i,* or "dance craziness."

The Kiowas modified the Feather Dance when they held the dance apart from the other tribes. The Kiowa Proper introduced an assembly for worship and included a giant tipi in the ceremony.

Dance meetings were held in an extra large tipi entrusted to the priest, Afraid-of-bears, who became its keeper. The members assembled in a circle with a cedar tree (altar)—the symbol of everlasting greenery and eternal life—on the *west* side of the assembly floor. The priest occupied the center of the sanctuary on an elevated platform in the back of the Yellow Cross. This cross symbolized the extensive power of the Creator over all *four corners of the universe,* clearly indicating that mankind falls under a divine power of salvation. The men sat in a circle in front of the cross; the women and children were behind the cross and to the rear.

The women's buckskin dresses, free of ornaments and beadwork, had only a moon and stars insignia painted on the front of the blouse. The men had no special costume, but used hand bells and rattles made of the tips of deer hoofs tied together.

The priest, with the ten ordained elders to help him, sought a message from the spiritual world. Since the first meeting on the South Canadian River in 1890, trances and visions were associated with the Feather Dance. Trances usually occurred only after many hours or days of dancing. The Kiowas put their hearts into the dance, praying for a vision. Sometimes an authorized and consecrated elder went into a trance and communicated with a departed spirit. After all, the individual spirit never dies, but merely passes to the spirit world.

Kiowa Voices: Ceremonial Dance, Ritual and Song,
Maurice Boyd, 1981, pp. 93-94

The Feather Dance of the Kiowas illustrates the extent to which the Ghost Dance spread to tribes far distant from the Prophet Wovoka in Nevada. And yet the four directions are acknowledged with the pipe prayers and with sacred movement in the dance steps. The cedar tree and the cross and the circular seating pattern appear to be hybrid forms that speak of both traditional Kiowa spirituality and Christian spirituality.

———————————— + ————————————

AFTERLIFE BELIEFS
IOWA

They think the soul goes to a place of rest, where it lives in the body as it does here, knows former friends and is happy.

They address the dead after death. They put on them their best attire, paint their faces, and then some one of the same tribe who is called upon by the oldest son, if a father, or some near relative, then makes a formal address to the body. In burying, the old practice was to bury in a sitting position with the face to the *east.* The body was put in the ground and over the top was raised a small mound ... no opening was left in the grave for the spirit to reenter ... for *four nights* after the burial it was customary to build a fire on the grave. With the body they buried food, and weapons and personal articles of the deceased in the belief that they would be useful to him on the journey.

They also believe that the souls of those who are killed in battle or that are killed in a village, do not go to heaven immediately, but are transmuted into thunder birds. That it is the souls of these departed warriors who make the thunder and lightning, and they are represented as having the form of birds. I did not learn whether their solicitude to carry away the bodies of the slain for burial was caused by this notion on the ground that those who remain unburied are the ones only who become thunder birds, which I presume is the fact.

Lewis Henry Morgan: The Indian Journals 1859-62,
Leslie White (Ed.), 1959, p. 69

Morgan, who had done much personal study of Iroquois folkways, travelled further into "Indian Country" and commented on the People that he met along the way. He had some specific interests that he wanted to learn more about, like language of families and clan systems. Though he was limited in his understanding of the complexity of each Peoples' customs, he nevertheless left a written record of what he experienced. Here he records eastward pointing of the seated corpse and the four-day ceremonial vigil fire.

—————————— + ——————————

PIPE CEREMONY FOR THE HUNT
OMAHA

... a pipe ritual prior to a bison hunt: The party having approached as near the herd as they suppose the animals will permit without taking alarm, they halt to give the pipe bearer an opportunity to perform the ceremony of smoking, which is considered necessary to their success. He lights his pipe and remains a short time with his head inclined. The stem of the pipe extends towards the herd. He then smokes and puffs the smoke towards the bison, towards the heavens, the earth, and finally to the *cardinal points* successively.

Offering Smoke: The Sacred Pipe and Native American Religion,
Jordan Paper, 1988, p. 21

Prayer before a hunt was always a necessity, and the pipe would naturally be carried along to help ensure success. This account of the Omaha pipe ceremony before a bison hunt was witnessed by Stephen H. Long some time in the 1820s. It manifests an ancient veneration of the cardinal directions.

———————————————— + ————————————————

BLESSING OF A YOUNG CHILD
OMAHA

The name of this ceremony was Thiku'wi'xe *(thi,* a prefix indicating action by the hand; *ku'wi'xe,* "to turn")....

All children, both boys and girls, passed through this ceremony, which is a survival of that class of ceremonies belonging to the lowest, or oldest, stratum of tribal rites; it is directly related to the cosmic forces—the wind, the earth, and the fire. Through this ceremony all the children who had reached the period when they could move about unaided, could direct their own steps, were symbolically "sent into the midst of the winds"—that element essential to life and health; their feet were set upon the stone—emblem of long life upon the earth and of the wisdom derived from age; while the "flames," typical of the lifegiving power, were invoked to give their aid toward insuring the capacity for a long, furitful, and successful life within the tribe. Through this ceremony the child passed out of that stage in its life wherein it was hardly distinguished from all other living forms into its place as distinctively a human being, a member of its birth gens, and through this to a recognized place in the tribe. As it went forth its baby name was thrown away, its feet were clad in new moccasins made after the manner of the tribe, and its *ni'kie* name was proclaimed to all nature and to the assembled people. . . .

The ceremony . . . took place in the springtime, after the first thunders had been heard. . . .

The tent was always a large one, set facing the ***east***, and open at the entrance, so that that the bystanders, who kept at a respectful distance, could see something of what was going on within. . . .

In the center was a fire. On the ***east*** of the fire was placed a stone. There was also a ball of grass, placed at the ***west*** of the fire-place near its edge. It was the mother who led the child to the tent. At the door she paused, and addressed the priest within, saying: "Venerable man! I desire my child to wear moccasins." Then she dropped the hand of the child, and the little one, carrying his new moccasins, entered the tent alone. He was met by the priest, who advanced to the door to receive the gifts brought by the mother as fees. Here she again addressed him, saying: "I desire my child to walk long upon the earth; I desire him to be content with the light of many days. We seek your protection; we hold to you for strength." The priest replied, addressing the child: "You shall reach the fourth hill sighing; you shall be bowed over; you shall have wrinkles; your staff shall bend under your weight. I speak to you that you may be strong . . . you shall live long and enjoy many possessions; your eyes shall be satisfied with many good things." Then moving with the child toward the fireplace in the center of the lodge, and speaking in the capacity of the Thunder . . . he began to sing the Invocation addressed to the Winds:

Duba ha ti no'zhi' ga she no'zhi' ga
Duba ha ti no'zhi' ga
She no'zhi'ga! She no'zhi' ga
I' I'

Literal translation: *Duba*, four; *ha* signifies that the number four refers to groups; *ti*, from *ati*, come ye; *no'zhi'*, stand; a, from *iga*, word of command given to a number; *she*, from *shethu*, a definite place near by; *ga*, a command, and end of the sentence; *I'*, the rolling thunder. The "four" refers to the four winds, to which the invocation is addressed by the Thunder priest.

Free translation
>   Ye four, come hither and stand, near shall ye stand
>   In four groups shall ye stand
>   Here shall ye stand, in this place stand
>   (The Thunder rolls).

At the close of this ritual song the priest faces the child to the *east*, lifting it by the shoulder; its feet are allowed to rest upon the stone. He then turns the child completely around, from left to right. . . . When the child had been turned, its feet rested on the stone as it faced the *south*. The priest then lifted it by the arms, turned it, and set its feet on the stone as it faced the *west*; then he again lifted the child, turned it, and set its feet on the stone as it faced the *north*. Lastly the child was lifted to its feet and placed on the stone as it again faced the *east*. During this action the following ritual song was sung: . . .

>   She gakuwi'xe akithe tha
>   She gakuwi'xe akithe tha
>   Baxu duba ha te tade duba ha te
>   Tade baco' the akithe tha
>   Tade duba ha te
>   I'I'

Literal translation: *She*, from *shethi*, going yonder, implies a person speaking; *ga*, to strike by the wind; *kuwi'xe*, to whirl; *tha*, oratorical end of the sentence; *baxu*, ridge or hill; *duba*, four; *ha*, groups; *te*, descriptive suffix indicating standing; *baco'*, in the midst; *the*, goes (third person); *akithe*, I cause him; *tha*, end of sentence; *tade*, winds; *duba*, four; *ha*, groups; *te*, standing; *I'*, rolling of the Thunder.

Free translation
>   Turned by the winds goes the one I send yonder;
>   Yonder he goes who is whirled by the winds;
>   Goes, where the four hills of life and the four winds are standing;
>   There, in the midst of the winds do I send him,
>   Into the midst of the winds, standing there.

(The Thunder rolls)

The winds invoked by the priest stand in four groups, and receive the child, which is whirled by them, and by them enabled "to face in every direction." This action symbolizes that the winds will come and strengthen him as hereafter he shall traverse the earth and meet the vicissitudes he must encounter as he passes over the four hills and completes the circuit of a long life. . . .

The priest now puts the new moccasins on the feet of the child, as the following ritual song was sung. Toward its close the child was lifted, set on its feet, and made to take four steps typical of its entrance into a long life. . . .

The ni'kie name of the child was now announced, after which the priest cried aloud: "Ye hills, ye grass, ye trees, ye creeping things both great and small, I bid you hear! This child has thrown away its baby name. Ho!"

The Omaha Tribe, Alice Fletcher & Francis LaFlesche, 1992, pp. 117-121

This account illustrates a particular kind of familiarity with the four winds that come from the east, the south, the west, and the north respectively. The People knew about their different kinds of velocities, temperatures, strengths, and gifts. What better way to introduce a child to the gifts of life than to envelope him or her with the winds that come from each direction and to have the child step on rocks that bespeak the ancientness of our life on Mother Earth!

---------------------------------- + ----------------------------------

IMPORTANCE OF THE FOUR WNDS
OSAGE

The Earth was called *Mon-Shon* and *Honga* (Sacred One). All animals, waters, plants, rocks, the things upon which the Osage depended came through the grace of the Mother Earth. The Little Ones viewed themselves as the caretakers of the land on which they lived and hunted; responsible, through their thoughts and actions and ceremonies, for the health and well-being of the life around them.

There were also many powers that dwelt in and around the Earth: The Thunders, the Waters, the Rocks. The **Four Winds** brought the seasons and the weather, as well as good or bad fortune. As messengers of the High Beings, they were appealed to so that they might carry the People's prayers to the Gods. The animals of the Earth had different powers, according to their nature and could impart to frail men their great strengths and abilities. Among the animals thought to possess much "medicine" were the bear, buffalo, hawk, eagle, otter, beaver, as well as the spider. The plants and trees lived long and useful lives and had the power to heal and nourish. Besides these, there were also many unseen powers that inhabited the Earth, though in a different plane of existence. Such were the elementals that dwelt in dark forests, certain springs and other mysteroius places. Some could take on the form of animals or of strange and frightening beasts, like the water monsters of ancient tales.

Osage Life and Legends: Earth People/Sky People,
Robert Liebert, 1987, p. 45

The Osage, like all Native Peoples of this continent, always knew that "the world is charged with the grandeur of God" (Pick, 1966, p. 47). All plants and animals, as well as the directional four winds, even all beings visible or invisible, mediate the gifts of the Creator.

———————————— + ————————————

PRAYERS OF PETITION
OSAGE

To bring in the new year a round of sweat baths were taken, along with emetics, to purify minds and bodies. The two grand chiefs went to the lodge of a man that owned a shrine which signified the well-being of the people and prayed to the "gods" or powers that had control over the lives of the People, for peace and health in the tribe. The chiefs then went to the borders of the village and called loudly to the *four directions*:

Wah-Kon-Dah will cause the coming days to be calm and peaceful.
The Tzi-Sho and Honga have called to Wah-Kon-Dah
    to make the days calm and peaceful.
That the little ones may come to us in unbroken
    succession and we become a People.

Wah-Kon-Dah will make the days beautiful:
Toward the winds of the *rising sun*,
Towards the winds of the *south*,
Towards the winds of the *setting sun*,
Towards the winds of the Land of Cedars (the *north*),
Wah-Kon-Dah will make the days to be calm and peaceful.

Osage Life and Legends: Earth People/Sky People,
Robert Liebert, 1987, pp. 26-27

Such a beautiful prayer to the Creator (Wah-kon-dah) asks for peace, many healthy children, and happy days. It is prayed on behalf of all the People, but especially those of the village of the one offering it.

+

PIPE CEREMONY
PAWNEE

Among Missouri basin and Plains native cultures, ritual warrior societies were a major feature of religious life. In 1902, James Murie observed the Skidi Pawnee Two Lance Society's renewal of the lances ritual, which demonstrates the elaborate variations on basic Sacred Pipe ritual that may develop. Only the society's members, excluding Murie, would have been present. Following the lance preparation ritual per se, Known-the-leader announced, "It is now time to offer smoke to the gods to show that we remember them. . . . Knife Chief will now rise and take the pipe I have filled."

Knife-chief rose and took the pipe which belongs in a sacred bundle. It is very old; the bowl is large; the stem smooth and round and represents the windpipe through which the prayers of the people pass. Knife-chief walked around the fireplace with the pipe, beginning at the *south*. At the *northeast* he stopped and the *south* assistant lighted the pipe with a burning coal. He then walked around the fireplace by the *west* and then *south* with the lighted pipe and stopped successively at the *south* and *north* entrances and blew smoke in those directions. He next halted at the fireplace and blew smoke on its rim towards the *northeast* and the *northwest*. *West* of the fireplace he stopped and blew smoke *southwest* and *southeast*. Then he passed *north* and stopped at the *west* facing *east*. He blew smoke *east*, *west*, and then *east* again. Then he directed smoke towards the heavens;

three times to the *north,* once to the *south,* faced about and blew smoke *west.* He turned again and blew towards the ground and the drums.

The pipe was then passed to those on the *north* and the *south* sides, each person taking four whiffs. Knife-chief then strewed the ashes from the pipebowl *west* of the fireplace and facing *west* passed his hands over the pipe-stem, then over his own body, and handed the pipe to Known-the-leader who said, "Nawa." All the rest of the people said, "Nawa." This ended the first smoke ceremony.

Offering Smoke: The Sacred Pipe and Native American Religion,
Jordan Paper, 1988, p. 32

The one praying blew smoke at points illustrative of each of the cardinal directions and also to the intercardinal directions. This pipe ceremony took into account all the directions that were important to the People.

--------------------- + ---------------------

GHOST DANCE HAND GAME
PAWNEE

Filling the Horn Spoon: The offerer with the horn spoon held in his right hand proceeds clockwise as he leaves the altar, until he reaches the buckets of corn *east* of the fireplace. Here he fills the spoon. To do so, for an arrangement of the buckets of corn in an arc, he comes inside the arc, that is, between the food and the fireplace. There are then two alternatives: a complete ritual method, and an abbreviated form. In the former, he dips the spoon into each bucket individually, from left to right down the row (or, from *north* to *south*), until with the dip into the bucket at the extreme *south* of the row, he has about filled the spoon. In the shorter form he takes corn from the bucket in the middle of the row, and from the one at each end. The order is middle bucket, extreme right or *south* bucket, and (turning completely around before proceeding, in order to maintain the clockwise ceremonial circuit) the extreme left or *north* bucket. The body turn for ceremonial purposes is here equivalent to a circuit around the fireplace.

In the arrangement of nine buckets in a cross, or "five-pointed star," the offerer first stands *north* of the buckets, and leaning over dips some from the central one, then moves to the *east* of the buckets and dips from the extreme eastern bucket—the one at the outer point of the cross-bar directed eastward; then moves to the *south* and dips from the extreme south bucket; then to the *west,* between buckets and fireplace, where facing *east* he dips from the extreme western bucket; and finally to the *north* where he dips corn from the extreme northern bucket. He has thus made a complete circuit, and dipped corn from five of the nine buckets, the central one, and the four outer ones. In a complete ritual form, he would now repeat his circuit, taking dips of corn from each of the four inner buckets.

After the spoon has been filled with corn, the offerer comes around to a position behind all the food. There are several ways in which he reaches this position. If he has followed the briefer form of filling the spoon, he finishes standing at the *north* end of the row of buckets, facing *east*; with the cross arrangement of the buckets he finishes at the *north* facing *south*. In both these cases, he may either come clockwise around the food to the *east* behind it and stop, or proceed through this position and then through a complete circuit of the fireplace clockwise until he again reaches *east* of the food facing *west*. On the other hand, if the complete form has been followed in filling the spoon from the row of buckets, the offerer finished at the extreme *south* of the row. From here he must proceed with the spoonful through a clockwise circuit of the fireplace, coming back outside or *east* of the assembled food to a position between food and *east* where he faces *west*.

In this position, the offerer makes two motions. The first is with the right hand, while the left holds the spoonful; the second, after changing the spoon to the right hand, with the left.

Motion: The free hand is extended out to the side; the right hand out to the right or north as the offerer faces *west,* at about normal shoulder height, the left analogously. At the constant height with the palm open and directed downward the hand is then swept inward around over the food until just past a position straight forward. The hands are changed and an analogous movement made with the other.

In the words of an informant, speaking of these motions, "this brings everything together," and implies that the offering is of all the assembled food.

The Pawnee Ghost Dance Hand Game: Ghost Dance Revival and Ethnic Identity, Alexander Lesser, 1978, pp. 221-222

As one can see from this ceremonial feast, great attention is paid to the ritual movement in a clockwise manner and the positioning at certain directions. These details bespeak much care in the observance of ancient traditions. Nowadays our prayer or etiquette might be simple, but nevertheless one can learn a lot from other, even ancient, ways of doing things.

———————————— + ————————————

PIPE CEREMONY
ARAPAHO

As with church choirs, the leaders, both men and women, frequently assembled privately in a tipi to rehearse the new or old songs for the next dance. During the first winter spent among the Arapaho I had frequent opportunity of being present at these rehearsals, as for a long time the snow was too deep to permit dancing outside. After having obtained their confidence the Arapaho police invited me to come up to their camp at night to hear them practice the songs in anticipation of better weather for dancing. Thenceforth rehearsals were held in Black Coyote's tipi almost every night until the snow melted, each session usually lasting about three hours.

On these occasions from eight to twelve persons were present, sitting in a circle on the low beds around the fire in the center. Black Coyote acted as master of ceremonies and opened proceedings by filling and lighting the redstone pipe, offering the first whiff to the sun, then reversing the stem in offering to the earth, next presenting the pipe to the fire, and then to each of the *four cardinal points*. He then took a few puffs himself, after which he passed the pipe to his next neighbor, who went through the same preliminaries before smoking, and thus the pipe went round the circle, each one taking only a few puffs before passing it on. The pipe was then put back into its pouch, and Black Coyote, standing with his face toward the **northwest,** the messiah's country, with eyes closed and arms outstretched, made a fervent prayer for help and prosperity to his tribe, closing with an earnest petition to the messiah to hasten his coming. The others listened in silence with bowed heads.

The Ghost-Dance Religion and the Sioux Outbreak of 1890,
James Mooney, 1991, p. 918

This pipe ceremony, celebrated at a song practice for the Ghost Dance, shows that the four directions are acknowledged. Facing northwest, an intercardinal direction, is significant in that it becomes a body-posture prayer anticipating the coming of the Messiah.

---- + ----

RITUAL PLACEMENT OF PEOPLE
IN HEALING CEREMONY
POTAWATOMI

Another "remedy" society, called the Snake Society, was led by a Shamaness, Mrs. Obínig. . . .

The Snake's formula treated bites by snakes, insects, men and dogs. Snakebite was considered the commonest and most dangerous of all; its cure was the society's chief business. . . .

The public spring rite and feast were given in the Obínig house, to which guests come on tobacco or verbal invitations. Places were formally set in this way: at the *southwest* side of the room sat the two male singers, Obínig and Joe Hale, who put himself *north* of the old man. Along the *west* side, on the ground before the three men were laid "powerful" sacks made of snake, weasel, and mink hides. Each belonged to a member, who put his down when entering the room from the *east*. Older members, such as as the Obínig couple, had the more "powerful" hides, and laid them at the extreme *south* end. Weaker sacks of younger people, such as the sons and their children, were laid *north* of these. A large cloth was spread before the hides, to their *east*, for tobacco dropped there by entering members and guests. . . . Along the *westerly* half of the *south* wall sat members who, as the side filled, then took places along the western half of the *north* wall. Guests sat at the *east* wall. . . . Mrs. Obínig sat before the members on the *south* side. In front of the tobacco-heaped cloth, towards the *south* end, appeared four dishes of food. The ritual placements expressed purposes, high respect, and ethics of design. . . .

When all were seated, the two singers intoned a general account (only generalizations were offered at public meetings, to preclude theft of "power" secrets) of their Medicine's history. Then, or in later afternoon after the feast, members performed a "snake dance" (this was suppressed by the Agency). The dance represented Snake movements, as if members blended with the Snake Spirit, dancing single file in coiling routes after the leader, who followed even smaller circles until the whole line bunched in a dense knot—the rattler's pose of huddling and rearing to strike. Suddenly the bunch uncoiled, people flinging themselves in all directions, running swiftly. Then again they formed a straight row, dancing in place. It was said that, at times, formerly they handled rattlers to show mastery, a sight that onlookers, patently, never forgot.

The Prairie Potawatami: Tradition and Ritual in
the Twentieth Century, Ruth Landes, 1970, pp. 72-75

In this account it seems that there are varying strengths for the sacks of hides. The "stronger" ones (snake, weasel, and mink hides) are placed at the west side and south side, while the "weaker" ones are deposited at the north. The ritual placement of people, food, and other items expressed the spiritual ways of the Potawatomi People.

+

SHIELD, WIND, AND DIRECTIONAL SYMBOLISM
CHEYENNE

... there is another well-documented Cheyenne shield in the collection of the Foundation for the Preservation of American Indian Art and Culture, Chicago.... The origin story of this shield is as follows:

... a young man, Whistling Elk went to a certain lake, and out on a rocky point running into the water. He carried with him a buffalo-skull, and putting it on the ground, lay down by it, and there fasted and prayed for five days and five nights. On the morning of the fourth day, a buffalo raised its head above the water and sang a song, directing Whistling Elk to make this shield and describing how it should be made.

The painting on the shield consists of a pair of long, slender, upward-directed horns, a little above the center of the shield; below them is a large disc surrounded by dots; between the horns is a red disc also surrounded by dots, and there are four dark discs evenly distributed near the border of the shield. These discs on the outer rim represent the *four directions;* the disc below the horns is the moon;

the red disc between the horns, the sun; and the dots are stars. The horns represent the animal that took pity on Whistling Elk and taught him how to make this shield. The moon is the spirit that during the night protected the brave who carried the shield, and the sun protected him during the day. The upper round spot to the left of the horns represents the *wind which comes from the setting sun*. The upper spot at the right of the horns represents the *wind from the north*, the lower spot on the right, the *wind from the east*, and the lower spot on the left, the *wind from the south*. The spirit which controls the *south wind* is supposed to have the greatest power when prayed to for help.

"Cheyenne Shields and Their Cosmological Background,"
American Indian Art Magazine, Imre Hagy, Summer 1994, pp. 40-41

The holy winds and the respective directions from which they come are never forgotten, even in battle. They are the powers which help with protection for the warriors and their unique gifts offer the man in battle possibilities for special moments of strength and valor.

———————————— + ————————————

COSMOLOGICAL INTERPRETATIONS
CHEYENNE

The Cheyenne universe might be arranged along a vertical axis and two horizontal axes, each perpendicular to the other. At the zenith of the vertical axis, within *Otatavoom*, the Blue Sky-Space, is the spiritual realm of *Ma'heo'o*, the All-Father, while the nadir within *Nsthoaman*, the Deep Earth, embodies *Heestoz*, the female principle. The female principle is emphatically not spiritual, however, for the vertical dialectic of cosmology is played out between spirit/maleness at the zenith and the matter/femaleness at the nadir. The spatial zones between zenith and nadir are tiered, and all witness, in various ways, the interaction between male energy and female substance. Male energy is represented by such spiritual entities as *Atovsz*, the Sun; *Ameonito*, the Moon; *Nemevota*, the Rain; *Nonoma*, the Thunder; and *Vovetas*, the Tornado. The material manifestations of femaleness include not only the sterile Deep Earth, *Nsthoaman*, but also the zone of fertile soil, *Votostoom*. The next tier above *Votostoom* is *Taxtavoom*, the atmosphere, then follow *Setovoom*, the Nearer Sky-Space, and

Otatavoom, the Blue Sky-Space, at the very top of the cosmos. All entities of the universe, except *Ma'heo'o* (all spirit) and *Nsthoaman* (all matter or substance) represent some organic composition of spirituality and substance. Entities within zones are entitled to more or less respect depending on how much spirit and how much substance they embody. For example, three categories of birds occupy the three upper zones of the upper world—the Atmosphere, the Nearer Sky-Space and the Blue Sky-Space—depending on their sacredness and role in Cheyenne cosmology.

The horizontal axis of the universe, the *four directions,* are related to respective colors, social structure and personal ritual paraphernalia, so the symbols related to these directions are more ambiguous than those of the vertical axis.

. . . we must understand that native artists converged the elements of the horizontal plane and vertical axis on only a single plane, the circular surface of the shield. Thus, we may reasonably suspect that elements belonging to both the horizontal and the vertical panes can be found among the painted designs. Further, we should not forget that these designs often have a "polysemic" function. This phrase, borrowed from linguistics, indicates that a certain element is capable of expressing many meanings at the same time.

"Cheyenne Shields and Their Cosmological Background,"
American Indian Art Magazine,
Imre Hagy, Summer 1994, pp. 39-40

The horizontal axis of the universe, the place where most human activities seem to take place, was always understood to be an orderly place by the Cheyenne. Color and ceremonial and personal things always took into consideration the universe and the direction points of contact with Maheó, the Creator.

———— + ————

SHIELD POWER
CHEYENNE

. . . it becomes clear that Cosmic Power, the Thunder and the Guardians of the *four directions* are the primary forces involved, which in a permutating system of associations means that the bearer of the shield is capable of repelling the thunders and bullets of his enemies throughout the *four corners* of the world.

"Cheyenne Shields and Their Cosmological Background,"
American Indian Art Magazine, Imre Hagy, Summer 1994, p. 45

A shield used in battle at a particular moment and at a particular place allows the warrior to experience battle on a cosmic level as he repels the "thunders and bullets of his enemies throughout the four corners of the world."

+

INTERCARDINAL SIGNIFICATION
CHEYENNE

The Cheyenne Indians also use the sacred circle and *the Cardinal Directions* as an educational tool and refer to it as the Medicine Wheel. In their lore, the *southwest* is the place of innocence and growth. Its color is red, and its totems are weather and the little mouse spirit. The *northwest* is the place of introspection, perfection, beauty and harvest. Its color is yellow, and its totem is the bear spirit. The *northeast* is the location of wisdom, death and disease. Its color is black, which is associated with purification, and its totem is the buffalo spirit. The *southeast* is the source of illumination, life and renewal. Its color is white, and its totem is the golden eagle, who—because it flies so high and is so powerful and sharp eyed—is considered a principal intermediary between the Above Beings and humans.

In using the Medicine Wheel for teaching and meditative purposes, the Cheyenne seek to discover themselves, to perceive things and themselves, to find relationships with the world around them, and to "turn the wheel." They explain the latter by saying that all of life takes place in a continuous circle, whose center and source of power are the Above Beings. Life flows from Them into the hoop and keeps it turning. The life lived by any person is represented by marking a small place on the hoop. Using this as a focal point, that person's life is thought of as being the result of what has been inserted into the hoop by prior generations, including grandparents and parents, all of whom have transmitted themselves into that person either literally or figuratively. While the person lives, he or she benefits from the ancestors' contributions, builds upon them, reshapes them, and hopefully adds to them in a positive way. When people leave this world for the next, their own contributions, including their children, are left behind as additions to the hoop that will continue to do its part in nourishing future generations. Thus the hoop turns and continues, unbroken and unending.

Secret Native American Pathways: A Guide to Inner Peace,
Thomas Mails, 1988, pp. 211-213

The tradition of using the intercardinals, rather than only the cardinal directions is not so unusual. Many of the tribes, as with most peoples of the world, have migrated to other places and brought their traditions with them. At times the migration was forced! Many tribes, like the Cheyenne, were split up and forced to live in places far from their homelands. Today the Cheyenne have reservation homes in Montana and Oklahoma. Some spiritual traditions developed along the way as they met people with other tribal customs and beliefs. It is not unusual today to notice tribes living side by side who are similar in customs outwardly but who have their own unique ways of celebrating a common Plains ceremony (for instance, the Sundance).

———————————— + ————————————

MASSAUM CEREMONY OF RE-ENACTMENT OF CREATION OF THE WORLD
CHEYENNE

The annual Tsistsistas tribal ceremonies, held in the presence of Maheo and the spiritual powers of the universe, depict the ancient order, *wonoom,* of the creation and serve its preservation. Today the Tsistsistas, forced to live in an environment destroyed by others, view the physical destruction of the world as an episode nearing its frightful end.

In the Massaum ceremony the creation of the world and its order was ritually reenacted. The ceremony began with nonexistence before existence, the time before all time. On the second day of the secret part of the ceremony, in the seclusion of the wolf tipi, the priest knelt on the ground *west* of the center pole. Because the center of the tipi had been cleared from sod, he knelt on the deep earth. He gently pressed the thumb of his right hand into the smooth earth. He marked four more spots about five inches from the central one, on the *northeast, southeast, southwest,* and *northwest.*

The universe was created from the center. The priest who represented Maheo in this action, opened the ground with a digging stick at the location of his first thumbprint (the cosmological singularity). He broke earth from the opening four times and placed it on the markers of the *four ceremonial directions.* The round opening, now about three inches wide and deep, was in the center of four small mounds. Between these, extending from the opening, he painted on the ground a white cross whose arms extended in the *cardinal directions.* The cross and the four mounds of the corners delineated *hestanov,* the universe. He covered the *southeastern and southwestern* mounds with red powder and the other two with black. These represented the mountains of the *maheyuno,* the four sacred guardians at the corners of the universe.

The Wolves of Heaven: Cheyenne Shamanism, Ceremonies, and Prehistoric Origins, Karl Schlesier, 1987, p. 7

Ceremonies are often didactic; they offer elements of teaching as they are celebrated. In various ways throughout the year people had ample opportunities to consider their origins and the reception of the things needed for life that were given by the Creator (Maheo). Both cardinal and intercardinal directions figured into the telling of the stories that would teach the People.

———————————— + ————————————

MEANING OF THE DIRECTIONS
CHEYENNE/ARAPAHO

Each of the four Maheyuno or spirit keepers has a specific intelligence, and together they are known as the wisdom of the *four directions.* The Great Spirit Maheo is the source of wisdom and intelligence. All created things, spirit and matter, are images of Maheo and possess an intelligence of Source, which can be shared. When summoned, the wisdom and power of the *four directions* can be shared with human beings.

THE SPIRIT OF THE *EAST*

The power of the *East* is the power of enlightenment, wisdom, and spiritual vision, our highest goals in life. It is the place of the morning star, the only star which shines with the sun. The medicine of the morning star is wisdom, involving the light of discernment. We Cheyennes are the Morning Star People. . . .

The season of the *East* is spring, the awakening of life from winter and the birth of new life, new seeds, new buds. It is a season of planting seeds and new ideas, new beginnings. The time is sunrise when life awakens from sleep. The colors are yellow and gold and have the power of invoking spiritual vision, growth, and healing. Yellow is the color of natural wisdom. With new life the universe is illuminated. So it is with the sunrise, which gives a special power to those who greet its rays. The time of life of the *East* is birth and infancy, the newborn, and its quality is innocence. The power of the *East* is that of light removing darkness, of a seed sprouting, and of a flower opening to the sun. It is a magnificent awakening, a new light, a new life.

The plant of the *East* is the dandelion, which is a source of vitamins A, B, and C. These help purify the blood. The mineral is amber, which is actually neither jewel nor mineral but the petrified tree resin of an extinct coniferous pine. Amber beads, amulets, and charms have been found in sites that date from ancient times. The ancients called it the "tears of the sun, the perspiration of the earth." It is thousands of years old and contains the accumulated wisdom of the earth. As one of the most powerful healing agents in nature, it also contains the power of the sun.

Amber is used in ritual healing by shamans to invoke and embrace the healing powers. It contains elemental virtues and qualities useful in curing all sorts of disease. When mixed with honey and taken internally, amber has been prescribed for bad eyesight; worn externally it heals and protects the throat.

Light, the antagonist of darkness, the dispeller of gloom and ignorance, is a great focus of healing. Amber irradiates light in a peculiarly pure way and is a source of wonder and inspiration. Amber glows yellow as the sun and is shaded light to dark, with a smooth silk-like luster. It is the gift to us from another healing agent, the wood of a tree.

Amber not only attracts light; it has electricity. Golden as the sun, charged with its hidden electrical power, it is a testimony that nothing ends, that life renews itself in countless ways. Yellow amber, once a tree growing in a long-ago forest, has changed form and become a different substance. In it is found the living embodiment of the Creative Spirit.

The animal of the *East* is the golden spotted eagle. It flies highest of all winged ones, thus closer to Maheo, and is the messenger of dreams and visions. The vision of the eagle from high places is like consciousness elevated, so the golden eagle is regarded as Maheo's messenger. It is the sun bird with feathers as rays of the sun. When any part of it is carried or worn, it represents the presence of God and of the higher self. . . .

THE SPIRIT OF THE *SOUTH*

The power of the *South* is growth occurring so rapidly that trust is needed because there may not be time for evaluation. It is a time of extending out into the world, experiencing and investigating. It is the time of testing ideas and methods, of putting knowledge, vision, and wisdom to work in the world.

The season is summer, when spring is fulfilled. The sun is direct and hot; there is movement and nature is flourishing. It is the time of the sun dance to celebrate and commune with earth and sun.

The power of the living, breathing earth is conspicuous at this time. The newborn of spring now experience the fast growth of the summer. The warm winds of the *South* embrace and nourish. Life is brought together. New projects are in process. The power of the *South* and of summer is the primal power of mating. The corresponding time of day is noon, and in human terms it represents youth. The colors are the red of the strong sun and the green of plants rapidly growing. Red is vitality and the passion of flowing life; green is the color of growth and trust. It is the color of earth, a balancing grounding color, neither hot nor cold. During rapid growth there are many changes and several lessons.

A mineral of the *South* is pipestone, a red clay-like stone, which is the petrified blood of the people mixed with the soil of Earth Mother. Its source is a sacred quarry whose history teaches a lesson in embracing peaceful tools, such as the sacred pipe, over weapons. Of all carving stone, pipestone is the most sacred for fashioning prayer pipes. It is also associated with the heart of the earth, the blood of the people, and the color of the strong sun.

The animal of the *South* is the redtail hawk, who likes the sun and warmth and is active and adaptable. It is a fearless hunter and swift flier. . . . In our flight of life we are reminded to be continually steered on to the Red Road in harmony and balance.

The plant of this direction is the rose. The rose is a shrub with thorns which protect it only from those who would attempt to disturb it. As a strong source of vitamin C, it is used in remedies for sickness. Rosewater is used as a perfume and a hair rinse, as well as to invoke the medicine power of the *South* in ritual ceremony. The exchange of roses symbolizes love and trust. . . .

THE SPIRIT OF THE *WEST*

The medicine power of the *West* and of autumn is introspection and self-evaluation, from which realization and awareness develop. The growth of summer stops, and during autumn life prepares for the season of renewal in the North during winter. The time is sunset, when most life prepares to slow down or sleep. So, too, humans contemplate and evaluate the lessons of growth. The *West* corresponds to our middle years, a time of harvesting ideas matured through testing, experimenting, and investigating in youth. Although fresh new visions never cease, this is when one should discover and develop strength to sustain visions already received and lessons already learned.

The medicine power of this direction and time is that of knowing oneself, in the darkness of solitude and introspection. Withdrawing from outside reality and journeying inward provides a mirror which reveals reflections otherwise unseen . . . it is a time of preparation. Autumn represents the force of the spirit descending to earth, of material and physical experiences transformed into spiritual awareness and conclusions. . . .

The color of the *West* is black, like the night. It is the color of withdrawing to the temple within to focus on the formlessness from which all things begin. . . .

From the darkness of entering within comes new light. This seems contradictory. . . . There is a time when we should cease to gaze at the external multicolored reality and close our two eyes to the world, to view our inner qualities with the single intuitive eyes of discernment.

An animal of the *West* is the grizzly bear. . . . The lessons, power, and messages of the spirit of the *West* are not as straightforward as those of the *South*. . . . Basically the grizzly is gentle and humorous when left alone hunting, sleeping, and frolicking in high mountain meadows. When threatened, it stands on two legs as a "two-legged"; it is the bear that "walks like a human." The vibration, intent, and power of a grizzly standing up is quite different from when it is walking on all fours. So, too, there are instances in our lives when we should stand tall. The grizzly is strong, yet gentle. Its silver tipped black hairs are as the stars in the night. . . .

There are other animals of the *West,* such as the raven and the thunderbird, which is the protector of the pipe and of all things sacred. Lightning, thunder and hailstones are of the *West*. Hailstones represent several things all with much power. They are the spirit descending to earth, the transformation of physical experiences into spiritual conclusions. . . .

The thunder beings travel and move around, but they originate and reside in the *West* . . . they are always terrifying and they always bring good. They test you. They come inside the sweat lodge during ceremonies and sometimes come on a vision quest. . . .

The stone of the *West* is jet, "black amber." Like amber it is a plant substance, the fossilized tree mulch of leaves and bark in water. The beauty of most jewels is in their capacity to reflect light, and this is one of the purposes of faceting precious stones. But jet and amber share their beauty in the radiations of light which emanate from inside them and in their soft, silky luster. Jet is not heavy, yet it is tough in texture. The spiritual application of this characteristic is obvious.

Jet is a protective substance. . . .

Jet contains the elements of earthly substances and many resinous purifying ingredients, which neutralize the power and spread of some kinds of germs. Powdered jet is burned in a fire to insure a safe return from journeys. A jet amulet neutralizes any negativity projected toward one from the world. It does so non-violently—it "neutralizes" negativity, it does not "destroy" it. This is big medicine. Like amber, jet can be ground to powder and burned. The fumes are beneficial in repelling germs and fever. Women in childbirth are given jet to hold. Powdered jet mixed with water is used as a paste for aching gums or toothaches and as a cleanser for teeth. Ointments or salves and powdered jet compounded with beeswax have therapeutic uses in the treatment of some skin disorders.

Jet is a black gem, a color associated with mourning and death, but there is nothing morbid or lacking in hope about jet. It holds within itself forces compounded of wood, earth, vegetable, and mineral substances, all active sources of protection, light, and healing.

Mullein is the plant of the *West*. Its leaves are made into a tea that helps liver problems and nervous conditions. The leaves are also smoked in pipes or burned as an incense. One of the many lessons of mullein is the important ability to be able to shift and change.

The time of life of the *West* is death, life beyond the earth without the physical body. The sun sets and the rays of the sun for the day are gone. The light of that day is over forever. This sounds so final. It is! This is why the day, the month, the season is not to be taken for granted. We have the guarantee of a new beginning, a new growth, a new dawn, with the rays of the sun returning at sunrise for a new day. It is sacred to grieve for a period over a death. Tears are strengthening and cleansing. But to embrace and cultivate unceasing grief or despair is to steal life, your life, and to hold back what you can fully share with those still living on this earth plane of existence with you.

Death is transition. It is a change. It is a return. Death is "an" end, it is not "the" end. . . .

THE SPIRIT OF THE *NORTH*

The medicine power of the *North* is renewal and purity; its quality is objectivity. As there is a time of withdrawing from the external world and entering within oneself, there also is a time, a cycle, of withdrawing and rising above our multicolored, multidimensional reality to view our life in objectivity, for cleansing and renewal. This time of life is old age, which I prefer to call "elderhood." At this time we are slowed down in the things of the world but are quickened in spirit. So, too, are the Earth Mother and the animals of the forest. Think of the difference between water, steam, and ice.

The season of this direction is winter, when the earth seems to be asleep. The time of day is midnight, when we are in rest from the day. Life and the forces of nature renew themselves in sleep for the coming new growth of spring. As the snow falls, it covers the multicolored forms of existence with a white blanket. A walk in the snow is fresh, vitalizing, and crisp. The animals are either asleep or are ready to move out with a renewed vitality. Leaves are gone; seeds are dormant yet very much alive. . . .

This time in life and position on the wheel is sometimes difficult. The winter appears stark, naked, cold, harsh, barren. It is a time of testing, a time to clean up one's behavior—a time of purification. The color is white for purity, for snow, for ice, and the color of changing hair as it ages. . . . As we become elders, we are potential sources of counsel for the young. We pass on our stories, experiences, and wisdom to catalyze the growth of others. Such a sacred responsibility requires purity, clarity and objectivity to be a source of clear light for others. The quality of one's consciousness in old age is a testimony to his personal evolution and growth.

The *northern* winter time of life focuses on spiritual values. We become not so much retired from life as we are consultants, still there, still doing, "in" the world but no longer "of" the world. This is a valuable principle, not exclusive to this time of life and position on the wheel of life, though it is concentrated there.

The mineral of the *North* is quartz crystal, capable of elevating consciousness. It is the sacred ice mineral. The plants are birch and aspen. The animal is the white buffalo, strong, mystical, physically as well as spiritually nourishing to the people. The Great Spirit often assumes the form of the white buffalo. The wisdom of the *North* is a distilled wisdom, a wisdom distinct from the natural wisdom of the *East*. In this time and place in life, we can be in union with the medicine power of the white buffalo, being as a sacred messenger to the people. The gift of the sacred pipe came out of the *North* through White Buffalo Calf Maiden to the Sioux and to some other Plains tribes.

Often the lessons of winter and the *North* are referred to as "the cold winds of objective truth." Some truths of the experiences occurring in our life, with its relationships, attitudes, and priorities, may not always appear pleasant when viewed through the pure, renewed eye of objectivity. But such is essential if we are to see the forest as well as the trees. Purity, renewal, and objectivity require time, effort, and patience. So does creativity. . . . Folks are pushed closer together, deeper into themselves. Relationships are tested. Situations are dealt with. Patience may wear thin, revealing feelings that should no longer remain suppressed or hidden.

Purity is essential in preparation, but winter is a time of renewal, for preparation for the upcoming spring. The Medicine Wheel and its medicine power cannot be pigeonholed. It is circular, not linear. Its focus is on the importance of process beyond product. . . . Each season, each lesson learned, is a preparation for the next. The predominant force of the *North* is the power of purity and renewal. Purification is necessary before other things can be attempted or learned. Purification sensitizes and focuses one's perception. The rite of purification in the sweat lodge is performed before most ceremonies and undertakings can occur. Smudging of one's body and lodge with cedar and sweet grass is an act of purification before medicine bundles are opened, before the pipe is smoked, and it precedes many other sacred doings. Medicine objects are regularly smudged for purification and renewal. A person's vision and guidance from the invisible world must be kept pure and renewed, so that they will remain strong, vivid, clear, and not cluttered with ego or wishful thinking.

Breath of the Invisible: The Way of the Pipe,
John Redtail Freesoul, 1986, pp. 61-75

The Great Spirit, spirit keepers of each of the four directions, the seasons, plants and animals, and things from the mineral world: all are in relationship for this Plains People. From these various entities the People derive their spirituality. They look for the directions as they use their wisdom and gifts to inwardly work on enlightenment, harmony, balance, love, trust, awareness, discernment, healing of all kinds, personal growth, and maturity. The Medicine Wheel is the outward sign of many inner spiritual realities.

———————————— + ————————————

PIPE CEREMONY
ARIKARA

The fire is lighted by the Fire-tender, and from its early sparks is ignited the tobacco in the ceremonial pipes, where, beginning with the priest, smoke is offered to the *Quarters* and the Above and the Below— to all that abide with man in this world-frame.

The World's Rim: Great Mysteries of the North American Indians,
Hartley Burr Alexander, 1953, p. 27

The Arikara pipe ceremony, as all pipe ceremonies, was never hurried. The experiential world situation of the one praying was always acknowledged according to a time-honored pattern.

—————————————— + ——————————————

OKIPA CEREMONY
MANDAN

Those painting the Bull Dancers worked all morning and did not finish until noon. The two men with buffalo-hide rattles came out and took their places. The Okipa Maker came out dressed as on the previous day and placed the pipe and pemmican ball in front of the turtles. He proceeded to the *south* side of the sacred cedar, where he again wept as he prayed to Lone Man to bring the buffaloes near and keep bad luck away from the village. While he was praying, the drummers began to beat the drums and sing, which was the signal for the Bull Dancers to come out. The people would congregate on lodges and around the open circle to observe these elaborately painted actors who performed the dances which were the most colorful of the whole ceremony. The Bulls danced directly toward the sacred cedar and formed a circle around it, then formed in pairs to mark out the *four cardinal points*, and, finally separated to mark the *eight directions*. A change in rhythm was a signal for the Bulls to return to the Okipa lodge.

The drummers, rattlers, Okipa Maker, and the eight Bull Dancers came out eight times the second day and repeated the same performance. The fasters came out only once the second day, following the first appearance of the Bulls. They formed a row at the *south* side of the sacred cedar and were dressed in buffalo robes with the hair side out. They returned into the lodge last and did not come out again that day.

Mandan Social and Ceremonial Organization,
Alfred Bowers, 1991, pp. 133-134

All prairie tribes had their own ways of calling the buffalo in preparation for the hunt. Some were quite sophisticated ceremonies, and they usually involved the whole band. The four cardinal directions and the four intercardinals make up eight points of a sacred circle in this section of the Okipa Ceremony. It was a renewal ceremony, asking the

Creator to give an abundance of buffalo and other animals and plants to the People.

———————————— + ————————————

PIPE CEREMONY
MANDAN

Whenever a Mandan doctor (medicine man) lighted his pipe, he invariably presented the stem of it to **the north, the south, the east and the west, the four cardinal points,** and then upwards to the Great Spirit, before smoking it himself.

> *O-Kee-Pa: A Religious Ceremony and Other Customs of the Mandan,*
> George Catlin, 1976, p. 75

George Catlin, a painter from Wilkes-Barre, Pennsylvania, was priviledged indeed. He experienced many of the ways of the western tribes during a period of time (1830-1850s) when they were quite free to be themselves without too much negative American influence. He must have been a participant in many ceremonies in which the spirits of the four directions were invoked.

———————————— + ————————————

CONTEMPORARY FOUR WINDS PEACE PRAYER
CROW

In November 1986, two Crow Indians stood before the Pope in Assisi, Rome, as part of a world ecumenical gathering to pray for peace. *Time* magazine reported that a "peace pipe" was offered ceremonially, and

A Crow Indian medicine man from Montana in full-feathered headdress, recited, "O Great Spirit, I raise my pipe to you, to your messengers **the four winds,** and to mother earth, who provides for your children. . . . I pray that you bring peace to all my brothers and sisters of this world."

> *Religion in Montana: Pathways to the Present,*
> Lawrence Small, 1992, p. 1

A Crow couple, Carol and Junior Whiteman of Pryor, Montana, celebrates their 25th anniversary at an outdoor tribal eucharist

Burton Pretty on Top, the man who offered this prayer, is active in both his Native ways as well as Catholic ways. He was raised in the Crow traditions by his grandfather and has found wonderful opportunities for celebrating both ways together. He is an inspiration for many others as he demonstrates spiritual leadership on and off the Crow Reservaton.

———————————— + ————————————

HOUSE ORIENTATION
CROW

Our house was located about three miles south of Lodge Grass. At first we had a big one-room log house with a dirt floor, but when they closed down Fort Custer in 1906, Father got some boards and added another big room. . . .

My brother Robbie now lives in the old house although it has changed some from my childhood. In those days, all of our houses had the back door opening to the *east,* and that was the door we used. Houses were built with a front door facing *west,* but Crows never finished them with a porch or stairs. Winds blow mostly from the west and north, so it was better to have the door on the *east* side of the house. In the old days Crows always pitched the tipis to the *east* so they could greet the Sun with their prayers when they came out into the daylight.

They Call Me Agnes: A Crow Narrative Based on the Life of Agnes Yellowtail Deernose, Fred Voget, 1995, pp. 72-73

The back door of many Crow homes, even though it may face east (as in the older homes), is more often a gathering place for friends and neighbors than a front door. Protection from the cold winds as well as directional symbolism are equally important.

———————————— + ————————————

PIPE CEREMONY
TETON

Lewis and Clark noted the following details of the Sacred Pipe ritual when among the Teton in 1804:

They first pointed the pipe toward heaven and then to the *four quarters* of the globe, then to the earth, made a short speech, lighted the pipe, and presented it to us.

Offering Smoke: The Sacred Pipe and Native American Religion,
Jordan Paper, 1988, p. 21

Meriwether Lewis and William Clark came to be quite familiar with the ceremonies of different tribes as they slowly travelled to the Pacific Coast and back from 1804-1806. This particular account of the Teton ceremony is similar to pipe ceremonies of today.

—————————————— + ——————————————

ALTAR PREPARATION RITUAL
OGLALA

Just before dawn, the dance stopped, and at this time the dancers, or their relatives, placed offerings outside the sacred lodge at each of *the four quarters*.

At dawn the dancers again entered the lodge, and with them there was the keeper of the sacred pipe; this holy man had been asked by Kablaya to make the sacred altar, but he had replied, "This is your vision, Kablaya, and you should make the altar; but I will be present beside you, and when you have finished I will offer up the prayer."

Thus, it was Kablaya who made the sacred place; he first scraped a round circle in the ground in front of him, and then within this circle he placed a hot coal. Then taking up some sweet grass and holding it above him, he prayed.

"O Grandfather, *Wakan-Tanka*, this is Your sacred grass which I place on the fire; its smoke will spread throughout the world, reaching even to the heavens. The four-leggeds, the wingeds, and all things will know this smoke and will rejoice. May this offering help to make all things and all beings as relatives to us; may they all give to us their powers, so that we may endure the difficulties ahead of us. Behold, *O Wakan-Tanka,* I place this sweet grass on the fire, and the smoke will rise to You."

As Kablaya placed the sacred grass on the fire, he sang this song:

I am making sacred smoke;

In this manner I make the smoke;
May all the people behold it!
I am making sacred smoke;
May all be attentive and behold!
May the wingeds, and the four-leggeds be attentive and behold it!
In this manner I make the smoke;
All over the universe there will be rejoicing!

The knife which was to be used for piercing the breasts of the dancers was purified over the smoke, as was also a small stone hatchet and a small quantity of earth. Kablaya was then ready to make the sacred altar; but first he prayed.

"O Grandfather, *Wakan-Tanka,* I shall now make this Your sacred place. In making this altar, all the birds of the air and all creatures of the earth will rejoice, and they will come from *all directions* to behold it! All the generations of my people will rejoice! This place will be the center of the paths of the four great Powers. The dawn of the day will see this holy place! When Your Light approaches, *O Wakan-Tanka,* all that moves in the universe will rejoice!"

A pinch of the purified earth was offered above and to the ground and was then placed at the center of the sacred place. Another pinch of earth was offered to the *west, north, east,* and *south* and was placed at the *west* of the circle. In the same manner, earth was placed at the other three directions, and then it was spread evenly all around within the circle. This earth represents the two-leggeds, the four-leggeds, the wingeds, and really all that moves, and all that is in the universe. Upon this sacred place Kablaya then began to construct the altar. He first took up a stick, pointed it to the six directions, and then, bringing it down, he made a small circle at the center; and this we understand to be the home of *Wakan-Tanka.* Again, after pointing the stick to the six directions, Kablaya made a mark starting from the *west* and leading to the edge of the circle. In the same manner he drew a line from the *east* to the edge of the circle, from the *north* to the edge of the circle, and from the *south* to the circle. By constructing the altar in this manner, we see that everything leads into, or returns to, the center and this center which is here, but which we know is really everywhere, is *Wakan-Tanka.*

The Sacred Pipe: Black Elk's Account of the Seven Rites of the Oglala Sioux, John Epes Brown, 1989, pp. 88-90

Just as a guest is invited and received into a home, so the powers of the four directions are invited to come to a place of ceremony that has been properly put in order. The meeting place of the powers is where the People have gathered, whose hearts are ready "in a good way."

---- + ----

POWERS OF THE SACRED DIRECTIONS
LAKOTA

The Lakota believe that there are really distinct personal powers in the *four directions*. These are called *Tatiye Topa*, which is usually translated *"Four Directions."* The Lakota word for "strong wind" is *tate*. *Tatiye* is probably a contraction of *Tate-o-uye* (He sends the wind). Rather than being the wind itself, the *Tatiye Topa* are the cosmological powers *behind* the physical winds; they are the ultimate causes of the four-fold, significant events of the Earth. They are *wakan*. They know everything that happens. God put them where they are. He gave them their power, and this power is really their own to use, but they use it as God would use it. The lyric of a Lakota song says, "God is with you, beside you, and you are holy, but you are not the same as He but beneath Him." In a very respectful, indirect way, this song reminds these powerful spirits that they should use their *wakan* powers rightly, for our righteous God is greater than each and nearer to each of these *wakan* spirits than He is to ordinary persons. The words of this song quite clearly indicate the Lakota's belief that these spirits are free persons.

In the Pipe ceremony, a person takes the pipe bowl and pipe stem from a pipebag, which has been kept away in a respectful location. Sweetgrass is usually lit, and the pipe is incensed in its sweet smoke. Then a pinch of tobacco is taken in the fingers, incensed, and extended as an offering in turn to one of the spirits of the different *cardinal directions*: the *West,* the *North,* the *East,* the *South,* toward *Tunkasila Wakan Tanka* above, and to *Unci Maka* below. After each spoken or unspoken prayer, the tobacco is placed in the Pipe. If the Pipe is not filled by the six offerings, the remainder of the pipe is filled prayerfully but silently. Sometimes a Pipe-filling song is sung while the Pipe is filled. Once the Pipe is filled it may be pointed in the different directions so that the one praying can "shoot" their prayer and petition to the spirit(s) in that direction.

According to the theology of the Pipe, the **Four Powers** are distinct from one another but are also similar to each other and frequently work together, even though their ways differ greatly from each other. Lakota sometimes compare them to angels (perhaps to the order of Powers). They have intelligence and wills of their own. They are strong like rock, swifter and mightier than all things experienced on earth. They are as ancient as the world and full of wisdom. They care for the people and indicate to the people their ways, but they usually do this through messages carried by lesser spirits and by medicine men. They direct and teach what must be done for a full life. If people do anything wrong against them, they will punish. Usually people respect them, and in return, they send good things. They deserve to be called "Grandfather."

In the old days, there were many stories which helped children to picture these powers and to learn about them in an enjoyable way. Today there are few stories. . . . A real demythologization has taken place. The barest outline of the Lakota cosmology remains today.

The Lakota say that the homes of the Four Winds are in the mountains in the *four quadrants of the Earth*. More is meant here than physical mountains; these spirits have a special closeness to God so that while their feet are upon the Earth, they are closer to God than all others on Earth. Besides the wind, an ordinary rock is a sign of their presence. They sometimes "speak very fast" through the rocks in a sweatbath to a medicine man. When they are viewed as angels assigned by God to the *four directions* for the guidance and correction of the major events on the Earth, there is little incompatibility with Christian revelation. However, it is still important to appreciate appropriately the symbolic side of their descriptions and manifestations.

According to the theology of the Pipe, there is a Sacred Power in the *West,* and he and his companions are ancient. From the *West* comes the purifying water of the sweatbath and these powers guard the water that washes away evil and gives strength. From the *West* come the companion, *Wakiyan*. The word *kinyan* means "to fly"; the word *kinyanpi* is usually translated as "the wingeds." The *Wakinyan* are said to be the spirits who give men and women dreams and visions of lightning and thunder. So the name *Wakinyan* is variously translated as "The Flying One," the "Winged One," the "Thunder Beings," and most commonly the "Thunderbird." In Lakota mythology it is said that the *Wakinyan* comes in the thunderstorm as a bird. When his eye blinks, the lightning flashes. When his wings beat, the thunder claps. He is strong and frightening like the thunderstorm. He is at the beginning, and the beginning is always sharp and hard, but then comes the innocent joyful, early, tender growth. He guards against and corrects religious evil. He sees to it that the Pipe is used rightly. In the *West,* a sacred stone looks on and is black, which is the color of the *West*. There the Horse People are his companions. The black eagle is his messenger.

In the *North,* there is a sacred power. Some picture him as a great man who tests the people. He guards the health of the people. *Waziya* is his name, and he has become confused with Santa Claus in recent times. The Power of the North helps the people to grow right and tall, like a pine tree. He straightens out the wayward. God has placed him in the *North* to watch those who enter the Red Path that leads from *north* to *south*. The Red Rock looks on, and his color is red. The Maiden who brought the Pipe is there as well as the Buffalo People who pray and sing. The baldheaded eagle is his messenger. It is on the *north* of the sweatlodge that virgins sit.

In the *East* is a Power that resides where the sun rises. He watches over wisdom and understanding. The Morning Star that gives wisdom and the Moon that gives guidance come from there and bring many spiritual things, especially just before the dawn. From the *East* comes the sun that enlightens and enlivens the world. Through him, especially when a person is on the hill, one is able to see how different parts of the world fit together. From there a yellow stone looks on and yellow is his color. His companions are the Elk People. His messenger is the golden eagle.

In the *South* there is a Sacred Power who guards the place toward which humans always face and the generations walk. He controls the final destiny of all things. Some say there is a river there that only the good can cross. His breath gives life. He watches over the joy and happiness of the people whose ghosts gather there in the *Takte Makoce*, the Deer Killing Country ("Happy Hunting Ground" to the Whites). There the souls of deceased Lakota are peaceful relatives with all the animal people, *Wamakaskan Oyate*. In the *South* there is a Sacred White Rock, and so the color of the *South* is said to be white, the color of the brilliant fog. Its messenger is the white crane.

The Pipe and Christ: A Christian-Sioux Dialogue,
William Stolzman, 1986, pp. 193-197

The foregoing material is part of a dialogue between Lakota Sioux spiritual leaders and Catholic priests who serve the reservation. This section explains the Lakota way of speaking about the Four Directions. The dialogue is ongoing, and should be very fruitful as time passes.

The holy powers behind the winds of each direction are understood to be loaded with "wakan" ("holy") power. The directions are identified by a variety of symbols, each symbol being a mnemonic device which leads to a deeper appreciation of the spirituality of this northern Plains People.

---------------------------------- + ----------------------------------

TRIBAL SYMBOLISM OF EACH DIRECTION OF THE GHOST DANCE
LAKOTA

Valuable light in regard to the Sioux version of the doctrine is obtained from the sermon delivered at Red Leaf camp, on Pine Ridge reservation, October 31, 1890, by Short Bull, one of those who had been selected to visit the messiah, and who afterward became one of the prime leaders in the dance:

> My friends and relations: I will soon start this thing in running order. I have told you that this would come to pass in two seasons, but since the whites are interfering so much, I will advance the time from what my father above told me to do, so the time will be shorter. Therefore you must not be afraid of anything. Some of my relations have no ears, so I will have them blown away.
>
> Now, there will be a tree sprout up, and there all the members of our religion and the tribe must gather together. That will be the place where we will see our dead relations. But before this time we must dance the balance of this moon, at the end of which time the earth will shiver very hard. Whenever this thing occurs, I will start the wind to blow. We are the ones who will then see our fathers, mothers, and everybody. We, the tribe of Indians, are the ones who are living a sacred life. God, our father himself, has told and commanded and shown me to do these things.
>
> Our father in heaven has placed a mark at each point of the *four winds.* First, a clay pipe, which lies at the ***setting of the sun*** and represents the Sioux tribe. Second, there is a holy arrow lying at the ***north,*** which represents the Cheyenne tribe. Third, at the ***rising of the sun*** there lies hail, representing the Arapaho tribe. Fourth, there lies a pipe and nice feather at

the *south,* which represents the Crow tribe. My father has shown me these things, therefore we must continue this dance. If the soldiers surround you four deep, three of you, on whom I have put holy shirts, will sing a song, which I have taught you, around them, when some of them will drop dead. Then the rest will start to run, but their horses will sink into the earth. The riders will jump from their horses, but they will sink into the earth also. Then you can do as you desire with them. Now, you must know this, that all the soldiers and that race will be dead. There will be only five thousand of them left living on the earth. My friends and relations, this is straight and true.

Now, we must gather at Pass creek where the tree is sprouting. There we will go among our dead relations. You must not take any earthly things with you. Then the men must take off all their clothing and the women must do the same. No one shall be ashamed of exposing their persons. My father above has told us to do this, and we must do as he says. You must not be afraid of anything. The guns are the only things we are afraid of, but they belong to our father in heaven. He will see that they do no harm. Whatever white men may tell, do not listen to them, my relations. This is all. I will now raise my hand up to my father and close what he has said to you through me.

The pipe here referred to is the most sacred thing in Sioux mythology. . . . The sacred object of the Cheyenne is the "medicine arrow," now in the keeping of the band living near Cantonment, Oklahoma. The Crow and Arapaho references are not so clear. The Arapaho are called by the Sioux the "Blue Cloud" people, a name which may possibly have some connection with hail. The sprouting tree at which all the believers must gather refers to the tree or pole which the Sioux planted in the center of the dance circle. The *cardinal directions* here assigned to the other tribes may refer to their former locations with regard to the Sioux. The Cheyenne and Arapaho, who now live far west and south of the Sioux, originally lived north and east of them, about Red river and the Saskatchewan.

The Ghost-Dance Religion and the Sioux Outbreak of 1890,
James Mooney, 1991, pp. 788-789

In the years following the massacre at Wounded Knee (in 1890 the spirit of the People drooped very low indeed), Wovoka, a Paiute from Nevada, experienced a special call from God and many came to follow his teachings. Even now we are discovering the effects of his teachings as they were shared in varying ways and in varying degrees with Peoples of other tribes. In the above account, Short Bull, a Lakota, appears to be able to share the new religious spirituality in a way that is both intertribal and ecumenical. Though he was aware of the different tribal religious ways, he found a format that would bring them, even some former enemies, together in prayer. Symbols and activities of the four directions and the movements of the sun figured into the rituals and dances.

----------------------------- + -----------------------------

VISION QUEST PREPARATION
LAKOTA

After a pipe full of the *cansasa* has been consumed, the deputies address the candidate in substance as follows:

"You desire to seek a vision. This is a solemn matter. You should not undertake it from curiosity only. You must do this according to the forms which we will now teach you. You must find a high place where no one will interrupt you. You must take with you plenty of *cansasa* and a pipe. You must take with you good medicine which we will give you. You may take a robe with you. But everything else you must leave behind you, except a loin cloth and moccasins. When you have thus prepared yourself, go to the place you have chosen. When you come there, clear a place of every living thing. This place must be large enough for you to sit or lie upon. When you have cleared it of every living thing, then you must place the medicine wands, one at the *east,* one at the *west,* one at the *north,* and one at the *south* on the place you have prepared. When you have done this, you may enter upon it to seek a vision. After you have entered upon it to seek a vision, you must not step beyond its boundaries nor speak to any man, woman, or child until after you have seen a vision or until you know that you will not see one.

"When you have entered on this place, you should meditate only on seeing a vision. You may invoke the spirits in words or song and you must always address them in a reverential manner. First, you should make an offering of the smoke of the *cansasa*. Offer it first to the Spirit of the *East,* then offer it to the Spirit of the *North*. Then offer it to the Spirit of the *South*. When you offer the smoke to the Spirit of the *East,* ask it to send you a vision. Wait and meditate for a time and if this spirit does not send a vision, then call upon the Spirit of the *West* in the same manner. If it does not send a vision, then call upon the Spirit of the *North* and then upon the Spirit of the *South*.

"If these spirits do not send a vision to you, then offer smoke to the Spirit of the Earth and call upon it. If no vision is sent you by this spirit, then you may call upon the spirit of heaven, the Great Spirit. But do not offer smoke to the Great Spirit until after you are sure that the other spirits will not send a vision to you. When you offer smoke to the Great Spirit, you must stand and lift your face to the sky and when you have offered the smoke, you must bow your face to the ground. After this, you must not look upon anything until you have seen a vision or have given up the quest. If you are sleepy, go to sleep, for it may be the vision will come to you in a dream. The vision may come to you as a man, a beast, a bird, or as some form that is not known. Or it may come to you as a voice only. It may speak to you so that you will understand its meaning or it may be that you will not understand. If you have done something which the spirits do not like, then you will see no vision. If you know that you have done something of this kind, you [had] better not attempt to seek a vision, for you will not see one.

"Do not be discouraged when you seek the vision, for the spirits may wait a long time before they bring a vision to you. When you have seen a vision, do not call upon the spirits anymore but return to us and we will advise you about its meaning."

Lakota Belief and Ritual, James Walker, 1991, pp. 132-133

The Lakota vision quest (hanbleceya), *is a time when one is alone with the Great Spirit and the powers of the universe. According to the ancient ways, the place of fasting is prepared in accordance with four directions spiritual practice, and the faster prays in each direction throughout the four days. The solitude, exposure to the elements, and the going without food and water are difficult but not impossible. A person is "opened up" and the experience of the quest is never forgotten.*

———————— + ————————

PIPE CEREMONY SONG
LAKOTA

Friend to the Eagle,
To you I pass the pipe first.
Around the circle I pass it to you.
Around the circle to begin the day.
Around the circle I complete the *four directions*.
I pass the pipe to the Grandfather above.
I smoke with the Great Mystery.
So begins a good day.

Crying for a Dream, Richard Erdoes, 1990, p. 18

This short Pipe Song celebrates circular movement and at the same time acknowledges the four directions.

———————————— + ————————————

VISION QUEST SONG
LAKOTA

1. Ate, wiohpeyata   Father, to the *West*
   nawajin yelo.   I am standing.
   wamayanka yo!   Behold me!
   Ite Otateya   The wind blowing in my face.
   nawajin yelo.   I am standing.

2. Ate, waziyata   Father, to the *North*
   nawajin yelo.   I am standing.
   wamayanka yo!   Behold me!
   Ite Otateya   The wind blowing in my face.
   nawajin yelo.   I am standing.

3. Ate, wiohiyanpa ta   Father, to the *East*
   nawajin yelo.   I am standing.
   wamayanka yo!   Behold me!
   Ite Otateya   The wind blowing in my face.
   nawajin yelo.   I am standing.

4. Ate, Itokagata   Father, to the *South*
    nawajin y elo   I am standing.
    wamayanka yo!   Behold me!
    Ite Otateya   The wind blowing in my face.
    nawajin yelo.   I am standing.

Lakota Ceremonial Songs, John Around Him, 1983, p. 18

The hanbleceya olowan, *or vision quest song, is especially important because it centers the one fasting on the importance of the gifts of God present* (Wakan tanka, Tunkashila) *in all creation. The wind from each of the directions is called in to the fasting place so that the faster might come to a greater knowledge of what is to be expected in response to the gift of life.*

———————— + ————————

SWEAT LODGE CEREMONY SONG
LAKOTA

1. Wiohpeyata etun wan yo!   Look towards the *West!*
    Nitunkasila   Your Grandfather
    ahitunwan yankelo.   is sitting there looking this way.
    Cekiya yo! Cekiya yo!   Pray to Him! Pray to Him!
    Ahitun wan yankelo.   He is sitting there looking this way.

2. Waziya takiya etun wan yo!   *Look towards the North!*
    Nitunkasila   Your Grandfather
    ahitunwan yankelo.   is sitting there looking this way.
    Cekiya yo! Cekiya yo!   Pray to Him! Pray to Him!
    Ahitunwan yankelo.   He is sitting there looking this way.

3. Wiohiyanpa ta etun wan yo!   Look towards the *East!*
    Nitunkasila   Your Grandfather
    ahitunwan yankelo.   is sitting there looking this way.
    Cekiya yo! Cekiya yo!   Pray to Him! Pray to Him!
    Ahitunwan yankelo.   He is sitting there looking this way.

4. Itokaga ta etun wan yo!   Look towards the *South!*
    Nitunkasila   Your Grandfather

ahitunwan yankelo.	is sitting there looking this way.
Cekiya yo! Cekiya yo!	Pray to Him! Pray to Him!
Ahitunwan yankelo.	He is sitting there looking this way.

5. Wakatakiya etun wan yo!   Look up above!
   wakantanka   The Great Spirit.
   heciya he yankelo.   He is sitting above us.
   Cekiya yo! Cekiya yo!   Pray to Him! Pray to Him!
   Ahitunwan yankelo.   He is sitting there looking this way.

6. Maka takiya etun wan yo!   Look down at the Earth!
   Nikunsi K'un   Your Grandmother
   heciya he yunke lo.   is lying beneath you
   Cekiya yo! Cekiya yo!   Pray to Her! Pray to Her!
   Anagoptan yunkelo.   She is lying there listening
      to your prayers.

Lakota Ceremonial Songs, John Around Him, 1983, p. 14

The sweatlodge ceremony (inipi) *is at once a sacred place and a sacred time. During the ceremony certain sweatlodge purification ceremony songs* (inipi olowan) *are sung. They always acknowledge the gifts that come from the four directions.*

———————————— + ————————————

YUWIPI CEREMONY FOUR DIRECTIONS SONG
LAKOTA

FOUR DIRECTIONS SONG

LAKOTA
1. Kola hoyewayin kta ca namah'un we.
2. Kola hoyewayin kta ca namah'un we.
3. Kola hoyewayin kta ca namah'un we.
4. Wiyohpeyata tunkan sapa wan kolatakuwayelo.
5. Kola hoyewayin kta ca namah'un we.
6. Kola hoyewayin kta ca namah'un we.
7. Waziyata tunkan lluta wa kolatakuwayelo.
8. Kola hoyewayin kta ca namah'un we.

9. Kola hoyewayin kta ca namah'un we.
10. Wiyohiyanpota tunkan zizi wan kolatakuwayelo.
11. Kola hoyewayin kta ca namah'un we.
12. Kola hoyewayin kta ca namah'un we.
13. Itokagata tunkan ska wan kolatakuwayelo.
14. Kola hoyewayin kta ca namah'un we.
15. Kola hoyewayin kta ca namah'un we.
16. Maka akanl Inktomi wan kolatakuwayelo.
17. Kola hoyewayin kta ca namah'un we.
18. Kola hoyewayin kta ca namah'un we.
19. Wankatakiye Wanbli Gleska wan kolatakuwayelo.
20. Kola hoyewayin kta ca namah'un we.
21. Kola hoyewayin kta ca namah'un we.

ENGLISH
1. Friend, I will send a voice, so hear me.
2. Friend, I will send a voice, so hear me.
3. Friend, I will send a voice, so hear me.
4. In the *West*, I call a black stone friend.
5. Friend, I will send a voice, so hear me.
6. Friend, I will send a voice, so hear me.
7. In the *North*, I call a red stone friend.
8. Friend, I will send a voice, so hear me.
9. Friend, I will send a voice, so hear me.
10. In the *East*, I call a yellow stone friend.
11. Friend, I will send a voice, so hear me.
12. Friend, I will send a voice, so hear me.
13. In the *South*, I call a white stone   friend.
14. Friend, I will send a voice, so hear me.
15. Friend, I will send a voice, so hear me.
16. On Earth, I call Spider friend.
17. Friend, I will send a voice, so hear me.
18. Friend, I will send a voice, so hear me.
19. Above, I call a Spotted Eagle friend.
20. Friend, I will send a voice, so hear me.
21. Friend, I will send a voice, so hear me.

After the lights have been turned off, this song is sung to invoke
the powers from the whole universe. All respondents agree that this is

one of the most powerful of all Yuwipi songs, and one of the most pleasing to the spirits.

The Four Directions song is unique among all Oglala songs inasmuch as seven renditions (an unusually large number) are sung, each rendition being sung to the same melody with slight textual modifications specifying the directional sources of power. While it is called the *Four Directions* song, actually six directions are named; in order, *West, North, East, South,* Earth, and Above. The first rendition does not specify any direction but is included to herald the whole universe.

The order in which the powers are invoked is the same as in offering the pipe. Walker ascribes this sequence to the order in which the Four Winds were born in Oglala mythology.

Each direction is identified by name, its corresponding sacred object (in this case a sacred stone), and color (corresponding to the *wanunyanpi,* placed around the *hocoka* in the meeting). The power of Inktomi, the spiderish culture hero, is invoked from Mother Earth, and the Spotted Eagle, messenger of Wakantanka from above.

Each rendition is comprised of three lines: lines 1-3, and the second and third lines of each rendition are identical. Plenty Wolf has been directed by the spirits to address each one of the directions by the term *kola,* friend. He tells the spirits to hear his intentions.

Beginning with the second rendition, and the first line of each following rendition, Plenty Wolf addresses each direction with the term *kolatakuwaye* which I have translated as "I call a friend." The meaning however, is stronger than simply "friend." The term literally means to consider one *related* by the term *kola.* While *kola* is the generic word for "friend" today, it is said to have meant a near-blood relationship in the olden days.

The Four Directions song is called *tatetopakiya olowan* 'toward the four winds song', and is accompanied by rapid tremolo drumming. It is rendered only once. Since it is the first song addressed to the spirits to entice them to come, Plenty Wolf also calls it *wicakicopi olowan,* 'They Call Them Song'.

Sacred Language: The Nature of Supernatural Discourse in Lakota, William Powers, 1986, pp. 80-82

This is a marvellous example of a Four Directions Song that includes Earth and Above. It is usually sung during a Yuwipi ceremony, a curing ritual conducted by a medicine man.

—————————— + ——————————

MEANING OF THE DIRECTIONS
LAKOTA

It is the belief of the Indian people
that to the **west**
the Great Spirit put holy people
and they are known as thunder beings.
We pray to them
that through their help
the Great Spirit will bring rain
or put it off
according to our needs.
To the **north**
we pray to the buffalo nation
who adopted the redman
to be his younger brothers.
The buffalo said to him:
"Look at the prairie.
You see all the food
so that I will not be hungry.
So, when you become my little brother,
you will not be hungry.
And look at the fur on the fore part of my body,
so thick and warm.
In the greatest blizzards
I can face into it and eat grass and live.
And so, little brother, you shall not be cold."
And to the **east**
is the elk nation,
known for its medicine.
To the **south**
is the crane nation.
To the Indian people
that direction is the spirit road.

Author and friend sport their Blackfeet capotes, full-length blanket coats

After we leave this world
our spirits travel that way.

Meditations with Native Americans: Lakota Spirituality,
Paul Steinmetz, 1984, p. 36

Spiritual leader Peter Catches, Sr., gives us instruction. Here each direction is mentioned along with its appropriate being. The west with the thunder beings who offer rain, the north with the buffalo who offer food and life sustenance, the east with the elk who provide healing, and the south with the cranes who mark the path that all people must travel after death.

----------------------------- + -----------------------------

MEANING OF THE DIRECTIONS AND CIRCLE AND FOURNESS
SIOUX

The Sioux obtain things from the *Cardinal Directions* when they pray to them. In their minds, *South, West, North* and *East* hold fixed positions on the great circle of hoop around which life moves in a clockwise direction.

The *East* is the abode of the Sun and the Morning Star, both of whom are sources of wisdom and understanding. The stone that marks this direction is yellow, which is also the color of its animal, the elk, and of its bird, the golden eagle. Yellow is the color of love—which the elk represents in Sioux lore—and the wisdom and understanding which comes from the *East* centers in true love, both physical and spiritual.

The *South* is the source of knowledge and power regarding life and destiny. Questions and prayers regarding these issues are addressed to the *South*. Its stone is white; it is the home of the Animal Spirit Peoples; and its totem and symbol is the white crane.

The *West* is associated with purifying water. It is the home of the Thunder Beings. Its stone is black. The Horse People also reside there, and their spirits are called upon to empower the participants in the Horse Dance. Its totem and symbol is the black or immature golden eagle.

The *North* is the source of knowledge regarding health and control, both of self and of other things. Its stone is red. Calf Pipe Woman, who in ancient times brought the first Sacred Pipe to the people and taught them how to use it properly, lives in the *North*. So too do the Buffalo Spirit People. Their totem and symbol is the bald eagle.

Sun Dance pledgers who hold a sage or fur-wrapped hoop in their hands as they dance are praying to the *Four Directions*. When the medicine people and the tribal elders want to teach adults, youth, or children about traditional life and how they should live so as to be pleasing to the Above Beings, they use a circle upon which the *Four Directions* are marked with their colors. As they move clockwise from one direction to the next, they talk about the things associated with each direction. Part of the education is learning how to call or draw in the power from each direction.

The circle is also used when a person wishes to reflect and meditate upon the four stages of life: birth at the *South*; youth at the *West*; middle age at the *North*; and old age, death, and the life-after at the *East.* . . .

As the person pauses in his thoughts at each of these Directions, he asks to help him think wisely about how life should best be lived, and the Directions give him guidance. The Sioux say that those who diligently practice this ritual become the wisest of their people.

Secret Native American Pathways:
A Guide to Inner Peace, Thomas Mails, 1988, pp. 209-212

The four directions are not just fixed objective points somewhere on the earth's surface. The hoop of the earth is vast. As each person prayerfully focuses on a particular direction, a lot can be learned and experienced. An individual's particular time of life, or daily problems or feelings, might be the reason that the gifts or powers of a certain direction are requested. The ways of prayer have no limits. Each culture has its own way of talking about and experiencing God's action in our world.

——————— + ———————

CONTEMPORARY PRAYER
LAKOTA/CHRISTIAN

CHRIST IS THE CENTER

Leader I: We will act out the ceremonial, recalling that Christ is the center of creation, the central reality of God's plan for the world, the central reality of our lives as Christians. As we face each of the *four directions*, we will respond in prayer. Following each prayer, we will return to face the center, reminded each time that it is Christ who is able to bring healing and salvation and who by his Spirit is able to renew the face of the earth.

Leader II: First, let us all face a center point. (All face center, pause)

Leader I: From the *East,* the direction of the rising sun, come wisdom and knowledge.

Leader II: Let us face *East* (all face *East,* pause) and let us pray:

All: **Enable us, O God, to be wise in our use of the resources of the earth, sharing them in justice, partaking of them in thankfulness.** (all face center, pause)

Leader II: From the *South* comes guidance, and the beginning and end of life.

Leader I: Let us face *South* (all face *South*, pause) and let us pray:

All: **May we walk good paths, O God, living on this earth as sisters and brothers should, rejoicing in one another's blessings, sympathizing in one another's sorrows, and together with you renewing the face of the earth.** (all face center, pause)

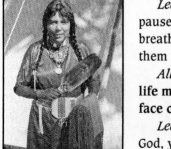

Leader II: From the *West* come purifying waters.

Leader I: Let us now face *West* (all face *West,* pause) and pray that the Spirit of God may again breathe over the waters making them pure, making them fruitful. Let us pray:

All: **We pray that we too may be purified so that life may be sustained and nurtured over the entire face of the earth.** (all face center, pause)

Leader II: From the *North* come purifying winds. O God, you have been called breath and wind of life.

Leader I: Let us face *North* (all face *North,* pause) and let us pray:

Maria Onion (Crow), 1996

All: **May the air we breathe be purified so that life may be sustained and nurtured over the entire face of the earth.** (all face center, pause)

> *Voices: Native American Hymns and Worship Resources,*
> Marilyn M. Hofstra, 1992, pp. 65-66

This is taken from a recent hymnal of the United Methodist Church. It is a wonderful coming together of spiritual songs and hymns from many tribes and parts of the country.

——————————— + ———————————

PIPE CEREMONY CLOSURE
BLACKFOOT

When the tobacco was burned out, the Pipe was returned to Bird Rattle, who carefully cleaned it, depositing the ashes in the *four corners* of the little box before him. We were told that this was to show that our tokens of friendship had been taken to the *four corners* of the earth by the four winds, and so could never be recalled.

> "Bird Rattle and the Medicine Prayer," *Montana: The Magazine of Western History*, Roland Willcomb, Spring 1970, p. 45

Here, in this Medicine Pipe Ceremony which took place near Browning, Montana, a few decades ago, the box momentarily becomes a microcosm of the universe with its four directions.

——————————— + ———————————

PIPE CEREMONY
BLACKFOOT

The pipe is offered to the *four directions, east, south, west* and *north,* in that order. The pipe is offered above to the Creator and down to Mother Earth. There are spirits in each of the directions who are guardians and watch over the things that are attributed to that direction.

In the direction to the *east,* for example, some tribes believe the rising sun symbolizes the Creator

Headdress (roach) with feathers, beadwork, and a medicine wheel

who begins the day. The sun is not considered the Creator, but is symbolic of the power of the Creator.

The *south* is looked upon as the direction of youth and where things are made to grow. As the sun goes across the sky then the plants turn in that direction.

The *west* is the direction from which the storms and water comes. The water is sacred and a precious gift the Creator has given to all life. We can not live without water.

The *north* is the direction of our old age. It is white. It symbolizes the wisdom that is borne by the elderly, the generations gone before us. It is also looked upon as the direction the winter weather comes to put things to rest for awhile to be born again in the spring.

Ni-Kso-Ko-Wa: Blackfoot Spirituality, Traditions, Values and Beliefs, Long Standing Bear Chief, 1992, p. 48

This pipe ceremony is also a teaching. The four directions have spirits who watch over the things and beings that are in that respective direction. And yet it is (the) Creator who watches over all.

——————————— + ———————————

BUFFALO SOCIETY CEREMONY
BLOOD

As I started toward the lodge of Little Dog where Apikuni awaited me, I mused as in a dream:

I had entered the lodge of the Matokiks.
I had been transported to a world of magic beauty.
I had been "at one" with the rhythmic ritual of the Matokiks
    each song, each mimetic dance, each beat of drum and
    rattle a dramatic prayer of gratitude for answers to prayers
    of last year, of supplication for the good of all the people
In beauty the ritual had been conceived by the Ancient Ones
In beauty it had been enacted "the right way" by Living Matokiks
It had called on the magic of the *Four Winds* for help,
    on the mystic power of Sun, Moon and Stars,
    on the miracle of Earth Mother and all her children.
It had expressed the Oneness of all Creation.

It had merged the Spirit of the Matokiks with
the Spirit of the Universe.

Lifeways of Intermontane and Plains Montana Indians,
Leslie Davis, 1979, p. 32

The Matokiks were women of the Buffalo Society who participated in an annual four-day ritual. This is a portion of an account of the ceremonies held in 1931 in the Canadian Rocky Mountains. The Matokiks were responsible for preparation of the camp site and the ceremonies within the teepee. They offered prayer on behalf of the People. The four winds are representational of the four directions. In the ceremonies the buffalo, the snake, and birds were remembered in special dances. It was a ceremony calling for an increase of the buffalo and other birds and animals so that the People would have plenty.

———————————— + ————————————

SACRED PIPE BUNDLE CERMONY
BLOOD

One priest now gets up with man and boy, man with fancy stem in his hand; all face *South,* then *West,* then *North* and dance a minute to slow time in each direction, at which there is great applause. [In the form of shouts and war cries. We clap our hands only to accent our talking, not to applaud. The "applause" is to cheer the new Medicine Pipe Man during his first ceremonial act as Owner.] Women do same, that is, candidate's wives and two other women. All morning, relations of candidate have been bringing in household articles such as dishes, fry pans, cups and saucers, pails, also blankets, guns, and etc. and piling them up at the entrance. These are now distributed by vendor and his wife to their relations, probably giving those who contributed when they were buying the pipe years ago.

Pipe is now rolled up and the newly made medicine man's wife carries it home on her back.

The Blood People: A Division of the Blackfoot Confederacy,
Adolf Hungry Wolf, 1977, p. 131

Many prairie tribes have the tradition of sacred bundles which contain personal and holy items (like sacred stones and eagle or hawk feathers) wrapped in cloth and animal pelts. Some are passed down in families, while others are given over to people who are attracted to their special medicine power. Some, like this sacred bundle, contain pipes of special repute. A ceremony, brief or long, is always needed for the transfer of a bundle. In this particular ceremony the four directions are acknowledged and danced to.

+

SWEAT LODGE CONSTRUCTION
BLOOD

The sweat lodge was constructed. There are one hundred willows to a holy sweat lodge. The entrance is on the *east* side and the exit is on the *west* side, just like the daily path of the Sun. The fifty willows on the *south* side were colored with real paint [red earth] and the other fifty willows were colored with black paint. The real paint represents the day; the black paint represents the night. The buffalo hides used to cover the sweat lodge were also colored, the hides on the *south* side with real paint, the hides on the *north* side with black paint. In recent years the willows and the canvases are not colored anymore.

In legends of the long-ago, only one rock was used in the sweat lodge. Lately, one hundred rocks were used. In this sweat lodge the rocks were not heated red hot. It was a sweat lodge just to reinforce the spiritual powers.

The buffalo skull, which is offered to Sun, was laid on a small pile of dirt that had been scooped out from a hole inside the sweat lodge.

The Blood People: A Division of the Blackfoot Confederacy, Adolf Hungry Wolf, 1977, p. 47

The sweat lodge is a special kind of holy place. It is always constructed and blessed according to the traditions. It is for purification. Here, during the time of the Sundance, the sweat lodge is prepared with special attention given to the four directions and symbolic coloration.

+

Turk Plainbull riding to camp at 1994 Crow Fair, Crow Agency, Montana

PIPE CEREMONY
PLAINS CREE

. . . the pipe ritual of a bear feast for another Algonkian speaking culture, the Cree—here the Plains Cree of Saskatchewan. Bear is the most powerful of the earth spirits for many native people, and, although all hunted animals are accorded rituals, those for Bear are particularly significant.

On the evening of June 16, 1913, Neil Sauwustim shot a bear. The following day at noon the writer visited [Four-cloud's] camp where Sauwustim was staying and there partook of the Bear feast. The skin has already been removed and was lying folded up, head outermost [marked with yellow ochre and given a gift of red cloth], in the place of honor. [After the meat was cooked and distributed], Four-clouds filled the pipe, gave it to Spotted-one, and lighted it while he puffed. Spotted-one, then, as master of ceremonies, for he is a distinguished old man, smoked a few puffs and then offered the mouthpiece skyward praying that the day should be propitious and that no one should be injured while the sun shone. He then offered it to the ground with a prayer that the powers of darkness should be equally kind to men, then to the *four world quarters* with prayers to the winds, and last of all to the bear, telling it that it had been slain to furnish food, and begging its good will and future abundance of bears. He then passed back the pipe which was relighted and passed to the rest. Next Spotted-one raised the dish of bear meat before him above his bowed head as an offering to Gitce Manitou to whom he prayed. Lowering the dish he cut off some tiny morsels of each kind of flesh thereon, and cast them in the fire as a sacrifice.

Offering Smoke: The Sacred Pipe and Native American Religion,
Jordan Paper, 1988, p. 29

The Cree are a large tribe with many bands living in both Canada and the United States. Some are on the prairies and have adapted their culture to it. This prayer, also addressed to the four world quarters and to the winds, tells us that this pipe ritual prayer at a bear feast was a solemn thanksgiving for the gift of the bear. It was always prayed in thanksgiving with petitions of various kinds.

———————————— + ————————————

GHOST DANCE SYMBOLISM
INTERTRIBAL

To allay fears on the part of the whites, the dancers tied an American flag to the top of the small pine tree erected in the center of their dance space. Cloth streamers, eagle feathers, stuffed birds, claws, and horns were fastened to the tree, too. The tree itself was referred to as the "sprouting tree," another symbol of renewed life. At the *"four corners of the world," four points* on the edge of the dance circle representing the *cardinal points*, were placed other ceremonial objects. On the *west* was a pipe, representing the Sioux nation. . . .

On the *north* was placed an arrow, symbol of the Cheyennes, whose most important tribal medicine is the Medicine Arrows and who formerly lived north of the Sioux. On the *east* was a symbol of hail, representing the Arapahos, who formerly lived east of the Sioux and were known by them as the Blue Cloud people. To the *south* was another pipe, with a feather attached, representing the Crows, former enemies but now at peace.

The dancing started about noon. The leaders, or priests, sat near the sacred tree in the center of the dance circle. The dancers sat on the ground around the edge, intermixed men and women instead of men on one side and women on the other, as was the usual Indian custom. All the dancers wore eagle feathers tied in their hair, near the crowns of their heads, something else that had never been done before. A mournful chant was sung and a bowl of sacred food was passed around for everyone to partake of.

A company of men, as many as fifteen, then began another song and marched abreast, others falling in behind, parading all around the camp before returning to the dance circle and taking their seats.

A young woman next entered the circle and, taking her place near the tree, started the main ceremonies by shooting four arrows, one to each of the *four directions,* in Sioux order, *west, north, east* and *west.* The arrows had bone tips, which had been dipped in steer's blood. No doubt this young woman represented the Buffalo Ghost Maiden, legendary bringer of the pipe and of important ceremonies. The arrows were gathered up and hung, with the bow, on the center tree. Also hung upon the tree were a hoop and four sticks used in the old hoop game, which had sacred significance to many tribes.

On a signal from the leaders, everyone arose to his feet and a line was formed, all facing the sun, while the chief priest waved a ghost stick over their heads. He then turned and faced the sun himself, making a long prayer, while the young woman, or sometimes a different one, came forward carrying a pipe, which she held toward the *west,* from where the Messiah was to come.

The ghost stick was a special wand, peculiar to the Sioux Ghost Dance, to the upper end of which were fastened two buffalo horns, painted red, forming an upright crescent. At upper and lower ends of the staff were sorrel horse tails, fastened in such a way as to look as if they were growing out of it. The staff itself was ornamented with wrapped beadwork and trimmed with red cloth. It, too, was later hung from the tree.

As the priest continued his prayer, the line of dancers closed in a circle around him. Most of them wore blankets and shawls, which they now wrapped around their waists, so that the fringe nearly touched the ground. The brilliant paintings on the ghost shirts and dresses now came to view. The dancers turned to the left, each one placing his hands upon the shoulders of the one in front, and all walked in a sun circle, singing, "Father, I come."

At the end of the song, all faced the center again, wailing and crying in a most fearful and heart-rending manner. Some clasped their hands above their heads, standing straight and still, asking the Great Spirit to allow them to see their loved ones who had gone on. Some grasped handfuls of dust and threw it over their heads. Then all sat down once more, to listen to another address by one of the leaders.

Indian Dances of North America: Their Importance to Indian Life,
Reginald Laubin & Gladys Laubin, 1977, pp. 60-61

This eyewitness account of a version of the Ghost Dance is replete with Plains symboism, some symbols of which would be understood by members of other tribes quite distant from the Plains.

———————— + ————————

THE DIRECTIONS AND THE HUMAN BODY
INTERTRIBAL

This primary projection of the physical world is of course not uniquely a product of American Indian thought. The quaternity of the cardinal directions and the trinity of heaven, earth and hell belong to many lands and peoples. It is a mathematical construction, but it is one developed not from chance but from a reason universal to mankind, and that reason is to be found in the human skeleton itself. Man is upright, erect, in his active habit, and he is four-square in his frame, and these two facts give him his image of a physical world circumscribing his bodily life. In the Indo-European and in many other languages of the Old World and the New the primitive orientation of man is indicated by those root-names for the directions which are, in meaning, for the *east,* "the before," for the *west* "the behind," for the *south* "the right hand," and for the *north* "the left hand." That the heavens are figured as the crown and front, earth's middle as the navel and the bowels, and earth's base as the footing of creation is symbolized in the image of that Titan who adorns the symbolic art of many peoples. The axial dimension of the universe is thus deduced from the standing position of a man. So standing, there at the middle, the human skeleton yields a world-frame with its *four quarters* and its three bodily divisions. Certainly it is no matter of merely idle imagination to note that the intellectual feat which our conception of a "world" implies is profoundly associated with just those physical traits which most mark off man from his fellow mammalians; for had we remained quadrupeds with horse and elephant, ox and dog, it is only to be assumed that (had any world been possible) our cardinal points must have been six and not four. Heaven could never have been so high nor hell so low for creatures whose mouth gives the main source of tactile definition. Geometry is the most human of sciences, clearly derivative from that bodily frame and carriage from which we formulate the dimensions of the world and the structures of that space which we are willing to call the real space.

The World's Rim: Great Mysteries of the North American Indians,
Hartley Burr Alexander, 1953, pp. 10-11

From the dawn of human history people have tried to understand themselves in relationship to their environment. As they were most familiar with their own bodies, it is not so unusual that they would see the human body as a reference point for connecting with the larger world. The four directions would be somewhat natural for people to work with as they lived out life in their bodies.

———————— + ————————

Tipis, Crow Agency, Montana

PIPE CEREMONIALISM
INTERTRIBAL

... there are universal features which indicate the primary symbolism and lead us into certain matters of human understanding and of the mind's radical metaphors which should enlighten us not only in the field of American Indian thought but also in the ideas and symbols of all mankind.

In the ceremonial gesture of the smoke offering, the several puffs may be directed to three, four, five, six, or seven points; but in every case these points belong to the one general system which in full is defined only by all seven. The smoke may be directed to the Above, the Below, and the Here; it may be directed to the *four cardinals* of the compass—*East, South, West,* and *North,* for it usually moves sunwise in sequence; it may be offered to the Quarters of the Earth and to the Above or to the Here, and this would yield a five-puff rite; or again to the Quarters, the Sky and the Earth, and this would yield six; and finally, in the full form, smoke will be blown to the six points which define the plane of earth's horizon and the zenith and nadir of its axis, and to that Middle Place where the axis cuts the plane to form the site of the ceremony and the ritual center of the World. Conceptually these seven points define man's primary projection of the universe, his World Frame, or cosmic abode, within which is to be placed all the furniture of creation. For it is only necessary to connect the *four cardinals* with a line marking the circle of the visible horizon, and, following the courses of the sun and stars, to draw the line of the wheel of day, circumvolent from sunrise to zenith, from setting to nadir and again downward and onward to returning dawn, in order to complete the great circles drawn upon the face of the abyss which yield us the terrestrial and celestial spheres. It is clear that the Indian, after the manner of our compass, not only organized the plane of the earth with respect to the radical *four of the cardinal points,* but that he also subdivided the Above and the Belows into zones and latitudes. First it is important to perceive that the red man's projection of his universe, incipiently at least, is a circumscribing sphere with axis and equator, longitudes and latitudes, and that the

Arapaho Peyote Ceremony rattle and Cheyenne Men's Society rattle

ritual of the pipe is schematically a recognition of the points from which the great lines of the sphere are generated. . . .

The World's Rim: Great Mysteries of the North American Indians,
Hartley Burr Alexander, 1953, p. 9-10

All human beings ponder the meaning of life. Number and distance and the use of the number four were found to be helpful in the ancient Americas.

———————————— + ————————————

SACRED PIPE AND
RELATEDNESS TO ALL THAT EXISTS
INTERTRIBAL

In communal smoking, the ritual also indicates the cosmos of social relationships. At the center is the self, the one holding the pipe. Next comes the circles (in cultures with circular dwellings) of human relationships: family, clan, and "nation." Further outward is the sphere of animal relations: those who walk on the earth in the *four directions,* those who fly in the sky above, and those who crawl through the earth below or swim in the sea. Finally there is the sphere of the most powerful spirits: the *Four Directions* (Winds), the Sky and the Earth (Sea). Together these four spheres of beings form "all my relations."

Fundamental to cosmological understanding is the pairing of female and male spiritual powers that when combined, result in creation. . . .

Once one goes beyond the basics of the directions, one is involved with monocultural understandings. Specific symbolic and mythic understanding of the meanings of the directions vary from culture to culture, even subculture to subculture. However, *east* and *west* are generally understood from the significance of the sun's path, symbolically equated with the path of life, as is the pipe stem itself. Accordingly, the ritual leader in a pipe ceremony normally faces *east,* the direction of the rising sun. The commonality of a fundamental cosmological understanding over most, if not all, of North America, despite major linguistic and cultural-ecological differences, helps explain why different Native American cultures could so readily borrow rituals from each other as well as maintain the common ritual of the Sacred Pipe.

Offering Smoke: The Sacred Pipe and Native American Religion,
Jordan Paper, 1988, pp. 39-40

Nobody needs to be permanently alone. We are always related: to the Creator, to the created ones who are visible or invisible, to the cosmos and all its life forms, and in special ways, to one another as human beings. Ceremonies express these relationships.

———————————— + ————————————

COSMOLOGICAL LIFE FORCES AND SYMBOLISM
INTERTRIBAL

The primary spirits can be divided into two categories: Earth and Sky, and the *Four Directions*. Mother or Grandmother Earth and Father or Grandfather Sky are often found in myths represented by their symbols. As specific celestial beings, they are, respectively, Grandmother or Mother Moon and Grandfather or Father Sun. . . .

Earth and sky together form the powers of creation. The second aspect of the primary spirit, the *Four Directions* or Winds, are the power—and life giving forces—of the created. They represent the world around us, the progression of the day, the rotation of the seasons, and the stages of life. Symbolized by colors, animals, and plants, these details vary from culture to culture, even sub-subculture to subculture.

Offering Smoke: The Sacred Pipe and Native American Religion,
Jordan Paper, 1988, pp. 59-60

Here is a theological description of the primary spirits that are invariably addressed at most indigenous ceremonies.

———————————— + ————————————

PIPE CEREMONY
INTERTRIBAL

Pére De Smet, one of the most wide-wandering of the Jesuit missionaries in North America, makes repeated allusions to the ritual use of the pipe. "On all great occasions," he says, "in their religious and political ceremonies, and at their great feasts, the calumet presides; the savage sends its first fruits, or its first puffs, to the Great Waconda, or Master of Life, to the Sun which gives them light, and to the Earth and Water by which they are nourished; then they direct a puff to *each point of the compass,* begging of Heaven all the elements and favorable winds." Elsewhere De Smet remarks: "It was really a touching spectacle to see the calumet, the Indian emblem of peace, raised heavenward by the hand of a savage, presenting it to the Master of Life, imploring his pity on all his children on earth and begging him to confirm the good resolutions which they had made."

The World's Rim: Great Mysteries of the North American Indians,
Hartley Burr Alexander, 1953, p. 5

Though he came to the Peoples of the West with some 19th-century European attitudes that would be unacceptable today, Father De Smet grew in many ways as he served the People. Early on, he learned the importance of the pipe and the four directions. His time among the People is still felt today.

——————————— + ———————————

GATHERING OF SPIRITUAL ELDERS (1993)
INTERTRIBAL

"May we find in the ancient wisdom of the Indigenous Nations, the spirit and courage to mend and heal," said Arvol Lookinghorse (19th Generation Keeper of the Sacred Pipe, Lakota Nation) at the Cry of the Earth conference, a historic gathering of Indigenous Spiritual Elders, which took place in the EcoSoc Chamber at the United Nations on November 22, 1993, the Year of the World's Indigenous Peoples.

There, 400 people, representing seven delegations from North America (the Algonquin, Mi'qmaq, Hopi, Lakota, Iroquois, Maya and Huichol nations) came together to share their traditional prophecies and earth-based values with the international community.

The 28 Elders presented their urgent messages with respect to the environment and humanity.

Many other Indigenous elders and community leaders came great distances to witness this unprecedented gathering. Members of the

Hawaiian Ohana Council, Chiefs and Clan Mothers from Canada, the United States, and Mexico attended, as well as Spiritual leaders and diplomatic leaders from as far away as Australia came to witness this event and to support the elders who were speaking.

Since the founding of the UN in 1948, the Hopi Spiritual Elders had been working toward a gathering of Indigenous leaders from the **Four Directions**. They recognized the United Nations as the "House of Mica" [House of Glass] spoken of in their prophecies. This is where they were instructed to deliver their warning to world leaders. "We are at a most critical time in human history. It is a crossroads at which the outcome of our actions will decide the fate of all life on earth," said Martin Gashweseoma (Hopi Traditional Spiritual Elder). . . .

The purity of emotion with which the Elders spoke was extremely moving to all who attended. As they spoke it became apparent that many of their prophetic concerns and warnings are the same. They spoke of the need for spiritual realignment and consciousness. They also spoke of the changes in the Earth that have occurred during their lifetimes; the deterioration of the family; the degeneration of our leadership and values; the poisoning of the water and the air. They spoke of the need for a return to natural, simple ways of relating with one another; with the animal kingdom; and with the planet. They spoke of the need to heal these relationships. They spoke of their hope that these warnings will reach the youth, as they are the future caretakers of the earth.

"Cry of the Earth," *Wind Messenger: A Newsletter of Wings of America*, Carina Courtright, Spring 1994, p. 8

To recognize that People come from the four directions to any kind of spiritual or social gathering is to say that one understands the world in the ancient indigenous way. One can be contemporary and traditional at the same time. This Cry of the Earth gathering at the United Nations was put on by Cresentera, a not-for-profit corporation committed to the preservation and presentation of traditions and values that promote a respectful relationship between humanity and the natural world.

Traditional dancers enjoy fellowship through music

Maya

MESOAMERICA CULTURAL AREA

PEYOTE DANCE
TARAHUMARA

The Tarahumara Peyote dance may be held at any time during the year for health, tribal prosperity, or for simple worship. It is sometimes incorporated into other established festivals. The principal part of the ceremony consists of dances and prayers followed by a day of feasting. It is held in a cleared area, neatly swept. Oak and pine logs are dragged in for a fire and oriented in an *east-west* direction. The Tarahumara name for the dance means "moving about the fire," and except for Peyote itself, the fire is the most important element.

The leader has several women assistants who prepare the Hikuri plants for use, grinding the fresh cacti on a metate, being careful not to lose one drop of the resulting liquid. An assistant catches all liquid in a gourd, even the water used to wash the metate. The leader sits *west* of the fire, and a cross may be erected opposite him. In front of the leader, a small hole is dug into which he may spit. A Peyote may be set before him on its side or inserted into a root-shaped hole bored in the ground. He inverts half a gourd over the Peyote, turning it to scratch a circle in the earth around the cactus. Removing the gourd temporarily, he draws a *cross* in the dust to represent the world, thereupon replacing the gourd. This apparatus serves as a resonator for the rasping stick: Peyote is set under the resonator, since it enjoys the sound.

Incense from burning copal is then offered to the cross. After facing *east,* kneeling, and crossing themselves, the leader's assistants are given deer-hoof rattles or bells to shake during the dance.

186

The ground-up Peyote is kept in a pot or crock near the cross and is served in a gourd by an assistant: he makes three rounds of the fire if carrying the gourd to the leader, one if carrying it to an ordinary participant. All the songs praise Peyote for its protection of the tribe and for its "beautiful intoxication."

Plants of the Gods: Their Sacred, Healing and Hallucinogenic Powers,
Richard Evans Schultes & Albert Hofmann, 1992, pp. 137-138

Dancing around a fire is ancient and practiced by many cultures. Light and sound coming from the inverted gourd appeal to the senses. The circle speaks of unity while the cross in the dust reminds the worshipers that the prayer is for the inhabitants of all quadrants of the universe. The fragrant smell of copal incense both purifies the area and carries aloft the prayers of the People. The rattles and bells beckon those gathered to become part of this danced prayer.

—————————— + ——————————

ACKNOWLEDGMENT OF THE CARDINAL DIRECTIONS
HUICHOL

While chanting or curing, the shaman waves his *muvieri,* or plumed wand, in the **direction of the four cardinal points,** thereby acknowledging the corners of the world which are believed to be upheld by four gigantic Brazil trees. In addition he addresses a fifth point (five is a sacred number among the Huichol), the *axis mundi* or central pole that pierces the several layers of the universe.

Of Gods and Men: The Heritage of Ancient Mexico,
Anna Benson Gyles & Chloe Sayer, 1980, p. 204

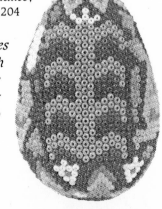

The Huichol waving the plumed wand recognizes each direction and the gifts that flow from each direction and prays them to the center of any particular religious ceremony. Divine healing power is brought to the patient by those who believe.

————— + —————

Huichol beaded egg with corn design

RELATIONSHIP OF CARDINAL DIRECTIONS
TO INTER CARDINALS
HUICHOL

The Huichols have made the *Nierika* or prayer offering into a sacred art form. The word *Nierika* means also the 'face' of the deity; a mirror; and the threshold through which one passes into the transpersonal realms . . . the five sacred directions, the ***sacred four cardinals*** and infinite center, intersected by the ***intercardinals,*** are depicted in the field of purifying fire. The absolute center point is the gateway to the infinite field of the divine.

Shaman: The Wounded Healer, Joan Halifax, 1982, p. 71

The relationship between the cardinal directions and the inter-cardinal directions allows the Huichol to describe the world in great detail. No part of the physical world can be left out; everything is important.

———————————— + ————————————

RELATIONSHIP OF CARDINAL DIRECTIONS
AND CROSS
TOTONAC

Religious belief is also linked with the natural habitat where local hills or springs may be thought of as holy, and even the cross—the symbol of Christianity—has an ancient significance. In use long before the arrival of the Spaniards, the cross is still linked by many Indian groups with rain, the growth of maize and with the *four cardinal points,* as well as with the Tree of Life which has its roots in the Underworld and its branches in the Heavens.

Of Gods and Men: The Heritage of Ancient Mexico,
Anna Benson Gyles & Chloe Sayer, 1980, p. 18

To those who know how to see deeper than only with the eyes, a spiritual sign speaks of holy things to the seeker. The cross is one such sign. Perhaps the cross, which was common to both Native Peoples of the Americas and to European Christians, spoke eloquently to both communities as they shared what was spiritually important to them.

Even today the cross as sign has the capacity to bring people together in dialogue.

—————————————— + ——————————————

PERSONAGES OF THE DIRECTIONS
LACANDON

. . . the Lacandons have lived in isolation ever since the Conquest. They worship *Hachayium,* the god of creation; *Kisin,* the lord of the underworld; *Nojoch Yum Chac,* the 'Old Lord of Rain'; *Yantho,* god of the **north**, and *Usukum* and *U-yidzin,* gods associated with other **cardinal points** that are not now distinguished.

These gods are represented by incense burners and clay figurines, which are placed in the ceremonial hut of each *caribal* where various ceremonies and rites are performed. The incense burners are renewed each year during a ceremony in which the men stay in the ritual hut for several days, abstain from sex, and pay homage to the used burners with offerings of *pozol, balché* and tamales (steamed cornbread).

Ethnic Groups of Mexico, Lilian Scheffler, 1987, p. 35

Incense and clay sculptures along with ritual isolation and sexual abstention express the ancient devotional way of life of the Lacandons.

—————————————— + ——————————————

FOUR-QUARTERED UNIVERSE
NAHUA

There were, at least among the ancient Nahuas, thirteen celestial levels and nine underworld levels, each inhabited by diverse gods and supernatural beings, often depicted as conjugal pairs. The top level (in some sources there are nine celestial levels) was inhabited by Ometeotl, the God of Duality.

Each of these realms, which in the Nahua imagination were divided into smaller, powerful units, were permeated with supernatural powers circulating up and down the cosmic levels through spiral-shaped passages called *malinallis.* Some levels, especially the lower terrestrial and aquatic levels, including the mountains, were filled with abundant, valuable forces such as seeds, water, and precious stones upon which farmers, families, and craftsmen depended. One Mexican scholar notes that the ancient Nahuas

> believed this earthly and aquatic world to be contaminated by death and jealously guarded by the dangerous "lords" of springs and woods. Even today, the places from which wealth derives—fountains, forests and mines—are thought to be points of communication between the worlds of men and that of death, guarded by the Ohuican Chaneque, "lords of the dangerous places."

In some versions of the universe these supernatural entities and forces flowed into the human level through giant ceiba trees, which held up the sky at the *four quarters of the world* and stood at the center of the universe. As we can see when we look at the ideal image of the universe as pictured in the *Codex Fejérváry Mayer,* the *four-quartered universe* is structured by four flowering trees, each with a supernatural bird on its crown. In some cultures a flowering tree or a sacred mountain stood at the center of the universe linking up, like a vertical shaft, the upper, middle, and lower worlds.

Religions of Mesoamerica: Cosmovision and Ceremonial Centers,
David Carrasco, 1990, pp. 51-52

Vegetative life, especially trees, are points of contact with the holy. Here four ceiba trees have the responsibility of holding up the platform of life. The birds symbolize contact with the heavenly realm.

———————————— + ————————————

QUETZAL DANCE
NAHUA

Every year at the Feast of St. Francis the ancient Quetzal dance is performed by the Nahua Indians in the small mountain town of Cuetzalan. In Aztec times this ceremony was probably connected with agriculture and astronomy; now too it is performed to ensure a successful harvest—and also to honor the saint. On the day of the feast the courtyard in front of the church is packed with people who have come from all the surrounding villages. Many of the women wear their traditional costumes, piling their hair high with skeins of purple wool which was a feature of pre-Hispanic dress. Bobbing above the crowds are the extraordinary head-dresses of the Quetzal dancers, immense circular frameworks of reeds interlaced with multicolored paper and strips of ribbon. Each huge colored wheel is attached to a small conical cap which is tied onto the dancer's head. Small feathers on the tips of the spokes are the only reminders that once the whole head-dress was made of the glorious iridescent plumes of the Quetzal bird. For the rest the dancers wear bright red trousers and a red top, all fringed with yellow, and in either hand they carry a gourd rattle and brightly colored handkerchief. Each dancer makes and pays for his own costume with the help of his family.

Before the performance begins, the dancers visit the church to offer prayers and seek the blessing of the saint. Then they return to the courtyard where, accompanied by a musician playing simultaneously on a reed flute and small drum, they begin their strange and ancient ritual. Each dancer marks out the *four cardinal points of the compass* with his right foot, then stamps and rotates to symbolize the passage of time and the cycle of the seasons. Their timing is so precise that all the vast colored head-dresses twirl backwards and forwards in unison. The dance continues on and off for many hours, and the weight of the head-dresses reduces nearly all the dancers to complete exhaustion.

Of Gods and Men: The Heritage of Ancient Mexico,
Anna Benson Gyles & Chloe Sayer, 1980, pp. 81-82

In the dance Nahuas have found it possible to bring together and express their double heritage: their own Mesoamerican ways and the Christian way. A place of respect is made in their being for both spiritualities, a feat that remains a challenge to many People of our own times.

———————————— + ————————————

RELATIONSHIP OF DIRECTIONS TO OTHER COSMIC ELEMENTS
AZTEC

One of the fundamental concepts of the Aztec religion was the grouping of all beings according to the *four cardinal points of the* compass and the central direction, or up and down. Therefore, in the Mexican mind the numbers 4 and 5 are very important, just as in Occidental magic the number 3 is significant.

The divine pair represented the central direction, or up and down, that is, the heaven and the earth, while their *four sons were assigned to the four directions, or the four cardinal points of the compass.* For that reason, three of them were characterized by different colors: red, black and blue, corresponding to the *East,* the *North,* and the *South,* respectively, while Quetzalcóatl occupied the place that a white Tezcatlipoca, corresponding to the *West,* must have held in the primitive myth. . . .

This fundamental idea of the *four cardinal points of the compass* and the central direction, up and down, which made the fifth or central region, is found in all the religious manifestations of the Aztecs and is without doubt one of the concepts they inherited from the old cultures of Mesoamerica.

Not only were colors and gods grouped in this manner. Also animals, trees, days, and men, according to the day on which they were born, belonged to one of the four regions of the world. Man was given the name of the day of his birth within the ritual calendar of 260 days. . . . The calendar was divided into four parts of 65 days each, one part corresponding to the *East,* one to the *North,* one to the *West,* and one to the *South,* and these parts were repeated an infinite number of times.

The Aztecs: People of the Sun, Alfonso Caso, 1967, pp. 10-11

Gods, colors, the calendar, and the four cardinal points all seemed to fit together in the cosmology of the Aztecs. One could wake up in the morning and know one's place in the universe temporally as well as spatially. All of created life was brought into a unity as it was seen to be related to the directions. Human life took on meaning as it related to the north, to the south, to the east, or to the west.

———————— + ————————

SACRED DIRECTIONS AND THE HUMAN BODY
AZTEC

The most pervasive type of sacred space where elaborate ceremonies were carried out was the human body. The human body was considered a potent receptacle of cosmological forces, a living, moving center of the world.

Consider, for instance, the elaborate image of the cosmos from the *Codex Fejérváry Mayer*. It reflects the typical Mesoamerican worldview divided into five sections. We see the *four quarters,* each containing a sacred tree with a celestial bird on top, surrounding the central region where XIUHTECUHTLI, the Fire God, is dressed in warrior regalia. According to scholars the body of Tezcatlipoca has been cut into pieces and divided over the *four directions of the world,* with his blood flowing into the center. The divine blood is flowing into the axis of the universe, which redistributes the divine energy to animals, body parts, vegetation, and the calendar, which is divided by the *four quarters of the cosmos*. Each quadrant shows two of the Nine Lords of the Night in ritual postures next to the cosmic tree. The dots surrounding the edges of the design represent the 260-day ritual calendar divided by the spatial structure of the universe.

In order to understand the religious power of the human body . . . let us focus on the importance of two body parts in Aztec religions, the heart and the head.

The Mesoamerican cosmos was conceived as a series of thirteen celestial and nine underworld layers, each layer inhabited by gods, supernatural beings, and forces. These powers and beings entered the earthly level through a series of openings or avenues of communication including the *four cosmic trees* at the edges of the world, mountains, caves, the rays of the sun, the motion of the wind, and so forth. These lines of communication were pictured as two pairs of heliacal bands, called *malinalli,* which moved in constant motion, allowing the forces of the underworld to ascend and the forces of the overworld to descend. In this way the Turquoise World (sky) and the Obsidian World (underworld) were dynamically connected to the terrestrial world of nature, human beings, and society. These supernatural forces emerged each day from the sacred trees and

Contemporary inlaid jewelry evokes the Mayan past

spread across the landscape. They could be introduced into the human body by either ritual means or through the action of nature.

Religions of Mesoamerica: Cosmovision and Ceremonial Centers,
David Carrasco, 1990, pp. 66-67

The sacred connections of the human body with the universe is played out in the cosmic imagery of the Aztecs. Life is dynamic and not at all static. It is multiform in being, and holy power is everywhere.

———————————— + ————————————

THE DIRECTIONS AND PASSING OF THE AGES
AZTEC

During each age, or Sun, of the earth, one god prevailed over the others, and he symbolized one of the elements—earth, air, fire, or water—as well as one of the *four quadrants of the universe*. Each god's period of ascendancy constituted one of the ages of the world. But at the end of each age, war broke out and destruction followed. Tezcatlipoca and Quetzalcóatl battled, each subdued the other, then both returned to the field of battle of the universe. The elements of earth, wind, fire, and water then came suddenly upon the scene from the *four directions* and clashed violently.

Aztec Thought and Culture: A Study of the Ancient Nahuatl Mind,
Miguel Leon-Portilla, 1982, p. 36

Not only directional spatiality, but temporality, was understood to participate in the flux of events that affected the Aztec universe.

———————————— + ————————————

THE GODDESS COATLICUE AND
THE FOUR SPATIAL DIRECTIONS
AZTEC

Coatlicue emerges powerfully as the concrete embodiment in stone of the ideas of a supreme cosmic being who generates and sustains the universe. It adumbrates the cruciform orientations of the quadrants of the universe, as well as the dynamic quality of time, which creates and destroys through struggle; this is the central category of Nahuatl cosmological thought. Perhaps of all the symbols of the Nahuatl universe, the most marvelous is the tragically beautiful image of Coatlicue. . . . To each of the four fundamental gods, to each of the *four directions,* a specified period of time within the Fifth Age was allotted for domination and subordination. This division of time gave rise to the years of the *East,* of the *North,* of the *West,* and of the *South.* In abstract terms, motion appeared as a consequence of the spatialization of time and of the orientation of the years and the days toward the *four directions.* . . . in a Nahuatl century of fifty-two years, each of the *four directions* was allotted a thirteen-year period of predominate influence. In a similar manner, with each year, the days of the *tonalámatl* (sacred calendar) were divided into sixty-five-day series of five thirteen-day "weeks." In a year of 260 days, there were four of these 65-day groups, and each carried a sign which related it to one of the *four cardinal directions.* . . .

The most important Indian manuscripts demonstrate a clear distribution of twenty day-signs among the *four directions:*

EAST
Cipactli, Alligator
Acatl, Reed
Cóatl, Serpent
Ollin, Movement
Atl, Water

NORTH
Océlotl, Tiger
Miquiztli, Death
Técpatl, Flint
Itzcuintli, Dog
Ehécatl, Wind

WEST
Mázatl, Deer
Quiáuitl, Rain
Ozomatli, Monkey
Calli, House
Quauhtli, Eagle

SOUTH
Xóchitl, Flower
Malinalli, Herb
Cuctzpalin, Lizard
Cozcaquauhtli, Vulture
Tochtli, Rabbit

Thus, not only in each year, but also in each day, the influence of one of the *four spatial directions* predominated. Space and time, combining and interpenetrating, made possible the harmony among the gods (the four cosmic forces) and, consequently, the movement of the sun and the existence of life. The profound significance of movement to the Nahuas can be deduced from the common Nahuatl root of the word movement, heart, and soul. To the ancient Mexicans, life, symbolized by the heart *(y-óllo-tl),* was inconceivable without the element which explains it, movement *(y-olli).*

The Nahuas, therefore, believed that movement and life resulted from the harmony achieved by the spatial orientation of the years and the days, in other words, by the spatialization of time. So long as this harmony continued, so long as the *four directions* of the universe

were each allotted thirteen years in every century and their supremacy unquestioned during the specified time, the Fifth Sun would continue to exist—it would continue to move. Should this balance some day be disturbed, another cosmic struggle for supremacy would be initiated. There would be one final earthquake—one so powerful that "with this we shall perish."

Aztec Thought and Culture: A Study of the Nahuatl Mind, Miguel Leon-Portilla, 1982, 53-55

Coatlicue, a goddess, was the mother of the god Huitzilopochtli. Statues which depict her are at the same time pyramidal, cruciform, and human in form. She embodied, even sculpturally, what most Aztecs understood about their universe.

———————— + ————————

DIRECTIONAL MOVEMENT OF THE EARTH-BEARERS
CHAMULA MAYA

The underworld is also the point from which the universe is supported. Opinions vary on the nature of this support, but most Chamulas think that either a single earth-bearer carries the universe on his back, or four earthbearers support the universe at the *intercardinal points*.

The whole cosmological system is bounded and held together by the circular paths of the sun and the moon, who are the principal deities in the Chamula pantheon. Each day they pass by the *eastern* and *western* edges of the earth on their trips to the sky and the underworld. These deities effectively represent most of the fundamental assumptions made by Chamulas about order, for they define both temporal and spatial categories that are critical for the maintenance of life.

Chamulas in the World of the Sun: Time and Space in
a Maya Oral Tradition, Gary Gossen, 1974, p. 22

Though a certain sense of syncretism seems to be evident here, it is a unity as it is experienced ceremonially by the Chamulas.

———————————— + ————————————

RITUAL CIRCUITS
CHAMULA MAYA

Chamula cosmological symbolism has as its primary orientation the point of view of the sun as it emerges on the eastern horizon each day, facing "his" universe, with *north* on his right hand and *south* on his left hand. This orientation helps to explain the derivation of the descriptive terms for *north* ("the side of the sky on the right hand") and *south* ("the side of the sky on the left hand"). Furthermore, the adjective "right" *(bak'i)* is positively evaluated in innumerable words and idioms in Tzotzil. By extension, it means "actual," "very," "true," or "the most representative," as in *bac'k k'op* ("Tzotzil"), which may be translated literally as "the true language," or in *bac'i k'ob* ("right hand"), which may also be read as the "real hand" or "true hand." *North* is on the right hand of the sun-creator as he traverses the sky.

This placement appears to be related to the belief that *North* is a direction of good omen and virtue. Chamulas often express this view as, *mas lek sk'aan yo'nton ta bac'i k'ob li htotike,* or, "Our Father's heart prefers the right hand way."

The fundamental orientation to the right also clarifies Chamula ritual treatment of space. In the first place, religious cargoholders themselves possess an aspect of deity in that they share with the sun and the saints (the sun's kinsmen) the responsibility and the burden of maintaining the social order. While acquiring for themselves a sacred aspect through exemplary behavior and language, as well as through constant use of sacred symbols and objects such as rum, incense, candles, fireworks, and cigarettes, most of which have actual or metaphoric qualities of heat, they metaphorically follow the sun's pattern of motion by moving to their own right through any ritual space in front of them. Thus, there is an overwhelming tendency of almost all Chamula ritual motion to follow a counterclockwise pattern. This direction is the horizontal equivalent of the sun's daily vertical path across the heavens from *east* to *west.*

This transformation of the sun's path according to Chamula premises could be derived by imagining oneself facing the universe from the eastern horizon, as the sun does each morning, and "turning" the vertical solar orbit to the right so that it lay flat on the earth. I should emphasize that no Chamula ever stated the derivation so simply. However, informants consistently said that *east* is the sun's position at *slok'htotik* ("the sun appears" or "dawn"); *north* is the horizontal equivalent to the sun's vertical position at *olol k'ak'al* ("half head," "half-day," or "noon"); *west* is *sbat htotik* ("the sun departs" or "sundown"); and *south* is the horizontal equivalent to the sun's vertical position at *olol'ak'obal* ("half-night" or "midnight"). This horizontal transformation allows cargo officials to "move as the sun moves," thereby restating symbolically both the temporal and spatial cycles for which the sun is responsible. Thus the beginning of any ritual (counterclockwise) circuit becomes the "conceptual *East.*" *North* in this system becomes the horizontal equivalent of the point of "maximum heat" of the sun at noon at the zenith of his orbit; *west* and *south* also follow the solar circuit. As a result, the *cardinal direction north* shares with the *east* the sign of good omen and positive orientation, while *west* and *south* are generally negative in the cosmological system.

The positive symbolic value of the *north* may also derive from Chamulas' awareness of the fact that the apparent position of the rising sun shifts northward on the eastern horizon during the increasingly longer days between the vernal equinox and the summer solstice. This period is also associated with the first rains of the wet season (in early May) and with the beginning (also in late April or early May) of the annual growing cycle for highland crops. *South* is also associated with the time of shortening days, from the autumnal equinox to the winter solstice, which marks the end of the growing season and the beginning of killing frosts and death in the annual solar cycle. These characteristics help to explain why the *south* is negatively regarded in some respects, for it represents both night and frost, dry weather and the nonproductive agricultural season. *West* represents incipient death in the life cycle and twilight in the daily cycle, as well as the period between the summer solstice and the autumnal equinox. The fact that the *inter-cardinal direction southeast* is the first point in the spatio-temporal symbolic scheme to represent an "upswing" or emergence of the sun from the negative nadir *(south)* of the system may be important in explaining why the *southeast* is frequently an alternate to the *east* as the initial position in ritual circuits and positions of ritual personnel.

Ritual circuits, therefore, carry a great deal more information than would appear at first glance. They proceed counterclockwise because that direction is the logical horizontal equivalent of the annual solar cycle and the daily solar cycle. Even though circumstances may not allow all individual circuits to begin in the actual *east* or *southeast,* the principles of the right hand and counterclockwise motion appear to serve as ritual surrogates for the eastern solar orientation and the solar cycle. Any initial ritual location can thus become "conceptual east." In this way men are better able to base their ritual orientation on the first principle of life itself, which is the sun.

> *Chamulas in the World of the Sun: Time and Space in*
> *a Maya Oral Tradition*, Gary Gossen, 1974, pp. 32-35

It is interesting to note that time of day figures into the Chamula Maya way of discerning the ritual movements of directionality for circling the sacred shrines. A highly developed sense of the calendar was, and is, central for the ceremonies.

———————————— + ————————————

DIRECTIONAL SUN SYMBOLISM
CHAMULA MAYA

The fundamental spatial divisions of the universe, its *cardinal directions*, are derived from the relative positions of the sun on his east-west path across the heavens:

East: *lok'eb k'ak'al,* "emergent heat (day)"
West: *maleb k'al'al,* "waning heat (day)"
North: *sokon vinahel ta bac'i k'ob,*
  "the side of the sky on the right hand"
South: *sokon vinahel ta c'et k'ob,*
  "the side of the sky on the left hand"

*Chamulas in the World of the Sun: Time and Space in
a Maya Oral Tradition,* Gary Gossen, 1974, p. 31

From their place in the physical world, this Mayan People describes directionality with both temperature and position in mind.

———————— + ————————

THE DIRECTIONS AND PYRAMIDAL SYMBOLISM
AZTEC & MAYA

Everything that we have come to understand about the builders of Mesoamerica's first metropolitan communities indicates that they lived in a universe pervasively alive from top to bottom, and when the architecture of those cities is examined with this style of perception in

*Contemporary Chicano architecture and mural work
at Chicano Park in the Barrio Logan, San Diego, California*

mind, their design can be seen to specifically reflect and address this condition of aliveness.

There appears to have been no arbitrarily placed pyramid in Mesoamerica; each face was constructed in reference to one of the *four cardinal points* in space—the same ones we know as **north, south, east,** and **west.** In our world these directions tend to function as convenient reference points but little more. We use them as relative designations, knowing that if we headed south long enough we would circle the globe and end up where we started. The ancient Meso-american did not think in such terms. For him or her, physical and psychological space, the outer and inner worlds, were not distinctly separable, and everything in the outer world, including something as seemingly vague as a direction, could be seen as an autonomous being that monitored the human community with watchful eyes.

> *This Tree Grows Out of Hell: Mesoamerica and the Search for the Magical Body*, Ptolemy Tompkins, 1990, p. 9

Even Mesoamerican pyramids expressed the four directions architec-turally. They became part of the ceremonial center complex which allowed for the celebration of the unseen mysteries inherent in the People's spiritual world. Like sacraments or religious buildings of other cultures, they became outward expressions of inward spiritual realities.

—————————— + ——————————

CONTEMPORARY POEM
AZTEC/CHICANO

FOUR DIRECTIONS

> *WEST*
> we are
> salmons
> looking for
> our womb

> *NORTH*
> eagles
> flying

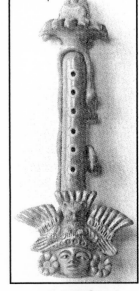

*Ceramic flute
(pre-Columbian)*

the Sun
in our beak

EAST
coyotes
calling
each other
in the Moon

SOUTH
we turn
into snakes
by eating
chile

*Costa Rican
Crocodile*

"Four Directions," *Snake Poems: An Aztec Invocation*,
Francisco Alarcón, 1992, p. 6

*This poem speaks of time and movement and some special elements of
creation. It seems to evoke an ancient Aztec dance of the four directions
and yet it is quite contemporary.*

———————————— + ————————————

HEALING SONG
CUNA

The Neles are the defence under the patient's hammock.
From the *east* the chiefs come, summoned
against the place of the Ancient Spirits they are the defence
making the whole place scarey.
From the *west* the chiefs come, summoned.
Nele Nettle with his men comes, summoned;
he comes with prickly leaf-cloths; comes stinging;
against the white-faced ancients they are the defence;
they are entangling the way, making the whole place scarey.
From the big sea the chiefs come, summoned.
Nele Small Peppers are the defence;
against the white-faced ancients they are the defence;
they are entangling the way, making the whole place scarey.

From opposite the big sea the chiefs come, summoned.
Nele Cabur Pepper with his men comes, summoned;
against the ancient spirits they come as the defence;
they are entangling the way, making the whole place scarey.
Nele Red Pepper with his men comes, summoned;
against the ancient spirits they come as the defence;
they are entangling the way, making the whole place scarey.
From below the chiefs come, summoned.
Nele Mupakkaopinale Pepper with his men comes, summoned;
Muppakka Oparpalele the chiefs come, summoned;
against the ancient spirits they come as the defence;
they are entangling the way, making the whole place scarey.

*Image of the New World: The American Continent
Portrayed in Native Texts*, Gordon Brotherston, 1979, p. 255

For thousands of generations this People has lived between the influences of Mayas to their north and Incas to their south. To their east they have always had Arawak and Carib neighbors. This healing prayer, the Serkan Ikala (Way of the Spirits of the Dead), calls upon all the healing forces to come from where they are to cure the patient who lies in a hammock with shamanic images, Neles, underneath and nearby. Two of the world directions are named, but it is understood that healing is to come from all the directions, even if they are called upon indirectly.

Kuna appliqued crab design

CARIBBEAN
CULTURAL
AREA

*A conch shell is used to call out
to Creator in the Taino way*

COLOR SYMBOLISM
OF THE FOUR DIRECTIONS
ARAWAKS OF
PUERTO RICO, CUBA, SANTO DOMINGO

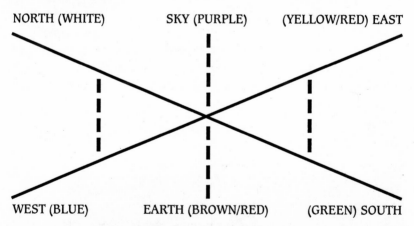

NORTH (WHITE)　　　SKY (PURPLE)　　　(YELLOW/RED) EAST

WEST (BLUE)　　　EARTH (BROWN/RED)　　　(GREEN) SOUTH

Interview with José Soto, Browning Pow Wow, Montana, July 10, 1994

*A surprise meeting with José Soto (of Tuscarora and Arawak heritage)
at a Blackfeet Powwow at Browning, Montana on July 10, 1994
enabled a good exchange of ideas to take place. José revealed the
traditional colors that are associated with the four directions (plus up
and down). Though today's indigenous island People also have African
and European blood and cultural ways, there is still much in the
ancient heritage that can be recognized and learned from.*

SOUTH AMERICA CULTURAL AREA

HEALING CEREMONY
MAPUCHE

Shamans use a specially made drumstick which also symbolizes their power, and some combination of gourd rattles and sleigh bells, also used at certain parts of almost every curing ceremony. The ritual consists of beating the drum over the patient's body and shaking the rattles over him. Shamans also suck and massage the affected parts of their client's body, if this kind of treatment is indicated by the diagnosis, and may also blow tobacco smoke or pour—or spray—from their mouth medicinal water (made from various herbal concoctions depending upon the illness to be cured) over the sick person's body in the *four cardinal directions* of the compass.

The Mapuche Indians of Chile, Louis Faron, 1968, p. 73

The movement of breath or smoke or liquid over a sick person's body, accompanied by prayer, is a common feature for many Peoples of the Americas, but there are also counterparts in the healing practices of other cultures around the world.

———————————— + ————————————

HEALING CEREMONY PARAPHERNALIA
MAPUCHE

To assist them in the curing rites—called *machitun*—the shaman or *machi* has a set of paraphernalia reminiscent of that used by Siberian shamans. The two most prominent pieces of equipment employed by shamans are the shallow drum *(kultrun)* and the carved

205

pole *(rewe)*. The drum, beaten almost continuously in some ceremonies, helps induce a trance state; the step-notched pole, which the shaman sometimes climbs during ceremonies, is a sacred symbol of office fixed in the ground outside the shaman's house. The kultrun is made of a shallow wooden bowl, about eighteen inches in diameter, and covered by velum. The cover is often undecorated but sometimes carries a symbolic design of the Mapuche universe depicting *four quarters of the world* and its center.

The Mapuche Indians of Chile, Louis Faron, 1968, p. 73

The drum of the Mapuche shaman is a symbolic microcosm of the universe and serves as a usual mnemonic device.

------------------------ + ------------------------

DIRECTIONS AND RAIN FOREST SYMBOLISM
KAIAPÓ

The Kaiapó maintain that the social organization of wasps is rather like that of people, since wasps' nests are round, just like the Kaiapó villages. A cross-section of a wasps' nest reveals further, different layers which accord with the Kaiapó's cosmological view of the existence of different earthly and sky levels. The Kaiapó say that once upon a time they inhabited a higher level (the sky) and descended to the present level (the earth). Some Kaiapó were left behind in the sky and the fires they light at night to keep themselves warm can be seen from the earth: they are the stars in the firmament.

In addition to the verticality of their world-image it is important for us to look at its horizontality. Contrary to what might be believed, the world is not round but consists of a somewhat rectangular, though rounded, part which represents the *kajkwa nhot* (the **West**). *Kajkwa*

Amazon

nhot roughly means the "end/tip of the sky." This part is flanked by two rounded extensions *(pa,* the "arms") that protrude on to a triangular extremity which represents the *kajkwa krax* (the *East*). This term means the "beginning/root of the sky." In the middle of all this is located a circular "center" *(ipok-ri)* which portrays the place of the circular Kaiapó village. Each Kaiapó community presumes it inhabits this real center of the universe.

Kaiapó, Amazonia: The Art of Body Decoration,
Gustaaf Verswijver (Ed.), 1992, p. 51

The Kaiapó look to the creatures of the world for instruction in life. They see themselves as somehow reflected in the mirror of other living beings. The West and the East are the predominant directions for them, West being the more positive direction. As an Amazonian People, perhaps the rivers and their tributaries bound them on the northern and southern sides and their usual mode of travel and operation is generally from east to west and vice-versa.

———————————— + ————————————

ADOPTION CEREMONY
HUNI KUI (AMAHUACA)

Several weeks after my arrival I was again presented in solemn ceremony before the assembled tribe. This time the ceremony was different. The chief began a chant I had not heard before, and the others responded and participated in a shuffling kind of dance without moving about. It was long and involved. In the end the chief took a branch of large leaves and carefully brushed them the full length of my body from the *four directions of the compass—east* first, then from the **west**, the *north* and the *south*.

Wizard of the Upper Amazon: The Story of Manuel Córdova-Rios,
F. Bruce Lamb, 1974, p. 21

The subject of this book was a Peruvian who travelled in Colombia and Brazil. While among this tribe he was brought into their life by adoption and learned much of the work of a curandero or healer. Here we are able to notice their form of honoring the four directions.

———————————— + ————————————

PARAMETERS OF THE EMPIRE
INCA

The Incas. Even now their very name conjures visions of imperial grandeur, of mountain strongholds and hidden citadels, of untold treasure in silver and gold, of alien invaders and slashing swords. The Incas dwelt in one of the last great secret wonderlands on earth; only among the stars may humankind again happen upon an unexpected continent and an empire unkown.

The empire ranged 2,500 miles along the western edge of South America, reaching across parched sands, over lofty snowpeaks, and into jungle without horizons. Royal roads threaded the land; heart-stopping suspension bridges spanned dark gorges.

Its emperor, the Lord Inca, believed the sun had founded his dynasty. "O Sun, my Father," he would pray, "let thy sons the Incas be conquerors and despoilers of all mankind," and he commanded subject peoples to honor the sun—servant of Viracocha, the creator—above all local gods. When he journeyed through his mountain realm, carried in a curtained litter by blue-liveried bearers and flanked by warriors with maces and slings, his people called down blessings from the slopes: *"Ancha hatun apu, intipchuri*—Great and powerful lord, son of the sun." "Little short of adoring him as God," a chronicler wrote.

His queen was his sister, and his harem of 600 included the fairest maidens from a hundred conquered nations. He lived in sumptuous palaces and wore robes of bat fur and hummingbird feathers, discarded after one wearing. He ruled a welfare state where everyone was looked after in return for unceasing toil; the punishment for brazen laziness was death. He called his empire Tahuantinsuyu, the *Four Quarters of the World*. Now we call all its inhabitants Incas. . . .

Lost Empires: Living Tribes, Ross Bennett (Ed.), 1982, p. 213

The Inca empire was vast indeed and the emperor had some sense that he was to rule it all in each of its quadrants as time would pass. Yet empires come and go no matter where they exist in the world. Anciently, this empire was called Tawantinsuwu by the People. The city of Cuzco was the center from which the roads going through the four quarters issued forth. Though they were not exactly aligned to each of the four directions, nevertheless these roads brought travellers to the uttermost regions of the commonwealth. Antisuyu was the name for the eastern part, while Cuntisuyu lay to the west; the third quarter, Collasuyu covered vast areas to the southeast of Cuzco, while the northern territorial enterprise bore the name Chinchasuyu.

———————————— + ————————————

PERSONIFICATION OF THE DIRECTIONS
ONA (SELKNAM)

North guards beautiful daughter against attempts by suitors (*Southeast* and *South*) to reach his country. Former gives up, but *South* and his men succeed after initial failure and strenuous effort. In subsequent wrestling contest between the opposing forces, *South* wins. He abducts *North's* daughter and flees, putting magic obstacles (storms) in way of pursuing *North*. Slippery mountain creates difficulties for both pursuer and pursued. Finally *North* is forced to return, defeated by violent storm sent out by *South's* father. *South* marries abducted girl.

> *Folk Literature of the Selknam Indians: Martin Gusinde's Collection of Selknam Narratives*, Johannes Wilbert (Ed.), 1975, p. 55

The Selknam (Ona) People of Tierra del Fuego on the most southern part of South America have been pretty much devastated during this century and the last because of epidemics, removal from their sovereign lands, and slaughter by European immigrants. Martin Gusinde, a priest from Germany and a great humanitarian, lived with them and tried to have others understand them. In a series of narratives, he recorded for posterity what he could of these gentle People. This summary of a story indicates a personification of some of the directions as they related to their homeland and history.

———————————— + ————————————

PERSONIFICATION OF NORTH AND SOUTH
ONA (SELKNAM)

The more important mythological and folklore cycles were those concerned with the adventures and deeds of: *Kenós*, the first man, agent of Temáukel, who gave the Ona their land; *K'aux*, the mighty hunter who divided their land into the 39 hunting territories and assigned one to each family; *Kwányip,* the hero who overcame the malevolent *Chénuke* and the giant cannibal, *Cháskels; North* and *South* and their struggles with each other for mastery; Sun and his wife, Moon; the mythical ancestors of the Ona; the primeval manlike being who later turned into mountains, lakes, rivers, and the like. . . .

Handbook of South American Indians, Vol. 1,
Julian Steward (Ed.), 1963, p. 124

The Ona of Tierra Del Fuego in Patagonia, a gentle People who were hunted almost to extinction in the late nineteenth century, possessed a homeland that was not vast, but the directions North and South were important to them both mythically and historically. It is more than lamentable that they are not with us in strength today. Perhaps, but only perhaps, we might learn from what was done to them so that we might let others live in all the quarters of our beautiful world.

———————————— + ————————————

RITUAL POSITIONING INSIDE THE HAIN
ONA (SELKNAM)

The *Hain,* a large wigwam, was usually about a quarter of a mile from the village or camping-ground, and always faced away from it, to prevent the prying eyes of the women from seeing through its ever-open door. Whenever possible, it was built near a clump of trees, which helped to screen the interior of the *Hain* from the other directions and served as a wing from behind which the actors could appear on the stage. The wigwam was always to the *east* of the village. Certain explorers have noticed these wigwams and have concluded that they were places of worship. It was not, however, any idea of religion of the cult of the rising sun that made them place the Lodge in that position, but merely because the prevailing winds came from the *west.* With the *Hain's* entrance facing *east,* there was more shelter from the weather. Another reason for having the meeting-place to the leeward of the village was the mystical nourishment with which the men were supposed to be supplied. The scent of roasting meat borne on the breeze to the village might have cast doubts on that story.

Aneki told me during that first discourse that, from the fire in the centre of the *Hain,* an imaginary chasm of untold depth, and with a flaming inferno at the bottom of it, ran out through the door and away *eastward* into the distance. Ages ago, when the *Hain* was new, this chasm had really existed and anyone trying to cross it had fallen in and been lost. Its presence now was only assumed, yet it was still not without its perils when a meeting was in session. Any man treading, however inadvertently, on the place where it was supposed to be would be thrown on the fire—though, added Aneki, he would not be held down there. This was a direct warning to me—and now I knew why my tutors had guided my footsteps so meticulously as we approached and entered the *Hain.*

This hypothetical chasm had another purpose. It divided the Lodge into two groups, according to parentage or place of birth. The *men from the north sat to the south* of the fissure, and the *men from the south sat to the north*. It also governed approach to the *Hain*. I, being from across the mountains to the *south* of Ona-land and having no connection, either by country or by blood, with the northerners, had to move out to the left when walking from the village, keeping the *Hain* on my right until I turned to go through the doorway. This I must on no account cross over, but must enter the wigwam with the wall close on my right and the fire on my left. There, half-way along, was *Kiayeshk,* which meant Black Shag and was the name of the pole darkened by burning. Beside *Kiayeshk* was to be my place at the councils, and I must not pass beyond it until the end of the proceedings, until directly called upon to do so.

If a man has two places of origin, inasmuch as his parents came one from the *north* and the other from the *south,* there were no such restrictions imposed upon him. Aneki himself was one of these privileged members. His father, Heeshoolh, came from the *south-west* and his mother was a northern woman, so he could pass the Lodge on either side when approaching from the village and take his seat *north* or *south* of the fiery chasm.

At the end of the meetings all these restraints were lifted and we could leave the *Hain* in any way we liked. When not in use as a Lodge, the wigwam served as sleeping-quarters and living house for bachelors, widowers ... and *klokten* who had passed their entrance examination.

Uttermost Part of the Earth, E. Lucas Bridges, 1988, pp. 414-415

In the Hain, teenage boys were instructed in the way of life of the People. The wigwam-like structure was also the place for the men to gather to tell the ancient stories. Directional seating arrangements followed a special protocol. It is amazing that the writer had such a fine understanding of the Ona ways, considering both language and cultural difficulties.

———————————————— + ————————————————

FOUR WINDS WRESTLING MATCH
ONA (SELKNAM)

The *four great winds* were once men and, as such, had difficulties amongst themselves, not knowing who was the strongest. They determined to settle their differences, once and for all, in a decisive wrestling match, as was the custom with the Ona when they wished to avoid the use of bows and arows. A great crowd having assembled, the usual ring was formed. The challengers stepped out and took on one or another of their opponents indiscriminately—and with varying success.

Wintekhaiyin, the **east wind,** though persistent, was far too gentle. After being thrown several times by each of the others, he realized his case was hopeless. Accordingly he resumed his robe and joined the onlookers.

Orroknhaiyin, the **south wind,** put up a much better show, as he was fierce and strong—a nasty, angry wrestler. But after a violent struggle and several falls, he had to give up and follow *Wintekhaiyin,* leaving the field to the other two.

Now came the real fight. *Hechuknhaiyin,* the **north wind,** was a trickly wrestler, powerful and bad-tempered. At last, however, he wore himself out against the tremendous strength of the untiring **west wind**, *Kenenikhaiyin,* and after a tempestuous bout was heavily thrown. On rising, being instantly challenged again, he drew back, thus acknowledging himself beaten.

This story describes, in a picturesque and remarkably clear manner, the characteristics of the four great winds, for after a warm morning in summer, when the others are sleeping or resting, *Wintekhaiyin* comes cautiously from his home in the **east** and blows with moderate strength till he wishes to rest, or sees the **north wind** threatening. Then he goes quietly home again. *Hechukn-haiyin,* still rough and ill-natured, often behaves badly until *Kenenikhaiyin* rushes down from the *west,* when he draws back, though most unwillingly, leaving the field to the champion. In the winter, *Orroknhaiyin,* the *south wind,* taking advantage of the fact that the others are resting, comes up fearlessly in full force to bring the snow.

Uttermost Part of the Earth, E. Lucas Bridges, 1988, pp. 440-441

What a great alternative to mortal violence: a wrestling match to show forth the victor! The personification of the four winds helped the People to understand more fully their own particular environment.

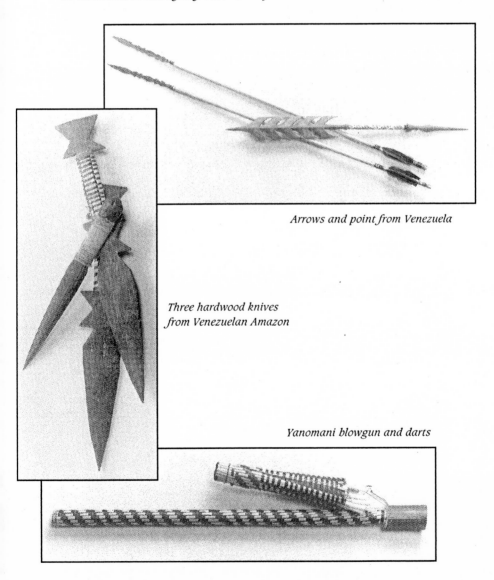

Arrows and point from Venezuela

Three hardwood knives from Venezuelan Amazon

Yanomani blowgun and darts

Praying with Eagle Feathers

INTERCULTURAL CULTURAL AREA

GIFTS OF THE FOUR DIRECTIONS
INTERTRIBAL

EAST
- light
- beginnings
- renewals
- innocence
- guilelessness
- spontaneity
- joy
- capacity to believe in the unseen
- warmth of spirit
- purity
- trust
- hope
- uncritical acceptance of others
- love that doesn't question others and doesn't know itself
- courage
- truthfulness
- birth
- rebirth
- childhood
- illumination
- guidance
- leadership
- beautiful speech

- vulnerability
- ability to see clearly through complex situations
- watching over others
- guiding others
- seeing situations in perspective
- hope for the people
- trust in your own vision
- ability to focus attention on present time tasks
- concentration
- devotion to the service of others

SOUTH
- youth
- fullness
- summer
- the heart
- generosity
- sensitivity to the feelings of others
- loyalty
- noble passions
- love (of one person for another)
- balanced development of the physical body
- physical discipline
- control of appetites
- determination
- goal setting
- training senses such as sight, hearing, taste
- musical development
- gracefulness
- appreciation of the arts
- discrimination in sight, hearing and taste
- passionate involvement in the world
- idealism
- emotional attraction to good and repulsion to bad
- compassion
- kindness
- anger at injustice
- repulsion by senseless violence
- feelings refined, developed, controlled

- ability to express hurt and other bad feelings
- ability to express joy and good feelings
- ability to set aside strong feelings in order to serve others

WEST
- darkness
- the unknown
- going within
- dreams
- deep inner thoughts
- testing of the will
- perseverance
- stick-to-it-iveness
- consolidating of personal power
- management of power
- spiritual insight
- daily prayer
- meditation
- fasting
- reflection
- contemplation
- silence
- being alone with one's self
- respect for elders
- respect for the spiritual struggles of others
- respect for others' beliefs
- awareness of our spiritual nature
- sacrifice
- humility
- love for the Creator
- commitment to the path of personal development
- commitment to universal life values and a high moral code
- commitment to struggle to assist the development of the people
- ceremony
- clear self-knowledge
- vision (a sense of possibilities and potentialities)

NORTH
- elders

- wisdom
- thinking
- analyzing
- understanding
- speculating
- calculation
- prediction
- organizing
- categorizing
- discriminating
- criticizing
- problem solving
- imagining
- interpreting
- integrating all intellectual capacities
- completion
- fulfillment
- lessons of things that end
- capacity to finish what we begin
- detachment
- freedom from fear
- freedom from hate
- freedom from love
- freedom from knowledge
- seeing how all things fit together
- insight
- intuition made conscious
- sense of how to live a balanced life
- capacity to dwell in the center of things,
    to see and take the middle way
- moderation
- justice

The Sacred Tree, Judie Bopp, 1989, pp. 42-72

A few years ago traditional Native People in Western Canada, many of whom were Christian as well as traditional, worked with university professors, clergy, and many other spiritual leaders to see how Native ways could be helpful in counselling situations, especially with drug and alcohol counselling. They reminded themselves that even now the gifts that come from the four directions and the medicine wheel continue to be good teaching tools.

———————————— + ————————————

TOBACCO AND THE DIRECTIONS
INTERTRIBAL

Although we have accepted a great deal of technology from the American Indian, we have not yet learned his more difficult lessons, lessons about mind and spirit. Some of the lessons concern the very things we have borrowed, as in the case of the most famous of Indian stimulants, tobacco. For the Indian, tobacco always had a sacramental meaning: the smoke was exhaled *east* and *west, north* and *south*, above and below, and then the smoker blew smoke on himself. In this way he joined the self with the cosmos. When we adopted tobacco we turned it into a personal habit, and we have overused it to the point where it has killed many of us. The final irony is that there should be a righteous public campaign against this sacred gift of America, as if there were something inherently wrong with smoking.

Teachings from the American Earth: Indian Religion and Philosophy,
Dennis Tedlock & Barbara Tedlock, 1975, pp. xi-xii

Nowadays it seems that most people who smoke are ignorant of tobacco's ancient sacred connections with the four directions. But there are many among the Peoples who do understand.

———————————— + ————————————

NATIVE CHRISTIAN PRAYER
INTERTRIBAL

(Face East)
L. From the *East*, the direction of the rising sun, we receive peace and light and wisdom and knowlege.
P. We are grateful for these gifts, O God.

(Face South)
L. From the *South* comes warmth, guidance and the beginning and the end of life.

P. We are grateful for these gifts, O God.

(Face West)
L. From the *West* comes the rain, purifying waters, to sustain all living
    things.
P. We are grateful for these gifts, O God.

(Face North)
L. From the *North* comes the cold and mighty wind, the white snows,
    giving us strength and endurance.
P. We are grateful for these gifts, O God.

(Face upward)
L. From the heavens we receive darkness and light, the air of Your
    breath, and messages from Your winged creatures.
P. We are grateful for these gifts, O God.

(Face downward)
L. From the earth we come and to the earth we will return.
P. We are grateful for Your creation, Mother Earth, O God.

ALL: May we walk good paths, O God, living on this earth as brothers
and sisters should; rejoicing in one another's blessings, sympathizing
in one another's sorrows, and together with You, renewing the face of
the earth.

Worship Resources, Juanita Helphey (Ed.), 1991, p. 32

*This prayer, though prayed by Christian Native
People and others, is a contemporary way of
addressing God while honoring the directions.*

——————— + ———————

CONTEMPORARY PRAYER
INTERTRIBAL

I am grateful to you Snowy Owl
Take me from the *West*, where the sun sets,
Where my mind sinks into its depths,

To your home in the **North**,
Cold northern winds that test and strengthen.
And on to the **East**, place of new light.
May I have the courage to make this journey

To face my tests with dignity and grace,
To see through my places of darkness
And release what is old and unneeded.
Snowy Owl, you are beautiful!
Fly by me with still, silent wings,
I know that you bring not death,
But spiritual rebirth—
May I be renewed as a child.

Winter is, after all, only a point
On the Great Circle of Life.
And whether it be difficult or easy
I know that it is good.

> "The North Wind,"
> *Creation Spirituality Magazine*,
> Ken Bear Hawk Cohen, Winter 1994, p. 40

*This Winter Prayer of someone who has come to learn of Native ways
focuses on one specific direction (North) without losing the wholeness,
of the others. The aspects of life that are associated
with each direction are made particular and concrete in this uniquely contemporary prayer.*

———————— ✛ ————————

FOUR DIRECTIONS PRAYER
INTERTRIBAL

(Facing **North**: Santa Cruz County)
Great God, our Creator, our eyes are turned towards where You speak to us from the **North**. You
are the power over the harshness of our lives. You
are the Great One who calms our fears and anxi-
eties. Give us strength to courageously walk the
difficult and dangerous roads and highways in life

with You. Thank You for your protection over all our diocesan brothers and sisters. . . .

Bless all of our spiritual relations in the County of Santa Cruz. Amen!

(Facing *West*: Monterey County) Creator of the setting sun, we send our prayers to You. Great Spirit, on our journey through life may we know the beauty of the setting sun. Help us to enjoy ourselves and to love You in one another. Bring to fulfillment the great work that You have begun within our Diocese.

(Facing *East*: San Benito County) O Creator, O Maker of all that is, You who have always existed, may the daily sun which rises in the *East* remind us of You who warms our lives with gentle strength and wisdom. Help all your people to share as we travel your sacred paths in our Diocese so that generations to come will also have light as they too walk your path

Bless all of our spiritual relations in the County of Monterey. Amen!

Bless all of our spiritual relations in the County of San Benito. Amen!

(Facing *South*: San Luis Obispo County)
O Maker of all, You send us soft winds from the *south* part of our Diocese. May goodness be always in our hearts and gentleness in our speech. We are reminded of those that make us happy in life: friends and family and birds and animals, You, O Great Power and Source of Life. Show us how to bring many others closer to You.

Bless all of our spiritual relations in the County of San Luis Obispo. Amen!

All One (That All May Be One): A Handbook for Ecumenical and Interfaith Worship, Scott McCarthy, 1996

Here is an example of a contemporary four directions prayer offered to Creator for the health and growth in life of those prayed for: all those living within the geographical territory of a Catholic diocese.

———————— + ————————

DIRECTIONAL SONG
INTERTRIBAL

From the corners of creation to the center where we stand,
Let all things be blessed and holy, all is fashioned by your hand;
Brother wind and sister water, mother earth and father sky,
Sacred plants and sacred creatures, sacred people of the land.

In the *east,* the place of dawning, there is beauty in the morn,
Here the seeker finds new visions as each sacred day is born:
All who honor life around them, all who honor life within,
They shall shine with light and glory when the morning breaks again.

In the *south,* the place of growing, there is wisdom in the earth,
Both the painful song of dying and the joyful song of birth:
As the earth gives up her life-blood so her children's hearts may beat,
We give back to her our rev'rence, holy ground beneath our feet.

In the *north,* the place of wisdom, there is holy darkness deep,
Here the silent song of myst'ry may awake you from your sleep:
Here the music still and holy sounds beneath the snow and night
In the ones who wait with patience for the coming of the light.

In the *west,* the place of seeing, there is born a vision new
Of the servant of the servants, who proclaimed a gospel true:
Let the creatures of creation echo back creation's prayer,
Let the Spirit now breathe through us and restore the sacred there.

"Song at the Center," *Agape* (sound recording), Marty Haugen, 1993

This contemporary Native Christian song was recently sung at an intertribal liturgy in the Convention Center at Anaheim, California. The directions were physically and vocally accented by different song sections in the congregation of several thousand people. Both Native and non-Native worshippers were energized by both the rhythm and the words about the four directions.

We must always see ourselves as part of God's creation, sharing the earth, indeed the whole cosmos, with fellow creatures: mountains, rivers, trees, birds, animals, and even beings invisible to our eyes.

Circles

CIRCLES

The Celts favored deasil, *or sunwise, as a direction; a fact which appears in many texts. It was contrary for many heroes to go* widdershins *(counter-clockwise) at all, and many kings were prohibited from making a circuit of their land in any way but* deasil, *while reciting prayers.*

The Celtic Tradition, Caitlín Matthews

My joy, my grief, my hope, my love,
did all within this circle move. . . .

"On a Girdle," Edmond Waller

. . . a circle existing in nature, and the idea of a circle existing, which is also in God, are one and the same thing displayed through different attributes.

The Ethics, Spinoza

Remember first of all that all human affairs move in a circle. . . .

Herodotus

Most cultures around our world have unique forms of circular dancing. Some build round houses according to the ancient ways while others group their dwellings in a circular pattern. There is also much archeological evidence for the praying by ancient inhabitants of Scotland's Orkney Islands at great monoliths set up in an enormous circle. The Ring of Ragnor is a case in point. And in Ireland it is still the custom to circumambulate certain churches or shrines while praying privately or out loud with other pilgrims. Many cultures use the circle as part of their experience of daily life. It would probably be very easy, even for a child, to enumerate the multiform uses of the circle, especially of the wheel. Even though the circle was well known throughout the Americas, one form of a circle, the wheel, was not ostensibly used, except on certain small ceramic wheeled toys. And yet, in the many and varied cultures of the Americas, the circle seems to have taken on an exalted significance: drums of every kind, the earth, a dance circle, a sacred ring of stones, designs upon the body of people or animals, earrings, headbands, the cosmos, carved pottery vessels and rounded baskets, the sun and the moon and the stars, ancient rounded kivas in the southwest of the United States, battle shields, round medicine lodges, and the circular homes of the Pawnee, the Arikara, and the Mandan: all these speak of a profound connection between the People and the created universe.

We see the circle in the design of the Sundance lodge, in the arc of the rainbow, and in the medicine wheel. It is like a mandala of unity inviting us to deeper participation in its design. The circle is indeed a sign of the unity of the People.

A circle speaks of inclusivity, of timelessness, of a People united in a common purpose; it expresses not a linear world view of things, but one that is dynamically cyclic; it speaks of the great round of the seasons and the gifts that each season brings to the People. The way of the circle is the way of interdependence, of tribal and personal unity. It is also the way of the sun in its daily cyclical manifestations: east, south, west and north are understood in the relationship between sun and Mother Earth.

The circle allows for color, variety, and movement, especially as it is prayerfully danced with in joy or in sorrow. The ancient petroglyphs scattered throughout the Americas show the circle of the sun to us even in our own time and speak of the People's ancient faith and spirituality. As the circle moves, as it rotates, it is descriptive of Life: what exists now and what might come to be.

Shrines like large medicine wheels made from rocks positioned strategically on the ground are found in many places, especially throughout the North American Plains region. They became places of pilgrimage for countless generations. Some medicine (sacred) wheels were drawn or worn as tangible spiritual reminders, much the same as someone might wear a cross or medal today. The sacred wheel became a teaching device to help the Peoples to live well. This is how it is used today, even though the interpretations vary from tribe to tribe and region to region.

From the Iroquois of the Woodlands we learn that they have always celebrated important healing ceremonies in the long house during the snowy cold of winter. Often they made circuits around a central fire, dancing counterclockwise (or counter sunwise). Like many others in their sphere of influence, they held the circle in high regard.

Many Peoples of the Southeast and other places throughout Turtle Island really enjoy a good game of lacrosse. Even today it grows in popularity with non-Native People, especially on college and high school campuses. Ritual circlings to draw in power are still part of the preparation for the game among the Creeks and Cherokees. Perhaps this reflects a more ancient appreciation for the circle, even as it was evidenced in the architecture of their ancestors. The Seminoles sang of the circle of life with their birthing songs. In the Southwest of a century or two ago the Texas Tonkawas had their own ways of bringing solace to the dying; circling the loved one was a part of this ritual. Their neighbors, the Karankawas, often danced around a blazing ceremonial fire to summon power. A few spectators have been privileged to observe a special Apache way of expressing solidarity throughout the night.

In California the Chumash were accomplished astronomers who understood well their place in the created universe. A People near San Diego, called by some the Luiseños because they lived near the San Luis Rey Mission, continue their dancing styles long after being influenced by the Spaniards. Even hunting practices (Nisenan, Shasta) did not miss out on the power of a circle of flames.

On the Plains the hoop of the nation is an important concept. Though there are tribal variations concerning some of the particular meanings, it is always about the unity of the People and that they might live and flourish. The medicine wheel reminds them of who they are for each other. In the old days a battle shield became a disk of sacred power to protect the bearer from the onslaughts of the foe.

The rite of encirclement is just as important for the Eskimo Peoples as it is for the tribes of South America. Circle dances are often around a fire, which is often understood to symbolize the sun. There is a wonderful scene which well illustrates this in the movie, *Dances with Wolves,* where the hero, a soldier, feels an inner call to build a huge bonfire and dance around it naked as an expression of his feelings after meeting some of the People and being invited to participate in their lives. Sometimes people or special objects were the focus of such ritual encirclement.

The wheel of the People continues to turn, despite encroachments from the dominant and other societies because it is a circle of Life.

He drew a circle that shut me out—
Heretic, rebel, a thing to flout.
But Love and I had the wit to win:
We drew a circle that took him in.

"Outwitted," Edwin Markham

"Chewing-gum break between dances"
San Juan Pueblo, New Mexico, June 13, 1992,
St. Anthony's Feast Day

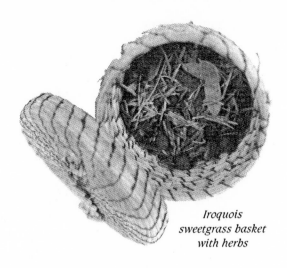

*Iroquois
sweetgrass basket
with herbs*

WOODLANDS CULTURAL AREA

MIDWINTER CEREMONIAL
SENECA

At the time when the Senecas return from hunting in January or February they annually keep a feast seven days; the professed object of which is to render thanks to the Great Spirit for the benefits which they have received from him during the preceding year, and to solicit the continuance of them through the year to come. . . .

The whole of this solemn season is spent in feasting and dancing. Two select bands, one of men and another of women, ornamented with a variety of trinkets, and furnished each with an ear of corn, which is held in the right hand, begin the dance at the Council-house. Both choirs, the men leading the way, dance in a *circle* around the council fire, which is kindled for the occasion, and regulate their steps by music. Hence, they proceed to every house in the village, and in the same manner dance in a *circle* around each fire.

The Iroquois Ceremonial of Midwinter, Elisabeth Tooker, 1970, p. 131

*Iroquois sweetgrass basket
from Oshwekan, Ontario,
Canada*

This excerpt describes a Midwinter Ceremonial which took place some time before 1812. It is similar to later and contemporary accounts. Circling with dance is one way to sacralize something.

——————— O ———————

229

FIVE CIRCUITS
ONONDAGA

You must perform the ceremonies and you shall make a *circuit* of the fire. You shall make a circuit of the fire in a certain direction. Do not ever let anyone make a circuit of it in the opposite direction; and do not even let it be that the left side of the body be on the outside of the *circle*. When one makes a circuit, the right side of the body shall be on the outside of the circle. And all persons shall make a circuit of the place where the two who shall sing will sit. . . .

Native North American Spirituality of the Eastern Woodlands:
Sacred Myths, Dreams, Visions, Speeches, Healing Formulas, Rituals and
Ceremonials, Elisabeth Tooker (Ed.), 1979, p. 272

Here is reference which underlines the fact that Onondaga dances, in fact, all Iroquois dances, are customarily danced in a counter-clockwise direction.

COUNTERCLOCKWISE DANCING
IROQUOIS

Iroquois dances are typically *round* dances, in partial *circles* of men and women, of men and women alternating, or of women alone, depending on the dance. The dance is always *counter-clockwise*, except for certain dances for the dead. Each dance has its proper step, but not all the dancers are equally proficient. Everyone may take part, and many do: infants may be carried by their fathers, young children just beginning to dance, adults, and old women barely able to shuffle around take part in the dance.

The Iroquois Ceremonial of Midwinter, Elisabeth Tooker, 1970, p. 29

Many circular dances of the Peoples are celebrated around a fire, a pole, or other sacred central items. Sometimes the drummers are in the middle; at times those who are being honored, for one one reason or another, are placed in the center.

POST MORTEM CUSTOMS
OTTAWA

Precontact burials discovered in North Carolina illustrate the early belief that highly reflective materials such as mica, used to cover an interred body's orifices, could block evil spirits from inhabiting the body and prevent the deceased's spirit from re-entering the corpse and lingering, not seeking the spirit world as it should. At the death of an Odawa (Ottawa) it was customary for close kin to paint *circles* around the corpse's eyes and mouth to obstruct the return of the deceased's spirit. It was believed that a spirit could not cross the line of an *enclosed circle* nor cross a line transposing it. This practice was also believed effective in forcing the soul to seek its way to the spirit land.

Silver in the Fur Trade, 1680-1820, Martha Hamilton, 1995, p. 50
Originally published in *Gah-Baeh-Jhagwah-Buk: The Way It Happened*,
James McClurken, 1991

Even at the death of a loved one, the People reinforced their belief in the other world by ensuring that the deceased travelled on to "the other side camp." Here the circle becomes a powerful protective sign for both the deceased and the rest of the People.

———————————— ○ ————————————

CIRCLE IMAGERY
ANISHNABE

Images of *circle upon circle* are evident in the design of many instruments. They may take the form of *painted rings* on a membrane, wooden disc, or vessel; or we may see circles of dots, each a multiplication of the last. The layers may be the multiple *rims* of a frame drum or carefully layered cloth wrapping a water drum rim or dressing a rattle handle or drum frame. Such images can be explained and interpreted in many ways. . . . In some instances, Anishnabe interpreters describe this image as "the one and the all."

Such images are also realized in performances of course. In some locations (at Chapel Island, Cape Breton, or Indian Island, New Brunswick, for example), the earth itself bears the imprint of a *ring of dancers,* moving year after year, generation after generation, over the same circle which is in turn a small dot on the sphere of the earth itself. At a powwow, a drum is surrounded by a *circle of drummers,* perhaps surrounded by a *circle of women* who are said to "hold the circle together"; the drum arbour is surrounded by a *circle of dancers* inside a circle of onlookers, who are probably ringed by food concessions and craft booths. . . .

Visions of Sound: Musical Instruments of First Native Communities in Northeastern America, Beverly Diamond, Sam Cronk & Franziska Von Rosen, 1994, p. 30

Generations upon generations of the People have joined in the great circle dance of the Creation. The constant movement expresses the ongoingness of all life.

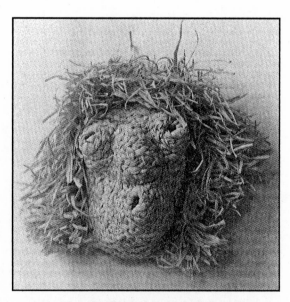

Onondaga braided corn husk false face mask from Six Nations Reserve (Iroquois), Oshwekan, Ontario, Canada

SOUTHEAST CULTURAL AREA

BIRTHING SONG
SEMINOLE

You day-sun
Circling around
You day-light
Circling around
You night-sun
Circling around
You poor body
Circling around
You wrinkled age
Circling around
You spotted with gray
Circling around
You wrinkled skin
Circling around

A Cherokee woman gives thanks for the gifts of water, plants, and rocks at her home in Carmel Valley, California

Seminole Music, Frances Densmore, 1956, p. 172

This Seminole birthing song sings of the path of the sun as it influences the movements of human beings at various moments in their life as they move about the earth.

———————— ○ ————————

LACROSSE GAME CIRCLINGS
CREEK

Lacrosse balls for use in certain ritual games continue to be surrounded with ceremony. For example, at the conclusion of the Oklahoma Creek Green Corn Ceremony, in preparation for the special lacrosse match marking the end of the summer ceremonial cycle, there is a special blessing ritual for the balls to be used in the games. After the players' final *circling of the ceremonial fire*, the medicine man leads the line of players away from the square while he holds two balls (about the size of golf balls) connected by a leather thong and dangling from a stick. The players form two lines behind him while he leads a call-and-response chant. The balls have been filled with herbal medicines especially prepared by the town chief or medicine-maker. The man holding the balls makes a wailing sound for a brief period. Then his assistant, with eyes directed to the ground, lets out a long, rising wail, which is concluded with all players letting out a war whoop. This is followed in unison by "huh, huh, huh, huh" exclamations, as players bang their lacrosse sticks together and depart for the ball field.

Upon arriving at the field, the medicine man, still holding the stick from which the balls hang, leads his team *counterclockwise around the goal* for several minutes, while beginning another call-and-response chant. After a few moments they stop behind the goal, and the medicine man holds the balls aloft as the team moves in front of the goal to line up on the field in preparation for play.

American Indian Lacrosse: Little Brother to War,
Thomas Vennum, Jr., 1994, pp. 74, 76

To ritually encircle an object is to sanctify it, to make it holy, to give it special sacred meaning. A game can also be a sacred event and the players' equipment as well as the playing field need to be blessed.

———————————— O ————————————

LACROSSE GAME CIRCLINGS
CREEK/CHEROKEE

The Creek custom of *circling the goalposts* just before a game, still practiced in the 1980s, has its parallel in their final *circling of the ceremonial fire* each year, carrying lacrosse sticks and equipment while leaders give out high-pitched wails to serve as a farewell to the fire and to honor the balls used in the game. When they arrive dressed for the game at the playing field, they repeat this performance at the goal to protect it and keep the players in a high mental state. (Victors *circle their goalposts* after a game, perhaps symbolically to suggest that the goal is still "safe"—that is, that it has survived being "attacked" or scored upon.)

Care was taken to bless, secure, and protect the equipment against evil spells before a game. . . .

On the day of the game, teams coordinated their arrivals at the field to occur simultaneously. Because of the distance of the agreed-upon field from the residence of the players, the journey often progressed in stages, with only part of the distance traveled the first day. This movement in stages was repeated ritually in the Cherokee game once players were actually on the field. Basil Hall described the arrival of Creek players at the field in 1828. Following a loud cry from the woods, one team suddenly emerged, "advancing to the ball play ground in a most tumultuous manner, shrieking, yelling, hallooing, brandishing their sticks, performing somersets [sic], and exhibiting all conceivable antics." They *circled* their goal in customary Creek fashion, then went to centerfield to await the emergence of their opponents—"squatted down in a thick cluster till their antagonists made their appearance." Once the other team arrived, "the two groups remained eyeing one another for a long time, occasionally uttering yells of defiance."

Like the Eastern Cherokee, the Oklahoma Creek today also advance in a line to midfield to meet opponents—a practice continued into the 1980s. After players *circle* their goals, the medicine man stands behind the goalposts, holding the two balls aloft on a short stick while the team divides into two columns behind him. A long wailing is punctuated by war whoops and concluded with all players noisily banging their lacrosse sticks overhead in the air, much like the final huddle before a football or soccer match. They then spread out across the field in front of the goal and behind the medicine man. He begins chanting rapidly in a monotone as he leads the line to centerfield, where the other team, similarly advanced, awaits.

American Indian Lacrosse: Little Brother to War,
Thomas Vennum, Jr., 1994, pp. 187-188

Even nowadays the circle and its importance are not forgotten by many lacrosse players.

———————————— O ————————————

CIRCULAR EARTH MOUND ARCHITECTURE
INTERTRIBAL

About five thousand years ago, monumental American architecture began to be created in *circular* or *half-circular*—D-shaped— forms, the largest of which are so striking that they justify calling the ensuing three millennia in American architectural history the Age of the Rings. Even more precise circles continued to be built thereafter, but they were now accompanied by the first appearance of square, hexagonal and octagonal ground plans on a large scale.

The first great expression of the Age of the Rings to descend to us in still recognizable condition lies just outside the southwestern sprawl of the little city of Monroe, on the opposite bank of the Ouachita River and eighteen miles south of Frenchman's Bend, at Watson Brake (a "break" is a breech in natural levee of a river, forming a backwater). This oldest monumental *circular* building yet discovered in North America was probably begun at about the time as the complex at Frenchman's Bend. Its primary form is a *circular embankment* three-fifths of a mile long, 820 by 650 feet across and about 3 feet high. The *ring* is punctuated by ten mounds, one of which rises nearly 28 feet higher. These punctuating mounds of earth atop the platform ring, confronting each other across a flat space or plaza, distinguish the Watson Brake earthworks from thousands of circular mounds of earth or shell across the Gulf Coast and along the rivers of the South and Midwest. . . .

Joe Saunders, an archaeologist who has been working at Watson Brake, Hedgepeth, and Frenchman's Bend, has found that several of the mounds in these complexes also appear to have "aprons" like those of the "falcon mound" at Poverty Point and Motley. All seem to provide for a choreographed movement: coming from the bayou or river one climbed the bank, probably by a graded way, to come out into a plaza. Then, before the great mound, there may have been a court of honor, and above it, on the first level, a place even more restricted. Finally, perhaps beside a pyre or beacon, one might be admitted into the presence of a person of the highest honor.

This use of earth to provide a succession of sacred spaces on ascending platforms persists in American architecture from 3000 B.C. through the creation of the immense structures of the period between A.D. 1000 and the arrival of the Europeans. The most prominent of these still to be observed today are at Etowah, in Georgia; at Emerald, near Natchez, Mississippi; at Moundville, in Alabama; and at Monks Mound at Cahokia, Illinois. At Cahokia, the sheer size of Monks Mound, with its many ramps and platforms, permits us to visualize easily a graduated ascent to sanctuaries of ever-increasing solemnity—with the sanctum sanctorum at the very top. The great pyramid at Cahokia is greater in extent than that at Gizeh, in Egypt. Well into the eighteenth century, the Indians—Natchez, Cherokee, Creek, and Caddo—were still building mounds of this sort.

Hidden Cities: The Discovery and Loss of Ancient North American Civilization, Roger Kennedy, 1994, pp. 9-10, 12

It is really quite amazing to consider that all the ancient earthworks were made by hundreds, or even thousands, of the People carrying earth in wicker baskets from one place to another. And they did this activity over and over again until each sacred edifice was completed and the ceremonies could begin.

Giving thanks to Creator for Life's special gifts while remembering that, indeed, Life is like a circle

SOUTHWEST CULTURAL AREA

NEAR DEATH COMFORTING CEREMONY
TONKAWA

Chaco Canyon, 1996

The Tonkawas emphasized and elaborated upon the final crisis of life—death. . . . When a person was thought to be on the verge of death his friends and relatives entered the tepee where he lay. Some of them formed *a circle around the ailing man* and put their hands on his body. Around these, *others formed a concentric circle* and placed their hands upon the shoulders of those in the first circle. If the tepee was a large one there might be *several such circles* around the pallet. Swaying and chanting, they hovered around the dying person throughout the night; in the morning the ailing one presumably died.

The Indians of Texas: From Prehistoric to Modern Times,
W.W. Newcomb, Jr., 1984, p. 146

Concentric circles of people praying around an individual in need of healing—physical, spiritual or emotional—is a powerful sign. This activity is shared by many cultures around the world.

———————————— O ————————————

DRUM DANCE
CADDO

The *cah-kit-em'-bin* or drum dance is always the initial dance of the night's cycle of dances for the Hasinai people. The dance retells the story of Hasinai origins. The men lead, carrying the drum. Some of these leaders are singers and some are drummers. They *circle the dance ground*, moving *clockwise*, in harmony with the earth's movement. Initially, there was a sequence of eleven songs, relating the origins and early heritage of the Hasinai. . . . In these songs, specific events are related about the Hasinai transition from the preceding world into the southwest, where they have lived now for centuries. Young boys are allowed to join the lead singers, so that they may become familiar with the songs, but they are not allowed to beat the drum. As the dance proceeds *around the dance ground*, other men and women join the singers and drummers, following their lead.

The second segment of the *cah-kit-em'-bin*, known as the *wah-sha-nee'-kee*, begins after a short pause. In this portion, the drummers are in the middle of the dance ground. The pace is faster than in the first segment. *The drummers rotate in the center of the dance area*; the dancers continue to *move in the direction of the earth around the center*. The *cah-kit-em'-bin* usually lasts about one hour. The Hasinai have moved through their history each time the dance is performed. It makes them one with their ancestors.

At the heart of Hasinai existence are the cultural traditions that carry the people through space and time. In the movement of dance and the language of songs, the reality of existence is projected into the future.

Hasinai: A Traditional History of the Caddo Confederacy, Vynola Beaver Newkumet & Howard Meredith, 1988, pp. 3-4

Like all the various Peoples, the Caddos know that the drum mysteriously and mystically contains their past, present, and future. The embodied circle is part of the expression of their existence.

———————— ○ ————————

Peyote-stitched beaded circular box

FIRE CIRCLING DANCES
KARANKAWA

They are very much given to dances they call *mitotes*. Some of these dances are festive and happy, and others funereal and sad, being distinguished from one another by the instruments which they play for them. For the festive ones they play a tamborine that is made of a tortoise shell, or of a half gourd, or with a French pot, and a whistle of reeds and an *avacasele,* for the sad ones they play certain instruments they call the *caymán.* This is very harsh and melancholy, and to the discordant notes they add sad and horrible cries, accompanied by gestures, grimaces and extraordinary contortions and movements of the body, jumping and *leaping in a circle*. For this *mitote* they light a fire, a big bon-fire and dance around it *circling around the fire* without ceasing day or night. These *mitotes* last three days and three nights.

The Indians of Texas: From Prehistoric to Modern Times,
W.W. Newcomb, Jr., 1984, p. 81.

The Franciscan Gaspar José De Solís toured his community's missions in Texas between 1767 and 1768 and spent some time among the Karankawas. He had quite a few opportunities to witness their festivities and took the time to note what he saw and felt. The circling of a sacred fire not only provided warmth and light, but also helped to center the dancers and their thoughts as they moved.

———————————— O ————————————

MEN'S CIRCLE AROUND
AN ALL NIGHT WARMING FIRE
APACHE

Here are a few of my observations while working with two companies of Apache firefighters during the Yosemite fire of August 1996.

In August 1996 I was assigned as a division Chief on the Yosemite Complex fires. I was assigned numerous engines, two companies of Apache firefighters, along with two companies of Hmong firefighters and a company of Eskimos. We were dispatched to a fire east of Cherry

Lake and hiked and drove into the deep wilderness to attack an isolated fire.

Late in the evening, as dark and cold approached, the crew boss of the Apaches asked permission to build a fire for warmth. I was frustrated to learn that the Indian crews had hiked into the wilderness without sleeping bags or blankets. Before we left I had given them directions to prepare to spend three to four days in the wilderness. The bosses told me that Apaches preferred to travel light. They again asked to build a campfire for warmth.

A rather large fire was built in our camp area and the Apaches gathered quite a pile of downed wood. I slept for a short time away from the crews and awoke an hour later to observe a beautiful campfire that was quite large and surrounded by a *circle of men*. The men stood facing the fire in such a tight circle that they leaned shoulder to shoulder facing inward; the circle was self-retaining. The men had eyes closed and appeared to be asleep. Their breathing was slowed and they appeared quite relaxed. Leaning against each other allowed physical relaxation and the fire warmed the fronts of all their bodies. I watched curiously. After some time, one of the men opened his eyes and moved slightly. The circle of men became more upright; all turned simultaneously so that their backs now were facing the fire and they became compressed back together in the shoulder to shoulder tight circle form, this time warming their backs to the fire. Again, after a period of time, the same man again wakened, straightened up, and the circle of men *rotated in place*, once again facing the fire, compressed shoulder to shoulder and again relaxing into the structure of the retaining circle. This pattern of rotation continued throughout the night. I observed no verbal or other communication. When there was a need to stoke the fire with fresh wood, the man who seemed to initiate the rotations would leave his place in the circle, obtain more wood for the fire and retake his place and the ritual of the warming circle would continue as before. The man who took the lead was the assigned crew boss of one of the companies.

I learned from the female crew boss, that these companies were Apaches from the San Carlos Reservation in Arizona. They were recruited by the U.S. Forest service as seasonal firefighters. They are trained on the reservation and then travel as a company for an entire fire season.

The Apaches were quite non-verbal and I did not notice much dynamic interaction, especially when compared with the Hmong and Eskimo companies. I was able to get some cursory information from the female crew boss when I gave her a ride in my vehicle. The man who I was told was a medicine man did not engage in any firefighting while I was there and was left in camp by his crew boss to guard our food from the bears.

Interview with Patrick Dowd, firefighter,
November 8, 1997, Carmel Valley, CA

This warming circle, not only allowed warmth for those who formed it, but permitted communal strength to be shared in a very unique way. This most likely could not have happened unless there already existed a sense of unity among the participants. On the one level it is practical; on another level it is spiritual. The medicine man/crew boss leader was vital to this activity.

Modern Kokopellis dance at the site of an ancient Anasazi circular kiva at Chaco Canyon, New Mexico

CALIFORNIA CULTURAL AREA

Drum at a Chumash memorial service in Seaside, California (1997)

CEREMONIAL DANCE
LUISEÑO

No one can dance without permission of the elders, and he must be of the same people, a youth of ten and more years. The elders, before doing the dances publicly, teach them the song and make them learn perfectly, because the dance consists in knowing the song, because they act according to the song. According to the song he makes as many kicks, as many leaps as the singers make, who are the old people, the old and others of the same people. When they have learned, then they can perform the dance, but before this they give him something to drink, and then that one is a dancer; he can dance and not stop when the others dance.

On this occasion the clothing is of feathers of various colors, and the body painted, and the chest is bare, and from the waist to the knees they are covered, the arms without clothing. In the right hand they carry a stick made to take off the sweat. The face is painted. The head is bound with a band of hair woven so as to be able to thrust in the cheyatom, our word. This cheyat is made of feathers of any bird, and almost always of crow and of sparrow hawk, and in the middle a sharp stick in order to be able to insert it. Thus they are in the house when immediately two men go out, each one carrying two wooden swords and crying out, without saying any word, and after stopping before the

243

place where they dance, they look at the sky for some time. The people are silent, and they turn and then the dancers go out. . . .

The dancers in this dance can be as many as thirty, more or less. Going out of the house, they turn their faces to the singers and begin to give kicks, but not hard ones, because it is not the time, and when the song is finished the captain of the dancers touching his feet cries, "Hu," and all fall silent. He again comes to the singers and sings, and all dance, and at last cries, "Hu," and the singers fall silent and they make the sound of the horse who is looking for his son. The sound hu means nothing in our language, but the dancers understand that it means "be silent." When the captain does not say, "Hu," the singers cannot be silent, and they repeat and repeat the song until the captain wants them to stop. Then they go before the singers and all the people who are watching them, and the captain of the dancers sings and dances, and the others follow him. They dance in a *circle*, kicking, and whoever gets tired stays in the middle of the circle and then follows the others. No one can laugh in this dance, and all follow the first ones with head bent and eyes toward the earth. Then this stops, all take off the cheyat to end the dance and holding it in the right hand they raise it to heaven, blowing at each kick that they give to the earth, and the captain ends the dance with a "Hu," and all return to the houses of the costumes, and at this the old men begin to suck or smoke, and all the smoke goes up to heaven three times before ending the dance. This done, it ends. The old man returns to his house tired, because the dance lasts three hours, and it is necessary to sing for three hours. It is danced in the middle of the day when the sun burns more, and then on the shoulders of the dancers appear fountains of water with so much sweat that falls. . . .

Indian Life and Customs at San Luis Rey, Pablo Tac, 1952, pp. 22, 24

A sacred fire circle for a Chumash ceremony

This account by the neophyte, Pablo Tac, of native life at a southern California Mission, describes a dance tradition as it was still practiced in the 1830s. One might easily recall some words of the Lord's Prayer: ". . . on earth as it is in heaven. . . ."

———— O ————

WORLD AXIS CONCEPT
CHUMASH

The keys to understanding their symbolism lie in the Chumash beliefs about the World Axis.

The World Axis first appeared at the beginning of the earth's creation, to maintain the cosmic balance. Anyone can confirm the existence of the Axis for themselves by simply stepping outside at night and looking at the stars. They revolve around a central pivot. The top lies at the apex of the sky, at the North Star. This is the most pure place in the physical universe. Below Polaris are realms of descending purity, leading downward to the level of the earth. The Chumash believed that the Axis cuts through Iwihinmu mountain, at the earth's sacred center northwest of Los Angeles and that its bottom lies in the underworld where the demons dwell. The *Encircled Circle* depicts the many layers of the physical world as manifested from the World Axis, with the outermost rings representing regions of increasing decadence.

A Circle Within the Aybss: Chumash Metaphysics,
John Anderson, 1994, pp. 4-5

The idea of a world axis is a helpful concept to grasp a People's understanding of their world. The encircled cross is one way of depicting to the interested person what is believed about the universe. Such a symbol was often etched or painted onto rock surfaces and, over time, served as a mnemonic device for opening up awareness in each ensuing generation of this People.

———————————————— ○ ————————————————

HUNTING WITH FIRE CIRCLE
SHASTA

The second method was used on the more open hills of the north side of the river, where the white oaks grew. When the oak leaves began to fall fires were set on the hills. . . . Then they came down . . . in the late fall. . . . It was at this time they had the big drive *encircling* the deer with fire.

"Shasta Ethnography," *University of California Anthropological Records*, Catherine Holt, 1946, pp. 310, 314

Here we have a good example of how the People related the time of fall in the circle of the seasons to their method of hunting deer with a circle of fire.

———————————— O ————————————

HUNTING WITH FIRE CIRCLE
NISENAN

In the fall brush burned toward center of large *circle* where frequently several hunters stationed in clearing who shot animals as driven in. Fire drives called *t'otsik.*

"Ethnology of the Nisenan," *University of California Publications in American Archaeology and Ethnology,* Ralph Beals, 1933, pp. 347-348

The Southern Maidu People, who live in the northern parts of the California Sierra Nevada, made sure that this spot burning was done in a circular pattern.

"Basket Weaver," charcoal drawing by Sister Jackie Graham P.B.V.M.

Piegan Tipi near Head-Smashed-In Buffalo Jump, Alberta, Canada

PLAINS CULTURAL AREA

MEANING OF SACRED WHEEL LANCE
CHEYENNE

Ox'zem, the wheel, is sacred to the Cheyennes, for the wheel figures in the traditions of how the people first received the corn and buffalo. The wheel takes the form of the *circle*, which has no beginning and no end. Thus it is also the symbol of eternity, the symbol of a universe that is filled with life pouring from the homes of Maheo and the four Sacred Persons.

"Ox'zem: Box Elder and His Sacred Wheel Lance," *Montana: The Magazine of Western History,* Peter Powell, April 1970, p. 32

This wheel is a symbol of everlastingness. God and the four holy intermediaries distribute life-giving things to the People who live on earth, that they might use them wisely.

——————————— ○ ———————————

MEDICINE WHEEL AND HUMAN BEINGS
CHEYENNE

In many ways the *Circle*, the Medicine Wheel, can be best understood if you think of it as a mirror in which everything is reflected. "The Universe is the Mirror of the People," the old teachers tell us, "and each person is a Mirror to every other person."

Any idea, person or object can be a Medicine Wheel, a Mirror, for man. . . .

Seven Arrows, Hyemeyohsts Storm, 1972, p. 5

When it was first published, this was a controversial book among the People. Some accepted it as truth, others did not. And yet some of the concepts within the book are helpful in a general way for many people of today.

———————————— O ————————————

MEDICINE WHEEL
LAKOTA

The "medicine wheel" is a common religious sign in Indian religion, not only among the Lakota, but among many other American Indian tribes as well.

Strangely enough, there is no common Lakota expression for "medicine wheel"; it is simply described as *cangleska na tate iopa* (hoop and four winds). Still it is a very common, highly regarded sacred artifact on the reservation, second only to the Pipe. The medicine wheel consists of a *circle*, through the center of which are drawn a horizontal and vertical line, to which an eagle feather is usually attached at the center. The *circle* represents the sacred outer boundary of the Earth; the horizontal and vertical lines represent the sun's and man's sacred paths, respectively; the crossing of the two lines indicates the center of the Earth where one stands when praying with the Pipe; the eagle feather is a sign of *Wakan Tanka's* power over everything. The medicine wheel is often marked with sacred colors, especially red, which is the color for something truly *wakan.* Only a few things are made of porcupine quills today; of these the medicine wheel is the most common. The medicine wheel is hung from the rear view mirrors of cars, worn as a necklace, hung as a wall decoration, attached to pipe bags, and used as a most sacred marking in Lakota religious ceremonies.

The *circle* has great religious and cultural meaning to the Lakota people. The Lakota teepee, its fireplace in the center, the sweatlodge, its pit, the Sundance grounds with its pole in the center—all are in the form of a *circle*. Whenever possible, the Lakota formed their camps into *circles*. When the elders gathered in council, they sat in a *circle*. In the *Yuwipi* ceremony and other ceremonies, the altar is made of or on the earth in the form of a *circle*. Not only the physical world but also the life of the Lakota people are considered to be like a hoop. When a person cuts through any living thing in its middle, he finds a *circle*. If the circle is broken, it is said that the person will soon die unless it is quickly healed. When the Lakota people are dying as a people, it is said that the hoop of the Lakota people is broken. In a *circle* there is equality for all, rather than the superior/inferior attitude found in lines, opposites, classrooms, and most White churches. In a *circle*, there are mutual responsibilities, sharings and respect. In the *circle* are found abundance, harmony, and tranquility. Religiously, the earth is conceived to be *circular* with a great, sacred hoop as its boundary.

The "center of the Earth" is not a geometric center. The "center of the Earth" is the center of life as realized in the heart of each individual. The "center" is wherever the believer stands, especially with the Pipe. As the Lakota walks the Sacred Red Path of the Pipe, he/she is always at the center. Only in death does the faithful one make that *wakan* passage to the Sacred Rim. The "center" is where the Four Winds are affecting and guiding the individual. Because the power of the Four Winds are always beyond the mountains that edge the world, they can never be reached by ordinary people in this life; this place is extraordinary and *wakan.* West is *always* west. Those who understand, know that West is beyond geometry, geography, climatology, and weather; these are but messengers of the West to the believer. The one holding and walking with the Pipe is in the center of the activity of the major forces guiding and shaping all major events on the Earth. Over this spot the eagle flies.

For the Lakota, the sacredness of the *circle* is extrinsic and secondary. Many Whites tend to find an intrinsic, primary holiness in the *circle*. When an area of the ground is cleared for an altar, not just anyone can draw the *circle*, only a medicine man is able to do this. His relationship to his spirits is communicated to the *circle* as he draws it. That is *his* altar because his spirits will come to it. Many people associate the Pipe Ceremony with the circle. Rarely is the word "*circle*" used in the Pipe Ceremony prayers. Rather the ceremony is directed toward the spirits in the cardinal direction. These four sufficiently *encircle* the one who prays and determines the magnitude and the *wakan*-ness of the **Great Circle**. The hoop of the Earth marks the boundary between the ordinary domain of man and the *wakan* domain of the *Tatiye Topa*. This hoop is sacred because of its relationship to those great *wakan* powers. One medicine man drew a *circle*. Pointing to the inside of the *circle* he said that this is where *we* live. Using his pointer to sweep around the entire area outside of the *circle*, he said that this was where everything *wakan* has its home. This was a very clear way of illustrating the smallness of our ordinary, *ikceya* world and the otherness and greatness of the *wakan* world. In the Pipe Ceremony, although the mouth of the Pipe is only swung through three quadrants between the four directions, it is still said that the Pipe has been moved in a *circle* because it has pointed at the four directions which define the *"encirclement."* At the Sundance, the sacred area is considered a *circle,* even though it is marked out ritualistically by only four pairs of flags placed in the four directions. In the vision quest, the seeker is surrounded by the flags in the four directions. The sacred area is *encircled* by the tobacco ties, even though the physical shape of the area is a rectangle.

Many different sacred and secular relationships produce Lakota *circles*. A particular *circle* is "ordinary" *wakan* depending upon whether the relational elements making the *encirclement* are "ordinary" or *wakan*, respectively. When a medicine man redraws the *circle* he is repeating a sacred action that is part of the religious tradition of the Lakota people. By redrawing the *circle* he calls for the re-actualization of the previous, *wakan* relationships. If the people do not wish to re-establish their *wakan* relationships, the leader says that the sacred hoop is broken. The medicine man could not say that the *"circle"* was broken if the *circle* was a paradigm of the Lakota universe. The *circle* is not a sign of a prescribed, *wakan* order, implying that it is the *circle* which *orders* right relationships. Rather, the *circle* is *a* symbol of *their* moral order. The frequency of the *circle* in nature and Lakota life makes the circle an awesome figure, but a secondary one. The *encircling* by the relatives is a sign of the virtue of the relatives. Therefore "walking the straight Red Path" is not inherently contradictory to "doing things in a *circle*" because value is not found in the physical form of the straight line or in the circle but in the practice of righteous, interrelational virtue. The *circle* is not archetype or a paradigm for the Lakota but a concrete consequence of their righteous social and religious virtues, especially respect and generosity. Respect is a virtue laced with fear that keeps the individuals in a society at their righteous distance from one another. Generosity is a virtue that shows itself especially in the filling of pitiful emptiness. From the practice of these two virtues alone, one can understand most of the *circular* distributions, actions, and figures of the Lakota. In summary, it is Lakota relational values that establish Lakota archetypes, paradigms, and geometries, and not the other way around.

The Pipe and Christ: A Christian-Sioux Dialogue,
William Stolzman, 1986, pp. 190-193

Nowadays the medicine wheel seems to be growing in popularity, even among those not raised with Native ways nor having Native blood. As with any sacred symbol, the medicine wheel, or hoop and four winds, can be misused or misunderstood. Perhaps in our own time it might yet become one of the integrating factors to bring greater unity among the Indian Peoples and between Indian Peoples and those who come from the dominant cultures of both North and South America.

———————————————— ○ ————————————————

SIGNIFICANCE OF THE CIRCLE
OGLALA

The Oglala believe the *circle* to be sacred because the Great Spirit caused everything in nature to be round except stone. Stone is the implement of destruction. The sun and the sky, the earth and the moon, are round like a shield, though the sky is deep like a bowl. Everything that breathes is round like the body of a man. Everything that grows from the ground is round like the stem of a plant. Since the Great Spirit has caused everything to be round, mankind should look upon the *circle* as sacred, for it is the symbol of all things in nature except stone. It is also the symbol of the *circle* that marks the edge of the world and therefore of the four winds that travel there. Consequently it is also the symbol of the year. The day, the night, and the moon go in a circle above the sky. Therefore the *circle* is a symbol of these divisions of time and hence the symbol of all time.

For these reasons the Oglala make their *tipis circular*, their *camp-circle circular*, and sit in a *circle* in all ceremonies. The *circle* is also the symbol of the tipi and of shelter. If one makes a circle for an ornament and it is not divided in any way, it should be understood as the symbol of the world and of time. If, however, the *circle* be filled with red, it is the symbol of the sun; if filled with blue, it is the symbol of the sky. If the circle is divided into four parts, it is the symbol of the four winds; if it is divided into more than four parts, it is the symbol of a vision of some kind. If a *half circle* is filled with red it represents the day; filled with black, the night; filled with yellow, a moon or month. On the other hand, if a half circle is filled with many colors, it symbolizes the rainbow.

One may paint or otherwise represent a *circle* on his *tipi* or his shield or his robe. The mouth of a pipe should always be moved in a *circle* before the pipe is formally smoked.

"The Sundance and Other Ceremonies of the Oglala Division of the Teton Dakota," *Anthropological Papers of the American Museum of Natural History*, J.R. Walker, 1917, p. 160

For those who would really see, the circle shows up in many places in the creation. To recognize the circle as one special sign among many is to develop a respect for the work of the Creator. Most tribes have incorporated the circle into aspects of their daily life.

—————————— O ——————————

SIGNIFICANCE OF THE CIRCLE
OGLALA

Everything the Power of the World does is done in a *circle*. The sky is round, and I have heard that the earth is round like a ball, and so are all the stars. The wind in its greatest powers whirls. Birds make their nests in *circles*, for theirs is the same religion as ours. The sun comes forth and goes down again in a circle. The moon does the same, and both are round. Even the seasons form a great *circle* in their changing, and always come back where they were. The life of a man is a *circle* from childhood to adulthood, and so it is in everything where power moves.

Black Elk Speaks, John Neihardt, 1932, pp. 164-165

Black Elk had great wisdom. He, in addition to knowing the ancient traditions of his People, was able to be open-minded to the ways of the Blackrobes as well. He lives on in the memory of his People.

PLAINS/ SOUTHWEST CULTURAL AREA

The drum carries prayers to Creator

SHIELDS AS CIRCLES OF POWER
INTERTRIBAL

Shields functioned as effective defensive weapons in Native American warfare, but European firearms, especially rifles, rendered them useless in terms of actual physical protection. Thereafter, Medicine objects attached to shields were employed in a variety of ways to keep Plains warriors in touch with the blessings inherent in the spiritual qualities of their shields. These spiritual qualities always remained paramount, and shields retained revered status, both on the Plains and in the Southwest, long after their value as objects of physical protection came to an end. Indeed, among Puebloans— especially Zunis and Hopis—shields still occupy an important niche in ceremonial life.

On the Plains, most shields surviving the desultory warfare of the 1860s and 1870s were buried with their owners. Others, such as those in the Southwest, became cherished relics from a vanished era.

Shields are rare, vital, and important parts of the American heritage. They speak of another time, when people strove for contact with the elemental forces of the universe and achieved that goal. Shields whisper of an age when prayer inspired power and murmur about the validity of the blessings conveyed to those in whose care they were entrusted. Though the people who dreamed the dreams and saw the visions have long since disappeared, some of the shields' Medicine cannot help but remain intact.

Throughout the Southwest and Great Plains, in all cases— whether Hopi or Navajo, Zuni or Apache, Keresan or Tanoan, Sioux or Cheyenne, Blackfoot or Arapaho, Kiowa or Crow—shields served as defensive weapons. But aside from their usefulness in parrying enemy blows before the advent of firearms, shields represented mystical forces, gifts bestowed upon worthy supplicants by the mysterious forces of the universe. Each shield was venerated, and each, above and beyond anything else it may have been, was and still is a *circle* of power.

Circles of Power, Ronald McCoy, 1988, p. 30

Even shields, which offered both spiritual and physical protection, are also expressions of the unifying power of the circle.

Rocky Bulltail's Crow Sweatlodge at Pryor, Montana, 1991

ARCTIC CULTURAL AREA

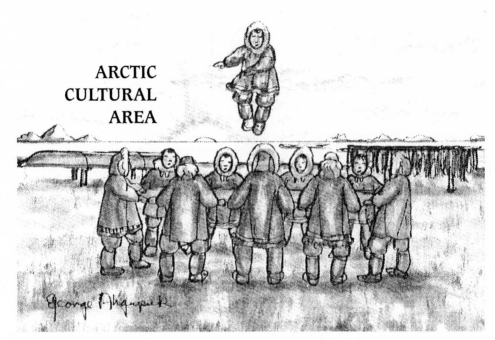

Originally a method for sighting game, but now enjoyed as entertainment, this circle of Eskimos holds a large skin while an individual bounces on it

ENCIRCLEMENT
YUPIK ESKIMO

. . . the act of *encircling* was also performed in various contexts to produce enhanced spiritual vision or as protection from spiritual invasion. For example, during the Bladder Festival, young men ran *counter clockwise* around the village before entering the men's house bearing bunches of wild celery needed to purify the bladders and "let them see" the gifts of the people. Likewise, when a man hunted sea mammals at certain times of the year, he had to *circle* his kill *in the direction* of the *sun's course* before retrieval. The boat itself was also ritually *circled* before launching in the spring, both in Alaska and in Siberia. Similarly, on the third or fifth day after the birth of a child in western Alaska, the new mother traditionally emerged from her confinement, marking her return to social visibility by *circling* the house, again *in the direction of the sun's course*. Finally, on the fifth day after a human death, the *grave* was *circled* in the direction of the sun's circuit by the bereaved to send away the spirit of the deceased. All of these ritual acts recall the magic circle ... whereby people walked in a *circle* around strangers who approached their camp so that their footprints would contain any evil spirits that might have accompanied the newcomers.

Crossroads of Continents: Cultures of Siberia and Alaska,
William Fitzhugh & Aron Crowell (Eds.), 1988, p. 265

Bering Sea Eskimos (Yupik) had a world view in which both humans and non-humans had "souls" and both needed to follow certain proscriptions and prescriptions in order to live well. Ritual circling was one of the ways of "doing things right."

George Turnmayer's seal skin, Angoon, 1975

MESOAMERICA CULTURAL AREA

Contemporary Chicano tattoo of an ancient Aztec four-directions circle

DANZA AND ITS SPIRITUAL RESPSONSIBILITIES
AZTECA/CHICANA

There was a note on the door at the MEChA office—it said, "Anyone interested in learning Aztec dance and participating in a ceremony for the Mother Earth, we will meet. . . .

It was 1980, and la Danza Azteca was new to Denver. A couple of months later as we sat and talked after a practice, we decided it was time to give individual responsibilities in the *dance circle*. These given responsibilities are known as palabras or words. When someone asked who would take the palabra (word) of the smoke, from behind me came Patricia's voice, "I will." I was surprised that she spoke up so quickly. "It was as if a voice came from inside of me," she said, "so deep that I knew it was right. . . . Like an outside force guiding me, putting me on this road." That was 17 years ago and today Patricia continues to carry the palabra of the Sahumero for Grupo Tlaloc, Danza Mexika en Denver, Coloraztlán.

Thinking back, she told me, "That first ceremony, it was the first sacrifice and the biggest sacrifice, so strong. . . . I've always looked for that strength, focus, and prayer again."

Patricial recalled the reason why we started the Danza. "So that our children would have something, be grounded to something, a strong road of prayer, to know who they are. What it has meant to me I wanted to give that to them."

Patricia at the center of the *circle*, has given that to all of us, that strong prayer and groundedness. At the center of the *circle* she is in the center of the universe with the sacred copal smoke embracing her, as she makes sure all of our prayers are equally embraced.

Carrying the smoke is a heavy responsibility," she shared, "but it is the prayers that the people are offering that maintain the smoke. It is the palabra that I hold, but it's the prayers from the *circle* that hold my palabra because this is where I learned to pray." Patricia has been a role model for all of our children and dancers in the *circle*. . . . "The Danza is me and I am the Danza, it's hard for me to separate, but I never thought I would be where I am, and I wonder where I would be if I hadn't taken the palabra of the smoke.". . .

The community gravitates to the Danza and at the center is always La Malinche with the smoke surrounding her head like a veil. "The smoke gives a visual connection. It is transparent and it embraces the prayers of our minds and hearts. When the smoke fills the air it captures all of these prayers and takes them up to the Creator and the people can embrace and understand the central energy force.

"Sometimes we enter into the *circle* coming from some real negative life situations; the smoke helps us to release some of that negativity and neutralizes it. Whether you're inside or outside the *circle*, the smoke binds us together; it is something you can understand on a lot of different levels."

All of our women are Malinches. We all represent the duality of our existence. We all carry the prayers of our families and the futures of our children. . . ."I'm not saying that I'm a major cornerstone in the *circle*. Everyone brings something valuable to the circle; it's like a puzzle. When someone with a palabra is not there, it is noticeable."

Let me say it to you, Comadrita. You are a major cornerstone in our *circle* and we love you very much. Gracias!

"The Woman Who Would Not Run,"
Razateca, Deborah Vigil,
March/April 1997, pp. 14, 31

Over the last thirty or more years I have noticed a renaissance among many of the People whose heritage is "south of the border." It

Ceramic drum

expresses itself in many ways: intellectually, spiritually, culturally, and also ceremonially. For many it is a way of life. Danza, indigenous dance, is a particular way that the People come together and share prayer in an ancient dance form. The above selection tells us of the special work of Patricia Sigala in the Denver, Colorado area. The circle, combined with honoring the four directions, is an essential aspect of this prayer.

——————————————— ○ ———————————————

CHICHA CEREMONY DANCING
CUNA

The ending ceremony at night was very interesting to me.

Everyone left the chicha hut at five p.m., went home, took a bath with gourds of water carried over from the river, ate, and returned to the chicha hut. The chief Kantule, still going strong (that was probably why he was chief Kantule) was emceeing the ceremony. A huge dance was performed. Several different variations were presented, the first of which interested me very much because the women's coin necklaces were clanging like hundreds of tiny bells on a Siamese temple, in tune to the rattles that each shook. *Two circles* were formed. In the center stood the form of the chief Kantule in all his glory with red cheeks, his nose lines, pelican bone necklaces, purple shirt, and red pants. On his left stood Ricardo, just as colorfully garbed, and at his right, Manitule another Kantule, who held the big ceremonial rattle. The Kantules sang and the women danced to a 4/4 beat sounding their rattles loudly on every other beat. Intermittent beats got a soft shake of the rattle. The ground literally shook with the force of their feet hitting it. I could feel the vibrations even where I stood. Gold nose and earrings flashed in the bright firelight as *round and round they danced* until the chief Kantule called out and the women broke into pairs and continued their mambo-like beat. The dance got wilder and wilder until at one point they were joined by a *third circle of men* who danced with as much vigor as the women. Flutes joined in the music of the rattles and soon nobody was standing still, including the Kantules or flute players. . . . i was hypnotized by the beat, and at one point felt my own body start to move with the beat of the rattles and flutes, almost of itself. I decided to go for a walk, then returned to watch the next offering of the evening. This second dance was a strictly male dance, during which time young men of the village strutted about and danced, imitating jungle animals. I was fascinated by the dignified yet earthly quality which the dance possessed.

Cuna, Joanne Kelly, 1966, p. 139

The writer, a woman of many experiences, describes this exciting dance that takes place during a fertility feast. Much chicha (a fermented reddish colored drink made from sugar cane, herbs, and corn) is shared by all, and lots of cigar-like rolls of tobacco are smoked and used as blessing smudges. Green pepper incense is also burned to keep the area clear of evil entities. Circular dancing as well as several circles of dancers are a feature of this sacred time.

Indigenous Mexican tripod circular vase

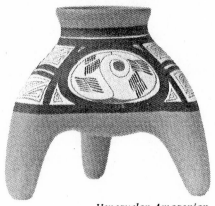

Venezuelan Amazonian
tripod ceramic vase

SOUTH AMERICA CULTURAL AREA

CIRCLE DANCE
TUCANOAN

In the circle dance, the participants line up outside the house in order of size, the tallest in the center. Each places his left arm around the next person's shoulder and in his right hand bears a hollow dance stave for pounding the rhythm. The entire group enters the house and, forming a huge *circle*, moves sideward a number of steps, then sways backward, then forward, and continues the side step. The dance rhythm is given by appropriate songs and emphasized with the dancing staves. The dance usually ends outside the house.

Handbook of South American Indians, Vol. 3,
Julian Steward (Ed.), 1963, pp. 792-793

In most cultures, a circle dance allows an increasing number of people to enter and feel one with the activity. As a circle grows and moves, it speaks well of the movement and inclusiveness of all life.

———————————— O ————————————

BABY BLACKENING CEREMONY *(WAICHEDN)*
KAINGÁN

This was the most joyful ceremony of the Kaingán. Every few years, whenever there were enough children to warrant a baby-blackening, a large number of the people of one extended family used to come together in a big camp. While the men with children to blacken went out with their brothers and first cousins to get honey for beer, the others made dance ornaments and hunted. The Kaingáng cannot restrain themselves as the day of the *festa* draws near, and night after night as the beer ferments the men walk back and forth across the *camp circle* carrying their babies on their backs and singing. When at last the beer is *tho,* the women paint their husbands with a black mixture made of charcoal and the sticky sap of a tree and stick feathers in it, and the men put little square hats of embira bark on their heads and wide bark belts around their waists, with bark tassels hanging down. Some of the belts are painted with black paint or animals' blood in crude designs that represent nothing at all. Now some men and women pass around the beer while the men stand or sit and sing, beating time by pounding on the ground with their clubs and lances. When the men have been singing awhile their wives come and stand or sit behind them, moving their arms slowly up and down in time to the music. Everyone sings as he chooses and as loud as he can, while clusters of young men stand around the older ones to try to learn the songs. There is no attempt to achieve harmony—everyone sings a different song, self-centered, musically oblivious to his surroundings. As they stand shaking their rattles or pounding their weapons on the ground—dancing, the Kaingáng call it—they stop from time to time to drink the beer. All day long and until late at night they drink while the women now stand, now sit, beside them, drinking beer, nursing babies, cooking food, eating, mourning, singing, quarreling. Every once in a while a group of men and women break out of the circle, grasp the *kondjáidn* and the *lu,* and walk across and around the *dance circle* in a confused singing knot, drunk, intense, and unsteady. This staggering around the *circle* is called dancing but bears not the slightest resemblance to the rhythmic artistic form usually called dancing. The Kaingáng make no effort to execute a formalized dance step. All they do is walk; yet their word for it is dancing, and they use the same term for the Brazilian polkas. What the word really means is something like "motion on foot while singing."

Jungle People: A Kaingáng Tribe of The Highlands of Brazil,
Jules Henry, 1964, pp. 195-196

Here is an example of the circular architectural form of the village influencing the circular mode of dance. Even though the author, an anthropologist trained under the noted Franz Boaz and Ruth Benedict, seems a bit prejudiced in his view about this form of tribal dancing, yet he reveals that the People lavish special ceremonial care on their chilren as they become initiated into a childhood phase of tribal life.

———————————— O ————————————

ARUANA DANCES
KARAJÁ

Karajá shamans have a soul that takes the form of a bird, and this allows them to fly to the place from which they derive their power. Given the important spiritual role of birds, it is easy to understand that feathers take on significance. The red tail feathers of the macaw are commonly associated with shamanism throughout Amazonia, and many other types of feathers are also used in a ritual context.

Masks worn during the aruana dances are an important ritual item made by the Karajá. Such masks represent the spirits of different fish, reflecting their importance to the Karajá. Although sting rays and many types of fish are represented, the most common mask depicts the aruana fish. . . . The dances are said to be rooted in the mythological origins of the Karajá, where it is said that a fish came to live with the people but then returned to its own element, the water. After that, the people imitated the fish by creating elaborate dance outfits, consisting of the fish masks, buriti palm-fiber skirts, and rattles carried in the hands of the dancer, which are hidden from view by the fringe of the mask.

The aruana masks themselves are considered very powerful and are never discussed with women, who are not supposed to recognize the men of the village dressed in the masks but are to believe that fish spirits are actually visiting their village. It is for this reason that the masks are often made in another village and assembled in secrecy, either inside or behind the men's hut. While being stored, they are the responsibility of one resident of the hut, the "master of ceremonies," who must above all protect them from the eyes of women. Only men of adult status may wear the masks in the dances.

Each different mask has its own set of songs, as well as its own characteristics, normally ordered on an agelike scale: some masks have youthful qualities reflected in energetic dancing and singing, while others appear to be older and require less vigorous dance steps.

The mask consists of a *cylindrical bundle of reed splints* decorated with tiny macaw feathers, which are applied in a mosaic pattern with beeswax. The pattern of this mosaic featherwork symbolizes the fish. Under this bundle of splints is a basketry frame that supports the mask on the dancer's head. Above the cylinder are long decorative feathers and bark wrapped projections also adorned with feathers. In preparation for ceremonies, the dancers are painted with red urucú and black genipa pigments, and they wrap their forearms with palm leaves.

The aruana dances are organized by pairs of sponsors, who, through their wives' kin, arrange to supply all the vegetable food for the ritual. Meat is obtained by communal hunting parties. Dancers often come from other villages to participate in an aruana cycle, which may last from several days to several months. . . .

The men put on the dance masks secretly behind the men's hut. They are occasionally assisted by the wives of the sponsors, who must keep their eyes toward the ground and under no circumstances actually look into the hut itself. When the dancers are dressed, a special pair of dancers wearing masks without feathers are sent down the dance track calling the women of the village to assemble by the row of huts.

The aruana dancers always leave the men's hut in pairs, shaking their rattles and singing songs while advancing along the dance track toward the women of the village, who have assembled near the huts or in the house of the wives of the sponsors. Once the masked dancers get near the group of women, they turn around and begin the journey back to the men's hut. Two women, their bodies painted in the geometric designs typical of the Karajá, follow the male dancers as they dance back toward the forbidden men's hut, never getting too close. When the masked dancers reach a certain point near the men's hut, they turn around and begin to dance back toward the village. The two women who had followed them begin dancing backward in the same direction, continuing to face the men's hut as they do so. When the male and female dancers get near the village, the two dancing females *turn around* and run to the group of women, ending the dance. The masked dancers, now far from the men's hut, walk back as another pair of men begin their trek. The aruana dances take place almost every day and they last late into the night, or even through it, until the end of the dance cycle, when the entire masks are either destroyed by burning or disassembled, the feathers being stored for further use.

Although children never participate in the aruana dances, boys and girls learn their respective future roles by creating a model dance in the sand with dolls. The boys stick tall hawk feathers in a *circle in the sand* to represent the forbidden men's hut. The aruana dancers are represented by wooden or ceramic figures, which are placed within this circle. A *second circle* is drawn in the sand by the girls to represent the assembled group of adult women. Into this circle the girls place painted ceramic litjoko dolls. The boys move their masked figures out of the men's-hut circle and make them "dance" toward the women while singing the aruana songs. The girls make their dolls "dance" replicating the movements of adult Karajá women in real-life ceremonies. By playing this game, the children rehearse important aruana dances and songs long before they are called upon to participate in actual ceremonies.

"The Feather Worker," David Fawcett in *The Ancestors: Native Artisans of the Americas*, Anna Roosevelt & James Smith (Eds.), 1979, pp. 37-38

Even in the ritual games of the children, the circle plays a key educational, and also spiritual, role.

———————————————— ○ ————————————————

CASSAVA DRINKING RITUAL
PIAROA

At seven o'clock in the morning the masked priests uncovered the two canoes of fermented cassava juice and the old sorcerer gave the order for the drinking to begin. A large space had been cleared around the two canoes. In the center of the tribal hut a small stool had been set up. It was carved out of one piece of some dark wood, and it represented the ritual seat from which the spiritual leader of the tribe officiated at the ceremony. The old man sat down on the stool. An old woman came forward and took the first calabash of liquid from the larger of the two canoes and brought it to him. A man was crouching on the ground before him. The old man slowly raised the calabash and made *three circles* with it round his head and across his chest and then *three circles* over the head of the man before him, to whom he then handed the calabash. The man drank the contents straight off and rose. A woman took the empty calabash from him and handed him a full one. In the meantime, a second man had advanced towards the old sorcerer to receive his first calabash. Then came a third and a fourth and so on and on until all the men had come forward. They were followed by all the women and their children.

The old sorcerer sat there stripped to the waist, performing his office impassively, repeating the same ritual gestures to each member of the tribe who came forward. When the last calabash of liquid had been handed over, he still did not move from his seat. Lighting one of his large cigarettes rolled in banana leaf, he began to smoke quietly. All around him and out in the square, which could be seen through the wide open door, the cassava-juice orgy began.

He was the only one who did not drink. He was the one who watches, the one who knows, the one who leads his people through the ceremonies of the scared day as he led them every night with his prayers and his invocation of the spirits.

The orgy gradually increased in vehemence as though in accordance with the slow movement of the sun as it rose higher and higher in the sky. Most of the tribe had now moved out into the square. Some of them drank standing up, others sitting or even lying down. Attentive women handed round brimming calabashes of cassava juice and saw to their replenishment as soon as they were empty, going swiftly backwards and forwards from the square to the two big canoes in the tribal hut. Each calabash held about a quart of liquid, and before long the stomachs of the drinkers could hold no more, and after each calabash they had to vomit before they could drink the succeeding one. They simply bent their heads forward to vomit, and then they bent them back to drink. Gradually the ground all around them turned into a shallow lake of yellowish liquid in which they stood or sat. . . . Women whose hair was decorated with strips of liana and glistening from the vegetable oil applied to it came up to us smiling and offered us calabashes, their fingers half in the liquid. They had stuck gaily-colored feathers in their hair and their shining faces were painted with complicated patterns. We could not always refuse to drink, and before long our stomachs began to swell too. Jean began to have difficulty in managing his camera at all. In the end we vomited also, and as we did so a great show of delight went up from the Indians. We went on with our filming.

The Impossible Adventure: Journey to the Amazon,
Alain Gheerbrant, 1953, pp. 142-144

Even within this apparent situation of intoxication, there is still a sense of order, and it is assured by the leadership of the shaman. This aspect of the ceremony leads to initiation within the People. It is definitely a controlled situation, and the participatns know its external boundaries as they individually become acutely sensitive to the super-natural realm of their common life and destiny.

──────────────── ○ ────────────────

RITUAL CIRCULARITY
MEKRANOTI

The women go to the gardens almost every day to collect sweet potatoes, manioc, and bananas or other fruits, as well as tobacco and cotton. Leaving in the early morning, they return to the village with the heavy loads by noon. Although the gardens are laid out by the men, the women own them. Like the village itself, they are *circular* in plan. *Circles* are the Mekranoti's most potent symbol. The courses of the sun and moon, both thought of as mythological beings, are understood to be *circular*. A great number of ritual artifacts are *circular,* as are such objects of daily use as baskets, spindles, musicals instruments, and ovens. Most dances and ritual are performed in *circular* configurations.

Mekranoti: Living Among the Painted People of the Amazon,
Gustaaf Verswijver, 1996, p. 117

It goes without saying that the circle is ever-important to this and many other Peoples of the Americas.

──────────────── ○ ────────────────

CONCENTRICALLY CIRCULAR GARDENS
MEKRANOTI

The surrounding forest blocked out any kind of view. Since arriving among the Mekranoti, the farthest away I had ever looked was from one end of the airstrip to the other. The view across the village plaza was even more restricted. The *inner circle of twelve houses* was so tightly packed that only a few inches separated some of the roofs. I longed to get out and see something, but there was nowhere to go. Finally I resolved to visit some gardens. Getting out of the village would be a good change from the daily routine. . . .

Keeping up with our guide required running at times. . . . Finally, we climbed a rocky hill and arrived at the garden's edge. . . .

The gardens were planted in *concentric rings:* in the center was a patch of sweet potatoes, surrounded by a *circle of manioc,* then *circles of bananas and papayas* on the outside. To get to the low sweet-potato vines in the center, we had to squeeze through the dense six-foot manioc plants. We hacked our way from one garden to the other.

> *Amazon Journey: An Anthropologist's Year Among Brazil's Mekranoti Indians,* Dennis Werner, 1984, pp. 45-47

Circles, circles, and then more circles. What a way to symbolize and celebrate our own part of the cosmos! Concentric circles speak of inclusivity while at the same time they allow for fresh additional growth. It would be interesting to apply this method to town and city planning in other parts of our world.

──────────────── ○ ────────────────

AYLLU CEREMONY
CANELOS QUICHUA

Just as soon as all hunters have returned, and it is known that the meat has reached both of the ceremonial houses, one of the ayudantes—who must have demonstrated his hunting skill by a large kill—picks up his drum and begins to *circle counter-clockwise,* beating the standard rhythm. Immediately other men shout the falsetto *juí juí,* and cry out *parihú, parihú, jistata ranuauuuu,* "togetherness, togetherness, the ceremony beginnnnnnnnnns" (literally, "is constructed"). Hardly does the circling drummer get started on his vision and thought-bringing shaman-power circling pattern than the women appear before him with large (quart capacity or more) mucahuas brimming with chicha. . . .

Usually he can't drink it all down fast enough, thereupon getting the remainder of a mucahua-full on his headdress as a chicha shampoo. *Ji ji ji jii,* cry the women and rush back to the chicha storage jars for more. . . .

A brief meal break takes place before the ceremony really gets under way. Women hastily place fowl, manioc, and plantains on banana leaves on the floor near the center of the house, and all grab, slurp, and gobble. Immediately afterward an ayudante or two begin their *drumming-circling* pattern, the prioste resumes his seat, and other ayudantes of the prioste arrive bedecked in skins and plumage, drumming as they come. All ayudantes now *circle round and round*, as their wives urge chicha on everyone else. Other members of the priostes' and ayudantes' families and visiting friends and relatives take seats on the long bancus around the house. Women go from one to another actively pouring chicha, fungus chicha, and vinillu down their throats. Sometimes four or five women converge on one person, each continuing her pouring as the selected receiver gulps, blows out liquid, and even stands on the bench in an effort to avoid the inevitable chicha shampoo.

By dark, identical behavior is taking place in both ceremonial houses. The central ayudante, who demonstrated great prowess in hunting, maintains his drumming and a calm demeanor in spite of the enormous amounts of chicha he is expected to drink. As visitors to the house begin to out-number the asua mamas and their daughters, other male ayudantes begin to serve chicha too. Their adult married and unmarried sons also help do this, undertaking the woman's primary role as chicha giver. Now the drummers turn outward, letting the distant and ancient souls of the drum and house sing out. From this point on the *circling pattern* shifts from clockwise to counterclockwise every ten minutes or so.

Sacha Runa: Ethnicity and Adaptation of Ecuadorian Jungle Quichua,
Norman Whitten, Jr., 1976, pp. 180-181

The Ayllu Ceremony brings together mythic time with present time through the enactment of mythic structure. Circular movement allows the participants to remain in a particular ritual area without wandering off and losing the impact of the sacred rites.

——————— ○ ———————

Yanomami basket from the Venezuelan Amazon

RITUAL ENCIRCLEMENT
MAPUCHE

Central to Mapuche religious belief is the concept of ancestral spirits. The most important of these are their former chiefs—those elders, lineage founders, military leaders, who walk the earth in the company of the sons of the gods. . . .

Spirits of ordinary ancestors may be active in the affairs of the living. If they are, however, it is often because their spiritual heirs have failed in some ritual obligation toward them. Whatever the case may be, the spirits who return to Mapucheland from the haven of the dead run the risk of contamination by a sorcerer-witch *(kalku)* and are, therefore, a threat to the well-being of the living. Indeed, during the first part of the funeral ceremony, there is a special activity called *amulpellun* which consists of the **encirclement** of the precincts in which the corpse is displayed (during the wake) and which is designed to drive away the evil spirits. This ceremony may be repeated on occasions when there is evidence of spirit return, even long after burial, in order to permit the ancestral visitor to depart without danger of contact with the forces of evil.

The Mapuche Indians of Chile, Louis Faron, 1968, p. 67

In this situation the Mapuche encircle not simply to bless, but to screen off anything evil that might draw near. Many cultures around the world have similar ritual observances.

———————————— ○ ————————————

COSMOLOGICAL CIRCULARITY AND
THE HUMAN BODY
INTERTRIBAL

Just as the hut and surrounding village can be seen in profile or in overhead, plane-view, so too can the body reflect vertically stacked and *concentric imagery*. The vertical zones of a standing profile human figure are obvious; in descending order, bicep ligatures, breastplate, belt, bracelets, below-knee ligatures and anklets. But for the spirit's eye plane-view one must imagine the body lying stretched out face-upward on the plaza, with arms and legs akimbo. In this view the innermost "ring" of corporeal art is the necklace of jaguar claws or teeth. The next ring out is the above-bicep arm ligatures and the breastplate, and the succeeding ring consists of the bracelets and the belt of jaguar skin, the below-knee ligatures and, lastly, the anklets. Thus, in a profile (vertical)-view, one's decorated body forms a stacked set of world levels, while in plane view it inscribes a series of nested *concentric rings of horizontal cosmic space* levels within levels, *circles within circles*.

Arts of the Amazon, Barbara Braun (Ed.), 1995, p. 123

Cosmological circularity may be seen in the body art of many Amazonian Peoples. It is a way of being in touch with life's cosmic forces and expressing solidarity with them.

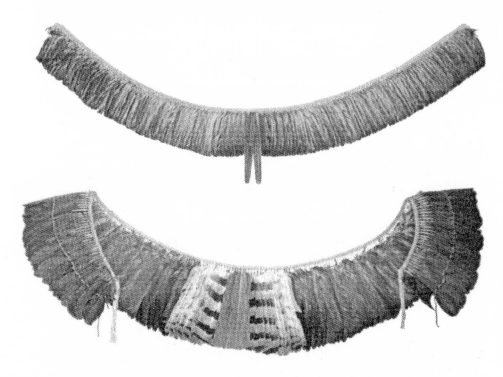

*Amazonian featherwork headdresses
to encircle the head during ceremonies*

A faster praying before a night fire

HOOP AND POLE GAME
INTERTRIBAL

Hoop and pole, another game played widely among North American tribes, replaces dice with human players on a three-dimensional field, but the need for control over cause and effect continues. The game, in which opposing teams battle to spear a stone or rawhide-covered ring, was a practical athletic contest as well as an occasion for gambling; it tested a player's fleetness, eyesight, and skill in throwing the stick, and it also served to strengthen the sense of community. A triumph meant salvation for the victor as well as for the group the player represented. To some tribes the hoop or wheel symbolized the *eternal circle of day and night*.

Gambler Way: Indian Gaming in Mythology, History and Archeology in North America, Kathryn Gabriel, 1996, p. 14

This game, and many others across the Americas, not only developed and demanded good skill, but was an invigorating way of expressing sacred belief as well.

———————— O ————————

PRAYER POEM
INTERTRIBAL

Warrior Jesus would be proud of the People
Finally honoring his teachings.
Fighting greed and selfishness
with Giveaways,
Fighting lies and abuse
with songs of gratitude,
Fighting apathy and uncaring
with prayer and community.

"I am the Way"—this is our trail
through the woods, brushed by the cedar trees;
this is our path through the wilderness—
the black unknown.
"I am the Truth"—this is our vow,
our commitment and dedication,
our love for the Creator.
"I am the Light"—this is the Red Road,
the blood of Mother Earth, smoke we send out
for seven generations.

Warrior Jesus
dances the *round dance* with the People.
His kingdom is already on Earth
For those who have eyes to see it.

"In the Name," Ken Bear Hawk Cohen, 1991

This poem "In The Name" is by one who has been exposed to a variety of indigenous traditions. The round dance, popular among the People throughout the Americas, is expressed here in a multicultural and multiethnic form so as to include all who step to the Kingdom dance with Jesus in sincerity and truth.

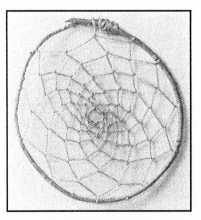

Dream catcher of willow and sinew

Crow Naming Ceremony

Baptism of a young child of the People

Number 4

NUMBER 4

"Four Mighty Ones are in every Man: a Perfect Unity cannot exist but from the Universal Brotherhood of Eden."

"Vala or the Four Zoas," William Blake

Each culture and religion has an understanding of numbers which are considered to be "lucky" or sacred for one reason or another.

The European and American missionaries who came to the Peoples already had sacred numbers in their faith agendas: the numbers 1 and 3. They symbolized unity within the Divine Trinity of Father, Son, and Holy Spirit. Trinitarian designs had traditionally been displayed in church and cathedral architecture for many centuries. They already permeated the cultures across the Atlantic which had received Christianity many centuries before.

But 4 was the dominant sacred number in the Americas. Though there were other numerical configurations that were important, like 7 or 6, 4 and its multiples took pride of place in a great many of the indigenous cultures, as witnessed by those described in this book. Though many Peoples throughout the Americas have become extinct because of disease or domination and some of their sacred ceremonies and ritual uses are lost to us forever, nonetheless there are survivors who today still carry on many of the ancient ways as they utilize the number 4 in praying privately or communally.

My father always told me when I was growing up that if a thing was worth doing at all, it was worth doing well. I suppose that if we expanded this saying a bit and explained it in the Native way, it might go like this: If it is worth doing at all, it is worth doing four times. I say this to express the fact that for many of the People it is still customary to hand over a sacred object like a pipe only after three feints and then the final presentation. This puts a sacred emphasis on what is happening; it also alludes to the situation of personal unworthiness on

277

the part of the receiver. It is a humbling action for both giver and receiver.

Doing something in sets of four is important in Native spirituality. Why is this so? We probably will never really know, but I would like to suggest that perhaps it is related to the four directions, north and south and east and west. These directions (or the intercardinal directions, northeast and northwest and southeast and southwest) are four in number. When all four directions are considered there is a fullness happening in the minds of the People. It is also four points of the sun on its daily journey: morning, afternoon, evening and night. With this kind of core thinking, it is fairly easy to give special meaning to 4 or its multiples in sacred planning. There are other explanations besides these.

Although much of Indo-European culture is based on triads, sets of three being expressed in religion, art, and culture, the indigenous Peoples of the Americas embodied their spirituality and culture most often in the form of tetrads: thinking and doing in sets of four.

The prime spiritual triad of Christianty, wherever it is lived out on Mother Earth, is based on an understanding of the one God who is also trinitarian: Father, Son, and Holy Spirit. Though the theological interpretation and expressions of this trinity abound in the historical and contemporary scene, still, perhaps for the sake of spiritual dialogue, the triad of the Trinity plus the Creation (all that exists apart from God) might be considered as a whole because of their direct relationship to one another. This kind of tetrad, though it may be considered a bit contrived, might serve as the basis for a greater exchange of ideas.

In the next few pages we will come to understand how the Woodlands Peoples by means of both dreams and experiences expressed fourness in their concept of four special beings who were responsible for bearing up the earth at special places (Algonquian) or four messengers speaking on behalf of the Creator (Seneca). Cherokee and Creek ceremonies were replete with the ubiquitous 4, even in the gathering of sacred herbs. Over and over again this special number will come up in a girl's puberty ceremony and Apache etiquette. We will recognize it in a contemporary Zuni poem for Mother Earth.

How our hearts will be happy as we hear and follow the sound of the drum and notice some California tribes (Ohlone, Hupa) using 4 ritually as they dance. We will also learn how the Washoes of the Great

Basin area near Reno, Nevada, used to fast for four days as they prepared to gather pine nuts in the autumn.

The harvesting and eating of fish in the Northwest allowed for certain creative uses of 4 in the blessing and dance ceremonies as reminders of the source of all sustenance (Kwakiutl, Nooksack Salish). We will see how, on the rolling prairies of Canada and the United States, for centuries the People healed one another (Comanche, Crow), prayed with tobacco and the pipe (Crow, Blackfeet) or peyote (Cheyenne), with eagle feathers (Blackfoot), in the sweatlodge (Crow) or considered the spirit world as part of everyday existence (Osage, Arapaho, Cheyenne, Teton Sioux, Crow, Peigan, Cree). They would also bless a child (Omaha) into its tribal inheritance.

In the Arctic, the Eskimo men had some special ritual and hunting symbolism based on the number 4. The Peoples of Mexico (Aztec, Seri) were able to connect the number 4 with water, while a Caribbean People's origin story succinctly speaks of the "four" twins of one birth (Taíno). At least one South American People, if not many, knew how there is a sacred fourness to a particular hallucinogenic cactus that is employed to heighten their awareness during unique prayer experiences. A good number of the People had surprising curing ceremonies whose ritual base was 4 (Mapuche).

Contemporary Taínos from Borikén (Puerto Rico) get ready to dance at a California intertribal powwow

WOODLANDS CULTURAL AREA

A riverside prayer with four branches in hand

BEARERS OF THE EARTH
ALGONQUIAN

And the Great Spirit made the Earth
in the form of a flat oval,
and he made *four beasts*
and *four serpents* and placed them
in the water under the Earth
to hold it firm;
but the *Four Winds* blew
and the Earth shook.

Indians of the Woodlands: From Prehistoric Times to 1725,
George Hyde, 1962, p. 2

Here, once again, we find guardians who hold firm the four parts of an oval-shaped earth. The four beasts and the four serpents have their particular tasks to perform, but it is the four winds who move about the earth to create movement and change. The fourness of beasts and serpents and winds is related symbolically. This use of 4 allows the storyteller and the People to group items into an easy way of remembering.

———————— :: ————————

BEAR CEREMONY
MUNSEE-MAHICAN

The skin of the sacrificed bear was tied around the center pole beneath the red and white face masks. . . .

During the ceremony *four male drummers* were stationed on the men's (west) side. During the second part of the ceremony they used a deerskin stitched into a rectangular cushion with the hair side in, serving as a drum. One half of this unique drum was painted red, the other white. A bear painted black was superimposed on the red, facing a black crescent moon in the white field. *Four drum beaters* were paddle-shaped, painted white and red, with a star in the white field

> *The Wolves of Heaven: Cheyenne Shamanism, Ceremonies, and Prehistoric Origins*, Karl Schlesier, 1987, p. 177

This ancient ceremony is not lacking in its symbolic use of four special drummers and four special drumsticks.

—————————— :: ——————————

CREATION STORY
MOHAWK

The woman sets off toward the sunrise, which in American Indian tales generally is the way to be followed by anyone setting out for the House of the Sun. We may therefore suppose that the mysterious one whom she is destined to marry will be in some way a personification of the sun. His dwelling is discovered at the place of the axial Tree, and this would seem to confirm that supposition. Moreover, when he later loads the basket that is to be carried by his wife to her people, he fills and shakes it down *four* times. *Four* is the number of the quarters of space.

> *The Way of the Seeded Earth/Part 2: Mythologies of the Primitive Planters: The Northern Americas*, Joseph Campbell, 1989, p. 154

Here is a creation story that tells of a mystical marriage between sun and moon. Four times and four directions figure into it as well.

—————————— :: ——————————

Iroquois moccasins, bag, and turtle medallion

MESSAGE FROM THE FOUR BEINGS
SENECA

Now the beings spoke saying, "We must now relate our message. We will uncover the evil upon the earth and show how men spoil the laws the Great Ruler has made and thereby made him angry. . . .

"*Four words* tell a great story of wrong and the Creator is sad because of the trouble they bring, so go and tell your people.

"The *first* word is *One'ga'* [Whiskey or Rum]. It seems that you never have known that this word stands for a great and monstrous evil and has reared a high mound of bones . . . you lose your minds and one'ga' causes it all. Alas, many are fond of it and are too fond of it. So now all must now say 'I will use it nevermore. As long as I live, as long as the number of my days is, I will never use it again. I now stop.' So must all say when they hear this message." Now the beings, the servants of the Great Ruler, the messengers of him who created us, said this. . . .

Now spoke the beings and said, "We now speak of the *second* word. This makes the Creator angry. The word is *Got'go'* [witchcraft]. Witches are people without their right minds. They make disease and spread sickness to make the living die. They cut short the numbered days, for the Creator has given each person a certain number of days in which to live in this world.

"Now this must you do: When you have told this message and the witches hear it, they will confess before all the people and will say, 'I am doing this evil thing but now I cease it forever, as long as I live.' Some witches are more evil and can not speak in public so these must come privately and confess to you, Handsome Lake, or a preacher of this Gai'wiio'. Now some are most evil and they must go far out upon an abandoned trail and there they must confess before the Creator alone. This course may be taken by witches of whom no one knows. . . ."

Now the beings spoke again saying, "This is the *third* word. It is a sad one and the Creator is very sad because of this third word. It seems that you have never known that a great pile of human bodies lies dead because of this word, *Ono'ityi'yende,* the niga'hos'säa', the secret poisons in little bundles named *Gawen-nodus'hä* (compelling charms). Now the Creator who made us commands that they who do this evil, when they hear this message, must stop it immediately and do it nevermore while they live upon this earth-world. It matters not how much destruction they have wrought—let them repent and not fail for fear the Creator will not accept them as his own. . . . Now another word. It is sad. It is the *fourth* word. It is the way *Yondwi'nias swa'yas* [meaning 'she cuts it off by abortion'].

"Now the Creator ordained that women should bear children.

"Now a certain young married woman had children and suffered much. Now she is with child again and her mother wishing to prevent further sufferings designs to administer a medicine to cut off the child and to prevent forever other children from coming. So the mother makes the medicine and gives it. Now when she does this she forever cuts away her daughter's string of children. Now it is because of such things that the Creator is sad. He created life to live and he wishes such evils to cease. He wishes those who employ such medicines to cease such practices forevermore. Now they must stop when they hear this message. Go and tell your people. . . .

"Now another message for you to tell your people.

"It is not right for you to have so many dances and dance songs. . . .

"Tell your people that these things must cease. Tell them to repent and cease. . . .

"Now another message to tell your people. *Four words* the Creator has given *for bringing happiness.* They are amusements devised in the heaven world, the *Osto'wägo'wa* [Great Feather Dance], *Gone'owo'* [Harvest Dance], *Ado 'we* [Sacred Song], and *Ganäwe 'gowa* [Peach Stone Game]. . . .

"Now another message to tell your people.

"The Creator has sanctioned *four dances* for producing a joyful spirit and he has placed them in the keeping of *Honon'diont* who have authority over them. The Creator has ordered that on certain times and occasions there should be thanksgiving ceremonies. At such times all must thank the Creator that they live. After that, let the chiefs thank him for the ground and the things on the ground and then upward to the sky and the heaven-world where he is. Let the children and old folk come and give thanks. Let the old women who can scarcely walk come. They may lean against the middle benches and after listening to three or four songs must say, 'I thank the Great Ruler that I have seen this day.' Then will the Creator call them right before him.

"It seems that you have never known that when Osto'wägo'wa was being celebrated that one of the four beings was in the midst of it, but it is so. Now when the time for dancing comes, you must wash your faces and comb your hair, paint your face with red spots on either cheek, and with a thankful heart go to the ceremony. This preparation will be sufficient. . . ."

Parker on the Iroquois: Iroquois Uses of Maize and Other Food Plants, the Code of Handsome Lake, the Seneca Prophet, the Constitution of the Five Nations, Arthur Parker & William Fenton (Eds.), 1968, pp. 27-30, 39-41

Handsome Lake, Ga-nyah-di-yoh (1735-1815), is said to have received a message from Creator to his People through four beings who helped him come back to life. He was a controversial figure among his People and some feel that he is responsible for changing many of the more ancient ceremonials. His Code (Gai'wiio') was annually recited in September and at all mid-winter festivals of the Iroquois. The recitation would take place over a three-day period. Four was used several times in the Code to group together important items. This religion is still important to many of the Iroquois People today.

———————————— :: ————————————

MEDICINE DREAM
OJIBWA

They slept in the wigwam, Starkmann accepting Louis's invitation to spend the night. Reed mats covered the dirt floor, and the musty darkness smelled of woodsmoke and unwashed wool blankets, but, tired from his long walk, emotionally drained, he slept one of the soundest sleeps of his life.

Wawiekumig dreamed.

In the dream, magizi clutched him and the young man in its talons, its mighty wings carrying them beyond the crack between night and day to a far place neither man recognized, a beautiful forest of towering cedars. There, Wawiekumig built a small fire, and the smoke of the cedar wreathed the young man, this grandson's brother-friend. He brushed his head with an eagle feather *four times*, singing a healing song. He sang in the ancient tongue, but the young man understood every word. He understood everything: the significance of the purifying cedar, of the eagle feather, each strand representing what was beautiful in the world, magizi's feather, the instrument for curing diseases of mind and spirit. The young man understood this;

there were no barriers of language or concept in the beautiful forest. When his song was done, Wawiekumig took his pindgigossan and shot a megis shell into the young man, who fell. While he lay as one dead, Wawiekumig offered a prayer to the manitos: I have cleansed him with the eagle feather and with cedar. Let him sleep nights and no longer reproach himself. Let him come back to himself, let him come home. Show him how to get through life as a man. It is I, Wawiekumig, who asks this, asks this. Then he raised his pindgigossan and shot the young man with life-restoring power. The young man sprang to his feet, in outward appearance the same, but not as he had been before. Then magizi took them in its talons once again, and they soared down the winds of heaven back to earth.

So vivid was this dream that Wawiekumig, upon awakening from it well before dawn, knew it had not been a dream of sleep but a medicine vision. It had actually happened, the event occurring in the world of manitos. In sleep their spirits had been taken there, and there Wawiekumig had once again, perhaps for the last time in his life, practiced his ancient arts and healed human suffering. For that he was grateful, and whispered a thanksgiving. Then he wrapped himself tightly in his blanket and fell back asleep, happier that he could remember.

Indian Country, Philip Caputo, 1988, pp. 426-427

This section of a contemporary novel about a Vietnam veteran offers some knowledge of Ojibwa ceremonies. Wawiekumig ("Round Earth") is an old man trained in the medicine ways from his youth. His medicine bundle (pindgigossan) might have been made from weasel skins or from the hides of beaver, muskrat, or bear. It is used to throw white cowrie shells (megis) at an initiate. The eagle (magizi) takes an active part. The supernatural powers (manitos) are the ones who, from ancient times, taught the People about everything that came to them from the Great Spirit.

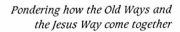

Pondering how the Old Ways and the Jesus Way come together

A doorway at an Oklahoma Cherokee tribal center

SOUTHEAST CULTURAL AREA

HERB GATHERING RITUAL
CHEROKEE

The Cherokee herbalist generally gathered his herbs just before they were to be used. When he found the plant he was searching for, he walked around the plant either once or *four times*, reciting the proper verbal formula.

The Southeastern Indians, Charles Hudson, 1976, p. 342

A four-fold circular movement around the plant honors and respects it. It is a holy action performed before receiving a gift from Mother Earth. This gift of an herb would then reveal a later gift of health for the patient prayed over.

———————————— :: ————————————

RITES OF THE BUSK (GREEN CORN CEREMONY)
CREEK

The square ground, its shelters, and the ritualized movement of males through them expressed Creek ideas about the structure of the tribal universe—of which the square ground was a symbolic micro-cosm—and the proper place of human beings in it. The passage of a man's life from birth to warriorhood to old age was indicated by his shifting seating assignment in the clan arbor. This symbolism was most explicit during key ritual periods, especially during the intense four to eight days of the annual Busk.

Among the rites of the Busk—the animal dances, the use of the emetic Black Drink, the ritual bloodletting—was the Creek version of a new-fire ritual. Like the Cherokee, the villagers in preparation for the festival would douse their home fires, clean up the ashes, sweep their floors, and throw out refuse. Then, using a drilling technique until a tendril of smoke appeared, the signal to add dry tinder, spiritual leaders would ignite a fire in the middle of the square ground. The flame, which represented the sun itself, was believed to renew the vitality of their homesteads, town, and cosmos. . . . The square ground was the summer location of the sacred fire and the traditional center of a town's political and religious activities. *Four shelters*, called "clan beds," were situated around a square plaza. . . .

On the *fourth day* of the festival the sacred fire was rekindled and camp fires were relit from it.

Color was symbolic in the square ground. Red clan beds (war) were built astride the male axis, the white beds (peace) on the female axis. A man's seating assignment reflected his change in age and role from boy, to warrior, to old man. It suggested the male passage from the world of his mother to the world of men and finally, as an elder, a return to the female domain.

> *Native American Architecture,* Peter Nabokov & Robert Easton,
> 1989, pp. 110-111

Architecture joins with ritual to describe and celebrate the changes in life, as illustrated in Creek ceremonial life.

Anasazi doorway

SOUTHWEST CULTURAL AREA

ETIQUETTE
MESCALERO APACHE

The stress on activities occurring in their appointed spaces in the Ceremony is evident daily in adult and children's activities. The politeness-decorum system lays stress on not wasting words: this leads to an economy of speech that strikes outsiders as being conversation punctuated by silences. To a Mescalero it is conversation punctuated by time for reflection, framing the next statements, being sure that the previous speaker is finished, and showing proper respect for language. Formal meetings are arranged into *four* spatially distinct sections; speeches have *four* parts.

"Singing for Life: The Mescalero Apache Girls' Puberty Ceremony,"
Claire Farrer in *Southwestern Indian Ritual Drama*,
Charlotte Frisbie (Ed.), 1980, p. 155

A desire to reflect the rhythms and designs of the cosmos enters into this People's sacred ways of activity. Even daily conversation does not escape the call to be part of all that exists because of the Creator.

———————————— :: ————————————

GIRLS' PUBERTY CEREMONY SYMBOLISM
MESCALERO APACHE

Directionality gives rise to both the concept of *"four"* and its related concept of balance. Together the latter two may be said to establish the harmony essential to existence. The Creator God created the world in *four days*; examination of the creation sequence reveals that not only did he *call* entities into being, but also that balance was present. Two days were devoted to the creation of the inanimate (sun, earth, sky elements, and earth elements) and two days to the animate beings (winged insects, crawling things, four-legged animals, humankind). *Four sets of entities* occur within each of the two sequences, as balance is further present in the juxtaposition of the above and below.

Creation is recapitulated in the holy lodge as the Singers sing the first night to the first Grandfather and what he represents, the second night to the second Grandfather, and so on. The singing is structured to bring together male principles (the structure itself, the dancing hides, the Singers) with female principles (the fire-pit, Godmothers, those impersonating White Painted Woman)—balance again. Within the holy lodge, then, is the visual and verbal manifestation of balance and *four*. It is a visual and oral transformation of the base metaphor.

Both concepts are given further visibility in the costuming of the portrayers of both White Painted Woman and the Mountain Gods. The girls' costumes consist of an overblouse and a skirt. Each item of clothing has two areas, front and back, on which decorations are placed. Thus, there are *four fields*; blouse front, blouse back, skirt front, skirt back. The beaded designs balance: that is, what appears as decoration over the left shoulder will also appear over the right shoulder. What is painted on the side of a girl's face will be painted on the other side. Similarly, the designs on the moccasins balance each other and, most of the time, they are composed of *four elements*. When not composed of *four elements,* balancing each other in sets of two, the design is composed of two elements, each of which is seen to balance the other.

The Mountain Gods provide an even more striking reminder of the importance of balance and the number 4. A Mountain God is *quadrilaterally symmetrical* both above and below the waist. The design, in evidence by facing him forward and dividing his painted areas on both midsagittal and lateral planes, can be replicated *four times* to reconstruct his image front and back. Likewise, by so dividing his costume from the waist down, he can again be seen to present a *quadrilaterally symmetrical* picture. His back is perceived as being in balance with his front, as each side of his front and back balance each other. Each of his arms balances the other. His sash, headdress, and even his kilt and moccasins present a balanced picture. It is number and arrangement that create this balance rather than area, just as it was number and taxonomic equivalence that provided the balance in the creation.

The basket around which the girls run contains *four items*: grass, pollen, tobacco, and eagle feathers. Both grass and pollen are earth items while feathers and tobacco are sky items: that is, they mediate between the below and the above in that both eagle and tobacco are viewed as communication channels to the Powers. Thus, the *four items* in the basket are seen as being in balance and hence contributing to the harmony and rightness of the world.

The girls take *four steps* on the painted skin before running around the basket. Each step represents a stage of life with the first (infancy) and the last (old age) balancing the two in the middle (childhood and adulthood). Infancy and old age are seen as time of dependence when one must rely on others to fulfill needs and often to help one move about. Childhood and adulthood, in contrast, are times of free movement, independence, and self-reliance.

Eight evergreen trees balance each other as *four* line each side of the runway/entrance for the holy lodge. The lodge itself is balanced with the *four* powerful *Grandfather poles* balancing the other eight poles.

The Ceremony abounds in additional examples of *four* and balance: activity spans *four days* with the middle two days presenting the "same" picture and the two days on either end balancing each other, partially by reversal. *Four varieties of dance* are performed with the dancing of the Mountain Gods (and the women dancing in their support) balancing that of the girls; the two kinds of social dancing provide balance to the two kinds of ritual dancing. Even the physical site is balanced in that the dance arena for the girls is balanced by the dance arena for the other dancers; and the girls' camp area balances the general camp area. . . . The girls' *four days* of exemplary existence and their journey through the *four stages* of life are emblematic of White Painted Woman's journey through the eons.

"Singing for Life: The Mescalero Apache Girls' Puberty Cermony,"
Claire Farrer in *Southwestern Indian Ritual Drama*,
Charlotte Frisbie (Ed.), 1980, p. 148-150

Such a demonstrative use of four strikes one as especially beautiful and clever. It would be indeed difficult to say exactly when this fourness first began to be used by the People; it is hidden in the mists of the ancient past.

CALIFORNIA CULTURAL AREA

Entrance to partially underground ceremonial roundhouse, Esselen Tribe, Carmel Valley

VARIETAL USE OF 4
CHUMASH

The number four is the sacred number which
regulated Chumash rituals. Four brings balance.

Four is a universal sacred number, probably dispersed to all the continents in a period beyond human reckoning. *Sku'mu* means *four* in Chumash, and it is greatly honored in their culture as the basic organizing tool for measuring a wide spectrum of proper behavior patterns. It is a basic unit in their counting system, as shown in the Chumash terms for five, six, seven, and twelve which all use *Sku'mu* as a base.

. . . a *four-fold* symmetry is suggested in the well-documented solar calendar, which was divided into four by the two solstices and the two equinoxes.

The earth is universally divided into four, representing the cosmic division which Europeans called the *four 'quarters'* of the world. This metaphysical organization of quartered space is probably the ancient conceptual root for the Chumash term *Sku'mu,* literally meaning to divide in four pieces. The suffix *-mu* means to occupy space, and it may be that all space was orignally conceived as ritually divided into four. Such geographical terminology expresses the *four-fold division* of the Middle World, and is one of the most significant examples of the sacred

291

number four in Chumash numerology. The poppy with its *four petals* has been an important symbol of this spatial division in Chumash folk tales.

The Chumash also adopted the *number four* as the dominant pattern of action in ritual behavior. Three feints would routinely precede a successful motion or action in both public and private ceremonies. A dancer, for example, might approach the central pole of a dance arena three times before finally touching it on the *fourth* (successful) *approach*. Endless variants can be found in Chumash folk tales where a character will fail to achieve a goal until the *fourth try*.

Examples of *four-fold warnings*, or *four refusals to take advice*, or *four scoldings* of children is a popular motif of traditional Hokan storytellers who were especially fond of plots organized around *four attempts of a hero* to complete an adventure. The four-fold divisional model thus appears many times in Kitsepawit's stories. In one example, he states that a Chumash will be overcome with terrible fear if he hears a coyote make a long howl three times in a row. The *fourth cry* warns of disastrous results, typically death to a loved one. Faced with such prospects, the listener often takes datura to counteract impending misfortune.

A Circle Within the Abyss: Chumash Metaphysics,
John Anderson, 1994, pp. 17-19

Each People has its own heritage of numbering; the Chumash also have theirs, allowing 4 to predominate. The datura plant (Jimsonweed) is a kind of hallucinogen that was used at certain times by many California Peoples.

---------- :: ----------

HIWEYI DANCE
OHLONE

The shaman wore an elaborate costume while performing the *hiweyi* dance. . . .

Chiplichu wore a feather boa called *hichli,* which passed across the back of his neck and was drawn back under his arms from the front, the two ends being joined behind to form a tail. He carried a cocoon rattle, called *wasilni,* in each hand, and a third cocoon rattle was fastened in his hair. He wore a wreath on his head, made of stems and leaves of mugwort *(Artemisia vulgaris)* twisted together, and his hair was held firmly by a net. *Four bunches of split crow feathers* attached to sticks completed his headdress. Each of these feather ornaments was about two feet long and tied with deer sinew. They were thrust in his hair, one sticking out in front, another in back, and one on each side. The cocoon rattle which he wore on his head was fastened at the back, with the rattles up. A tule mat, said to be six inches thick, with armholes, was worn very much like a skirt and reached to the knees. It was held by a string around the neck, tied in front. Under the mat, Chiplichu wore a piece of deerskin about his middle. He was not decorated with paint.

As he danced, he held a cocoon rattle upright in each hand. He held the rattles away from him at about the level of his breast and swung them together from side to side. While the ceremony was going on, the people were supposed not to smoke. Whenever Chiplichu saw anyone smoking while he was dancing, he turned around *four times*, then danced up to the offending individual. He went on dancing, but rubbed his hands *four times* down the arm of the offender that held the pipe. After the fourth time he took the pipe away from the man. Then he danced up to the fire, and made *four passes with the pipe over the fire*, and finally threw it into the blaze. He did this because he was told in his "dream" to allow no one to smoke when he danced (Gifford 1955:302).

The *hiweyi* was danced in curing ceremonies, especially for those caused by the sighting of a ghost.

California Indian Shamanism, Lowell John Bean (Ed.),
1992, pp. 171-172

Though Ohlone, the missionary Chiplichu brought a form of this Ghost Dance teaching to neighboring Miwoks. The hiweyi *dance was usually celebrated on a hilltop with 12 men. They sang four special songs. Later a special ceremony was held in a gathering house for four nights beginning at sunset and lasting until midnight. The dance itself allowed for the ritual use of four in a variety of ways.*

::

RITUAL USE OF 4
MIWOK

Four is the Miwok sacred number. His ritual is repetitive, usually performed *four* times: the dance stage contains *four* parts; a dancer passes a piece of regalia over his head *four* times before putting it on; ritual acts are performed *four* times consecutively; each dance is in *four* parts: the ceremonies last *four* days.

Miwok Means People, Eugene Conrotto, 1973, p. 89

This citation leaves no doubt that the ritual use of four governed many actions for the People in California.

—————————————— :: ——————————————

BRUSH DANCE
HUPA

... the ritual begins well before the dance itself, as she gathers the plant substances that will be needed, going without food or water and speaking prayers as she collects the medicine. On the first night of the public ritual, she builds a fire in a particular way. ...

"You have *four sticks*. It has got to be tan oak and madrone, when you're baking that pitch, and then you got to *put tobacco on each corner*. I always put Bull Durham under here [where the sticks cross each other]."

She emphasized that all of her prayers were spoken in the Hupa language.

... and then she makes medicine over the baby for three days in much the same way as it has been done for at least one hundred years.

One important element is the waving of burning sticks of pitch-wood over the baby. The wood must be sugar pine, and a certain song is sung while this is done. Mrs. Pratt described the fire waving in these words:

First we take that salal brush and we throw it on our fire, and it just burns. It goes click, click, click. My father used to call it firecrackers because it crackles like that. Then you stick your pitch on the end and get it started, and it's got to be rotten. Used to be some nice ones but they've logged everything out and it's getting hard to find. You stick it in the fire and it blazes. So that's what we go this way with [she sings, swinging the sticks at waist level as if waving them over the baby]. If the baby is sick or not doing well, that is why we wave that fire. It scares away things. It helps the baby to grow stronger.

She also used the bark of the sugar pine, pounding it up and mixing it in water that the child will drink. Other medicines are used to steam the child at various points in the three-day ritual.

This is my medicine basket. We put herbs in it, and we steam it with hot rocks. You put it underneath the blanket and steam the baby. It cleans them out, and it works on them so they grow up healthy. Some of the same stuff goes into these [other] two baskets, only it's not steamed. It's Colt's Foot, and you put that in there, and you put a pine, a *new* growth of pine bough, on top. I pick them about three o'clock in the morning. Both of them. And I dance.

On the last night of the dance, Mrs. Pratt speaks a medicine formula which is perhaps the single most important element in the ritual.

About three in the morning I pick up both of the medicines and I dance. Towards Mount Shasta. That's where we call for our medicine. There's a sharp rock, and you pound on the rock and you talk. Then you hit it again twice. No answer. Talking in Indian all the time. You pound three times, and the third time he's giving it to you.

Cry for Luck: Sacred Song and Speech Among the Yurok, Hupa, and Karok Indians of Northwestern California, Richard Keeling, 1992, pp. 24-25, 293

The Brush Dance was originally held any time to cure a sick child. Nowadays it is an annual spring event. During the ceremony, medicine substances that were previously gathered are prayed with and fire on a stick is waved around. Alice Pratt led this dance on August 24, 1979 and offered this foregoing information.

A Miwok roundhouse in the California Sierra

GREAT BASIN CULTURAL AREA

BIG TIME GATHERING
WASHOE

By far the most important part of the annual round for most Basin dwellers was the early autumn pine nut harvest, referred to by the Washoe as *Gumbsabai,* or the Big Time. It was a big time, indeed, not only for the amount of food gathered but also for the chance it gave otherwise scattered family groups to socialize and celebrate. This was an opportunity for elders to meet in council, for youngsters to fall in love, and for people of all ages to thank the bountiful spirits. . . . For Washoes, the fall ceremony was the culmination of a ritual that began earlier in the year when people buried branches laden with young pine cones by a stream and prayed and danced for a good piñon crop. A ritual leader consulted with spirits in his dreams as to the timing of the harvest, then sent out a messenger with a rawhide thong tied in knots that denoted the number of days before the Big Time. The messenger would carry this string calendar from camp to camp and announce the coming assembly, untying one knot each day.

On the appointed date, Washoes gathered near pine nut groves their ancestors had harvested for centuries and embarked on *four days of labor, prayers* and *celebration*, four being a sacred number to them as it was to many other tribes. Each day the men went out to hunt, while the women ritually bathed themselves before gathering pine nuts. Later in the day, there were races and gambling, as well as prayers and dancing. The dancers often carried piñon gathering tools—long hooked poles for shaking down the pine cones and baskets for holding the harvest in the hope that those implements would absorb the blessings summoned by the prayers and songs. The leader who had called the group together *fasted during the four days*, consuming only small portions of cooked pine nuts and cold water while he prayed for a rich harvest.

After the four days, elders gave to each family a share of the pine nuts collected by the women and the game taken by the men. No family was to eat its own portion, however. After preparing the food, each family gave its share to another as a gesture of hospitality, receiving a portion in turn. As the meal began, elders prayed over the food and encouraged the people to be peaceful and charitable. After the ceremony, entire families set out for the grove and began the real pine nut harvest, which often lasted for weeks.

American Indians: Indians of the Western Range,
Henry Woodhead (Ed.), 1995, pp 39-40

The Washoe traditional lands are not too far from Reno, Nevada. Four days of fasting are really four days of prayerful preparation.

Idaho lava rocks

NORTHWEST CULTURAL AREA

Totem pole

SPIRIT DANCING
NOOKSACK SALISH

Another important instruction given to the new dancers requires their active participation during the winder dance season for at least *four years*. Four years is probably a good average of the number of winter seasons required to fix the trancing pattern permanently in the dancer's responses. *Four,* of course, is a ritual number and there are undoubtedly other symbolic associations as well. On a social level, the four-year requirement will assure a goodly number of at least relatively experienced dancers at the large parties every winter who will help to integrate each year's crop of new dancers into the dancing community. In addition, there is a series of supplementary rituals for the dancers to undergo even after initiation. Second-year dancers must have a ritual painting of the face. If a dancer is to have a "uniform"—special dance paraphernalia—it is ordinarily put on sometime during the first four years if family finances will permit it. When he is four years old (that is, four years past initiation), a dancer is considered strong enough to help initiate new dancers.

Coast Salish Spirit Dancing: The Survival of an Ancestral Religion,
Pamela Amos, 1978, p. 135

Spirit Dancing is in the process of making a comeback, both in Canada and the United States. Winter is the time setting for this series of prayerful dance ceremonies that include trance states as a means of getting in touch with the realm of the Spirit. It offers a complement to the religious styles of Christian Pentecostalism and Native Shakerism.

———————————— :: ————————————

FIRST SALMON CAUGHT THANKSGIVING CEREMONY
KWAGIUTL

When the *first four silver salmon* (coho) were caught by trolling, the fisherman's wife met her husband's canoe at the beach and said a prayer of welcome to the fish. She brought them up to the house and butchered them according to custom, leaving the heads and tails still attached to the backbones. These she set in the roasting tongs to cook by the fire. When the eyes of the fish were blackened, the family group was assembled in the house, and they sat behind the fire. The tongs with the roasted fish were laid on new mats spread before the people, who were given water to drink. The one of highest rank then prayed to the food before it was eaten:

"O Friends! thank you that we meet alive.
We have lived until this time when you came this year.
Now we pray you, Supernatural Ones, to protect
us from danger,
that nothing evil may happen to us when we eat you,
Supernatural Ones!
For that is the reason why you came here,
that we may catch you for food.
We know that only your bodies are dead here,
but your souls come to watch over us when we are going to eat
what you have given us to eat now."
"Indeed!"

After eating, the family wiped their hands on shredded cedar bark, but did not wash them. The wife gathered up the bones and all that was not eaten into the mat, and threw it into the sea, including the mat, thus ensuring that the salmon would become whole again and return to the land of the Salmon People. Other of their species seeing them knew they had been treated with due respect and honor, and so they too would follow up the river. It seems the custom of all the tribes to return the bones to the water, with the exception of the Tsimshian, who burned them in the fire.

Indian Fishing: Early Methods on the Northwest Coast,
Hilary Stewart, 1982, pp. 165-166

The first four salmon of the catch were important and treated in a special way. The represented all the coho that came to feed the People; therefore, thanks needed to be given to them in a prayerful manner.

—————————— :: ——————————

FISH HARVEST RITUAL
KWAGIUTL

Eulachon, so important for the rendered oil, was also recognized with a ritual when the run began. A chief, with the privilege of catching the first of the eulachon, went in his canoe to a special place in the river, tying the canoe up to a particular overhanging branch. It was always the same place. Taking up his dip net, he addressed it in prayer that it might be successful:

"Go on, friend,
on account of the reason why you came,
placed in the hands of my late ancestors
by our Chief Above, our Father,
and go and gather in yourself the fish,
that you may be full when you come back, friend.
Now go into the water where you may stay, friend."

He then partially lowered the dip net *three times*, and pushed it right down for the *fourth*. When it was hauled up he prayed to the shimmering mass of fish writhing in the net.

"Now come, fish, you who have come
being sent by our Chief Above, our Praised One,
and you come trying to come to me.
Now call the fish to come and follow your magic
power that they may come to me."

The chief then poured the hundreds of slender, silver fish from the net into the canoe. *Four times* over he did this to complete the ceremony, and then returned home. All fishermen were then allowed to start harvesting the oil-rich fish that came in millions every year. When each man pulled up the first in his dip net, he offered a prayer of gratitude to the eulachon. There were different ways of saying it, but a common prayer was:

> "Thank you, Grandchildren, that you have come to me
> to make me rich as it is done by you, fish,
> your Dancers. You will protect me
> that I may see you again next year, Grandchildren.
> Thank you that you do not disdain trying to come to me,
> Supernatural Ones."

Indian Fishing: Early Methods on the Northwest Coast,
Hilary Stewart, 1982, p. 170

Dipping the net four times into the water and then four times pouring the fish into the canoe were significant for this People; it was at the same time a sign of fullness and also symbolic of the greatness of this water harvest.

Grateful to his hosts who nursed him in illness, this elder painted totem designs on their dining room wall (Bear and Raven).

Praying with four bundles of burning sage

PLAINS CULTURAL AREA

HEALING CEREMONY
COMANCHE

The formal contract occurs when the patient initiates the ritual involved with his request for Sanapia's aid. . . .

The patient then produces the demanded items of payment which he has been instructed to bring by his liaison-advisor. This approach ritual payment consists of a piece of dark green cloth, a commercially obtained 5/8-ounce bag of Bull Durham tobacco, and *four corn shuck cigarette "papers."* The patient rolls a cigarette, takes *four puffs* and hands the cigarette to Sanapia. When she takes it, the contract is made. . . .

After Sanapia has taken the cigarette, thus agreeing to the contract, the patient places the green cloth in front of her and lays the Bull Durham and the corn shuck leaves on the cloth.

Sanapia states that the requirement of the piece of dark green cloth follows from the nature of the major medicine which she employs in the treatment of ghost sickness. This type of payment can no doubt be connected with the ritual involved in her collection of *bekwinatsu,* or "swelling medicine." It is necessary for Sanapia to pay the plant with a piece of green cloth before extracting from the earth.

> The medicine I use, that swelling medicine, got green leaves. The cloth goes with that. That's what the meaning of the dark green goods supposed to be. It stand for that, you might say. That kind of medicine get them well and they paying for it.

302

When Sanapia has accepted the cigarette and taken the required four puffs, she says to the patient, "Tell me your troubles." The patient then begins to inform Sanapia of the specific reasons that he has sought her aid and generally to unburden himself concerning any and all varieties of "trouble" which he is experiencing. . . . It is during this outpouring that Sanapia makes her diagnosis or decides exactly what course of action she will pursue regarding the patient.

Sanapia: Comanche Medicine Woman, David Jones, 1972, pp. 73-74

The four cigarette papers and the four puffs of the cigarette initiate the healing work to be done.

———————————— :: ————————————

ORIGINS SYMBOLISM
OSAGE

When they came across the cedar, whose boughs remained green even in the depths of winter, they were impressed with the life-power and wonderful fragrance of this tree that clung even to the bare rock of the bluffs, making of it a symbol of everlasting life:

On the brink of a precipice stood a cedar,
Sighing where she stands in her chosen place,
Saying: "Here upon this precipice I stand,
In order that the Little Ones may make of me their medicine."
*In the midst of the **Four Winds**,*
Whichever way the wind blew,
She sent forth a pleasing fragrance,
Saying: "Behold my roots,
Which I have made to be the sign of my old age;
When the little Ones make of me their symbol,
They shall live to see the toes of their feet gnarled with age.
Behold the wrinkles of my ankles and my outspreading branches;
When the Little Ones make of these their symbols,
In their ankles and limbs there shall be no cause of death.
See the downward bend of my branches;
With these as symbols, the People shall live to see their shoulders
Bent with age.

See the feathery tips of my branches,
These are the signs of my old age.
When the Little Ones make of these their symbols,
They shall live to see their hair whitened and feathery with age,
As they travel the Path of Life."

Besides being a symbol of long life, the Osage made the female cedar to be the Tree of Life itself, a symbol common to peoples throughout the world. . . .

As the cedar was the symbol of continual growth, so the rocks symbolized the enduring and unchanging. The Osage saw the rock as the very foundation of life; in the creation of the land, the Elk called to *the Four Winds* to expose the ancient rock upon which he created the vegetation of the Earth.

The Osage say that their ancestors came upon *four large rocks* in their journeys. The rocks also gave themselves as symbols of endurance to the Little Ones:

Even the great gods themselves
As they move over the Earth pass around me
As I sit immovable as the Great Red Boulder.
When the Little Ones make of me their bodies,
Even the gods shall pass around them
In forked lines
As they travel the path of life.

The rocks were also used for healing, when heated and used in purifying sweat baths. *Four rocks* were used in the sweat bath that preceeded the Naming Ceremony. Although it is hard for the white man to conceive of, the Native Americans also gave to the rocks the power of thought and the ability to transform themselves and appear to the People in dreams. The very rocks were thought to be alive with power.

Osage Life and Legends: Earth People/Sky People,
Robert Liebert, 1987, pp. 80-81

The four winds and the cedar tree are ancient origin symbols for the Osage People. The four rocks speak of endurance and are ceremonially related to the rocks used in the sweatlodge.

———————————— :: ————————————

WIND CONTROLLING PERSONAGES
ARAPAHO

We believed in a power that was higher than all people and all the created world, and we called this power the Man Above. We believed in some power in the world that governed everything that grew, and we called this power Mother Earth. We believed in the power of the Sun, of the Night-Sun or Moon, of the Morning Star, and of the *Four Old Men* who direct the winds and the rains and the seasons and give us the breath of life. We believed that everything created is holy and has some part in the power that is over all.

The Arapaho Way: Memoirs of Carl Sweezy, Althea Bass, 1966, p. 68

In a short and concise manner this spiritual leader of the Arapahos offers a tribal cosmology that includes the guardians of the wind directions.

———————————— :: ————————————

FOUR WINDS SIGNIFICANCE
ARAPAHO

The connection of *four* with the conception of the circle is wonderfully keen in the Indian mind, and finds full expression with the Arapaho. Of course, this connection is given in nature by *the four quarters* determined by the sun, whose manifestations form the greatest visible phenomenon in the world, and there probably is more or less causal relation; but the connection extends to human matters not in any direct relation with nature . . . but it may safely be said that the idea of four is almost invariably inherent in the idea of the circle, at least in the mind of the Arapaho. A circle is to him *a four-sided or four-ended thing*: it is *per se four determined and four-containing*. The rhombus, the rectangle, the cross, are all equivalents of the circle; and when, as often, the connection or identification is not directly made, it is almost always not far away. Where we think geometrically, the Indian thinks symbolically; where we are realistically visual or spatially abstract, he is pictographic. . . . Of course, the connection of this tendency as regards the conception of the circle, with the straight-lined character of American (what we falsely call geometric) as contrasted with the overwhelming preponderance of the curve in the Old World, is not far to seek.

From the prevalence in North America of color-direction symbolism, and the extent among the Arapaho of direct color-symbolism, of world-quarter and of *four symbolism*, it might be expected that they, too, connected certain colors with certain directions. There is as yet apparently no trace of any such color-direction symbolism. While there may be instances of it, they are certainly sporadic, and contrary to the general trend of Arapaho symbolism, and would only prove the innate deep-seatedness of such an association.

There is a certain connection of different colors with *the number four*, especially in ghost-dance ornamentation. A typical quill-embroidery in white, yellow, red, and black has also been described as referring to *the sacred four*. In the few cases of ghost-dance objects observed, the colors have always been black, red, yellow, and green, blue sometimes replacing black. There is, however, no fixed order in which these successive colors come, so that it is evident, that, while taken collectively they may contain the idea of *the four-directional world*, there is no definite attribution of particular colors to certain directions. Taking the colors as they occur from left to right, or in sunrise circuit, their order in the several cases is black, yellow, green, red, black, green, red yellow, with white as the central fifth; black, green, red, with white as the fifth; and blue, red, yellow, green. So that, whether the several series are read forward or backward, the same order cannot be obtained. One of these cases is that of *four different winds* represented by lines of different colors. The winds are often equivalents of the world-quarters in America, so that we are here apparentlly not very far from association of colors with directions; but the only idea in the mind of the maker of this piece seems to have been that of *four*, and the colors served only to emphasize this idea as such.

The Arapaho, Alfred Louis Kroeber, 1983, pp. 413-415

For a First Nations person of the Americas, indeed for any human being, the cosmos speaks of the marvellous works of the Creator. Shape and color and direction conspired to help the Peoples express their deep sense of the spiritual. The holy part of this mix was directionality and it was expressed in four unique ways. Some of the early settlers, artists, travellers, and ethnologists were quick to notice the tribal ways and to draw conclusions about those ways. Early on, they recognized the multiple use of the number four in everyday Native life.

—————————— :: ——————————

SACRED PERSONAGES IN RITUAL
CHEYENNE

Four is the sacred number among the Cheyennes, five the unifying number that pulls together all the power resting in the others. Maheo, the All Father, made *four* Sacred Men who live at the semi-cardinal directions of the universe. These are the Maheyuno, the Sacred Persons who guard all creation. Maheo's home is the fifth direction—the center or heart of the universe. Thus, throughout the Cheyenne Sacred Ceremonies, sacred actions are performed in groups of four or five.

"Ox'zem: Box Elder and His Sacred Wheel Lance,"
Montana: The Magazine of Western History, Father Peter Powell,
Spring 1970, p. 32

In art or ceremony the fourness of life comes up always; it is a constant religio-cultural reference point of the People that they share with other tribes.

—————————— :: ——————————

PEYOTE CEREMONY POEM
SOUTHERN CHEYENNE

our smoke has gone *four ways*
it calls for us

my brothers smile with tears
we may never meet again

eagle of fire whose
wings are scented cedar

moon of forever who
guards the sacred seed

keep us strong
to meet the
coming days.

"Our Smoke Has Gone Four Ways," Lance Hensen in
Carriers of the Dream Wheel: Contemporary Native American Poetry,
Duane Niatum (Ed.), 1975, p. 59

*Lance Hensen, in his poem "Our Smoke Has Gone Four Ways," seems
to suggest aspects of the Native American Church peyote ceremony.*

::

NUMBER AND LANGUAGE OF PRAYER
TETON SIOUX

When *Wakan Tanka* wishes one of mankind to do something he
makes his wishes known either in a vision or through a shaman. . . .
The shaman addresses *Wakan Tanka* as *Tobtob Kin.* This is part of the
secret language of the shamans. . . . *Tobtob Kin* are *four times four
gods* while *Tob Kin* is only the *four winds*. The *four winds* is a god and
is the *akicita* or messenger of all the other gods. The *four times four*
are: *Wikan* and *Hanwikan; Taku Skanskan* and *Tatekan* and *Tob Kin*
and *Yumnikan; Makakan* and *Wohpe; Inyankan* and *Wakinyan;
Tatankakan; Hunonpakan; Wanagi; Waniya; Nagila;* and *Wasicunpi.*
These are the names of the good Gods as they are known to the people.

Wakan Tanka is like sixteen different persons; but each person is *kan.*
Therefore, they are all only the same as
one. . . . All the God persons have *ton. Ton*
is the power to do supernatural things.

"The Sundance and Other Ceremonies of the
Oglala Division of
the Teton Dakota," *Anthropological Papers
of the American Museum of Natural History*,
J.R. Walker, 1917, p. 153

*To multiply 4 by itself is to mystically
describe power or fullness of being.*

::

Hunter-warrior in wolfskin

CREATION STORY
CROW

In the beginning, water covered the earth. Itsi, He First Made All Things, wandered about on the water, hunting for thoughts, looking for land. He called to a loon flying overhead: "Come here, my brother; dive under the water and see if you can bring up mud. With that, we will make land." The loon dived three times unsuccessfully, but the *fourth time* he came to the surface with a little mud in his bill. Itsi laid it in the palm of his hand and kneaded it; then he blew it out of his hand, and it scattered over the water and it became land. With his thoughts he created streams and mountains.

Itsi pondered deeply, and from a lump of the newly formed land he made *four small images, which he rocked four times*, singing slowly.

The *fourth time* he sang the song, he cast the images from him, and as they struck the earth, they sprang up living creatures of human form and size, two men and two women. The two pairs were placed in different valleys and commanded to multiply. Thus the human race began.

For food, Itsi made plants, roots, and berries of many kinds to grow. Then he molded clay in the shape of animals with *four legs* and with a hump on the back. "Live!" he commanded, and buffalo filled the prairies. The Deer People and other animals he made in the same manner, and the birds, to whom he said, "You shall give songs to the people, and supernatural strength to those who fast and cry."

Then the creator thought, I have made everything, but out of this earth come creatures that I do not know. He looked closely and saw that they were ants, and their bodies became tobacco seed. He thought, the People I am making shall live over all the earth, but those to whom I give this plant shall be few, and it shall make their hearts strong.

As the people multiplied, he scattered them and gave them different tongues and a desire to fight with one another. To the Apsaroke, he gave tobacco seed, saying, "When you meet the enemy, this plant will make you as strong as the powerful little ants from whom these seeds came."

Prayer to the Great Mystery: The Uncollected Writings and Photography of Edward S. Curtis, Gerald Hausman, 1995, pp. 128-129

This story tells how Itsi, the Creator, made the world. Edward Sheriff Curtis (1868-1952), the photographer, spent some time taking pictures of many Peoples of the continent and interviewing them in regard to their cultural and spiritual ways. This is one story that he recounted. The importance of the number 4 is often encountered in stories of the origins of everything.

---- :: ----

HEALING
CROW

My mother and father grew up in the Indian way of worshipping. They fasted and belonged to the Tobacco society, as did many Crows in their day. . . .

A person became a member of the Tobacco Society by adoption. I was adopted by Packs The Hat and his wife when I was twelve. I miss them, as they were really good to me. . . . The Packs the Hats first asked my parents if they could adopt me, and when my parents agreed, they set a time in the spring. They took me into the adoption lodge and sang medicine songs for me three times, and the *fourth time* they adopted me. I didn't have anything to do except sit and let them sing and pray for me. They fixed a lunch for me each time they sang, with oranges and bananas, which were special at that time.

At the adoption *four couples* (a man and his wife) sang for me, and each couple gave me a medicine song. After they *sang it four times* it became my song. When Packs The Hat sang his special song, all the other couples joined in, and then they made me get up and dance along with my adopted father and mother, the Packs The Hats. Then I was adopted. I selected *four medicines* that the couples had out on display because that was part of the adoption.

> *They Call Me Agnes: A Crow Narrative Based on the Life of Agnes Yellowtail Deernose*, Fred Voget, 1995, p. 106

To this day the Tobacco Society is important to Crows. The singing of special holy songs four times by four couples and the choosing of four special medicines is also highly significant in this northern Plains ceremony.

---- :: ----

TOBACCO SOCIETY MEMBERSHIP
CROW

As in all Crow worship, tobacco signified the promise of good health, luck in war, and a long and productive life. However, tobacco was noted especially for the wealth it would generate. Tobacco seeds multiplied in the pods, and tobacco became a prime symbol of a numerical increase of any kind, in buffalo, horses, and humans. The ceremony consisted of a ceremonial planting in the spring, followed by the transmission of Tobacco medicines to candidates adopted into the bundle groups. Membership usually was by invitation, but a man might become a member by vowing to join were he successful in a horse raid or if he or a relative recovered from an illness. Adoption symbolized the birth of a child, and the ceremonial "father" and "mother" dressed their "son" and "daughter" in new clothing. The "children" reciprocated with lavish gifts, including horses. Adoption with payment formalized a candidate's right to acquire *four Tobacco medicines*, songs, and dances and to participate in the planting.

"Mixers" of the various chapters held rights to prepare the tobacco seeds and to supervise planting. The medicine dreams of mixers determined the location of the garden and the time of planting. A medicine woman led the procession to the garden, making *four stops along the way* to sing to the earth. She wore a wreath of ground cedar to drive away evil spirits bent on blocking their prayers and carried an Otter or Beaver medicine to ensure that the seedlings would have sufficient water to grow.

Before planting, each mixer started a warrior with a push on a run across the narrow width of the garden to stimulate and protect the growing plants. The run symbolized the path of a successful war party; on the return journey, the warrior would report that he had seen plenty of buffalo, groves of ripened berries, and tobacco seedlings pushing vigorously through the ground. Mixers initiated the planting by *feinting three times before thrusting a painted chokecherry digging stick into the ground*. Women imitated the mixer in their movements, while their husbands followed, dropping seeds in the holes. Before departing the garden, each chapter erected a miniature lodge in which Tobacco Man could sweat. Within it they burned Tobacco's bear root incense to assure him that they had followed sacred procedures.

Throughout the ceremony they expressed the reverence and respect they felt for sacred tobacco and Morning Star, its owner.

*They Call Me Agnes: A Crow Narrative Based on the Life of
Agnes Yellowtail Deernose*, Fred Voget, 1995, pp. 15-16

The Tobacco Society exists for contemporary Crows and their children's children. The four-fold sets of actions are significant and give special emphasis to the prayers.

—————————— :: ——————————

TOBACCO RITUALS
CROW

Crows always were fearful that a baby or a youngster would get sick, especially with pneumonia. If that happened, they called in a medicine man who was known for his cures. He used an ash or chokecherry tube to suck out the bad stuff, and he usually received a horse and several comforters as payment. When I was about six years old, I took sick with double pneumonia, and my parents took me to an Indian doctor by the name of Gros Ventre. My mother said I was just skin and bones by then. He sucked all the bad blood out and cured me. In those days Indian doctors were great. They could do almost anything and even could put bones together. People always tried to pay them well with *four things*, for the cure worked better with the spirit helpers that way. And that's the way it works today, too, if you go to a medicine man for a cure. For four things today, Crows like to give a Pendleton blanket, dress goods, tobacco, and money.

*They Call Me Agnes: A Crow Narrative Based on the Life of
Agnes Yellowtail Deernose*, Fred Voget, 1995, p. 39

As in any segment of the human family, it is important to protect newborn children. As medicine persons need to make a living too, it is only fair that they receive payment in a practical but symbolic manner.

—————————— :: ——————————

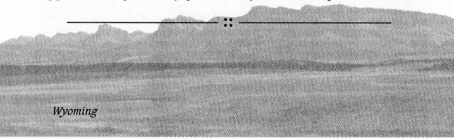

Wyoming

TOBACCO SOCIETY ADOPTION CEREMONY
CROW

The procedure was carried out in *four sessions*, at each of which the initiate was presented with the larger amount of food to take home.

These preliminary sessions during the winter initiated the adoption with feasting, and the selection of *four songs* that were given to the "child." The "father" usually chose the medicine songs displayed by members of the adopters society. At the fourth meeting, following the Tobacco procedure, "the father asked some man to sing a certain one of his songs, saying, 'I want my child to have that one.' He thus selected *four songs*. As each song was chosen, the owner sang it, and then rising took the candidate's arm and danced with him while the other members sang. The candidate was now pledged to pass through the initiation in the ensuing spring."

The formal adoption and transfer of medicine usually took several days. The procedure was divided into eight stages: (a) consecration of the novice(s) and medicines in a special tipi; (b) ceremonial exit from the consecration tipi and procession to the adoption tipi; (c) consecration of the adoption tipi with coup blessing and prayer smoke with a pipe by the adoption-lodge owner or pipe lighter; (d) public transfer of songs and dances, with the novice dancing between or with donors; (e) payment of wealth to adopters and to fraternal brothers who have contributed wealth or services for the novices; (f) invocative purification and good-wish blessing of the novice through a "washing" or sweating, including the medicines; (g) display of medicines and the taking hold of the medicines by the initiate presented by the "father" or secondary donor-sellers, thereby indicating that he is not afraid and can manage the power within; (h) feasting of the medicine-sellers and ceremonial parents by the initiate and his relative, to terminate the proceedings.

The Shoshoni-Crow Sun Dance, Fred Voget, 1984, pp. 66-69

This unique Crow tribal ceremony entails the invitation for adoption followed by the sharing of special songs and dances and the actual adoption into the society and proper passing over of the medicines. Doing actions four times is important.

—————————— :: ——————————

COLOR SYMBOLISM FOR THE SEASONS
CROW

Crow customarily base their symbolism on straightforward connections. Both form and color carry the burden of meaning, and both may hold mulltiple significances within a standarized system of meanings. Variability stems from the subjective experience of the visionary. . . . A seasonal symbolism commonly associated *green* with *spring, red* with *summer, yellow* with *autumn*, and *white* with *winter*.

The Shoshoni-Crow Sun Dance, Fred Voget,
1984, pp. 297-298

The four seasons, all important in Crow spirituality, have their own identifying descriptive colors. Often these seasons and colors are expressed in the beaded and painted designs of the People.

———————————— :: ————————————

SACRED PIPE ADOPTION CEREMONY
CROW

In the Sacred Pipe preliminaries, two pipestems were stuck in the ground about a foot apart and an ordinary calumet was laid before them. A pipe bundle containing the pipe to be transferred was displayed also in the middle of the "father's" tipi. Other pipe holders came on invitation, and one acted as pipe lighter. He was an important ceremonial figure, since he initiated prayer and consecrated the paraphernalia. Smoking together in prayer was an essential preliminary to acting together in any enterprise, just as the "smoking" of pipe and drums in the fragrant incense of sweetgrass was a prerequisite to their use. While the drumming and singing of *four medicine songs* went on, the "father" and "mother" gently swayed the "son" and "daughter" from side to side as if handling babies, for adoption called up the notion that the initiate and his wife were about to be born.

A childbirth theme was pervasive in much of the adoption ritual. "We will let this boy be born" was a signal for building the adoption tipi in the Tobacco ceremonies. In the Sacred Pipe, a warrior feigned with awl in hand the ear-piercing normally carried out on the *fourth day* when an infant was named with a coup blessing. At the feast given by the initiate in gratitude to the adopters, the adopter came as a father to greet his newborn and brought choice meat, along with fine moccasins and leggings. The "father" fed the initiate as if he were a young eagle, as the "novice throws out his hands as wings and *four times* moves his mouth in imitation of the young birds." *On the fourth try*, he actually took the meat and all then partook of the feast.

The painting and dressing of the candidate and his wife in accordance with ceremonial rights owned by the adopted took place in a special tipi. In the Sacred Pipe, the novice escaped from his "father's" tipi to the consecration lodge, where he was finally tracked down. *Four warriors* recited their deeds, and the first must have struck coup on the enemy inside a tipi; otherwise, no one could enter. Tobacco members assembled in the consecration lodge, resplendent in their finest dress and ornamentation, with medicine bags slung down their backs. Those with the right to paint the tobacco plant insignia, validated by dream, vision, or inheritance-purchase, set to work. Women usually painted women and men painted men, but there were some members who had the right to paint both sexes. At the request of the "father," a member painted the initiate, and then the "father" undressed his "child" and reclothed him in a fine outfit. Now they were ready for the procession to the adoption lodge, led by the wife of the owner. She feinted leaving at each of the three songs, and exited on *the fourth*. At each of *four stops along the way* they sang a medicine song and then they entered the adoption lodge with its centered altar-replica of the original tobacco planting ground. . . . The sacred tobacco was coming up, there were plenty of berries, and everyone was free of sickness.

A pipe lighter circulated a pipe in prayer among the men and the candidate to solemnize the occasion and bring good luck to the transfer. Following a brief interlude of singing and dancing by women, the candidate arose and danced to each of his four songs. This was the moment for payment, and a herald told relatives to bring the wealth forward—stick tokens for horses, blankets, quilts, money, and other valuables for the "father." The lodge owner usually claimed two pieces of the red cloth preferred in offerings to the Sun. All ended this portion of the Tobacco adoption drama by taking up a green branch and, to the accompaniment of a special song, moving the branch up and down to make the leaves dance as if growing.

In the Sacred Pipe the "father" brought his "child" into contact with growth and the continuous renewal of life by placing him on crossed blades of grass, symbolic of spring. The candidate's birth was dramatized in a ceremonial washing and by the feigning of ear piercing by a warrior who offered a coup-blessing. The washing and ear piercing were repeated *four times*, in accordance with the Crow ceremonial number. The "father" symbolized the good luck and wealth that would follow his "child" by drying his head with quilts, blankets, strips of red calico, and even money, each of which was thrown away to the assembled guests after use. Prayer sweating in the Tobacco adoption was the counterpart of the baptismal-cleansing of the Sacred Pipe. Both ceremonies expressed good wishes for the newly adopted.

A "child" furnished willows for the sweat lodge according to instructions of the "father." The number was in *sets of four*. Perhaps as many as ninety-four willows or more, according to the rights of the sweat-lodge owner. He also brought stones from the mountains. *Four warriors*, who buiilt the sweat lodge, received *four pieces of red calico* from the wealth brought by the candidate's relatives.

Medicine bags of members sweating were placed on top of the buffalo hides or quilts covering the sweat-lodge frame. Usually the owner began the singing after *four cups* of water were poured on the *four heated stones*. This was a time for singing medicine songs and telling good dreams. From four cups of water they went to seven, then, ten and finally paid no attention to the count. At each interlude a respected warrior handled the water and *four songs* were sung. Before each start the cover was raised with a good wish—for life until winter, for plenty of berries, or a spring free of sickness and death. The "father" had a special wish for his "child." After washing him with bear-root and water, or rubbing him down from head to foot with the sage sacred to the Sun, the "father" wished a full life for his "child." "All you above, let him live to be an old man."

Before the *fourth* and last good wish, the medicine bags were taken down and faced to the mountains. The men plunged into the water after the prayer-sweating to assure that sickness or any other thing which threatened well-being or life would be carried downstream away from them. All that remained was for the candidate to claim his medicines from the bags placed atop the sweatlodge by members of the adopting society. The timing of the prayer sweating usually determined whether the newly adopted claimed his medicines in the afternoon or the next day.

The newly-adopted Tobacco member selected power tokens from medicine bags displayed in a large tipi. He chose mystic tokens from any bag, a choice that usually included *four bags* of the sacred tobacco itself. Frequently the *four who gave songs* during the preliminary instruction were ready with sound advice on the stronger medicines. Whatever was chosen—eagle tails, a shell, a wolfskin, a whip, or an otter skin—was paid for with a horse or other valuable. Each item was accompanied by a song, which would be taught to the initiate.

The Shoshoni-Crow Sun Dance, Fred Voget, 1984, pp. 69-73

Adoption in any form is a good thing, both for adopter and adoptee, no matter the occasion, because it is about making room in one's life for another's life to achieve its potential.

———————————————— :: ————————————————

SWEAT LODGE CEREMONY
CROW

Now we are ready to bring the rocks into the lodge. Everyone is quiet and prayers are being said by one and all. A man is selected to bring the rocks from the fire into the lodge. This man makes a vow or request in his heart and does not speak. No one talks during this time, but everyone is making his own vow in his heart. So the rock man carries the first stone to the lodge. The man who will put the water onto the rocks is already seated inside the lodge by the side of the pit. He has two forked sticks with him to place the rocks correctly. The rocks are brought to the lodge one by one. The *first four rocks* are placed in the bottom of the pit, *one for each of the four directions*. During the time the first four rocks are being placed, everyone remains silent and praying. After the fourth rock is placed, everyone says, *"Aho, aho, thank you for hearing our prayers."* Now everyone can talk again, and the rest of the rocks are brought in and placed into the pit. Now the red-hot rocks are glowing brightly as they fill the hole to form our altar. Then the water bucket and dipper are brought in and switches are placed for everyone. The switches can be made of sweet grass or other grasses such as beaver grass. The participants will tap themselves with the switches to help bring out the sweat and purify their bodies.

Everyone is now ready to enter. As I said, we all bathe ourselves with water before we enter. This reminds us of our purification but it also helps to prevent burns when the steam from the rocks first hits us. We have nothing on when we go into the lodge. Some men may wear a loincloth, but generally we are naked. Then men always go together, and the women can go together after the men are through. Remember, each person faced Acbadadea alone, and our nakedness represents our return to Him in the same manner in which He sent us into this world. We should not be ashamed of our nakedness but rather remember the holiness of our creation and our humility before our Maker.

The first group will now enter the lodge, each person going clockwise until the lodge is full. A helper generally stays outside the lodge and helps with covering the doorway and lifting the covers at the door at the end of each "*quarter*." We take the purification in *four different periods*, called "quarters," each of which is ended with a break, as we come forth out of the lodge. All things are done in four in the Indian way. This reminds us of the *four directions* that complete the circle of life. . . .

Yellowtail, Crow Medicine Man and Sun Dance Chief: An Autobiography,
Thomas Yellowtail with Michael Oren Fitzgerald, 1991, pp. 107-108

The sweatlodge ceremony is an ancient sacrament of the People from time immemorial. The first four hot rocks are placed inside the pit individually and there are four different "rounds" or quarters to the ceremony.

---------------------- :: ----------------------

DROPPED EAGLE FEATHER RECOVERY RITUAL
BLACKFOOT

In one of the Grass Dances, Night Gun lost an eagle-feather from his war-bonnet: but there was tabu against the owner recovering it himself. According to custom he chose Bear Chief (Ninochkyaio), a famous warrior, who first related *four tales* of his own brave deeds and then led forth the dancers. In single file they circled the feather *three times* without touching it; but the *fourth time*, Bear Chief picked it up and gave it to Night Gun.

"Dances of the Blackfoot Indians," Walter McClintock, 1937, pp. 12-13

Four tales of bravery are recounted first and then, after four times circling the eagle feather, it is picked up. Today at pow wow gatherings across North America similar ceremonies attest to the importance of eagle feathers for the People.

———————————————— :: ————————————————

PIPE CEREMONY PRAYER
BLACKFEET

When the tobacco was burned out, the Pipe was returned to Bird Rattle, who carefully cleaned it, depositing the ashes in the *four corners of the little box* before him. We were told that this was to show that our tokens of friendship had been taken to the *four corners* of the earth by the *four winds*, and so could never be recalled. . . .

The ceremony was carried out with dignity and perfect decorum. One did not have to understand the Blackfeet language to feel the ardor, the faith, and the depth of feeling in those old hearts as they intoned their prayers. . . .

THE MEDICINE PRAYER

Oki, Si pol si me! Listen oh *Sweetgrass*!
We are about to send your spirit
To the Great Above All Person.
Your ashes we will return to the Earth.
As your spirit passes through this lodge
Let it purify, and make this place inviting
For all friendly spirits who may be near.
Purify this Medicine Lodge
And drive away all evil spirits.
Purify our hearts and bodies
And cleanse them from all taint.
Purify our minds

Crow women at parade dance ask Creator's blessings for the coming year on the Crow People of Montana

And make our thoughts toward our friends
As sweet as your fragrance.
Your spirit ascends, oh Sweetgrass!
Carry our prayers to the Great Above All Person:
As sweet incense to his nostrils
May they be acceptable to Him.

Oki, Tshak u may tah pi! I greet you, oh *Mother Earth*!
It is you who have given us our food.
You have fed and protected the green grass,
The sweet foods, the berry bushes, the trees,
With rich grass you have fed the buffalo,
The deer, the antelope, the elk and all creatures.
All these things, you have given us
That we may make pemmican to eat;
That we may have clothes to warm us;
That we may build ourselves lodges
Where our friends may visit us
And warm their hearts.
It is you who feed and protect us.
And when the Great Spirit shall call us
To follow after the buffalo,
You will take into your arms our tired bodies,
Like the ashes of this sweetgrass.
And give them rest,
We invite you, oh Earth Spirit,
To smoke with us in our Medicine Lodge.

Oki, Na to si! I salute you, oh *Sun Spirit*!
Great gift of the Great Above All Person!
It is you who first planted the seed
In the heart of Mother Earth.
It is you with your great power
Who called the seed into life,
And with light and warmth caused it to grow.
When you go away the grass dies;
The Storm Spirit leaves his lodge in the north
And rages over mountain and plains,
Seeking to devour us.

But when you return we are glad:
The earth becomes green again;
All the wild animals grow fat
Enter this lodge, oh Sun, that we may share your strength.
Our friends are before us.
They have purposed great things.
They have undertaken difficult tasks.
Make plain their trails before them.
Bring them health and strength and good fortune.
Keep their minds and hearts toward all people
As straight as this pipe stem:
Their deeds and thoughts as fragrant
As the incense of this sweetgrass;
Give their eyes the vision of the eagle
To see the needs of all people;
Their ears the alertness of the deer
To hear the cries for help and understanding:
Put into their minds the will to serve
And into their hearts the courage of the bear.
To speed to the relief of distress
Swift as the flight of an arrow;
Make them strong like the bull buffalo,
That swerves from its course
But overcomes all obstacles
That stand in its path.
As the smoke of our pipe spirals upward
So are our thoughts in prayer.
We invite you oh Sun Spirit,
And all friendly spirits
To enter this Medicine Lodge
And smoke with us the Medicine Pipe.
Kimoki, Kimoki.
Have pity on us. Have pity on us.

"Bird Rattle and the Medicine Prayer," Roland Willcomb,
Montana: The Magazine of Western History, Spring 1970, pp. 45-47

*A surprise downpour does not
interfere so much with a Blackfeet
Powwow at Browning, Montana, 1995*

In this 1930s personal prayer, four entities are addressed. Later, after the pipe ceremony, the four directions are symbolized by depositing the tobacco ashes in the four corners of the box. Here the box becomes, at least for the moment, a microcosm of the earth and the directions and the winds that come from those directions.

—————————— :: ——————————

SACRED RITUAL ITEMS
PEIGAN

Four items that were sacred and always accompanied each ceremony were the pipe, sweetgrass, the sacred red paint and sage. Honour, respect, sacredness, and all that was good were symbolized in the pipe. It cleansed the body and mind of the bad spirits surrounding the smoker's universe. Sweetgrass was used as a personal blessing during ceremonies. The burning of sweetgrass symbolized respect for the Creator. Sacred red paint was used on the face and body and all sacred objects that were associated with special ceremonies. It was the reflection of the earthly prayers for inner strength in overcoming all that was bad. A person purified body and mind with sage. It was laid beside each sacred object and was used within ceremonies as a decoration. It symbolized what was taken from Mother Earth and what must go back to her. These *four* elements were essential in each ceremony, and could be used separately when praying, either in the morning or at night.

The Peigan: A Nation in Transition, Bernadette Pard, 1986, p. 69

Most People of the northern Plains often used these four sacred items together, either personally or communally, so much that they could be considered to be a set.

—————————— :: ——————————

CEREMONIAL ETIQUETTE
PLAINS CREE

Their ceremonial number, *four*, was repeatedly used. Thus *four* smudges were built, *four* songs sung, *four* offerings made, *four* preliminary rituals held *four* puffs taken upon lighting a pipe, and so on through each part of every ritual. When *four* objects or activities could be spatially oriented, they were laid in the *four cardinal directions*.

The Plains Cree: An Ethnographic, Historical, and Comparative Study,
David Mandelbaum, 1985, p. 235

Four was so common on the prairies as a ritualistic element that it is not unusual to see it ritualized among the Plains Cree.

———————————— :: ————————————

PIPE CEREMONY SIGNIFICANCE
INTERTRIBAL

In the Indian calumet ceremony, the lighted pipe is addressed first to *each of the world quarters*, then held elevated, stem upward, so that the sun may take the first puff. And so there again we have the *four of space* and in the middle the place of the sun, the axial center, place of the axial Tree: T.S. Eliot's "still point of the turning world. . . . Where past and future are gathered."

The Way of the Seeded Earth/Part 2: Mythologies of the Primitive Planters: The Northern Americas, Joseph Campbell, 1989, p. 154

The pipe ceremony always speaks of oneness through the ritualized progression of the four directions with the circle and the favoring of action in a four-part motion. The one praying with the pipe is always physically bounded by the four directions.

Crow traditional beadwork design

Alaska

MEN'S HOUSE RITUALS
YUPIK ESKIMO

When young boys came to live in the men's house *(qasgiq)*, they entered the social and ceremonial center of the Yupik world. It was in the men's house that they would receive technical training as well as careful instruction in the rules that they must follow to become successful hunters ... the performance of these tasks had both practical and ritual implications. For instance, the water bucket must be kept full at all times to attract the seals, who were always thirsty for fresh water. Likewise, boys were required to keep the water hole constantly free of ice and to take care to drink from it only in a prone position to please "the old woman of the hole," who would subsequently send them good luck in the hunting. Here the water hole was explicitly designated the window of the world below.

In stories such as "The Boy Who Went to Live with the Seals," the male seal spirits were depicted as living in an underwater men's house from within which they could view the attention of would be hunters by watching the condition of the central smoke hole in their underwater abode. If hunters were giving them proper thought and care, the smoke hole would appear clear. If not, the hole would be covered with snow and nothing would be visible. When their visibility was obstructed in this way the seals would not emerge from their underwater world or allow themselves to be hunted.

The performance of a number of important ceremonies in the men's house dramatically reinforced the notion of the ice hole and smoke hole alike as passageways between the human and nonhuman worlds. For instance, one of the most important traditional ceremonies was the Bladder Festival, held annually to insure the rebirth of the *yuas,* or spirits of the seals, which were said to be located in their bladders. During the closing performances of the Bladder Festival, the shaman would climb out through the skylight to enter the sea, visit the seal spirits, and request their return. Likewise the inflated bladders were removed through the *qasgiq* smoke hole at the end of the festival and taken to the ice hole. There they were deflated and sent back to their underwater *qasgiq* with the request that they return the following year.

In addition to serving as a passage permitting movement and communication between the world of the hunter and the hunted, the central *qasgiq* smoke hole was also a passageway between the world of the living and the dead. For example, in the event of a human death, the body of the deceased was pulled through the smoke hole, after first being placed in each of its *four corners*. By this action the deceased, on the way from the world of the living to the dead, gradually exchanged the mortal sight that is lost at death for the supernatural clairvoyance of the spirit world. Although both the smoke hole and the ice hole were rectangular rather than round, this does not undercut the significance as spiritual eyes. One variant of the circle-dot motif is, in fact, a rectangle with *four* small *projections*, one at each corner, within which was carved a dot surrounded by concentric circles. In fact, the numbers *four* and five figure prominently in Central Yupik ritual, representing among other things the number of steps leading to the underworld land of the dead. The Bladder Festival rituals use *four corners* and *four sets* of hunting and boating gear. At one stage in its performance, the bladders were presented with tiny spears, miniature pack baskets, and other tiny tools *in sets of four* to enable them to capture the food that they were given. Painted bentwood bowls and incised ivory made for the occasion have spurs that occur in *units of four*. The reference to square or rectangular holes and the quadrangle functioning like a circle and dot may form a logical symbolic complex with this added sacred dimension.

Crossroads of Continents: Cultures of Siberia and Alaska,
William Fitzhugh & Aron Crowell (Eds.), 1988, pp. 264-265

This men's house is a gathering place which has spiritual windows between the world of human beings and the world of the animals. When certain ways are followed, animals allow themselves to be hunted. The circle dot motif which is popular in much Eskimo decoration illustrates a desire for clairvoyance, for clear seeing that is both ordinary and extraordinary, depending on which kind of seeing is needed at a given time. The circle dot design is like an eye of awareness for the beholder. The number four figures well in Yupik natural and ceremonial culture.

---------------------- :: ----------------------

ORIGIN STORY
ESKIMO

It was the time when there were no people on the earth. For *four days* the first man lay coiled up in the pod of a beach pea. On the fifth, he burst forth, falling to the ground, and stood up, a full-grown man. Feeling unpleasant, he stooped and drank from a pool of water, then felt better. Looking up, he saw a dark object approaching with a waving motion until it stopped just in front of him. It was a raven. Raven stared intently at man, raised one wing and pushed up its beak, like a mask, to the top of its head, and changed immediately into a man. Still staring and cocking its head from side to side for a better view, Raven said at last: "What are you? Whence did you come? I have never seen the likes of you." And Raven looked at Man, surprised to see that this stranger was so much like himself in shape.

Then Raven told Man to walk a few steps, again marvelling: "Whence did you come?" To this the Man replied: "I came from the pea-pod," pointing to the plant nearby. "Ah!" exclaimed Raven, "I made that vine, but did not know anything would come from it." Then Raven asked Man if he had eaten anything, to which Man replied he had taken soft stuff into him at a pool. "Well," said Raven, "you drank some water. Now wait for me here."

He drew down the mask over his face, changing again into a bird, and flew far up into the sky, where he disappeared. Again Man waited *four days*, when the Raven returned, bringing *four berries* in his claws. Pushing up his mask, Raven became a man again and held out *two* salmonberries and *two* heathberries, saying, "Here is what I have made for you. Eat them." Then Raven led Man to a creek where he took clay and formed two mountain sheep, which Man thought were very pretty. Telling Man to close his eyes, Raven drew down his mask and waved his wings *four times* over the images, which became endowed with life and bounded away. When Man saw the sheep moving away, full of life, he cried out in pleasure. Next Raven formed two other animals of clay, but because they were not fully dry when they were given life, they remained brown and white. Thus originated the tame reindeer. Raven told Man they would be very scarce. In the same way a pair of wild reindeer, or caribou, were made, being permitted to dry and turn white only on their bellies before being given life. These, Raven said, would be more common, and people could kill many of them.

Inua: Spirit World of the Bering Sea Eskimo,
William Fitzhugh & Susan Kaplan, 1982, pp. i-ii

Here is a wonderful creation story of the first man. The first woman is created a few days later. The four days of being covered up wanting to burst out of the beach pea pod, another four days waiting for Raven the Creator to return with four berries, and the flapping of the wings four times is highly significant for the People. The rest of creation then follows.

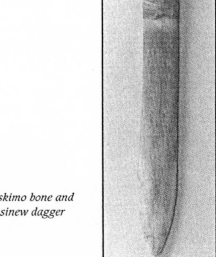

*Eskimo bone and
sinew dagger*

*Children dance in the ancient way to honor
the Virgin Mary, while the pastor and a visiting
Lakota Catholic priest look on*

MESOAMERICA CULTURAL AREA

NEQUATEQUILIZTLI (CHILD'S WATER CEREMONY)
AZTEC

Aztec parents sent for a *tonalpouhqui* ("he who can discern the fortune of those who are born"), who consulted his book, the *Tonalamatl,* or book of destiny, to determine the sign of the child's birth to see if the day was propitious or unlucky. *Four days* later the child was baptized; if the day of birth was unlucky, custom allowed for a religious fiction that postponed the ceremony until a more favorable date.

In the third section of the Codex Mendoza we find an account of the ceremonial bath and baptism *four days* after a child's birth. It describes how

> ... the midwife took the naked baby in her arms and took it out to the courtyard of the mother's house ... and the midwife bathed the creature ... and at first when they took the baby out to bathe it, if it was a boy they put its insignia in his hand, and the insignia was the instrument with which the baby's father practiced his military art or a trade ... and if the creature was a female the insignia with which they took her out to bathe was a distaff and spindle and a little basket and broom, the things she would practice when she reached the age. And the boy's umbilical cord, together with a shield and an arrow ... was taken to the place where war

was waged against enemies, and buried in the earth. . . . The girl's umbilical cord was buried underneath the *metate,* a millstone used to grind cornmeal.

This was followed by a banquet at which guests strewed food and *pulque* upon the sacred fire, which had been lit since the beginning of labor as an offering to the ancient god of fire; after the banquet the old men and women could devote themselves to the pleasure of drinking, after which the midwife gave the baby its name.

Boys were often named after the date of their birth: One cane, Two flower, Seven deer; or named after an animal, as in Nezahualcoyotl (hungry coyote); or named after a remembered forebear or some present-day event. Girls' names were based upon the word *xóchitl,* meaning flower; for instance, Matlalxóchitl (green flower), Quiauhxóchitl (rain flower).

Citing Sahagún (Bk. VI, Ch. XXXII), Soustelle describes with certain variations—while maintaining its essence—the ceremony of baptism with *four rites of water,* in which the midwife deposited a few drops of water in the child's mouth and said:

"See with what you will live upon the earth, so that you might grow and flourish, receive it." Then with her wet hand she touched the child's breast so as to cleanse and purify its heart.

Then she sprinkled several drops upon its head while reciting:

". . . receive and take the water of the lord of the world, that this clear blue celestial water might enter your body and live there."

And finally she washed the child's entire body while reciting a blessing to ward off all evil. After this, again *four times,* the midwife presented the child to the sky while invoking the sun.

Finally, she begged of the gods that the boy should be a valiant warrior. The last two parts of the ceremony were omitted for girls.

The Pre-Columbian Child, Max Shein, 1992, pp. 29-30

This ancient water ceremony, which has some similarities to Christian baptism, was obviously an important rite for the People in pre-Contact times. The fourfold use of water was expressed in different ways: bathing, giving a drink, touching with a wet hand, sprinkling, and a final full bathing of the child.

—————————————— :: ——————————————

SACRED WATER VISION
SERI

With three other medicine men I went to the Sacred Cave of the Big Mountain. For *four days* before we visited it, and for the *four days* we were there, we ate no food and drank no water. When we got inside it was all dark, and all the time we were there it was like night. We lay down together where it was smooth and slept for *four days* and *four nights*, after which the Spirit which lived there came to see us.

He lives in a little cave inside the big cave. I could see through him when he walked toward us, yet I was conscious he was coming closer and closer, until he was a hand's length from my face. It was dark as night, but I could see him. His arms were stretched out and his hands were hanging down, and from their tips water dripped. It was like ice. He came to me very slowly, and held his fingers over my head. He came again and spread his hands over me, and from the finger-tips I caught water in my palms.

This water is very strong medicne. I give it to a sick man or woman and in three days they are well. If you make this trip to the Holy Cave you never get old like other men. I have none of the holy water now, but if anyone gets sick I can go and get some. Sometimes the color of the water changes.

From his *first* finger the water comes clear.
From his *second* finger the water comes yellow.
From his *third* finger the water comes red.
From his *fourth* finger the water comes blue.

The Last of the Seris: The Aboriginal Indians of Kino Bay, Sonora, Mexico, Dane Coolidge & Mary Coolidge, 1973, p. 94

It is interesting to note that these four water colors are the same as the Seri Creator's wind direction colors. Four-day fasting both before and after entering the sacred cave expresses the emptying of oneself in order to be filled by the divine presence so that one becomes a fitting vessel for the healing of others.

Costa Rican
crocodile

CARIBBEAN CULTURAL AREA

Travesia Taína night-time dance (Jayuya National Indigenous Festival), Puerto Rico

ORIGINS STORY
TAÍNO

Mythologies of the Hero Twins are prominent throughout the world, but emphatically in the Americas, where the two appear under many guises; in cosmogonic myths as the Sun and Moon or, as in the Navaho legend Where the Two Came to Their Father, as the twin sons of the celestial lights. In that Navaho tale, the two, when fully empowered, become *four*, representing the *four quarters* of the earth and sky. In the following Taino legend, the Exploits of the *Four* Twins of One Birth, recorded by Pane c. 1494, the mythological twins are *four* throughout.

THE EXPLOITS OF THE *FOUR* TWINS OF ONE BIRTH

There was a man called Yaya, whose name we do not know. He had a son called Yaya-el, who wanted to kill him, and so, was exiled. For *four* months he was exiled, after which his father slew him, packed the bones in a mortuary urn, and hung the urn from the roof, where for some time it remained.

Then Yaya one day said to his wife, "I would like to see our son, Yaya-el." She was pleased. So, taking down the urn, he turned it upside down to have a look at the bones, but what fell out were fishes, large and small. And seeing that the bones had turned into fish, the couple ate them. . . .

When one day Yaya had left his house to go to inspect his gardens, the *four* sons arrived of a woman who had died in giving birth to them.

Itaba Cahubaba, she was called, The Blood-bathed Old [Earth] Mother. She had been cut open and the *four* taken out. The first was called Deminán Caracaracol; the other three were nameless. And when Yaya had departed from the house, these *four* entered to get the mortuary urn. Only Deminán dared to take it down, and all were gorging themselves on the fishes it contained when Yaya was heard returning. In haste to hang the urn up, they hung it badly. The urn fell, broke, and out poured so much water that it flooded the earth. Many fish came too. The origin of the sea was from that urn. And the brothers, terrified, fled.

They came to Bayamanaco's door and perceived that the old man had been cultivating cassava. "Bayamanaco," they said, "is our grandfather." And determining to learn from him the art of preparing food from that plant, Deminán decided to go in. . . .

Now when Deminán entered Bayamanaco's house and presented his request, the old man put a finger to his nose and blew at him a charge that struck his back between the shoulders. It was full of the powdered tobacco that he had been using that day as snuff, and when Deminán returned to his brothers, his back was in great pain. He told them what had happened. They looked and saw that a tumor had

appeared. It was swelling to such a size that Deminán was on the point of death. The brothers were unable to open it, until they gave it a blow with a stone axe, and out came a living female tortoise. So in that place the *four* built their home and reared the tortoise.

The brothers, . . . having ended their cosmic escapades, settled down at last in a definite place, built a durable house, and set themselves to the task of engendering mankind. . . . They had acquired fire, cassava, and tobacco, and had passed from the primitive stages of a wandering foraging band to the position of a settled agricultural community with a situated

Giving thanks at the river

population, liberated living conditions, and customs relatively advanced. They had passed . . . 'from the raw to the cooked,' from the
natural to the civilized state. As the *four* children of Mother Earth and
as personifications of the *winds* of the *quarters*, they were now to
become the patriarchs and civilizers of mankind—the ancestral
founders of the Taíno culture.

*The Way of the Seeded Earth/Part 3: Mythologies of the Primitive Planters:
The Middle and South Americas,* Joseph Campbell, 1989, pp. 314-315
Originally published in *Mitología y Artes Prehispanicas
de las Antillas,* José Arrom, 1989

*The story here tells of the four brothers who are really the winds that
emanate from the four directions. The myth is interesting because it
also mentions some of the life staples of the Caribbean cultures: fish,
tortoises, cassava and tobacco, the sea and its treasures.*

Giving thanks for the gift of water in the Taino way

SOUTH AMERICA CULTURAL AREA

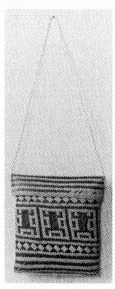

Piaroa woven bag

CURING CEREMONY
MAPUCHE

While addressing herself to anyone in the room the shaman went outdoors to her *rewe* and offered a prayer to her *pillan*. This ended the curing ceremony. Before we left her, however, she gave each of us a bottle of water from the herbal tray and told us to drink a little of it morning and night for the next *four days*.

The medicine was bitter. We poured it on the ground on the *fourth day* and returned the empty bottles to the shaman, feeling more than a little dishonest. Before the month was out, my wife and I moved away to take up residence on another reservation farther south and did not see the shaman again for many months. In the meantime my wife became pregnant and had a miscarriage. When we finally related this to the shaman she immediately said that we had not followed her directions. Before leaving Chile I was able to see her once again and tell her that my wife was at last carrying a child and had returned to our country. The shaman said that she was happy for us. She also said that her power was so strong that it worked even though we did not follow her advice carefully. She suggested that I make her a gift of a bag of sugar because payment, in these circumstances, always assured success.

The Mapuche Indians of Chile, Louis Faron, 1968, pp. 74-75

The shaman's Rewe *is a carved and notched pole upon which she or he stands while drumming and singing the prayers. It is a symbolic center of the world, and perched from there, the shaman leads ceremonies. Units of four days enter into the Mapuche ritual way of doing things.*

SYSTEM OF FOUR
WAYAPÍ

Wayapí had no numbers beyond *four*. They had a glorious way of indicating 'a lot' or 'a very large number' which was to hold out all the fingers and thumbs of both hands and say a long word that you might translate: 'All-our-hands-together-very-good'. But four was where the strict computation stopped.

You might have thought that they would at least have gone on to five, given the digits on our hands, or even get as far as ten to account for all our fingers and thumbs. But it's not an accident that stopping counting at four is found all over the world. Four is a kind of completeness. And Wayapaí indicated it like this: stick out your fingers of one hand, fold in your thumb, and separate your fingers two and two, like a sort of heavy V sign. 'Two and two make four' we say, making it sound like a platitude, but in fact we're at the heart of human logic. . . .

It's no accident that Pythagoreans associated the number four with harmony and justice. It's no accident that in the psychoanalysis of Carl Gustav Jung those mandalas, the circles divided into four that people dreamed or designed, were seen as expressions of the person's striving after the unity of self and a sense of completeness, just as they were used in Buddhist traditions of meditation. Binary systems, systems of twos, dual organizations, great elaborations of contrasts like the *yin* and *yang* of the Dao, systems of left and right, the oppositions and contradictions of Marxist thought; all these seem amateur in the face of thinking in fours. . . .

It is no accident that Wayapaí numbers stop at four. The number four is fundamental and elemental.

Getting to Know Waiwai: An Amazonian Ethnography,
Alan Tormaid Campbell, 1995, pp. 119, 137

In the lifestyle of this tropical rainforest People, things made a lot sense, especially human social organization, when they are expressed in units of four.

———————————— :: ————————————

Vase design, Chimbote, Peru

RATTLE DESCRIPTION
UMUTINA

The young men from the Umutina village on the upper Paraguay have taken up their position in two lines. Those in the back row have an animal skin hanging down behind and are wearing bunches of foliage in their ears. The ones in front are dressed in palm-leaf skirts. There is a palm strip covering their eyes. The rattles . . . are made from calabashes or pottery. In his raised right hand the master of ceremonies is holding an instrument made from a *cujete,* the Crescentia fruit so widely found in Brazil. . . . As they have no stalks, a wooden rod is usually driven through the calabash to provide a secure grip. The stem is often attached with wax . . . *four holes* are bored at the place where the handle is to be attached and it is tied on with thread or sinews. The rattles, which are meant to exorcise and drive out harmful spirits, are often adorned with feathers. In many tribes the feathers are regarded as the soul of the bird assisting the shaman. The contents of the rattles are very varied—dry seed grains, gravel, pieces of shell, etc. The differences in the material used play no part as a rule—the only decisive factor is the sound effect. But in certain cases the rattling objects inside the capsule are credited with magic powers, especially if they are the gift of a mighty wizard or some other being with supernatural abilities.

Music of the Americas: An Illustrated Music Ethnology of the Eskimo and American Indian Peoples, Paul Collaer (Ed.), 1973, p. 164

This is a description of a circular rattle of the Bororo People who live in the Brazilian Mato Grosso. Fourness plays into the construction of their spherical rattles.

—————————————— :: ——————————————

MEANING OF SACRED CACTUS
INTERTRIBAL

Shamans specify *four* "kinds" of the cactus, distinguished by the number of ribs: those with *four* ribs are rare and considered to be the most potent, with very special super-natural powers, since the *four ribs* represent *the "four winds" and the "four roads."*

The cactus is known in northern coastal Peru as San Pedro, in the northern Andean area as Huachuma, and in Bolivia as Achuma; the Bolivian term *chumarse* ("to get drunk") is derived from Achuma. Aguacolla and Gigantón are its Ecuadorian names. . . .

Four-ribbed cacti . . . are considered
to be very rare and very lucky . . . to have special properties
because they correspond
to the *"four winds"* and the *"four roads,"*
supernatural powers associated with **the cardinal points**. . . .

Plants of the Gods: Their Sacred, Healing and Hallucinogenic Powers,
Richard Evans Schultes & Albert Hofmann, 1992, pp. 155 & 157

Whether it be species of cactus or the "fourness of ribs," or the four winds or the four roads, Andean symbolic reference to the four directions cannot be easily dismissed.

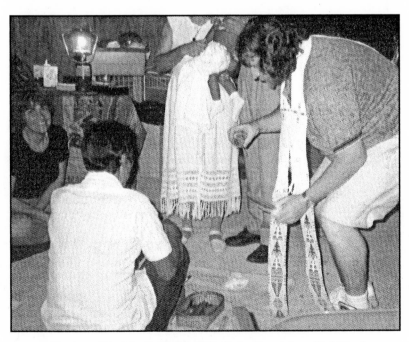

*Blessing of Huaykuni, "Spirit of the Forest," one-year-old child of
Santiago and Nanci Obispo of Puerto Ayacucho, Venezuela,
by Shaman Joseluis Piaroa and Father Scott McCarthy*

INTERCULTURAL
CULTURAL
AREA

Arapaho youth at St. Stephen's Mission, Wind River Reservation, Wyoming

FOUR RACES OF HUMANKIND
ALGONQUIN/MESTIZA

THE ORIGINAL PLAN OF CREATOR, LIFE-GIVER

We are One People, on One Earth;
All life is sacred; The Earth is sacred;
We must cherish and protect our Mother Earth,
Father Sky above and Sacred Oceans [Waters] below;
The *Four Races of Humankind* will live in
Harmony with all Living Things, so that as many
as Seven Generations to follow each Generation—
Our Future Generations—will live.
The Seven Eagle Feathers represent these Future
Generations and our Sacred Ceremonies.
These Sacred Feathers carry our prayers to God,
Whom we call Grandfather, Wakan-Tanka,
Tunkashila; That All Our Relations may live.
It is One Prayer:

PEACE

Through the Eye of the Feather: Native American Visions,
Gail Tuchman, 1994, p. 94

338

Elaine Bluebird Woman Reyna is known to many of the People in California, especially those near San Juan Bautista and Monterey. Like some people today, she interprets that there are basically four races: black, white, red, and yellow, and these (as well as any others) are called to live in harmony within the earth circle. She calls for one Earth—one People. It is her own special vision that is to be shared with everyone. Perhaps the anthropologists would differ with her as to the exact number of races in the world, but nevertheless, she prays daily for a greater unity and healing of all people on Mother Earth. As I interviewed her, she preferred the more inclusive word "Waters" to be used rather than "Oceans" that is used in the original quoted text.

———————————— ∷ ————————————

SACRED RECITATION
INTERTRIBAL

Song and dance are intrinsic to religion among Indians. Words—chanted, sung, or spoken—are valued by an Indian primarily for the reaction they produce within himself rather than for any effect they might have on others. The first stage of Indian ritual is almost always the rise of the singer on his own song to a plane of power—a place of contact with the forces that move the universe. In many tribes this power is obtained by reciting words or sounds *four times*, four often being a sacred number. The words and sounds are only the small visible aspect of a far greater mystery, which lies beneath speech.

Ritual of the Wind: North American Indian Ceremonies, Music and Dance,
Jamake Highwater, 1984, p. 119

The sacredness of the number 4 is manifested in the ceremonies of many Native Peoples of the Americas. Sometimes it is related to honoring the four directions in some way; at other times it has to do with the four seasons; while in other instances it might have to do with the recognition of a four-part universe, either four levels or quadrant sections. Always it was and is understood that an aspect of divine or sacred presence is somehow related to a particular aspect of the cosmos.

———————————— ∷ ————————————

INTER-RELATEDNESS OF COLOR AND FOURNESS
INTERTRIBAL

... it is notable that ... for the American Indian, numbers possess strongly a geometrical significance. They are symbols of order, and especially of the order of space, rather than indicators of class or quantity; and to certain of them there attaches also the glamor of fortune or fate, as reflected alike in tale and ritual. In the main, it is the number *four* that to the red man carried the notion of luck or charm which the European associates more readily with three; and this luckiness of four is perhaps because this most geometrical of all the numbers—symbol of the plane of Earth—accords with the vividly spatial and visual form which nature takes on for the Indian's eyes. *Four-part* and *cruciform emblems, crosses* of every style and *quartered designs* are extremely common in Indian art, giving expression to the quaternities of his thought, and in his metaphysical moments the whole realm of distinguishable things is apt to be organized in fours or in multiples of fours. The kinds of living things, animals, birds, insects, plants are organized into fours; so are the meteorologicals, the winds and the stars and the heavenly bodies; so the hills and waters; and so also the storeys or regions of the world above and the world below, which for many of the native people are four. But perhaps the most significant and individual symbolism of all is that of color. Here again a fourfold order is established, each cardinal direction having its own color (not invariable for all tribes or societies), while the above is the realm of the union of the radical colors and the below the realm of their deprivation. Such primarily symbolic colors are associated with the living kinds of plants and animals, with beads and with minerals, and intricately with ceremony and costume. ...

The World's Rim: Great Mysteries of the North American Indians,
Hartley Burr Alexander, 1953, p. 11

Native cultures are rich in so many ways; undoubtedly the use of four is a unifying factor for many of them.

Ceremonial Combinations

All things considered. . . .

"All Things Considered, " Gilbert K. Chesterton

Indigenous People have always been familiar with their place in the "grand scheme of things." Their sense of space and place has always been made manifest in their ceremonial relationship to the earth, the sun, the moon, and stars. These ceremonies of spatiality, often celebrated at equinoxes and solstices, are also observed at other times, but always in relationship to the rest of creation.

As one observes or participates in a Native American ceremony, one often notices the recognition of the four directions by means of voiced prayer or ritual or dance while the People are gathered in a circle. It has been this way from ancient times. Sometimes the ceremony is embellished by a four-fold doing of something important. Even present-day pow wows (Native gatherings) are not without their sacred elements, though often they may be less obvious to the casual visitor.

For instance, at pow wows there are different tribal customs for ceremonially retrieving an accidently dropped eagle feather. When it is noticed, all usual activity is postponed as four men, often war veterans, surround the feather in four directions. A prayer is offered and after three feigned attempts to pick it up, it is actually retrieved on the fourth attempt. A cry of victory is often heard and the pow wow announcer then allows for an instruction for all the gathered People concerning the sacredness of the eagle feather and the ancient ways. Though each tribe does the ceremony a bit differently, these are the essential aspects of it. But the gathering in a circle, the honoring of the four directions, and the feather being picked up on the fourth attempt are all sacred signs that are in harmony with one another. There are literally hundreds of examples of this similar ritual behavior to be appreciated. I include here a representative sampling of these combinations.

Wyoming beaver lodge

Four Directions & Circles

FOUR DIRECTIONS
& CIRCLES

We put things in order—God does the rest. Lay an iron bar east and west, it is not magnetized. Lay it north and south and it is.

Horace Mann

With this combination we go back in time to observe how in the Southeast the ancient Natchez and Cherokee pipe ceremonies very often included the whole village as they quite dramatically circled about the sacred area or ritually passed the holy pipe among themselves. In this their directional awareness was primary. On the Great Plains a selection of Pawnee poetry of the sky magnificently recounts the People's important connection for their spiritual life. Then a modern day spiritual leader of Northwestern Yakima and Cowlitz ancestry speaks to us of the medicine wheel, while way down in Ecuadorean South America, the Canelos Quichua share with us their own special cosmology.

John Plainfeather and daughter at roping practice. Even here the circle is evident

WOODLANDS CULTURAL AREA

CIRCULAR AND FOUR DIRECTION IMAGERY
ANISHNABE

In other Anishnabe instances, circular designs were associated with direction, the *four cardinal points* on the axes which defined the *circle,* or Medicine Wheel. For Anishnabek, the *four directions* symbolize concepts which are fundamental to spirituality. They take many forms, sometimes emphasizing the sectoring of the *circle,* sometimes the directions themselves or those in-between the cardinal points, and sometimes representing floral petals, hearts, or elements of the natural world to cite only a few examples. Occasionally, the *four directions* merge with other symbols. . . .

Within Anishnabe music, the symbolism of directions is represented not just in instrument design and decoration but also in some of the processes of construction and use . . . the four curved wooden posts, each placed at a cardinal point, and cross-lacing, especially on frame drums. . . .

While the Medicine Wheel and its four-direction symbolism has been widely discussed at Elders Conferences, and in both scholarly and "popular" publications by both Native and non-Native writers, two aspects rarely mentioned are the *motion* of the wheel and instances when the directions are *unequal.*

For Anishnabek, there are patterns which visually represent the *four directions* in motion. In some cases, however, this aspect is represented by the fact that the directional axes in design are not quite aligned with the cardinal points . . . the force of the cardinal directions may be so great that ceremonial gestures (within the pipe ceremony, for example) may be performed a little to the side of North, South, East, or West. By analogy, the alignment of patterns on the membrane of a drum or the position of a snare may be slightly off-axis.

In the non-judgmental ideal of Native discourse, we have most often heard that the different peoples around the circle are not hierarchically arranged, nor are different stages in the cycle of life. Each is valued and necessary. There are , however, some contexts in which the directions are not equal. Drumsticks which are made from two pieces of wood at right angles may represent one direction as longer and more powerful than the other three.

> *Visions of Sound: Musical Instruments of First Native Communities in Northeastern America*, Beverly Diamond, Sam Cronk & Franziska Von Rosen, 1994, pp. 130, 132

Even in construction techniques the circle and the cardinal directions are not forgotten. The People have always carefully bodied forth their age-old heritage in such ways that it mirrors or describes the natural order of creation.

———————————— ⊕ ————————————

PIPE CEREMONY SIGNIFICANCE
OJIBWA

The pipe ceremony is not merely a framework for an address to an unknown God. It is a sacramental act of communion with the Great Consensus.

Seated in a *circle*—the form which symbolizes the unity and wholeness of the cosmos itself—the participants invoke the two bases of existence, Grandfather Sky and Mother (or Grandmother) Earth. Then they invoke the spirit powers of the *four directions*, the Grandfathers who preside over birth, growth, old age, and death of nature and human beings. The keeper of the pipe points the stem in *all the directions*. Then the participants pass it from mouth to mouth around the *circle*. The communion is consummated in the life-breath of the participants. . . .

Yet it is misleading to speak as if the individual participant's experience of communion were most important. The pipe ceremony is above all the group's celebration of itself in its aspiration to be a small consensus. Although this act can be celebrated on a variety of occasions, its most legitimate use is as a prelude to a council or conference. The pipe ceremony is the group's celebration of its own automony, its power to determine, as a group, its course of action. . . .

Shall We Gather at the River?, George Van der Goes Ladd,
1986, pp. 70-71

The author, a United Church of Canada minister, spent a lot of time with the Anishinabe band on the Peguis Indian Reserve in Manitoba. It is an area that was once part of the great Métis (mixed blood) territory, whose inhabitants in the last century sought independence from Canada. Many pipe ceremonies, replete with circular and directional symbolism, helped the People to draw closer to each other, especially in the more difficult times of transition.

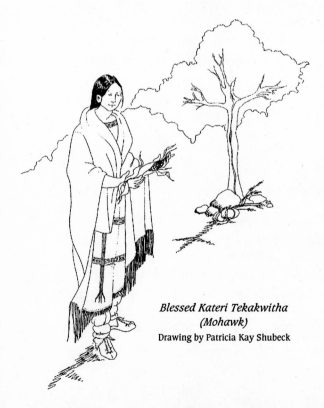

*Blessed Kateri Tekakwitha
(Mohawk)*
Drawing by Patricia Kay Shubeck

SOUTHEAST CULTURAL AREA

PIPE CEREMONY
NATCHEZ

The day the Ambassadors are to make their appearance, all the Nation assembles. The Masters of Ceremony conduct the Princes, Chiefs of the Villages, and Old Chiefs of quality, to special seats near that of the great Chief. And when the Ambassadors arrive, they stop and chant the song of peace. The ambassage consists ordinarily of thirty men, followed by six women. Six of the handsomest men, with the finest voices, march in front, followed by the rest, all chanting and marking time with the *sicicouet* [which is an Algonquian word, denoting the rattle or small drum commonly used by shamans for their incantations].

When the great Chief invites this party to approach and they advance, those bearing the calumets come chanting and dancing with marvelous agility, now *circling about each other*, now presenting themselves frontwise, and always with the most violent movements and extraordinary contortions. When they have entered the great Chief's circle, dancing about the chair on which he is seated, they stroke him with their calumets, from his feet even to his head, and then retire, returning to the others of their company, where they fill with tobacco one of their calumets and with one of their number holding in hand a flame, advance all together before the Chief, and, upon lighting the pipe, direct the first puff toward the *Heavens*, the second toward the *Earth*, and the rest *around the horizon*, after which without further ceremony, they offer the pipe to the Prince and the other Chiefs.

This ceremony concluded, the Ambassadors in token of the alliance rub their hands over the Chief's belly and then all over their own

349

bodies, after which they set their calumets on a small forked stick before his throne, while the one especially charged with the representation of his Nation delivers an address that lasts for about an hour. This finished, a sign is made to the visitors to be seated on benches near the great Chief, who responds with a discourse about equal length; after which the Master of Ceremonies lights the great calumet of peace and offers this to the visitors. Puffing, they all swallow their smoke, and the great Chief then inquires whether all have arrived safely (which is to say, whether all are in good health), whereupon those who are seated near the Visitors, one after another, perform the same courteous office, after which they are conducted to the cabin prepared for them, where they are feasted. . . .

After this ceremony, which is repeated, night and morning, for four days, the great Chief returns to his cabin, and when then he pays his last visit to the Ambassadors, these set a stake before his feet about which they seat themselves, and the Warriors of the Nation, dressed in all their finery, dance around this, each striking it in turn while recounting his exploits. There follows then a presentation of such gifts to the Ambassadors as kettles, hatchets, guns, powder, and shot.

The Way of the Seeded Earth/Part 2: Mythologies of the Primitive Planters: The Northern Americas, Joseph Campbell, 1989, p. 235

The preceding narrative, recorded by the Jesuit priest Lepetit in 1730, describes a calumet ceremony which took place during a peace-making visit by ambassadors of another tribe. Note the use of song and dance and stylized sacred movement with the great pipes.

PIPE CEREMONY
CHEROKEE

At this dance, we saw something we had not seen before—ritual smoking. In the wintertime and at monthly meetings, ritual smoking is done during the day, but in the summer it is done in the evening at the monthly meeting and prior to the stomp dance. The ground chief usually prepares the pipe, but he was absent on this occasion, and Robert Bush did it. The pipe and a bag of tobacco had been placed on the mound near the upright iron rod. As Robert said a reverent prayer, he picked the pipe and bag up, filled the pipe, then lighted it with a coal taken from the fire. While he did this, the members remained seated in their clan beds, but at the conclusion of the prayer they quietly arose and began to form a huge *circle* in the square. Members of one clan led off, indicating that they are the main clan at the ground, and as they passed the next clan bed its members fell in behind them, and so on until the beds were empty and a single line had formed around the square. Robert stood to the *east* of the fire, and smoked seven puffs on the pipe while holding the bowl level and pointing *east*. He then *rotated the pipe in a counterclockwise movement* and handed it to the person behind him, who moved up to take his place. The pipe itself never moved from its position. Instead, the *circle of people moved slowly counterclockwise* until everyone who wished to smoke had come to where the pipe was and smoked it, including women and children. When the pipe ran out of tobacco, Robert refilled it and relit it just as he had at the beginning of the ceremony.

Some of the people drew in deep drafts, and you could see the smoke rising very clearly from their mouths. Others, especially children, drew short drafts. After each person had smoked his seven puffs, he turned to his right and resumed his place in the circle. The last man returned the pipe to Robert, and Robert turned to face the fire. He knocked the pipe's remaining ashes onto the fire as a sacrifice, said another prayer, and returned the pipe to its prior position on the ash mound. The line of people walked counterclockwise until the clan members had reached their beds. They stood here until the chief said another prayer, then they sat down, and the ritual smoking was completed.

While it is often noisy at the ground, with everyone visiting, dancing, running, yelling, and talking, it was extremely quiet during the tobacco ritual. Even the children kept silent, and it became a truly beautiful moment. Everyone knew this was tobacco that had been ritually treated by the medicine men, that it was supposed to cement peace and friendship, and that it would bring good luck to the people who belonged to the ground.

The Cherokee People: The Story of the Cherokees from Earliest Origins to Contemporary Times, Thomas Mails, 1992, pp. 312-314

Once again we see ritual circling, but it is in a counterclockwise direction. The people smoking move more often than the pipe actually does. Among many other tribes it is the pipe that moves around the People and not vice-versa.

*Pre-Columbian
ceramic bowl*

SOUTHWEST CULTURAL AREA

BLESSING POEM
YAQUI

The clear moon arcs
over the sleeping Three Sisters,
like the conchos that string
the waist of a dancer.

With low thunder, with red bushes smooth
as water stones, with the blue-arrowed rain,
its dark feathers curving down
and the white-tailed running deer—
the desert sits, a maiden with obsidian eyes,
brushing the star-tasseled dawn from her lap.

It is the month of Green Corn;
It is the dance, grandfather, of open blankets.

> I am singing to you
> I am making the words
> > shake like bells

Owl Woman is *blessing all directions.*
This corn—with its leaves that are yellow
in the sun, with the green of small snakes,
with its Mother Earth's hair and even teeth,
with its long leaves, its dark stem,
and the small blue bird that drinks from its roots—

you are shaking purple in dusk,
you are climbing the rims of the world.

Old grandfather, we are combing your hair
for blue stars and black moons.
With white corn, with cloud feathers,
you are crossing dawn with the Dream Runners.

    I am closing your blanket
    I am making the words
    speak in *circles*.

"Red Rock Ceremonites," Anita Endrezze in *Carriers of
the Dream Wheel: Contemporary Native American Poetry,*
Duane Niatum (Ed.), 1975, p. 164-165

*This poem by Anita Endrezze entitled "Red Rock Ceremonies" alludes to
both directional and circular symbolism. One can almost see the
dancers moving about in one great prayer of thanksgiving.*

*Navajo child grinding
corn with cradleboard*

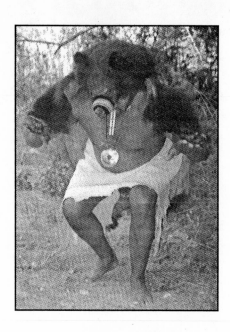

CALIFORNIA CULTURAL AREA

BEAR DANCE
CHUMASH

As the dance began, *Samala's* companion used split sticks of elderberry to keep time as he sang, *"Huyuhuyuna. Huyuhuyuna. Huyuhuyuna. Huyunuyuna."* When he had finished, *Samala* was announced by a clown who cleared a path for him and recited:

"Greetings, fellow countrymen, kinfolk and everybody! I beg of you: the bear will enter to dance, bringing with him all the fierceness of the wild, so if anyone even makes a noise, the bear could pounce on him and bite him."

Entering the ring from the **south**, *Samala* crouched down and imitated a frightened bear. He then pointed his feather staff or *plumero* to the **east**. In his left hand, he held a headdress ringed with feathers and topped by long magpie plumes. Three singers accompanied him with turtle shell rattles with asphaltum and filled with pebbles. They sang:

Listen to what I am about to sing.
Listen to my breathing on high.
Listen to my stamping.
I tear up the ground.
Listen to my groaning.

Look! Listen!
    He grunts on high.
The ground shakes.

In the night he makes a noise
　　like a thunderclap,
'I yaka mi ha mi.

Clear the way!
Clear away the dirt which obstructs
　　when I step forth with pride.
The feathers fold up.
I am a creature of power.
I stand up and begin to walk to
　　the mountain tops, to *every*
　　corner of the world.
I am a creature of power.

*Ohlone people of the
Monterey area*

Samala had painted his face and he wore a short grass skirt. From a cord around his neck hung a bear paw, an honor reinforced by his having incised bear-paw petroglyphs at a remote shrine which he visited only at the winter solstice. He *circled the dance area* and shook his *plumero* in *all corners*. If anyone got out of order, he lunged at them, sometimes biting them on the shoulder.

As a dancer, *Samala* had been initiated as an *'antap* and was considered knowledgeable in astronomical, pictographic, and datura lore. He was also a faithful Catholic, having been baptized and buried with church ceremony.

The Temescals of Arroyo Conejo, Thomas Maxwell, 1982, p. 124-125

Samala, also known as Rafael Solares, not only was a dancer, but was a very helpful informant concerning his People's ways. The four corners of the world, places that the directions pass through, were an essential part of this danced story.

————————————— ⊕ —————————————

TRANSFORMATION STORY
WINTU

Many people came into existence somewhere. They dwelt long and no one knows what they did. And then one of them dreamed. So he said, "I dreamed; of a world wind I dreamed." And they said, "You have

Ohlone territory shoreline near Monterey, California

dreamed something bad." Then they all dwelt there a long, long time. And after that it blew, and the wind increased. They had an earth lodge, so they said, "Let us go into the earth lodge. The world is going bad." So they all went in. And they said, "Let all the people together enter the earth lodge; the world is going bad." So at noon they all entered the earth lodge. Then it blew. It blew terribly. Every kind of tree fell down *westward*. And the one who had dreamed, that man who had dreamed, stood outside and did not come into the earth lodge. Standing outside he spoke, "It is raining, O you people, and the trees are falling *westward* all at once." And he went on speaking, "The water is coming; the earth will be destroyed." And all the houses outside were blown away; none remained. Then, coming into the earth lodge, he said, "It must be that my dream is coming true. I dreamed of wind, and I must have been right about the destruction of the world." He stood alone, leaning against the post of the earth lodge. And all the people went. He remained thus for a while and then the post he was leaning on came loose. Then this person went; the one who had dreamed went last after all the people were gone. So the world was destroyed and water alone was left.

Thus it was for some time, and then He-who-is-above (Olelbes) looked down from the *north*. He looked for a long time everywhere, *west,* and *east,* and *south*; he looked all around in a *circle*. And in the *north,* right in the middle of the water, something was barely visible. Then while he was looking, it moved to the *west* and to the *east*. He could scarcely see it. Then it seemed to him as if it swam around a little. It was lying there before him on the bedrock. He-who-is-above knew. It was a lamprey which lay there all alone. That lamprey had come first into existence, and lay there alone. In the meanwhile, there on the rocks, lay a little mud. The water lay there long, very long, no one knows how long it lay there, and finally the water began to recede, to go down *south* and as it receded it turned into a multitude of creeks. Then at last there lay a little earth that had come into being, and that earth turned into all kinds of trees.

This is all. It has been transformed.

"Wintu Myths," *California University Publications in American Archaeology and Ethnology*, Cora DuBois & Dorothy Demetracopoulou, 1965, pp. 286-287

In this recreation of earth we are able to notice the importance of the directions. Creator sees things from the point of view of the directions and the circle. It is as if these aspects of cosmic life were purposefully remembered once again in this act of creation.

A reconstructed but active Wintu tribal roundhouse near Wintun, California

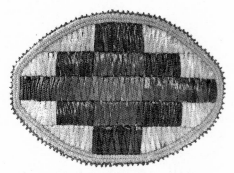

*Shoshone-Bannock porcupine quillwork
belt buckle from Fort Hall Reservation
near Pocatello, Idaho*

PLAINS CULTURAL AREA

SKY POEM
PAWNEE

CIRCLE OF THE SKY

Remember, remember the *circle* of the Sky
the stars and the brown eagle
the supernatural winds
breathing night and day,
for the *four directions*
Remember, remember the great life of the sun
breathing on the earth,
it lies upon the earth
to bring our life upon the earth
life covering the earth.

*By the Power of Their Dreams: Songs, Prayers and Sacred Shields
of the Plains Indians*, Maureen Mansell, 1994

This contemporary poem celebrates the larger cosmos from the perspective of the poet in such a way that circularity and directionality are special components.

358

PLATEAU CULTURAL AREA

Directional prayer with eagle feathers

MEDICINE WHEEL
YAKIMA/COWLITZ

I have presented a basic comparative study revealing relationships between my Native American spirituality and that of Judaism and Christianity, with a little sprinkling of a few other ancient concepts. The *Medicine Wheel* encourages you to continue this exciting journey by adding insights from your spiritual life experience, whether that may be of Christianity, Buddhism, Islam, or any other. We need to continue looking for the many other relationships that exist. The Creator has revealed herself to all people in all cultures throughout the entire catalogue of the human race.

The Medicine Wheel also urges you to bring your own personal life experiences to it. Allow the Wheel to act as a mirror to this diary of events. These personal life experiences may come from your own rites of passage, or from encounters in your family life. They might be experiences you have entertained in your larger circle of social awareness.

Allow the Medicine Wheel to become a daily mirror to your life. Begin each day pondering the teachings of the Wheel as you turn to the *East* and begin your prayer time to the Creator in each of the *Four Directions*.

Always attempt to remain well centered as you endeavor to walk the Red Road. Allow yourself to soar high spiritually or theologically as well as philosophically, and yet be ever mindful of the necessity to remain well grounded.

Medicine Wheels: Ancient Teachings for Modern Times,
Roy I. Wilson, 1994, p. 160

The writer is both Native and Christian (a retired Methodist minister) and knows well both spiritual traditions. And yet he is also open to sharing his sacred ways with people of other faiths. This is a good thing.

The mystery and gift of a circle of fire

Amazon

SYMBOLIC COSMOLOGY
CANELOS QUICHUA

The transition from earth to sky is a continuous one for the Canelos Quichua. As fog, *puyu,* swirls and rises, it carries aspects of earth life upward toward the sky, and also to the rivers. Aspects of sky life and river life are carried downward by rain, *tamia.* There are many possibilities for metaphor based on movements of celestial bodies. . . . White clouds are regarded as high fog, and long, dark clouds streaking across dawn and dusk skys, or seen on bright moonlit nights, are regarded as high river—*jatun yacu.* Parakeets, *ucupachama manda huichu,* come and go between earth, sky, and underworld, carrying songs and mediating between the souls of spirits and souls of humans. Women, mediators between soil and water, are able to send human and spirit songs upward through fog or by parakeets to the sky rivers, and along these rivers to their destinations. Such songs are sung to absentee men to give them comfort or do them harm. . . .

Beyond the *four cardinal points*—upriver, downriver, and either side, *chimbajta*—there are two other basic directions—straight up, *cusca,* and straight down, *ucumu.* The center of the sky is "straight up." The most acceptable Jungle Quichua term for what we call sky is simply *jahuama,* from *jahua* or *ahua,* high. The sky is also called *silui* or (plural) *siluguna.* Sky and earth domains join at cardinal points of the horizon.

Indi, the sun, is yellow, and he symbolizes light and warmth: he is regarded as a predictable sky Runa. Two other predictable sky Runa (when they are in their own sky domain) are the morning star, *Cuillur,*

361

who appears in the *east*, and the evening star, *Docero,* who appears in the *west*. Both of these sky Runa are positioned near the earth since they are just above the *east-west* cardinal axis. When they descend to earth they become completely unpredictable and generate variety and transformation in mythic structure. There are many stories about these star Runa, and about the sun; they are often used in Runa metaphor as people. The rest of the stars are also regarded as Runa with their own system of directionality, determined by the movements of the moon. The Milky Way is their fog, and the dark streaky clouds their rivers. Every celestial body is regarded as a night sun, *tuta indi;* though stars are white, in this sky context they symbolize life, an extension of the sun's yellow.

The most important celestial body is the moon, *Quilla,* for he links predictability, and provides a charter of Canelos Quichua continuity through original incest. Both phase and directionality are important in conceptualizing the moon. The "new," "green," "unripe" moon, *llullu Quilla,* is feminine but prepubescent. It cannot have children or make chicha or pottery. Only when the moon is "ripe," *pucushca Quilla,* from half to three-quarters full, is it regarded as adult male, ready to perform its various mythical sexual relationships, including incest. Because the moon does not rise at the same time or in the same place, a second set of concepts related to positioning are applied to Canelos Quichua cosmology. The moon is strongest when it is *eastward, southward* or *northward*, and weakest when it is *westward*. Stated another way, I think it safe to say that it is at its metaphorical best when it is strongly masculine in either the clear female sector, *east*, or potential female sector, *north*, or *south*, or when it is cusca—straight up—in the dimension which cuts through the center of a *circle drawn around the perimeter of the cardinal points*. It is at its metaphorical worst when it is a weak male in the *west*, the undisputed male sector.

Two Venezuelan Amazonian rattles, a turtle shell rattle (Yanomami), and a large rattle (Rikmaktsa) from the Brazilian Mato Grosso

Peruvian motif

Eventually, in its movement across the heavens, Quilla enters into the sun's special place over the Andes—*Indiaycushca*—and passes on down into the underworld. Weakness and fatigue overtake both Quilla and Indi as they move to the Andes at the end of a visible tour.

The underworld, *ucupachama,* is thought to be inhabited by small Runa and animals, just as this world is. But these Runa, the *ucupachama manda* (manda = of, from) are very powerful shamans, and they forever question the sincerity of the Canelos Quichua Runa. Their world is also divided into day, *pucha,* and night, *tuta,* but the times are reversed, for when there is night on earth, Indi is bringing yellow warmth to the underworld, and when it is day on earth the stars, and often the moon, are bringing their night sun to the underworld. *Directions*, too, are reversed in the underworld. Again, Quilla is anomalous, for he may be above the earth during the day, and also in the underworld during its day.

> *Sacha Runa: Ethnicity and Adaptation of Ecuadorian Jungle Quichua,*
> Norman Whitten, Jr., 1976, pp. 44-45

The sky and the underworld are understood by this People as being in relationship to their earthly world, even with respect to the four directions. Runa, People, either human or cosmological, are also in direct relationship with each other.

Children's prayer circle at Our Lady of Refuge Catholic Church, Castroville, California, summer 1988, incorporating Native and Catholic prayer ways

CONTEMPORARY FOUR DIRECTIONS PRAYER
INTERTRIBAL/INTERFAITH

Everyone gathers in a *circle*. All share in a time of holy silence. Then drum or flute music is softly played throughout the blessing. One leader recites the following prayer, another recites the next, and so on.

PRAYER

Loving, Creator, we owe our existence to you.
All living creatures come from you.
Today we find ourselves coming here to remember the gift of life.
As we look around ourselves we recognize the life of trees and
    all other life forms to which we and they are related.
We bless you this day. Amen.

All Face *EAST*

From the *East* the sun comes everyday and spreads light
    over all things.
It speaks to us of your love.
As we think of all the people and things that live to the *East* of us,
    we ask for wisdom and understanding that what is done at
    this place may be for the benefit of everything and everyone.

All Face *SOUTH*

The *South* makes us think of warmth.

We thank you for all the gifts that come to us from the *South*.
Help us not to waste them.
Help us to remember the needs of all our relatives,
    especially those which cannot speak for themselves.
May what we do here and what is done here in the future
    be a blessing.

All Face *WEST*

The sun sets in the *West* and our day comes to an end.
Give us abundant waters to fill our rivers, lakes, and oceans.
Help us to value the gift of water.

May there be an abundance for our land and its wildlife
    and peoples for generations to come.

All Face *NORTH*

As we look *North* we think of cool winds,
    cleansing breezes that cause leaves to fall to the earth to rest.
As we are gathered here, teach us patience and endurance.
May we lighten one another's burden.

ALL: Amen.

Holy Silence

Final Blessing

Bless this holy place.
May the redwoods and all other trees abound.
May all people enjoy the goodness that we now experience.
May the birds sing.
May beauty be always before us and behind us.
May all that is beautiful be above and below us.
May we be surrounded by beauty and immersed in it.
In our youth and in our old age, may we walk the path of beauty.

ALL: Amen.

SONG

All spend some time looking at, admiring, touching, experiencing the uniqueness of the redwood trees. This blessing, with adaptations, could be offered whenever certain kinds of trees and plant life are scarce or are facing extinction. It should remind the people gathered in prayer that all humans have a responsibility before the Creator-Redeemer to care for all other life forms on planet earth.

Celebrating the Earth: An Earth Centered Theology of Worship with Blessings, Prayers and Rituals, Scott McCarthy, 1990, pp. 267-270

The original occasion of the circle blessing ceremony in the midst of redwood trees was the lamentable bulldozing of some ancient giant redwood trees at a university campus in Northern California in order that room be made for new student housing. The ceremony was celebrated in an interfaith manner.

*A joyful prayer of thanks to Creator
for a blessing received*

Circles & Number 4

CIRCLES & NUMBER 4

Tous pour un, un pour tous (All for one, one for all)

Les Trois Mousquetiers, Alexandre Dumas

This basic combination is typified by circular symbolism included within some type of four-fold action. As we shall see, from the materials in this section, throughout the Americas the People embody this kind of activity through wonderful, communal dances (Cherokee, Tubatulabal, Maidu, Crow, Seri, Txicao, and Canelos Quichua). At other times it is expressed by a food thanksgiving ceremony (Tsimshian) or another kind of festival (Omaha, Mapuche). This combination could even be shown through the wearing of certain trade brooches.

As we vicariously experience any of the events or rituals mentioned within these pages it is important to keep in mind that color, sound, movement, indeed all sensory perception, was and is a normal part of Native spirituality, just as it is for any other gathering of human beings.

A northern California seasonal waterfall reminds us of the directions we might take in the Circle of Life

369

*Praying at the river with tobacco
and eagle feathers*

WOODLANDS CULTURAL AREA

CIRCLES OF LIFE
ONEIDA

NOW
It came to be part of the Great Celebration . . .
so that this one or that
would choose the *circle* to walk
which was most appropriate
for their learning that year.

As the People saw the value
of this *circle of circles* . . .

IT CAME TO BE
that the *center circle* was understood
as that which contained
the learning and resident Wisdom
of the Whole People,

WHEREAS
those *four circles* dancing at the edge
became the personal circles
of each of those
who together constitute that People.

AND IT WAS SEEN AND UNDERSTOOD
THAT THE CENTER CIRCLE
NOURISHED THE WHOLE PEOPLE . . .

370

WHEREAS
  FOUR-CIRCLES-AROUND
    NOURISHED INDIVIDUAL GROWTH
  WHICH—RETURNING TO THE CENTER CIRCLE—
  NOURISHED, IN TURN, THE WHOLE PEOPLE.

AND IT CAME TO BE
  That an understanding grew among them
    of a double circle,
      constantly walked

The first of these
  the Whole People
    walked in a continuous direction.
The second of these
  was walked,
    as appropriate and needful to each one,
    as if it spun off from the Center Circle
    —which indeed was so—
so that
  it was walked in the opposite direction,
    returning each such individual
      once more to the Center Circle.

AND FOR A LONG TIME
  The People kept this Pattern on the Earth
    as a recognition of their understanding . . .

The needs of each,
The needs of all,
  are appropriately walked
    in a continuous direction,
      each circle leading to the other
  so that all and each
    may continuously dance
      the Circle of the People
        and the Circle of Growth within.

Contemplating the "New Way"
with the "Old Way"

AND FOR THIS REASON
   You and I walk today
     this continuous double circle
      at the Turning of the Seasons,
     when Earth Begins to turn again
      toward light of growth.

AS IT IS SO . . .
   SO LET IT CONTINUE . . .
     SO THAT THE CHILDREN'S CHILDREN
     MAY LEARN THIS WISDOM.

The Walking People: A Native American Oral History,
Paula Underwood, 1993, pp. 234-235

The above is a section from a large work concerning the oral history of a People, in this case the Oneida, a tribe within the Iroquois Confederacy. The writer sees herself as sharing the historical wisdom of her grandfather's grandmother with a new generation of listeners. She has a unique way of speaking about life's circle.

Shawnee house (reconstruction in Ohio)

SOUTHEAST CULTURAL AREA

DANCE ETIQUETTE
CHEROKEE

A prayer before making camp on the trail

As the leader begins, he walks once *counterclockwise* (all movements take this directions around the *circle)*, shaking the rattle as he decides what songs he will perform. . . . Although the duration of an animal dance averages ten to fifteen minutes, some leaders may prolong the dance to as much as twenty minutes. . . . A dance almost always deviates in some details from the form of other occasions. This may be due to the ability, mood, or caprice of the leader, and may provoke laughter by adding an unexpected element to the play. Partial intoxication, error, forgetfulness, confusion, and inexperience all add to the variation.

Even the simplest dance unit, when complete, comprises *four song periods*, punctuated by the leader's signals. A characteristic instance is as follows:

1. Walking period in which the leader beats a tremolo, *walks once around the dance circle*, and shakes the tremolo again.

2. The dancing begins and the song is repeated seven times.

3. The leader signals with his rattle, the dancing continues, and one or two women wearing leg-rattles enter the column behind the leader, who holds his rattle at a greater height. The song is repeated *four times*.

4. The leader holds the rattle aloft, shakes it in tremolo, and the dancers face center, stomping heavily *(a'stɑyi:'disti:yi:'*, "faster and

373

harder") in one position. At the termination of this high point of the dance the leader rattles in tremolo and the men whoop *(a't'ohi:stįyi:'*, [habitual cry or shout]) or yell, and all break rank.

The gait is the simple, alternating, shuffle common to eastern North America, with the knee bent a little and the body relaxed and inclined forward. The dancers keep in close formation one behind the other. The leader may vary the pattern by advancing sideways to the left, and is imitated by the rest of the company. The women move their feet in a shuffle of 3 or 4 inches, with rather more grace than the men. The arms hang limp at the sides except when the men imitate the hand motion of the leader at the turns of the song, by raising the hands to the shoulders or to the head. The only attempts at dramatic gesture are as specified in the appropriate places, and if the Cherokee dance performances are witnessed in the style of the Plains Indian it may be interpreted as recent acculturation from Western sources.

Although feather ornaments and masks are worn, no face painting has been observed among Eastern Cherokee dancers in recent times.

Cherokee Dance and Drama, Frank Speck &
Leonard Broom, 1993, pp. 23-24

There are certain elements that are common to most Cherokee dances (and perhaps are held in common with other Southeastern tribes). Two of these elements are the movement in a counterclockwise circular direction and the division of the dance into four song periods.

*A prayer
for peace . . .*

*but to pray
is also
to be joyful*

Entrance to Esselen underground sweat lodge, Carmel Valley

CALIFORNIA CULTURAL AREA

HOME-MAKING
CHUMASH

"Tomorrow, we will begin the framework," *Maqcip* agreed. "We will use willow for the uprights until we establish the general outline of the hut; then we will use sturdy sycamore saplings for the rest of the uprights and the lower *four tiers* for horizontals. We will use the willow bark to lace the poles together along with rope and twine made from the leaves and stalks of yucca. *Weqcum*, you and *Timiyaquat* begin looking for good straight poles about seven to ten centimeters in diameter. *To'goch* and *Ksen*, you two begin peeling bark in long strips as soon as they begin bringing in the poles. *Tule,* you can supervise *To'goch* and *Ksen;* that way you will be here on site to oversee the construction of the hut. . . ."

'Ese'es was sent to cut yucca and his middle boy went along to help carry the bundles back to camp. *'Ese'es's* wife and daughter offered to do the digging for the *fire circle*.

"*Kakanupmawa* and I will begin the hole for the poles. *Tule,* help us mark out the *circle* so we will get the first ones in the right places. By the time we have them done, some of the poles will have been peeled and ready to set. We can measure the other holes from these after we see how hard or easy the saplings bend and how big the circle must be for the size poles they bring. If the hut is ten meters in diameter, then it should be planned for about four and a half meters high. The poles must be longer than that for we will need some leeway in making the smoke hole."

"Your father and I will clean the circle and begin hollowing out the center where the fire pit will be," added *'Ese'se's* mother as she searched for a leafy branch to use as a broom and a sharp stick with which to root out the plants within the marked circle. "We should be able to construct the basic framework today and tomorrow. In fact, tomorrow morning, the first party can begin cutting tules so we can start thatching by evening. The old hut's not only too small but the dust from the dried tule is getting so bad, I suspect we will not be able to endure them during the hot spell which will surely begin any day now."

It took twenty-four poles to form the circle of the new hut. Once they were in place, the men tied the heaviest bendable sycamore saplings they could manage at one-third meter intervals horizontally around the circle of poles trying to alternate inside and outside the uprights. It wasn't always possible to bend the long poles sharply enough but by placing some poles mostly on the outside, and others mostly on the inside, strength was given to the structure, not against earthquakes, but against the strong winds and against the torque which results from the bed frames being secured against the house posts. It took *four* long sycamores for each circle around the hut and there were to be *four circles* in ascending rings before they switched to smaller and more supple willow branches. In addition, some perpendicular poles were planted inside the circle and tied to the bent poles to help hold them in position and later to serve as bedposts. By evening, all this had been accomplished. As they sat in the firelight, the next day's plan was laid.

The Temescals of Arroyo Conejo, Thomas Maxwell, 1982, pp. 94, 96

Family members always worked together to make a circular house-home that matched the terrain and climate of the Central California coast and inland areas. Items in sets of four found themselves built into the structure itself.

———————— ✪ ————————

Dining lodge roof, Esselen Tribe, Carmel Valley

MOURNING CEREMONY
TUBATULABAL

When Elemgil made a fiesta, he told his messenger to go tell everybody. Dick went to the Monilabal at Tejon, Porterville, and to the Kawaiisu, and told the people to come to cubka-yl. Before the fiesta began, Kawicina, the dance manager, told the boys to make a brush enclosure for the people to camp in. Some of the Monilabal and people around here went over to cuhka-yl in groups. Before they got to Elemgil's, the men who had feather headdresses put these on, and then they lined up in single file and the line advanced like a snake, the men singing and hollering. When they got to the enclosure, men, women, and children lined up straight; the men and boys did a piston-rod step, lifting one foot in front of the other, the women walked sideways. Kawicina stood in the middle of the line, calling "tak-e-e?" to Elemgil; he was calling for money. Then all the people went into the enclosure and two men clowned to get money. One man put ashes all over the other man's face. Elemgil brought his money out, the people held out their hands and he gave each person a ten- to twelve-inch string of beads.

After that Kawicina showed the people where to camp. The fiesta lasted six days and nights. Elemgil supplied all the food for the people and hired girls to cook; his relatives and friends helped him. They brought food, piñons, rabbits, seeds, anything. None of the visitors brought food, they were there to eat.

At night two male dancers, dressed in feather skirts and feather headdresses, danced; they just lifted one foot in front of the other, and went *around the fire* inside the enclosure, slowly. *Four old men* sang for them and rattled splitstick rattles. Some women would dance too, apart, not holding hands. The dancers held the dead person's clothes in their hands, and they cried as they danced. Elemgil or his relations, or anybody would pay the singers and all the money was put in a pile near the singers. It was divided among the singers and the muluwin (male dancers) the next morning. When some other people wanted to dance, the first dancers quit and the others would dance all night, until daylight. If some of the women didn't want to dance, the mulluwin would go over to them and pay them to dance. The muluwin had black stripes painted down their faces; the women had red dirt daubed on theirs.

Grown people and children watched the dancing; the messenger tended the fire; Elemgil looked on every night for a little while, then he would lie down and go to sleep. Some people would be playing hand games, too; men and women would play. The Monilabal women played hand games a lot.

In the daytime they'd play dice and hand games and hoop-and-pole games. . . .

They kept up the dancing for five nights. On Sunday, Elemgil made a tule image and they burned it before noon.

Besides the image, feather wands and yellowhammer banners were also carried while *dancing around the fire* and thrown in with the image.

The feather wand carried at the burning was made from a stick two feet long. The stick was first wrapped with mud-hen feathers at the bottom, next mountain quail crests were tied to the tips of the mud-hen feathers. On the top were two eagle feathers. This wand was tied on the end of a long stick and carried in the procession by just anyone, then thrown into the fire. . . .

Yellowhammer bands were worn around the waist of dancers or carried aloft on poles. Yellowhammer bands or banners were sometimes hung on doors of the houses to keep the ghosts away. These bands were made by men and bought for about two dollars apiece in shell money by the one giving the fiesta.

The dancer or muluwin wore a feather dance outfit. He also carried a bunch of eagle feathers tied around his wrist. Some dancers wore the hair the women giving the fiesta had cut off in mourning. They tied the hair around both legs like garters.

When the image was thrown into the fire, the men and women lined up and the one giving the fiesta threw beads over the heads of the people; anyone catching them could keep them. After all the dead person's belongings had been burned, they filled the hole with dirt as if they were burying the dead person.

Indian County of the Tubatulabal, Bob Powers, 1981, pp. 86-87

Here is a description of an 1870 mourning ceremony held at Hot Springs Canyon for the wife of Elemgil. Though the weather would perhaps have been very hot, the dancers would have been faithful to their commitment to step to the drum beat to honor both the Creator and the deceased woman and family. As with many of the People, circling the dance floor is the practice, as is the preferred number of singers: four.

——————————— ☉ ———————————

USE OF CONDOR FEATHER CLOAKS IN DANCE
MAIDU

In the 1960s, Chico Maidu elder Henry Azbill recalled the importance of the condor at his village of Mikchopdo, now part of the city of Chico. He described the Moloko'mkasi, a dance last given in February of 1906 that was danced by two male dancers. Each wore long, enveloping cloaks of condor feathers which had been attached to a net foundation. Unlike the smaller capes used in other dances, these capes covered the dancer from head to foot, and were open in the front. They were topped with white swan feathers and a number of feathered pins, and long bands of flicker feathers hung down from the top of the dancers' heads. As the dancers approached the ceremonial round-house from their dressing area a half-mile away, they stopped *four times* with their accompanying singer, dancing and whirling in time to his song. Their cloaks lifted away form them as they spun, revealing their red-painted bodies. Upon reaching the roundhouse, they *circled* it *four times counterclockwise*, and *four times clockwise*. They then ran up the roof of the roundhouse and disappeared into the smoke hole. While the entire village came to view the approach of the dancers, only members of the dance society were allowed inside the roundhouse to view the dance itself. The Moloko'mkasi was one of a handful of dances considered to be endowed with supernatural power and thus dangerous for common people. After the village religious leader died late in 1906, the condor cloaks were destroyed and the condor dance was never given again.

"The California Condor and the California Indians,"
American Indian Art Magazine, Craig Bates,
Janet Hamber & Martha Lee, Winter 1993, p. 44

Circling the roundhouse four times both clockwise and counterclockwise is a way of blessing it more fully, more powerfully. Nothing is ritually left out or missing in this manner of hallowing something for special use. How many times one repeats an action often tells us of the importance of both object and action.

Argillite box

NORTHWEST CULTURAL AREA

FIRST SALMON CAUGHT THANKSGIVING CEREMONY
TSIMSHIAN

When the Tsimshian people of the Northwest caught their first salmon, for example, they immediately notified several of their oldest shamans, who went down to the river to greet the salmon. While one shaman donned fisherman's clothing, the others spread a cedar-bark mat on the ground and placed the salmon on it. Taking up the mat by its corners, the shamans carried the salmon to the village chief's house. The fisherman-shaman led the procession, shaking a rattle in his right hand and waving an eagle's tail in his left. Only selected members of the village were permitted to enter the chief's house and attend the remainder of the ceremony. Inside, the shamans placed the salmon on a cedar board and walked around it *four times*. When it came time to clean the fish for the ceremonial meal, the shamans used a mussel-shell knife; to cut with a stone or metal knife could bring on a violent thunder-storm. They cut the salmon's head first, then the tail, addressing the fish in honorary terms as they did so.

American Indians: The Spirit World,
Henry Woodhead (Ed.), 1992, p. 75

Ritually circling an object or person four times is a way of simultaneously honoring and blessing. It is a way also of giving thanks or of preparation.

380

PLAINS
CULTURAL
AREA

A danced prayer within a sacred circle of stones

FESTIVAL OF JOY CEREMONY
OMAHA

In the ancient Omaha ceremony the people had the vast expanse of the prairie at their disposal, yet each tribal group kept its appointed place, not only during the dance, wherein they made *four approaches* toward the sacred tree, but when all the groups formed into *two great circles* the tribal order of their relative positions was still preserved. The two circles were made up according to sex. The women and girls danced in *one direction next to the pole*; the men and boys formed the *outer circle* and danced in the *opposite direction*. This dance was the occasion of much hilarity and fun. Old and young danced with vigor, and great was the delight of the tribe as it spun around the emblematic tree, carrying branches. At the close of the dance all tossed the branches at the foot of the pole, leaving a mound of green on the wide spreading plain.

Indian Games and Dances with Native Songs,
Alice C. Fletcher, 1994, pp. 61-62

The Hé-de Wa-chi, or Festival of Joy Ceremony, was celebrated in late summer to renew tribal unity. As the Omahas were made up of ten distinct groups, the tree with its twigs and branches was understood to be an appropriate symbol for the People in their unity and diversity. It must have always been a really beautiful ceremony.

———————————— ☻ ————————————

SANCTIFYING OF WHISTLER-PLEDGER
FOR ANCIENT SUNDANCE CERMONY
CROW

The process of sacramentizing the "whistler," carried out by the bundle owner, probably began right after the first hunt and was repeated at each ceremonial stop enroute to the dance ground. The whistler's own tipi provided the staging for the consecration process. Ground cedar was brought in to carpet the floor, and sage was used to make up a bed in the rear. The bundle owner seated himself to the right of the whistler and received old men who inquired about the whistler's intentions, tested the strength of his convictions and the validity of the dream that sanctioned the ceremony. With pipe they added their prayer smokes and blessings.

The visitation of the old men undoubtedly was designed to get at the truth or falsity of the dream. If false, a man probably withdrew and waited for a clearer signal. If the interpretations of the old wise men agreed with a pledger's conviction, he reaffirmed his intention to go ahead with a simple statement to his ceremonial father: "Sing for me tonight, and I will dance for you." This set the bundle owner in motion to get together the kilt, moccasins, buffalo robes, eagle-bone whistle and other gear required. The owner's wife assembled a tanned deer-skin for the kilt, an unused buffalo robe, and buckskin for the moccasins. Before the manufacture of any item, the owner purified with incense the materials, tools, and persons involved. The ceremonial father himself cut the hide for the kilt, *feinting three times before putting the knife to the hide*. A virtuous woman prepared the kilt and the woman who sewed the moccasins qualified only if her husband had killed and scalped an enemy. The moccasins were blackened with charcoal as a sign of victory and were decorated with buffalo hair to represent a scalp taken from the enemy.

Consecration of the whistler was symbolized in the ceremonial drama of painting and dressing for the Sun Dance, undressing, and sleeping beside a buffalo skull. This ritual called for *four singers* with their hand drums and two women accompanists. All dress paraphernalia were assembled within easy reach by the effigy owner, including a cup of white clay, ground cedar, eagle-bone whistle, buffalo-hide rattle, two feather plumes, skunk-hide necklace, kilt, robe, moccasins, and sage. Taking some clay, the ceremonial father began to sing, accompanying himself with the rattle. His wife, who acted as his assistant, sang along with him and put cedar on the fire of smoldering buffalo chips. After the *fourth rendition of the song*, the owner carefully smoked the kilt. He then repeated the *four songs* and gently raised the whistler, grasping only his thumbs. As the whistler became erect, he extended his left foot over the cedar incense and stepped into the kilt. The wife then raised the kilt into place and tied it with a leather cord. During the donning of the kilt, the drummer-singers offered prayer smokes.

The whistler next was painted with the white clay in the manner of a buffalo when rolling in a wallow. First, however, the best drum was purified in fresh cedar incense by the bundle owner's wife, while her husband sang a medicine song. In returning to his place, the consecrated drummer with his drum made a (clockwise?) *circuit* to avoid crossing in front of the whistler. After consecrating his rattle, the ceremonial father sang softly and with the fourth song sang aloud, at which time the dummer-singers joined in. After smoking his hands in the cedar incense, the father outlined the whistler's body from head to toe. *He did this three times*, and then, *on the fourth song*, feigned the painting of the whistler with white clay—*first from the front, head to toe, then the back*, followed by the left and right sides. Following the same order (*E, W, N, S*), the wife-assistant applied the paint to the whistler, using a bundle of sage. Next the ceremonial father drew a square cross on the whistler's breast and back, to signify Morning Star. With a zigzag line from each eye, he symbolized the whistler's tears. A zigzag lightning mark applied to the forehead imitated the painting used by the Sun himself.

To complete his "son's" dress, the ceremonial father hung a skunk-hide necklace around his neck, tied a feather to the back of his head, and attached eagle plumes to the little fingers of each hand. Both the skunk skin and the feathers were daubed with the clay. The moccasins were smoked in fresh cedar and put on, the first left (N) and then the right (S). This was done by the owner's wife. After smoking the buffalo robe, the owner *three times feigned placing it* on the ground. *On the fourth song* he put the robe in place and guided the whistler to his seat. The wife adjusted the robe and drew the ends around the pledger.

The bundle owner next smoked and daubed the final item of dress, the eagle-bone whistle, with white clay. To the accompaniment of song, the "father" danced in a squatting position before his "son." *Three times he feigned* the insertion of the whistle, and *on the fourth song* he inserted the whistle into the pledger's mouth. The pledger then danced in imitation of his mentor. To end this drama, the owner took the whistle and draped it around the whistler's neck.

Upon completion of the ceremonial dressing, the drummers ended their singing, took up a pipe, and offered prayer smokes. All during the dress-consecration the cover of the tipi was raised for all to see. *Four warriors* now entered *from the left,* and *four from the right.* Each carried a wolfskin to indicate that he had served as a scout, and each had moccasins tied to his belt as if in readiness to set out on a war expedition. Only the weaponry of war was missing, since it was forbidden at this stage of the ceremony. Two women sang a song that indicated return from a successful war venture. . . . As the drummer took up the song, the men sounded a war whoop and flirted with the women. After the *fourth rendition*, the warriors individually recounted war deeds and left. Thus began the mobilization of the mystic powers of renowned warriors to overwhelm the enemy.

To the accompaniment of prayer smokes and songs by the drummer-singers, the bundle owner ceremonially undressed the whistler. *Feigning three times* in each case, he removed the head plume, skunk-skin necklace, little finger plumes, whistle, and moccasins. The kilt was not removed. At the call, "Bring in his quilts!" two bundles of sage and cedar were brought. After shapng the cedar into a pillow and the sage into a mattress, the owner lowered the whistler to his bed, with feet to the fire and with palms up. *Following three feints and songs, the owner on the fourth song, covered the whistler with the buffalo robe*. Now he called out, "Bring in the buffalo bull!" This horned skull he set close to the whistler's head, facing the fire and the *east*.

Consecration of the pledger now was ended, and he soon was left alone to sleep and, it was hoped, to dream of power. The owner and his wife-assistant made public where they would next encamp, perhaps only a few miles away. . . .

At the second, third, and *fourth camps* the police awaited the people, and as they arrived, directed them into a *circle* with the pledger's tipi and the shade structure. . . . At each stop the bundle owner repeated the ceremonial dressing and undressing of the whistler and more warriors recounted their coups. With the *fourth* consecration the preliminaries ended.

The Shoshoni-Crow Sun Dance, Fred Voget, 1984, pp. 87-92

An observer visiting would easily come to understand the protocol of fourness in this and other Crow ceremonies.

––––––––––––––––––––––––– ⊕ –––––––––––––––––––––

HOME CUSTOMARY RITUALS
CROW

Old men used to get together regularly in the evening to smoke and pray. When we were living in our winter house, Pete Lefthand's grandfather, Bird Tail That Rattles, would come over every evening. He was a Sioux and lived just a little ways from us. George No Horse came often, too. The men always sat toward the back and the women and kids up by the door. This was the way it was in the old days in the tipi. The place of honor, and the place where a man hung his medicine, was in the back of the tipi. Here he received his guests, and whatever they had to do together, they first opened with a smoke-prayer. When Father and Bird Tail That Rattles smoked, they pointed the pipe to the Star People and to Mother Earth and the Earth People. Each one would say, "You, whoever is up there, take a puff." Then they pointed to where the winds came from, first the **north**, then **south**, and said the same thing. I never saw them go to the *east* or *west* with the pipe. I think this tobacco smoking to the stars and cold and warm winds was meant to take care of everything, to keep us strong and healthy and to protect us from harm during the winter. . . .

Kids were around the old people a lot, and we learned to respect them and what they were doing and saying. When they were smoking and praying, they were pretty strict, and we were not allowed to walk in front of them but had to pass around at the back. We noticed how the old men would make a *circuit to the left* of the stove when they were leaving, the same as they used to do when leaving the tipi. I think kids today would be smart if they listened more to older people and learned from them. Now, young people are busy running around in cars, and they don't want to listen or pay attention to older people.

They Call Me Agnes: A Crow Narrative Based on the Life of
Agnes Yellowtail Deernose, Fred Voget, 1995, pp. 74-75

Prayerful smoking was and is an everyday responsibility and activity for many Apsaaloka, or members of the Crow Tribe. The four winds, rather than the four directions themselves, are points of spiritual contact and though they dwell in modern houses, the ancient custom-ary circuit upon leaving a tipi is often very important as a tie with the past.

———————————————— ☺ ————————————————

WOMAN CHIEF'S DANCE
CROW

One time the Crow had a woman who was an outstanding fighter and leader. She was an Atsina captured when she was a little girl. She could hunt like a man, and she struck first coup twice and was good at horse raiding. She had *four wives* to take care of the tipi and the hides. They called her Woman Chief. It was her own Atsina people who killed her in 1854.

When I was growing up, they had a dance called Woman Chief named after this woman. A Crow man married to an Atsina woman introduced the dance around 1902, making use of the Owl Dance and whippers. Whippers came in with the Omaha or Grass Dance back in the 1870s, and the Hot Dancers of that day took it up. . . .

My sister, Amy, used to go and watch them rehearse the Woman Chief's dance when she was about five. *Four women* carried war-bonnets, two owned buggy whips, and two women chiefs carried a hooked or a lance staff wrapped with otter. The hooked sticks were like the ones carried by brave men of the military club when we Crow fought the Piegan, Sioux, Cheyenne, and Arapaho. Two men also belonged to the group and were the parade leaders. A pipe lighter started the dance with a smoke-prayer while the drummers drummed out *four songs*. When the drummers sang another set of *four songs*, the dancers had a parade dance *circling* the dance hall. After the parade dance, each of the women asked, "Who will take care of my stick?" Men volunteered to make their own parade dance with the stick, warbonnet, or whip. For that public honor each had to hold a small giveaway at the dance hall.

They Call Me Agnes: A Crow Narrative Based on the Life of Agnes Yellowtail Deernose, Fred Voget, 1995, pp. 184-185

Here it seems that four is a mnemonic device which helps to bring to mind the fact that this female chief had four "wives" to care for her domestic concerns. Yet four is also emphatic and ceremonial in the dance.

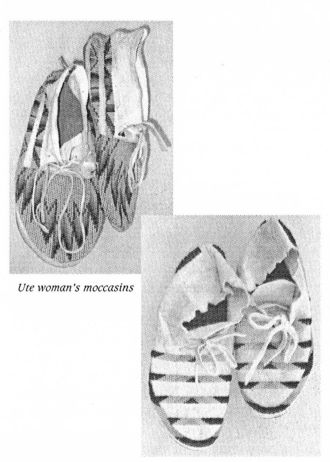

Ute woman's moccasins

Sioux woman's moccasins

Quiché Mayan priest/elder at Los Cimientos in the Guatemalan highlands

MESOAMERICA CULTURAL AREA

CIRCLE DANCE
SERI

In the month of May, when all the flowers are in bloom, the women give their *Circle Dance*. None of the men are allowed near—they must sleep and stay far off. During the *four days* of the dance, each woman takes the part of a certain flower, which is painted on her face afresh every day. While she is dancing she wears flowers in her hair, interwoven with a wreath of green leaves.

At sunrise baskets of flowers—all the kinds of which the fruit is not eaten—are *laid in a circle* outside the dance-ground. In its center is the singer, an old man—the only man allowed to look on. Around him is a *small circle of little girls*, then a *larger circle of older girls*. The *third circle* is composed *of young married women*, and in the *outside circle* are *all the old women*.

At the end of the *four days* the baskets in the outside ring are turned over, covering the flowers, which are left there for *four days more*. Then the women bathe in the sea and wash off all the paint from their faces.

The Old Man who sings wears *four kinds of cactus-flowers*—*Pitahaya, sahuaro, sahuesa* and *cina* . . . and standing in the center of the circles . . . sings the . . . stanzas. Each time he has sung ten a woman tells him. They are given in the exact order of the sequence. . . .

While the dance is going on each girl leaves the circle and dances to her particular plant. When she returns she brings its fruit or flower in her hand.

The Last of the Seris: The Aboriginal Indians of Kino Bay, Sonora, Mexico,
Dane Coolidge & Mary Coolidge, 1973, pp. 231, 233

The Seri Women's Fiesta Dance is a blessing dance of the flora of creation. It is replete with fourness and circular symbolisms as each plant is recognized and blessed.

————————————— ☻ —————————————

WAR DANCE FIRE
SERI

A blue fire is used as a war signal, to summon the men when they are going to war. It is made by burning dry wood which has been soaked in salt water along the beach, and they make a very large fire. Many men *encircle* it, dancing slowly; while on the outside, with their backs to the flame, *four* big men keep watch. The fire blinds their enemies, while it reveals their approach to the watchers. If there are a hundred men there is one fire—four hundred men, *four fires*.

The Last of the Seri: The Aboriginal Indians of Kino Bay, Sonora, Mexico,
Dane Coolidge & Mary Coolidge, 1973, p. 211

Even going to war was regulated with a circle dance around fire. The four men watching (either the dancers around the fire or the enemy) perhaps express a directional symbology that is in common with most other Mesoamerican Peoples.

Quiché Mayan priests/elders praying for health and the harvest at Los Cimientos in the Guatemalan highlands

Piaroa shaman's headdress,
rattle, paraphernalia box,
and smudging cigars

SOUTH AMERICA CULTURAL AREA

TRIBAL NEW YEAR CELEBRATION
MAPUCHE

A large number of Mapuche Indians live in Puerto Dominguez and the invitation I got was in connection with their celebration of the *We xipantu,* the start of their new year on the eve of June 24th, the feast of St. John the Baptist.

For the Mapuches, the celebration of the *We xipantu* has a great importance. It gives them the opportunity to appreciate their world and the realities in which they live. It marks the start of new ventures and the beginning of their new year.

The renewal of nature, the start of the new year, the reawakening of their relationship with mother earth, with their family, their culture and their friendships are all experienced in the celebration.

For the Mapuches, their calendar year is not counted in terms of days but in the rhythm of nature. Their year starts in winter, *Puken,* which for them is the rainy season, the months of June, July and August. This is followed by *Pewu,* which means the period of flourishing.

The third season is *Walug,* a period of harvesting. The fourth season is *Rimugen,* which for them is the time for thanksgiving, the months of March, April, and May. Last March while I was new in the regions I was able to witness the thanksgiving celebration in one of the Basic Christian Communities in the rural area. The fruits of the earth—including a big jar of honey—were brought up at the Offertory.

The New Year celebration that I attended was very interesting. The vigil started at 8:00 in the evening with the presentation of the different groups or clans. All the speeches were in *Mapudungu* (the

Mapuche's dialect); luckily I had an interpreter with me so I managed to follow them. Their musical instruments were played. The local fruit-bearing tree called *maqui* (one of the sacred trees of the Mapuche) was placed at the center part of a *circle of people*.

Each of us took a branch from the tree and then we formed into *two circles*. The men and children playing their instruments, formed the inner circle and the women, the outer. As soon as the circles had been formed, we began the Mapuche prayer dance, in slow rhythm one step at a time. The first two times around, we held the branch with our right hand; the third and *fourth time*, we held it with our left hand. The *four rounds* of *dancing* and praying are symbolic of the *four seasons*.

After the prayer dance, the children presented a short drama and the adults recited poems and sang songs. Instead of clapping hands after each number, we shouted as a gesture of appreciation. For them, clapping hands is a foreign custom!

We were given a drink of *modai,* a mixture of corn, wheat and honey. Then, we had our meal at 3:00 A.M.!

The vigil ended at sunrise with the people greeting one another with the expressions, *"Akui we xipantu"* (the New Year has arrived) or *"Winoi xipantu"* (the setting sun has returned).

Returning back to Loncoche on the bus, I thought of the experience I had just gone through and the song of the Psalmist, "From the rising of the sun to its setting, great is the name of the Lord."

"Mapuche New Year," *Columban Mission,*
Virgie Mozo, December 1994, pp. 20-21

The narrator is a Filipina, a missionary sister who shares her life and faith in Chile. Here is an example of two faith traditions coming together to celebrate the earth's seasons as well as the great circle of the Creator's temporal gifts.

---------------------------- ⊕ ----------------------------

COMMUNAL DANCE
TXIKAO

The Txikao we met . . . were having a small party themselves when we arrived. A few women, two or three grown men, but for the most part, children, were doing a sort of conga in and out of the main hut.

Stamping on *every fourth beat* with the right foot—around which bells made from pigs' trotters had been tied—the fifteen dancers wheeled merrily along, turning around to go backwards for a step or two, and then turning again and *circling a pole* stuck in the ground before chanting and dancing back into the hut from which the muffled sounds of the continued dance emerged.

A Question of Survival for the Indians of Brazil,
Robin Hanbury-Tenison, 1973, pp. 50-51

The Txikao live in the Xingu Park, a Brazilian Amazonian area set aside in 1961 at the urging of Orlando, Claudio, and Leonardo Villa Boas, three men who sadly came to know the disastrous effects of "development." This tribe once faced extinction because of exploitation and disease. For some years now they have had a chance to once again self-determine their lives. Xingu Park offers some semblance of protection from outside interests.

———————————— ☉ ————————————

FIRE DANCE
TIRIÓ

That night we never cooled down. As the heat of the day passed we sat in close to the fire, passing around the fish meat and *kasila*. The fire shot sparks at us, and took so much of the air in the clearing that we were lightheaded. I wanted to widen the *circle* so we were further back, the flames were high and were making the leaves of the trees crackle.

"No, you start dance."

I knew I should not have shown weakness. "Why me?"

The women were already applauding the idea. While I jogged a few *circuits around the fire* Pim stuck out his feet, so that to avoid tripping I had to swerve even closer to the flames. I collapsed back on my log and drank so much *kasila* to cool down I became as drunk as the others.

Every visible object was tinged red in the fire-glow, the moths, the tubular roots, even our eyes. Our clothes and skin were an even deeper red from the dye. The leaves curtaining us trapped the sparks and smoke as if we were in a cave. The Indians looked into the flames with vacant expressions and seemed to relish the scorching heat, as if wanting to forget the cold world outside, as if they believed it was against them.

As the *men wheeled around the fireside* in the first major dance, the *four women* stared into the flames through the gaps made by their legs. Then they slipped inside the men's *circle* and formed their own, on the very edge of the fire. The women were loose-limbed and raring to go. They spun holding hands, so near the fire the sparks were zipping through their hair. The men stood still and watched in an *outer circle*. For the first time ever I was entreated to stand with the men to dance.

The women closed their eyes, upturned their heads and let their hair fall back down their shoulders. The men were beating a rhythm with their feet, but their eyes were glazed and fixed on the heart of the fire. The women seemed to be melting in the flames in front of my eyes. They strutted round with their backs to us, their toes brushing the embers. This was a fire dance. The women were worshipping the fire with their bodies. They stopped skipping and took a stance with their feet wide apart. They let the flames lick over their skin and wriggled their hips at the fire, wailing. We watched and chanted as they bent forward almost straddling the fire core. I thought they must be in terrible agony; they sang in high, conclusive screams, like gulls, above the furnace roar. Through the flames I saw tears running down the women's cheeks, spilling over their breasts. I winced at their pain.

Then I knew there was no pain. We men were all now pressed in there amongst them. The women's skin seared mine at first contact, then we were intertwined. We were clinched together, our arms fastened in a tight *circle*. We began moving in a *solid ring* around the fire. A moment before I would never dare approach a fire this close, but now the circle was tightening and shrinking. We were coming in closer still. I couldn't get away, and I didn't want to.

We were fused together, smelted by the fire, and this was complete unity; acceptance by the Carib Indians. I felt tears brimming in my eyes and saw them trickling down my chest and dropping into the fire. The teardrops, like everything else, were bright red.

Who Goes Out in the Midday Sun: An Englishman's Trek Through the Amazon Jungle, Benedict Allen, 1986, pp. 189-191

In this somewhat contemporary first-hand account we are able to vicariously experience an interesting circle dance around a central fire. It opened up the participants to a trance-like state whereby they were unharmed either by the heat or flames. Such a dance led to an experience of oneness with all that was before and around them. The four women were essential to this dance.

────────────────── ✪ ──────────────────

NIOPO AND STINGING ANTS CEREMONY
PIAROA

All these Indians were preparing themselves for the coming test.... During the night all the men of the tribe had followed the example of the old sorcerer and taken niopo, and at dawn their spirits had not entirely returned to their bodies. . . .

They had gone beyond their ordinary, everyday world and were feeling their way forward into the unknown spaces of their tribal destiny under the guidance of the tranquil old sorcerer who was in charge of their souls. And part of his task was to guide the boys safely through the initiatory rites of the great culmination which would make them into men.

I looked around for the young neophytes, and after a while I saw them.... It was just midday and there were no shadows on the ground. The puddles of yellowish liquid steamed in the sun. Then the sound of maracas came from the tribal hut and the five masked priests appeared again. They **gathered round** the three boys who were soon to be men and took them by the arms, leading them, half carrying them towards the hut. The boys' legs dragged along the ground between the long fringes of the costumes of the tiger priests. The priests made their way across the village square, dancing backwards and forwards slowly, and then they went into the hut. Men crowded forward to meet them and took the boys from their arms. Across their backs the boys each carried a package done up with liana. The package contained the hammock which an Indian always takes with him on a journey. Three hammocks were now unfolded and slung to the nearest posts in the hut, and the boys were laid in them by the masked priests. Then the priests left the hut. The old sorcerer had sat down on his stool again to the right of the canoes, which were now almost empty. To his side, on the floor, were various accessories: two flat pieces of wickerwork, long cigarettes of green tobacco rolled in banana leaf, and a calabash of cassava juice. The five masked priests reappeared. On the forehead of each one, in place of the usual painted design, was a rectangular piece of wickerwork containing 200 imprisoned and wriggling ants, black and shining. Facing the old sorcerer, they danced from one foot to the other whilst their acolytes detached the five pieces of wickerwork containing the ants from their headdress and placed them at the feet of the sorcerer. Then the tiger priests retreated a couple of paces and began to chant louder and louder. This was the original chant of the tribe, the chant of the tigers who had brought the first infant Piaroas to the earth in their claws.

One of the boys got out of his hammock and went toward the old sorcerer with a firm and assured step, and sat down facing the old man on a second stool which had been placed there. He looked into the old man's face and, leaning forward, he placed his hands on the old man's knees. The ceremony of initiation was about to begin.

The old man picked up one of the squares of wickerwork with the ants. . . . In the absolute silence which now prevailed one could hear the wild clicking movements of the legs and pincers of the ants. But apparently the insects were still not sufficiently excited to sting at once and altogether as the ritual required, so the old sorcerer dipped the wickerwork square into the calabash of liquid at his side. Then, taking a lighted cigarette, he gently blew the smoke over the ants. The blue fumes filtered through the wickerwork and rose up to the roof of the hut. The wild excitement of the ants caused the sound of their struggles to increase in volume like the crackling of a fire as it flares up. Holding the square in his hands, the old man described *three circles* round the head of the seated boy. Up to then the old man had held the square so that the heads of the ants were facing the boy. Now he turned it round. Several men stepped forward and seized the boy by the wrists and the head, and the old man then placed the square on the boy's chest. This time 200 abdomens of the giant ants touched the boy's flesh and 200 stings penetrated simultaneously, injecting their venom. The boy's body suddenly contracted and he forced himself back. A large hand closed over his mouth firmly to prevent him from crying out.

Slowly the old man moved the wickerwork square over the most sensitive parts of the boy's body. He performed the operation with great care and a minimum of movement. It went on for two, three, four minutes, and then finally the ants were passed in a last slow, caressing movement over the cheeks and forehead of the boy. The men released their grip. The boy's body straightened. He still sat there with his hands on the old man's knees without moving. In the eyes of all he was now a man. . . . A woman came forward and bathed his chest, his arms and his back with a little of the liquid which she scooped out of the calabash with the palm of her hand. The old man had taken up his cigarette again and now he puffed great clouds of bluish smoke over the body of the tortured boy.

Until then the lad's eyes had been half closed; now they opened wide. He looked around slowly, as though astonished. He seemed to have returned from another world, or to have entered a world which was completely new to him. He stood up, walked back to his hammock and lay down. From all parts of the great hut now wreathed in smoke rose a long, shrill cry. It was a shout of triumph from a community which now had another man in its ranks. . . .

If this Indian ritual is hard for the boys, it is no less hard for the adults. It demands that those who watch must also suffer, and therefore, after the last of the three boys had gone through the initiatory ritual, all the men came forward one by one and then all the women, to sit before the old sorcerer and submit to the imposition of the wickerwork ant screens, though the squares used for the women were not so large. When Mario's turn came, the old man took particular care to see that his ordeal should be greater than that of the others, because he was the chief. In the middle of it he fainted. *Four men* sprang forward at once to raise him up again. Imperturbably the old sorcerer continued to pass the ants over the flesh of Mario's inert body. We knew that on our account Mario had not drunk so much as the others, and now he had not the same resistance to the torture. He had to suffer his ordeal to the very end.

Then came the turn of the women. . . . Instead of putting their hands on his knees, they put them behind their heads, their elbows raised high and spread wide to lift their naked breasts proudly and present them in the most favorable position. Whilst the ant screens were being applied to them they affected a complete indifference to the pain. They even seemed to be very proud to be the center of attention. Not a muscle of their faces twitched and they had no need of any assistance. They did not even wink an eyelid, but continued to chat in high-pitched tones with their friends during the whole ordeal, and not once did their voices break. One would have said that they felt nothing at all. When it was over they walked back to their hammocks with a firm tread and then collapsed into a coma.

I rose, covered with sweat and dust, for I had spent the whole ceremony lying flat on the ground holding the battery of accumulators whilst Pierre lit up the various phases of the torture with our lamp and Jean took reel after reel of film . . . but we had been able to record all the details of the initiatory rites suffered by the three boys and the subsequent ordeal of the men.

The next morning the life of the Piaroas went on as though nothing at all had happened.

The Impossible Adventure: Journey to the Far Amazon,
Alain Gheerbrant, 1953, pp. 145-149, 152.

This is a common ritual throughout the Amazon, though some of the specific details and interpretations may vary from tribe to tribe. Blessing individuals with three circular motions is also common, as is the ritual surrounding of the candidates at times. This age-old ritual reenacts the ancient stories of the People and causes them to participate in what is often called "sacred time."

———————————————— ☻ ————————————————

AYLLU CEREMONY
CANELOS QUICHUA

While the lanceros busy themselves being as unpleasant as possible, other men and women join in the activities described above, playing havoc with the remains of the Nunghui—and Sungui—derived soul power of the pottery and chicha. Tinajas are dragged to the central plaza still half full of chicha, which is flung around in a general free-for-all. The jisteros continue their ***drumming round and round in a circle*** near the camari table, and many women dance as a unit, throwing their hair to and fro. Then the lanceros leave this scene and go to the house of one of their members, where they drink chicha until a little before 5:00.

Dominario. At 5:00 the lanceros go to the priest and tell him that they wish a "benediction" for their *dominario,* a ritual to terminate the ayllu ceremony. . . . A powerful shaman imbued with ancient knowledge comes quietly to the church. . . . He moves to the front of the church, faces the square, and begins to play a melody on his three-hole flute while softly beating a rhythm on his drum. Inside the church several men prepare a ten-foot-long bamboo pole with *four notches*, into which they place copal to form the basis for *four torches*. The pole represents the great anaconda from Ancient Times. It is the corporeal representation of Sungui or Yacu mama, master of water and spirit master of the Yacu Supai Runa. The copal fire burning in the ancient amarun represents the powerful central red color of the rainbow, sky-earth symbol of the ancient water spirit.

The *four lanceros* assemble in front of the powerful shaman, and on his signal begin the last of their dances until the next ceremony. First they dance shoulder to shoulder, back and forth, swinging their wooden knives in a set pattern to the rhythm of their bells and the drum. Then the jistero drummers come back into the picture and *circle* the dancing lanceros, moving clockwise. Women break into the *circle* and dance as a group, tossing their hair.

Next the lanceros break into two groups and dance toward each other, moving back and forth, as the women continue their dance and the soul-bringing drummers continue their beat. On another signal from the flute-and drum-playing powerful shaman the lanceros put their backs to one another and work through a different *quadrangular* pattern. Then, on another shaman signal, they begin to dance back and forth, weaving in and out in a square dance-like pattern. . . .

Inside the church the *four copal torches* in the bamboo log are lit; some jisteros, themselves descendants of the ancient jaguar ayllus, pick it up and assume the "dress," churana, of the ancient anaconda spirit on their shoulders. Then, with the dream-bringing drumming jisteros, they begin to *circle the entire plaza*. The ancient yacu supai is ritually freed from the water domain and for a moment "dominates" the land, flooding it with ancient water power. The shaman leader, imbued with ancient knowledge, maintains his melodies and rhythm, the lanceros (as taruga pumas) keep up their *quadrangular dancing patterns*, and the women continue their dancing adjacent to them. The women's dance is to Nunghui, ancient garden and pottery-clay giver. The jisteros, led by the jaguar-borne anaconda, then begin to run around the plaza and then back and forth around the square and through the church, knocking aside the flimsy partitions and crashing around in a jaguar-determined serpentine course, before running off, still carrying the burning amarun pole, first to one ceremonial house and then to the other, and finally breaking up into respective cai and huarmi units. The lanceros remain in the plaza, dancing for a while, and then ask the priest for a special benediction for them alone.

Sacha Runa: Ethnicity and Adaptation of Ecuadorian Jungle Quichua,
Norman Whitten, Jr., 1976, pp. 193-194

Copal incense is used in prayers by many Peoples in Mesoamerica as well as in some South American territories. In this part of the Ayllu Ceremony, which also expresses tribal affinity with the supernatural and natural worlds, four torches and people dancing in circles and quadrangle patterns align their ceremonial patterns with those of many other Peoples in North and South America.

––––––––––––––––––––––– ☉ –––––––––––––––––––––––

HUASI RITUAL
CANELOS QUICHUA

A ritual context—a setting in which stylized behavior takes place—is often established by a man within his own huasi. In its simplest form this basic huasi ritual brings power to the individual and household. While resting during a return from a hunt a man weaves a basket-like headpiece from split vine or reed. On entering his household he walks to the center, gives the game to his wife, and, after drinking chicha for ten minutes or so, begins to weave feathers and animal skin into the head-piece. Particularly favored are a combination of monkey skin and the entire plumage of the giant toucan, curassow, cock of the rock, or guan. Should the hunter be fortunate enough to have killed all of these, he may make a really elaborate headdress of monkeyskin with the toucan on top, beak sticking out over the man's face, two or three large black birds arranged down behind, and the cock of the rock on the bottom on a frame, so that when the man moves rapidly the bird seems to fly.

When the headpiece is ready the man plays a private soul song on his transverse flute, dons the rig, takes up his drum, and begins to *move counterclockwise around the house*, beating the peccary-skin side and allowing the monkey-skin side, with attached chambira-fiber snare, to resound inward toward the center of the room. The beat is always the same, 1-2-3-4/1-2-3-4, with the *fourth* beat either absent or distinctly diminished to allow the snare to"sing" out its buzzing *mascuyu,* soul-dream, sound. This ritual walking, where the man takes about one step *every four beats*, is called *yachajuí.* The sound of the drum beat represents Amasanga-controlled thunder, and the snare buzzes the spirit helpers' dream song. Thoughts of distant living and dead relatives come to the man and to other household members as he continues *to circle*. The souls of other animals awaken and also sing their own songs, which the man and women think-hear.

Sacha Runa: Ethnicity and Adaptation of Ecuadorian Jungle Quichua,
Norman Whitten, Jr., 1976, p. 165

The ritual structure of this huasi ritual expresses the sensitivity of this People's sacred circularity and the use of a four-beat rhythm with the drum expresses their solidarity with other Native Peoples of the Americas.

——————————————— ✪ ———————————————

NAMING CEREMONY
MEKRANOTI

Four days after our return to the village, the women started preparing big earth ovens, so I realized that this was the final day of the ceremony. One by one, the tortoises' meat was removed. While the women did the butchering and prepared the festive meal, I entered the houses to watch the dancers being decorated. Unfortunately, the men didn't wear elaborate decorations this time. Their bodies were only smeared lightly with red annatto dye, and each man put on a small feather headress, a necklace, and a back feather pendant. Those who were ready for the dancing gathered at the small campsite of the initiates. By the late afternoon, all of the men were there, as were the women and childeren who'd come to watch the scene. Women were allowed to enter the men's house only on such specific ritual occa-sions. People started insisting that I participate, by dancing for Mengra, Kamkra's newborn son, who was therefore also my son. When I was told that the dancing would insure that all the newborn children became strong and healthy, I gave in, saying that I'd need to take time out to take notes and photographs. My body was quickly painted red all over, and Kokoket, Kamkra's wife, fetched a feather headdress for me to wear. She also brought an extra-long palm pole for me to use.

Late that afternoon, the men all went to the landing strip and rehearsed briefly. Forming one big *circle*, they all held long poles. Moving *counter-clockwise*, they sang while vigorously stamping their right feet on the ground. . . . The women and children gathered to watch. The gleam of the fires made the dancers look like shadows emerging from the emptiness. During the first hour or so, the configuration of the dancers changed frequently. Groups were continuously formed and reformed, each group representing all the "fathers" of a newborn child. Since both biological and "classificatory" fathers participated in these groups, I had to dance in several such blocks. Those men who didn't belong to the category of fathers of newborn children danced at the rear. We stopped briefly every 15 minutes or so, when a man personifying a jaguar symbolically attacked the children being honored, who stood behind us with their ritual friends. We also briefly stopped at about 2:00 a.m. to eat the meals the women had prepared earlier.

Mekranoti: Living Among the Painted People of the Amazon,
Gustaaf Verswijver, 1996, p.80

The tábák, or naming ceremony, of this Brazilian Amazon People has as its purpose the bestowal of names on children after they have been instructed in special songs and the ancient ways. But the ceremony also expresses overtones of future marriage as well.

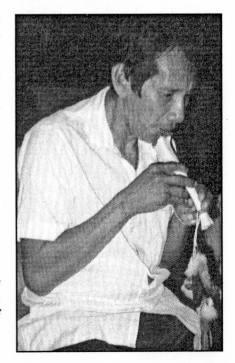

*José Luis Piaroa, a shaman from
the Amazon region of Venezuela,
playing on a deer bone flute*

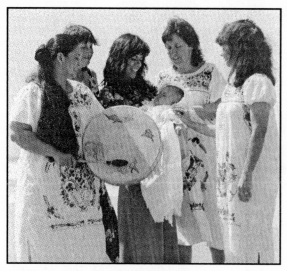

Celebrating a baptism at a beach near Santa Cruz, California

INTERCULTURAL CULTURAL AREA

CIRCULAR BROOCH SYMBOLISMS
INTERTRIBAL

Small **round dots** were often depicted by native peoples. The dots appear as body tattoos and on garments, lodges, horses, pipes, and drums. . . .

These dots, when expanded into *circles*, as ring brooches, also symbolized celestial entities such as stars and the concept of eternity, the cycle of life, and the sequence of the *four seasons*. Native Americans dance in a sacred circle, and they draw circles on the ground around their homes, burials, sweat lodges, and certain spiritually significant areas. To native peoples, the circular brooch represented more than a geometric form; it embodied many powers and represented nature's many cycles.

Silver in the Fur Trade, 1680-1820,
Martha Hamilton, 1995, pp. 51-52

Even trade items, in both ancient and post-Contact times, bore spiritual significance among the Peoples. The circle had a certain preeminence among the myriads of designs.

Number 4 &
Four Directions

NUMBER 4 &
FOUR DIRECTIONS

There are three things beyond my comprehension, four, indeed, that I do not understand: the way of an eagle through the skies, the way of a snake over the rock, the way of a ship in mid-ocean, the way of a man with a girl.

Proverbs 30:18-19

It is fairly easy to see a connection between four directions and four items or personages which relate to these directions. It is an almost automatic coordination.

The Menominee and Ojibway of the Woodlands sing and dance to the winds of the directions and design appropriate accoutrements to match. They associate guardians with these four quarters of the universe. The Southeastern Creeks and Seminoles offer annual dances for all the ceremonies that have to do with the gift of corn. The directions figure greatly in their overall planning for the activities. In dancing or healing ceremonies, the Cherokees and others know how to address the four personages.

In the Pueblos of the Southwest the whole community comes alive with the sounds of drumming and singing and dancing on a regular basis. Often outsiders are invited to be present. Each direction is venerated in a variety of ways throughout the festive days, and every one has a part. The Apaches have their Gan dances and puberty ceremonies while the Navajos acknowledge the four sacred mountains as they enter the sweatlodge for healing or to welcome a girl into womanhood.

The Californians all have their origin stories and often the cardinal directions are described (Pomo). The Northwestern Peoples would never think of entering a ceremonial house without the proper directional etiquette (Wanapum), nor of eating salmon without first offering the right prayers (Tsimshian).

Many is the Plains ceremony that calls on the directions and ritually has something done four times, often over and over. It is safe to say that all the prairie Peoples could not let a day go by without expressing some prayer or action that included this combination. Even the sub-arctic Cree and Eskimo of Canada know the appropriate religious lore regarding the taciturn winds.

The Peoples of the vast regions of Mesoamerica always considered these themes in architecture and dance and ritual, no matter where they lived. Even South America is not exempt from such action.

Kuna delegates from Panama at Indigenous Encounter in
Puerto Rico, April 1998

WOODLANDS CULTURAL AREA

Praying to the Four Directions

BAG WITH STRAP
MENOMINEE

This bag made of deerskin, worn with the strap around the neck, was designed to hold many useful items. It was made by a woman who lived in the forests of Wisconsin, very likely of Menominee ancestry. All the materials used for the bag came from nature. She tanned the deerskin carefully and darkened it with a brown dye derived from black walnut hulls. She braided yarn spun from nettle fibers for the strap. The designs visible on the bag were created with porcupine quill embroidery. The artist softened the quills in water, dyed them with plant and mineral dyes, and then sewed them to the surface of the bag using a variety of techniques for different effects. The linear elements of the design were produced by wrapping quills around a thin, thread-like strand of sinew, the dry, stringy tendon of animals, and then stitching the quills down into place. The six four-petal "flowers" at the top of the bag were created with this method. The broad, solid band of color beneath the "flowers" was accomplished by flattening the quills and folding them back and forth to fill a horizontal "lane." with the quills sewn down at the edges of the lane. Two lanes make up the horizontal band in the middle of the bag. The artist created the cross and diamond design below with both "wrapped" and "folding" techniques.

The designs appear to be geometric and abstract in the sense that they do not represent the likeness of anything. They are nevertheless symbolic. The *"equal-arm" cross* in the center is an ancient symbol in

North America. Its arms point to each of the *four cardinal directions: north, south, east,* and *west.* Because these dimensions define the terrestrial earth in a Native American worldview, the *number four* is considered sacred. The *four corners* of the diamond that surrounds the cross restate the number four. The *four-petaled "flowers"* in the upper panel are also equal-arm crosses with references to "four" and the terrestrial earth as well . . . the patterning is symmetrical, meaning that one side mirrors the other. Each area of decorations on the bag— the upper panel with the six crosses, the central with its alternating colors, and the low panel with the cross and diamond—is "radially" symmetrical, the same from side to side and top to bottom.

These are all characteristic features of women's art of the Great Lakes region. The designs are non-representational, and yet symbolic of cosmological principles, i.e., the sacredness of the earth and the number four. The radially symmetrical patterns create equivalences between "up," "down," top," and "bottom" in a manner that also symbolized *"four"* as a principle by which both the designs and the earth are organized. Color shifts, for example, the way red and blue alternate in the four-petal flower patterns, are another convention tied to a philosophical ideal that attempts to reconcile or harmonize polar opposites.

Art of the American Frontier: A Portfolio, David Penney, 1995, pp. 7, 9

The author describes a bag that was fashioned in the early part of the last century. Recently it was on display at an exhibition. Once again we are able to recognize the primacy of both the cardinal directions and symbolic fourness in a practical but beautifully thought out and executed object of art.

———————————— ✢ ————————————

WINDS OF THE FOUR DIRECTIONS
OJIBWAY

The *Four Winds* and Flint, for instance, are quintuplets. They were born of a mother (unnamed) who, while given human characteristics, lived in the very distant past . . . this character . . . may have anthropomorphic characteristics without being conceived as a human being. In the context she, like the others, is an *atiso'kan*. The Winds were born first, then Flint "jumped out," tearing her to pieces. This, of course, is a direct allusion to his inanimate, stony properties. Later he was penalized for his hurried exit. He fought with *Misabos* (Great Hare) and pieces were chipped off his body and his size reduced. "Those pieces broken from your body may be of some use to human beings some day," *Misabos* said to him. "But you will not be any larger so long as the earth shall last. You'll never harm anyone again."

Against the background of this "historic" event, it would be strange indeed if flint were allocated to an inanimate grammatical category. There is a special term for each of the *four winds* that are differentiated, but no plural for wind. They are all animate beings, whose "homes define the *four directions*."

The conceptual reification of Flint, the Winds and the Sun as other-than-human persons exemplifies a world view in which a natural-supernatural dichotomy has no place. And the representation of these beings as characters in true stories reinforces their reality by means of a cultural device which at the same time depicts their vital roles in interaction with other persons as integral forces in the functioning of a unified cosmos.

> *Teachings from the American Earth: Indian Religion and Philosophy*,
> Dennis Tedlock & Barbara Tedlock, 1975, p. 153

Each wind has a home in a particular direction. In not having a plural word for "wind," the Ojibway language is perhaps saying that each wind deserves special respect and is unique and therefore deserves a more personal name.

✵

SACRED DANCE
OJIBWA

Today he would dance in honor of the north wind manitos, for **north** was the direction of wisdom. Tomorrow his dance would be to the spirits of the **south**, direction of trust; then to the **east**, direction of enlightenment; then to the **west**, gateway to the future and the Afterworld. After each day's dance, he would lie down beneath the branchless pine and fast, starvation of the body nourishing the spirit. By the end of the *fourth day,* he hoped his spiritual senses would be heightened as never before. . . .

Facing north, he danced, toe-to-heel, his feet moving to the rhythm of drumbeats summoned from memories of ceremonies long ago. He danced singing a hymn to Wayndanhimuk-nodinjoon, the *Four Sacred Directions*, the circle in which all things moved. *Four directions, four seasons to the year, four seasons to a man's life*. *South* summer childhood, Wawiekumig sang. *West* autumn maturity. *North* winter old age and death. *East* spring rebirth.

Indian Country, Philip Caputo, 1988, pp. 157-158

In this passage from a contemporary novel, aspects of the seasons are related to the four directions. Dance allows a person to stay close to this power of the earth while at the same time opening up the spirit to offer prayer.

---------------------------------- ✸ ----------------------------------

INTERCARDINAL DIRECTIONS
CHIPPEWA

Nowadays it is clear to me how important ideals picked up from those I dearly loved stuck with me.

If I might, some of these ideals can be set forth in *four quarters*: the *northwest* brings to mind my tipi (home), the Prayer or Council Lodge, and the place where the Medicine Man mixes and administers medicinal concoctions—all fundamental to the welfare of the people. Moreover, the tipi is supported by seven poles, seven council fires of the Sioux Nation, an ideal of representative council that solidified in the minds of the Sioux about the year 1868.

The *northeast* recalls to us the stalwart and brave, the fearless and the fearful; it brings to mind the tribes' progressive sense joined with attentiveness to disciplined family life and the need, at times, to fight for God-given rights.

The *southeast* suggests the urgent need we have to pay homage to the Great Spirit with great thankfulness for His care and many blessings granted the people. . . .

Finally the *southwest* quarter brings to mind the elements that compose a spiritual system: the *four cardinal directions*, the *four winds*, the heavens and earth, the sacred place, the sacred way along which each man meets what is sometimes soothing and refreshing and fruitful to life, but at other times what is disastrous to man.

We might feel today, that this form of inner life training, a spirituality, is strange and foreign to our modern way of thinking. But, in fact, we of 1974 can become familiar with and highly challenged by it, in this modern context of life.

Quest for the Pipe of the Sioux: As Viewed from Wounded Knee,
Wilbur Riegert, 1975, pp. 117-118

Here is a personal understanding of the four directions by a bicultural Chippewa who also spent a lot of time with Sioux.

A young Onondaga prays at a lakeside

A prayer at the beginning of the day

SOUTHEAST CULTURAL AREA

STOMP GROUNDS PREPARATION
CREEK

In the years following the federal resettlement of the 1830s, most Creeks built log or frame houses after the fashion of their white neighbors, but back in the hills they established more than fifty separate "stomp grounds," recreating their old Southeast township names and their square grounds. Here the Creek and Yuchi medicine men observed traditional summer ceremonies and revived rites that harked back to the ancient mound festivals of Mississippian times.

Early in spring 1978, we were guided into the Cookson Hills of eastern Oklahoma for a look at a few of the twenty or more remaining stomp grounds where Creek and Yuchi Indians still hold the Green Corn rites. Our escort was Archie Sam, the grandnephew of Watt Sam, the last speaker of the Natchez tongue. Archie Sam led us into the humid woodlands between the Canadian and Arkansas rivers, where Creek who were moved from the Southeast initially re-established their town centers. Outside the town of Gore we drove to the site of his family's old grounds, once known as Medicine Spring. It had become a weedy pasture where farmers dumped their garbage; less than a century ago it was the setting for games, dances, and curing rituals.

Recently some Creeks near Gore had petitioned Sam to "bring back the fire" of the Medicine Spring ground. First he established a "re-

412

hearsal ground" for them to practice the old dances. Its *four clan benches*—Wind clan at the *north*, Alligator to the *east*, Bear to the *south* and Bird to the *west*—surrounded the hearth of a *four-log* fire. . . .

Native American Architecture, Peter Nabokov &
Robert Easton, 1989, p. 113

Many People of Native American heritage are seeking to understand the old ways, especially the ancient spiritual ways. Architecturally putting into place the building and ceremonial fire area of the Creeks is one kind of attempt to do this. Of course, the spiritual wisdom calls also for those who live it, to tell it and share it. It is nothing short of a miracle that in many tribes and groups, despite many attempts at cultural and religious destruction, there still exist those who can lead ceremonies and pass on knowledge.

GREEN CORN CEREMONY FIRE
CREEK

Among the Creek Indians, who lived originally in present-day Georgia and Alabama before being displaced to Oklahoma, the Green Corn Ceremony reaches a peak in the so-called Busk, a ritual that is performed to this day. Traditionally, in preparation for the ceremony, women and children scoured the dwellings and even extinguished the household fires that had been kept burning continuously since the preceding year's Busk. In the meantime, the men prepared the square where the Busk would be held, scraping away a layer of earth and sprinkling fresh soil, or sometimes white sand, over the area. *Four* logs specially chosen for a ceremonial fire were laid in the center, with a timber pointing in each of the *cardinal directions*. (From this blaze, the women would later take coals to rekindle hearth fires.) After the consecration of the *square,* no one could enter who had not fasted.

The day of a Busk, which usually lasted *four days*, was one of purification. Gathering in the square, the men settled or forgave all debts and quarrels of the preceding year; no substantial harvest could be expected in the absence of harmony among tribe members. Shirkers and tribe members guilty of antisocial behavior atoned for their acts by confessing and asking forgiveness. Even a murderer who had escaped execution by fleeing into the forest would be absolved if he could reach the square unharmed during a Busk.

American Indians: The Spirit World, Henry Woodhead (Ed.), 1992, pp. 102-103

Four logs, four directions, four days, and a square: these are some of the lived-out symbols of this important ceremony of life.

--------------------------------- ✦ ---------------------------------

HARVEST CEREMONIAL PREPARATIONS
CREEK

Various species of the animal kingdom came into the homes of the Creeks for protection and food. The bear, the deer, the panther, the snake and birds. By the sanction and purpose of the Great Spirit the Indians accepted them and claimed relationship with them as a clan. Though at one time there were a dozen or more clans there are only seven today, namely: Bear, Deer, Bird, Wind, Potato, Raccoon and Panther (Tigers). This happened due to the dying out of the ancient ways. So according to the instructions of the *four angels,* a Chief and his assistant built their square or in our language the Big house (Chukorako). Its foundation, spiritually, were *four logs* cut the same length and laid in the direction of the *four cardinal points, east, west, north* and *south*. In the center, space is left for the fire which as yet they had not performed the method of creating it. With all things, the Creeks were told, there must be a ceremony or ritual as we taught you. One man had been pointed out as the Master of Fire. He and his assistants found the tinder (tokpvfka) in Sycamore wood. On a block of dried and seasoned Elm, a dried and hard stem of Cane (Kohv) was used to drill on it and cause spontaneous combustion onto the tinder. No other method was to be used to obtain fire as it was a holy thing and considered a gift of the Great Spirit. The fire was not to be started until the plan and layout of the bighouse was completed. On each side of the fire a brush arbor was built. The one on the *west* was considered the Chief's bed which was partitioned off for the notables such as the vice chief (e'mapoktv), the medicine man (Hilishvya), the precious person (hemeha) and the judge (Fvcechv). The seats were primitive with logs across blocks. The Chief's bed was elevated, covered with bark and Cane. In the first section *north* were seated the Wind and Bear clan, and in the *south* the medicine man (hilishaya) the hemecha who was of the Bird Clan and the Beaver clan. The Chief was of the Bird clan. In the *north* arbor were the messengers called Big Emathla and Little Emathla. On the *east* was the Warrior's bed called Tustenuke. The *south* arbor was for the rest of the clans and visitors called este coloke. At the *northeast* corner of the Chief's bed were placed two pots of medicine. A little north of the emathla arbor was the house of precious articles. The women entered the grounds from the *southwest*. The ball ground was usually a little *northeast* of the square. Outside the square were brush arbors for families and their children.

Now it is in the month of the Big harvest moon (hayothlakko) or August, and the green corn is at its best. As per the wish of Yahola it is the Creeks' new year and they will have their first celebration or "Busk" as it is referred to by the Anglo-Americans. The square is ready for the fire to be built—the tribe is ready for the fast. . . .

The master of the fire feeds to it the wood brought up by his assistants, then he *makes a circle* around it about twenty-five feet in diameter, which makes the area sacred and holy. No one is to enter it except the master, the medicine man and the person who supplies wood to the fire. If a child or a person unknowingly trespasses the limits, the spirit and the holiness of the fire is desecrated, so that a new one has to be built. Being true to their belief, it has never happened. . . .

The fast begins in this manner; no food or water is taken in. The medicine man sends *four men* out to find and bring to him the roots of (Mekohoyemecv) or redroot, its properties are highly emetic. Along with that, some spicewood (kapapaska). These are made into tea in separate pots. The medicine man (Hilishaya) sings a prayer and blows it into the concoction through a hollow reed. He does this *four times*. At around 10 o'clock the men come with containers (gourds) to drink the warm tea of the redroot (which by the way, its botanical name is Hex Vomitoria). Each person knows just how much to take in before the urge to vomit happens. For some it takes alot, for others very little.

Chasers of the Sun: Creek Indian Thoughts,
Louis Littlecoon Oliver, 1990, pp. 5-7

Growing corn

We are clearly able to recognize a three-fold pattern at work here: the teaming up of the directions with both fourness of action and circularity.

—————————————— ✳ ——————————————

CEREMONIAL FIRE AND RITUAL WALKING
CREEK

The day of the beginning of the celebration was determined by the chief, or *mika,* and his council, and the opening ceremonies took place in the great town square. . . .

Fifth day: The *four* logs of the original fire having lasted only *four* days, another four were similarly arranged and the Fire kindled as before, after which the men drank the black drink. . . .

Eighth day: In the square and outside of it the most solemn ceremonies were conducted. A concoction supposed to have virtue as a physic, made by beating and stirring into water fourteen kinds of plant, was drunk by the men and rubbed over their joints, after priests conducting the ceremony had blown into it through small reeds. Another mixture composed of the ashes of pine boughs and old corn cobs stirred in water was prepared in a pot by *four* little girls, after which two large pans of a mixture of water and clay were prepared by the men. The chief and the warriors all rubbed themselves with portions from each of these mixtures, after which two men, especially appointed, brought to the chief's house flowers of the old men's tobacco, of which everybody present received a share. The chief and his counselors then walked *four times* around the burning logs, throwing into the fire, each time they were at the *east*, portions of the old men's tobacco, and each time they were at the *west*, pausing, facing *west*, before going on. After all of which, the following concluding ceremony was performed:

At the chief's house there had been displayed for some time a cane with two white feathers at its tip. At the moment of sun-set, a man of the Fish clan took this down and, followed by all present, began walking toward the river. At halfway, he **uttered a death whoop**, which he repeated **three times more** before arriving at the water's edge, where he stood while the company following congregated along the bank. Everyone present placed a grain of tobacco on his own head and into each ear, and at a signal *four times* pronounced, threw tobacco into the river. At a like signal, announced again ***four times***, every man dove into the river to fetch from the bottom ***four stones***, with which they crossed themselves on their breasts ***four times***, throwing one stone back into the water with each crossing, uttering at each the death whoop. They all then washed themselves and, with the cane with its two feathers held aloft, returned to the square, where it was planted. Then everybody walked through the town visiting, and after nightfall came the mad dance with which the celebration ended.

The Way of the Seeded Earth/Part 2: Mythologies of the Primitive Planters: The Northern Americas, Joseph Campbell, 1989, pp. 238-239

In the late eighteenth century Benjamin Hawkins described this harvest busk ceremony (Green Corn Ceremonial) in his book, A Sketch of the Creek Country, in 1798 and 99. *Notice that four logs are used, there is a four times ritual walking section, honor is given to the four directions, there are four loud cries, four signals for the offering of tobacco to the river, and four stones are brought up from the river's bottom and they bless themselves with the stones four times before throwing them back into the river at the sound of a four-fold whoop.*

⁜

CEREMONIAL SQUARE GROUNDS AND SACRED FIRE

CREEK

An 18th-century Creek village . . . reflects the highly organized nature of tribal life. Houses were arranged in clusters, each cluster including airy summer shelters and well-insulated winter lodges. The focal point of the village was the game field, often used for a rod-throwing contest called chunkey. The 40-foot pole at its center was sometimes topped with an object used as a target for archery and spear-throwing. The two poles at its rear were usually decorated with scalps or skulls, trophies of military triumphs. Next to the field is the ***square ground***, a quadrangle of open-work structures where tribal elders met beneath the shade of the thatched roofs during the warm months.

America's Fascinating Indian Heritage, James Maxwell (Ed.), 1978, pp. 90-91

Not unlike the Spanish plaza or the Italian piazza, the square ground of the Creeks was bounded by buildings. The People could gather to light the ceremonial four-log fire and know that they were centered and flanked by the four directions.

───────────────── ✢ ─────────────────

SQUARE GROUNDS POEM
CREEK

Of that which is natural
   is the key to our belief.
Strike the flint—rub the wood
   to create fire was the law.
Look to the sun and moon
   which without there's no life.
Four is our sacred number
   so the arbors are that many
On the *square*—star measured;
   east, west, north and *south*
Make the trees fall eastward
   Trim the limbs for the arbors,
Set up the pole—the sacred one
   which is called Pok'Kabe
and was carried by *four men*
   to the mystery hole prepared;
At the top, the Buffalo Skull.

Chasers of the Sun: Creek Indian Thoughts,
Louis Littlecoon Oliver, 1990p. 43

This poem about the preparation of the Koweta (Creek People) ceremonial grounds in Oklahoma is replete with directional symbolism as it acknowledges fourness in this logistic design and ritual activity. The poet was born in 1904 and has had little formal education, but he was well-versed in the ancient ways of his People.

───────────────── ✢ ─────────────────

HEALING CEREMONY
CHEROKEE

... ritual strategies and devices may be seen in the following Cherokee ceremony used to treat rheumatism or arthritis, an illness which afflicted many Southeastern Indians and which they greatly feared. ...

Prior to treating his patient the priest prepared his medicine by boiling the roots of "bear's bed" fern *(Dryopteris Adams.),* "Crow's shin" fern *(Adiantum pedatum L.),* and at least three other kinds of fern. Both the priest and his patient had to fast for the duration of the therapy.

The first ceremony began just as the sun came up. A terrapin shell containing two white beads was placed near the patient. After the patient took off his clothes and lay down, the priest rubbed the warm medicine on his body while reciting the following formula.

Listen! Ha! In the Sun Land you repose, O Red Dog. O now you have swiftly drawn near to hearken [sic]. O great *adáwehi* you never fail in anything. O, appear and draw near running, for your prey never escapes. You are now come to remove the intruder. Ha! You have settled a very small part of it far off there at the end of the earth.

Listen! Ha! In the Frigid Land you repose, O Blue Dog. O now you have swiftly drawn near to hearken. O great *adáwchi,* you never fail in anything. O, appear and draw near running, for your prey never escapes. You are now come to remove the intruder. Ha! You have settled a very small part of it far off there at the end of the earth.

Listen! Ha! In the Darkening Land you repose, O Black Dog. O, now you have swiftly drawn near to hearken. O great *adáwchi,* you never fail in anything. O, appear and draw near running, for your prey never escapes. You are now come to remove the intruder. Ha! You have settled a very small part of it far off there at the end of the earth.

Listen! On *Wáhala* you repose, O White Dog. O now you have swiftly drawn near to hearken. O great *adáwchi,* you never fail in anything. O, appear and draw near running, for your prey never escapes. You are now come to remove the intruder. Ha! You have settled a very small part of it far off there at the end of the earth.

Listen! On *Wáhala* you repose, O White Terrapin. O now you have swiftly drawn near to hearken. O great *adáwchi,* you never fail in anything. Ha! It is for you to loosen its hold on the bone. Relief is accomplished.

The priest recited this formula in a low whisper or murmur uttering *Ha!* in a louder tone of voice. After reciting the fomula and rubbing the medicine on his patient's body, the priest blew his breath on the affected parts. He repeated this ceremony three more times, replicating it exactly, with the only variation coming after the *fourth performance* when he blew his breath on the affected parts *four times*. The priest repeated this entire *four-part-performance* again after the sun was above the horizon, and again at mid-morning, and a fourth time at noon.

In the formula recited by the priest *east* is called "the Sun Land," *north* is called "the Frigid Land," *west* is called "the Darkening Land," and *south* is called *"Wáhala,"* after a mountain of that name which they believed was located in the south. An *adáwchi* was a human or spiritual being with great power. Only the very greatest priests and spiritual beings were regarded as being *adáwchi.* Since the illness was caused by a deer, the priests invokes from the *four quarters* spiritual dogs, natural enemies of deer, flattering them by calling them "great *adáwchi* who never fail," Each is called in from afar to come and take away a portion of the illness. Finally, the white terrapin, who had great influence in curing illness, is called in to loosen the illness from the patient's bones. The white beads in the terrapin shell symbolized relief and happiness.

The Southeastern Indians, Charles Hudson, 1976, pp. 346-348

Four complementary ferns were used in this healing ceremony. The healer repeated the sections of the prayers four times and the whole ceremony was repeated three more times before afternoon. The four quarters were referred to by special names. Throughout the ceremony use of the number 4 was a unifying factor.

---------------------- ✤ ----------------------

GIFTS OF THE FIRST AMERICANS
CHEROKEE

Long before the coming of the European missionaries, the natives inhabiting North and South America had their ceremonies honoring God, the Creator. Sadly the missioners felt these ceremonies were pagan and did not allow them to be incorporated into the Catholic liturgy. Since Vatican ll, there has been an attempt to include traditions of native people in the liturgy.

Native Americans in western North Carolina are predominately Eastern Cherokee, and few are Catholic. The early missionaries in this area were Baptist and Methodist, so many of the Cherokees joined these churches. . . .

The Cherokees and other Native American people have brought many gifts to the Catholic Church. They have a rich history of traditions and symbols, many compatible with the Catholic Church. I am proud to use some Native American traditions and symbols in the church in North Carolina.

In addition to the altar cloths and sacred vessels with Native American designs on them, we have tried to incorporate Native American spirituality into the liturgy by using "smudging" and the "four directions prayer" during Mass.

Native Americans use smudging for purification of one's self, dwelling or space. Smudging is similar to burning incense in the Catholic Church. Different tribes use various things for smudging— weed, grass, sage, cedar or sacred tobacco—all gifts from mother earth. The shell used to hold the offering is a gift from the water.

The *four directions prayer*, one of the traditional Cherokee prayers, includes the *four directions* and the *four races*: *East* being red; *North* white or blue; *West*, yellow; and *South*, black. The prayer is for all those who have gone before, for all who are with us now, and for all yet to come. This inclusiveness and caring for all is certainly what Jesus must have had in mind when he said, "Love one another as I have loved you." We also sing a few hymns in the Cherokee language.

Another similarity is the Cherokee have seven clans and the number seven is very sacred to them, just as we have the seven sacraments.

One of the talents of Native Americans is that they use the gifts of the earth, and their art is an expression of thanks to the Creator. Many of the Cherokee are noted for their artistry in pottery, carving and basket making. There is life in the rock, wood and earth from which these beautiful crafts are made. . . .

The Native Americans have great faith that God will provide for them. They have a tradition of giving gifts instead of receiving. When someone has a birthday or special occasion, friends and family are invited to a "giveaway" where gifts are given to others from the person celebrating. . . .

Another gift the Cherokee bring to the parish is their sense of community—what belongs to one, belongs to all by tradition. . . .

Working with Native Americans is a gift as well as a challenge to us. We must learn to trust in the Holy Spirit by living more simply and in the now, as our Cherokee brothers and sisters do.

"Gifts of the First Americans," *The Glenmary Challenge Magazine*,
Tom Field & Mary Hess, Winter 1996, pp. 13-14

In a wonderful way, the writers speak of the blending of worship forms for the sake of the People. Though these directional colors are specific to the Cherokee People, they also speak of the four main groupings of humanity that have come into the Cherokee experience.

——————————— ✤ ———————————

SOUL TRAVEL DURING SLEEP
SEMINOLE

The Seminoles believed that when a person fell asleep his soul left his body through his anus and went to the ***north*** where it had dream experiences. Normally it returned when the person awoke, but sometimes it refused to come back and this caused a person to fall ill, particularly when the soul went from ***north*** to ***east***. A priest was called in to coax the soul back to its owner. If a person's soul went all the way ***east***, and thence to the ***west***, the person would die. But the person was not completely dead until ***four days*** later, when a second soul left his body and went to the ***west***.

The Southeastern Indians, Charles Hudson, 1976, p. 344

Even sleep and the activities of one's spirit have a relationship to the four directions.

——————————— ✤ ———————————

GREEN CORN CEREMONIAL ACTIONS
SEMINOLE

... with the assistance of the same two "sighters" *four* regular *sections of oak log*, each approximately a foot and eight inches in length and *four* inches in diameter are placed in position on the mound by the ground's medicine man. These are the *four logs for the sacred fire*. First the *north* log is placed, then the *south*, then the *west*, and finally the *east* log. The medicine man places the logs slowly and deliberately, praying all the while. The cross formed by the logs, resting on the circular mound, is emblematic of the sun, and the sacred fire is, in fact, considered to be the earthly embodiment of the sun. Next the medicine man is handed *four perfect ears of the new corn crop* by the chief, and he places these next to the logs. . . . He blows and prays over each ear for about five minutes before putting it in place, moving his mouth from one end of the ear to the other as he does so. When he has finished, tinder is placed where the four logs meet, and it is ignited with flint and steel. As it blazes up, more tinder and larger dry sticks are added until the fire is blazing nicely and has consumed the four ears of corn, which are thus sacrificed to the fire and the sun. The sacred fire will continue to burn until the end of the ceremony. About 9:30 a.m. *four* young men, using shovels, carry coals from the new fire to the cooking fires in the various camps, which have been extinguished.

Now the Green Corn medicines are prepared. At Oklahoma Seminole grounds today these are the *pasa (Eryngium yuccifolium Michx., Button snake root)* and *hoyvnijv (Salix humilis Marsh., Small pussy willow)*. Two young men are sent to secure these plants, and each returns with a supply. The entire plant of the *pasa* is used, but only small roots of the *hoyvnijv*. . . . The *pasa* is merely placed in a large earthenware crock and worked slightly with the hands as water is poured over it. Later it is "bubbled" by the medicine man using his bubbling tube. The *hoyvnijv* roots are first bruised by pounding them on a log, using a wooden mallet, then placed in a washtub with water and "bubbled." All of this work is done in the *east* arbor (at some grounds outside the *paskofv,* east of the ground). The medicine man, as he bubbles or blows into the medicines, prays that they will be efficacious. They are ready for use by 9:45 a.m., but are allowed to steep until perhaps 10:30. . . . Before the medicine taking begins, an assistant to the medicine dips up a quantity of the *hoyvnijv* in a dipper and *circles the ground,* sprinkling medicine to the right and left as he follows his counterclockwise course. He spirals inward gradually and what remains he pours on the sacred fire as an offering. The men intone *"Matoooo!"* (Thanks!) as he does this.

Medicine taking and scratching of the women and children take place next. A tub of *hoyvnijv* is taken to the *east* edge of the *paskofv* and placed just inside the trash mound circling the ground. Women, girls, and small uninitiated boys come here with various containers. First they drink and wash their heads, arms, and legs in the holy liquid a number of times. They are then scratched if they choose, after which they wash and rinse their mouths *four* times, facing *east*, and retire to their camps.

The scratching ceremony today is done with an ordinary steel needle, not the older implement involving several thorns or pins set in a wooden frame or bent buzzard's quill. *Four* scratches are made on each upper arm, *four* on each lower arm, and *four* on the back of each calf. A woman may select an elder male relative to scratch her and her children. Small children, even babes in arms, are sometimes scratched, however lightly, because the rite is considered beneficial to the health. Red licorice candy is given to small boys and girls after their scratching to produce a positive association, but even with this inducement some of the small children cannot hold back a whimper as the needle bites and the blood wells up. After they have been scratched and rinsed in water the women and children, who have been fasting since midnight, can break their fast.

It is now the men's turn to take medicine. For this part of the ceremony the medicine man and his assistant sit in the *east* arbor, facing *west*, the two containers of medicine in front of them. The members of the ground, in pairs, approach from the *west* and, when they reach the place where the two are sitting, kneel before them. Each communicant has a dipperful of *hoyvnijv* poured over his head. He is then handed a dipperful of *pasa.* Holding the dipper in his left hand and using the first two fingers of the right, he dips out a small amount and, with a flipping notion, sprinkles a small amount to the *north, west, south,* and *east*, an offering to the deities of each of the *four cardinal points,* Then, still using the same two fingers, he applies a small amount to the tongue *four times* in succession. He then drinks the remainder of the dipperful. He returns the dipper to the medicine man or assistant, and it is returned filled with *hoyvnijv*. Each communicant swallows an enormous draught, and perhaps a second, then rises and walks past the *east* arbor to the eastern limits of the ground and vomits. Men from the chief's or *west* arbor take medicine first; and when they have finished, men from the *south* arbor; and then men from the *north* arbor. There are no men or boys in the *east* arbor except for the two men dispensing the medicine. The *pasa* is administered only to initiated men, and to them only during the first episode of medicine taking, not during the last three, when only *hoyvnijv* is employed.

Oklahoma Seminoles: Medicines, Magic, and Religion,
James Howard, 1984, pp. 131-132,134-137

The Seminoles, a People who are the descendants of several tribal groups who moved to Florida at different times during the last two centuries, still continue many of the ancient ways. The four directions, circular movement, and the ritual use of four times in succession are all marks of many of their ceremonies.

--------------------------------- ✳ ---------------------------------

FEATHER DANCE
SEMINOLE

The Feather Dance involves as many dancers as there are feather wands, plus the three musicians. The principal singer, usually the medicine man of the ground, carries the crock drum, and his two assistants carry coconut shell rattles. The feather dance is performed *four times* during the Green Corn, each of the *four episodes* involving *four circuits* of the square ground. At some grounds three episodes are danced on the third day of the ceremony, then a fourth the following morning. At most grounds, all four episodes take place on the third day.

The dance begins with each of the dancers taking a wand from the bunch at the front of the chief's arbor and moving to form a cluster around the three musicians, who face toward the *east*. They wear no special costume except for the shaved crane feather stuck in the hat or cap mentioned earlier in connection with the Ribbon Dance. Most of the men, in fact, are probably wearing second-best clothing, since they are in the midst of taking medicine, which involves kneeling in the mud before the tub of *hoyvnijv* and pouring some of the medicine over their heads, and also vomiting up the medicine they have imbibed.

In the dance they hold the lower end of the feathered wand at waist level and dance in place, patting the left foot on the ground before them, drawing it back, and then patting the right foot and drawing it back, and so on. As they execute this step they also manipulate the wand, moving it back and forth at the top. The dancers sing in unison with the musicians. The head singer calls out the words *"apiu, apiu,"* and all the dancers whoop. He then begins to sing. Once he has sung the key phrase and the song is recognized, all who know it join in. In spite of the shabby dress of the dancers, the Feather Dance is strangely compelling and beautiful. The swaying of the feathered wands in time with the music creates the odd illusion of a flock of small birds hovering just above the dancers' heads. The songs are quite melodic and attractive as well. Each episode has *four parts*, and each part employs only one song, which is sung and danced to at *four stations*. The first station is in front of the **west arbor**, the second in front of the **south arbor**, the third in front of the **east arbor**, the fourth in front of the **north arbor**. These locations vary from one ground to another, however, and at some grounds there is a station at the *tajo* or mound. At some grounds the dancers and singers march slowly from one station to another, intoning the cry "Hi-i-i" as long as they can hold their breath, then ending with a whoop. At others the dancers run pell mell from one station to the next. During the fourth episode the dancers do not stop at the last three stations but merely march slowly around the ground, dancing and singing.

Oklahoma Seminoles: Medicines, Magic, and Religion,
James Howard, 1984, pp. 140-141

The Feather Dance is a good example of a dance that holds together and expresses in sacred movement the four directions and the use of the number 4 to stress fullness and unity both in rhythm and in architectural planning.

SOUTHWEST CULTURAL AREA

Prayer for deer

KATCHINA CEREMONY
HOPI

Standing to the *east* of the hatch facing the opening, he bows down *four times* very slowly, saying "ha-a-a-a-a" in a falsetto which lasts to the limit of his breath. After this he takes a handful of the finely ground white corn from his sack and, bending down, pastes it on the lower side of the hatch. The kiva chief then comes out and sprinkles corn meal toward him *four times*, gives him *four prayer-sticks* which the men in the kiva have made for him, and receives one of the nine bundles of corn (and beans) carried by Ahül.

"Notes on Hopi Ceremonies in Their Initiatory Form in 1927-1928," *American Anthropologist*, Julian Steward, January/March 1931, pp. 61-62

This description comes from the notes taken at some observed ceremonies between 1927 and 1928 by Julian Steward, an anthropologist. A particular Kachina (a spirit being who brings crops, blessings, along with the much needed rain, good health, and who opens a fertile path for patients) Ahül, was being honored with corn meal, a special symbol of life. The east, a symbolic direction of beginnings and newness, is honored in this reminiscence of the ceremony, as well as the important fourfold prayer sticks and corn meal sprinklings.

SNAKE DANCE
HOPI

Six days before the public dance, the Snake Priests go out after the snakes, spending most of *four days* at this task. The first day they go *north* of the village, the second day *west*, the third day *south*, and the fourth day *east*. Bodies painted red, they travel in loincloth only, their nakedness being an additional prayer that rain may cool their sunburned bodies. On the fifth day they make the "man medicine," and on the morning of the sixth, which is really the fifteenth day of ceremonies, an Antelope race is held. Actually, anyone can participate. The race is started by a special officer, who himself sometimes runs as much as three miles to a certain spring, where he fills a gourd with water and ooze from its bank. This he smears on the left foot of each runner, then he smashes the gourd, which is the signal for the race to start. The racers represent the rain gods bringing water directly to the village.

In the afternoon, the Antelopes gather green boughs and construct a *kisi,* a sort of circular shade or booth, and in front of it they dig a shallow pit and cover it with a cottonwood board. It represents the entrance to the underworld. At sunset the Antelope Dancers come out of their kiva and march *four times* around the plaza. Each time they pass the board they sprinkle corn meal on it and stamp on it with the right foot, the sound representing thunder; the rattles they shake, made of antelope skin, are the sound of rain. The sound of their stamping on the cottonwood board also lets the dwellers in the underworld know that the ceremonies are being properly performed.

The Snake Priests appear and repeat the same performance. The two fraternities then line up, facing each other and singing, first softly, but gradually louder, shaking their rattles harder, simulating an approaching storm.

An Antelope Priest of the Corn Clan and a Snake Priest of the Cloud Clan go into the *kisi,* returning with green stalks and vines with which the Antelope Priest dances around the plaza, just as the Snake Priests will dance with the live snakes on the following evening. He drapes the greens around his neck and carries them in his mouth, while the Snake Priest dances behind him with his arm around his neck in positions similar to those of the coming snake ritual, except that the role of the Snake Priest will be reversed. After *four times around,* the Antelope Priest gathers up a second bunch of greens from the *kisi* and dances around *four times more*, after which the fraternities return to their respective kivas and the Antelopes are served food by the women. The Snake Priests also eat, but it is their last meal until the ceremonies are ended. After the meal the Assistant to the Antelope Chief gathers up the greens from the *kisi* and carries them out to the corn fields in supplication for mature crops.

On the morning of the sixteenth, or last, day, another race is run, similar to the Antelope race of yesterday, but this time to honor the snakes. A preliminary race seems to be an important part of many of the dances of the Southwest. Also that morning in the Snake kiva the Snake Chief makes a medicine of certain roots, including soapweed, or yucca, for washing the snakes. The actual washing, done early in the afternoon, is conducted by a man of the Cloud Clan. . . .

Following the washing of the snakes, the Snake Priests paint for the ceremonial dance, mixing the paints with the "man medicine" made two days before. Pink clay is smeared on moccasins, forearms, calves, and the upper right side of the head. The chin is painted white and the rest of the face, black.

The snakes are carried in two bags, one for rattlers and one for other kinds, taken to the plaza, and deposited in the *kisi.* The Antelopes come out of their kiva, dance *four times around*, each time stamping on the board, as they did the day before, scattering meal upon it. The Snake Priests, each wearing a turtle-shell rattle below his right knee, follow in like manner, and both fraternities line up facing each other for a period of singing. Then the Snake Priests, each accompanied by a whipper and a catcher, or gatherer, dance over to the *kisi,* where each Snake Priest is presented with a snake, which he first carries in his hands, then places about his neck and in his mouth, holding it with his teeth, imparting to it his prayer. The whipper dances behind him, with left arm around the dancer's neck, calming the snake with movements of his feathered wand, as if stroking it, and preventing it from coiling. Each snake is danced *four times* around the plaza, then tossed aside, and the catcher picks it up. These catchers thus hold all the snakes that have been discarded until all have been danced with, when an Antelope Priest draws a circle of meal on the ground and casts meal to the *six directions (four world quarters, up and down).* The catchers then throw the snakes inside the circle, and the Snake Priests scramble wildly to grab handfuls of them, then run swiftly over various trails out of the village to turn the snakes loose to carry their messages to the dwellers of the underworld. It was decided the night before which trail each Snake Priest would take and at what place he would deposit his snakes.

While the Snake Priests are engaged in freeing the snakes, all men and boys of the village who have not taken active part in the ceremonies march around the plaza *four times*, followed by the Antelope Priests, who do likewise. The Snake Priests then bathe in a special medicine which has been brewing all day and drink some of it too. It is an emetic and purgative, used to purify themselves and overcome any evil influence of the snakes. So the Snake Dance ends; it will not be given again for two years in this village. The rain is sure to follow, bringing grass for the game and livestock, maturing the corn, ripening the orchards, revitalizing the people both materially and spiritually.

Strange as the Snake Dance is in comparison to Indian rituals elsewhere, there are yet some interesting comparisons. The number *four is sacred here*, as everywhere, among Indians. We have also seen the Priest make *offerings to the six directions*. At many intervals during the Snake Dance and its time of preparation such offerings are made, using the fluffy "breath feathers" of the golden eagle. Many tribes have similar terms for these and put them to similar ceremonial use. They represent the breath of life, life itself. The idea of dancing for power, to signify unity of purpose, to establish harmony with all creation, is not strange to Indians all over the country.

Indian Dances of North America: Their Importance to Indian Life,
Reginald Laubin & Gladys Laubin, 1977, pp. 420-422

The snakes are brought in from the four directions. The ritual circling of the plaza is done in sets of four during the dances. The Snake Dance is a powerful yet stimulating way to learn and pray about each person's participation in the great dance of life.

---------------------- ✳ ----------------------

FOUR DIRECTIONS DANCE
TEWA

Shadeh is the Tewa word for dance. Translated literally, shadeh means "to be in the act of getting up, of waking up." By dancing, one awakens, arises in a heightened sense of awareness to the dance and participation in its meaning. To dance is to move with the song and sound of the drum and, hence, to participate in an ageless cosmic movement. The dance honors and recognizes the interactive role of human beings with the natural world. Songs entreat clouds and animals to come with their blessings into the human place, the village. The drumbeat is the heartbeat of the earth, which is thought about and made alive in dance. The heartbeat of the earth is physically felt when the Pueblo plazas vibrate with moccasined feet moving on the earth to the beat of the drum.

The moccasined feet are counterbalanced by the adornment of heads with feathers of birds and tablita headdresses graced with cloud and mountain symbols. Birds and clouds are of the sky, while mountains are of the earth, with summits that also touch the sky. Cloud, mountain, and bird symbols are sewn onto the women's mantas and men's kilts. Evergreen branches are placed within belts and headdresses and held in each dancer's hands. The boughs bring to the dance the everlasting life-strength of the encircling hills and *four* world-bounding mountains. Skins of animals—deer, antelope, buffalo, turtle, skunk, fox, coyote—carry the strength of the hills and mountains; the skins also symbolize the cyclic nature of life because they recall the animals who give themselves to the physical sustenance of human beings.

As they dance between female earth and male sky, connecting essential opposing elements of Pueblo philosophical thought and being, dancers evoke the human condition. Cycles of life—fertilization and the coming together of opposites in order to create life—are continual themes of Pueblo dance. Male dancers shake gourd rattles full of seeds. In certain dances, participants hold ears of mature corn, which represent the fullness of fertilization. In other dances, women hold baskets in front of them, as the male dancers move back and forth with lightning or zigzag wands.

On a larger scale, the shadeh connects the human place to the movement in the sky, to other simultaneous worlds below, and to the horizontal directions that embrace mountains, plants, and other animals. As such, the dance drama is of the middle place—between up and down, *north, west, south,* and *east.* The plaza, or *bupingeh,* is the "middle-heart-place." It is the central communal space where the community gathers to observe the ritual dance/drama of asking for, and receiving, life.

Native American Dance: Ceremonies and Social Traditions,
Charlotte Heth (Ed.), 1992, p. 93

This dance (shadeh) *is celebrated as those present experience ever-awakening sensitivity to what the Creator is doing even now. The dancers, representing the whole of life actually, are between the "up and down" of the world and are bounded within the four directons.*

——————————————— ✣ ———————————————

SACRED BALL GAME
TEWA

The blessing of the seeds is called "putting the mark of the spirits on them." The seed-filled ball used in the game is colored half yellow and half black. The black is symbolic of the rain-laden cumulus clouds of the spring and summer, while the yellow symbolizes sunshine. At noon on the day of the game the Summer chief emerges from his home wrapped in a blanket, his face painted, and the ball carefully hidden from view. He climbs a home which overlooks the "earth mother earth navel middle place" in the middle of the *south* plaza. Below, the men of the village, from teenagers to the elderly, have already gathered and been divided up into two teams. The Summer chief then utters a short prayer, throws the ball toward the earth navel, and the game begins.

The players must complete *four sunwise circuits around the village*, although one team always attempts to move the ball in the opposite direction. During this time any woman or girl may grab the ball and carry it into her home to invoke its blessing for the household. The players wait outside in the meantime, and when the ball is returned it is accompanied by a basket of food, both of which are thrown to the players. The ball is usually punctured on the same day, but the game could last as long as *four days*. If after four days the ball has not yet spilled its contents, it is returned intact to the Summer chief by the head *Towa é*. In any case, the buckskin cover is always carefully picked up after the game and returned to the Summer chief, to be used again the following year.

The Tewa World: Space, Time, Being and Becoming in a Pueblo Society,
Alfonso Ortiz, 1969, pp. 173-174

Here is an interesting blessing which includes participants from the whole village. Four times the ball filled with seeds moves around the village and is even brought into individual homes that they too might be blessed. Four is a number of fullness. A circular object (the ball containing roundish seeds) is ritually moved around the pueblo in a circular fashion four days in a row during one of the four seasons (Summer) to call forth blessings for the People, especially for their agriculture.

✽

DIRECTIONAL SONG
ZUNI

Cover my earth mother
four times with many flowers

Cover the heavens
with high-piled clouds

Cover the earth with fog
cover the earth with rains

Cover the earth with great rains
cover the earth with lightnings

Let thunder drum over all the earth
let thunder be heard

Let thunder drum over all
over all the *six directions* of the earth

*Dancer, San Juan Pueblo, New Mexico,
Saint Anthony's Feast Day, 1992*

The Magic World: American Indian Songs and Poems,
William Brandon, 1971, p. 47

This piece of poetry, "Storm Song" (adapted from Matilda Coxe Stevenson, "The Zuni Indians," 1904) is beautifully descriptive. Flowers, clouds, fog, rain, lightning, thunder: this song celebrates the plant life and all the elements of the sky which give fertility, which are life-giving. The four directions and the zenith and nadir are to be filled with the power of the Creator.

✽

PRAYER POEM
LAGUNA

I
I traveled to the ocean
    distant
        from my *southwest* land of sandrock
        to the moving blue water
    Big as the myth of origin.

II
Pale
pale water in the yellow-white light of
        sun floating *west*
          to China
        where ocean herself was born
Clouds that blow across the sand are wet.

III
Squat in the wet sand and speak to Ocean:
    I return to you turquoise the red coral you sent us,
        sister spirit of Earth.
Four round stones in my pocket I carry back the ocean
        to suck and to taste.

IV
Thirty thousand years ago
    Indians came riding across the ocean
    carried by giant sea turtles.
Waves were high that day
    great sea turtles waded slowly out
        from the grey sundown sea.
Grandfather Turtle rolled in the sand *four times*
    and disappeared
        swimming into the sun.

V
An so from that time
    immemorial
        as the old people say

Canyon de Chelly Anasazi ruins,
Navajo Reservation, Arizona

rainclouds drift from the *west*
    gift from the ocean.

VI
Green leaves in the wind
Wet earth on my feet
    swallowing raindrops
        clear from China.

"Prayer of the Pacific," Leslie Marmon Silko in *Carriers of
the Dream Wheel: Contemporary Native American Poetry*,
Duane Niatum (Ed.), 1975, pp. 226-227

*In this "Prayer to the Pacific," the contemporary woman poet Leslie
Silko reflects on her southwest heritage while spending some time at
the Pacific Ocean. She brings into the poem some ancient origin stories
and traditional ways of interpreting the past as she reflects upon
Grandfather Turtle, the bringer of the gift of rain.*

--------------------------------- ✳ ---------------------------------

CHILD BLESSING CEREMONY
APACHE

When old enough, the baby is allowed to roam freely and crawl
about the *gowa* (home) with all of the adults taking care that he or she
does not get into trouble or fall into harm's way. This freedom to
explore and learn continues throughout childhood.

The first spring following the time when the child left the cradleboard
was the occasion for the first hair cutting ceremony. Such a ceremony
still takes place, the spring after the child is crawling. The child's face
is brushed with sacred pollen by the di-yin following which the di-yin
cuts the hair closely. This ceremony is repeated for *four springs.*

To give the child a good start on the sacred lifeway, an elaborate
first moccasins ceremony is held sometime between leaving the
cradleboard and the second birthday. This is a cause of great rejoicing
for the entire family and many gifts are prepared to honor all who
come. The rites begin at Sunrise with the prayers and the marking of
all present with pollen. The child is lifted by the di-yin *four times to
the East, four times to the South, four times to the West*, and *four
times to the North.*

Four footprints are made on buckskin with pollen and the child is led by the di-yin through the footprints as prayers are said for the future of the child.

After the child is fitted with the first moccasins *(ke'iban)*, gifts are blessed and distributed. Celebrations of singing, dancing, and feasting might continue far into the night. Again, Blessing Songs are often adapted for this celebration. Several times, the child might be lifted to the Moon with prayers that he or she grow tall and strong.

These rituals conducted early in life have always been considered to leave a great imprint preparing the child for the sacred journey along the Lifeway.

> *When the Earth Was Like New: Western Apache Songs and Stories,*
> Chesley Goseyun Wilson & Ruth Longcor Harnisch Wilson,
> Bryan Burton, 1994, pp. 66-67

As in all Indian blessing ceremonies, the di-yin *(medicine man) honors the sacred directions: east* (ya'ai Hanadahge), *south* (hayaago), *west* (ona'it'aahyu) *and north* (hadag). *The child, as time goes by, learns to do the same throughout her or his lifetime.*

------------------------------ �֎ ------------------------------

CROWN (GAN) DANCE
WHITE MOUNTAIN APACHE

In White Mountain Apache religious ceremonies, both music and dance are inextricably intertwined with fundamental beliefs concerning the profound reality of divine power. While they are invocations to specific powers, almost all sacred songs recall the very fact of creation and the design of the universe, most notably through repeated references to the *four cardinal directions*. In traditional White Mountain Apache religious thought, the *east, south, west,* and *north* are holy, and the colors associated with them (black, blue or green, yellow, and white, respectively) and the number *four* and its multiples have sacred connotations. Emphasized throughout sacred songs, these references invoke an awareness of the divine origin of the universe and the spiritual powers that sustain all life. The following verse, from a Crown Dance song transcribed and published by the ethnologist Pliny Goddard in 1916, is illustrative:

Earth was holy,
Sky was made,
Earth was made,
The Gan young people lighted on the sky *four times*
Their lives, *four directions* they heard me.
With pollen speech,
With my mouth speech,
It moves within me.
The holy Gans were in line *four times* with me.

Native American Dance: Ceremonies and Social Traditions,
Charlotte Heth (Ed.), 1992, p. 66

How a People prays in a ceremony nowadays is usually directly related to the way it has prayed in ancient times, unless, of course, their ways were so devastated by others that they have had to "borrow" ceremonies from others. Even now, this dance is important to the People and it reminds them of their daily life within the four directions.

--------------------------- ✢ ---------------------------

MEN'S HAT
WHITE MOUNTAIN APACHE

The *four cardinal colors*—the *east* is black, the *south* blue, the *west* yellow, and the *north* is white—can be seen in this hat. This hat also shows *four things* that hold great significance for the Apache: the eagle feather, turquoise, deer thong, and the yellow pollen. Each individual Apache has an eagle feather that has been blessed by the medicine man for each person when they were young. The eagle feather is for protection and must be kept with us wherever we go. A turquoise stone is for boys and a white bead is for girls and women—these represent the power of the earth. The deer, representing the power of the animal world, is very sacred. For Apaches, the deer is an object of prayer and respect. The deer, a source of clothes and food, has also been important for our survival. Yellow pollen represents the power of the water world, and is used to pray and bless with. All these sacred items must be together with you at all times.

All Roads Are Good: Native Voices on Life and Culture,
Edgar Perry, 1994, p. 77

The hat, belonging to a White Mountain Indeh (Apache) man, is illustrative of a richly symbolic heritage. This description offers a sense of completeness, of wholeness, expressed in the use of the directional colors and the four sacred items.

----------------- ✳ -----------------

HOOP DANCE
WHITE MOUNTAIN APACHE

Another dance that is being revived at Holy Ground, a new ritual for White Mountain Apache, is the Hoop Dance. Like the Crown Dance, the Hoop Dance is performed as part of a healing ceremony. The following description of a Hoop Dance is from a 1936 account. A sick person is seated on a blanket in the middle of a dance ground facing *east*. One boy and one girl stand on the *east, south, west,* and *north* sides of him. All the boys are holding hoops and the girls are holding crosses. (This can be reversed.) When the medicine man starts to sing, the youngsters dance toward the patient, the boys placing their hoops over the patient's head and the girls holding their crosses just over his head. The hoops and crosses are raised and the youngsters dance back to their original positions. This dance is repeated as the medicine man sings *four* songs. Next, another man sings while the medicine man takes the hoop from the boy standing on the *east* and places it over the patient; the patient is then turned toward the *south* and the medicine man takes the *south* hoop and places it over the patient; the patient is then turned toward the *west* and the procedures are repeated until all the hoops are placed over the patient. The patient then stands up and steps out of the hoops. Similar procedures are repeated with the crosses. This entire ceremony can be repeated anywhere from one to *four* times that night.

Native American Dance: Ceremonies and Social Traditions,
Charlotte Heth (Ed.), 1992, p. 80

The hoop dance, at the same time a curing ceremony, utilizes the spiritual power of children. Once again we see a sacred movement with circles and crosses and positioning in each sacred direction. Four times, a number which expresses fullness, is also the norm.

----------------- ✳ -----------------

GAN DANCE SONGS
APACHE

1.
When the earth was made
when the sky was made
when my songs were first heard
the holy mountain was standing toward me with life.

At the center of the sky, the holy boy walks *four ways* with life.
My mountain became my own: standing toward me with life.
The dancers became: standing toward me with life.

When the sun goes down to the earth
where Mescal Mountain lies with its head toward the sunrise
black spruce became: standing up with me.

2.
Right at the center of the sky the holy boy with life walks
        in *four directions*.
Lightning with life in *four colors* comes down *four times*.
The place called black spot with life,
the place called blue spot with life,
the place called yellow spot with life,
they have heard about me
the black dancers dance in *four places*.
The sun starts down toward the earth.

3.
The living sky black-spotted
The living sky blue-spotted
The living sky yellow-spotted
The living sky white-spotted
The young spruce as girls stood up for their dance in the way of life.

When my songs first were, they made my songs with words of jet.
Earth when it was made
Sky when it was made
Earth to the end

Sky to the end
Black dancer, black thunder, when they came toward each other
All the bad things that used to be vanished.
The bad wishes that were in the world all vanished.
The lightning, the black thunder struck *four times* for them.
It struck *four times* for me.

4.
When my songs first became
when the sky was made
when the earth was made
the breath of the dancers against me made only of down:
when they heard about my life
where they got their life
when they heard about me:
it stands.

> "The Masked Dancers of the Apache," Pliny Earle Goddard in
> *Holmes Anniversary Volume*, F.W. Hodge, (Ed.), 1916, pp. 133-135

The four songs of the Masked Dancers, often call Gan dancers, accompany a girl's puberty rites. In a wonderful way they bring out the importance of sacred directionality and the ritual use of the number 4.

———————————— ✳ ————————————

FOUR SACRED MOUNTAINS
NAVAJO

In the beginning, Navajo medicine men say, there was darkness, black mist and water. June Bug formed the earth by gathering mud. Navajo legends say the Diné, the People, emerged through a reed from *four* colorful **underworlds** and found themselves between the *Four Sacred Mountains.*

> *Navajo: Portrait of a Nation*, Joel Grimes, 1992, pp. 19, 119

For the Diné (Navajo) People the four sacred mountains visibly speak of other realities that are expressed through holy directionality.

———————————— ✳ ————————————

KINAALDA CEREMONY
NAVAJO

In the chilly month of April, 1984, I participated in a very special five day ceremony for young Navajo (Dine) women. Since the day of my birth my relatives have been preparing for the *Kinaalda* ceremony which blesses women for their sacred existence to ultimately bring forth life. The history of the *Kinaalda* is extensive. It upholds the traditions of the Dine and promotes the special essence and responsibilities of womanhood.

Upon reaching 14 years of age my family and clan relatives gathered to plan for the ceremony. They worked collectively every day to symbolize the unity that will forever surround my family.

The setting of the *Kinaalda* was my family's homeland in Tse-Ya-Toh, New Mexico. The event occurred in a traditional Dine home known as a hogan, a one-room octagonal dwelling with a round roof. Although the days and nights were cold, I kept warm by the wood stove in the center of the hogan and thought about my journey into womanhood. . . .

The first day established the foundation for the ceremony. My family chose a female relative to brush my hair with the traditional brush, *beezho*. She tied my hair with a strip of buckskin while blessing me with prayers and songs. I was dressed in a traditional blouse and skirt that would remain on me until the end of the ceremony. I was adorned with family bracelets, rings, necklaces and two concha belts which stayed on me throughout the full five days, never to be taken off regardless of the massive weight!

I was told to eat, sleep, breathe and embrace the spirit of the ceremony. Each day I rose and ran on a path to greet the dawn and the rising sun toward the *east*. I was told to run without stopping, regardless of what little rest I may have had or how heavy my jewelry weighed. I ran a further distance each morning and on the last morning I ran the farthest, approximately one mile.

While I ran a group of relatives, young and old, ran behind me continuously teasing me. However irritating it was I was told to remain focused on my path, never looking back, always looking forward while not being distracted. I ran as the sun travels, going *west* and then began the tasks of the new day. The five days entailed hard work: preparing meals for visitors, grinding corn, hauling water and wood. I was not allowed to eat salt or sugar and had little time for rest, sleeping only 4-5 hours per night.

On the final night I was surrounded by my family and several medicine men who blessed my passage into womanhood. I was instructed not to sleep on the final night and remained alert and attentive throughout the evening. The medicine men blessed me with *Hoozhooji* (Beauty Way) chants and prayers. I sang the songs simultaneously and repeated the prayers so that I could reflect upon them throughout my life. This lasted until dawn when my hair was washed with yucca plant in the ceremonial basket and tied with a *tsiyeel* (Dine traditional hair-style).

I completed the last morning run of the five days and returned to the hogan. I went outdoors to the *alkaan,* cooked corn cake and, while surrounded by family members, blessed it with *Taadidiin* (yellow corn pollen) in *four directions*. After the blessing the corn cake was divided amongst the family. During the remainder of the morning I honored all who came to celebrate my *Kinaalda* by a "giveaway" of gifts, food and candy, symbolizing that I would continue to have a charitable spirit. This concluded the ceremony. Yet, I did not change my ceremonial clothing for *four more days* in order to complete the nine day cycle of the *Kinaalda.* I reflected on the ceremony and thought about my future as a woman.

I feel the *Kinaalda* enriched my life and am honored to have been given the opportunity to fulfill my family's dream of completing the ceremony. Each day I strive to remain healthy, physically, emotionally, mentally and spiritually, through the *Kinaalda* teachings of lifeways. I am sustained by the sacred essence of the teachings and hope to pass them on to future generations. I have faith that the legacy of this special celebration of womanhood endures and enriches the lives of young Dine women.

I wish to leave you with this thought written by an unknown author: "Pure faith fails never, it continues forever." May you keep the faith within yourself and you will achieve your goals in life!

"Kinaalda: Running to Womanhood,"
Wind Messenger: A Newsletter of Wings of America,
Chenoa Bah Stilwell, Spring 1994, p. 2

There are some striking similarities between the Diné (Navajo) puberty ceremony and that of the Indéh (Apache) People. Directionality is prime and so is the use of the number 4 in the rituals.

---- ✳ ----

SWEATLODGE
NAVAJO

The sweathouse is a miniature conical hogan with the doorway structure omitted. The "sudatory" is used in various ceremonies. In the Night Chant *four* sweat houses are erected at *each of the cardinal points*. On *four consecutive days* the patient enters one of the sweat houses starting on the *east* and finishing on the *north* by way of *south* and *west*. During this process the singer decorates the lodge with a figure representing the rainbow. When the drawing of the rainbow is completed the patient enters the sweat house.

Big Eyes: The Southwestern Photographs of Simeon Schwemberger, 1902-1908, Paul V. Long, 1992, p. 53

This healing ceremony does not omit the importance of directional symbology nor the ritual use of the number 4. Both healer, patient, and others who participate in the prayers become very aware of their ceremonial importance as the story and prayers are sung out and enacted.

---- ✳ ----

CONTEMPORARY SONG
NAVAHO

Within the *four sacred seasons*, going the *four directions*, I lost myself yet I found myself returning and learning affection for the plain and simple good things.

I learn to touch the sky, paint a butterfly, cry with the rain, learn to take pain, to study the order of things and sing of beauty on hummingbird's wings.

Within the *four sacred colors*, going the same direction, I found myself just to lose myself in caring and sharing affection for the plain and precious true things.

Now I have to touch the sky, follow the butterfly, walk in the rain, master the pain, staying with the order of things, and sing of beauty of eagles on wings.

And I learn to touch the sky, follow the butterfly, walk in the rain, master the pain, staying with the order of things, and sing of beauty of eagles on wings.

"Plain and Simple," *Encircle* (sound recording),
Arliene Nofchissey Williams, 1987

In a contemporary manner this song expresses aspects of both Navajo and Christian spirituality. Colors and directions especially remind both singer and listener of Native tradition; praise for the ordinary and unique aspects of God's creation echoes much of the Christian heritage, while the actions within the song marvelously combine both ways.

———————————— ✳ ————————————

DIRECTIONAL PRAYER CEREMONY
INTERTRIBAL

Cantors begin: *"Veni, sancte spiritu"*—assembly picks it up . . . procession begins. Then

OPENING PRAYER
Presider: *Great One, Spirit of all who gather here in the* **southwest,** *whose voice we hear in the winds and whose breath gives life to all the world. Great One who has created the light of day and the light of night to give direction to our lives, you as our Maker gather us here in this place. Make of this gathering a holy people where truth is spoken in love. As we journey together this week, even though we come from many places and backgrounds, may we be blessed with unity and understanding.*

"Veni, sancte spiritu" continues. . . .

INDIAN BLESSING OF THE FOUR DIRECTIONS

(The *four* dancers with candles enter down the *four* aisles. When reaching her place in the center . . . she faces *east* and holds her candle high while the prayer is said.)

PRAYER OF THE FOUR DIRECTIONS
Reader 1: *Spirit of light and of life . . . blessed are you, Lord God, Our Father. . . . As the sun rises in the **east** and lights up our day . . . may we learn to love you more. Graced by your companions from the flowing Atlantic, the rolling Appalachians, and the beautiful coast-lines . . . together we reach out in the arms of the horizon, blessed by the light that guides us through each day.*
(Dancer places her candle in the stand)

"Veni, sancte spiritu" continues. . . .
(Second dancer faces **north**, holds her candle up high)

Reader 2: *O Spirit of wisdom and truth. . . . We welcome all of you from the **north**, from the mighty great lakes, the ski-country of New England to the springs, lakes and rivers filled with fish in the great northwest.* You come to light our footsteps on the road of peace! Help us drawn to this place by the Spirit to be one holy people united in peace and justice. May we share our gifts in this gathering, intent on building a more beautiful world.
(Dancer places candle in candle stand)

"Veni, sancte spiritu" continues. . . .
(Third dancer faces **west** and holds candle high)

Reader 3: *O Spirit of beauty and the setting sun. . . . We welcome all of you from the **west** . . . from the roaring blue Pacific to the majestic snow-covered peaks of the Rockies. You come to bring your gifts to this gathering in the desert. In humility and peace may we tear down our hills of pride and fill our valleys of despair with hope. May we straighten the winding ways of our lives with truth and let bloom in our midst this week . . . the fruits of your joy.*
(Dancer places candle in candle stand)

"Veni, sancte spiritu" continues. . . .
(Fourth dancer faces **south** and holds candle high)

Reader 4: *O Spirit of goodness and warmth. . . . We welcome all of you from the sun-warmed sun-belt, through the ranch and oil country to the water-surrounded Gulf coast communities. With your gifts of warmth and hospitality may we all together praise the Lord of Heaven. We praise Him in the rising and the setting sun. Bless us this week with eyes to see, ears to hear and a heart to appreciate You in our brothers and sisters.*
(Dancer places her candle in the candle stand)

Veni, sancte spiritu" continues. . . .

Presider: *Great Spirit of wisdom and unity . . . every part of these great United States reflects your goodness to us. We give thanks always for the gifts of light and life, of wisdom and courage, of warmth and concern. Guide us this week that we may blend this gathering into one. Great Spirit, enlighten and bless our mission so we may truly benefit your priests and your church through out our beautiful country. We ask this through your Son and our brother Jesus Christ.*

"Monday Gathering Prayers during 16th Annual NOCERCC Convention,"
People of Reservations around Phoenix, Arizona, 1989

I was present at this ceremony a few years ago. Though the Catholic priests and others concerned with the clergy on-going education seminar were from a variety of ethnic backgrounds, a great unity was

felt. The prayer brought everyone together. In particular, it showed the openness with which the Native People of the Southwest around Phoenix welcomed Catholic spiritual leaders from many other places on Turtle Island (this continent). It was definitely a time for touching the sacred, as well as for learning.

*Taos Pueblo,
New Mexico*

CALIFORNIA CULTURAL AREA

A prayer facing west, giving thanks in Esselen traditional territory, Carmel Valley, California

BOATING PREPARATIONS
CHUMASH

The next morning, before dawn, the crew gets up and goes down to the embarcadero. The three men who are going out to sea bring along their blankets. Many Indian men went about naked, even in winter, and the rowers of the *tomol* always went naked. . . . I have seen islanders from Santa Cruz Island painted. . . . They paint . . . with their fingers just before going to sea, but . . . also . . . when they are coming back from the sea. In their ears, they wear little sticks an inch long and 1/4 inch in diameter. These are blackish in color. Their hair is worn loose, falling down all around, and is about 6 inches below the shoulders.

When these men reach the embarcadero a *fourth man* is already there to help them. They all lift the *tomol* and carry it in the same manner as before. At the surf's edge they set the boat down. The Indians then chant a prayer, addressed to the world, as they prepare to launch the *tomol* through the surf:

> *Tiluinaga* (**4 times**)
>> Give room!
> *'Alishtaga'an* (3 times)
>> Do not get discouraged!
> *Shushulishi'it* (3 times)
>> Help me to reach the place!
> *'Ayaya* (**4 times**)
>> Hurrah!
> *No'o.*

They now wait for a calm spell, which may not come for 15 minutes. While they are waiting, the captain goes down to the water. There, he takes a stone and enters the surf, waiting for a wave. When the wave comes and is about to break, he throws the stone at its hollow and looks carefully to see what movement the stone will make. If the stone moves **westward**, the captains say that a **south wind** is going to come up. This is the *smolho,* a dangerous wind. If the stone moves **eastward,** a **north wind** will blow and they will not venture out into the sea.

When the proper time arrives, which is the calm spell or *tsmeme,* they prepare to put out past the surf. . . . If conditions are good, when the *tsmeme* comes the signal is given by the captain and all pick up the *tomol* and carry it through the surf. They take the boat out just so far that the bottom of the canoe does not touch the sand.

> *Tomol: Chumash Watercraft as Described in the Ethnographic Notes of John P. Harrington*, Travis Hudson, Janice Timbrok & Melissa Rempe (Eds.), 1978, pp. 131-134

Entering the sea at any time can be a perilous thing. Such travel preparations are necessary. Praying before leaving to go somewhere is common to all cultures. Here the directions are considered and the opening and closing words of the chant are sung four times: a way of beginning and ending with a sense of completeness.

———————————— ✤ ————————————

COYOTE CREATES
PIT RIVER

After Coyote had made the world and designed the animals and other creatures to live on it, he decided the world should have people too. Old Coyote told his wife Pelican Woman, that if he made people that they would not be able to live with them but would have to go away. Pelican Woman agreed to leave for the she wanted the people to live on the earth.

Coyote tried and tried to make people but had no luck. First, he carved them out of little oak sticks but there was no life in them. Next, he tried sticks of pine, but still nothing happened. He used sticks from all the different trees but they did not become people. He became very angry and scattered the many kinds of sticks all over the world. He cried, "When the fleas bite you, you will become people."

He then carved all kinds of people from sticks of the buckeye tree and placed them in his ceremonial house. He put some on the *north* side, some on the *south*, some on the *east* and some on the *west*. He then cut some milkweed plants and poured the milk over the sticks and said, "You will now become people."

The next morning when Coyote entered the ceremonial house he heard the people talking and saw them walking around. He called them all together and gave each group a name and a language that was different from all others. He said, "The *four lands, north, south, east,* and *west* now have people who are different from each other. They will live in those places and be happy." Coyote then told the people that he and his wife were going away and that the people could not go with them.

He said to the people, "When you die you will come to my new home to live. Only dead people can come to my land; only dead people."

Before he left, Coyote gave names to all the trees and plants, and to all the birds and animals. He said, "From now on you will be called by the names I have given you." And he set everything in order as we know them today.

He then told his people, "When you die, after *four days* your spirit will come to my new home in the *west*, beyond the horizon, and there you will live with me."

He then called Pelican Woman and they left for their new land in the west. They went away to their new home beyond the ocean where they live today. When the people die, their spirits stay for *four days* and then go to the land beyond the western horizon to be with Coyote and Pelican Woman forever.

Where Is the Eagle?, William Coffer, 1981, pp. 210-211

This northern California People, like many of their neighbors, included Coyote in many stories. This trickster/creator/foolish character gives us many ways to understand both ourselves and our environments. The fullness of four days and the variety of the directional lands and territories of the Peoples are also allowed for in this particular creation story.

✳

ORIGINS STORY
POMO

He lived in the *north*, the Old Man, his name was Marumda. He lived in a cloud-house, a house that looked like snow, like ice. And he thought of making the world. "I will ask my older brother who lives in the *south*," thus he said, the Old Man Marumda. "Wah! What shall I do?" thus he said. "Eh!" thus he said.

Then he pulled out *four* of his hairs. He held out the hairs. "Lead me to my brother!" thus he said, Marumda the Old Man. Then he held the hairs to the *east*; after that he held the hairs to the *north*; after that he held them to the *west*; after that he held them to the *south*, and he watched.

Then the hairs started to float around, they floated around, and floated toward the *south*, and left a streak of fire behind, they left a streak of fire, and following it floated the cloud-house, and Marumda rode in it.

He sat smoking. He quit smoking. And then he went to sleep. He was lying asleep, sleeping, . . . sleeping, . . . sleeping. . . . Then he awoke. He got up and put tobacco into his pipe. He smoked, and smoked, and smoked, and then he put the pipe back into the sack.

That was his first camp, they say, and then he lay down to sleep. *Four times* he lay down to sleep, and then he floated to his elder brother's house. His name was Kuksu. This Kuksu was the elder brother of Marumda.

The Kuksu, his house was like a cloud, like snow, like ice, his house. Around it they floated, *four times* they floated around it the hairs, and then through a hole they floated into the house, and following them the Marumda entered the house.

"Around the *east* side!" said the Kuksu. Then around the *east* side he entered the house, and he sat down, he sat, and he took off the little sack hung around his neck. He took out his pipe and filled it with tobacco, he laid a coal on it, and he blew, he blew, and then he blew it afire. Then he removed the coal and put it back into his little sack. After that he smoked, *four times* he put the pipe to his mouth. After that he offered it to his older brother the Kuksu.

Then Kuksu received it. "Hyoh!" he said, the Kuksu. "Hyoh! Good will be our knowledge, good will end our speech! Hyoh! May it happen! Our knowledge will not be interfered with! May it happen! Our knowledge will go smoothly. May it happen! Our speech will not hesitate. May it happen! Our speech will stretch out well. The knowledge we have planned, the knowledge that we have laid, it will succeed, it will go smoothly, our knowledge! Yoh ooo, hee ooo, hee ooo, hee ooo, hee ooo! May it Happen!" Thus he said, the Kuksu, and now he quit smoking. . . .

Then Marumda sat up, he sat up, and they both stood up. They stood facing *east*, and then they stood facing *north*, and then they stood facing *west*, and then they stood facing *south,* and then they stood facing the zenith, and then they stood facing the nadir. And now they went around each other both ways, they went around each other *four times* back and forth. Then Marumda went to where he had been sitting before, and he sat down; and then Kuksu went to where he had been sitting before, and he sat down.

Then Marumda put tobacco into the pipe that he took out of his little dried-up sack. He felt in his little dried-up sack, he brought out some tobacco and filled the pipe with it. Then he felt in his little dried-up sack and brought out a coal, he put the coal on top of the tobacco, he put it on top and he blew, he blew, and blew it afire. *Four times* he blew, and then he offered it to his brother Kuksu. *Four times* he made as if to take it, and then he received it. Four times he blew and then he offered it back to Marumda. He received it, and put it back into his little dried-up sack.

He blew out the smoke *four times*. First he blew it towards the *south,* then he blew it toward the *east*, then he blew it toward the *north*, then he blew it toward the *west*, then he blew it to the zenith, then he blew it to the nadir. . . .

Then Kuksu poked him with the pipe, and Marumda received the pipe, he received it and put it back in his little dried-up sack. And then the Marumda scraped himself in the armpits, he scraped himself and got out some of the armpit wax. He gave the armpit wax to the Kuksu. Then Kuksu received, he received it, and stuck it between his big toe and the next. And then he also scraped himself in the armpits, he scraped himself, and rolled the armpit wax into a ball. His own armpit wax he then stuck between Marumda's toes.

Then Marumda removed it and blew on it, *four times* he blew on it. Then Kuksu also removed the armpit wax and blew on it *four times*, and after that he sat down. Then Marumda went around the Kuksu *four times*, and then he sat down. And then the Kuksu, he got up, he got up, and *four times* around the Marumda he went. Then they both stood still.

Now they mixed together their balls of armpit wax. And Kuksu mixed some of his hair with it. And then Marumda also mixed some of his hair with the armpit wax.

After that they stood up; facing *south*, and then facing *east*, and then facing *north*, and then facing *west*, and then facing the zenith, and then facing the nadir: "These words are to be right and thus everything will be. People are going to be according to this plan. There is going to be food according to this plan. There will be food from the water! There will be food from the land. There will be food from under the ground. There will be food from the air. There will be all kinds of food whereby the people will be healthy. These people will have good intentions. Their villages will be good. They will plan many things. They will be full of knowledge. There will be many of them on this earth, and their intentions will be good.

"We are going to make in the sky the traveling-fire. With it they will ripen their food. We are going to make that with which they will cook their food overnight. The traveling-fires in the sky, their name will be Sun. The one who is Fire, his name will be Daytime-Sun. The one who gives light in the night, her name will be Night-Sun. These words are right. This plan is sound. Everything according to this plan is going to be right!" Thus he spoke, the Kuksu.

And now the Marumda made a speech. Holding the armpit wax, holding it to the *south*, he made a wish: "These words are right!" Thus he said, the Marumda. And then he held it to the *east*, and then he held it to the *north*, and then he held it to the *west*, and then he held it to the zenith, and then he held it to the nadir: "According to this plan, people are going to be. There are going to be people on this earth. On this earth there will be plenty of food for the people! According to this plan there will be many different kinds of food for the people! Clover in plenty will grow, grain, acorns, nuts!" Thus he spoke, the Marumda.

And then he blew tobacco-smoke in the *four directions*. Then he turned around to the left *four times*. Then he put the armpit wax into his little dried-up sack. After that he informed the Kuksu: "I guess I'll go back, now!" Thus he said, and then he asked the Kuksu: "Sing your song, brother!" And then the Kuksu sang. . . .

After that Marumda floated away to the *north*, singing the while a wishing song. . . .

With this song he traveled *north*, the Marumda, riding in his house, in his cloud-house. He was singing along, holding the armpit wax in his hand and singing the song. Then he tied a string to the ball of armpit wax, passed the string through his own ear-hole and made it fast. Then he went to sleep.

He was lying asleep, when [suddenly] [the string] jerked [his ear]. He sat up [and looked around] but he did not see anything, and he lay down again to sleep. It went on like that for eight days, it went on for eight days, and then it became the earth. The armpit wax grew large [while] Marumda was sound asleep, and the string jerked [his ear]. At last Marumda sat up, he sits up, and he untied the string from his ear-hole. Then he threw the earth [out into space].

"Creation Myth of the Pomo Indians," Anthropos,
William Ralganal Benson & Jaime deAngulo,1932, pp. 264-267

This origins story, told by William Ralganal Benson, sets the four directions at the beginning of things. The repeated mention of "four times" expresses completeness.

✳

STORY OF THE FOUR WINDS
YUROK

As one can see, all forces of nature, the waves, the trees, and all things that grow, the Te Paw (spruce tree), the T'pererner (fir tree), the Keelch (redwood), the animals, the fish and the birds, everything was endowed with spirit. So also was the wind.

The winds came from a place above Point St. George called by the Indians "K'-Nay-Ah-Wit," a spot about three or four miles above Crescent City. There in the beginning lived seven brothers and two sisters. At low tide one can still find some of the beads they wore if you scrape the sand. After talking with Wah-Peck-oo-May-ow, the Great Spirit, the eldest and the third oldest went *north* to Haw Gone, whence they controlled the north winds. The second and fourth children went *south* to "Per-Wer-Ich." The next two went *west* to "Tay-Wallah-May-Ow" and there stayed to make their home. The younger brother and younger girl went to the *east* to "Hay Skeek-May 'Ow" (meaning "inland") to make their home. The elder sister, however, stayed home at "Knay-Ah-Wit" to see that no other winds came into being. The winds as so established were controlled by these spirits from their homes.

These winds were revered by the Indians, and why shouldn't they be! Haw Gone brought the fish "Hay-Scoos-Lak" to the people in the early fall. After being smoked and dried they are called "Key-Gess" (smelt). The *east wind* brought warm air from inland to comfort on cold summer days when the fog of the sea clutched at the land. The *south wind* brought the "Quo-Roy" (candle fish), followed by eels (Kay Win) and sturgeon (Cah Cah). But the best wind was the *west wind* for the west wind brought salmon, the staff of life to the people on the Klamath.

The older sister who had stayed at home at "K'-Nay-Ah-Wit was to be envied. Her home was close to the beach where she was always assured of plenty of crabs, mussels, clams, seaweed, periwinkles, sea urchins, rock oysters and many kinds of fish. She loved to go in the water to swim on days when the wind and waves were not fighting, and to run on the beach to meet the wind and to run its fingers through her hair. As old Nachutre (Jennie Scoll) used to say, "En maket feel goot en dats why he stay home dat girl, en he neffer likes to go somblace."

Indian Lore of the North California Coast,
Austen Warburton & Joseph Endert, 1975, pp. 18-20

The origin stories of the People always have to do with their present reality. In this narrative we are able to notice the connection between the cardinal points and their guiding spirits. Each wind brings a different set of gifts for the People.

A Chumash ceremonial willow hut put up for a memorial service in Seaside, California under the guidance of medicine woman Adelina Contreras in 1997

GREAT BASIN
CULTURAL
AREA

SYNCHRONIZED
HEALING CEREMONY
NORTHERN PAIUTE

Willie, my brother, was pitching hay with the Indian doctor, George Calico, down on Carpenter's ranch. Willie was talking to him about Mamma's being so

A Shoshone woman praying with sage, tobacco, and a hawk feather

sick, and the doctor said he would like to treat her. He said she was too young to die, that he might not be able to cure her, but he wanted to try. When Willie came home that night he told us sisters what the Indian doctor had said. The family talked it over and decided we would have him treat her.

Only certain people can talk to the Indian doctor and we got our cousin, Ben Charley, who knew how to do it and what to say. He had to go and talk to him just before the sunrise. He said he would do what he could for Mamma and gave Ben Charley a willow stick with two eagle feathers tied to it. One feather is the longest in the eagle's tail, the other is a short fluffy one from under the tail. We put the stick in a bucket of dirt and placed it at the head of Mamma's bed so it could wave all day above her head. Nobody was allowed to touch the feathers.

After working all day in the field, the Indian doctor came and started his cure at seven o'clock. Mamma had to be put on the floor, and it took *four men* to place her there, for she was such a big woman. He started working her head, giving it a massage for almost half an hour, then he stopped and would sing. The neighbors came in and watched, and everyone there joined in the singing. He sang the most beautiful songs, then he massaged again. We had to give Mamma clean handkerchiefs often, for she seemed to blow her nose and spit lots. Alternating the massage and the singing, he worked until twelve o'clock—not before twelve nor after, but exactly at twelve. We had a little lunch prepared—well, it was a big lunch—cakes, roast, salad, mashed potatoes, and coffee. The doctor would smoke a little and rest besides eating food. Then he started massaging and singing again. About two o'clock, he told us what was the matter with her. He said she had a clot on the brain. He kept up the massage and the singing until sunrise the next day. He told Willie to cut a good strong willow stick, one Mamma could use for a walking stick. He told him to fix it up nice and to hide it in Mamma's room. She was to know nothing about this.

Willie cut the stick and hid it in the closet. Next morning, when we got Mamma on the bed and cleaned up, we found the handkerchiefs she had blown her nose on were pink with bloody streaks on them. We were awfully scared of that blood but did not say anything. We were afraid we would break the spell or kill the power. That day she was better and could eat. The second night, the doctor came and went through the same routine as on the first night, massaging her and singing at regular intervals.

The third night, he told us to get five rocks out of the water. They must be clean rocks, not to come from dirty water. Willie went to the river over by Ruddel's ranch where he could wade in fresh water, and got the rocks. They had to be placed against the wall opposite Mamma's bed, beginning in the *northeast corner,* a few feet apart, equidistant. At intervals during the day, say at nine, eleven, and so on, the rocks were moved, one at a time. About five, the *fourth rock* was moved. The rock left in the corner was moved exactly at sunset. We had Sister watch from the *west window* to say when, and then we moved it. We knew that it made no difference how far the rock was moved— that it needed only be picked up and set down again.

On the *fourth night,* exactly the same procedure was followed. Each day we picked up a rock, one every day until the fifth day, then we took the five rocks to the river and put them where they came from.

On the morning of the fifth day I came from my house, just twenty feet away, and entered Mamma's house through the kitchen. I opened the door into her room, and I could not believe what I saw. In the doorway stood Mamma, who only days before had been paralyzed!

There she stood. She had the cane in her hand and was watching the sunrise. Mamma, who had been helpless for weeks and was blind, standing in the door, watching the sunrise.

"Mamma, Mamma. What is the matter? Sit down."

I dragged her old rocker up and she sat down. I got slippers for her bare feet and she looked up at me and smiled. I got her breakfast, and after several hours she let us help her to bed. Every day she improved, and began again to do her work. She lived for eighteen years afterward. She never could tell us how she got up or remembered where she found the cane.

Karnee: A Paiute Narrative, Lalla Scott, 1966, pp. 108-111

The Paviotso (Northern Paiute) came to experience newcomers only more recently in their ancient history in the Great Basin desert region. From the mid-1800s until now they, like others of the People, have had to take on many new and different things, some of which were are not so helpful for them and their cultural ways. But here we recognize the ancient ways of healing within a modern-times context: both direction and number are synchronized with the sun's movements to effect a miraculous cure.

Lava rocks, southern Idaho, Shoshone-Bannock traditional territory

Whale design cedar box

NORTHWEST CULTURAL AREA

FIRST SALMON CEREMONY
TSIMSHIAN

The pattern for the Tsimshian First Salmon Ceremony was laid down in a myth, as were many of the codes of behavior that governed certain aspects of life, and from this it is not difficult to envision the solemnity and joy of the celebration of the return of the salmon.

When the first salmon of the season were caught, *four elderly shamans* were called down to the fishing platform at the water's edge from which the fish had been caught. They brought with them a cedar bark mat, freshly made for the occasion; eagle down, symbol of peace and friendship, and red ochre. One of the shamans put on the garment worn by the man who had caught the fish, and painted his face with the ochre. In his right hand he held his ceremonial rattle, and in his left an eagle tail, the long black feathers tipped with white.

The four shamans carefully placed the salmon on the new mat, and *holding it by the four corners* carried it up to the chief's house, the place where special guests were always taken. The shaman wearing the fisherman's raiment led the procession, shaking his rattle and swinging the eagle tail, eagle down on his head floating to the ground. Eventually they reached the big plank house of the chief, where young people having recent contact with birth and puberty (the ritually unclean who might offend the salmon), were required to leave.

Old people led the procession into the house, and they were followed by all the shamans of the village dressed in colorful ceremonial regalia.

Amid the continued singing of special songs, the honored fish was placed on a cedar board, and *four times* the shamans *encircled it*,

458

rattling their beautifully carved rattles and swinging the eagle tails. The singers finished the songs and seated themselves in the proper place around the house. The fire crackled, making light and shadow patterns along the room beams and the sturdy walls.

All was hushed. The shaman wearing the fisherman's garment called upon two old women shamans to cut the fish, for butchering fish was traditionally women's work. With a mussel shell knife the salmon head was first severed, then the tail, followed by a cut along the ventral side to remove the inner parts. All the people assembled maintained silence, and as the fish was being cut, the women shamans called the salmon by honorary names of great significance: "Chief Spring Salmon ... Quartz Nose ... Two Gills on Back ... Lightning Follow One Another ... Three Jumps."

The giving of names bestowed high social privileges, and the first salmon of the season was thus being honored. Finally the fish was cooked in the prescribed manner and shared among the guests. When they had finished, all the bones, entrails and any uneaten parts were gathered up carefully into a clean mat and ceremonially put into the fire. This ensured the fish's revival and return to its home in the Spring Salmon village out in the sea. Since it had been well treated and duly honored, the other salmon would follow up the river.

With the ceremony concluded, the catching of great quantities of the fish could then proceed.

Indian Fishing: Early Methods on the Northwest Coast,
Hilary Stewart, 1982, pp. 166-167

Four shamans carrying the salmon by the four corners of the mat and encircling the salmon four times is a unique way of expressing thanksgiving and honor to the life-giving fish.

✳

CEREMONIAL HOUSE DIRECTIONAL SYMBOLISM
WANAPUM

There was a small open space to the *North* of the larger house, which was Smohalla's residence and the village assembly room as well. This space was enclosed by a whitewashed fence made of boards which had drifted down the river. In the middle was a flagstaff with a rectangular flag. . . . Smohalla explained: 'This is my flag, and it represents the world. God told me to look after my people—All are my people. There are *four ways* in the world—*North* and *South* and *East* and *West*. I have been all those ways. This is the center. I live here. The red spot is my heart—everybody can see it. The yellow grass grows everywhere around this place. The green mountains are far away and all around the world. There is only water beyond, salt water. The blue is the sky, and the star is the *North Star*. . . .'

A Good Medicine Collection: Life in Harmony with Nature,
Adolf Hungry Wolf, 1990, no page number

Smohalla's flag was a symbolic representation of the world that he knew. His perception of the directions was also based on personal experiences in travelling. He saw himself as a definite part of the world. The colors in the flag spoke of a cosmology that he knew and was comfortable with. His Dreamer religious movement grew especially during the 1860s and helped to maintain a strong traditionalist identity among the People for many years.

Tree root on shore of lake near Usk, Washington

PLAINS CULTURAL AREA

VISION QUEST
COMANCHE

To be a success in life—to gain repute as a warrior—a man had to have the aid of some supernatural force. This assistance came to a person in a vision, a mystic experience. It might come unsought, but ordinarily a young man who had about reached puberty tried desperately to have a psychic experience. A shaman prepared the youth for his quest by talking to him and making him bathe, symbolic of purification. The vision-seeker *carried four things* with him: a buffalo robe, a bone pipe, tobacco, and materials for lighting the pipe. Thus equipped, and dressed only in a breechclout and moccasions, he left camp and sought an isolated hill or other special place to await his vision. On the way he *halted four times*—the Comanches' mystic number—to smoke and pray. When the youth had found a suitable place, not so far from camp that he could not return when weakened, yet isolated and lonely, he smoked and prayed for power. During the night he kept himself covered with the robe, his face to the *east*, but as the new day dawned he rose to face the sun and to absorb its beneficial rays. And throughout his quest he fasted. The attitude of the supplicant was one of awe and respect for the omnipotent powers, but not of groveling before them. The spirits were glad to give their power and the supplicant was happy and grateful when it was bestowed upon him. Usually a vision was received within the customary *four-day* and *four-night* vigil,

461

although occasionally the quest was extended and sometimes it was unsuccessful.

The Indians of Texas: From Prehistoric to Modern Times,
W.W. Newcomb, Jr., 1984, pp. 185-186

It is fairly easy to imagine a medicine person walking with a vision quest candidate and stopping four times along the way. Perhaps the four halts were also a way of symbolizing a desire for spiritual progress in life. Facing east (a strong power direction) allowed the faster to receive the morning light and gradual warmth on four different occasions during his ordeal. He would accompany these occasions with prayer.

---- ✳ ----

BALL GAME
OMAHA

This ball game was known to a number of tribes that formerly lived on the prairies, and called by different names. The game as here given is as it was played among the Omaha. The opening of the game was ceremonial. The person who performed the opening ceremony had to belong to the tribal group that had charge of the rites pertaining to the Wind, for the figure outlined on the ground by the movements of the ball in the opening ceremony was one of the symbols of the Wind. The Wind when spoken of ceremonially was called the *Four Winds*, one for each of the *four points of the compass*. These Four Winds were regarded as the messengers of the Giver of Life, known as Wakon'da by the Omaha and kindred tribes. The recognition of man's connection with the forces of Nature did not disturb the pleasure of the Indian when entering upon a game; on the contrary, it tended to enhance his happiness by bringing to his mind his dependence upon Wakon'da, together with the feeling of being in accord with the power represented by the Wind.

Indian Games and Dances with Native Songs,
Alice C. Fletcher, 1994, p. 102

"Ta-bé," a ball game played with goals at east and west, was always quite lively. The four directions were ritually recognized in this sport.

---- ✳ ----

CORN PLANTING RITUALS
OMAHA

.... corn was held and regarded as a gift from God. Every stage of its growth was ceremonially observed and mentioned in rituals and songs.

Among the Omaha tribe when the time came for planting, four kernels from a red ear of corn were given to each family by the keeper of this sacred rite. These *four red kernels* were mixed with the ordinary seed corn, that it might be vivified by them and made to yield an ample harvest. Red is the symbolic color of life. In this ceremony is preserved a trace of the far-away time when all the precious seed corn was in the care of priestly keepers. The ceremony of giving out the four red kernels served to turn the thoughts of the people from a dependence solely on their own labor in cultivating corn to the life-giving power of Wakon'da dwelling within the maize.

In the Omaha Ritual Song of twenty-six stanzas which preceded the distribution of the four red kernels, the Corn speaks. It tells of its roots reaching in the *four directions* (where dwell the messengers that bring life), of the growth of its jointed stalk, of the unfolding of its leaves, of the changing color of the silk and of the tassel, of the ripening of the fruit, of the bidding of the people to come, to pluck and to eat.

Indian Games and Dances with Native Songs,
Alice C. Fletcher, 1994, p. 10

Corn was common to many Tribes as a staple food. The People were always thankful for it. In this ceremony the four directions reach out to the source of the Creator's life-giving power.

---------------------------- ✢ ----------------------------

ORIGINS STORY
OSAGE

The People chose Elk to go below, for he was a mighty being and a strong swimmer. The Elk went below and dove into the waters; with powerful strokes he made his way, but at last grew weary and began to sink beneath the waves. In desperation Elk cried to the *four directions* and gave the breath of life to the *Four Winds*. The Winds came together with a mighty crash that sent the water upward in a fine mist to become the clouds. Now rocks and dry land began to appear from the beneath the waters and soon a broad land stood above the seas. In his great joy Elk laid down and rolled over and over. Like waves, *soils of four colors* began to cover the rock. Again and again Elk rolled on the ground, and wherever a hair fell from his body there sprang up the grasses and trees and fruiting bushes upon which all life depends. Now the spirits of the animals, large and small, from the mighty black bear to the smallest insect, took on their forms and began to walk and crawl and fly over the new Earth; each with the wisdom of how to live and feed, taking their places within the great round of life.

When the Earth was made ready by the action of the Elk, and the trees and grasses were as thick as the hairs of his hide, the spirits of the Little Ones made ready to descend. There was only one being that could lead them in their descent to the Earth, so the People made their appeal to the Great Red Eagle (red for the color of dawn). The Red Eagle gave to the People bodies of eagles and led them as they soared down through the *four divisions of the heavens*, landing with wings outspread in the uppermost branches of the Red Oak, the sacred tree that upheld the heavens. As the People landed they loosed a great torrent of acorns that clattered down and covered the roots of the tree. This was a prophecy and a promise of the many children that would be born into the tribe and of the fruitfulness of the Earth.

WI-GI-E OF THE ELK

In the midst of the *East* Wind,
In the midst of the *North* Wind,
He threw himself upon the Earth.
As he stood the sky became calm and peaceful
As though touched by gentle hands.
Throwing himself upon the Earth in the midst of the *South* Wind.
He cleansed the land,
Every part of the Earth
Of all anger.

Again he threw himself down upon the Earth,
When he rose to his feet

He had left the Earth covered with hairs of his body.
The Elk spoke, "These are the grasses of the Earth;
I have scattered them so that the animals may appear
    in their midst."

He stood with his rumps toward the People
Saying, "These ball-like muscles of my rumps,
They are the hills of the Earth.
Behold the ridge of my back;
It is the ridges of the Earth.
Behold the tip of my nose;
It is the peaks of the Earth.
The knobby base of my antlers;
They are the loose rocks of the Earth.
Behold the branches of my antlers;
They are the branches of the rivers.
The small tines of my antlers are the creeks of the Earth.
The large tines are the rivers
Dotted here and there with forests."

Osage Life and Legends: Earth People/Sky People,
Robert Liebert, 1987, pp. 74-76

The number 4 and the directions predominate in this origins story. It is amazing how each People, through story-telling and ceremony, makes their own the mystery of the beginning of all things at the hands of the Creator. Here the elk is the giver of the things of creation to all the People.

---------------------- ✵ ----------------------

LODGE AND VILLAGE
PAWNEE

Over the flat, unaccented landscape of the Great Plains, the stars shine at night with an enveloping brilliance. To the Pawnee Indians, a seminomadic people centered in Nebraska, this majestic display was nothing less than divine. The shining vault above them was the dome of the lodge that had been built by their heavenly father, the god Tirawahat. And the stars themselves were revered spirits. When the

Pawnee died, they entered this heavenly company, traveling through the Milky Way, past the flickering campfires of their departed tribesmen.

The circular lodge inhabited by the still-living Pawnee was covered with a thick layer of earth, but a wide smoke hole in the roof afforded the people inside the dwelling a glimpse of the stars, from which they drew their strength. *Four inner support poles* reaching from the floor to the ceiling around the firepit were aligned to the *northeast, southeast, southwest*, and *northwest*, and painted black, red, white, and yellow, respectively—colors that were associated with star gods who, according to legend, supplied Tirawahat with the invisible posts that hold up the *quadrants of the sky* vault. The Pawnee lodges were built with the entryway facing to the *east* so that the inhabitants could see the morning star—the god of light and fire—that would shine on the hearth as a manifestation of the daily miracle of renewal.

Pawnee legend held that each of their villages was founded by a particular star, who told one person how to assemble a bundle of sacred objects related to its worship. This knowledge was then passed down from generation to generation. The hereditary Pawnee chiefs kept the star bundle hanging from a buffalo-hair rope in the sacred, western portion of their lodges—the section that was associated with the evening star and reserved for priests during the performance of ceremonies.

American Indians: The Spirit World, Henry Woodhead (Ed.), 1992, p. 166

The Pawnee People celebrate the intercardinal directions and, with colors, speak of their ancestral connections with the stars. Though times have changed, they have never forgotten their unity with the stars, that part of the creation that was singled out by the Creator (Tirawahat) for special relationship with the Pawnee People.

ORIGINS STORY
ARAPAHO

In the beginning, according to Arapaho accounts, the First Pipe Keeper floated on a limitless body of water with the Flat Pipe. He fasted and prayed to the Creator, who inspired him to send the duck to search beneath the water's surface. The duck emerged with a little bit of dirt, which the First Pipe Keeper put on the Pipe. Then he sent the turtle to the bottom, and it, too, returned with dirt. The First Pipe Keeper put this dirt on the Pipe and blew it all off toward each of the *four directions*. In doing so, he created the earth. Then he made the sun and moon, man and woman, and vegetable and animal life, followed by day and night and the *four seasons*. He then taught the first people the religious rites that they would need. The duck and turtle were placed with the Pipe into a bundle, and the Arapaho—descendants of that first man and woman—have been responsible for them ever since. For the Arapaho the contents of the bundle are symbols of the creation, and their custody of the bundle a sacred trust. . . .

All Arapaho traveled through *four stages*, or "hills of life"— childhood, youth, adulthood, and old age. The duties, responsibilities, and privileges of males and females changed at each stage. The Arapaho symbolically equated the life cycle with the movement of the sun, the *four cardinal directions*, and the progress of the seasons.

The Arapaho, Loretta Fowler, 1989, pp. 13, 23

Here is a prime example of how a People relates the fourness of things to their daily life.

———————————————— ✳ ————————————————

INTERCARDINAL PERSONIFICATIONS AND SPECIAL PERSONAGES
PAWNEE & ARAPAHO

The various divine hierarchies can be typified by two examples in particular. One is the Pawnee tradition, the other the Arapaho, two tribes known for their broad and profound religious temperaments. The Pawnee place Tirawa, the Father, as Creator of all beings, and below Him the Evening Star (female) and the Morning Star (male), who beget the first human being, a man. Below these are *the Four World Quarters*: the sacred personified winds of the *northeast*, the *southeast*, the *southwest*, and the *northwest*. Next are the three deities of the *north*, led by the North Star Chief, and below these Father Sun and Mother Moon, who give birth to the second human being, a woman. These humans are the progenitors of the race.

. . . . when Indians come together for a ceremonial smoking of the pipe, they use it to incense the *Four Quarters*, thus, by retracing the orderly shape of the universe, reminding themselves of their place as creatures in this sacred house called earth.

The People of the Center: American Indian Religion and Christianity,
Carl Starkloff, 1974, pp. 36-37

Here we see that, like other tribes, the Pawnee and the Arapaho Peoples have an orderly way of relating to the cosmos, though their explanations differ from one another. The use of the number 4 and the cardinals and intercardinals figure greatly in their teachings and ceremonies, even after the introduction of Christianity.

——————————————— ✤ ———————————————

SWEATLODGE SYMBOLISMS
CROW

This belief that the sweatlodge is central to Crow identity is brought out by the often-heard Crow concept that there are *four things* which make up the Crow: the Sacred Pipe, the clan system, the Tobacco Society, and the sweatlodge. The Sacred Pipe is seen as a symbol of leadership and peace, and the vehicle that conveys prayers: the clan system defines the individual's place within the social fabric of the Crow, with the mother's clan providing for the physical needs of the individual and the father's providing for the social recognition and religious needs; the Tobacco Society is the only religious organization that is specific to the Crow, and, in fact, is seen by Crow people as the ritual expression that differentiates them from all other nations. And, last is the sweatlodge, which provides for the physical and spiritual cleansing of the individual. Taken together, these *four* things are at the heart of what it means to be Crow. . . .

The ceremony of the sweatlodge also reinforces Crow concepts of the cycle of life, and of time in general. The Crow perceive time as cyclical, always repeating *four stages*: summer followed by fall, followed by winter, then spring, followed by summer again. The sweat ceremony, with its *four "rounds,"* is said to mirror the *four seasons* of the year.

At the beginning of the first round, water is splashed on the heated rocks to represent the rain storms of the fall or spring, what Crows call *xaláachke,* "the long rains." Termed *iihkupche,* this symbolic gesture represents the desire that all participating in the "sweat" may see those rains.

During each round a set number of ladles full of water is poured on the rocks: four, seven, ten, and finally the uncounted number, *chimmíssuua,* what Crows using English often call the "thousands" or "millions." To conclude each round, a participant must say a prayer to "raise the door." Usually these prayers are a recital of a sleep dream that predicts some coming season.

This is because the Crows firmly believe that dreams are predictive in nature. The events or seasons of the year that are seen in dreams are thought to be vision of things to come. . . .

Much more symbolism, beyond dreams, is included and incorporated into the sweatlodge. As an example, the Crow say that the world is composed of *four elements*: air, *huché:* earth, *awé:* water, *bilé* and fire, *bilée.* All four elements are present in the sweat: the air that carries the searing steam: the earth, our mother, that is sat upon: the water that is poured on the hot rocks or drunk after the second round: and the fire, the red hot rocks that have been heated in a fire. . . .

With all of this symbolic investment, the sweatlodge is also seen as a personal cleansing, both physical and spiritual.

Usually the right to conduct a sweat ceremony, or "sweat rights," are passed from father to son. In most cases this is actually a classificatory father, what Crows call "clan fathers," or members of one's father's clan, since religious training and knowledge generally comes from individuals via this relationship. But the manner of performing a sweat is personally owned, since Crows generally consider religious rites to be personal property. A payment is made to recompense the individual for whatever they endured in order to gain the knowledge and right to perform the ceremony.

When inquiring about sweat ways, my own Crow family had me seek out one of my father's clan brothers who is known for his sweat rights. Through our lengthy discussion, I learned of the role of the stars in his "sweat way." Later, . . . he built a sweatlodge for me and my family and passed that on to me. . . . I gave him *four "good" physical gifts* for his spiritual one.

This was the "star way" of conducting a sweat. Here the *four pours* of the first round represent the *four seasons* and *four directions of the winds*, the seven represent the Seven Brothers, or the Big

Dipper, the ten represent the Gathering of Stars, the Pleiades, and the uncounted pours stand for all the stars in the sky.

In discussing his way to pour, he said there are *four seasons, four directions of the wind*. "Each wind means something else. A *south wind* means warmth, a *west wind* means a chinook, a *north wind* means cold is coming, an *east wind* means success, life, where light comes from, like that."

The Stars We Know: Crow Indian Astronomy and Lifeways,
Timothy McCleary, 1997, pp. 74-77

The contemporary Crow sweat lodge is an important "sacramental" way of communing with the Creator as a sharer in the creation. Past and present are one as the participants give thanks and look forward to life in the seasons to come. The symbolic four is present in many ways in the Crow universe but especially in the much celebrated Crow sweat tipi.

✳

CLEANSING
NORTHERN CHEYENNE

The evil tendencies that lie within a person's own heart need also to be dealt with. Wesley referred to these tendencies as "evil wishes." To dispel them, an individual must find "man" sage growing in a place where it has not been contaminated by any previous human presence. While the penitent stands facing the sun, he passes a handful of the sage away from himself, twice over the right shoulder and twice over the left. He then passes it with a sweeping motion over his forehead. Lastly, he points the sage away from himself *four times* in a *clockwise direction* and lowers it to the ground with *four downward movements*. The expression Wesley gave for this or for any similar act was nasez, meaning, "I clear it off."

The Last Contrary: The Story of Wesley Whiteman (Black Bear),
Warren Schwartz, 1988, p. 60

Wesley Whiteman, who lived from 1897-1981, shared much of his spirituality with those who would seek to understand it. Though he was a believer in both ways, Native traditional religion and Catholic, he had no difficulty making the connection for himself, nor of talking about it with others. Here we can recognize the familiar circular four-fold action schema, but this time in an act of penitence.

------------------------------- ✳ -------------------------------

GHOST DANCE
NORTHERN CHEYENNE

. . . the Ghost dance among the northern Cheyenne had several features not found in the south. *Four fires* were built outside of the dance circle and about 20 yards back from it, toward each of *the cardinal points*. These fires were built of long poles set up on end, so as to form a rude cone, much as the poles of a tipi are erected. The fires were lighted at the bottom, and thus made high bonfires, which were kept up as long as the dance continued.

> *The Ghost Dance Religion and the Sioux Outbreak of 1890,*
> James Mooney, 1991, p. 915

During the Ghost Dance spiritual movement many ancient ways of praying were revised and adjusted by the Peoples to express the truth of the movement. Symbolism that was both local and, to some extent, able to bridge the differences among the tribes, was utilized, but it was a symbolism that was also ancient, the building and lighting of the four fires in a certain way, for instance.

------------------------------- ✳ -------------------------------

SCAR SYMBOLISM OF
KEEPER OF SACRED ARROWS
CHEYENNE

The structure of the ritual and its shared symbolic forms give some insight into the religious and moral meanings that filled the experience of the Cheyennes during their high culture period. Rich indeed was the symbolism of form and color; and in important ways it is possible to view the Sweet Medicine tradition as being a general text for the ritual. A more detailed examination of the ritual process will bring these points into sharper focus.

The theme of sacrifice . . . is embodied symbolically and literally in the flesh of the arrow keeper—at least this was the custom in traditional days. The symbolism of the *cardinal directions* was evident on the arms, shoulders, thighs, back and loins of the man performing this sacred role. From these areas of his body strips of flesh were cut; and in each of these body areas the number of cuts equaled the symbolic number *four*, evoking the powers of the *cardinal directions*. In addition, a strip of flesh was cut from the outside of each arm, extending from each wrist and passing up over the shoulders, from there to extend down each side of the chest until the cuts met in the center of the sternum. At the point where the cuts met, a round piece of flesh was extracted and immediately above this cut another crescent shaped piece of skin was taken out. Powerfully symbolizing the sun and moon, these scars reminded the people of the virtue of the person who kept the sacred arrows and of their power among the people.

Renewing the World: Plains Indians Religion and Morality,
Howard Harrod, 1992, p. 103

The ritual of the Sacred Arrows has undergone some modifications over the years, but its core remains the same. The human body became the canvas upon which the ancient truths were painted. As with many other cultures that used scarification and the art of tattooing, so did the Cheyenne utilize the body of the keeper of the Sacred Arrows as a permanent sign of the powers of the four directions.

NUMERICAL AND DIRECTIONAL SYMBOLISM
TETON SIOUX

In former times the Lakota grouped all their activities by *fours*. This was because they recognized *four directions*: the *west*, the *north*, the *east*, and the *south; four divisions of time*: the day, the night, the moon, and the year; *four parts* in everything that grows from the ground: the roots, the stem, the leaves, and the fruit; *four kinds* of things that breathe: those that crawl, those that fly, those that walk on four legs, and those that walk on two legs; *four things* above the world: the sun, the moon, the sky, and the stars; *four kinds* of gods: the great, the associates of the great, the gods below them, and the spiritkind; *four periods* of human life: babyhood, childhood, adulthood, and old age; and finally, mankind has *four fingers* on each hand, *four toes* on each foot and the thumbs and the great toes taken together form *four*. Since the Great Spirit caused everything to be in *fours*, mankind should do everything possible in *fours*.

"The Sundance and Other Ceremonies of the Oglala Division of the Teton Dakota," *Anthropological Papers of the American Museum of Natural History*, J.R. Walker, 1917, pp. 159-160

Often, as we look for the celebration of the four directions in a culture, we also come upon the ritual use of four. For eons these two elements have helped the People to pray and understand life.

———————————————— ❋ ————————————————

HORSE DANCE
SIOUX

Among the Sioux a Horse Dance was also associated with Thunder. This was a very elaborate ritual and usually in charge of *Heyoka* members. It was described by both White Bull, of the Minikonjou, and Black Elk, of the Oglalas, who had Heyoka dreams while just youngsters.

Sixteen horses were used—*four bays, four buckskins, four blue roans*, and *four blacks*. The colors related to the *four directions*; ... the black was probably for the *West*, blue for the *North*, bay for the *East*, and buckskin for the *South*. These colors are somewhat different from those given by White Bull and Black Elk. Both used black for the *West*, white for the *North*, sorrel for the *East*, but Black Elk had buckskin for *South* and White Bull had light roans. Apparently, as in most Sioux ceremonies, there was some liberty in details.

The horses were painted with red zig-zag lines with forked endings down each leg, and the riders' paint matched the horses. The riders wore hood masks of cloth or buckskin, with long eagle primary feathers attached to look like horns ... there were *four singers*, each carrying a hand drum, each singer and his drum painted in one of the *four horse colors* ... there were ... virgins, ... Black Elk stated four, wearing red-dyed buckskin dresses, with faces painted red. They were important characters in the dance, one representing *East* and carrying a pipe; one *West* with a hoop symbolizing the nation; one *North* carrying a "healing herb" and a white goose wing; and the one *South* carrying a wand—a "flowering stick"—symbolizing the growing things of the world. These *four* maidens thus held in their hands the life of the Sioux nation. Each wore a wreath of sage; from it hung a long spotted-eagle tail feather.

. . . a brush arbor was erected for the center of activity, but Black Elk used a specially painted tipi . . . the leader rode a black horse and was himself painted black, with white spots representing hail. But Black Elk rode a bay horse and was painted red, with black lightning down his arms and legs. Either way, it must have been a spectacular and impressive thing to watch. The horses also had the long eagle-feather primaries inserted in their bridles in such a way that they looked like horns.

The painting of the leader, riders, and maidens was all done inside the sacred tipi. In Black Elk's ceremony there were six singers, all old men, whom he called the Grandfathers, for they represented the *Four Directions*, the Sky, and the Earth.

First the riders went out. When the Grandfathers began to sing about the *West*, the black-horse riders mounted and lined up, *four abreast*, on the west side of the lodge, facing *West*. Next they sang of the *North*, and the white horses and riders lined up on that side of the tipi. Then followed the sorrels, with their red riders to the *East*, and the buckskins, with yellow riders to the *South*.

The leader sang now along with the drumming and singing of the Grandfathers while the virgins stepped outside, carrying their sacred emblems. They were followed by the leader, who mounted his horse and stood behind them, facing *West*. After the leader came the Grandfathers, standing abreast behind the leader on his bay horse. They sang again of each direction and of the horses representing them, and as they did each troop in turn wheeled and fell into position, four abreast—first the blacks, then the whites, sorrels, and buckskins, and all pranced in time to the song.

The procession started out, the maidens running ahead a pace, pausing, running and pausing, while the lines of horses moved into position. First the black horses circled around to take the lead and headed for the *West* side of the camp circle. There they wheeled, came back, and followed the buckskins, while the white horses went around the maidens to take the lead to the *north* side of the camp. This procedure was followed also by the sorrels leading to the *eastern* side and the buckskins to the *southern* side, when the blacks once more took the lead. Each time a troop reached its side of the village, the singers sang about that direction and its power. This parade, with its wheeling and changes of position, circled the village *four* times. On the second time around many of the people, mounted on their own horses, joined in the procession, bringing up the rear, so that it was a great festive occasion for everyone.

After the *fourth time* around, the procession stopped again on the *west* side, all facing back toward the sacred tipi in the center. The virgins were first again, *four abreast*, then the leader, followed by the six Grandfathers, also abreast, and the horsemen lined up in a company front on either side of them, the blacks and whites on their left, the sorrels and buckskins on their right. The leader raised his hand and called out *four times*, the fourth time being a signal for all to charge the sacred tipi. All endeavored to count coup on it, the *first four* expecting to receive special good luck as a result.

. . . just previous to this final charge, which ended the public ceremony, the painted riders dismounted, holding their horses by their halter ropes, and danced . . . they circled the camp twice, but, four being the sacred number, we feel that four was the customary number of times . . . this ceremony was given in preparation for war, but Black Elk said he gave it to fulfill his vision and to bring good fortune to his people. Just before the Grandfathers left the sacred tipi, they smoothed the ground within. On returning after the ceremony they found tiny horse tracks all over the interior—the tracks of the spirit riders who had guided the ceremony.

. . . during the parade a guard was posted over the ceremonial arbor, but . . . after the ceremony horse and moccasin tracks were found all over the ground inside. A holy man then predicted the fate of the next war party by studying these tracks.

Indian Dances of North America: Their Importance to Indian Life,
Reginald Laubin & Gladys Laubin, 1977, pp. 360-362

Four teams each of four horses with the four sacred colors of the directions, four singers, four virgins, four riders, circlings, the whole ceremony done four times: these are some of the ways that the Horse Dance was able to celebrate the People's spirituality. This was a dance for power, as well as for healing.

�֍

DIRECTIONAL AND NUMERICAL
RELIGIOUS ASSOCIATIONS
OGLALA

In cosmology as well as ritual, we find exhaustive references to the number 4 in both static and dynamic representations. For example, if we look at other symbols of the *Four Winds*, we can see that new modes of analysis can help unlock potential meaning. In the past we would have been likely on "logical" grounds to see the members of the *Four Winds—West, North, East,* and *South*—as constituting a category. At the same time, the relationships between the directions and, say, colors, animals, and birds that symbolize each of the respective directions were syntagmatically related. A syntagmatic chain hypothetically would be produced by the association of, say, *West* Wind, representing the paradigm "direction"; fall representing the paradigm "season"; black representing the paradigm "color" associated with the direction; buffalo representing the "animal" symbolizing the direction, etc. The entire series may be schematized in the following way:

DIRECTION	SEASON	COLOR	ANIMAL	BIRD
West	Fall	Black	Blacktail Deer	Swallow
North	Winter	Red	Buffalo	Magpie
East	Spring	Yellow	Whitetail Deer	Crow
South	Summer	White	Elk	Meadowlark

The above schema may be considered the Western inclination to arrange topically and paradigmatically, that is, into things that go together. It produces a group of static categories. From the Lakota point of view, however, the schema makes more sense if we view it in the following way:

1	2	3	4
West	*North*	*East*	*South*
Fall	Winter	Spring	Summer
Black	Red	Yellow	White
Blacktail Deer	Buffalo	Whitetail Deer	Elk
Swallow	Magpie	Crow	Meadowlark

From this perspective, we see that all members of paradigm 1 are interchangeable—that is, in the language of semiotics, they are metaphorically related—while the relationships expressed between paradigmatic sets express metonymical relationships. The point is, in the first schema, there is a tendency to see each paradigmatic set as static, while in the second schema there is a sense of movement. The two schemas are, of course, two aspects of a singular analytical perspective, a perspective based on the notion of a two-dimensional rather than a one-dimensional model. One model produces a static or synchronic representation of the number 4; the second produces a dynamic or diachronic representation.

The second schema also represents what we might regard as a mechanism for breaking the mythical code. Any reference to a singular member of a paradigmatic set is implicitly a reference to all other members of the set (by definition) as well as a reference to the relationship between all four paradigmatic sets. Hence, when a medicine man sings that he is calling a "red stone friend," he is really making a reference to a totality whose aid may be sought by addressing only one of its parts. "Red stone," then, is really a referential marker that signifies the *north*, winter, buffalo, and so on. Any reference to one member of the set is a reference to all of them. Therefore, a prayer or song that addresses specifically, say, the magpie, a red stone, a whitetail deer, and summer has in fact made a general reference to the *four directions*.

We should not be so dazzled by analysis, however, that we overlook the quality of fulfillment in sacred numbers—that, in fact, a recitation of the numerical components of the series does lead somewhere. For example, in the creation story, we find metaphorical references to personified gods whose actions result in the creation of a viable universe from a static matrix. The investment of movements in static objects ultimately causes the creation of the universe as the Lakota now see it. During the process, a quadripite plan unfolds in which (1) days and nights are distinguished, (2) the month is established, (3) the year and the seasons (that is, space) are established, leading up to the present "time" period, the fourth generation, which is (4) the present time.

Beyond the Vision: Essays on American Indian Culture,
William Powers, 1987, pp. 68-71

As we live we must learn to associate things and people and the work of the Creator. This is, I believe, how we develop a spirituality. There are many ways of doing this, from memorization to annual feasts and holidays. The Oglala and many other Peoples of the Plains often associate particular directions with certain seasons or colors or animals or birds or minerals. Such mnemonic customs help them to order their world spiritually.

---- ✳ ----

MEANING OF FOUR
LAKOTA

Tunkan, the stone spirit; Wakinyan, the thunder spirit; Taku-skanska, the moving spirit; Unktehi, the water spirit—they are all *wakan:* mysterious, wonderful, incomprehensible, holy. They are all part of the Great Mystery. These are our *four* great supernaturals, which brings us to yet another form of symbolism—the magic of a number which we share with many other peoples.

Four is the number that is most *wakan,* most sacred. Four stands for Tatuye Topa—*the four quarters* of the earth. One of its chief symbols is Umane, which looks like this:

It represents the unused earth force. By this I mean that the Great Spirit pours a great, unimaginable amount of force into all things—pebbles, ants, leaves, whirlwinds—whatever you will. Still there is so much force left over that's not used up, that is in his gift to bestow, that has to be used wisely and in moderation if we are given some of it.

This force is symbolized by the Umane.

Lame Deer, Seeker of Visions: The Life of a Sioux Medicine Man,
John Lame Deer & Richard Erdoes, 1972, p. 115

Just as the Judaeo-Christian tradition speaks of angels (Gabriel, Raphael, Michael, etc.) which uniquely mediate the Divine Presence, so in the Lakota way, four main spirits express power that is available to human beings who take the time to ask for it.

---------------------------------- ✸ ----------------------------------

ANNUAL RELIGIOUS CEREMONIAL
MANDAN

The Mandans believed that the earth rests on the backs of *four* tortoises. They say that "each tortoise rained ten days, making forty days in all, and the waters covered the earth.". . .

Their annual religious ceremony lasted *four* days; *four* men were call for by *Nu-mohk-múck-a-nah* . . . to cleanse and prepare the Medicine Lodge, "one from the **north**, one from the **south**, one from the **east**, and one from the **west**." *Four* was the number of tortoise-drums on the floor of the Medicine Lodge; there were also *four* buffalo and *four* human skulls arranged on the floor of the Medicine Lodge. There were four couples of dancers in the bull-dance, and *four* intervening dancers in the same dance, as has been described; the bull-dance was repeated *four* times on the first day, eight times on the second day, twelve times on the third day, and sixteen times on the fourth day , adding *four* dances on each of the *four days*, which added together make forty, the exact number of days that it rained upon the earth to produce the Deluge.

There were *four* sacrifices of various-coloured cloths raised on poles over the Medicine Lodge. The visits of *O-ke-hée-de* were paid to *four* of the buffaloes in the bull-dance; and in every instance of the young men who underwent the tortures explained, there were *four* splints run through the flesh on the legs, *four* on the arms, *four* on the body, and *four* buffalo-skulls attached to each one's wounds. And, as has been related in the tradition above given, *four* was the number of bulls given by the medicine child to feed the Mandans when they were starving.

O-Kee-Pa: A Religious Ceremony and Other Customs of the Mandan,
George Catlin, 1976, pp. 75-76

George Catlin, who travelled among the Mandan in the 1830s before their great decimation through imported diseases and other "gifts" of the visitors from the East, wrote much about their ceremonies, especially this one. He was alert to the importance of the four directions.

---------------------- ✳ ----------------------

BUFFALO BULL DANCE
MANDAN

From where I sat, this little mystery-thing, whatever it was, had the appearance of a small tortoise, or frog, lying on its back, with its head and legs quite extended, and tasselled off with exceedingly delicate red and blue and yellow ribbons or tassels, and other bright colored ornaments. It seemed, from the devotions paid to it, to be the very nucleus of these mysteries—the *sanctissimus sanctorum,* from which seemed to emanate all the sanctity of these proceedings, and to which all seemed to be paying the highest devotional respect. . . .

There were also *four sacks of great veneration* lying on the floor of the lodge, each containing some three or four gallons of water. They were made with great labor and much ingenuity. Each one was constructed from the skin of the buffalo's neck and most elaborately sewed together in the form of a large tortoise lying on its back, with a bunch of eagle's quills appended to it as a tail. Each of them had a stick, shaped like a drum-stick, lying on them, with which, in a subsequent stage of the ceremonies, they are beaten upon by several mystery-men as a part of the music for their strange dances. By the side of these sacks, which they call *Eeh-teeh-ka,* are two other articles of equal importance, which they call *Eeh-na-dee* (rattles), in the form of a gourd-shell also made of dried skins and also used in the music of their dances.

The four sacks of water have the appearance of very great antiquity. By enquiring of my friend and patron, the medicine man, after the ceremonies were over, he very gravely told me that "those *four tortoises* contained the waters from the *four quarters of the world*— that these waters had been contained therein ever since the settling down of the waters!"

There were many curious ceremonials enacted in the open area in front of the medicine-lodge by members of the community. One of these, which they call *Bel-lochk-na-pic* (the bull dance), is repeated *four times* during the first day, eight times on the second day, twelve times on the third day, and sixteen times on the fourth day; and always around the frame, or "big canoe."

Eight men, with skins of buffaloes thrown over their backs, with the horns and hoofs and tails remaining on, their bodies in a horizontal position, imitated the actions of the buffalo. The bodies of those men were naked and all painted in the most extraordinary manner: their limbs, bodies, and faces with black, red, or white paint. Each carried on his back a bunch of green willow-boughs about the usual size of a bundle of straw. These eight men, being divided into *four pairs*, took their positions on the *four different sides of the frame*, or big canoe, representing thereby the *four cardinal points*.

Between each pair was another figure with his back turned to the big canoe, engaged in the same dance, keeping step with them, with a similar staff in one hand and a rattle in the other, and (being *four in number*) answering again to the four cardinal points. These *four young men* were also naked, with no other dress upon them except a beautiful kelt (or quartz-quaw) around the waist, made of eagles' quills and ermine, and very splendid head-dresses made of the same materials. Two of these figures were painted entirely black with pounded charcoal and grease. They were called the "firmament or night," and the numerous white spots dotted all over their bodies were called "stars." The other two were painted from head to foot as red as vermilion could make them. These represented the day, and the white streaks painted up and down over their bodies were "ghosts which the morning rays were chasing away."

These twelve are the only persons actually engaged in the bull dance, which is repeated each time in the same form, without the slightest variation. There are, however, a great number of characters engaged in giving the whole effect to this strange scene, each one acting well his part.

The dance takes place in the presence of the whole nation, who are gathered around on the tops of the lodges, or otherwise, as spectators. On the first day the bull dance is given once to each of the *cardinal points*, and the medicine-man smokes his pipe in those directions. On the second day, *twice* to each, *three times* to each on the third day, *four times to each on the fourth.*

Letters and Notes on the North American Indians,
George Catlin, 1975, pp. 194-195

The honoring of the compass points, the ritual use of the number 4 in both personages and amount of ceremonial days, along with highly illustrative painting of the dancers, exemplifies the ordered importance of this People's spirituality.

———————————— ✣ ————————————

PATRONAGE OF THE INTERCARDINAL DIRECTIONS
ARIKARA

In the Arikara concept of the universe each of the semi-cardinal quarters of the horizon is consecrated to one of the *four elements,* four guardians, under God. Thus the *southeast* corner (of the lodge) is consecrated to the sunrise, the *southwest* corner to the thunder, which implies water, necessary element of all fire. The *northwest* quadrant is consecrated to the wind and movement of the air, and the *northeast* is consecrated to night. In addition, each of the four quarters had a secondary significance, and in this second grouping of power or elements the *southwest* quarter is dedicated to the guardian spirit of the genius of the bison. . . .

"The Arikara Buffalo Society Medicine Bundle," *Plains Anthropologist, Journal of the Plains Conference*, James Howard, June 1974, p. 245

Circularity and aspects of the four directions fit together well in the cosmology of this northern plains People.

———————————— ✣ ————————————

SUNDANCE LODGE PREPARATION
BLOOD

The construction of the Medicine Lodge began with the placement of twelve upright cottonwood logs. These posts stood in a circle about thirty-five feet in diameter; in the center was the large hole into which would go the Center Pole. The posts, long enough to extend about nine feet above the ground, forked at the top end. Eleven smaller logs, each about twelve feet long, were laid so that their ends rested in the forks of adjacent uprights, thus forming a circle. The remainder of the Holy Lodge was constructed the following day, the most important day of the ceremony.

Wilson observed in his notes:

> That morning as I neared the camp I saw that most of the lodges had sacrifices or offerings of some garment or blanket elevated upon an extra lodge-pole leaning against the lodge; these were tied to cross sticks. . . . At each of *the four lodges* occupied by the O-Kon people an extension rite was, in the forenoon, begun.

Wilson did not often explain the spiritual meanings of the details of ceremonies he recorded. For instance, the customary purpose of an offering is to give every family an opportunity to participate in building the sacred lodge. A gift of fabric, fastened to a small frame, is presented to the holy people, who are acting in behalf of the Spirits, just before the main construction of the lodge takes place. The frame is made by tying two scraped willow sticks in the shape of a cross, representing the *Four Holy Directions* of the Universe. Bunches of sage tied to the cross represent the gifts obtained from our Mother Earth. The cloth is added to share our material wealth with the Holy Powers.

The Blood People: A Division of the Blackfoot Confederacy,
Adolf Hungry Wolf, 1977, p. 25

Preparations for this medicine lodge of the Sundance always follow a time-honored pattern. Here the Blood People of the Canadian Plains honor the four directions with offerings of both sage and colored cloth.

✤

SUN DANCE
BLOOD

A strange sight next appeared. *Four processions* of young men approached from the lodges, one from each of the *cardinal points*. Each procession was made up of pairs of young men, walking, each pair behind the other. Each man held aloft a lodge pole, which was strongly connected at the top to the pole of his companion. So in all 4 of the processions, the poles of every pair of young men were tied together, a foot and a half or two feet apart. They approached a few yards at a time until, when within 50 or 60 yards of the Sun-Lodge, they changed their formation from column to line. This resulted in the ends of their 4 lines uniting so that they, as a whole, formed a large circle, the center of which was the half erected medicine lodge. The completion of the lodge by raising the heavy timbers in place [with their lodge poles] was the errand of all these young men.

We are here in the midst of a symbolic battle. The young men with their lodge poles represent the warriors of the tribe, the tribe's defenders, carrying their weapons. The warriors are about to converge upon the Center Pole, representing the enemy, and overpower it by raising it up. This is symbolic of the People's power to triumph in battle. The holy people wait by the Center Pole to lend their spiritual power to the victory. The husbands wear the black paint worn by a victorious war party.

Completing the Medicine Lodge follows:

The A-Kax [holy party] now left their positions and entered the circle; the black men each carried the scalps tied to a short stick, climbed upon the resting center pole and, all bending their heads close to the top and covering their heads with their blankets, prayed silently. At the end of this prayer, they jumped down and the circle of young men closed in amid deafening yells and attacked the center pole with their poles. Each pair worked together. Placing the connecting cord against the pole, most of them pushing from the under side, they soon had it upright in its hole, being assisted at first by some other men who put their shoulders to it. Next they attacked the rafters which were lifted up. The butt end of one of them was placed upon the center of each stringer and all the small ends bearing offerings were resting in the fork of the center pole. The butts were tied in place with raw hide, the whole being completed in a very short time to the satisfaction of the Indians, who consider the completion of the lodge a cause of joy.

The Blood People: A Division of the Blackfoot Confederacy,
Adolf Hungry Wolf, 1977, p. 33

The preparation and construction of the medicine lodge for the Sun Dance was virtually a ceremony in itself. The four processions from each of the cardinal directions acknowledged the power that came from the directions, while the circular architecture reminded them that the People were in unity as they prayed together during this holy time.

———————————————— ✦ ————————————————

DIRECTIONALITY
PLAINS CREE

"Directions" are *north, east, south, west*, up and down. To Native Americans, however, they are also instructions for our path and involve a certain way of doing ceremony and ritual. We all have our own directions, road or path, to follow.

The grandfathers sit in the *four directions*. We call on the grandfathers in the *east*, where the sun comes up; in the *south*, where the moon is; in the *west*, where the sun goes down; and in the *north*, where the grandfathers sit in darkness.

The *four* winds and the *four* seasons are directions. The *four* races of people are in the *four directions*. I believe the red man is from the *west*, the yellow man is from the *east*, the white man comes from the *north*, and the black man is from the *south*.

When early Native Americans set up their lodges in which to live, depending on the direction of the winds, they ideally placed the opening to greet the morning sun in the *east*.

> *Center of the World: Native American Spirituality*,
> Don Rutledge, 1992, p. 21

A direction indicates a way to go, a way to move. Four of them open up paths, not only of physical travel, but also of orientation which help with giving thanks to the Creator and living life well.

─────────────── ✤ ───────────────

SMOKING TIPI CEREMONY
PLAINS CREE

Ranking next in importance to the Sun dance among the sacred ceremonies, was the Smoking Tipi *(pihtwowikamik)*. As with all vowed ceremonies, it was given in fulfillment of a pledge made to the supernaturals; in order to give it a man had to acquire the right either in a vision, or by purchase, or through inheritance.

This ceremony consisted of a night-long singing session during which many prayers were said, offerings given, and pipes ritualistically manipulated. It was usually held in the spring in an enlarged tipi. This structure differed from the ordinary enlarged tipi in that it was built on a four-pole foundation. The *four poles* were laid on the ground, *one pointing to each of the cardinal directions*, their tops laid one over the other. . . . The tipi was then set up by the men.

In the center of the lodge a round altar was made by excavating the sod to a depth of about three inches and a diameter of four or five feet. The depth of the excavation was increased each successive time that the host gave the ceremony. *Four* pegs were planted in the altar flush with the surface at opposing points on the circumference. A fire was built in the center of the altar. At the *north* side of the lodge, near the wall, *four* cloth offerings were draped over short upright stakes.

The pledger had *four* assistants. He also chose two young men who had to sit close to the fire, not moving throughout the ceremony. The ritual began after food had been served and eaten by all those in the lodge except the host, who neither ate nor drank during the rite. Two of the assistants came up and sat beside the two young men, each assistant near one of the pegs in the altar. The two smoked in unison, prayed to the spirit powers, and then passed their pipes along the perimeter of the altar just as was done along the rectangular Sun dance altars. Two men sat at the other two pegs, received the pipes, smoked them, and passed them on along the edge of the excavation. The pegs symbolized the thunders, one in each cardinal direction.

When this part of the ritual had been completed, two pipes were passed around the assembled company. Then *four* rattles were held over sweetgrass smoke and one handed to each of the pledger's assistants. The head assistant received the "chief" rattle. He sang his power songs aided by a chorus of the other assistants and of the women who were present. The other men in the lodge did not sing until they had received rattles. After the head assistant had sung through his power songs, he passed the chief rattle to the assistant sitting next to him, who then led the singers in his songs. Thus the chief rattle was passed around until every man who possessed songs of his own had an opportunity to sing them. The other three rattles were also passed around. Soon after the start of the ceremony, boys daubed with white clay entered the lodge, wailing. They carried offering cloths which they presented to the host.

The singing continued through the night. At dawn, the chief rattle was given to a man who sat near the door. This was the *"manito person,"* so called because he was well versed in all the songs and procedure for the ceremony. The pledger had also confided to him the circumstances under which the vow was made. He sang a special set of songs connected with the office. As he sang, the servers shook the *four cloths* which were draped over poles at the back of the lodge, as though to wake them. The ceremony ended after the *four* assistants took places beside the pegs on the altar and passed the pipes as before.

The ceremony is replete with ritualized manipulations of pipes and rattles.

> *The Plains Cree: An Ethnographic, Historical, and Comparative Study*,
> David Mandelbaum, 1985, pp. 199-201

Fourness takes the symbolic forefront in this ceremony: a four-pole foundation tipi set up (one for each direction), four pegs in harmony with the tipi foundation bounded the altar (symbolizing the cardinal direction thunders), four cloth offerings, four assistants, four rattles. Perhaps each of the songs would have been sung four times as well or would have had a four-part sequence.

✦

SUN DANCE MEANING
INTERTRIBAL

From the latter years of the eighteenth century, until it reached its apex in the 1880s, one ceremony loomed above all the rest as typical of the transformative process and worldview of those who had left behind their woodland traditions and re-created themselves into the peoples we know today as the Plains tribes. That ceremony is known by many names by different tribes—the Sun Dance, They Dance Staring at the Sun, the Thirst Dance, the Medicine Lodge, and the Dance for the World.

The whole ceremony is not technically a dance. While dancing in place or bobbing to the sound of the drum and sacred songs over an extended period of time does take place, this aspect is only part of a series of other complex and profound rituals that make up the Sun Dance.

At the appointed time of year, in the summer, sometimes near the summer solstice, the tribe (or, in some cases, several allied tribes) would gather in great camps on the Plains. After selecting sacred leaders and associates, the participant would enter into a *four-* or eight-*day period of fasting* from food and water. Practicing ritualized behavior and restraint, the people would demonstrate awesome respect for the sacred drama of re-creating the world and all that is in it in a miniature version of the cosmos. This miniature version took the form of a sacred lodge, circular in shape, walled in and roofed over by some tribes, but always made of natural materials (posts and beams of newly cut trees, foliage, vines, and reeds).

A sacred tree, or *axis mundi,* is placed at the center and the lodge is demarcated into the *four quarters* of the universe, which are marked by smaller decorated trees or sacred altars. Offerings of precious animal skins—and, in modern times, brightly colored yard goods, a once-precious trade item—adorn the sacred tree and those of the *four quarters*. Other esoteric offerings (almost always including tobacco) are placed on the crotch at the top of the sacred tree.

In solemn procession, the accoutered participants, sacred leaders, singers and drummers, and audience enter these sacred worlds and proceed to offer themselves up as sacrifice to the ancient gods, in thanksgiving for life itself and all that sustains life. In due time, each individual's vow to undergo this sacrifice becomes part of a great collective prayer for the life of all things and all peoples of this world.

The elements of the Sun Dance are simple—dancing in place, the sound of an eagle-wing bone-whistle blowing in rhythm to the great drum (or drums), and the ancient voice-prayer-music of the singers as they address the Sun and other powers of the universe: "Oh, holy powers, we honor you this day that we may live. Have pity on me. Accept my suffering this day in reciprocation for all you have given us."

The essence of the prayer rises out of the teachings of the shamanic tradition of communion with the gods via sacred acts: music, dance, visual-arts compositions, and projection of one's will into the heart of the experience of relationship. First and foremost in this relationship is the recognition that humans are but one of many beings among all the plants, insects, reptiles, birds, other animals, minerals, and hidden mysteries of the earth itself. Tribal teachings emphasize that all are children of an infinite and ongoing process that transcends our most basic understanding of time itself.

At the heart of the Sun Dance prayer is a cyclical view of time and process, this great circle of life that various tribes call "That Which Moves," "The Great Holy," "The Great Spirit," or "The Great Mystery."

It is this concept, or its perceived parts, that the tribes in their sacred lodges have demarcated and manifested as symbol in their visual arts, music, oratory, poetry, dance, drama and vernacular architecture.

Native American Dance: Ceremonies and Social Traditions,
Charlotte Heth (Ed.), 1992, p. 135

The sun dance, as it is commonly called, clearly expresses the People of the Plains tribes' ways of centering themselves and celebrating the powers of the directions. Wherever they gather, they know that they are centered and have placed themselves in a position to receive the gifts of the Creator through the four directions.

*Cree sundance arbor left standing, a few weeks after ceremony,
Rocky Boy Reservation, Montana*

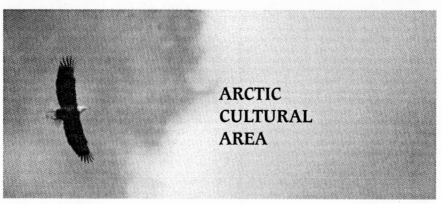

Bald eagle in Alaska

ARCTIC CULTURAL AREA

WIND PERSONAGES
JAMES BAY CREE

For the Cree, the relationship of the wind persons to animal gifts is constantly confirmed by everyday experience. The wind persons bring cold or warmth and snow or rain, and with the coming and going of predominant winds the seasons change. They are responsible for the variable weather conditions to which animals and hunters each respond. The bear hibernates and is docile only in winter when the *north* wind is predominant. The geese and ducks arrive with the increasing frequency of the *south* wind and leave with its departure. In a myriad of other ways, the animals and hunters, and the success of the hunt, depend in part on the conditions brought by the winds.

Each of the *four wind persons* resides at one of the *four points* on the compass, and each has specific personal characteristics related to particular seasons, weather and animal patterns, hunting conditions and success. When a hunter is asked by young men and women who have been away to school why he says that the animals are given by the winds, he often answers that they must come and live in the bush to see for themselves. It is demonstrated in the daily and yearly experience of the hunters, and it can be shared with anyone who will spend enough time in the bush. . . .

The concepts of the wind persons mediate and link several series of ideas that serve to order the Cree world in space and time. The wind persons are said to live at the *four corners* of the earth, thereby orienting space on a *four-point compass*. The wind persons also link God to the world. They are part of the world "up there," but they affect the earth down here. They thus link the spirits and God who are up there to the men and animals who live their lives on earth.

Native Peoples: The Canadian Experience, Bruce Morrison & Roderick Wilson, 1989, p. 176

The four wind persons who care for each quadrant of the earth relate themselves to the birds and animals that are at the center of the life of the Cree People. Experience and day to day knowledge tell them how to order their world with the wind persons in mind.

———————————— ✤ ————————————

WIND ORIGINS
ESKIMO

The characteristic feature of Eskimo religious thought is its anthropomorphic view of the universe. Deities, stars and natural phenomena have their origin in human adventures, often of an anecdotal nature and full of prosaic details. The Eskimos have given relatively little thought to the birth and elaboration of the world. The earth is depicted as a tent resting on pegs, with a cover over it—the vault of heaven—which was slashed by a knife in *four* different places to allow the ***north, south, east*** and ***west*** winds to escape. Beyond is another world, the sky, which resembles the earth. According to a fairly general belief, the earth tilted at one time, and its former occupants now live underneath.

Larousse World Mythology, Pierre Grimal (Ed.), 1977, p. 441

A good knowledge of the winds is essential to the nomadic Eskimos. Though their homeland territory is vast, they nevertheless know how important the winds are no matter in what part of the northern hemisphere they live. Winds commonly come from certain directions. A knowledge and respect for these directions is always important, not only for survival, but for religious celebration.

View from a plane of the Arctic snows

Four directions family prayer (Mexican-American)

MESOAMERICA CULTURAL AREA

THE FOUR BACABS
MAYA

Besides their true gods or deities the Mayas' mythology contained *four BACABS*, who were known as Kan, Muluc, Ix and Cauac, considered semi-deities or genii, who were symbolical of the *four cardinal points of the compass* and were thought to support the *four corners of the sky*. Each had its own color by which it was identified, Kan being yellow; Muluc white; Ix black and Cauac red.

America's Ancient Civilizations, A. Hyatt Verrill & Ruth Verrill, 1953, p. 45

Here color and direction join together to identify the bacabs *who hold up the sky*.

———————————— ✴ ————————————

THE DIRECTIONS AND PYRAMIDAL SYMBOLISM
MAYA & AZTEC

Throughout Mexico and Guatemala, as well as in the bordering Indian regions of the American Southwest, the *four directions* were held in particularly great esteem. The *Maya* believed that in each direction stood a deity called a Bacab, a mythological being responsible for supporting his particular quadrant of the cosmos. The sky stood above the earth thanks to these creatures, and numerous ritual devotions were offered to them in order to sustain and reward their efforts on behalf of humankind. The *Aztecs* believed that each direc-

492

tion had a "personality" of its own, which manifested particular aspects of the journey of human life. *East,* the direction where the sun emerges each day from the bowels of the underworld, was characterized as the direction of youth and potency. From there a person moved *south* into adulthood and *west* into old age, the direction of the sun's daily fall back into the underworld. *North* was the direction of death and decay. To face or travel north had grave implications, for it was there that a soul could lose itself forever and not be able to return back to the *east,* which often served as a fifth as well as first direction—the place not only of birth but of rebirth.

The Mesoamerican pyramid served not only to mark these *cardinal points* and the life journey they represented, but also, through its existence in physical space with them, allowed its makers to enter into communication with the *four quarters* and the aspects of human destiny they contained. Time and space thus blended magically together to form a single element in which the soul played out its fate.

But the fate of humankind did not end at death, and so the cosmic stage on which the human drama was enacted did not stop at the terrestrial plane. The *four quarters* were thought to lie at the midpoint of a many-leveled cosmos that stretched down into a fearful region of hells and up into a glorious celestial realm, which the pyramidal structure, standing at the midpoint of both vertical and horizontal space, addressed as well. A pyramid could have nine tiers because heaven possessed nine levels; it could have 365 steps leading to the summit because the year possessed 365 days, each of which had a personality and temperament of its own.

> *This Tree Grows Out of Hell: Mesoamerica and the Search for the Magical Body*, Ptolemy Tompkins, 1990, p. 10

It is, perhaps, difficult for contemporary human beings to relate to the personification of a direction, especially since, in our modern times, we have "thing"-ified the universe and pretty much recognize only ourselves and plants and animals as being alive; we often say that rocks and other inanimate things have no spiritual substance; and yet, these bacabs, who cared for the four quarters of the universe, were considered to be personalities who could be addressed without poetic apostrophe.

———————————————— ✤ ————————————————

CHAPEL BLESSING
Q'EQCHI MAYA

The community of Semuy II in the Diocese of Verapaz in northern Guatemala celebrated a big day on July 26, 1992. People from the different communities came from far and near to participate in the solemn blessing of the new barrio chapel. They braved the rainy weather and the slippery paths of the mountains, some for more than three hours, as they walked to the remote barrio. This was not to be an ordinary gathering. It was the *wa'tesink,* the Q'eqchi blessing for the new chapel. It was unique. As the parish priest of El Calvario Parish in Coban, I was invited for the Christian blessing, but this was to be an experience in the Q'eqchi way of doing things. . . .

The celebration began about noon when the early arrivals were served a simple meal of black beans, tortillas and a drink made from corn. There was singing and dancing. An afternoon shower sent everyone for cover into the newly finished chapel, but when the rains ended the music of the marimba brought everyone outside again. More singing and dancing, including the ever-popular Dance of the Deer.

The celebration of the *wa'tesink* started about 11:00 p.m. with a procession of the whole community. At the lead was the new Mayan cross. Then the elders were followed by women with gifts: cacao, boiled chicken and corn and candles. The cross was placed in the front of the altar. Recalling the age-old tradition of the Q'eqchies at planting and harvest times, the meaning of the Mayan cross was explained by the catechist: There were five candles and a prayer was said over each. The white candle, symbol of purity, was then placed on the **northern** tip of the cross. The yellow candle, for the good and bad, was placed opposite the white one. The red candle stands for life and was placed on the **eastern** tip. The black candle is for death and darkness. It was placed on the **western** end of the cross. In the center a green candle was placed. Green is the color of Mother Nature. It stands for life and for everything that woman or man may receive from Nature. The first *four colors of the candles* coincide with the *four principal colors of Mayan corn*: *saki hal*—white corn; *kan hal*—yellow corn; *kak lich*—red corn; and *g'eq waj*—black corn.

The *wa'tesink* was done by a team of five elders. The **cardinal points** were incensed with *kopal pom,* made from evergreen oak. At each point the elders enshrined a mixture made from ground cacao, blood of two young roosters and the water used to wash the meat. The place is covered with earth and a candle is lighted on the spot. The Christian blessing was performed by me. I sprinkled the *four cardinal points* of the chapel with holy water and prayed the prayer of blessing. In the prayer we expressed our trust in God, the heart of heaven and earth; giver of the sun which warms us and makes all things grow with life; the moon to be able to measure the days; the rain which refreshes and gives vitality to Mother Earth. We prayed that God may bless this cross which has called all of us in Christ to follow his way in this community. We prayed that this chapel might be a place where we encounter the meaning of life, of death and suffering, and that we may build a better community where peace, brotherhood and love abide.

Following the blessing, some women distributed a drink made from cacao. Drinking the cacao is a sign of reconciliation. Then all present received some boiled corn and a piece of chicken—a sign of communion with all sharing a common meal. . . .

"Blessing of the Chapel in Semuy II,"
Missionhurst Magazine, Melchor Villero,
February 1993, pp. 16-18

This contemporary celebration is a wonderful joining together of two ancient spiritual traditions. The blessing speaks of the oneness of both ways under the smiling eyes of the Creator.

--------------------------------- ✳ ---------------------------------

WIND DIVINITIES
MAYA/LACANDON

In some parts, the winds are thought to be under the control of the rain gods. Thus, in Mopan-Maya folklore the mischievous servant of the Chacs opens their windbag and lets loose the winds. . . .

In modern Chorti belief, the winds seem to have hived off from the rain gods, taking some of their functions and attributes. Their chief duty is to ride horseback across the skies distributing the rain beaten out of the clouds, . . . a duty which in Yucatan falls to the horse-borne Chacs, but the Lacandon call on the wind to distribute the powder over the clouds to cause rain. The Chorti winds are called Ah Yum Ikar, "Wind Lords."

A passage in the Chilam Balam of Chumayel reads: "The *[four]* angels of the winds [*cangeles ik*] which were set up while he created the star, when the world was not yet lighted, when there was neither heaven nor earth: the Red Pauahtun, the White Pauahtun, the Black Pauahtun, the Yellow Pauahtun." The Pauahtuns are now accepted as Chacs, but they could have been winds, servants of the Chacs who later were merged with them.

The Lacandon believe that wind gods are set at the *four points of the compass*. Under the name Chaob *(Ch'aob,* "carriers off"?) they, in conjunction with an earthquake, will bring about the destruction of the world when the last Lacandon dies, and . . . they will blow so hard they will blast the monkeys out of the trees. Their leader, the god in the *east* is called Hunaunic.

. . . there are six of these beings assigned to the four points of the compass plus *northeast* and *southeast*. All bear merely the names of those directions, except the one in the east, who is called Bulhacil u Talkin, "Inundation of the East." *Bul ik* . . . is "wind storm with earthquakes" and is qualified by the colors red and white. It is probable that there were four, each with its world color and direction. . . .

Maya History and Religion, J. Eric Thompson, 1990, pp. 270-271

Even today the Mayas and other Peoples throughout Mexico and Guatemala honor the sacred directions, often in reference to the wind directions. Their ancient cosmology and stories found no problem with naming the personages in charge of these winds as coming from the cardinal or intercardinal directions.

———————————— ✤ ————————————

TIME AND SPATIAL INFLUENCE IN REGARD TO THE SACRED DIRECTIONS
AZTEC

It was also necessary to reckon with the influence peculiar to the year itself, and likewise that which the cardinal points of space might have upon the signs. For the Mexicans thought of the world as a kind of Maltese cross, the *east* uppermost, the *north* on the right, the *west* below and the *south* on the left. The twenty signs for days were divided into *four sets* of five, each ruled by one of the cardinal points: for example, the signs *cipactli* and *acatl* belonged to the *east, ocelotl* and *tecpatl* to the *north, mazatl* and *calli* to the *west,* and *xochitl* and *tochtli* to the *south.*

After this, each cardinal point in succession ruled one day, following the order *east, north, west, south;* and also one year, also following the order *acatl (east), tecpatl (north), calli (west) and tochtli (south).* Because of this the day or the year was imbued with the qualities ascribed to each quarter—fertility and abundance to the *east,* barren aridity to the *north,* falling-off, old age and death to the *west* (setting sun), and a neutral character to the *south.* . . .

Thus the spatial influences which ruled time fitted into one another like so many hollow wooden Russian dolls: or rather it may be said that Mexican philosophy did not conceive one abstract space and one abstract time, homogeneous and separate media, but rather on the other hand concrete multiplicities of time and space, single points and happenings, disparate and unique. The qualities peculiar to each of these 'moment-loci', expressed by the sign which indicated the days in the *tonalpoualli,* follow one another cyclically in an abrupt, total change according to a determinate rhythm, in conformity with an everlasting order.

Daily Life of the Aztecs on the Eve of the Spanish Conquest,
Jacques Soustelle, 1961, pp. 111-112

Just as we have no great difficulty in recognizing four seasons in a single year, so the Aztecs had little problem ordering their world temporally and spatially with four directions, events, and qualities of life.

--------------------------------- ✦ ---------------------------------

THE SACRED DIRECTIONS AND
CALENDRICAL DAY SIGNS
AZTEC

This page is divided into *four quarters,* each surrounded by the image of a serpent with its head near the center of the page and its body all but enclosing the *four sides* of a rectangle. In each case the serpent's belly forms the outer edge of the rectangle border and its back forms the inner edge. At the center of the page is a little spiritual beast known as a *tzitzímitl*. Within each rectangle is the image of a deity who is physically connected to five of the day signs.

Beginning at the lower left corner and proceeding counterclockwise, the deity assigned by Seler to the *East* is Tláloc, the god of rain and storm; he has attached to his body the day signs for Alligator, Serpent, Water, Reed and Movement. The deity of the *North* is Tlazoltéotl, the goddess of the earth, filth and the moon; she has attached to her body the days signs for Wind, Death, Dog, Jaguar and Flint. The deity of the *West* is Quetzalcóatl, the god of the wind; he has attached to his body the day signs for House, Deer, Monkey, Eagle and Rain. The fourth deity, the deity of the *South,* is Macuilxóchitl, 5 Flower, the god of games and pleasure; he has attached to his body the day signs for Lizard, Rabbit, Grass, Vulture and Flower.

The astute reader will have noticed that these day signs are regularly spaced in the series of 20. They follow the arrangement of the columns of day signs in the first representation of the *tonalpohualli* in the codex. . . . If they are to be assigned directional significance here, as Seler has done for the quarters of the *tonalpohualli* when arranged as five rows of 52 days, the five day signs associated with the *East* are found in the first column of the *tonalpohualli,* the days of the *North* are in the fourteenth column, the *West* in the twenty-seventh column and the *South* in the fortieth column. In each case the five day signs are found in the first column of the quarter of the calendar assigned to the appropriate direction.

The Codex Borgia: A Full-Color Restoration of the Ancient Mexican Manuscript, Gisele Díaz & Alan Rodgers, 1993, pp. XXX & 6

Iconography is an important way for those of us living in the twentieth century to see how Aztecs participated in the four directions. It is nothing short of miraculous that we have extant early illustrations and paintings which tell us of the Aztec way of life and belief, especially when we consider the destruction wrought by many of the early European invaders.

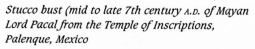

Stucco bust (mid to late 7th century A.D. *of Mayan Lord Pacal from the Temple of Inscriptions, Palenque, Mexico*

DIVINITIES AND THE DIRECTIONS
AZTEC

In a mysterious way Ometeotl also existed as Tezcatlipoca, "Smoking Mirror," the all-powerful god of the Aztecs who, unlike Ometeotl, could be depicted in mythic images and addressed in ritual. But just as Ometeotl, the ultimate ground of being, is at once unitary and dual, similarly Tezcatlipoca is mysteriously unitary, dual, and quadripartite. As half of a duality, Tezcatlipoca, "Smoking Mirror," finds his opposite in Tezcatlanextia, "Mirror Which Illumines." Tezcatlipoca is thus associated with the night, with its obscured vision, while Tezcalanextia is linked to the day, illumined by the sun. ... Tezcatlipoca is both created by and identical to Ometeotl. He is a manifestation of the divine essence characterized as Ometeotl on another plane. Significantly, perhaps, the Ometeotl duality used the union of the male and female as its metaphor for creativity, while the Tezcatlipoca duality used the union of day and night. These are, of course, the two clearest manifestations of cyclical rebirth in human life.

The unfolding continues. According to the *Historia de los Mexicanos por sus Pinturas,* Ometeotl and Omecihuatl (the female aspect of Ometeotl), known in that account as Tonacatecuhtli and Tonacacihuatl, begot *four sons*, each an aspect of Tezcatlipoca. Thus each of the *four deities* who unfold from him share with him the creativity characteristic of Ometeotl; together they constitute the cosmic powers necessary for the world to exist. These *four gods*, each of whom exalted himself over the others by assuming, in sequence, the role of the sun, another manifestation of the creative essence of the cosmos, are the red Tezcatlipoca, who is Xipe Totec, or Camaxtli-Mixcoatl, a god associated with the *east* and sunrise who embodies the creative power that provided the corn as man's sustenance; the black Tezcatlipoca, a god commonly known simply as Tezcatlipoca, the warrior of the *north* and of the nadir, or midnight, position of the sun, who was in many ways the most powerful and the most dangerous to man, or, as the *Historia* puts it, "the biggest and the worst"; the blue Tezcatlipoca, who was Huitzilopochtli ("Hummingbird on the Left"), the warrior of the *south* and the zenith, or high-noon, position of the sun, who was responsible for the creation and maintenance of the Aztec state; and Quetzalcoatl, probably a white Tezcatlipoca, a god also known as Yohualli Ehecatl ("Night and Wind," by extension "Invisible and Intangible," an appellation given also to Ometeotl), who was associated with the *west* and sunset and was widely considered to be the creator of human life.

The Flayed God: The Mesoamerican Mythological Tradition,
Peter Markman & Roberta Markman, 1992, p. 66

Gods and special colors associated with each direction only strengthened the ability of the Aztecs to see themselves as being daily involved in a life that is at the same time terrestrial and celestial.

------------------------------ ✦ ------------------------------

CHILD'S WATER CEREMONY
AZTEC

... the father would send for the *tonalpouhqui,* or soothsayer, a specialist in the study of the sacred books. This person, who was offered a meal, as well as his fee of cloth and turkeys, began by asking the exact moment of the birth, so that he might decide what sign the child was born under. He then consulted his *tonalamatl* to find the sign of the day of the birth and the set of thirteen days to which it belonged.

If the sign of the day were considered good and fortunate, he could say 'Your son is born under a good sign. He will be a lord or a senator, rich, brave, pugnacious; he will be courageous and he will shine in war; he will reach high rank among the commanders of armies' And then one could go on to the naming of the child the next day. But if the sign of the day proved to be calamitous, then the *tonalpouhqui* exercised his wit to find a better sign in the same set of thirteen, as nearly as possible in the *four following days*. 'The child is not born under a good sign,' he would say, 'but in this series there is another, a reasonable sign that will diminish and correct the unfortunate influence of the principal sign. . . .'

The naming itself was carried out not by the soothsayer, nor by a priest, but by the midwife. The ceremony had two parts, the ritual washing of the child and the actual naming. They began by getting ready a great deal of food and drink for the family feast that would follow the baptism; they also made a little shield, a bow with *four arrows*, each corresponding to one of the *cardinal points*, if the child were a boy, and little spindles, a shuttle and a box if it were a girl. All the relatives and friends gathered in the mother's house before sunrise.

As soon as day broke they arranged the symbolic objects in the inner courtyard or in the garden. The midwife, provided with a full water-jar, addressed the baby, saying 'Eagle, jaguar, valiant warrior, oh my grandson! here you are come into this world, sent by your father and mother, the great god and the great goddess. You have been made and begotten in your own place, among the almighty gods, the great god and the great goddess who live above the nine heavens. It is Quetzalcoatl, who is in all places, who has done you this kindness. Now be joined to your mother the goddess of the water, Chalchiuhtli-cue, Chalchiuhtlatonac.' With her wet fingers she set some drops of water on his mouth. 'Take and receive this, for it is with this water that you will live upon the earth, and grow and grow green again; it is by water that we have what we must have to live upon this earth. Receive this water.'

After this she touched the baby's chest with her wet hand and said, 'here is the heavenly water, the very pure water that washes and cleans your heart and that takes away all stain.' Then she threw some drops on his head. 'Let this water enter into your body, and may it live there, this heavenly water, the blue celestial water.' Lastly she washed the child's whole body, saying the formula meant to keep off evil. 'Whatever you may be, you who might do this child a mischief, leave him, go off, go away from him; for now this child is born again—he is new-born and new-formed by our mother Chalchiuhtlicue.'

After the *four water-rites*, the midwife presented the child *four times* to the sky, invoking the sun and the astral gods. In this way the traditional gestures were regulated by the holy number. The last formula also invoked the earth, the divine spouse of the sun. And, taking the shield and the arrows, the midwife begged the gods that the boy might become a courageous warrior. . . .

The ceremony for naming the girls was similar, but the baby was not presented to the sun, which was the god of men and warriors: after the ritual washing the midwife and the relatives, in a touching ceremony, spoke to the cradle in which the little girl would lie, calling it Yoalticitl, 'the healer by night', and saying, 'You who are her mother, take her, old goddess. Do her no harm; watch over her kindly.'

When these rites were over, the name of the child was chosen and announced. . . .

The ceremony closed with a family banquet, at the end of which the old men and women might give themselves up to the pleasures of drink.

The Daily Life of the Aztecs on the Eve of the Spanish COnquest,
Jacques Soustelle, 1961, pp. 165-167

A four-fold washing, ritually connected to specifics in the Aztec cosmology, express some of this People's beliefs. Such beliefs situate a child, indeed anyone, in the midst of eternal sacred activity. There is satisfaction in knowing that we are indeed a part of all that exists.

————————————— ✤ —————————————

FOUR-QUARTERED UNIVERSE
NAHUA

There were, at least among the ancient Nahuas, thirteen celestial levels and nine underworld levels, each inhabited by diverse gods and supernatural beings, often depicted as conjugal pairs. The top level (in some sources there are nine celestial levels) was inhabited by Ometeotl, the God of Duality.

Each of these realms, which in the Nahua imagination were divided into smaller, powerful units, were permeated with supernatural powers circulating up and down the cosmic levels through spiral-shaped passages called *malinallis*. Some levels, especially the lower terrestrial and aquatic levels, including the mountains, were filled with abundant, valuable forces such as seeds, water, and precious stones upon which farmers, families, and craftsmen depended. One Mexican scholar notes that the ancient Nahuas

believed this earthly and aquatic world to be contaminated by death and jealously guarded by the dangerious "lords" of springs and woods. Even today, the places from which wealth derives—fountains, forests and mines—are thought to be points of communication between the worlds of men and that of death, guarded by the Ohuican Chaneque, "lords of the dangerous places."

In some versions of the universe these supernatural entites and forces flowed into the human level through giant ceiba trees, which held up the sky at the *four quarters of the world* and stood at the center of the universe. As we can see when we look at the ideal image of the universe as pictured in the *Codex Fejérváry Mayer*, **the four-quarterd universe** is structured by *four flowering trees*, each with a supernatural bird in its crown. In some cultures a flowering tree or a sacred mountain stood at the center of the universe linking up, like a vertical shaft, the upper, middle, and lower worlds.

> *Religions of Mesoamerica: Cosmovision and Ceremonial Centers*,
> David Carrasco, 1990, pp. 51-52

Vegetative life, especially trees, are points of contact with the holy. Here four ceiba trees have the responsibility of holding up the platform of life. The birds symbolize contact with the heavenly realm.

--------------------------------- ✣ ---------------------------------

TEMPLE ORIENTATION
TOLTEC

Said to be fabulous artists and artisians, they built a wonderous capital at Tula to the north of the Valley of Mexico. Sahagún's informants regaled him with tales of the magnificent temples of Quetzalcoatl and its *four precincts*, one of gold facing *east*, another of turquoise facing *towards the sunset*, and white and red shell-decorated shrines facing *south* and *north*. This temple, wrote Sahagun, stood as the ultimate symbol of a people of learning and genius, the inspiration for all that was best in Aztec life. The Tolteca loom larger than life in Aztec legend.

> *The Aztecs*, Brian Fagan, 1984, p. 39

Bernardino de Sahagún arrived in New Spain in 1529, about 10 years after the fall of Tenochtitlán. He learned the Nahuatl language and studied with Aztec elders and youths to provide a number of works that are helpful to our understanding of ancient Mesoamerican cultures even to this day. From him we learn that the giant Toltec rulers became mythical heroes for the later Aztecs whose nobles often claimed descent from one of the Toltec heroes.

--------------------------------- ✣ ---------------------------------

Copal incense wrapped in leaves from southern Mexico

COSMOLOGY
HUICHOL

In traditional Huichol discourse the world, *Tatei Urianaka*, is conceived as a shallow gourd which rests on its bottom and is surrounded by five seas. This gourd, conceived as a female deity, is also used to represent the idea of fecundity and is sometimes referred to as a metaphor for the womb *(urianada*, literally, stomach, abdomen). The female earth is imbued with motherly attributes as suggested by the prefix *tatei*, mother.

Over the gourd earth lies another semi-circular area called *Taheima* which is reigned over by another female deity, *Tatei Werika Wimari* (Our Mother Young Eagle Girl). At the highest limits of the sky exists a door which leads to the land of the dead.

Under the gourd is a dark cavernous underworld known as *WatetUapa*. These are the only three vertical levels that the universe is commonly said to be divided into.

The three levels are circumscribed by the movement of the sun, *Tau*, which passes through the ellipse of the sky and descends over the sea to return under the earth's concavity and rise again by a magical staircase, *ununui*, over *Rreunar*, a sacred mountain to the *east*.

The Huichol world has definite boundaries which are marked by *sacred rocks placed at each of the four cardinal points aligned along an east-west and a north-south axis*. The region thus inscribed is known as the Middle Region of *Heriepa* which translated as "sierra". This corresponds to the habitat of the Huichol but sometimes also includes the area occupied by neighbouring peoples. The boundaries of this region were chartered by the voyage of *Watakame* when he together with *Nakawé,* the creator, were carried in a canoe first to the *western rock*, *Washiewe,* just off the coast of Nayarit facing the village of San Blas in an area called *Tukamerishe* the "Line of Shadows". Following this the canoe drifted to the *eastern rock* known as *Tomana Tinika* and probably located somewhere in the desert regions of *Mahakate* near Lake Chapala, Jalisco and then to the *northern-most extent* marked by the rock *Rauramanaka* in the north of Nayarit.

The *four cardinal points* which radiate out from the region inhabited by the Huichol, "The Land of Clarity", aligned by the *four pivotal rocks*, are most often referred to by the name of the deity under whose care each segment is committed.

The *west* is referred to by the name of the deity *Haramara* and the *east* that of *Nariwame.* The **north** is refered to as *Tzakaimute* and the **south** *Rapaviemeta.* Each of these deities is said to hold jurisdiction over the region to which they correspond. In addition, each is associated with the rock that marks its domain.

Within the boundaries of the middle Kingdom there exist five holes which lead inside the earth. One of these is located at the **eastern mountain** of *Rreunar* or what the mestizos call *Cerro Quemada* while that to the *west* is found to the edge of the Pacific Ocean. By means of the **western** hold the sun gains access to the underworld, *WatetUapa.* After travelling underground it exits to the *east* at Rreunar. A third hole is said to be located in the centre of the territory inhabited by the Huichol which is associated with the place where the ancestors emerged from *WatetUapa* and began the work of creating *Heriepa.* The remaining two holes are said to lie to the **north** and **south** but uncertainty surrounds their whereabouts and significance.

In summary, the Huichol world is composed of three levels; a dark cavernous underworld, sometimes thought of as being aquatic and known as *WatetUapa;* a concave earth called *Heriepa;* arched by an elliptical sky called *Taheima. Heriepa* itself is surrounded by five seas and divided into five regions each under the jurisdiction of a deity through whose name the dominion is known. The Huichol occupy the centre of this divine topography at the point of creation. The universe is delineated by the movement of the Sun through *Heriepa* and its nocturnal sojourn through *WatetUapa.* . . .

The earth is said to have feminine attributes. In the primordial time of creation *Tatei Urianaka* offered herself voluntarily to be sacrificed to form the earth. She had sexual intercourse with *Kauyumarie,* a deer deity affiliated with the Sun, which caused her womb to increase in size, stretching it until it was large enough to provide the land mass of *Heriepa.* She is usually limited to the area inhabited by the Huichol but is sometimes thought of as constituting a larger area which includes all of Mexico.

The earth was divided into five regions by *Tatewari,* the old fire deity associated with shamanism—who then appointed the Sun as governor. The Sun assigned *four deer deities* to the **cardinal regions** and invested them with jurisdiction over them. These were *Kauyumarie* in the **east**, *Ushikuikame* in the **south**, *Watemukame* in the **west**, and *Narihuame* in the **north**.

The earth is thus conceptualized as female, but governed by four male deer deities. Despite this, for most purposes it is the feminine attributes to *Tatei Urianaka* which are emphasized over the masculine characteristics of its governors.

> "Huichol Natural Philosphy," *Canadian Journal of Native Studies*,
> Anthony Shelton, 1987, pp. 341-343

The Huichol structure of the world is quite interesting and, in some ways, similiar to a few cultures on the outer reaches of their domain. The directions have a certain kind of pre-eminence, as do certain animals. A balance of female and male energies is also manifested.

✣

SANTO STATUE BLESSING
MAYO

To San Juan in particular the paskolam and masom have a special ritual relationship dramatized on San Juan's Day. This ceremony took place as follows on June 24, 1961 in Banari. Upon approaching the empty church in the cool of early dawn, I was startled by the eerie reverberating sound of crowing roosters which were tied to the pillars in the church. About mid-morning a procession formed, headed by the paskome carrying two of the birds and followed first by the ceremonial dancers and musicians from the ramada, then by San Juan's image, the church group, and the women and men of the pueblo. The matacin dance society, a group of ceremonial dancers closely connected with the church organization, should have been leading the procession but many members, including the dance leader, were ill. As the procession left the church and moved down the konti bo'o it made thirteen stops. Each pause involved the reading of a section of sacred Christian scripture by the maestro, and the singing of traditional hymns by his women assistants. This ritual was complete by the time the procession reached the pueblo boundary, marked by the pueblo cross. Then the group marched quickly to the river's edge where San Juan originally jumped into the river and near the hill where the San Juan kurus yo'owe stands under the oak tree. On a low spot at the river's edge the paskola and maso dancers and their musicians began singing and dancing. The image of San Juan was placed upon a large square cloth facing the river. The mo'oro (ceremonial advisor of the hosts) of the Santa Kurus paskome partially undressed the little santo, taking from him the characteristic water gourds and the little straw hat with a red feather in it that the santo customarily wears. The santo retained his red robe and still clung to the tall round metal cross that is his other insignia. In front of San Juan the sacristan placed a plate for small contributions. Also on the cloth were placed a large cup-shaped iridescent shell, the two drums of the mo'orom, one for each of the two sets of paskome, and the insignia of the paskome, their fox tails and rosaries and ribbons. Before the paskome put their insignia on the cloth they knelt on the downriver side of San Juan, to his left, and addressed prayers *eastward* toward the river.

One Paskola who does the speaking for the ramada group in rituals, the paskola Yo'owe (head paskola) made a short speech (hinabaka) in Mayo addressing himself not to the congregation, not to the paskome, but to the river. Then he and another paskola took San Juan, carried him to the river, and waded into the water. They lowered the image three times to each of the *four directions*, laid him face down and lowered him three more times, each time nearer the water, and the last time put his face in the water. They made this ritual also toward each of the *four directions*. Finally they put San Juan back on the cloth. The Santa Kurus mo'oro adjusted San Juan's neck scarf, rose and took the head paskola with his own left hand, led the paskola into the water, and with his right hand made the sign of cross with his first finger in the river water. He made a sign of the cross upriver, across river and downriver, and with each sign said: "In the name of the Father" [*cross*], ". . . the Son" [*cross*], "the Holy Spirit" [*cross*]. Then the mo'oro baptized the paskola by taking water three different times and patting him on the head with it. Then the other paskolam baptized the paskome and vice versa. The maso also took part in this baptizing. The men baptized in the manner described above, but the women members of the paskome cupped both hands and dropped water on the heads of the paskolam. Then the sacristan was baptized and baptized the paskolam in return. The head maestro and others in the procession also joined the baptizing by patting water on their own heads, and children who were in the procession now jumped into the river in their clothes and swam and played in the water. This ritual is performed in remembrance of the baptism of Itom Acai Usi, and the paskolam are said to be like San Juan Bautista, companions of Cristo.

The paskome put on the insignia, sandals and other items of clothing which they had shed for the rituals. The sacristan filled the shell near San Juan with river water and the paskome dipped their fingers in it and *crossed* themselves. Then the paskola and maso began to dance again, in their positions upriver from San Juan and to his left. After a sort dance the procession reformed and started back....

The Mayo Indians of Sonora: A People Who Refuse to Die,
N. Ross Crumrine, 1988, pp. 27-28

Here we have a sharing of traditions and a new way of regarding both the directions and the cross.

———————————————— ✤ ————————————————

DIVINITIES IN SACRED CAVE
SERI

The Seris have two little wooden gods which they hang up in the sacred caves, tied together with a string, and when people are sick they put them on their breasts.... The two-legged god stays eight days in the cave, the one-legged god stays twelve days.

They go to the caves of the gods, but they are not gods. They can be painted in any color—red, blue or black. The hats on their heads show they are men. If they were gods they would have a cross on them.... When someone is sick we put the two-legged figure in some cave in the mountains, the higher up the better, and he is left without food and water for eight days. He gets tired of that and the man will get well, because the god will come out to get food and water.

The two-legged god can only stand it eight days in the cave—the one-legged one can go twelve days. They hang up the two-legged god first, in the hope that the sick people will get well quick. If they do not, they put the other one in the cave. As they approach the cave they sing to the figure, and if the person is going to get well the spirit of the little figure will come out.

Anybody can take the sick person to the cave, and when the sick one gets well they know that the spirit of the figure has come to them. They leave the figure in the cave then. There are several caves, but the high ones are best. For *four days* they sing songs to these figures, called:—I Am Singing That You May Cure.

The figurine is held out to the *four directions*, while the eyes are fixed upon it. Then, at the end of the song, the image is held at arm's length. If it trembles, the medicine is no good. When they sing to the one-legged god and the patient is getting well, the wind begins to blow. If it does not blow, he will not get well.

The Last of the Seris: The Aboriginal Indians of Kino Bay, Sonora, Mexico,
Dane Coolidge & Mary Coolidge, 1973, pp. 128-129

The carved images represent the Creator's spiritual power which can be called into a person's life. Singing spiritual songs for a four-day period and holding out the image to the four directions are, for the Seris, ways of drawing in God's healing power.

———————————— ✤ ————————————

SONG OF THE WINDS
SERI

Below the sea there is the mouth of a cave
In which all the winds are born.
He comes below the sea and mounts up
To where there is no sun.
But the cave is light, like the sun.

Another mouth is smooth and slippery
And hard, like ice.
He stands erect with his arms outstretched
And from each finger there comes a wind.

First he blows the White Wind
Then he blows the Red Wind
Then he blows the Blue Wind
And from his little finger
He blows the Black Wind,
Which is stronger than them all.

The White Wind comes from the *north*
And is very hot.
Blue comes from the *south*.
The Red Wind comes from the *west*

Contemporary Aztec dancers
share the ancient ways

In the middle of the day, and is soft.
The Black Wind comes from beyond the mountains
And is strongest of them all.
The Whirlwind comes from the *east*.

The Wind God makes them come
From the points on his fingers—
White from his *first*
Red from his *second*
Blue from his *third*
Black from his *fourth*.

The Last of the Seris: The Aboriginal Indians of Kino Bay, Sonora, Mexico,
Dane Coolidge & Mary Coolidge, 1973, p. 82

This Song of the Winds expresses the timed movement of the four winds as they relate to the cardinal directions. Wind symbology plays an important role for this coastal People, as does the use of special colors for both the winds and the four directions.

———————————————— ✤ ————————————————

ORIGINS OF CLANS
SERI

After First Man and First Woman married and had children . . . for six generations a brother married a sister. Then there was no brother and the girl married the son of another pair who had moved away. Her name was Kee-meé-kay ahn kó-ahn, Woman with Many Children— and from her twelve daughters sprang all the Seri Clans.

Kee-meé-kay is the mother's family name. Each of the daughters carried that name—the rest is just for her. The first daughter was:

*Kee-meé-kay ah pay-ket-ee—**First** Girl*
*Kee-meé-kay ee-quop—**Second** Girl*
*Kee-meé-kay ee-kee-quop hah—**Third** Girl*
*Kee-meé-kay ee-kee-só—**Fourth** Girl. . . .*

Tahm was the father of the twelve girls—and the same word is now used for Man. From these *four daughters* are descended the *four Seri Clans*, and until lately they lived separate from each other:

The Coyote People lived at Poso Pina in the mountains
   on the mainland.
The Pitahaya People lived on the flats of the mainland.
The Turtle People lived on the **southwest** point of the Island.
The Pelican People lived on the **southeast** point of the Island.

The Last of the Seris: The Aboriginal Indians of Kino Bay, Sonora, Mexico,
Dane Coolidge & Mary Coolidge, 1973, pp. 126-127

*The four Seri Clans trace their descent from four mythic time ancestors.
The places that these clans occupy seems to indicate directional
symbolism, even though they are both a mainland and island People.*

*Contemporary Chicanos remember their indigenous heritage
and celebrate it in an urban setting at
Chicano Park, San Diego, California*

SOUTH AMERICA CULTURAL AREA

*This Catholic lay leader is also an Aymara Yatíri (a shaman),
Titicaca, Capacabana, Bolivia*

AYLLU CEREMONY
CANELOS QUICHUA

Once or twice a year a large-scale ceremony is held in and near the administrative locus of each Runa territory.... It is also a pivotal point of articulation between the stipulated antiquity of Canelos Quichua culture, the vicissitudes of contemporary penetration of outside forces and the adjustments necessary to insure a future through social adapability.

The structure of this ayllu ceremony is partitioned into two parts, a female huarmi jista and a male cari jista. These are also known, respectively, as jilucu jista and quilla jista. The two parts are symbolically joined by both consanguineal and affinal ties, reflecting the mythic union of the male moon and his sister, the female jilucu bird.

Other participants in their varous houses are arranged around the two parts, as descendants from an ancient brother-sister union, each related to others by stipulated common descent, from Mythic Time, from Ancient Times, and from Times of the Grandparents. All participants in this unified, partitioned ceremony are known as jisteros. In structural opposition to the jisteros are the lanceros, *four dancing warrior men* representing affinal attack power, which both complements and opposes the mystical power symbolized by the jisteros. . . .

At least two male priostes (organizers) are chosen at the end of an ayllu ceremony and charged with the responsibility of carrying out the basic obligations of the next ceremony. . . . The ayudantes are known as cajoneros uyariungui, sound-making (and dream-bringing) drummers. . . .

The priostes agree to a site for the cari jista house in the *west, north,* or *south*. They and their ayudantes then either build large new oval houses in these areas or borrow existing houses that are well situated for the ceremony. The ayudantes, a few of whom come from distant territories, also move their actual residences so as to be on the side of their respective ceremonial partition. People from whom the house borrowing is done also move around, either to get themselves in one or the other partition or to get more or less out of the partitioned structure itself.

> *Sacha Runa: Ethnicity and Adaptation of Ecuadorian Jungle Quichua,*
> Norman Whitten, Jr., 1976, pp. 167-169

The Ayllu Ceremony not only has its complementary male and female dimensions, but it also is enacted with specific symbolic fourness and allows for the ritual use of the four directions.

Peruvian pottery motifs

A prayer for healing

INTERCULTURAL CULTURAL AREA

LACROSSE AND EMETICS
CHEROKEE, OJIBWE,
IROQUOIS, YUCHI

The spiritual aspects of the game extended beyond the equipment used to the location and orientation of the field itself. For religious and symbolic reasons, Cherokee fields were usually adjoining or at least near rivers or streams to facilitate the "going to water" ritual. Ojibwe lacrosse fields were laid out *east* to *west*, possibly to conform to the ritual orientation of the medicine lodge and ceremonial drums; the latter were oriented *east* to *west*, with a yellow stripe down the middle of the drumhead to represent the "path of the sun."

The use of emetics, or vomit-inducing liquids, by lacrosse players is widely reported. In addition to fasting and bathing before a game, Iroquois players drank an emetic decocted from the bark of red willow and spotted alder. The Yuchi town chief prepared a special emetic made from red root and button snakeroot boiled in water to render their juices. The potion was believed to be the gift of the sun, whose symbol was used as decoration on the pots holding the liquid, and all males of the town drank from the pots, *four at a time* facing *east* and beginning at noon, when the sun was at its highest point in the sky.

American Indian Lacrosse: Little Brother to War,
Thomas Vennum, Jr., 1994, p. 46

Not only in lacrosse, but in many other games as well, the playing field took into account the four directions, especially east and west, the path of the sun. The emetic taken by the players to purify themselves was given to four players at a time as they were oriented toward the east, the direction of new beginnings.

A contemporary Taíno wedding of Luis and Esdras Ramos Santana

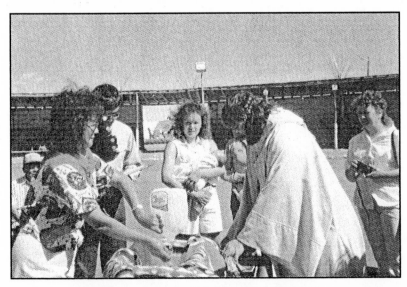

Baptism ceremony of Christine Bird (Blackfeet)
at North American Indian Days Powwow, Browning, Montana, 1994

Feather rattle in hand and adorned with the pelt of a bear cub,
a young man faces the sun as he prays a springtime request to Creator

Four Directions, Circles & Number 4

FOUR DIRECTIONS, CIRCLES & NUMBER 4

Out of intense complexities intense simplicities emerge.

Winston Churchill

They say that variety is the spice of life. This is so true in regard to the rituals and activities of all Native People. The themes described in this book have been combined in the most creative and intriguing ways in the major cultural areas. Original ancestry stories of the People had their influence on architecture, music, choreography, artistic design, and daily and festive lifeways: "As it was in the beginning, is now, and ever shall be," to quote from part of a prayer from my own spiritual tradition. Some ceremonies are a result of acceptable religious borrowings from other nearby Peoples. Centuries of individual and communal spiritual growth and practice have provided us with these ancient ways in our own time. Individuals and spiritual leaders must always consider well the past ways of doing ceremony before adapting too hastily to present needs.

All the elements of this combination are to be found in the holy rites of the Ojibwa, especially those of the Midewiwin. No matter the cultural area or the tribe, it is the same with all the other selections that I have included in this section. The reader needs only to take the time to ponder for a while what is happening in the cited pages.

I find it very interesting that both the People in general and especially the spiritual leaders can adapt the ceremonies for difficult situations. I recall being part of a rally for a peace and justice issue for an individual that was held outside a court house. As the lawyers and defendants and others passed by they could not help but notice how almost one hundred individuals were being gathered into a large circle. Not all were Native. The spiritual leader called for an inner circle to be made up of relatives and special friends of the incarcerated defendant. Then he began a pipe ceremony and directed his prayers to the four directions. The pipe was then ritually passed around the inner circle. Some took four puffs and passed it to the next person. More prayers were offered and words shared and then this ceremonial part was over with. I could not help but be aware of all of the elements of the combination taking place before my eyes: a circular gathering, a four-directions prayer, and the usual four puffs of smoke.

As we gather with the People may we look and listen and come to understand.

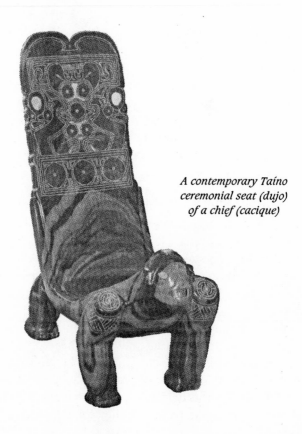

A contemporary Taíno ceremonial seat (dujo) of a chief (cacique)

WOODLANDS
CULTURAL
AREA

Lakeside directional prayer

CREATION STORY AND
PEACE DRUM
ANISHNABE

... the Creator, he had put all of his powers in that place. He had already put in motion the **sacred circle**. We use that word "the circle" a lot of times, in many ways. The drum is a circle. It's not only because it's round. There's more to it than that. The circle, it's not only because of its shape; there's more to it than that. The English word "circle" can only define its shape.... But the Anishanabe description ... is much more than that, much more beautiful, much more meaningful, and much more spiritual. But we use this language because it is the language of the day.

The Creation story ... is that at a certain time after the Creator had finished the Earth and the Earth was teeming with our relatives, the ones that run about on the Earth, the ones that swim in the water, the ones that fly in the air, this Earth—is a womb. Therein lies the teaching that woman was here first, then man. The Earth she is the Mother of all living things. And water is her lifeblood. If there was not water there would be no life. It courses through her veins in the rivers that run over the surface. The Earth was given instructions by the Creator. And the Earth Mother she has been following those instructions without fail ever since the beginning. We do not know the spans of time—maybe it was ten million years—that this Earth Mother existed in peace and harmony and beauty before man started. ...

She was beautiful, the greatest beauty that you can imagine. But at a certain time the Creator said, "I should like to send my children to the Earth," and where did he turn, where did he look? (When I use the term "he," I do not know if that's correct because the Creator is neither man nor woman. He is both.) At that time, when the creation begins, he reached out to this beautiful Earth and he took four handfuls, *four handfuls of the earth*. . . . In those four handfuls, he took that, and he moulded it . . . he knew that [in] what he was creating, what was going to be set on Earth, what was going to have tracks on the Earth, there would be physical sickness. And so all of the things, of those things he held in his hand, that fell back down through his fingers, are all the medicine you will ever need.

When he had finished moulding that figure he took the sacred megis shell, the megis shell that is still in the centre of the Midewiwin lodge, and through that shell he blew his breath upon it, he blew the breath of life. And he gave him, that figure, that spirit/man, that figure that was part spirit and part physical of the Mother Earth, he gave it instructions. "I'm going to lower you to the Earth." He was told his instructions. All of that is right here in this world. It is said that as that being was coming down to the Earth from the reaches of the Creator, he looked down and saw this most beautiful, beautiful Earth. Today when you look at true traditional dancers—and I'm talking about true traditional dancers—you see them, if you go to a big drum ceremony someday, if you go to sun dance, you will see them—the traditional dancers when they lift their feet and when they set their feet down ever so gently on the earth, that was the act of that man who was lowered to the Earth. . . . It was so beautiful that he didn't want to disturb one blade of grass. Because it was so beautiful. And so he touched the Earth lightly like a feather. . . .

After the world was populated, there came the time among the Anishanabe people when anger came among us. Anger appeared among us; it's not part of our original make-up. The Creator did not give us anger; he gave us love, kindness, sharing, faith. That's what he gave us. He did not give us anger. He didn't give us conflict. He didn't give us the mentality of war. It's something else he gave us. And what this original man saw when he was coming to make his tracks upon the Earth, he saw this whole creation living in harmony. He saw the yellow flowers existing by the purple flowers in peace. He saw the birch and the maple existing side by side, each taking of the abundance of the sun as it was needed. He saw the rivers flowing where they needed to flow. He didn't see conflict. He didn't see the pine trees trying to take over the little trees. He didn't see the birds of one feather chasing off the birds of another feather. God's plan is not for conflict, war, destruction. That's man's. These are the things upon which our philosophy builds. From that, what this being saw as he was lowered to the Earth he was filled with that harmony, and as he walked off with his relatives, as he came upon the deer, he greeted them. As he came upon the different species he greeted them. He called them by their names.

That's what he saw. That's harmony. That's peace. And that's how we were to live here on this Earth. We were not to take all, only that which we were to use. We were not to wholesale slaughter all of the moose, only that which would help us. But a time came when anger came, manifested itself. And conflict. And war. And this war among the Anishnabe people themselves, we don't know how long it lasted but it lasted a long time—created divisions among people. But at the same time, the maple still stood side by side with the birch. The yellow flower still existed with the red flower, each taking of the sun and the earth. The rest of creation did not war. Man did. Man made war. It wasn't God who made war. Man. He wasn't given that instruction: "bring war and conflict to the earth, that's what I want." It was the exact opposite of that. And this conflict that I talk about, when I heard that these conflicts were so terrible that it would make the largest rivers run red, whole families were decimated; whole clans were wiped out; that's how terrible it was. Then at a certain point in time, God the Creator looked down and he saw one Anishnabekwe sitting alone at the top of a hill. And she sat there for many many days without food, without water. She had tobacco in her hand, cedar in her hand. She had sage and sweetgrass. And it is said he looked down and he bent down close to her so he could hear her and she was praying. She was praying for the end of the bloodshed, the end of what was taking place among her people. She prayed for Anishnabe man to come to his senses, for Anishnabe man to get back to what he was supposed to be—a man of peace, a man of honour. That's what she was praying for. And it is said that he took pity on her and he gave her—and he said to her, "I will give you something that will bring peace. If you will take what I am going to give you and in turn give it in the way that I instruct you, what I shall give you will bring peace and the end of bloodshed. And it will always be a symbol of peace." That's the drum.

And there's a whole beautiful story about how that drum was given. And he manifested it for her so that she could see it and it hung above the Earth—suspended above the Earth. And one of the instructions to her was that it sould be suspended always. And when you see these traditional drums, those ceremonial drums, you see those *four stakes* upon which that drum hangs, that's what that symbolizes. That it should hang suspended above the earth. That's what that drum symbolizes. And from that grew other drums. But that drum that was given to that woman, she brought that. . . . We must remember that. We must remember that the drum came to us through woman. . . .

Anishnabekwe in turn gave it to us with those instructions. And one of the commandments was that we, as Anishnabe men, was that we should sit around that circle, that we should circle that circle, and that it should be a *circle of peace*. No conflict. That we are to guard that circle. That certain way that we are to prepare for that drum, a certain manner that we are to gather ourselves around that drum. And from that grew many other kinds of society. But that first one [was] that Peace drum. And there are [as many] stories about other drums as there are other drums. And that [Peace] drum as we know—true ceremonial drums that we don't see at Indian Days, powwow, or at the grand opening of Canadian Tire, or on TV—they have certain markings on them. Those markings have great meaning. . . .

Across the middle you will see, on some of the drums, a series of stripes like that. It has a lot of meaning. It says when you put this drum in place to begin your ceremony, that this road must always be *east* to *west*, because that's what it means, the road of life. And that there are two halves to this *circle*. That's why I was saying earlier today, "Anishnabekwe"—that she's a part of it. This drum also by its colours and shape has other meanings. Some drums will be blue on one side and red on the other. Those two colours also represent something. They represent some part of that teaching. But this half is dependent on this half; otherwise you only have half a drum. This colour stripe depends on that colour stripe because it has something to do with something we hear so often—walking in balance. Another way that the teaching goes is that this represents the night side of life, the dark side of life, and this represents the good side of life. But in order to walk in balance, you must know of this side as well as this side. Because if you walk only on one side—only on the dark side—you're out of balance. That if you walk only with the knowledge of this side of life, you're out of balance, we are told. That's what those symbols, those colours they represent.

They also have stakes on which the drum is suspended. Each one is a different colour. Each one of those represents one of the sacred directions. At the top of that pole, at the top of that stake, which is generally shaped like that, there's a little hook here where this loop will go on this stake. And thereby the drum is suspended just as it was in the beginning. Each one of those poles, it will be coloured in different colours, nowadays wrapped in coloured yarn—long ago they simply dyed the wood. That wood is a certain kind of wood for a certain purpose. . . . Each one of those poles sits in one of the *four sacred directions*. And there's a spirit in each of those directions that is represented by this feather on each stake. This **stake which is the west** is a certain colour. This **stake which is the east** which is the source of light and knowledge is a certain colour. That's a general description of a drum. And in the beginning, the drum was made a certain way. . . . But one head had to be male, and the other side had to be female. And so generally, the one side was the female of the animal you were using. If it's moose hide, one side had to be from the female of the animal and the other side male, for a very specific reason. It was tied in a certain way. . . . There were a certain number of these [lacing points] that were cut into that hide so that they formed a pattern. There was also a certain way in which it was laced so that it formed a pattern and in that pattern you could see the four directions in-between. See these diamonds. That represents the *four directions* again. So everything about the drum symbolizes [something]. But it is the meaning of that drum that is the most important. Nowadays we have drums of every description. The drum society to which I belong, that drum will never leave that reserve because that's where it's given, that's where it will stay. Only woman could say it could be moved. And the drum represents one drum. There's only one drum, even though there are many.

Visions of Sound: Musical Instruments of First Native Communities in Northeastern America, Beverly Diamond, Sam Cronk & Franziska Von Rosen, 1994, pp. 35-38

This powerful description by Eddie Benton-Benai concerning the Anishnabe peace drum, shared at a drum workshop in Canada in 1986, manifests this People's rich heritage concerning the drum. Just the sight of the drum calls to mind the depth of spirituality of the People and in particular the woman's role in handing on the spiritual ways.

———————————————— ⊕ ————————————————

MEDICINE LODGE SOCIETY RITES
OJIBWA

In the morning, he dressed in his best buckskin, decorated with quillwork especially for the occasion. He went first to the sweat lodge, where he again joined his tutor and the priests. They sat together, chanting songs and prayers and smoking. The candidate prayed and made offerings of tobacco to the bear spirit. He asked it to compel the dangerous spirits to draw away from the entrance of the ceremonial lodge so he could enter safely. After the prayers and singing had ceased, the group left the sweat lodge and walked solemnly to the large ceremonial lodge, the candidate leading the way, and the priests chanting as they walked behind. When the group reached the main entrance, they stopped. The candidate's sponsor and one of the priests stepped forward and took positions on either side of the candidate. The other priests entered the lodge and sat down. A drummer began to drum and sing. Starting to the *south*, the candidate and his escorts walked around the lodge *four times*. His relatives and people from the encampment watched. Sometimes, *four people*, representing *four benevolent bear spirits*, accompanied the three as they *circled the lodge*. *Four evil bear spirits* challenged them during their circuit, but the benevolent bears always overpowered the evil ones and allowed the candidate to complete his journey.

When the group reached the entrance on the *fourth round*, they stopped. The candidate asked to enter. "Let me come in!" he shouted. "I come for death, I come for life!" The priests said prayers. The candidate entered and the priests led him around the inside *four times*. He shuffled slowly with the beat of the drum, his body and knees bent forward. Others fell in behind until everyone was dancing. After *four circuits* the dancing stopped, the priests returned to their places, and the candidate moved to the *west end* of the lodge. *Four priests* approached him. The drumming slowed, and the priests prayed. The drumming stopped altogether. In the silence, the chief priest stepped forward, holding a bear-paw medicine bag. A cowrie shell shot out of the bag and hit the candidate. He collapsed as if he had been shot with an arrow. The priests danced around him, each holding a medicine bag and taking a turn touching the apparently lifeless body. At last the chief priest commanded the man to stand. He stood and began singing. Again, the priest chanted prayers and made offerings. They gave a medicine bag to the man, now a newly initiated member. He carried it as he *circled the lodge* and thanked the priests.

> *Giving Voice to Bear: North American Indian Myths, Rituals, and Images of the Bear*, David Rockwell, 1991, p. 21

The Medicine Lodge Society (Midewiwin) stresses after death birth into a new life in another form. With the bear as the patron animal spirit the People gather in the spring to harvest maple sugar or in the fall to harvest wild rice. The sacred geometry of the four directions and ritual circling are key to experiencing important aspects of the ceremonies.

⊕

MIDEWIWIN CEREMONY
OJIBWA

Inside, Mide priests sat in their assigned places along the reed-and-bough sides of the lodge, their faces painted according to their degrees, wingbone necklaces around their necks, dancing bags slung over their shoulders, their pindigigossans—medicine bundles made of otter and weasel skins, hides of beaver, muskrat, and bear—in their laps. The sacred pole occupied the center of the Midewegun, the center of all things, a smooth rock at its base. The Grand Mide . . . stood before the pole, arms folded over his broad chest, a rattle in each powerful hand, a bearskin pindgigossan hanging from his belt, his face painted in the colors of the *four quarters* of the universe: *north*, white; *south*, blue; *east*, green; *west*, red. The fourth-degree cross-pole was sewn on the front of his deerskin shirt. The Grand Mide was powerful of body and spirit. . . . Even his name was formidable; Manito-bijiki, Buffalo Spirit. . . .

Someone blew a wingbone whistle. Its sharp cry silenced the crowd outside. The waterdrum sounded *four times*. The waterdrum—the voice of the *Sacred Circle* in which all nature moved, voice of the *four-winds* manitos. The priests rose and began to dance to the drumbeat, their feet tracing patterns meant to ward off and confuse any evil that attempted to enter the Midewegun. They danced and sang songs they had heard in dreams, each singing his own song, an interweaving of different voices, yet not unmelodious. Necklaces clattered as the holy ones danced around and around the lodge, rattles hissing and whistles shrilling. These sounds, the chants, the throb of the drum, the tread of feet, the movements of the dancers at the edges of Wawiekumig's vision had a strange effect. A looseness came to his knees, a lightness to his head. The strain of standing with eyes fixed on the pole, of resisting the impulse to look at the holy men, some of whom were breaking off and rushing at the initiates, pelting them with white shells from the pindigigossans, made Wawiekumig dizzy. The peculiar spinning in his head was like a childhood dream of tumbling from a high place. . . .

Four blasts from the bone whistle brought the drumming, singing, and dancing to a sudden halt. The grand Mide swept his arm in a call for total silence. . . .

Indian Country, Philip Caputo, 1988, pp. 152-153

This short fictional version of a particular Mide ceremony is replete with some of the important symbolism concerning the four directions and the manitos. Face-painting and dancing and whistle-blowing serve to express aspects of this time of personal and communal prayer.

———————————— ⊕ ————————————

HEALING RITUAL
OJIBWA

Nevertheless, even the lay Indian believes in specially powerful *manidos* operating in certain spheres, whom he reverences or dreads according to their supposed beneficence or malevolence. They are the personifications of nature's mightiest forces, the sun and the moon, thunder, the storm winds, the awful power that lurks in water, particularly in the water of the great lakes, and the beneficent power of grandmother earth working silently, but influencing everything that dwells upon its surface. Grandmother earth and the water *manido* perhaps, too, the sun and the moon, have many lesser *manidos* at their command. . . .

The sun *manido* travels **west** across the sky and passes under the earth to the **east** again. Without him the earth would have no daylight and no warmth; man's life would be wretched in the extreme. . . .

The sick could entreat the help of the sun *manido*. . . . A man who had been ailing for a long time might pitch his wigwam toward the **east, walk four times sunwise around the fire**, then, standing at the entrance, pray to the sun *manido* for healing and throw a little tobacco into the flames.

The Ojibwa Indians of Parry Island: Their Social and Religious Life,
Diamond Jenness, 1935, p. 32-33

A campfire or homefire relates to the sun. This homefire ritual circuit of four times and the facing of the sunrise direction honors the manido of the sun and prepares the sick person for healing.

*A young Onondaga ponders
the natural beauty of a lake*

A prayer facing the setting sun

SOUTHEAST CULTURAL AREA

FOUR CORNER DANCE (KVNAWA OPVNKA)
SEMINOLE

This dance is still performed on occasion. Men and women form a long file, holding hands. The leader, a man carrying a coconut-shell rattle, sings and takes the group in a counter-clockwise direction, using a simple walking step. When he reaches the *east* side of the square ground he gradually winds the group into a tight *spiral*, like a watchspring. His song is: *"Wehe yahaiyo-o"* and the answer, sung in unison by those following him, is *"wehe yahaiyo, wehe yahaiyo."* This is *repeated* over and over. When the group is tightly coiled the leader sings *"oho oho,"* reverses and uncoils the spiral using the first song again. When the line is straightened out he leads the group to the *north* side of the ground, where he coils and uncoils the group as before, and then does the same at the *west* and *south* sides of the ground—hence the name "Four Corner Dance." The dance ends at the *south* side.

The dance is performed in honor of the *four Giant Horned Snakes* that reside at the *four corners* of the world, and the coiling and uncoiling of the line of dancers represent the coiling and uncoiling of snakes.

Oklahoma Seminoles: Medicines, Magic, and Religion,
James Howard, 1984, p. 170

The Oklahoma-based Seminoles who maintain this ancient dance are acting out the movements of a snake. They celebrate their tribal mythology, especially the origin of things, in songs, dances, and stories.

---- ⊕ ----

LENTEN SWEAT LODGE
CHEROKEE

For *four hours* flaming stubby logs surround the smooth river rocks that glow orange-hot like fiery balls. The closely tended camp fire cuts the cold night air and lights the way to the igloo-shaped lodge. A half moon of stones provides a safe *perimeter around the fire*, while a *smaller stone circle* encompasses the pipe, tobacco, herbs and other elements for the ritual. In the evening darkness eleven Cherokee people and friends assemble for the spiritual ceremony of the sweat lodge.

I reverently approach the sweat lodge with apprehension and self-doubt. Can I endure the physical ordeal of intense heat? Will I renew my spirit by this sacred ritual? Can I connect with the spirituality of native peoples? The questons haunt me on my pilgrimage through another culture in my search for cleansing and renewal.

"You need rebirth every day, especially in this society of abuse," Cleto Montelongo instructs me as I nervously prepare for this strange liturgy. "The sweat lodge is our church. It represents the womb of Mother Earth, the center of the universe."

Cleto, a husky man in his mid-forties with black hair hanging down the full length of his back, works with the American Indian Center in Atlanta. He explained: "My mission is to be who I am. I have a responsiblity not to change things, but to keep the message alive. Spirituality is a way of life. It is how you conduct yourself with God and Mother Earth. 'All my relations' means that I am connected to the trees and the grass and the snake and the earth."

Stripped except for swimsuit and towel, Cleto, as spiritual leader, enters the lodge first. Through prayer he prepares the place for ten more to join him in the *circular room* where they will sit cross-legged on mats covering the cold earth. A reverent silence opens the heart for communal prayer.

Using a pitchfork, an assistant brings in a glowing rock and places it in a shallow trough dug out in the middle of the dark lodge. My mind races back to the prophet Isaiah whose lips were purified by a burning ember: "Now that this has touched your lips, your wickedness is removed, your sin purged" (Is. 6:7). I meditate about my own unworthiness. I think about the centuries of sin committed against Native Americans.

Others join Cleto, chanting in their native tongue and rhythmically beating a drum. Cleto sprinkles cedar shavings on the fiery rock. They sparkle on contact and give off an aromatic smell. It is like incense rising.

Another rock is introduced and another—seven in all to symbolize the *four directions*, plus the Great Spirit, the earth and the people. Cleto, using a dipper, splashes the rocks with water which hiss and sizzle and emit powerful steam. I feel every pore of my body open as more water is poured onto the rocks. Slowly the heat intensifies and the sweat continuously trickles off me. My entire body is crying for my sins, and the sins against the earth, and those against whole races of people. I am living Psalm 51: "Thoroughly wash me from my guilt and of my sin cleanse me" (Ps. 51:4).

Each quarter hour Cleto opens the lodge flap and the smoke and steam escape, a symbol that our sins and imperfections dissipate before the Great Spirit.

The ceremony links me to the sufferings of others. My mind flashes between prayer, physical discomfort, and thoughts about the sufferings of native peoples. In the first half century after their arrival, according to the saintly Catholic missionary, Father Bartoleme de las Casas, the Spanish had murdered fifty million Native Americans. In the U.S. between 1776 and 1900, Native American land holdings were reduced ninety-five percent, because settlers wanted gold and farmland, and corporations wanted mineral or railroad rights. Today, for many of the remaining million-and-a-half Native Americans, poverty, addiction, and loss of identity continue the oppression.

Images of the mistreatment of people and the abuse of land imprint themselves on my mind. A cobweb of sorrow, outrage and indignation entangles my heart. Could the lament of Jeremiah be more pointed? "Our fathers, who sinned, are no more; but we bear their guilt" (Lam. 5:7).

In the lodge, chanting and drum beating mingle with the heat and incense. Participants have an opportunity to pray.

"Grandfather, I give you thanks for this life and this good earth," prays one. Another remembers that "our community needs to heal; all races need to heal." Prayers include sincere contrition for past abuses, requests for strength for future struggles.

After an hour I emerge from the lodge. In the cold night air, stream emanates from my exhausted body as I see the stars and trees in a different light. I look around the campfire and realize a new connectedness with others. Can I ever again be indifferent to the earth or other cultures, I muse, since I have been purged and reborn?

"A Unique Lenten Sweat Lodge," *The Glenmary Challenge*,
John Rausch, Spring 1992, p. 12

In this ceremony all the elements are present: the circle, the directions, the fourness of things. Because it is based on Creator and creation, all human beings can feel connected with the communal experience of it.

--------------------------------- ⊕ ---------------------------------

WORLD SEGMENTS AND COLOR SYMBOLISM
CHEROKEE/CREEK

The Southeastern Indians believed that the universe in which they lived was made up of three separate, but related, worlds: the Upper World, the Lower World and This World. In the last lived mankind, most animals, and all plants.

This World, a round island resting on the surface of water, was suspended from the sky by *four cords* attached to the island at the *four cardinal points* of the compass. Lines drawn to connect the opposite points of the compass, *from north to south and from east to west*, intersected This World into *four wedge-shaped segments*. Thus a symbolic representation of the human world was a *cross* within a *circle*, the cross representing the intersecting lines and the circle the shape of This World.

Each segment of This World was identified by its own color. According to Cherokee doctrine, *east* was associated with the color red because it was the direction of the sun, the greatest deity of all. Red was also the color of sacred fire, believed to be directly connected with the sun, with blood and, therefore, with life. Finally, red was the color of success. The *west* was the moon segment; it provided no warmth and was not life-giving as the sun was. So its color was black, which also stood for the region of the souls of the dead and for death itself. *North* was the direction of cold, and so its color was blue (sometimes purple), and it represented trouble and defeat. *South* was the direction of warmth; its color, white, was associated with peace and happiness.

The Creeks held a similar conception of the *four segments* of the world, though they differed somewhat from the Cherokees in the attributes and colors assigned to the directions.

America's Fascinating Indian Heritage,
James Maxwell (Ed.), 1978, p. 83

This World, the one we all live in now, was seen as being suspended by cords to the Upperworld. The relationship of heaven and earth was understood in a manner reminiscent of the early Hebrews' explanation of a three-fold universe (the heavens, the earth, the netherworld) with the exception that this world was at the lower level rather than in between the two others.

———————————————— ⊕ ————————————————

SOME CUSTOMS AND WAYS
UNITED LUMBEE NATION OF NORTH CAROLINA AND AMERICA

Among some of the Southeastern Indians there is a belief that all living beings have *four souls*, or *life energies*. One has to do with the personality and memory. This is the soul that lives on after death and it is located in the head. Another is the life force that is located in the liver. Another is the spirit or essence of being which makes us uniquely human and distinguishes us from animals and other beings. It resides in the heart. A *fourth* is the energy that is our bodies and it resides in the bones. At an individual's death, it is a custom to sit up with the dead body, just like keeping a vigil at an Irish wake. This comes from an ancient belief that at a person's death certain evil conjurors would come in the form of ravens or owls to steal the life force located in the liver, thus adding to their own life force. In the past, people used to make their own burial clothes. Today some people have the practice of draping the coffin with a black cloth, or burial shroud. Another practice still common today is the placing of certain items in the coffin with the deceased to be carried into the spirit world. Other than these special customs, our funerals are very similar to most other funerals in this country.

Also, like many Southeastern Peoples, the Lumbees understand that there are *four spirit beings* at each of the *cardinal directions* who hold up the *four corners of the earth*. Often these spirits are referred to as "men." It is also understood that these beings may take the form of spirit animals or spirit birds. Colors are also associated with the four directions, the most common being red, white, black, and blue. Most prayers and dances are done in a *counterclockwise* direction: *east, north, west,* and *south*, counterclockwise being the direction for receiving positive blessings.

Interview with Knowles Walking Bear,
Lubbock, Texas, January 27, 1997

The Lumbee Nation is made up of many Peoples originally from the southeastern United States. Smaller tribes and bands, many mixed with European and African blood, as well as those of some of the larger tribes like the Cherokee, the Creek, the Cheraw, the Hateras, and the Tuscarora, share in their heritage. By telephone I interviewed Walking Bear, the Director of the United Lumbee Nation Hawk Society, who enlightened me regarding some unique features of Southeastern customs and practices. Though the United Lumbees do not have specific reservation lands and are living in many places in the country, nonetheless, they feel their tribal unity and share it in each generation. They are the one of the largest tribes east of the Mississippi River.

Pottery by Hopi elder, Ethel Youvella, at Second Mesa, Arizona

SOUTHWEST CULTURAL AREA

GIRLS' PUBERTY CEREMONY
MESCALERO APACHE

At Mescalero the Girls' Puberty Ceremony is an annual event celebrating the initial menses of selected girls, as well as the perpetuation of the tribe. During the event, the Singers recount tribal history from the time of the beginning by the shores of a big lake far to the *north*.

While the Ceremony celebrates womanhood and focuses on women, it is conducted by men; not just ordinary men, but powerful holy men who are beyond reproach. Each Holy Man/Singer *(Gutaat,* One Who Sings) must be intelligent and able to memorize and interpret songs in a special form of Mescalero Apache. Each must sing 64 different songs on each of the *four* nights of the Ceremony. Additionally, the Singer must memorize long stories of the people, their travels, and accounts of tribal interactions from the beginning to the present. The Ceremony is thus a reenactment of events from the beginning of cosmological time and a recitation of ethnohistory.

The Ceremony and its attendant rituals are seen by the Mescaleros as *the* crucial factor in their ethnicity and their success in coping with the rigors of survival as a people in a pluralistic society not of their making. The Singers sing women into their adult roles, sing tribal history, and sing the people into their concerted existence.

Our Ceremony, the puberty rites, is the most important religious rites that we adhere to today. . . . The female—the woman of the tribe, when she

536

reaches womanhood, this elaborate Ceremony is held over her. Not, not because she has reached puberty, but because she is a *woman*. And, then, everything is done—for her that a people might live. That a people will *always* live. Every year we have this to regenerate ourselves as a people— That we will make her strong, and generous, and kind, and proud so that she will bring forth a *strong* warrior child that . . . will protect the people.— This is the way a people perpetuate themselves. . . .

At the same time, the Ceremony is a reunion with the primary life force, the Creator God *(Bik'egudindé,* Because of Whom There is Life), and his consort, Mother Earth or White Painted woman *(Isdzan-atl'eesh,* Woman Painted White). . . .

The Girls' Puberty Ceremony, then, is a ritual drama, a reenactment of creation. . . .

THE CEREMONY

THE FIRST DAY

The few spectators who have braved the predawn chill sit on the **north** side of the ceremonial area directly opposite the large cooking arbor. Several Singers and Painters *(Anaagu'liin,* One Who Makes Them) emerge from behind the cooking arbor. They have been singing and praying near the girls' quarters while each Godmother *(Naaikish,* They Who Direct [the girls]) begins to dress her charge from the left, the side of the heart and, therefore, the side closest to the Creator God. First comes the left moccasin, then the right. Next comes the soft buckskin skirt made heavy with its fringe, each strand of which ends in a handmade tin cone. The buckskin overblouse with its elaborate beading and more tin cones follow. Finally, the scarf is added. . . . Finishing touches are provided by jewelry: beaded work, porcupine quill work, turquoise, and silver. . . .

As the final items (scratching stick, drinking tube, pollen bag, and sometimes a medicine bundle) are put in place on the dresses, the Singers come to the **northwest** side of the Ceremonial grounds and stand near the spectators. The Painters array themselves behind the Singers. The lead Singer begins to chant a prayer to the Powers.

Strong, young men assemble the poles for the holy lodge *(Isaane-bikugha,* Old Age Home), inside which the actual ritual will take place. The 12 evergreen poles are arrayed in a **circle**, bases toward the center, behind the Singers. Grasses are tied to the tops of the *four* primary poles, the grandfathers; they are then blessed with cattail pollen *(te, Typha latifolia)*. The circle opens to the *east* and has a basket at its center. The Singers pray as they sprinkle pollen from the base to the tip of each Grandfather.

Prayers continue as the mothers, grandmothers, and Godmothers of the girls join the Singers. As the Singers chant to each Grandfather, the women "send forth a voice," a high-pitched ululation of reverent praise and pride. Meanwhile, the young men who are raising the poles pause *four times*, once for *each cardinal direction*, before bringing the poles to their full upright position.

The first Grandfather represents the moon and the stars; he stands in the *east*. The second Gradfather represents the sky elements (wind, rain, lightning, clouds, thunder, rainbows, mountains) from his position in the *south*. The third Grandfather represents the animals; he stands in the *west*. And the fourth Grandfather represents man, humanity; he stands in the *north*. "And since man is a frail being, it takes all the other three to hold him up." The four Grandfathers remind the people of creation. . . .

When the 12 evergreen poles are in place and lashed together at their tops, a young man climbs up the frame to secure the lashing and then cover the top third with white canvas. Other men cover the bottom two-thirds with freshly cut oak branches. Soon the holy lodge is completed on the outside. At the very top are tufts of boughs left on when most of the trunks were stripped of their branches and greenery. In the middle is the white canvas and, finally, the bottom is composed of tighly interwoven oak boughs.

> The main Ceremonial lodge is made of 12 evergreen fir trees. These poles . . . represent eternal life for us. And the 12 represent the 12 moons of the year. . . The 4 main structure poles . . . correspond to the 4 directions of the universe, the 4 seasons, the 4 stages of life—for in the natural world everything is based on 4. . . .
>
> These 12 poles that form the tipi, to us represent the balance of Power, goodness, generosity; all that is good in this world comes from this tipi, this holy lodge. . . . It says to us, "Come forth, my children, enter me. I am the home of generosity, pride, dignity, and hope. . . .
>
> The 4 Grandfathers hold up the universe for us. . . . These poles are heavy; it takes many men to lift them. . . . When these poles are being raised, the mothers of the daughters put their hands on the poles. And that

signifies that the home is not a home without the woman; and even though this Ceremonial structure is going up, it also has to have the help of the woman even though she is physically not able to put it up.

The basket that had been in the center of the circle formed by the poles is now brought out in front of the holy lodge. It is a hand-made basket containing gramma grass, pollen, eagle feathers, and tobacco.

[The] basket represents the . . . heart of a people: it has all the important things. It has grass in there: food for all that we live on, the animals. The feathers represent eagle. . . . We get our authority to live as a people from Eagle. He is God's earth authority. That's why we wear the feathers . . . feathers are our authority and pride. . . . Tobacco is man's hope and his prayers . . . the basket is industriousness.

Activity intensifies as men labor to form a runway of fully boughed evergreen trees, *four* on the *south* and *four* on the *north* of the *east*-facing entry to the holy lodge. Other men begin to bring in freshly cut tules *(Scirpus lacutris)* to carpet in front of and inside the tipi. Simultaneously, a fire-pit is dug in the tipi's center.

The fire-pit . . . signifies the woman and the poles represent the man. Men are the shield; they protect. The woman is the center, being protected. . . . Everything revolves around the tipi . . . it's a people. The cover is men. The fire is woman, warmth, love, and perpetual labor for a family to live. If there's no woman in here, there's no rhyme or reason to it. . . . Everything is male in that lodge except the women and the fire.

Outside the holy lodge the Singers are facing *east* and praying. The lead Singer slowly raises his left hand as he sings. His palm faces outward; painted on it, in red, is a sun with rays emanating outward to the four directions. The Godmothers lead the girls to their places on buckskin mats placed on the quilts and blankets on top of the tules just as the Singer completes his last song and his arm is fully extended. As if on command, the sun tops East Mountain, striking his upraised palm. It is a moment of breath-taking beauty, requiring an exquisite sense of timing and precise attention to minimal light cues as well as the manipulation of the songs so that the last line of the last song coincides with the sunrise.

When men offer red paint to the sun—red signifies male and men. That's the background of the sun. The two basic colors of the universe is yellow and red, yellow for women. . . . And the sun is the physical representation of God. . . . [As the sun rises] goodness washes over you.

The girls kneel, facing *east*, on their skin mats while a line forms to the *southeast* of them. The girls' mothers stand behind them holding burden baskets filled with food; their fathers and uncles stand to either side, inside the runway and directly in front of the holy lodge. Each Singer applies the yellow cattail pollen to the girl for whom he is singing: a tiny sprinkle to the *east, south, west, north*, thence from the *west* to the *east* (from the crown of her head to her forehead), to the *south* (on her right shoulder), to the *north* (on her left shoulder), and from the *south* to *north* (across her nose). The movements form a cross, linking the *four directions* with the girl as the center.

Pollen is applied to them. They are blessed with pollen. Pollen is the color of yellow. The yellow color represents God's generosity. It also represents the *south*, from which the warm winds bring rain that a thirsty land might drink and bring forth its bounty of fruit and meat. And they are . . . blessed that they will be fruitful and bring forth strong sons that they will be mighty warriors . . . that they will bring forth strong daughters that will become the mothers of a warrior race; that they will perpetuate themselves in a good way, a holy way, with the Powers of the *four directions*.

The Singers step to the front of the line that has formed and are blessed by each of the girls, beginning with the one kneeling on the *south* and proceeding to the *northernmost* girl. Then the people in line pass before the girls. As the girls complete the blessing sequence for those kneeling in front of them, they are, in turn, blessed by the person's reaching into the pollen bag and repeating the sequence that the Singers had performed. Babies too small to move their own hands have them moved by the parent or relative bringing them through the line. Those who have specific complaints linger to rub some of the pollen on the afflicted area. Anyone who is sick or troubled will go through the line as will those who seek to remain well and partake of the blessings of God as mediated through the girls. . . .

The Lead Singer motions away those still in line as the Godmothers assist the girls in going from their knees to their abdomens. Each girl lies face down with her head to the *east* as her Godmother presses and "molds" her into a fine, strong woman. The hair is smoothed over the girl's shoulders and back before molding begins: first the left shoulder, then the right; next the left and right sides of the back; the left hip and the right hip; then left then right thigh and calf; the left and right foot.

As the Godmothers near the feet, a man takes the basket, that had been present since the morning began, out to the *east*. While the Singers chant and the Godmothers ululate, the girls run along the *north* side of the dance arena, around the basket, and back on the *south* side of the arena. The basket is moved closer to the holy lodge three more times; and the running girls *encircle* it three more times.

The *four* runs around the basket symbolize the *four* cycles of life: infancy, childhood, adulthood, and, as the basket nears the Old Age Home in the *west* again, old age. As the primary characters in the ritual drama, the girls reenact the legendary journey of White Painted Woman who walked to the *west* as an old woman only to return from the *east* as a young woman once again.

At the conclusion of the *fourth* run the girls return to the entrance-way of the holy lodge where their uncles or brothers invert the burden baskets, spilling tobacco, candy, piñons, fruit, and money over them.

The spilling from the baskets signals the end of the public rites and triggers massive give-aways by matrilineal members of the girls' families. Relatives throw candy, oranges, apples, and cigarettes from the beds of pickup trucks. People of all ages dash to pick up the gifts, for this is special food and tobacco that has been blessed.

While the assembled crowd, many of whom arrived with the sunrise, scampers for the distributed gifts, the girls return to their camp-out homes. There each girl's Godmother talks to her of sex and her responsibility for motherhood. The Singer gives his "daughter," as he will refer to the girl for the rest of her life, Indian bananas *(husk'ane, Yucca baccata)* and says, "Be fruitful all the days of your life; obtain food and not be lazy." He repeats this, and the feeding twice more. The *fourth* time, the Godmother feeds the girl; as she does so, she tells her, "May you bring forth in this world strong male children so they will protect your people."

Even before the Singer and Godmother finish, those who were not yet blessed form a line outside the camp-out home. At the conclusion of the feeding, they are admitted. Each kneels in front of the girl, who is sitting on a bed or a chair, and pollen blessings are exchanged. . . .

Everyone who comes to a Ceremonial is fed all meals free. . . .

While Ceremonial participants rest in the afternoon, the spectators are entertained by contests. Some members of the audience of the ritual drama become perfomers in these events. An all-Indian rodeo, with competitors from many states, takes place on a mesa to the northeast of the Ceremonial grounds. Prizes are generous and points are earned for the annual all-around Indian cowboy championship. . . .

Meanwhile, in the dance arena there are dance contests in the pan-Indian Powwow style.

The mounting tension is almost tangible as darkness begins to descend and the huge bonfire is prepared and lit in the center of the dance arena. When the sun no longer colors the mountains and deserts to the *west* and when the fire is roaring, jingling noises can be heard from the *east* as the Mountain God dancers *(Ga'he)* prepare to enter the dance arena. Their Painter and his assistants have been busy for the past few hours praying, drumming, and chanting while the entire group of Mountain God dancers *(Baanaaich'isndé)* has been painted and dressed.

The designs that appear on the Mountain God dancers are different each night . . . the elements are combined in a different manner for each of the *four* nights. The combinations follow the precepts given long ago when the first Painters were given their dancers, songs, and symbols, as well as curing power. While the designs appear different to outsiders, they are said to be the "same thing" as the previous night. . . .

Each dance group is identifiable by its design set, distinctive sashes, and headdresses. The general costuming is the same—kilts, paint, head covering, headdresses, and red streamers with *four eagle feathers* attached and tied to each upper arm. There is no mistaking a Mountain God dancer or the group to which he belongs.

Each dancer wears an A-line wraparound buckskin kilt that is fringed and fitted with beaded or skin decorations as well as "jingles" cut and shaped from tin cans, which jingle each time the dancer moves. Worked leather belts, often with bells attached, and red sashes hold up the kilts. The mid-calf length buckskin moccasins are decorated with bells either at the top or at the ankle. If there are no bells on the moccasins, leather straps with bells are worn around each leg.

A head covering of black fabric (canvas, heavy cotton, dyed buckskin, or heavy doubleknit), with round openings cut for each eye and the mouth, is topped by a bilaterally symmetrical headdress made of yucca and wood. The headdress of each group member is the same and is painted with designs matching or repeating an element of the design painted on the dancers' bodies. Thus, with the exception of the palms of the hands, a dancer is completely covered with clothing or paint from the top of his head to the soles of his feet. He becomes the anonymous personification of a Mountain God.

Usually there is a dance set (*four* Mountain God dancers and one or more clowns) for each girl, although at times two girls will share a set of dancers. Sharing is most apt to occur when the girls are sisters or first cousins.

The spectacle is awesome as the fully costumed Mountain God dancers converge on the dance arena, jingling rhythmically as they move, their headdresses piercing the darkness above them. The dancers pause from a trotting step just outside the dance arena. There the lead dancer gets the others in step by striking the sticks he carries in each hand against his thighs. The clown *(Libąyé)* mimics each movement of the lead dancer, but always a bit late.

All being in step, and all noises from the bells and the tin cones—as well as the strident note from the cow bell slapping against the clown's derriere—being in synchrony, the lead dancer moves his group into the dance arena. They raise their arms and sticks as they approach the fire and emit a hooting sound resembling that of an owl or a turkey. They are said to be praying as they make this noise. Their movements and vocalizations are said to be "blessing the fire." When the lead dancer is within a few feet of the fire, he lowers his arms and sticks and bows his head before the line steps backward still facing the fire. The approach, hooting, lowering, and retreating sequence is repeated three times. On the *fourth* approach the dancers dip their bodies first to the left, then to the right as they approach the fire; they move so quickly in their *four dips* to each side that their arms seem like windmills. This time as they retreat the lead dancer again slaps the sticks on his thighs as he guides the group once around the fire to the *south* side of the dance arena. The blessing sequence is repeated again from here, thence from the *west* and *north* each time with one complete *circuit of the fire* between stops for the *cardinal directions*.

After the fire has been blessed, the group moves to the holy lodge where the sequence is repeated from each of the directions in order (*east, south, west, north*).

When the blessings are completed the Painter begins his drumming and chanting from a position in front of the holy lodge. The Mountain God dancers and their clown now dance with dramatic posturing, stamping, and gesturing around and around the bonfire, always *moving in a clockwise direction*. Even when there is no singing or drumming, they keep moving. . . .

As the Painter begins his drumming a large cardboard is placed on the ground in front of the benches where he and the chanting men sit. Young boys congregate around the cardboard carrying evergreen sticks they have gathered from near the holy lodge. They join the adult drummers and chanters by beating in rhythm with their sticks and, occasionally, also join in the singing of the choruses of a song. Once again, a part of the audience becomes performers.

The regular dancing of the Mountain Gods signals the women to join in the dancing as well. Their dance path is several feet away from the bonfire and the path of the Mountain Gods. Some of the first women to dance are the girls for whom the Ceremony is being held; they are accompanied by their Godmothers who dance in front of them. Their mothers and close female relatives dance behind them: ". . . while the men are dancing, the women dance around them. . . ."

The girls for whom the Ceremony is being held wear their Ceremonial attire. All other women wear everyday dress without jewelry that might make noise. Only the Mountain god dancers, the clowns, and the girls make noise in the dance area; those sounds are perceived as music. . . . Only the women's legs move in performing the dance steps used; however, the execution of the steps moves the body toward, then away from, the fire; and that movement produces a swinging motion of the fringing on the shawls. . . .

The girls make only a few *circuits of the fire* before retiring to their arbors to rest before their strenuous dancing begins. . . .

While the Mountain Gods and the women dancing in support of them hold the attention of the spectators, the girls are led into the holy lodge by their Godmothers. During the leading-in portion of the Ceremony, the girls are said to be inviting in life and magnanimity for their people and for themselves.

Cowhide dance mats are awaiting the girls around the inside periphery of the holy lodge. The Godmothers spread blankets for themselves and the girls to sit on while resting; it is here that they await the arrival of the Singers.

Before recounting the tribe's history through chants accompanied by the deer hoof rattles, the lead Singer offers smoke to the Powers. The other Singers follow his lead. As soon as the Singers begin to chant, the girls rise to dance.

Two dance steps are used by the girls. The more common one involves keeping the body rigid while only the feet move. By pivoting alternately on the balls and heels of their feet they take *four* "steps" to the left, then *four* to the right. The cowhide on which they dance is just wide enough to allow *four lateral movements*. They hold their arms in front of them by bending their elbows, raising their forearms, and making their hands from relaxed fists with the palms outward while the knuckles rest lightly on the shoulders. The position and step create movement of the girls' clothing and cause the tin cones to strike one another, adding another sound to that produced by the men's voices and the percussion of the rattles. The other dance step the girls use is designed as a rest; it, too, however, is strenuous. Again the body is held still while the feet move. With their hands on their hips and while standing in place, they kick one foot and then the other straight out in front. Between songs the Godmothers will massage the girls' shoulders, backs, or legs if it appears they are showing sign of fatigue. Alternating the two steps with short rest periods, the girls will dance for several hours while the Singers chant. . . .

The girls dance while 64 songs are sung . . . from about 10 p.m. to midnight before retiring to their camp-out homes. Social dancers replace the Mountain God dancers between 11 p.m. and midnight. Sometime between 2 a.m. and dawn the social dancers leave the dance arena. The first day ends.

THE SECOND THROUGH FOURTH DAYS

There is no morning ritual on these days. Afternoons are filled with Powwow-style dance competitions and the rodeo.

After supper, but before the bonfire is lit for the Mountain God dancers, the war dancers appear in the Ceremonial arena. . . .

The bonfire . . . is lit at dusk in preparation for the Mountain god dancers and the social dancing that will follow them. Around 10 p.m. the girls will again dance for two hours or so in the holy lodge as the Singers continue their chanting recitation of tribal history, keeping track of the songs with *sticks placed in a circle around the central fire-pit.*

THE FIFTH DAY

Since time is reckoned from sunrise to sunrise and since the fifth day's activities begin when the *fourth day* is almost complete, the activities are considered to be a part of the fourth day: this despite a fifth sunrise coming in the midst of the fourth day's final activities. They may also be viewed, and indeed are, as the beginning of the second four days when the girls will remain on the Ceremonial grounds with only close female relatives and their Godmother—when the public aspect of the ritual is over and the private aspect begins.

Again, people assemble before dawn for the final ritual activities. . . .

The jingling of the girls' dresses and the percussion from deer hoof rattles are also heard just before dawn on the fifth morning, for the girls have been dancing all night while the Singers sang and the Godmothers counseled.

> These girls have been dancing for *four* nights. On the fourth night they dance from when it gets dark to daylight with a break around midnight. It is a physical ordeal for them. But they must go through it. . . . It is a sacrifice they make . . . their physical contribution that they make that a people can be strong and healthy.

On the previous three nights the lead Singer placed song *tally sticks in a circle* around the fire: this morning the sticks make a pathway, replicating the form of the holy lodge and its runway. As the last stick is planted, the Singers rise, signaling the Godmothers to take the girls back to their living quarters where their hair and bodies will be washed in yucca-root suds, repeating the actions of the first day when the girls were cleansed and dressed. This ritual foreshadows activity which will take place at the end of the eighth day.

All tules are taken out of the holy lodge and replaced with fresh ones. The folding chairs for the Singers are placed so they face *east* and are behind the girls, whereas previously they had faced *west* toward the girls.

Before the girls reappear in the holy lodge they will have their faces painted with white clay by the Singers. Their arms, from fingertips to elbows, and their legs, from thighs to feet, will also be painted.

> The girls' faces are painted white signifying that they have achieved; they have done their ordeal. They have lived four good days and they will be

running. Running signifying a physical effort that they must do in order to prove themselves that they are worthy mothers. . . . That white paint is the sign of purity and of the Mother Earth. . . . They are called White Painted Woman, because white is the color of purity, these four days.

But before their final ordeal, that which was given form by the males must be destroyed by them.

The young man who had placed the white covering on the holy lodge once again shinnies up the poles to disengage the lashing and lower the covering. While he is working, other men on the ground take away the oak boughs that had covered the bottom of the lodge. Meanwhile, inside, the girls are being blessed and sung to. People crowd in, even though the poles are beginning to fall. As the last of the poles falls, save the Grandfathers, the girls are revealed sitting on the ground, each with her Singer and Godmother kneeling in front of her. People form lines in front of one or another of the girls; the Singers take seats to the left of the girl for whom they sang while the Godmothers stand to the right. The girls sit with their eyes downcast as the Singers bless each one in line; this time there is no hurry—all who so desire will be blessed. Rather than pollen, the blessing is performed with white clay and red ochre. Each singer paints the faces of those in line a bit differently from the other Singers. Males are painted on the left side and females on the right side of their faces; each singer used his own marks. When all have been painted and blessed, each girl is led out of the holy lodge with an eagle feather by her Singer.

> Now they have been brought out of the tipi after the four days of religious functions.—They have been brought out. They have been brought by an eagle feather. They tell them,

>> Four days you have walked your land and done good. Now hold this eagle feather, the symbol of authority and walk out of your home. Go forth into the world.

The girls are escorted to a white buckskin that has been placed on the ground in front of the runway, now lined by their fathers and close male relatives. *Four crescent moons*, painted with colors evoking the *directions* and said also to represent life's stages, form the stepping-stones each girl walks on, left foot first, before her final run. As the girl under the tutelage of the lead Singer steps on the first crescent, the first song is sung: one additional song is sung for each of the other three crescents.

> And she will be told,
>> Now you are entering the world.
>> You become an adult with responsibilities.
>> Now you are entering the world.
>> Behold yourself.
>> Walk in this world with honor and dignity.
>> Let no man speak of you in shame.
>> For you will become—
>> The mother of a nation.

At the end of the final song, she is pushed off the buckskin by her Singer and Godmother. The other girls follow the first one by quickly stepping on each of the four crescents and, like her, running to the *east* around the same basket that was used on the first day's run.

They are singing to them as [they are] running and they are telling them,

> You will be running to the *four corners of the universe*;
> To where the land meets the big water;
> To where the sky meets the land;
> To where the home of winter is;
> To the home of rain.
> Run this! Run!
> Be strong!
> For you are the mother of a people.

Three times the girls run around the basket; each time it is placed farther from the frame of the holy lodge (the four Grandfathers). On the last run, each girl takes from the basket the eagle feather with which she was led into and out of the holy lodge, and, instead of returning to the holy lodge as she had on the three previous runs, she runs to her quarters behind the cooking arbor. Simultaneously, the four Grandfathers crash to the ground.

> During their last run they are running to their destiny; they are running into the hard world of adulthood . . . the hard world of a hunting world, a war world. . . . When the last run is completed, food will be thrown out that a people might be fruitful and multiply to many.

What began five mornings ago with the erection of a holy lodge and the distribution of food, ends with the destruction of the holy lodge and the distribution of food. In between have been goodness, holiness, the affirmation of the essential rightness of the world, and the place of humans in it. . . .

"Singing For Life: The Mescalero Apache Girls' Puberty Ceremony,"
Claire Farrer in *Southwestern Indian Ritual Drama*,
Charlotte Frisbie (Ed.), 1980, pp. 126-145

This beautiful and lengthy ceremony, having some similarities to the Navajo Kinaalda Puberty Ceremony, is really a celebration of the whole Apache People. Over and over, life is ritualized in the ceremonial components of four, circles, and the cardinal directions.

⊕

GIRLS' PUBERTY CEREMONY
MESCALERO APACHE

Directionality seems to have primacy in Mescalero Apache life. It underlies both circularity and the number 4. Following "the natural order of the universe," we go from *east* to *south* to *west* to *north* to *east*, and so forth, thus describing a *circle* with four named points. As the girls bless themselves and others, they sprinkle pollen, following the directional circuit, and create patterns of *circles* within which are contained *crosses,* thus duplicating the visual form of the base metaphor. The erection of the holy lodge, a tipi, with its *four Grandfathers, one for each direction*, again underscores the importance of the cardinal directions in describing a *circle* and orienting the Ceremony.

Dancing provides the most obvious instance of *circularity* during the ritual drama. The primary dance pattern is *circular* and follows a "sunwise" circuit, clockwise, beginning in the *east*.

Traditional dwellings (tipis, arbors) are also *circular*. Today the rectangular pattern of a commercial tent is often appended to a more traditional camp-out home. But all ritual activity occurs either in a traditional, *circular* structure or outside in the world that is also perceived as being *circular*.

Perhaps the most pervasive aspect of *circularity* during the Ceremonial is time—cyclic and endlessly *circular*. Human existence has been so short in terms of time in general that we are unable to comprehend fully the magnitude of the wheel of time, it is believed. The girls provide a visual reminder of the *circularity* of time by running around the basket *four* times to symbolize infancy, childhood, womanhood, and old age. Simultaneously, this indicates human existence through time and time's ever constant cycle. Although each girl will die, she allows the tribe to live through her and her offspring: the tribe endures through the cycling of time as White Painted Woman herself endures by ever cycling from *east* to *west* and by ever appearing as an aspect of each girl participating in the ritual. The cyclical nature of time is said to be represented through the daily circuit of the sun, from which is taken the "proper" movement while in the holy lodge, or any ceremonial structure where entrance is from the *east*. Movement should properly follow the sun's circuit: *east, south, west, north*.

Circularity is engendered and maintained by following the "natural" order. Even salt sprinkled on food during the meals at Ceremonial time is distributed in a *circular*, clockwise motion.

"Singing For Life: The Mescalero Apache Girls' Puberty Ceremony,"
Claire Farrer in *Southwestern Indian Ritual Drama*,
Charlotte Frisbie (Ed.),1980, pp. 147, 149-150

Both the circle and the four directions are constant symbols for meditation and prayer in Apache ceremonies and yet the fourness of things in life is not forgotten. They tie in the individual and the community with the cycle of all life and the gifts that help one live life well. Time and space are perceived as one throughout human and planetary existence.

———————————— ⊕ ————————————

NIGHT CHANT HEALING CERMONY
NAVAJO

... the first *four days* of the ceremony swing *clockwise* (the preferred term is "sunwise") through the *four world-quarters—east, south, west,* and *north*—completing the familiar circle that symbolizes nature in its entirety.

The colors of the jewels—white, blue, black, and yellow—are the colors of the *four cardinal points, east, south, north,* and *west.*

Four Masterworks of American Indian Literature,
John Bierhorst, 1984, pp.285, 335

In this Night Chant Healing Ceremony the oneness of the creation is illustrated by the circle, while the movements and prayers that one makes in life are conditioned by one's response to the directions when they are thought of as containing the gifts needed by everyone.

——————————— ⊕ ———————————

GAME SYMBOLISMS
NAVAJO/PUEBLO

Their playing fields were mandalas—literal maps of the universe. The *circuits* on which the Navaho and Pueblos played stick-dice, for instance, were often *circles of pebbles* in the dirt with a striking stone in the center. The stone symbolized the island through which the ancestors emerged from the underworld. The ring of pebbles, usually arranged in *four groups* of ten, represented the sacred mountains in the *four directions*, and inside the ring lay the great body of water that flowed away through the breaks in the circle. Contenders struck the center stone with *four sticks*, black on one side for thunder and red on the other for lightning. The very act put the players simultaneously in touch with their origin and their ultimate destiny. Just as the object of the Hindu dice game of *pachisi* is to enter the gates of heaven, the object of the Navajo stick-dice game is to return to the underworld through the place of emergence.

Gambler Way: Indian Gaming in Mythology, History and Archeology in North America, Kathryn Gabriel, 1996, p. 13-14

In ancient times the games of other world cultures often had religious meaning as well as practical value. Native People were no strangers to this realization.

Ancient Pueblo
ceramic bowl

Esselen brothers praying in the direction of the west

BOY'S PUBERTY CEREMONY
LUISEÑO

The chief initiation of boys, which is said to have followed the ant ordeal, was accompanied by the drinking of a decoction of jimsonweed roots, Spanish toloache. This plant was called mani. The period of stupefaction lasted two or three days, or sometimes *four* days, but this was regarded as too heavy a dose. The boys to be initiated were caught in the evening and given the drink in the *wamgush,* the ceremonial enclosure, the same night. Any adult man who might happen to be uninitiated on account of having lived elsewhere in his youth, would also be made to take the drink. The boys were instructed to be good and kind-hearted and not to steal. . . .

A part of the inititation ceremonies was connected with a ground-painting in the *wamgush.* The painting was made with red and yellow paint, *paesul* and *navyot,* ashes for white, and charcoal for black, on the ground which formed the background of the painting. The entire picture, which was **circular** and represented the world, was called *torokhoish.* The circle was bisected from **north** to **south** and from **east** to **west**. At each end of the two diameters were represented the bear and the rattlesnake. The *four radii* formed by the intersecting diameters, and pointing as it were to the **cardinal directions**, were called *tamaiawot pomo,* the hands of the world. Parallel to the circle on one side, and apparently outside of it, was a representation of mountains, *tota-kolauwot,* literally, rock-wood or stone-timber. This representation may have consisted of no more than a line. In the two quadrants of the circle farthest away from this mountain symbol, were placed representations respectively of the raven, of the spider called *kuikhingish,* or the tarantula. In the center of the circle, where the two diameters intersected, was a hole perhaps a foot and a half across, called the navel. This is said to have had reference to death, to have represented the grave, and indicated to the initiates the fate that would overtake them if they disobeyed. (The ceremonial feathers of an initiate were buried in this hole after his death.) The world is thought to be tied at the *north, south, east,* and *west* with hair-ropes, *yula-wanaut* or a rod or cane, *nakhat,* to which one of the *four hair ropes* is tied. . . . The entire *torokhoish* painting "filled the *wamgush,"* being apparantly about twelve or fifteen feet in diameter . . . the old man instructed the boys.

A short rope . . . was laid next to the hole in the center of the painting. The boys went to the *wanaut* and, holding their feet together, made three jumps along it. Thereupon they spat into the hole, thereby ending the ceremony.

When one of the initiated, the *pumalum,* dies, the ground-painting is again made. In the hole in the center are buried his head-dress, *cheyat,* and similar articles. At the end of the ceremony the initiates squat in a *circle*, with their hands stretched forward, growl or blow three times, and erase the painting. . . .

The ceremonial structure or *wamgush* . . . is an open enclosure of brush. It is only a few feet high, so that it can be looked over from the outside. The *eastern* end is left open. At the *north* and *south* are small gaps used as entrances. A little distance to the *east* is a small brush enclosure in which the dancers put on their ceremonial dress. When there is dancing in the *wamgush* as in the *tanish* or dancing in connection with the *toloache* ceremony, the *pumalum* or initiated dancers stand at the *western* or closed end. A fire is in the middle. The singers, old men, sit at the open or *east* end, and behind them are women who sing. The people who are looking on are behind these. Half of the dancers proceed from the small enclosure around the *southern* side of the *wamgush* and enter at the *north*, while the other half pass around the *northern* end and enter from the *south*.

"The Religion of the Luiseño Indians of Southern California," *University of California Publications in American Archaeology and Ethnology*, Constance Goddard DuBois, 1908, pp. 176-180

A combination of three ancient ways is found in this ceremony: the four directions are honored, the circle is celebrated, and the number four becomes prime. This must have been a very beautiful ritual; the sand painting would be well worth seeing, I am sure.

———————————————— ⊕ ————————————————

WORLD BINDING SNAKES
CHUMASH

The unifying symbol of Chumash cosmological lore is the encircled cross, consisting of a *circle* with a *cross* in the center. The cross divides the circle into *four equal sections*, corresponding to the *fourfold divisions of the cosmos*. The vertical line represents the linking of the divine powers of the *north* and *south*, and the horizontal line represents the *east-west* solar path. . . .

Piliqutayiwit reports that that Chumash called these deities *Ma'aqsiq Itasup,* two divine beings holding the earth so that it remained in a fixed position. This appellation means Binders of *Shup,* the earth, and they were symbolized as two giant serpents. . . . Eagle . . . rules the upper world under the directions of the Creator, so these *Ma'aqsig* did not replace the Eagle's control of the heavens but instead served . . . as the guardian snakes of the sacred *north* and *south mountains*. They were earthly representatives of the powers that maintained order in the larger cosmos. It is possible, therefore, that the North Star was the patron deity of the Chumash *northern Binding Snake*, while Sirius was the patron of the *southern Binding Snake*.

The *east-west* line had a mirror-image symbolism. It connected the rising and setting sun. Piliqutayiwit says there were only two Binding Snakes, ruling the north and south, so we might conclude that the east-west line of the Chumash did not have binding spirits to hold it in place. This would explain why the solar deity wanders along a wide arch on the horizon during its annual pattern of rising and setting. There were no *Ma'aqsiq* to force the sun to rise and set every day at the *cardinal points of east and west*.

The responsibility for keeping the sun from wandering all over the horizon probably fell to the two Binding Snakes from the north and south, who alternately pushed the sun back and forth in conflicts of will. Thus, as the sun approached its extreme northern sunrise point at the summer solstice, the northern *Ma'aqsiq* resurged and pushed it back south to moderate the summer heat. Each day thereafter, the sun rose farther and farther toward the south on the horizon and reduced the southern sphere of influence. Finally, at the winter solstice, the southern snake reasserted itself and pushed the sun back north to renew its rule during spring and summer. Through this endless cycle of the seasons, the east-west line of the sun constantly changed its rising and setting positions.

A Circle Within the Abyss: Chumash Metaphysics,
John Anderson, 1994, pp. 21-22

Piliqutayiwit is a contemporary Chumash who enjoys sharing the ancient ways of his People. Here he offers an explanation of how special beings care for the world's daily round so that the People may live.

———————————— ⊕ ————————————

ENCIRCLED CROSS DESIGN
CHUMASH

Chumash astronomers, like those of ancient Europe, looked around them and wondered why the earth did not revolve like the sky. It seemed fixed in place, unmoving. To express this ordering of life on earth, the Chumash used the Encircled Cross to symbolize the cosmic forces which seized the earth in mythic times and stopped it from revolving with the upper worlds. Supernatural powers dwelling in Polaris (in the **north** sky) and Sirius (in the **south** sky) were the dominant forces of order, maintaining the **north-south** line of the cross. The changing path of the sun, moving from **east** to **west,** regulated the weaker east-west line. Combined they divided the earth into *four quarters*.

A Circle Within the Abyss: Chumash Metaphysics,
John Anderson, 1994, p. 5

Each People developed its own unique way of recognizing the directions and giving honor to them. It is sad that so much has been forgotten in regard to their knowledge of ordering the

Ancient petroglyphs near Bishop, California

universe in which they lived. But happily, in our own time, many are coming together to reexplore and promote the ancient ways.

———————————————— ⊕ ————————————————

HEALING CEREMONY
CHUMASH

Recently I had the opportunity to prepare for a healing ceremony held at a home of a family member in Seaside, California. I was asked by Adelina Alva Padilla, a Chumash spiritual leader/medicine woman, to arrange for certain items to be in readiness.

Two years ago a hut was constructed on the family property. It is considered to be a holy place like a church: a place to pray anytime. The hut is left up throughout the year, but during ceremonial times, twelve 12-ft.-tall willow poles are set in the ground standing straight up a few feet away from the base of the hut surrounding it, providing a *circular walkway*. These poles represent the twelves brothers and sisters of a deceased brother. When the poles become too weathered they may be replaced with fresh ones. The ones that were too weathered are then broken and burned in the outside firepit along with any weathered branches and leaves. One time the local city officials wanted the hut to be taken down because it was visible to the nearby traffic. However, miraculously, the willows that are part of the hut structure sprouted new leaves and continue to be alive. Adelina indicated that this structure is living and, like any living trees, by city ordinance they cannot be cut down indiscriminately. There is a *circular firepit* in the center of the floor and outside there is another *circular sacred fire* for ceremonies. Rocks are placed around the base of the hut's circumference. During the year individuals may paint these rocks or leave a written message of some kind. The outdoor fire pit has rocks lining it. Those present surround it during ceremonial times. The hut is made of willow poles. There is an *eastern* entrance and a *western* exit.

Four directional colors are maintained. Yellow is for the *east*, red for the *south*, black for the *west*, and white for the *north*. Blue represents the sky and green represents the earth.

Herbs are important in the ceremonies. I gathered mugwort which was used for the floor covering. Also, some of the stalks are bound together for tossing into the fire as offerings and some are placed around the hut. She also asked me to mix sage with the mugwort to make certain stalks. Some of these were burned in the fire, others were placed around the hut, while others were given away. I also had to cover *four* of the upright poles with loose mugwort and sage all the way up the pole to represent the *four directions*.

The firekeeper began the sacred fire the night before (Saturday) and it was kept going until midnight the next day (Sunday). I also made prayer ties of wild tobacco (from the Chumash Reservation area near Santa Barbara) mixed with other commerically available natural tobacco and sage in 3-inch cotton squares in the colors of the *four directions*.

Adelina shared lots of wisdom and did two ceremonies: one beginning at 1:00 p.m. Sunday and the other at about 5:30 p.m. The first ceremony was for remembrance of our family's deceased relative. She burned herbs and tobacco in the outside fire, talked, prayed, and drummed. Singing standing up, she *circled the drum* during the songs. Then she gave a blessing with eagle wings. She herself also had tied extra sage and cloth to *four* poles behind the outdoor fire in full view of the participants. These were in the colors of the *four directions*. Another woman assisted her this time, but at other times a year previous she had been accompanied by *four female helpers*. On Saturday night she had also set up an altar which contained a picture of the deceased family member and was used to hold her sacred ceremonial items. Sometime later I was directed to place *four* eagle feathers, two on each side of the deceased relative's photo as well as prayer ties and sage and mugwort which I positioned decoratively.

Oh, yes, during the 3:00-5:30 p.m. time period when others were taking a break she had a chair draped with a multicolored blanket and sage and mugwort placed nearby. An elderly gentleman sat down for a healing blessing. She doctored him. From the outside I brought to her burning sage in an abalone shell. She lit sage and mugwort and dropped them into the unlit interior firepit of the hut. She honored the *four directions* each time that she gave an offering.

During the second ceremony she shared much wisdom and teachings with everyone. At this time my mother (an elder who is close to death) was brought out for a special blessing. Adelina acknowledged her. Then her assistant passed out mixed tobacco and sage prayer ties to those present and directed them to take a pinch of tobacco and one at a time *circle the fire* and drop the tobacco offering into it. Adelina would speak, sing, or drum during this time. Then she asked each person to pass by the *east* side of the fire, approach my mom, show respect, and place a prayer tie on her lap or other place on her body and then go back to their place by way of the *west* side of the fire. My mother was placed within the *circular walkway* able to face the *south* side of the outside fire. Adelina sang to her special comfort songs. My mother responded to her, even though she is in the last stages of Alzheimer's disease.

During this second ceremony she asked my niece to bring inside the hut all the children present for them to listen to teaching, and they spoke about the deceased relative to keep him present in their lives. The year before, my niece had been given a drum to help teach the children.

We were told that a *clockwise circling* of the fire or other sacred place is for the living, while a *counter-clockwise circling* is for those who have passed on. Adelina then "sent things ahead to the spiritual world" for my mother to have them waiting for her when she passed on. Some of these items were a beautifully painted gourd dipper, a sheathed carved bone knife, several empty woven baskets, a herb-containing basket, etc. She sang many times and the participants made one more offering of tobacco to the fire and the ceremony was over. A feast followed, but Adelina continued to fast.

Interview with Mary Ann Chioino Kline, Seaside, CA, July 12, 1997

This ceremony took place on June 29, 1997 and was the second in honor of the deceased relative. Though the setting was urban, the People were able to marvelously celebrate their ancient ways in regard to prayerfully honoring the directions, gathering in the circle, and expressing a unified fourness of activity.

—————————— ⊕ ——————————

SWEATHOUSE
TUBATULABAL

Each hamlet had its sweathouse. To build a sweathouse a spot was picked near a spring or live stream so that a pool could be made. A *round hole* was then dug about *four feet deep* and fifteen feet wide.

Three oak posts about fifteen inches in diameter and seven and one half feet long were cut. These posts, which forked at one end, were set in the ground in a straight line, *east* and *west*, inside the hole. A pole eight inches in diameter and fifteen feet long was then set in the forks of the three posts. A series of smaller poles were laid side by side from the ridgepole to the ground on both the *north* and *south* sides. The same kind of brush they used to cover their dwellings was then piled on top and the whole building completely covered with about one foot of dirt. A doorway three and one-half feet high and two feet wide was then formed in line with the center upright post on the *south* side by lashing a pole *four feet* long across the top of the door area and cutting of the poles below. From the door a dirt ramp led down into the house and at the end of the ramp a small fire would be built. Two fire tenders with their piles of oakwood sat on either side of the fire. As many as 30 bathers could be accommodated in the sweathouse, and they sat with their backs to the four foot dirt walls. Both men and women usually sang and smoked sparingly or chewed tobacco mixed with lime while bathing. The women always took their sweat baths first and the men stayed in longer, sometimes as long as three hours. When the sweat bath was finished, all bathers ran out and plunged into the cold water. Boys and girls usually were about fifteen years old before they were considered old enough to stand a sweat bath.

Indian County of the Tubatulabal, Bob Powers, 1981, p. 9-10

Alignment of posts according to the four directions was a time-honored architectural activity for this People. A circle is by nature inclusive and allows for many expressions of unity among those gathered.

———————————————— ⊕ ————————————————

MARU DANCE
POMO

By 10:30 p.m. about 100 people had assembled in the Dance House, an approximately *circular structure* about 45 feet in diameter. It is built of lumber, entirely above ground, has eaves about six feet high, and its shake-covered roof is supported by rafters whose upper ends rest on a massive center pole probably 12 feet in height. There are no side posts. The floor is hardpacked earth with no covering of any kind. A bench of planks against the wall provides seating for the audience.

Entrance to the Dance House is through a tunnel about 10 feet in length facing toward the *southwest*. A few feet directly in front of the inner end of the tunnel is the fire, with a smoke hole in the roof directly above it. The fire is, as of old, presided over by the usual official Firetender.

Everyone present was attired in ordinary clothing, except that the skirts of the women participating in the dances were extremely long, sometimes touching the floor and concealing almost completely the bare feet of the dancers. Both men and women performers were bare-footed. . . .

At about 11:00 p.m. the singers took their places on a bench just behind the center pole and began the first song. This was led by the prophet, Essie Parrish, as were all other songs. . . . Several preliminary songs were sung, accompanied by *four* men as burden singers. The prophet and two of the men used clapper rattles. No drum of any kind was used.

After the opening songs a woman took her place immediately in front of the center pole and spoke at some length in the local dialect, interspersed from time to time with some expressions in English, and with several references to "our Leader." This speech ended with a very Christian phrase, which left no doubt that it was definitely intended as an invocation. The prophet then took her place before the center pole and made a stirring exhortation to all present. This was followed by more singing. . . .

Then through the tunnel came the first file of dancers, 11 in number (nine women and two men), to perform the flower dance. The woman leading the group carried in her right hand a "baton" 18 inches long made of flowers. In her left hand was a flower *circlet* or wreath about a foot in diameter. About her neck hung a tremendous flower wreath. Each of the other dancers was similarly bedecked except that each had a floral wreath in each hand. . . . One woman without flowers brought up the rear. . . . All flowers in these decorations were fresh garden flowers. . . .

The line of dancers marched in a *counter-clockwise* direction *four times* around the fire and finally to a position behind the center pole and the singers, who sang continuously throughout the entrance of the dancers. After a short interval the singing resumed and the dancers moved out and danced *four times* around the fire, in a ***counter-clockwise*** direction.

One feature reminiscent of aboriginal patterns was the use of the hands. Dancers, especially women dancers, formerly carried in their hands certain objects, such as tassel-like pendants of tules or rushes, which they brought alternately up and down in time to the rhythm of the music. The floral pieces carried by these dancers were manipulated in the same manner.

The end of this set of dances concluded with dancers divided into two lines on either side of the Dance House, facing toward the audience. After a short interval the dancers quickly faced inward toward each other, where they danced in place for a short time. The lines then advanced, each dancer passing through the opposite line and coming to a position facing the audience. Immediately the dancers whirled so that the two lines again faced each other. This action was repeated *four times*. Finally the dancers passed in single file, in a ***counter-clockwise*** direction, *four times* around the center pole and fire, and out through the tunnel entrance, thus concluding this first cycle of dances. As they passed through the tunnel they left their floral ornaments on some shelves on either side of the tunnel.

"The Stewarts Point Maru of 1958," S.A. Barrett in *The Maru Cult
of the Pomo Indians: A California Ghost Dance Survival*,
Clement Meighan & Francis Riddell (Eds.), 1972, pp. 112-114

Essie Parrish, a Kashia Pomo from Stewarts Point Rancheria, was a well-known leader of the Bole Maru religious movement in the 1950s. The Dances of July 3, 1958, which in part are described here, expresssed the People's contemporary spirituality. She led ceremonies that blended both aboriginal and Christian elements. But the counter-clockwise circling within the round house and the musical accompaniment of four men as well as southwest directionality attests to the importance and continuance of the ancient ceremonial ways.

*Esselen traditional tribal
territory, Carmel Valley*

Ancient petroglyphs near Bishop, California

GREAT BASIN CULTURAL AREA

PINENUT DANCE
WASHOE

One special man, says Hank Pete, dreamed about pinenuts and prayed for them. He was not a shaman but he had power. . . . He prayed that the pinenuts increase in number and not be full of worms. This man was the leader of the pinenut dance and was the person who decided whether the pinenuts were ready for picking. If people were to pick the pinenuts without the leader's consent, says Pete, the nuts would be wormy and rotten.

Pinenuts were probably the most important single food of the Washo. The pinenut dance (gumsabá'ai) was held in the fall of the year before the pinenut harvest. The leader called the people together in Double Springs Flat by sending around a knotted cord. The knots represented the number of days remaining before the ceremony was to begin. The messenger untied a knot every day as he traveled about calling people. As the people assembed, the leader of the communal rabbit hunt gathered as many people as possible for a large rabbit drive, and outstanding hunters would organize communal deer hunts. The hunting drives lasted *four days* after which the Washo began the pinenut dance.

The pinenut dance lasted *four nights*. Each morning everyone had to take a bath. During the day the Washo engaged in a variety of games and races, all accompanied by heavy gambling. People of different moieties opposed each other in the games. The most popular games were men's footall, a ball race, foot races, archery contests, the hand game and women's shinny. Usually teams from the different moieties played each other in all the games.

Men's football was played on a field with goals at either end. The object was to kick a small buckskin ball between the two sticks forming the goal. Five or six men played on a side. The games began with the throwing of the ball between the two teams in the middle of the field. Wreslting was allowed in the football game. One goal won the game.

The ball race was also played by men. Two teams arranged themselves in straight lines at right angles to a line between the paired sticks forming the goal. Each team had a ball which at the start of the game was in the possession of the team member at the end of the line farthest from the goal. The object was to kick the ball from man to man down the line and through the goal. The first team to kick its ball through the goal won the game. . . .

The foot races of both the men and women began with a challenge. One moiety challenged the other by individual members running to the center of the *camp circle*, depositing bets which were tied onto sticks, and retiring. People then dashed from the other moiety, which was camped on the other side of the camp circle, and called the bets in the same way. All of the betting was man to man. The identities of the runners were kept secret until the race began because shamans might have attempted some sorcery against a contestant. The race was to halfway point and return and usually took several hours. Runners adorned themselves for the race: Indians of the *East moiety* painted white marks on their bodies and wore an eagle feather; those of the *West moiety* painted red marks. . . . The winner of the race was bathed by a female relative, and the basket was thrown into the crowd. . . . Also, anyone from the losing side could come and take the clothes the winner had been wearing.

Archery contests began with a challenge. The targets were two round sticks about 4 ft. high set at opposite ends of the course. *Four men* competed, two on a side. At each end of the course stood a member of each team. These two men shot three arrows apiece at the opposite goal. A hit scored *four points*; an arrow placed nearer the goal than any of the opponents' arrows counted one point. Eight or 10 points won the game.

The hand game was played by men and women. The game was played with *four bones*, two of which had black wrappings around them, and 10 tally sticks. The tally sticks were divided five to a side. Two men from one side hid a bone in each of their hands. A person from the other side who had the reputation of being a good gambler tried to guess the location of the bones marked with the black wrappings. The side hiding the bones scored a point if the man guessed incorrectly. Only the team in possession of the bones could score ponts. The game ended when one side had captured all of the tally sticks. The side with the bones sang, and the men hiding the bones sometimes played tricks such as putting both bones in the same hand to confuse and rattle the guesser.

A similar game was played by old men. They used *four long sticks*, two of which were wrapped as in the hand game. The sticks were hidden behind a winnowing basket, and eight tally sticks were used. . . .

Women played shinny on a field from 50 to 100 yards long with *circular goals* about 7 ft. in dia. drawn at each end. Betting was carried on. . . . Each player had a stick with which to propel a braided rope of deer hide toward the goal. The game began with the braided piece of hide thrown between the teams in the middle of the field. The women tried to knock the rope into their goals with the sticks. The rope could not be stepped on or picked up with the hand. Four to seven women played on a side. One point won the game.

The dancing took place in the evenings. Both men and women danced and sang, carrying the tools they used to gather and prepare the pinenuts: the burden baskets, hooked poles for drawing the cones closer, straight poles for knocking down the cones, manos and metates for grinding the nuts to flour, and the paddles for stirring the mush. . . . People *danced clockwise in a circle*. During the dancing, the leader moved about talking and praying for pinenuts and all other Indian foods. The leader told people to be good, to treat children and old people with kindness, and to be good to their wives. . . . On the *fourth night*, women laid out pinenuts and all other food and prayed over it. After the dancing on the fourth night, the people bathed and scattered to their pinenuts plots to harvest the crop. When a family had piled up the first batch of the new crop for cooking, a woman threw some small stones over the pile of cooking pinenuts and prayed that the crop be good and not make people sick. . . .

People still go to the hills in family units to gather pinenuts; although pinenuts are no longer a staple, they remain an important food for many families. The attempted revival indicates an interest in the pinenut ceremony, but no one seems able or willing to arrange the dance. Its revival in 1952 will probably be one of the last attempts at holding an annual pinenut dance.

"The Persistence of Aboriginal Ceremonies Among the Washo Indians,"
The Washo Indians of California and Nevada,
Stanley & Ruth Freed, August 1963, pp. 34-36

This special time for the People offers examples of the unique use of four items (days, nights, individuals, bones, sticks), the grouping of the People into east and west moieties, and the gathering in a circle and dancing clockwise to make a sacred circuit area, expressing many of the external forms of Native spirituality.

Desert witness to Creator's gifts

Reconstructed Mandan circular dwellings in North Dakota, beside the Missouri River

FOUR POLE CEREMONY
PAWNEE

This ritual of the Skull bundle symbolized the forming of the Skiri federation and the organization of the bundle scheme, which is its objective expression. Unfortunately the ritual is lost beyond recovery, but portions have been related by the few who knew about it. The central idea, as taught by the priests, is that First Man was placed in Center Village. The Evening Star bundle had been given to him and the people of this village. Later, out of the *west* came *four* villages associated as one, Old Village. There were *four sacred bundles* in Old Village, *each representing one of the semicardinal directions*. The leader of the bundles was the Big Black Meteoric Star bundle, and the head of its village insisted on being spokesman for the people of both Center and Old Village. Faced with this dilemma, First Man divided the functions of priest and chief, as directed by Evening Star in a vision. He gave the position of priest to the leader of Old Village and took the office of chief for himself. Then, as symbolized in the man's step, First Man received the bow, arrow, and other contents that formed the nucleus of the Skull bundle, which stood as a gift from Tirawahat to First Man and symbolized his chieftainship. The ritual associated with the Skull bundle is believed to have derived from the Evening Star bundle, a belief which historical analysis seems to justify. Among other functions, it presided over the meeting of the chiefs in late spring and became associated with the Four Pole Ceremony, symbolizing the

566

renewal of the original federation of the villages. At the same time the four leading bundles were given their ceremonies and ritual functions.

The bundle is now in the American Museum of Natural History, New York. The outer wrappings are now of black cloth, but were formerly of hide. Around the whole is the inevitable hair rope, the symbol of a priest. Tucked under the bindings are a wooden bow and three arrows. (It is said that there should be *four*.) These . . . symbolize the handing of these implements to First Man. They are very sacred because of this association. . . . When the Morning Star Village made the human sacrifice, this bow was used to shoot the victim. The reasons for this association are not known.

With the bow are two pipestems, one pipe stoker, and three sticks of unknown use. The skull is bound to a stick by which it is held securely to the bundle. Finally, there is a small bundle of buffalo skin containing a sacred pipe with a decorated stem. . . .

Inside of a wrapping of black silk is a buffalo skin and within this some white cloth. The contents of the bundle are the following: Mother Corn wrapped in buffalo skin; two ears of corn wrapped in cotton cloths; skin of a hawk with wrapper of deer and buffalo skin; a large mussel shell with painting outfit; an arrow-straightener of elkhorn; a pipe bowl wrapped in buffalo wool; an otter collar, regalia for a warrior, now in fragments; packages of red and white paints; native tobacco; a package of plumseeds; five braids of sweetgrass; and two swan heads.

The Four Pole Ceremony was held in a circular enclosure. For this an embankment was thrown up with an opening to the *east*. In front of this entrance was a small mound of earth taken from the centrally constructed fire pit. Within the enclosure at the *west* side was a raised altar. Around the inside of the ring of earth was a screen of green branches set up in the ground. Arranged around the fireplace were *four poles* bearing tufts of branches at their tops: a white pole of cottonwood, a red of box elder, a black of elm, and a yellow of willow. All of the bundles are brought to the ceremony by their keepers, who sit . . . according to their rank and the geographical relations of the respective villages. As will be noted, . . . most of the bundles are upon the *north* side of the enclosure; these lived on the *north side* of the Loup River, the others upon the *southside*. . . .

The leading bundles are associated with the four poles according to the colors, as stated in the color name of the bundle. These bundles, poles, colors, etc., represent the powers in the *four quarters of the world* and also stand for *spring, summer, autumn,* and *winter*, but in no fixed order, the season a bundle represents being determined by the order of the ceremony. . . .

When everything is ready for the ceremony to begin, the Skull bundle is opened and the skull placed in front of the bundle. Red paint is then mixed with fat and rubbed over the whole skull. With blue paint a circle is drawn around the face and a line down over the nose, the painting of Tirawahat. . . .

The first important procedure is the bringing in of the *four poles*, one for each of the leading bundles. Selected are *four warriors* who take positions corresponding to the *four directions*. Each wears full war regalia: the otter fur collar, the sacred ear of corn on the left shoulder, and the hawk on the right. Each warrior placed on his head a ball of down feathers, and transversely in the scalplock, an eagle feather. Their faces are painted red, streaked down the sides, and on the forehead is a bird's foot mark like the constellation in the Milky Way. Each carries a warclub and the pipe from one of the leading bundles.

Once outside, the *four warriors* dance while the people gather about them, forming *four groups*. Then each group follows its leader, who leads off in a known direction. Scouts have been sent out to locate the trees. Each scout now reports to his own party that he has found an enemy standing among the timber. The party then approaches as if stealing upon an enemy. All the warriors are dressed as if for battle. When the tree is sighted they rush it, and the first to strike it counts coup.

Each bundle requires a different kind of tree: willow for the Big Black Meteoric Star, elm for the Yellow Star, cottonwood for the White Star, and box elder for the Red Star bundle.

A virgin has been selected to chop the tree; but before she can approach, the leading warrior, who bears the bundle pipe, must make the regular smoke offering. For this he stands *east* of the tree; upon completing the offering, he deposits the ashes on the tree's *west* side. Then a second man comes forward and makes the regular meat offering.

The girl now takes the ax and, approaching from each of the *four directions*, strikes off a chip, each time with *four feints*. After this her uncles and brothers cut down the tree while the people shout. As the tree falls, they make all the noise they can symbolizing victory over the enemies. The warriors then bear the tree toward the village, the people following. *Four times* they pause to rest; the old women *circle* about the men and tree, making obscene jests and proposals, or rather, using words that can be so interpreted. . . .

As each party reaches the enclosure for the ceremony, the bearers of the tree make feints at the entrance and so continue until someone comes forward to count a coup, stating that the tree is entering the door of the enemy. As soon as this procedure is over, they enter.

During this pole gathering, the priests and a few old men remain in the ceremonial lodge. According to the proper formula, the *four holes* are dug to receive the poles. Then a secret ceremony is performed: Fat is taken from the bundle, made into cakes the size of each hole, and one placed in the bottom of each; then over it is sprinkled some pulverized native tobacco. The sacred knowledge is that the fat symbolized the earth; the tobacco, the people. Before the holes are dug the fireplace is excavated. First a stake is driven at the center of the enclosure and with a rope from the bundle the *circumference of the fireplace* is marked off. The stake is withdrawn and an offering of fat and tobacco placed in the bottom. The fat offering is then taken from all the holes and carried to the dumping place *east* of the door, and the earth from the diggings ultimately heaped over it.

As each party brings in its pole, the priest in charge fills the pipe and makes the smoke offering. The appropriate song rituals are sung; the warriors dance *four times* and then plant the pole. As the poles stand, they are trimmed to the very top where a few of the branches are left. The painting songs are then sung, as the priest paints each pole its proper color.

When the poles are all in place and painted, the vital part of the ceremony begins. The keeper, or chief, with the skull in his hands, stands facing the bowl, fixes his eyes upon the shell in the water, and recites a ritual recounting the creative acts of Tirawahat. Unfortunately, this ritual is lost and with it, the meaning of the whole procedure. This ends the ceremony proper.

During the following night certain doctors appear in skins of bears, loons, wildcats, and wolves, charging about through the camp fighting the people.

The final act of the priests is a ritual to "open the roads to the enemy's country and to the buffalo." As the priests sing the proper songs, the keeper of the Skull bundle dances with it and makes certain movements to each of the *four directions*. Then with loud shouting the people join in the dance. After this ceremony war parties can set out and the chief's council can plan the buffalo hunt. . . .

It is not certain at what time of the year the ceremony was held. The moving of the Pawnee to Oklahoma disarranged their whole cycle. The buffalo were gone and without them many of the rituals could not be given. The relations of the stars to the seasons, the direction from which the storms came, etc., were all different. Consequently, it is not strange that no one now knows the precise place of the Four Pole Ceremony in the yearly cycle. However, it has been put where those competent to have an opinion think it should be, i.e., before the autumn and winter hunt.

Ceremonies of the Pawnee, James Murie, 1989, pp. 107, 109-111

This ancient Four Pole Ceremony recounts the beginnings of the Pawnee People as a tribe and highlights their holy use of sacred bundles. The rituals would energize the People on a regular basis so that they would feel a greater sense of their unity and power. At the same time, they would be able to give thanks for the gifts bestowed on them by (the) Creator (Tirawahat). The cardinal directions, as well as the intercardinals, are symbolically very important in the ceremony as are the four seasons. Four poles made from four kinds of trees, four warriors, four groups of people, four attempts to chop the trees, four pauses to rest, four holes dug into the ground to receive the poles, dancing four times: all this made for a highly symbolic and didactic ceremony.

———————————— ⊕ ————————————

A MEDICINE WHEEL
BLOOD

He did not . . . die a young man because of weakened lungs. Rather, he had a long and productive career. He should have been appointed head chief of the tribe when his brother died in 1907, but in the minds of Indian Department officials, the stigma of the police battle still hung over his head and the position was denied him. So more and more he turned to religious matters. Eight times he was a member of the sacred Horn Society; *four times* he owned medicine pipes; and twice he was the owner of the beaver bundle, the most ancient holy object on the reserve. He also joined several religious societies, including the doves, brave dogs, braves, Black Catchers, and dogs.

When he died in the spring of 1940, he had become recognized as a leading holy man and warrior. He had been a member of the Horn Society that year and his tepee had been pitched to hold their meetings. Around it he had placed a *circle of stones* in addition to the usual pegs and had marked two stone fireplaces inside. He told his son Bob that after his death, the lodge was to be moved and *four lines of stones* placed on the ground, each extending from the circle to the *cardinal points*, thus creating a *medicine wheel*.

"The lines signify that he was a brave man," said his son-in-law, "a leader who had been to war. It was Steel's wish to have this done in tribute to him as a warrior chief."

The medicine wheel is still there today, an ancient tradition that stands as a reminder of a brave man who should have died in 1891, but didn't.

> *The Amazing Death of Calf Shirt and Other Blackfoot Stories: Three Hundred Years of Blackfoot History*, Hugh Dempsey, 1994, p. 160

Steel, whose People, the Bloods, are part of the Blackfeet Confederacy, lived in difficult but interesting transitional times. His familiarity with the ancient ways is expressed even after his death.

----------------------------------- ⊕ -----------------------------------

PIPE CEREMONY
CROW

. . . the first thing I do in all my prayers is to hold my smoke up high above me and offer my smoke and my prayer to Acbadadea with words like I just said. Then I will come down with the pipe, and I will offer a prayer to Grandmother Earth and the Medicine Fathers, who are represented by the *four directions* of space.

Grandmother Earth is a way of expressing that part of Acbadadea which is created in this world, because all that we have in this world is created by and from Acbadadea, but Acbadadea is also above all things. It is the same for the Medicine Fathers. When I move the pipe in a *circle* to all of the *four directions*, it also has a similar meaning, because all the winds, the powers, and Nature, wherever you look or wherever you go, come from Acbadadea. By recognizing this and by thinking about this, you can understand a great deal about who you are. So when you hear me pray to any of my Medicine Fathers or to Grandmother Earth or to one of the *directions of the Four Winds*, you will know the meaning of what I am saying. You might say that each of these things represents, in one way or another, part of Acbadadea, but always remember that Acbadadea is much more than all of these things.

> *Yellowtail, Crow Medicine Man and Sun Dance Chief:*
> *An Autobiography*, Thomas Yellowtail, 1991, p. 102

God, First Maker (Acbadadea), is always supreme in Crow worship, but other created beings are venerated with prayer. The pipe ceremony always acknowledges Acbadadea, Grandmother Earth, and the four spatial directions of the winds that are ritually remembered with the circular motion of the pipe.

⊕

SWEATLODGE CEREMONY
CROW

The sweat ritual had *four cycles*. First, after rocks heated over an open fire had been placed in a central pit and the participants had entered, the lodge was sealed, and *four dippers* of water were poured over the rocks to fill the lodge with steam. Prayers and songs were offered. After the door had been briefly opened to refresh the participants, the second cycle began. This time, seven dippers of water were poured over the rocks. Again, prayer and song were offered. In the third cycle, ten dippers of water were poured, and in the fourth, an uncounted number, again accompanied by prayer and song. With the completion of the fourth cycle, the door was opened, and the participants plunged into a nearby creek or river.

By undergoing the *four cycles* of the sweat bath, the participants came to recognize its association with the *four seasons, the four directions of the circle*, and the *four components of the world*—fire, rock, water, and air. In the sweat ritual, the participants merged their essence with the primal elements, facilitating prayer, sacrifice, and spiritual cleansing.

The World of the Crow Indians: As Driftwood Lodges, Rodney Frey, 1987

The sweat lodge ceremony constantly brings before the People the ancient beliefs in regard to the circularity and fourness of life as it comes from the hands of the Creator.

———————————————— ⊕ ————————————————

HEALING CEREMONY
GROS VENTRE

Yellow Man's father-in-law was told to call seven men and six women to sing Bull Lodge's medicine songs as he doctored. The seven men must take a place in the tipi to their right as they enter, and the six women must stand directly opposite to the seven men, going to their left as they enter. The patient must lie with his head toward the *east*, where the sun rises. A filled pipe with kinnickinnic is to be placed by his bed, with the stem pointing in the same direction. When this was done Bull Lodge was told the patient was ready.

Bull Lodge took his drum, his medicines, and the black cloth that he intended to use in his doctoring. Entering the tipi where the sick man was, he approached at the patient's left side. He sat down on the ground at the foot of the bed and took up his drum. Speaking to the men and women who were there to sing for him, he said, "I will sing my song three times. Then I will turn the drumming and singing over to you."

There was a man present named Many Tipis who was noted for his singing and quick memory. When Bull Lodge gave his song the third time, Many Tipis was singing it along with him. Many Tipis sang it himself the *fourth* time. Bull Lodge told the people that almost everything was done as it was supposed to be in the preparing of the tipi and patient. But one mistake was made. In the articles to be given to Bull Lodge for his services, he had told them he was commanded not to receive any weapons or anything that was sharp. This rule applied to the *first four times* that he doctored. But after the *fourth time*, he could receive weapons. Now Yellow Man's brother-in-law had given a gun, an arrow scabbard made of mountain lion's skin, an elk horn bow, and a robe with porcupine quill work in it, as well as seven horses. So the gun, scabbard and bow had to be replaced by two robes, to make it a proper gift for Bull Lodge at this time.

Bull Lodge stripped off his clothes, all but his breech cloth. Taking the red paint that is commonly used by the Gros Ventres, he painted all the scars on his arms, legs, and chest which had been made during his fasting experiences. He also painted his forehead and wrists. Then, taking the drum, he sang his song keeping time. He sang it *four* times, then he turned the drum and the singing over to the men and women who had come to sing as he doctored.

Bull Lodge placed a wooden bowl beside the patient. It was about six inches in diameter from rim to rim and about two or three inches deep at the center of the hollow. A rainbow design was painted around the edge of the rim. The inside was all black, and the outside was dark red. Bull Lodge had made this wooden bowl out of a Box Elder burl, especially for doctoring purposes.

Yellow Man had been covered with the black cloth, and Bull Lodge removed it. Then he began to draw or suck with his mouth on the patient's chest. After each time Bull Lodge drew, he would spit the stuff into the wooden bowl. After doing this *four times*, he had the patient turned over, back up. Then Bull Lodge drew on the patient's back with his mouth. Again he did this *four times*, then the singing stopped. The stuff he had drawn out of the patient's chest and back was a mixture of yellow, green and brownish-colored matter.

Then Bull Lodge lit the filled pipe that had been laid beside the patient before he entered. After he had finished smoking, he took the black cloth that had covered the patient and stroked him with it. He drew it from the patient's head along his full length and shook it gently. He performed this *four times*.

Bull Lodge took his drum and sang his song *four times* over the patient. Before turning the drumming and singing over to the seven men and six women, he again doctored the patient by drawing on the chest and back with his mouth. He told those who were there that if his uncle were really bad off, he would doctor him seven times, but that if he were not so bad off, he would cure him by doctoring him *four* times. Bull Lodge ordered the singers to start up again while he covered the patient with a black cloth. He lighted the filled pipe and began smoking. Occasionally he would blow smoke on the cloth covering the patient. He did this *four times*. Then the singers stopped.

Then Bull Lodge gathered up the black cloth with both hands and stood up, raising the cloth and praying. "Father Above Man, I am grateful for these powers to heal and cure. Look down on me. I will raise a body up again." Turning *east* he repeated this, adding the words, "I am using the painting on the shield that you gave me." He turned to the *south* and repeated the prayer. He turned *west* and spoke the same prayer again. Then lowering the black cloth, he blew on it *four times* and slowly spread it out. He prepared incense. Taking the black cloth by one corner with his left hand while holding the bulk with his right hand, he passed it over the incense smoke *four times*. He placed the cloth over the wooden bowl, which contained the stuff he had drawn from the patient's body. Then Bull Lodge lit the pipe again and smoked. He blew smoke on the covered bowl *four times*. Then he stood up with the bowl still covered with black cloth. Holding it up in a gesture of offering he prayed, "Father Above Man, I am grateful for this life you gave me and for these powers to heal and cure. Look down on me. I will raise a body up again." He put the bowl down again and uncovered it. It was empty. The matter in the bowl had mysteriously disappeared. The patient's head was now pointing toward the *west*. It had first been moved to the *east*, then to the *south*, and then *towards the final direction*. This entire ceremony was one day's doctoring.

Now that Bull Lodge had finished doctoring for the day, he turned his attention to the food which had been prepared for them. He asked for a small piece of meat. When it was given to him, he cut it into *four pieces*, each the size of a small mouthful. He then called for a small cup of broth. He held these up for the patient to see and asked Yellow Man if it looked inviting. "Yes," said his uncle, "Feed it to me." Then Bull Lodge made incense. Taking the plate which contained the *four pieces of meat* with his left hand, and the cup with broth in it with his right hand, he held the plate of meat over the incense, then the broth. He raised the plate and cup slightly in a gesture of offering and prayed, "Father Above Man, I am about to feed this food you gave us to a patient who is sick. Look down on us from above as I feed it to my uncle, Yellow Man." After this prayer he sat down and began to feed his uncle.

Bull Lodge took one piece of meat from the plate and held it over the incense, then he held it up for a moment before feeding it to Yellow Man. He took a horn spoon and dipped some of the broth from the cup. He held it up for a moment before putting the spoon to the patient's mouth. Bull Lodge did this until his uncle had eaten all *four pieces of meat* and drunk all the broth in the cup. Then he turned to the seven men and six women who sang and said, "All stand up." Bull Lodge stood up as well and told them to raise up their plates of food. While they held their plates of food up, Bull Lodge prayed. "Father Above Man, I am sharing this food you gave me with these people who are in this tipi. Put your kind thoughts into this food from above, that they may enjoy it and have a long life."

Then they all sat down and ate their food together. Now while all these people were eating, the patient was watching them and he thought he would like a little more to eat. So Yellow Man spoke up and said, "My nephew?" "What is it?" Bull Lodge answered. "These people eating makes me want more," said his uncle, "I wish you would give me something more to eat." And hearing this, Yellow Man's father-in-law said, "I am glad that my son-in-law is better already."

Then Bull Lodge took another piece of meat, and breaking a smaller piece off with his fingers, he dipped it in the broth and fed it to his patient. As he passed each piece to his uncle, Bull Lodge would say, "Father Above Man, look down on me as I feed the sick." He did this until Yellow Man had eaten the entire piece of meat he had in his hand. When the meal was over, Bull Lodge distributed the things that were given him for his services as a doctor.

First he gave one horse and one robe to his friend Sits Like A Woman. His niece, Counts Two Coups, received a horse and so did his sister Bird Woman, and his aunt Crane Woman also got a horse. Bull Lodge kept three head of horses and two robes for himself. After distributing the gifts, he said, "Now I am done, so we will all go home. I will go out first, then the men will follow, then the women. All of you will make a complete *circle* to the left as you go out of the tipi." So he went out first. Then the seven men followed him out, then the six women. When everyone was outside, those who had received horses from Bull Lodge took them away.

THE SECOND DAY

It was understood that Bull Lodge was to continue doctoring his sick uncle, and he notified Yellow Man's father-in-law to have the patient ready for him before the sun rose on the second day. So it was done. Before the sun rose, Yellow Man's father-in-law called Bull Lodge and told him the patient was ready. When Bull Lodge went to his uncle's tipi, Yellow Man said to him, "My nephew, I ask you to doctor me just as you were commanded to do. You are to apply the full force of the power given to you as a doctor." "All right, uncle," Bull Lodge answered, "I will do my best." Now the singers remained silent as Bull Lodge began his doctoring. The patient's head was pointed to the *west*, along with the filled pipe. After the patient was moved, Bull Lodge made incense. Taking his whistle, Bull Lodge held the mouthpiece of the whistle over the incense, then the opposite end, then the mouthpiece again, then the other end. He incensed both ends of the whistle twice, to make *four times*. Bull Lodge then *circled* the patient to his left and stopped at his feet.

Facing away from the patient to the *east*, Bull Lodge blew long on the whistle. Then he turned to the *south* without changing his position, and he again blew on the whistle. Turning to the *west* in the same position, he blew on it again. Then facing the patient, Bull Lodge knelt down, holding the whistle with his left hand as he blew on it once again. This time while blowing the whistle he tapped the sole of the patient's left foot *four times*. He performed this twice on each foot. After this Bull Lodge stood up and *circled* the patient, stopping at his head. With the whistle in his left hand he held it to his mouth and blew, meanwhile stroking the patient from his head down to his feet and also shaking his hand gently. He did this *four times*.

Then Bull Lodge *circled* the patient, moving to his left and stopped at his feet. He knelt down and took the little fingers of his uncle's hands in both of is own hands and gently shook them. He did this *four times*, and after each time he would shake the patient's hand and blow breath on him. Then Bull Lodge pulled on all of the patient's fingers, still holding both hands, and popped the joints. Then he pulled on his uncle's fingers once more and raised him to a sitting position, letting go of his hands.

Yellow Man raised his arms high up above his head, as if stretching. He drew his legs up and crossed them. Then the patient placed his hands on his knees as he sat and looked around the tipi. The singers had remained silent during the entire ceremony. . . .

THE THIRD DAY

The next morning before sunrise, Yellow Man's father-in-law called on Bull Lodge. Bull Lodge told him to prepare the patient by putting his head in the direction of *west*. The seven men and six women were already at the tipi of the sick man when Bull Lodge entered. He had his wooden bowl, whistle, and black cloth with him. He first made incense and incensed his drum. He held it over the smoke, tipping it down slightly in an *easterly direction*. Then he tipped it to the *south*, then to the *west*, and finally to the *north*. Next he incensed the bowl, the whistle, and the black cloth. Taking his drum and holding it above his head, he prayed, "My Father, Mountain Man, I am about to use these things that were supernaturally associated with the shield you gave to me. Look down upon me as I perform with them the way you showed me."

After this prayer, Bull Lodge began to sing. After doing the song once for the singers, he asked them to sing it while he doctored. Before they started, Bull Lodge said, "This time, I'll draw with my mouth three times on the patient's chest and three times on his back." As the singers began, Bull Lodge began to draw on the chest of the patient. After he had drawn three times on the chest he ordered the patient turned over, so he could get at the back. But his uncle said, "I don't need any help, I'll turn over on my stomach without help." He did this. Bull Lodge then drew on the back with his mouth. When he finished, the patient turned over again on his back.

Bull Lodge stood up and *circled the patient* completely, stopping by the patient's side. He took the black cloth and covered the patient with it. He took the wooden bowl and prayed. "My Father, Mountain Man, it was you who appeared to me on the Black Butte. Come to me now and be with me in my first experience as a doctor, I need your help." Then he repeated this short prayer three times with the wooden bowl upraised, and as he did so a slight breath of breeze struck the wooden bowl and his hands. As soon as the breath of breeze came he began to imitate the cry of an eagle. He did this *four times*. Then he told the patient to uncover his face. After this Bull Lodge placed the bowl on the ground before himself and sat down.

The matter he had drawn out of the patient's chest and back was in the wooden bowl he held as he prayed. But when he put the wooden bowl down, the matter had mysteriously disappeared, and three round objects lay in the bowl instead. Those three objects were only recognizable to Bull Lodge. One was yellow, one dark blue, and the other was red. Each was the size of a large marble, and they lay in a row at the bottom of the bowl. Bull Lodge passed the wooden bowl among the people so that they could inspect the mysterious objects.

Bull Lodge then asked that the patient be helped up, but his uncle said, "I don't need any help, I'll get up by myself." And he did. Then

Bull Lodge told the patient to lie down again and he covered him with the black cloth once more. He made incense, and incensed his hands and the wooden bowl while singing his medicine song. After putting down the bowl, Bull Lodge *circled the patient*, stopping at the left side of the bed nearest the tipi. Then he blew on the whistle *four times*. Going all the way around the patient's feet he stopped and blew on the whistle *four times* again, but on the fourth, he blew spasmodically. Bull Lodge *circled* around the patient's right side and blew his whistle in the same way. Then moving around to the patient's head, he stopped and blew on the whistle again *four times*. After this he *circled* around the patient's left side. Grasping the black cloth that was placed over his head, Bull Lodge drew it all the way down the length of his uncle's body, shaking it gently. While he was doing this he said, "Yellow Man arise." He did this *four times*. After the fourth performance, he said, "All right, Yellow Man, stand up." Slowly, Yellow Man turned onto his right side. Then he got onto his hands and knees, then he stood up in a stooped way, using his hands to brace himself on his knees. The strain of his effort was visible to everyone, but he did not fall. Bull Lodge got down on his knees and told Yellow Man to face *in the direction of the rising sun*. Then he told his uncle this: "As I move my hands on the ground, you move your feet, first using your right foot while I use my right hand."

Bull Lodge rubbed his hands on the ground gently. Rubbing his palms together he blew his breath on them. Then he said, "All right, Yellow Man, step." With both palms against the ground Bull Lodge moved his right hand forward towards the *east*, and Yellow Man moved his right foot forward at the same time. Moving his left hand, Bull Lodge said, "Now your left foot." Yellow Man moved his left foot. Then Bull Lodge said to the patient, "Now turn to the *south*." Yellow Man turned in that direction, and Bull Lodge said, "Now do the same thing again." He moved his right hand on the ground, and Yellow Man moved his right foot. This was done for each of the *four directions*, so that Yellow Man took two steps in each direction. Then the entire procedure was repeated. Then Bull Lodge told his uncle to sit down on the bed.

Bull Lodge made more incense, and incensed his hands. Kneeling before the patient, he took out one of the three round objects that had appeared in the wooden bowl. He chose the red one. Holding it in his right hand, he motioned away from himself with it and toward the patient. He did this twice with each hand, making it *four times*. Then he rubbed the object between his hands a few times and stroked the sitting patient from his head to the bed. After dusting his hands, Bull Lodge blew on them, then he stroked the patient with his left hand. He repeated this act twice with each hand to make it *four times*. And Bull Lodge said he was done.

The singers told him the food was ready, and he told them to distribute it, feeding him first. After everyone was served, Bull Lodge told them to stand up and hold their plates high as before while he prayed. Then they all sat down and began to eat. Before taking the first mouthful, each person broke off a small bit of food and placed it on the spot where Bull Lodge made incense.

Then the patient spoke up saying, "I want to eat with you." So Bull Lodge cut *four pieces of meat* from his share and placed them in his medicine bowl. After holding it up and praying, he gave it to the patient. Bull Lodge told him to pick up a single piece of meat with his right hand and say, "All Powerful, look down on the food your son has shared with me. Make it strengthen me as it comes from his hands." "Now use your left hand," Bull Lodge added, "and so on until you have eaten up all four pieces." The patient ate as Bull Lodge ordered. After everyone had eaten, Bull Lodge said, "We are going now, because I am done for this time."

Bull Lodge got up and started to leave the tipi when his sick uncle, Yellow Man, spoke up saying, "I want to go out with you." So he got up and followed Bull Lodge out of the tipi. When they were outside, Bull Lodge said, "Follow me." He led his patient around the tipi, going to his left and circling back to the entrance. Then both of them went back into the tipi. Before Yellow Man sat down he addressed Bull Lodge. "My nephew, you have given life back to me, and I will live it in gratitude to you." Putting his arm around Bull Lodge's neck, he embraced and kissed him. Then Bull Lodge took his leave.

FINISHING THE CURE

Now the three times Bull Lodge said he would doctor his uncle were completed, and Yellow Man was able to walk again. But not all the work was done. Bull Lodge had to give Yellow Man a drink of medicine *four times* before he would be completely well. So he went to his uncle's tipi once a day for *four days* to make the medicine and give it to him. On each of these mid-day visits, Bull lodge took with him his medicine and the three round colored objects which had appeared mysteriously in the wooden bowl. After making the patient's medicine,

Bull Lodge would take one of these objects and stroke him with it. Then he would have his uncle drink the medicine.

On the first of these visits, the medicine was colored yellow, on the second it was colored dark blue, and on the third it was made from hailstone water, which was green. The color appeared as soon as the medicine touched the water. On the fourth visit Bull Lodge made a colorless water, using the supernatural powers that were given to him. Each visit, he covered his wooden bowl with the black cloth and sang his medicine song *four times*. He raised the cloth from the wooden bowl and saw that there was now water in it. Taking a pinch of medicine between his thumb and forefinger, he sprinkled a little bit in *four different places* in the container of water. He said a silent prayer as he held up the medicine, then he dropped the rest of it into the water. It was now ready for the patient to drink. By this time, Yellow Man was far advanced in recovering from his sickness. After he had drunk the medicine on the *fourth day*, Bull Lodge pronounced him cured.

The work of Bull Lodge occurred when he had reached the age of forty, and it was the first of his doctoring experiences.

The Seven Visions of Bull Lodge (As Told by His Daughter, Garter Snake),
George Horse Capture (Ed.), 1992, pp. 68-77

This lengthy healing ceremony makes ample use of doing things in a four-fold pattern. The four directions are part of the healing process also as are the ritual circlings of the patient. Bull Lodge always tried to be ritually accurate when he performed a ceremony. This was his People's tradition.

———————————— ⊕ ————————————

PIPE CEREMONY
DAKOTA

Therefore, by *circling the pipe*, the offering is made to all the gods. The *circle* is the symbol of time, for the daytime, the night time, and the moon time are *circles above the world*, and the year time is a *circle around the border of the world*. Therefore, the lighted pipe moved in a complete *circle* is an offering to all the times.

When the Shaman has completed the *four quarters* and the time he should point the mouthpiece of the pipe toward the sky and say, "I pass the pipe to the father with the sky." This is an offering to the

Wind, for when the *Four Winds* left the lodge of their father, the Wind, he went from it, and dwells with the sky. He controls the seasons and the weather, and he should be propitiated when good weather is desired.

Then the Shaman should smoke the pipe. . . .

The World's Rim: Great Mysteries of the North American Indians,
Hartley Burr Alexander, 1953, p. 8

How prayerful and dignified is the pipe ceremony! It unites all present in solidarity and sends forth prayers that transcend time and space. An unhurried ceremony, it gives ample time for the participants to give themselves over to holy time with the Creator.

———————————————— ⊕ ————————————————

PIPE CEREMONY
DAKOTA

Probably the most instructive native account of the meaning of a ceremonial smoke-offering is that given by Sword, a Dakota shaman. According to this teacher, before a shaman can perform a ceremony in which deities participate, he must fill and light a pipe and say: "Friend of Wakinyan, I pass the pipe to you first. *Circling* I pass to you who dwell with the Father. *Circling* pass to beginning day. *Circling* pass to the beautiful one. *Circling* I complete the *four quarters* and the time. I pass the pipe to the Father with the Sky. I smoke with the Great Spirit. Let us have a blue day."

Beginning with the *West* the mouthpiece is pointed to the *four directions*, or rather to the *Winds of these quarters*. Wakinyan, in the Siouan tetralogies, is the Winged One, associated with the Rock, which is the deity of the West, and the Winged are the strong ones of the West. Next in turn the pipe is offered to the *North Wind*, the *East Wind*, and the *South Wind*. The *North Wind* is the companion of Wazi, the Wizard, "Beginning Day" designates the lodge of the *East Wind*, while the "beautiful one" is the feminine deity who is companion of the *South Wind* and who dwells in his lodge "under the Sun at midday." "It pleases the *South Wind* to be addressed through his companion rather than directly," said Sword. The *Four Winds* are the messengers of the gods, and for this reason should be first addressed. The shaman explained the meaning of the rite as follows:

When the offering has been made to the **South Wind** the Shaman should move the pipe in the same manner until the mouthpiece again points toward the **west**, and say, "Circling I complete the *four quarters* and the time." He should do this because the **Four Winds** are the *four quarters of the circle* and mankind knows not where they may be or whence they may come and the pipe should be offered directly toward them. The *four quarters* embrace all that are on the world and all that are in the sky. . . .

To smoke with the Great Spirit means that the one smoking is in communion with the Great Spirit. Then he may make a prayer. The prayer here is for a blue day. Ordinarily, a blue day means a cloudless or successful day. When a Shaman formally prays for a blue day, it means an enjoyable day and an effective performance of a ceremony.

> *The World's Rim: Great Mysteries of the North American Indians*,
> Hartley Burr Alexander, 1953, pp. 7-8

Circling movements, the four directions, and their respective winds, are recalled as People pray with the sacred pipe.

———————————— ⊕ ————————————

BEAR DANCE
LAKOTA

A man dreams of the bear and so he is very *wakan*. Also he belongs to the Bear Society. The man who dreams of the bear is leader of the whole society. . . .

When a man is wounded, a big tipi is set up in the middle of camp and the wounded man moves into the tipi. Inside the tipi the entire floor is completely covered with sage. And all those who consider themselves Bear, these and only these, move into the tipi with the wounded man. And when the Bears doctor, they all have **round** drums. They sing many very good songs. And so the Bear leader moves about. All those who have been wounded stand and move about. Those who have different types of medicine move about. They are all thought to be very *wakan*. There is a very white medicine and it smells very good. All men find it very pleasing. When they smell it, then the wounds do not fester. They are cured. So it is that for *four nights* the ones who were wounded will participate in ceremonies.

Then all those who had been wounded will come out. So an old man goes about proclaiming this aloud. Perhaps some of the women are menstruating, so none of them come near. The old man goes along. *Around the camp on the inside of the camp circle*, the crier goes along. So then the people stir about and men crowd all around the Bear tipi. Then, as the Bears sing, all of the people stand looking intently at the entrance to the Bear tipi. Suddenly the Bear leader begins to move quickly towards the tipi entrance. Growling ferociously, he comes out of the tipi. His body is painted entirely red and his hands white; he carries a knife. All of the onlookers flee. Then one of the wounded comes out after him, carrying a short staff painted entirely red. Slowly he comes out. The staff is forked at the end. And then the Bear singers come out, singing as loudly as they can. Therefore, the Bear leader and the one who was wounded bend down and move about furiously. . . .

Well now, the wounded begin to walk and they stand facing the *south*. Then they turn and stand facing the *west*. Again they turn and stand facing the *north*. Again they turn and stand facing the *east*. They all stand with their arms raised in prayer. Throughout, they sing songs. Therefore, the Bear leader moves about. And now when they have completed the *four directions* they go back to the tipi from which they came. Again they go inside. The doctors place the wounded at the *catku* [place of honor in the rear of the lodge]. At last they apply the healing root. . . .

Lakota Belief and Ritual, James R. Walker, 1991, pp. 157–159

The knowledgeable informant, Thomas Tyon, remembers this directional and circular symbolism at the Bear Dreamers Society healing ceremony. Sacred movement ritually expressed signed forth to both spectators and participants the power of communal prayer.

———————————— ⊕ ————————————

BLACK ELK'S VISION
LAKOTA

Black Elk looked ahead to a time when he saw the American Indian people climbing upward on a very treacherous journey. He saw *four levels* in the journey of his vision. Each level of ascent represented a generation.

At the end of the *first ascent*, the people camped together in a *circle* and in the center of this sacred circle stood a holy tree.

By the time the people reached the end of the *second ascent*, they became troubled, restless, and afraid. The leaves began to fall from the holy tree.

The journey to the third level was filled with many difficulties. Each person followed his own vision, people ran in confusion and were no longer together. The whole universe carried the sound of war in the winds. By the time the people reach the highest point of the *third ascent*, the nation's hoop was broken. It was no longer a circle. The holy tree seemed to be dying.

When the people began the journey of the *fourth ascent*, the holy tree was gone and the people were starving. This is what Black Elk saw and it made him very sad, so sad that he began to weep. As he wept, he saw on the *north side* of the starving camp a sacred man painted red. The sacred man walked into the center, reclined, and then began to roll: As he rolled, a fat bison took his place. And where the bison stood, a sacred herb sprouted and blossomed—right in the center of the nation's hoop, in the very same spot where the tree had been. *Four* bright and beautiful *blossoms*—one black, one white, one red, and one yellow—formed on the herb's single stem. The brilliant rays of each blossom "flashed to the heavens."

Before long, the flowering tree was back again at the center of the nation's hoop—right where the *four-rayed herb* had blossomed. In his vision, Black Elk was then given the four-rayed herb to carry with him as the people took the final, most difficult steps of all—the steps toward the fourth ascent.

It was dark and terrible. The whole world was screaming for the "winds of the world were fighting." After a time the earth became covered in a blanket of stillness. And out of this stillness a soft song emerged which filled the entire world and rippled the silence. It was so beautiful that the whole universe began to dance—nothing could remain still. The dark clouds passed over, blessing the people with friendly rain and a flaming rainbow. This is when Black Elk saw the hoop of the whole world.

It was a different hoop than the one that had broken. It was a *hoop of many interconnected hoops* that made *one circle*. It was as "wide as daylight and as starlight" and in the center of this hoop of many hoops grew one mighty flowering tree to shelter all of humanity.

It was a sacred hoop.

The Hoop of Peace, Jan Havnen-Finley,
1994, pp. 34, 36, 38, 40, 42-44

Black Elk (1863-1950) had a very full life. He saw many changes coming to his People, changes that seem to have been mostly harmful. He also was a receiver of visions. Here is one special vision that he is well known for sharing. This vision of the Sacred Tree includes elements of the four directions, circularity, and four ascents. As a Native Person and as a follower of Christ (he was a catechist among his People for many years) he was well able to put the Two Ways together in his own person so that others around him would be able to recognize the unity.

--------------------------------- ⊕ ---------------------------------

LAKOTA AND CATHOLIC SYMBOLISM
SIMILARITIES AND DIFFERENCES
LAKOTA/CHRISTIAN

In the Christian religion, the most common physical sign of faith is the cross. This can be seen everywhere among the followers of Christ: on walls, around necks, on books, but most of all, over every Christian church and altar. While the medicine wheel is most at home flat upon the Earth, the cross is most at home in a vertical position. The medicine wheel speaks of the blessing a person receives from the Sacred Powers of the Earth for his earthly survival; the cross speaks of man's being lifted up to God through the incarnation, death, and ascension of Jesus Christ. Through him, earth and heaven are united in a special way. Besides the vertical axis of the cross, the Fathers of the Church saw a special meaning in the horizontal axis of the cross. They saw in the open arms of Christ the beginning of a great circle, embracing all mankind in his death for the salvation and sanctifica-tion of all sinners. However, while the cross emphasizes the redemp-tive work of Christ, it does not of itself, incorporate the Trinity symbolically. It is only when the Christian marks himself in the form of the cross in the name of the Father, and of the Son, and of the Holy Spirit that he makes a miniature profession of the Christian creed. By this act Christians renew the blessing of the Trinity upon themselves.

This blessing recognizes and sanctifies the Christians, making themselves holders of divine life. The Sign of the Cross divinizes Christians and makes them part of the Church which Christ will raise to heavenly glory on the Last Day. By this action, Christians place a cross upon themselves, as Christ did. . . .

In the Bible it is significant that the *four-directional* spirit motif appears in apocalyptic passages pertaining to the End Times. Speaking about the Last Day, Jesus said, "Then the Son of Man will appear in the sky, and all the clans of earth will strike their breast as they see the Son of Man coming on the clouds of heaven with power and glory. He will dispatch his angels with a mighty trumpet blast, and they will assemble his chosen from the *four winds*, from one end of the heavens to the other." In (Rev. 7:1) one finds, "After this I saw *four angels* standing at the *four corners* of the earth; they held in check the earth's *four winds* so that no wind blew on land or sea or through any tree." In the prophet Zechariah the *four winds* of heaven are seen as chariots.

> Again I raised my eyes and saw *four* chariots coming out between two mountains, and the mountains were bronze. The first chariot had red horses: the second had black horses; the third, white; and the fourth chariot spotted horses—all of them strong horses. I asked the angel who spoke to me, "What are these, my Lord?" The angel said to me in reply, "These are the *four winds* of heaven which are coming forth after being reviewed by the Lord of all the earth."

This passage speaks of the winds in a fairly unimportant servant role.

There are other scriptural passages which speak of a different type of four-fold being, very close to God. Similar to this passage, the Lakota hold that each element of the *"four"* also is in *"four,"* etc.

> As I looked, a stormwind came from the *North*, a huge cloud with flashing fire (enveloped in brightness) from the midst of which (the midst of the fire) something gleamed like electrum. Within it were figures resembling *four living creatures* that looked like this: their form was human, but each had *four faces* and *four wings*, and their legs went straight down; the soles of their feet were *round*. They sparkled with a gleam like burnished bronze. The faces were like this: each of the *four* had the face of a man, but on the right side was the face of a lion and on the left

side the face of an ox, and finally each had the face of an eagle. Their faces
(and their wings) looked out on all their *four sides*; they did not turn when
they moved, but each went straight forward. (Each went straight forward;
wherever the spirit wished to go, there they went; they did not turn when
they moved.)

Human hands were under their wings, and the wings of one touched
those of another. Each had two wings spread out above so that they
touched one another's while the other two wings covered his body. In
among the living creatures something like burning coals of fire could be
seen; they seemed like torches, moving to and from the living creatures.
The fire beamed, and from it came forth flashes of lightning.

As I looked at the living creatures, I saw the *wheels* had the sparkling
appearance of chrysolite, and all four others looked the same; they were
constructed as though one wheel were within another. They could move in
any of the *four directions* they faced without veering as they moved. The
four of them had rims, and I saw that their rims were full of eyes all around.
When the living creatures moved, the wheels moved with them, and when
the living creatures were raised from the ground, the wheels also were
raised. Wherever the spirit wished to go, there the wheels went, and they
were raised together with the living creatures, for the spirit of the living
creatures was in the wheels. Over the heads of the living creatures,
something like a firmament could be seen, seeming like glittering crystal,
stretched straight out above their heads. Beneath the firmament their
wings were stretched straight out, on toward each other. (Each of them had
two covering their body.) Then I heard the sound of their winds, like the
roaring of mighty waters, like the voice of the Almighty. When they moved,
the sound of the tumult was like the din of an army. (And when they stood
still, they lowered their wings.)

Above the firmament over their heads something like a throne could be
seen looking like sapphire. Upon it was seated, up above, one who had the
appearance of a man. Upward from what resembled his waist, I saw what
looked like fire; he was surrounded with splendor. Like the bow that
appears in the clouds on a rainy day was the splendor that surrounded him.
Such was the vision of the likeness of the glory of the Lord (Ez. 1:4-28).

Later in (Ez. 10:8-21) these creatures are identified as cherubim.

In the Old Testament, the first commandment ordered that "You
shall not carve idols for yourselves in the shape of anything." (Ex.
20:4) Still God commanded that cherubim be carved and placed upon
the ark. Strange!? In ancient sculpture, cherubim were usually hy-
brids: e.g., a creature with the head of a man, the front quarters of a

lion, the hind quarters of an ox, and the wings of an eagle. In non-Jewish cultures, these images indicated the protective spirits of places, temples, and city gates. Despite the many negative commands forbidding Jews to become involved in pagan religions, a most ancient Jewish law directed that these hybrid spirits should be mounted on top of the most sacred object in the Old Testament.

There was one other image that God ordered Moses to make. When the people sinned, saraph serpents were sent to bite the people so that many would die. In response to Moses' prayer, God ordered him to make a bronze image of a serpent, mount it on a pole, and lift it up for all to see. Those who looked on it were healed (Num. 21:4-9). This image . . . was a pre-figurement of Christ, who was raised on the cross to bring salvation to those who turn to him. . . .

Now then . . . If the serpent which God specifically ordered . . . to make was an indication of a future, universal, salvific reality, then one is seriously moved to consider the cherubim on the ark to be also indicative of universal, naturalistic, hybrid realities around his heavenly throne. I maintain by this argument that the apocalyptic passages in Ezekiel and Revelations are not only talking about something symbolically, but they are also pointing to something real!!

In the book of Revelations, John speaks of *four living creatures* immediately around the throne of God.

> At the very center, around the throne itself, stood *four living creatures* covered with eyes front and back. The first creature resembled a lion, the second, an ox, third had the face of a man, while the fourth looked like an eagle in flight. Each of the four living creatures had six wings and eyes all over, inside and out. Day and night without pause they sing, "Holy, holy, holy." (Rev. 4:6-10) See also (Rev. 5:6-8,7:6-8)

. . . A person familiar with Lakota symbolism is immediately drawn to many meaningful and coherent religious understandings that are most difficult to put into words. While it cannot be said that the above Scripture passages prove that there really are four-sided creatures around God's throne now and at the ends of the earth, one begins to wonder when the same type of imagery emerges from the revelations of other religions. At least the Lakota and the Christian religions are compatible on this point. Still, a more profound comparison can me made. . . .

Many Indians have great difficulty with the doctrine of the Trinity. As one full-blood put it, "They say, 'In the name of the Father, the Son, and the Holy Ghost.' Now they cut off the 'Ghost' part and they say 'Spirit.' They say there are three persons in one God. To us Indians, God is not like a can of sardines, one head sticking out here, another there, and a third one there—three heads for one God." Many people have great difficulty with the notion of the Blessed Trinity because they are strongly influenced by the drawings in their catechisms where the Father is pictured as an Old Man in one corner of a triangle, the Son as a young man is pictured at another corner, and the Holy Spirit is pictured as a dove at the third corner. When this picture, made for children, is carried over into adulthood, it leads to the heresy called "tri-theism." It is wrong to imagine the Trinity as a family of three different people. There are not three gods but only One. The Lakota people are very strong monotheists. "We all believe in the same God (singular)." The Jewish people were trained by God to be very strong monotheists. Every Christian is a monotheist. If it is wrong to picture the Trinity as three separate people, how then can it be explained?. . .

From the beginning of my interest in the Lakota and Christian religions, I realized that if the two religions were to be recognized as truly compatible, they had to be compatible on the most fundamental level. The primal spiritual beings of the Lakota religion had to be clearly compatible with the primal spiritual persons in the Christian religions. The comparison of the *Four Winds* of the Lakota religions demonstrated significant similarities.

First, the Spirit of the *West* is like God the Father. They both mark the beginning of all things and help make them grow. The Father's work is predominately creative; the rains from the *West* bring new life. The *Wakiyan* and the God of the Old Testament reveal their will, especially on mountains amidst lightning and thunder. They establish definite rules concerning religious things. They strongly enforce ritual and religious traditions. When things are "done wrong," they both show their anger so that many people fear them. The Spirit of the *West* is feared most of all. The fear of God in the Old Testament and the fear associated with the *West* are very similar. They are both strong and demanding. They are just and will not let the evil doer go free. They require much purification especially before ceremonies, although the formal rules that each prescribes and the modes of purification that each orders are different.

Secondly, the Son of God, like the *North Wind*, shows what good comes from a life that is obedient and straight. Respect for the directives and teachings of one's elders are essential for a good straight life. They both show the tremendous good that can be accomplished by sacrifice for the sake of the people. Here *woman* has a special place, for the Maiden is pictured carrying the Pipe and Mary too is always pictured with her Son. The Pipe is the primary intercessory instrument in the Lakota religions. Through it prayers are sent to *Wakan Tanka Tunkasila* for the temporal welfare and material life of the Lakota people. Christ is the primary agent in the Christian religion. Through him prayers are sent to God the Father for the eternal salvation and spiritual life of all God's people. Jesus is called the Lamb of God who takes away the sin of the world so that we may live eternally with God in heaven. Similarly, the buffalo provided religious meat to the Lakota people. By the death of the buffalo the Lakota people overcame physical death and hunger. Each points to a straight and narrow path; for the Lakota it is the Sacred Red Path that leads to union with one's relatives in the *South*; for the Christian it is following Christ, carrying one's cross onto establishing God's heavenly Kingdom.

Thirdly, like the Power of the *East*, the Holy Spirit is associated with the obtaining of wisdom. He raises up leaders within the sacred community and gives to ordinary men understanding, courage, ability to pray, and effective communication in the spiritual order. Both spirits are related to "enlightenment." Charisms and the exercise of spiritual power, however, are received according to the religious and cultural tradition to which one belongs, for wisdom perfects and unites that which has already been given by God. The harsh, humble and personal outlook of the first direction is now replaced by a lofty, living and universal outlook. Strict obedience to traditions is now enlivened by one's own spiritual experiences and familiarity with what is *wakan/ holy*.

What of the *fourth stage* to which we referred earlier? There is no fourth person in the blessed Trinity obviously! This presented a great impasse for a time in the comparative study of the two religions. Some felt that perhaps the character of the fourth element in Lakota religion would give a clue to a fourth element in Christianity. In examining the Lakota mythology, it was noted that the peoples of the first three directions were very specific: the horse people, the buffalo people, the elk people. But in the *South* the Lakota spoke of *all* the animal peoples, *wamakaskan oyate*. It is to the *South* that all faced, *Itokagata*. The *South* is the *takte makoce* where one will live in ghost form in an earthly happiness with ones' relatives and all animals. The *south* was different from the others in that it was more corporate and dealt with the after-life more than with the present. Comparatively, the question arose immediately: Is there any divine Christian reality that will be universally corporate in the after-life? The immediate answer was: Yes, the Mystical Body of Christ!

So there are now, and will always be only three individual divine persons in God. But because of the incarnation there will be corporate reality, the Mystical Body of Christ, united to the Triune God in the End Times. Christian revelation points to some kind of divinization of believers within that corporate entity called the Mystical Body of Christ. Revelation says that in the final Kingdom, the faithful Christian will see God "face to face." There is definitely an aspect of equality indicated in that expression. In the Sign of the Cross, the Trinitarian formula is not expressed in a vacuum but *over* someone. When a person is baptized, his is marked in the *name* (singular) of the Father, and of the Son, and of the Holy Spirit. To be marked with a Jewish name is to be declared to be of the same "stock" and "household." Receiving a new name spiritually changes a person. By the power of God, man comes to have God's life in him somehow by gift; he is united to God, he is one with God. In the mystical Body of Christ, Jesus, under the aspect of his humanity, becomes the head of a corporate entity, with the Spirit sanctifying and raising all the members to the nature of their highest and pre-dominant member, the God-man Jesus Christ.

In the Lakota medicine wheel the *West* and the *East* are united in a special way. This is similar to the close relationship of God the Father and the Spirit of God, who have always been recognized as clearly active in the world in imminent and extrinsic ways, respectively. In the Lakota medicine wheel the *North* and the *South* are closely connected through the Sacred Red Path, which all are called to follow. This is similar to the Way that Jesus walked from the particular time of his incarnation to the particular time of his return at the parousia. Since the fourth element is transcendental, eschatological, and corporate, it is qualitatively different from the first "three," which are more established, existential, and individual.

Certainly the Lakota four-directional Spirits are not divine. The Lakota primarily speak of them as operating in the physical domain where they assist humans, animals, and Grandmother Earth. These spirits, like all the other Lakota spirits, act both as intermediaries between us and God and as independent agents of the special but limited *wakan* powers. So there are many differences between the Lakota "four" and the eschatological Christian "four." Still despite their differences, this three-plus-one comparison indicated a compatibility between the two religions on a most fundamental religious level.

The Pipe and Christ: A Christian-Sioux Dialogue,
William Stolzman, 1986, pp. 197-205

Perhaps it is helpful to compare and contrast other cultures' ways of relating to spiritual things. This somewhat complex theological discusson is one way to begin, but there are many other ways as well, like friendly discussion. Greater understanding can often be the result. It is good to see that there are those who would want to build bridges of dialogue so that future and present generations may benefit.

———————————————— ⊕ ————————————————

PIPE CEREMONY
TETON SIOUX

The pipe is used because the smoke from the pipe, smoked in communion, has the potency of the feminine god who mediates between godkind and mankind, and propitiates the godkind. When a shaman offers the pipe to a god, the god smokes it and is propitiated. In this invocation, when the shaman has filled and lighted the pipe, he should point the mouth toward the *west* and say, "Friend of *Wakinyan*, I pass the pipe to you first." Thus he offers the pipe to the *west wind*, for the *west wind* dwells in the lodge of *Wakinyan* and is his friend. The pipe should be offered to the *west wind* first, because the birthright of precedence of the oldest was taken from the firstborn, the *north wind*, and given to the second born, the *west wind*, and the gods are very jealous of the order of their precedence.

When he has made this offering the shaman should move the pipe toward the right hand, the mouthpiece pointing toward the horizon, until it points toward the *north*. Then he should say: "*Circling,* I pass to you who dwells with the grandfather." Thus he offers the pipe to the *north wind*, for because of an offense against the feminine god, the Great Spirit condemned the *north wind* to dwell forever with his grandfather, who is Wazi, the wizard. Then the shaman should move the pipe in the same manner, until the mouthpiece points toward the *east* and say: "Circling, pass to beginning day." This is an offering to the *east wind*, for his lodge is where the day begins and he may be addressed as the "beginning day." Then the shaman should move the pipe in the same manner until the mouthpiece points toward the *south*, and say: "Circling, pass to the beautiful one." This is an offering to the *south wind*, for the "beautiful one" is the feminine god who is the companion of the *south wind* and dwells in his lodge, which is under the sun at midday. It pleases the *south wind* to be addressed through his companion rather than directly.

The *four winds* are the *akicita* or messengers of the gods and in all ceremonies they have precedence over all other gods and for this reason should be the first addressed.

When the offering has been made to the *south wind* the shaman should move the pipe in the same manner until the mouth-piece again points toward the *west*, and say: "Circling, I complete the *four quarters* and the time." He should do this because the *four winds* are the *four quarters* of the circle and mankind knows not where they may be or whence they may come and the pipe should be offered directly toward them. The *four quarters* embrace all that are in the world and all that are in the sky.

"The Sundance and Other Ceremonies of the Oglala Division of the Teton Dakota," *Anthropological Papers of the American Museum of Natural History*, J.R. Walker, 1917, pp. 156-157

This explanation of an invocation during a pipe ceremony was given by a spiritual leader named Sword. Protocol must be followed because it maintains the purity of the ceremony and helps in its being passed on to other generations. It must not be intentionally "played with" because a sacred action is being performed and holy objects are being used. In this circular actitivy the four winds and the four directions complement each other and are often invoked in a variety of prayer forms, one of which is the pipe ceremony.

PLATEAU CULTURAL AREA

A Kootenai-Salish young woman preprared to dance at the powwow grand entry at the 1996 Crow Fair, Crow Agency, Montanta

SALMON FEAST
WY-AM

"La-wit" is the name of the worship pole that stands in front of the long-house door. "Pi-a-toot Ka-ke-a" is the name of "the holy bird" facing the eastern sky.

There is a high window above the **east** door in the long house. When the sun comes up in the **east**, the shadow of this little bird comes through the window and falls on the dirt floor in the center of the long house. This is a sign that the Almighty is reaching down to touch "the open heart of Mother Earth."

This morning at an hour after midnight, the chief saw the first trace of dawn in the eastern sky. It came as a sign that the Almighty had heard their prayers. Now he was sending them their answer.

He was speaking to them through these soft white clouds and the sunshine. The Wy-ams could hear His voice in the wind. He was coming to them through the spring. . . .

While the salmon is cooking out under the open sky, the tule mats have been placed down the center of the long-house floor. Platters of venison and bowls filled with roots and berries have been put on the mats. These are the *four Great Foods* that are always blessed at the salmon feast.

Chief Thompson is slowly *circling the floor* of the long house. He is *going from right to left as the earth turns*. He is asking the Almighty to bless the men and women who will help him serve "the sacred foods at the feast." These people have been chosen because they have "spirit power." Some of them are Warm Springs Indians, who also help with the huckleberry feast on their reservation. Others are from Rock Creek, where Chief Yallup and his people hold a root feast each April. The rest are Wy-ams.

Six drummers, standing in the *rounding west end* of the long house, ended the prayer-singing to the thundering roll of their drums. Then they hung their drums on the rounded wall and sat on the floor with the rest of the visitors. Two lines of Indians sat facing each other, clear around the great long-house floor. Every seat was filled. Out on the grounds, other visitors waited for the second and the third servings of salmon. . . .

When the chief's wife carried the salmon into the long house, she saw all of these people lining both sides of the tule-mat table-cloths. And, with more than two hundred "comers" waiting outside the long-house door, she knew there must be more food. So, she sent an Indian boy to The Dalles to buy many groceries. The boy took a big bundle of beautiful beadwork to help pay for this food. During the summer, she will pick cherries. It will take all and more than she can make to pay for the groceries that are being served at this feast in Chief Thompson's long house.

During the great salmon feast of 1951, three sittings of "comers" lined both sides of the tule mats. . . . Indians are eating along the *west* end and clear down the *south* side of the long house. After they are through, some of the visitors will file out again. Some will even start stick games out on the grounds. But "the true believers" will quietly take their places on the raised seats at the *east* end of the long house. There they will listen and pray while the old chief blesses the water and the salmon for each sitting of "comers."

No Wy-am ate until all of the visitors were served. During the serving, not one of Chief Thompson's helpers crossed over "the open heart of Mother Earth." Always they *circled* "from right to left as the earth turns. . . ."

On the day of the great salmon feast, when the people had eaten their fill, Chief Thompson rang his little bell. The old Indians stood. They turned to the *left*. They bowed to the bell and to the drum. Then they turned back to the *east* again. With their hands over their hearts they began to sing, "How Thankful Are We to the Almighty." After each verse, they stretched their hands higher toward the sky. By the end of the song, they were all standing with outstretched arms as they thanked the Almighty for sending them the Great Food, the salmon.

Come to Our Salmon Feast, Martha Ferguson McKeon,
1959, pp. 12, 36, 42, 44

To circle is to imitate the movement of the earth. It is to copy a timeless action. When it is done with holy purpose it becomes a sacred movement, even a sacred dance. The four directions can also be celebrated in this movement. This Salmon Feast Ceremony of a People in eastern Washington State illustrates how in ceremony these go together well.

A Quiché Mayan priest/elder prays to Creator for those who live in the community of Los Cimientos in the highlands of Guatemala

MESOAMERICA CULTURAL AREA

FLYING MEN OF PAPANTLA
TOTONAC

The town of Papantla, in the state of Veracruz on Mexico's Atlantic coast, is five miles away from El Tajin, the famous center for archaeological studies of the Huastec Indian culture. . . . It is in this region . . . that an impressive pre-Columbian ritual dance has been handed down from generation to generation and remains almost intact from the time when the Huastecs ruled the region. The "flying men" of Papantla continue to this day to launch themselves into the air held only by ropes, acting as intermediaries between the sun and the earth, in order to symbolically fertilize the earth. . . .

The brilliant rays of the hot Mexican sun reverberate off the white walls of the church at Papantla . . . in the main square, Totonac Indians, in their loose smocks and billowing white trousers, calmly stroll along under the tropical trees. . . . The muggy air is stirred by faint, rather shrill music. Five men move along the side of the square and up toward the church in single file. The first man in the line, the group's *caporal,* is playing a flute and a small drum. The men are wearing costumes made of red velvet fringed with yellow—their jackets embellished with motifs picked out in colored pearls, their hats adorned with mirrors in which the sun's rays dance playfully. The eyes of the passers-by are drawn to the group: these are the flying men, the *voladores,* guardians of an ancient rite handed down to them by their ancestors from before the coming of the *conquistadores.*

On the terrace in front of the church stands a concrete *circle* from the middle of which a metal pole stretches up out of sight into the sky. At the very top, forty meters above the ground, a frame from which *four ropes* are hanging sways gently in the wind. The five men reach the pole to the sound of the music which has been handed down to them from ancient times. On the circle around the pole, they perform a ritual dance, moving in turn to face the *four cardinal points* to salute the gods of the *four elements* so that the ceremony will be a success.

Four flying men start to climb the pole, which takes on a more pronounced sway under their weight. Three of the men place themselves on the sides of the frame while the fourth turns the frame in order to wind the four ropes uniformly around the pole. . . . The *manzana,* a sort of wooden disk forty centimeters in diameter perched right at the top of the pole, will serve as the caporal's stage. First seated, then standing, all the while turning respecfully towards the *four cardinal points*, the caporal plays his reedy music, which floats away on the air. Leaning first backwards, then forwards, he hops from foot to foot on the narrow wooden platform which sways from side to side at the top of the pole. He accompanies his movements on the *puzrol* (a flute with three holes) with a melodic line cadenced by rhythmical beats on the drum hooked over one of his fingers.

A few clouds pass behind the five men, momentarily blocking out the sun, to which the ceremony is dedicated. The caporal then sits down on the central platform, the four others surrounding him. There is a moment of silence. The caporal then takes up a new rhythm. The four men let themselves fall backward, head first, their arms stretched open. The multi-colored ribbons in their hair float in the air as they gradually descend in a spiral, the rope held fast between points, bowing first to the *east* to salute the sun, then to the *north* to the god of the winds, next to the *west* to the god of the earth, and finally to the *south* to the god of water. These birdmen were the earth's messengers to the sun. They climbed towards the sun to beseech fertility and protection. Before each ceremony, eight days of total abstinence were observed, and which are still observed to this day. The flying men must follow a starvation diet, avoid alcoholic drink, and have no sexual relations for one week beforehand. Since the men symbolize the sun's rays reaching down to earth, they must be pure.

In the past, the ropes were wound in such a way as to ensure that each flying man made thirteen turns around the pole on his way down. Thirteen turns multiplied by four birdmen make fifty-two, the number of weeks in the Totonac yearly cycle. At the end of each cycle, the renewal of the fire took place. The same figures are also to be found on the niches of the pyramid at El Tajin. Three hundred and sixty-four niches: the 364 days in the lunar year, giving thirteen 28 day lunar months, or 52 seven-day weeks. . . .

Young voladores are taught the traditional way of cutting down the "flying tree"—a tree with a very straight trunk, from the top of which they will learn how to fly. The tree is chosen in the mountains and stripped of its branches. A dance is performed around its base to ask forgiveness of the god of the forest for taking one of his children. After a long ceremony consisting of dances, invocations, and supplications, the tree is cut down and taken away to the dance site. A two-meter-deep hole is dug, into which are thrown offerings of alcohol, a variety of food stuffs, a black hen (which is either still alive or strangled on the spot), eggs (so that the pole will stick hard to the earth), and a candle (so that lightning will not strike the pole). Thus nourished, the tree will not be hungry and will not feel tempted to feed on human lives.

The Totonac Indians who practice these rites profess themselves to be Catholics. . . .

"Voladores: The Flying Men of Papantla," *Native Peoples Magazine*, Sabine Vendrely, Summer 1994, pp. 46-50, 52

Though something seems to be lacking in the proper interpretation of this ceremony, there is much that does make sense. The People have found a means to continue both Ways together. The "flying pole," tzakatquihui, is always respected and through the unifying circle and the veneration of the directions the People address the Creator.

———————— ⊕ ————————

PEYOTE GATHERING EXPEDITION
HUICHOL

Dwelling in the highlands of Nayarit, just below the Gran Chichimeca, exactly at the entrance to the Lower Sonoran corridor, where in pre-Conquest times there were settlements from the coast to the Sierra, the Huichols are the inheritors of a substantial Meso-american tradition. . . .

Their legendary place of emergence, *Wirikuta,* is the desert be-tween the Rio Grande and San Luis Potosi, where grows the plant of eternal life, *hikuri,* the desert-cactus peyote. Annually, pilgrimages are undertaken by small parties under the leadership of a shaman *(mara'akame)* to harvest this fruit of the knowledge of immortal being. It is a journey of some three-hundred miles each way, along a route punctuated by holy sites, a passage to be accomplished during the dry season between the harvest festivals of October and rain ceremonies of February. In December 1966, two anthropologists, Peter Furst and Barbara Myerhoff, joined such a party under the conduct of Ramón Medina Silva, who besides being a *mara'akame,* was an artist (creat-ing yarn paintings) and a musician (playing the fiddle). . . .

The party gathered at Ramón's little rancho and there engaged for three days in last-minute preparations. "Every *peyotero* works for weeks," states Furst, "to prepare his or her own prayer objects, ceremonial arrows, and decorated votive gourds, or even a miniature version of the large folk-art yarn paintings." While the others sewed, strung beads, adorned hats, and so on, Ramón occupied himself preparing Kauyumari's antlers, wrapping them with colored yarn, and attaching ceremonial arrows along with eagle and hawk feathers hanging freely to blow in the wind; every now and then he put his hands to his mouth to make the call, or whistle, of the deer.

To return to Wirikuta, all had to become gods, and on concluding his preparations, Ramón revealed the names he had dreamed for them. He would himself be Grandfather Fire, who in the beginning raised the heavens by placing *four great trees* in the corners of the world. His paternal uncle, Carlos, who had already gone on pilgrimage eight times, would be Our Father Sun, and another relative, Sebastian . . . would be Deer Snarer, patron of the deer hunt. Francisco, whose age was variously given as between 70 and 110, would be Our Great-Grandfather; Lupe, Ramon's wife, Our Mother Maize; Victoria, her niece, Our Mother of the Children; and Pablo, married to Carlos's daughter, Elder Brother Deer Tail. In a sense, this hunting god, Deer Tail, and the Sacred Deer Person, Kauyumari, are aspects of a single power: that represented as at once the hunter and the hunted. . . . Barbara Myerhoff, finally, was identified with the deity Eyebrow of the Peyote (a fuzz in the center of each peyote which senses the ritual condition of the seeker), and Peter Furst, as driver of the camper, became the Arrow that Guards Us.

In conclusion, a sort of Last Supper was served of water and tortillas, before, during, and after which everyone prayed, offering water and bits of tortilla to the *quarters* and to Grandfather Fire; following this event a number of restrictions were in effect—among others, abstentions from salt, washing, full meals, sexual intercourse, and ample sleep.

The first act of the pilgrimage was to gather food for Grandfather Fire, who would be kept alive during the journey by *four companions* remaining behind. Ramón prayed over the wood, holding each piece aloft to the *quarters*, while all chanted and the mood became very solemn. From his house Ramón then brought out a stone disk—about two feet across and two inches deep—meant to cover the sacred opening that goes down to the center of the earth, from which Grandfather Fire was born. Scooping a hollow in the ashes and covering it with this stone, he recited prayers to the fire for success and then covered all with wood arranged to point *east-west* and *north-south*, after which everyone, in single file, made a *ceremonial circuit* around the flame.

The next event was a ceremony of the restitution of innocence. *Around the fire*, each in turn arose, acknowledged the *four directions*, and in formalized speech named the names of all those with whom he had ever had illicit sexual relations. For each name Ramón tied a knot in a cord drawn from his quiver, and at the end of each revelation brushed the candidate down with his plumes and then shook them into the fire. Then the pilgrim shook and brushed himself, his clothing, and his gear into the fire, which he then *circled* back to his place. The knotted string was elevated, prayed over, and cast into the flames: and from this moment to the end of the course, the pilgrims knew each other as the Ancient Ones.

Ramón then placed one end of his deerskin-strung bow in his mouth and, holding the other between his toes, with a ceremonial arrow beat on the string a rhythm which told Grandfather Fire that all was well and in readiness. From his quiver he took a cactus-fiber cord that he passed twice around the *circle*, first in front of, then behind, the pilgrims, after which he scorched it in the fire and returned it to his quiver. At last, he blew a horn and took up his violin, and the company danced and sang through the night. . . .

The camper with its cargo of gods en route to the land of the knowledge of eternal life punctuated the adventure with stops at which Ramón recounted the related legends: tiny water holes, small caves, tree stumps, little clumps of rock, heaps of pebbles. On approaching a place called in Spanish La Puerta (but in Huichol, The Vagina), he required the curtains to be drawn, so that those on pilgrimage the first time (the *primeros*) should not see until properly instructed; and a short way beyond this portal he required the camper to stop. All descended and knelt in a *semicircle*, and with prayers for all and for each, he blindfolded the *primeros*. Here, in the Mythological Age, the First Pilgrims wept: some of those now present did so too. . . .

Proceeding . . . onward deeper into the natal zones of their lives, pausing here and there for little ceremonies, here and there to pass the night, at last the assembly arrived at the place called Where Our Mothers Dwell: a little cluster of water holes, from which a sacred water flowed that was to be drunk and sprinkled over each. In the First Peyote Hunt the female members met and joined the males at these springs, where even now they abide in the form of snakes.

Among those "Mothers" here to be brought to mind was old Nakawe, The One Who Came First, who, after the flood, remade the world. She is an old woman with very long hair, who, leaning on her staff, walks alone in the Sierras. With her staff, she recreated the animals and plants and, while the earth was still soft, sent the Macaw to scoop up mountains with its beak. In her canoe she had saved a single man, Watakame, and a little black she-dog, with which the man subsequently dwelt. . . .

At this very holy shrine, Where Our Mothers Dwell, Ramón removed the blindfolds from the *primeros'* eyes and, as they looked about in wonder, recounted legends of the Ancient Ones, pointing to places where they had stopped and rested on the First Peyote Hunt and had eaten, sung, or talked with the animals. The mood of the company here changed to banter, and a language of "reversals" came into play. Ramón told Myerhoff that her hair was now cactus fiber; himself, the Pope; his wife, Lupe, an ugly boy; Victoria, a *gringa;* and Francisco, a *nunutsi* ("little child"). . . . Someone sneezed, and the laughter was uproarious; for according to one of the conventional reversals, the nose had become the penis.

"When the world ends," Myerhoff was told, "it will be as when the names of things are changed during the peyote hunt. All will be different, the opposite of what it is now. . . . There will be no more difference. No more man and woman. No child and no adult. All will change places. Even the *mara'akame* will no longer be separate. That is why there is always a *nunutsi* when we go to Wirikuta. Because the old man, the tiny baby, they are the same."

. . . the company at last arrived at Real de Catorce, a former colonial mining town on the border of Wirikuta, which, as Myerhoff describes it, is "a flat stretch at the base of two sacred mountains . . . a featureless brush desert of creosote and cactus." The interior, where the cactus grows, can be reached only on foot, "for there are no roads or even paths into the center of the region." . . .

All went to look for deer tracks, for, according to the legend, the first peyote appeared, in the beginning, in the tracks of the first deer. When they returned, a brush fire was built, and after an interlude of praying, talking, and singing, Ramón drew from his quiver the scorched cactus-fiber cord for the ceremony of "knotting in." It was passed twice around the *circle*, first in front, then in back, of the *peyoteros,* while Ramón twanged his bowstring. Then he summoned each to his side, to kneel holding one end of the string, while he prayed and tied a knot in it. Carlos tied the knot for Ramón; then Furst and Myerhoff were knotted in. No one was to sleep that night. Remaining awake, all were to hold right thoughts, to be of one mind, and to ask Grandfather Fire and Our Father Sun for the strength they would be needing the next day in Wirikuta, whence they all had been born.

Leaving their fire burning by the camper, at dawn they crossed the railroad tracks to a little stand of stunted trees that marked the perimeter of the sacred land, where they made again a fire, to which each brought a stick. Then the company fanned out, searching for tracks. Their manner was of stalking, stooping, whispering, and moving through the brush on tiptoe. Ramón, discovering signs of the passing of earlier Huichol searching parties, bade his company move on, and in single file they walked for three hours, until he gave the sign for all to fan out. After a time, he again gave a sign. He had seen the deer.

All gathered behind him as he drew his arrow and readied the bow. All prayed as he stalked carefully to within a few feet, aimed, and shot into the base of the plant an arrow aligned *east-west*, then quickly another, *north-south*. The peyote-deer was secured. Ramón, approaching, placed beside it, to the *west*, the horns of Kauyumari; he then cleaned the ground around the flat-topped plant, which was about two inches in diameter, and beckoned all to sit around it. With his plumes sweeping downward, he combed back into the plant the multicolored rays of energy *(kupuri)*—to most eyes invisible—which had spurted upward when the deer was struck. The company then presented their offerings: decorated gourds of sacred water, ceremonial arrows, yarn paintings, antlers, beads, miniature deer snare, and lighted candles. Then naming in a long chant the gods they represented, they knelt in a *circle* and wept, while Ramón dipped the tips of his arrows into the peyote blood (which only he could see) and with this substance anointed the forehead, cheeks, eyes, and breasts of each god present. . . .

With his knife Ramón next dug the peyote carefully from the ground, leaving some of the root, "so that the deer might grow again from his bones"; then slicing from the center outward, he placed a segment of the plant in each pilgrim's mouth, after touching it to the recipient's forehead, cheeks, and eyes.

The hole was then covered with gifts, and the company, still whispering, fanned, stalking out over the desert. After several hours, they returned, their baskets heavy with cactus. "Now," Ramón said, "we must leave as quickly as possible. It is dangerous to remain longer." And they left at a run, as though in peril, arriving . . . to find the Old God, their fire, still aglow. The next day was spent searching for more peyote, then sorting, admiring, and packing the harvest; and that night, for the first time on the trip, much peyote was eaten, with laughter at first, but then a falling into silence, each alone, as Myerhoff tells, "engrossed in his private view of beauty and light."

The final ceremony occurred . . . back in . . . the yard of Ramón's rancho. The fire had been kept burning by the *four* who had remained and were now silently standing with lighted candles in their hands. All *circled* the fire, thanks were chanted to the gods, the baskets were set down, and peyote was distributed to be eaten. Then Ramón removed from the coals the stone disk he had put there, and each male of the company dropped in to the uncovered hole a small package of wild tobacco wrapped in maize husk and yarn; after this the stone was replaced and wood once more moved to cover it. Dipping some dried flowers into his gourd of sacred water, Ramón now touched with them the crown of the head, cheeks, and lips of each present, then took from his quiver the string of knots that represented their unity and passed it *twice around, once before and once behind*; then he summoned each to come and grasp the string to the right of the knot that represented himself while he slowly untied it from the other end. The string was then passed over the fire for the last time and returned to the basket of the *mara'akame*. A small bowl of salt was brought out, and Ramón, calling each before him, placed a pinch of salt in his mouth—which broke the fast, and with that the mystery play was ended.

There were two related ceremonies to follow the Peyote Hunt. The first, the Cleansing of the Spines, took place in the Sierra several weeks after the party had returned and involved among other rituals, the cleaning of a small field for planting of maize: one for Grandfather Fire, another for Our Father Sun, and so on, for all deities represented on the trip. The second would then be a Deer Hunt, in which the deer was to be caught in a snare and neither bow and arrow nor gun might be used.

The Way of the Seeded Earth/Part 3: Mythologies of the Primitive Planters: The Middle and Southern Americas, Joseph Campbell, 1989, pp. 294-299 Originally published in *Peyote Hunt: The Sacred Journey of the Huichol Indians,* Barbara Meyerhoff, 1974; "Peyote and the Mystic Vision," Barbara Meyerhoff and "The Art of Being Huichol," Peter Furst in *Art of the Huichol Indians,* Kathleen Berrin (Ed.), 1978

In making the pilgrimage, the Huichol recognize the necessity of hearkening back to the mythic time in order to be in proper alignment with the directionality of the present time. Only then will the pilgrims reach their goal and return safely to rejoice with their God-given cache of peyote.

———————————— ⊕ ————————————

CH'A CHAK CEREMONY
MAYA

Since Ch'a-Chak ceremonies are a community effort, the work and the materials were all contributed voluntarily. Don Pablo brought his knowledge, his prayers, and his sacred stones. The other men built the altar and dug the nearby fire pit where the sacred breads would be cooked. Their altar looked simple and improvised, a shaky table of poles held together with vines. During the ceremony, however, it would become the center of the cosmos. All the participants brought the dough made with corn ground by their womenfolk for the sacred breads that are layered, like heaven and the underworld, on the altar, as well as the cooked meats, and the "wine" made from honey and "virgin water" from a deep natural well.

That day, while I was studying the ancient cityscape and presiding over our excavation in the temple-mountain, the ceremony was well under way in the woods at the far side of the village. Don Pablo and his helpers had set aside three days for the prayers and preparations. The following day, all the villagers and archaeologists together attended the climax of the Ch'a-Chak ritual and witnessed the legacy of thousands of years of Maya devotion and ritual knowledge. This is the *Ch'a-Chak,* "Bring-Rain" ceremony.

Once we were assembled, Don Pablo began. With quiet dignity, he crouched down beside the altar and picked up a tin can nailed to a stick. Holding the handle of this homemade brazier, he rummaged in his pocket, pulled out a little bag of white powder—*pom,* dried fragrant tree sap—and sprinkled it on the coals that were burning inside the can. As the sweet smoke rose in billows, he raised his voice in prayer and began moving *counterclockwise* around the leafy green arbor of bound saplings and baby corn plants. The incense cloud undulated back and forth in the hot air.

Pitching his voice into a higher octave to show the proper respect, Don Pablo spoke softly to the Chak Lords, the rain gods. He *circled around* the tall, thin *cross* made of sticks that stood behind the altar and the *four young men* stationed at its *four corners*. These men were making the roaring sounds of thunder, *ruum-ruum-ruum.* They were clapping small wooden sabers and pistols together, and sprinkling fresh, clean water from little gourds onto the boys who crouched at their feet beside the corn plants of the arbor. The men embodied the Chakob, and the boys were the frogs of the rainstorm. The boys chirped and croaked, "whoa-whoa," imitating the many night sounds that are heard when the land and the crops are sated with the rains they were trying to bring with this ritual.

As Don Pablo passed in front of the altar, he paused to pray more loudly, shaking the arching branches the way the thunder shakes the roof of a house. He pulled on one of the six vines that radiated outward from the center of the arbor. Entranced, his eyes half closed, he raised his face heavenward and summoned the gods to save the crops of the farmers who stood anxiously around the altar observing him. The late-afternoon air hung heavy, still, and expectant over the fallow cornfield with its tangled thicket of new-growth trees. Clouds passed by above the treetops and suddenly everyone heard a distant rumble of thunder. Perhaps it would not come that day, but soon, they knew, the Chakob would bring back the rain. They had heard the *h-men's* prayers.

Every one of us, the men and boys of the village and the motley crew of American and Mexican archaeologists working nearby, was caught up in that moment. That hopeful rumble of thunder broke the tension caused by our hesitant, sympathetic attempt to believe and the mild embarrassment of the villagers caught between their faith in ancient knowledge and their aspirations to become "modern" people. Being present at this ceremony was like something glimpsed from the corner of your eye, something you're not really sure you've seen. For a brief time Don Pablo had gone a little beyond our view, into a place represented by an altar set with cooked breads, gourd cups of corn gruel, and magical stones. He talked to god in that place and god listened to him. Don Pablo is an *h-men,* a "doer," the shaman of his town.

> *Maya Cosmos: Three Thousand Years on the Shaman's Path,*
> David Freidel, Linda Schele & Joy Parker, 1993, pp. 31-33

This ceremony, which took place within the last few years, is typical of many contemporary Mayan cere-monials for the increase of the earth's bounty for the sake of the People. Circular movement is im-portant, as is recognizing the four directions so that the ancient teach-ings and prayers become a reality for the modern-day Maya who, even now, must suffer under government and military domination, and, more recently, North American funda-mentalist evangelical prosetylism.

Aztec drummer at ecumenical Thanksgiv-ing celebration, Our Lady of Mt. Carmel Church, Carmel Valley, California, 1997

SOUTH AMERICA CULTURAL AREA

SACRED SPACE
MAKUNA

*Ceremonial mask
from Venezuela*

The Makuna term for maloca, *wi,* means more than simply house. It also has the connotations of *wiro,* the coat of an animal or the skin of a human being; *he wi,* a sacred ritual, as in the ritual of the ancient Yurupari flutes; *bukua wi,* birthplace or a point of origin, procreation, and propagation, as in a place where animals are believed to breed and multiply; and *masa yuhiri wi,* the mythical birthplace and waking-up house of the clan. A maloca, then, is the protective skin of the clan, a sacred state of being, a space of procreation and rebirth, and a crossroad between this world and the *he* world.

In Makuna imagery the maloca is itself a model of the cosmos. Conversely the universe is conceived of as a cosmic house with doors, posts, beams, walls, and roof. The maloca's roof is the sky, the house posts are the mountains that support it, and the floor is the earth. The ridgepole under the roof is the path of the sun and the river of the sky. An imaginary river flows along the middle of the house, representing the Milk River of the earth, and below the earthen floor, where the dead are buried, is *bohori riaka,* the underground river of death and sorrow, where human corpses float through the Door of Suffering in the *west.* At the Water door in the *East,* contextually identified with either the men's or the women's door in the maloca, the Milk River flows out of this world and into the upper and lower layers of the cosmos. The three imaginary rivers are all connected in the maloca cosmos forming a great *circuit of celestial, terrestrial, and chthonic waters* embracing the entire world.

Every Makuna maloca is constructed according to the plan of the primordial maloca. The house in this world thus has its counterpart in the spirit realm where the exogamous group with all its spiritual knowledge and tangible possessions originated. In water Anaconda's underwater maloca, his descendents were taught the sacred dances and received the cultivated food plants and ritual goods—coca, tobacco, yage, and the dance regalia. Every post and beam of the original maloca is named after an ancestral anaconda. The *four central house posts* in the Makuna maloca are thus identified with the *four principal ancestors* of the Land and water people—*Yiba Hino* (Earth Anaconda, *Kome Hino* (Metal Anaconda), *Wai Hino* (Fish Anaconda), and *Ide Hino* (Water Anaconda)—all closely related by mythical ties of kinship and marriage.

Makuna: Portrait of an Amazonian People, Kaj Århem, 1998, pp. 85-86

"As above, so below. . . ." and again, "as it was in the beginning, is now, and ever shall be. . . ." seem to typify this People's communal dwelling symbolism and architecture.

———————————————— ⊕ ————————————————

HAIN HUT SYMBOLISM
SELK'NAM/HAUSH

The Hain hut encapsulated the whole of Selk'nam society as a reflection of the cosmos. The *four 'skies'* (designated by the main posts of the hut) represented the mystic axes of the universe and every adult male who participated in the ceremony had a special place inside the hut, as he had in the cosmos . . . the Hain was a large wigwam with a *circular base* and one entrance facing the *east*, away from the cleared area where the spirits (actors) performed. Its height and circumference varied according to the length of the tree trunks available, but every attempt would be made to build it as large as possible.

The *four principal posts* were aligned in a *circle* at the base of the hut at the *cardinal points*, called 'skies' (sho'on). These posts symbolized the 'centres' (oishka) of the 'skies', the 'wombs' (haiyen), the places of creation in the universe. Then three additional posts were put up, on the 'periphery' (shixka) of the principal posts. Each of the seven posts represented a number of territories and lineages. The three posts were situated between the four central posts, at the *north-east*, the *south-east*, and the *south-west*. Why there was no post for the *north-west* is a question that remains unanswered, except in so far as the number seven had a ritual significance. However, a few territories were assigned to the north-west, the 'peripheral' section which lacked a post, and the men born there stood and sat in this section of the Hain. Each of the eighty (or more) territorial units was assigned either to one of the *four principal 'skies'* or to an intermediate, peripheral, sky.

The pre-eminent post placed at the entrance to the hut symbolized the supreme significance of the *eastern sky*. The *east* and *west posts* were the first to be set up and were thought of as brothers-in-law. In a physical and symbolic sense they were mutually supportive, as were the *north* and *south posts*. As mentioned above, everyone among the Selk'nam and Haush together belonged to one of the *four skies* (or to a peripheral sky), according to the territory where they were born, which was usually the father's. In 1923 when Gusinde participated in a Hain the Selk'nam had no territory to assign to the *east sky*, and the Haush had no territories corresponding to the *west sky*. When the Selk'nam performed the ceremony without the Haush the *east post* was occupied by some men from the *north* or *north-east posts*. As skies were the exogamic units (marriage being forbidden between two people who were associated with the same sky), brothers-in-law had to be from different skies.

The *four skies* were thought of as 'invisible cordilleras of infinity'. The *east sky*, whose post was named Páhuil (a Haush word), was the most magnificent yet the most treacherous of all. Its great slippery cordillera was surrounded by a sea of boiling water. The magnificent cordillera of the *west sky* was the centre, or womb, of the wind (Shenu), for whom the *west post* of the Hain was named. The sun (Krren) was associated with the *west sky*, and Shenu was his brother. Shenu had assisted his brother Krren, then a powerful shaman, when they attacked the Hain of the matriarchy and its dominant leader, the female shaman Moon (Kreeh). In the beautiful cordillera of the *south sky* lived Owl (Sheit), for whom the *south post* was named. His mighty brother Snow (Hosh) also lived there with their sister Moon, once sovereign of the famed matriarchy, who had been defeated by her husband Sun. Finally, the cordillera of the *north sky* was the home of Sea (Kox) and his sister Rain (Chalu). Here the mystical Flamingo (Telil) was honored as the *north post* of the Hain. The souls (kaspi) of humans returned at death to these wombs, the skies, with which each person had been identified during his or her lifetime. In the wombs of the vast outer space the souls were reunited with the eternal forces of the universe.

Patagonia: Natural History, Prehistory and Ethnography at the Uttermost End of the Earth, Colin McEwan, Luís Borrero & Alfredo Prieto (Eds.), 1997, pp. 86-89

It is wonderful to see how these Peoples at the tip of South America symbolized and ritualized their cosmic habitat. Martin Gusinde, an Austrian priest, was welcomed by them to participate in their sacred ceremonies. History was not good to these People. There are few survivors.

———————————— ⊕ ————————————

AGRICULTURAL FERTILITY RITES
MAPUCHE

The formal preparation is handled by the ñillatufe and his assistants, the other chiefs and elders. . . . The ceremonial field is tidied up by the elders and helpers of the host reservation, and the main and secondary altars prepared, as well as the ramadas or cubicle-like shelters of boughs to be used by participants during the ceremony.

The main altar is either an old carved effigy post or simply a crotched tree trunk of recent origin. It is surrounded by boughs of trees which are considered sacred (cinnamon, apple, maqui) and which are renewed each year the ceremony is held. Now the field is ready for the ritual. The officials offer prayers to their ancestors and to ñenechen, the Supreme Being. A small sacrificial fire is made. . . .

When the sun is at about 9 o'clock, the participants and guests begin to flock onto the ceremonial field. Some of them occupy ramadas already set aside for them, others hastily construct windbreaks, others merely seat themselves next to their horses or ox-carts which, after everyone is settled, form a *ring or a semi-circle* around the ceremonial field. By this time the officials have staked out the sacrificial sheep or oxen, gathered wood for the special ceremonial fires (at the main and secondary altars), and have placed wooden bowls of sacrificial grains and libational offerings at the main altar. . . .

The second day of the ceremony draws many spectators, as distinguished from responsible participants, and is characterized by a good deal of visiting, gossiping, and often the drinking of wine or hard cider. . . .

The *four main parts of each day* of the ceremony may be separated into the *early morning*, the *mid-morning*, the *early-afternoon*, and the *late-afternoon* sections. These should be conducted unerringly by the ñillatufe, the chief-priest, who has the assistance of other ñillatufe, chiefs from participating reservations, and other ritual specialists. Sometimes shamans are invited to participate, since they may fill a gap in a knowledge about religious lore. Officials called captains and sergeants are present to help preserve order, curtailing drunkenness and preventing fights and any other disturbances which would pollute the ritual atmosphere and limit the effectiveness of the ceremony. . . .

The ñillatufe offers an opening prayer to ñenechen and ancestral spirits. . . . The priest stands near the main altar with his assistant priests to his right. The ñillataufe, upon finishing the prayer, commands his captains and sergeants to have the male participants commence the *encirclement of the ceremonial field* (awn) . . . the encirclement . . . is to clear the field of evil spirits who might otherwise contaminate the ancestral spirits present. The men who perform the awn are mounted on their finest horses and dressed in their finest clothes (usually of the Chilean buaso type), some of them wearing sheepskin masks, or painted faces, to hide their identity from the evil gods.

The awn or *encirclement* describes the ceremonial field. Sometimes the ceremonial field on a reservation is in the midst of farmland. When it is, it is frequently *squared*, indicating a place which should neither be plowed nor grazed. The manner of Mapuche plowing results in the square shape of the ceremonial field. The visible fact contradicts, however, the Mapuche statement that their ñillataun field is circular. The *circularity*, which has great symbolic value for the Mapuche, is actually seen only in the performance of awn and the disposition of the participants around the ceremonial field. The awn riders *make a circle* around the two altars, encompassing both of them. So tight is the riding circle of the horsemen and so great their speed, the horses are actually leaning inward as they gallop *counterclockwise* around the sacred ground. . . .

The awn envelopes the ceremonial field. The riders *encircle the two altars*. The main altar is called the rewe, as is the shaman's "sacred pole," which is what the word means; the secondary altar, as mentioned, is called the llangi, a bier, as in the wake and funeral ceremony, and stands about 100 yards from the main altar, in an *easterly direction* (the orientation of Mapuche ceremonies is toward the east).

The riders race around the perimeter of the field and from time to time raise cries to chase away the evil spirit. . . . The horsemen are most impressive and hold the full attention of the audience. They ride in a column of twos, led by standard bearers and their rear brought up by a sergeant carrying a long staff of office. Taking their cues from the captain and/or the ñillatufe, they dismount near the secondary altar where they tether their horses and begin a short *foot-dance around the llangi* before returning to the main altar. When they come to the main altar they participate in the purun (dance) which has started there.

The purun is a slow *dance*, again *of encirclement*, which takes place around the main altar and lasts for roughly fifteen minutes. The ñillatufe gives commands to the captains and sergeants to step up or decrease the dancing tempo. Both men and women dance in the purun, in a *counterclockwise encirclement* of the rewe (main altar). They wear sprigs of the sacred branches of cinnamon, apple, and maqui, which decorate the altar. They may also carry kernels of maize, wheat, and other domestic plants.

Music is provided by a number of players who know the traditional instruments, such as the whistles (pifulka), which are made of stone, pottery, or wood; the trumpets (trutruka), made of Chilean bamboo covered with leather and tipped by a cow's horn; and drums (kultrun), made of shallow wooden "bowls" covered by sheepskin or, sometimes, calfskin. All are native instruments, described in the earliest chronical reports more than 400 years ago, and all are homemade.

After the ñillatufe gives the command to end the purun, he orders the dancers to line up in a special manner. He lines up a row of men and a row of women. Each row extends *east* (toward the secondary altar) from the main altar. Now the men face the women, and the ñillatufe begins his second major prayer of the morning. During the intervals between stanzas of this prayer, the opposing lines of men and women are commanded to do in-place dancing. The dance ends after ten minutes or so, when the dancers, especially the older ones, are panting and perspiring heavily.

At this juncture, the ñillatufe, with the assistance of his captains and sergeants, as well as other officials, kills one of the sacrificial sheep, which has been staked near the main altar. This is a bloody episode in the ceremony, which is enacted at least once more during the ritual, and, if the ritual is traditionally perfect . . . the sacrifice will be made in the morning and afternoon of the first and second day. In this manner, *four sheep* are given to the ancestors and the gods.

The Mapuche Indians of Chile, Louis Faron, 1968, pp. 101-104

The agricultural fertility rite, ñillatun, is replete with circular and directional symbolism, as well as number 4 ceremonialism.

———————————— ⊕ ————————————

INTERTWINED INDIGENOUS AND CATHOLIC CEREMONIES
CANELOS QUICHUA

As the camari goes on the *drummers circle round and round* and powerful shamans and aspiring trained shamans play special camari soul songs on their pingullus. . . .

As the pottery trumpets begin to honk away in a non-musical male-female merged soul noise and as other gifts of special pottery figurines are given away, the racket and activity within the ceremonial house crescendo even more. Lanceros again enter, are quickly fed and given more chicha, and begin again to dance in the center of a *circling group* of as many as twenty drummers. Powerful shamans play their pingullus, others play transverse flutes, and people begin to wonder if, during this ceremony, too much enactment of mythic structure will occur and the great flood of antiquity will return. As hard rain comes people comment on the possible need to build a great raft with soil and manioc on which to travel *eastward*. Men and women assume the roles of Docero, Cuillur, Indi, Quilla, Jilueu. Young girls begin to serve guests in very special figurines representing the core aspects of mythology, including a special tree mushroom made by the prioste's wife. . . .

About 3:00 p.m. a more staid, formal camari is held near the front of the church, where the *four lanceros* and their families are fed, and where outside guests may also be invited to participate. The priest also marries several couples at this time, and, at least in Paca Yacu, a slow dance takes place for a few minutes, before the married couples return to their respective houses to give their own parties. Gifts of firewood, plantains, and a bit of black smoked meat are brought to the priest's house, and all drummers go **round and round in the central square**, women dancing within the **circle**.

Sacha Runa: Ethnicity and Adaptation of Ecuadorian Jungle Quichua,
Norman Whitten, Jr., 1976, pp. 190-191

The sound of the drummer and many feet in motion upon the sacred earth must be fantastic to experience. And yet, this People's particular relationship to different aspects of the universe is expressed by ritually utilizing the directions. Fourness is shown by the movements of the four lanceros.

⊕

CURING CEREMONY
QUECHUA

Apertura de la cuenta (opening of the account): Eduardo sets up the *mesa* in a special order: first, the *Campo Justiciero* artifacts; second, the *Centro Medio* artifacts; third, the *Campo Ganadero* artifacts; and last, the staffs from right to left. Then, while invoking the forces of nature along with the *four winds* and *four roads*, he fills his mouth with sugar and Tabu, and he sprays the mixture three times over the *mesa* to purify it. After a second invocation, this same operation is repeated three times with sugar and *agua florida*. This is followed by another invocation and three more blasts of spray composed of sugar and *agua cananga*. Finally, sugar and sweet-lime juice are sprayed three times over the *mesa*. (Usually the total number of blasts is twelve).

Oraciones (prayers) to the *Campo Justiciero* addressing God, the Virgin Mary, and the saints of the Roman Catholic faith. These prayers, mostly in Spanish with a little Latin and some Quechua, include the Hail Mary and the Our Father. . . .

Llamada (call) to the sacred mountains and lagoons, the ancient shrines, and to *curanderos,* alive and dead, so that they will attend the session in spirit. . . .

Raising of the *San Pedro* remedy. Eduardo pours *tabaco* into a shell, makes a **cross** with it over the *mesa,* and hands it to one of his assistants, who then bends down beside the can of San Pedro brew. The assistant then lifts up his shell alongside the can, makes a **cross** with it over the remedy, stands, and imbibes the *tabaco* through his nose. This is repeated twice more, once with *agua cananga* by itself and once with Tabu by itself; then this same procedure is performed by the second assistant—who is followed by everyone else present at the session except Eduardo (but only with *tabaco;* not the perfumes). If for some reason a patient cannot get the *tabaco* down his nostrils, he is allowed to swallow it. . . .

Sopla (blowing) and *chicotea* (violent shake) of the staff. An assistant or Eduardo now sprays the patient's staff three times with whatever liquid is indicated by the account. He then slices the air with the staff in whatever **compass direction** or **directions** are indicated, and he returns it to its proper position at the front of the *mesa.* . . .

Salto sobre el fuego (leap over the fire). After the curing acts are performed for all present, the victims of the witchcraft must then leap *four times* so that their movements form a **cross** over a small bonfire of straw lit by Eduardo's assistants. After the jumps, each must then stamp out the fire. Then, as each individual patient steps backwards, an assistant cuts the ground between his or her feet with one of the *mesa* swords. This appears to be a symbolic act indicating "mastery over fire" or "magical heat," a shamanistic attribute that is passed on to the patient in order to purge and purify him or her by exorcising evil spirits. . . .

Piaroa bat spirit mask

Refresco (purification, or "refreshment") or participants and locale. The two assistants orally spray a mixture of holy water, white cornmeal, white flowers, white sugar, sweet-lime juice, and powdered lime in the faces, on the necks (front and back), and over the hands (front and back) of everyone, including Eduardo and each other. While they are "refreshing" the patients, Eduardo gathers up his artifacts in the same order as he put them down at the beginning of the session. . . . All of his artifacts must be put away before sunrise to prevent sunlight from striking them, and any leftover *San Pedro* is buried for the same reason. Once he has packed everything up, he uses his dagger to cut a ***cross*** three times in the earth where the *mesa* was laid, and he then sprinkles the *refresco* mixture used by his assistants three times along the cuts in the ground and once in each of the ***four corners of the*** **mesa** ***area***, which must not be touched by anyone until noon of the day in progress. . . .

Eduardo el Curandero: The Words of a Peruvian Healer,
Eduardo Calderón & Douglas Sharon, 1982, pp. 80, 82, 84-85

This leader, like many in South America, uses the hallucinogenic San Pedro cactus along with a special blend of indigenous and Christian rituals performed over a mesa, *a table, replete with special shamanic power objects. Doing something four times and making crosses to represent both the cardinal directions and the Christian cross are important procedures in the work of a* curandero *a healer. Perhaps doing some things three times is in honor of the Holy Trinity.*

Llama, Creator's special gift to the People

INTERCULTURAL CULTURAL AREA

Morning prayer with water blessing by an Arapaho elder during an intertribal (Arapaho, Crow, Shoshone, etc.) youth retreat at Saint Stephen's on the Wind River Reservation in Wyoming (March 1991)

CIRCULAR, DIRECTIONAL, AND NUMERICAL RELATIONSHIPS
INTERTRIBAL

Color symbolism plays an extremely important part in the spiritual system of the Native American tribes. Each one of the *cardinal points* has its corresponding color, and each color its special symbolic meaning. When each Spirit, or Person, who lives at a cardinal point is invoked and called in, the Person brings with him to dispense to the individual or group in need all of the characteristics that were given to him in the beginning by the Above Beings. The Person is called, "The Red Man," etc.

For the Sioux and other Plains Indian tribes, the pipe is the main and most effective channel through which the Persons come when called upon. As the pipe is pointed at a Direction a prayer is sent forth and the powers of that Direction are channeled to the one who points the pipe. However, just the act of placing out a colored cloth, or of touching a colored cloth—especially on a medicine hoop—calls in a Person and his powers. In the Native American way, since the Above Beings are infinite and know all things, the act of making an offering of a particular color is sufficient, and as it is performed the Persons and powers become immediately present, although the addition of a spoken or meditated prayer enhances the supplicant's own part in communication, since it focuses, clarifies, sharpens and attunes the supplicant's consciousness. To put this another way, what the Above Beings ask us to do in our relationship with them is done more for our sakes than for His, since we are the ones who are always in need of better understanding.

Examples of placing a color and having the Person and attributes immediately present are: attaching colored cloths to the base of the Sun Dance tree, attaching the *four colors* to the rim of a medicine hoop and blue and green colors at the center, placing the *four colors* at the *four corners* of a questing place, and using the *four colors* to mark the place where a patient stands while the medicine person determines the cause of and cure for their ailment.

There is considerable diversity in the color and attribute systems of the various tribes, both as to the location and types of the powers. Non-Indians should not be troubled by this. The Native Americans remain faithful to what was given to them in the beginning of time, and they are not troubled by the variations. The Above Beings knew what was best for them, and arranged things accordingly. . . .

It is interesting, but not, since we are taught by the same God, surprising, that black is generally the symbol of death, while white symbolizes purity and peace, and red symbolizes the blood line, power and triumph in warfare. . . .

Movement around the *circle* is always in a clockwise direction, since this is believed to be the direction the benevolent sun follows as it travels.

Living in the Timeless Age, Thomas Mails, 1990, p. 25

The persons and powers of the cardinal directions are expressed through an ancient color symbolism which helps to express the uniqueness of each direction. This symbolism varies from tribe to tribe. But the fourness of things is ever important.

Taking time to pray,
remembering all our relations

⊕

MEDICINE WHEEL
INTERTRIBAL/CHRISTIAN

Look up and raise your heads, because your redemption is drawing near. Luke 21:28

When you look at a tree, you will notice that for every year it survives there is a *circle*. The next year another forms—and the year after, there is another. Eventually, the tree becomes strong.

The medicine wheel is like a tree. In the medicine wheel are the *four directions*—the *east*, the *south*, the *west*, and the *north*. The medicine wheel teaches us a holistic approach to life.

Knowledge of ourselves as human beings is a protection for us, a help to how we live. We must understand the medicine wheel teaches us a holistic approach to life.

All learning is on a path beginning in the *east*. The east is called the place of *illumination*. This is a simple word meaning seeing. Illumination represents physical sight as well as spiritual insight—the way of the soul.

South is where warmth comes from. This is the place of growth; we keep on growing—we never reach a place where we stop. *Trust and innocence*, accepting our humanness, becomes foremost in our minds as we journey through the place represented by *south* on the medicine wheel. Sometimes we judge each other harshly; we need to learn to be kind, to accept ourselves.

The *west* is a place of *introspection*. Here we learn to look at ourselves. It is important to be able to look at ourselves to see within. It is much easier to judge others—but we need to evaluate ourselves, to know our humanity.

Knowledge begins in the *north*. We can never start by seeing something and knowing. We must always start by seeing how something works. All learning takes time and work.

The more we understand about life, the deeper our roots grow. We must keep in balance these *four things*; illumination, trust and innocence, introspection, and knowledge. As we understand these things, moving in circles outward, always growing, always learning, we will become strong like the tree—the tree of life.

God works through people. People who are spiritually strong have a glow—a love of life. These are our Elders, the people who bring healing in our communities. They do not seek to gain personal power. Instead, they are kind people, channels for the healing which is carried out by our Creator.

PRAYER FOR MEDITATION

The sun of righteousness shall rise,
with healing in its wings.
Malachi 4:2

Creator,
we give thanks for teachings
which help us to know how to live.

May we set our eyes upon you
looking always for ways to serve,
bringing healing to our communities.

Lord, give us your words and your wisdom
that we may be instruments of your peace.

PRAYER FOR ALL PEOPLE

That we may do our work quietly and diligently, and not
weary of doing good,
let us pray to the Lord.

The Journey: Stories and Prayers for the Christian Year from People of the First Nations, Joyce Carlson (Ed.), 1991, p. 194-196

This Native Christian prayer by William Dumas, an elder from Thompson, South Indian Lake, Manitoba, is to be prayed on Sunday between November 13th and 19th during the feast of Pentecost, which celebrates the coming of God's Spirit in fullness upon all the Peoples of the earth. It is part of the Church's prayer cycle.

⊕

SACRED CIRCLE
INTERTRIBAL

The circle is called by various names—the Sacred Circle, hoop or medicine wheel. It is a natural and perfect form, a therapeutic form, a holy form. Within it is latent energy that comes alive when the circle is used. Into it all things are drawn and within it all things are bonded and renewed in the relationship with one another. It creates love, which is the bond of perfect unity. Above the circle is the Greatest Power for life. Its voice is the Thunder and the Rattle. Below the circle is the next greatest power, which is Mother Earth and procreation. Its voice is the drum.

*Four great power*s that were created by the Above Beings in the beginning are Persons who live at either the *Cardinal Directions* or at the *southeast, southwest, northwest,* and *northeast.* These powers are always active in the *four great winds*, the *four seasons*, the *four colors*, the *spirits of the four classes of humans*, and the *spirits of the four classes of all other created things*. When the powers are called upon and come into the Sacred Circle, they bring all of these brothers and sisters with them to make them available to the caller.

The circle brings about change and the Native Americans have always thought of change as a line bending back to reconnect with its beginnings, so that the circle is continually reestablished. When it is unbroken, the wheel is in motion—it turns. After the powers have seen your heart and listened to your meditations, they will send their messengers to you bearing baskets that are filled with promises, insights, comfort, strength, guidance and hope.

Exploring the Secret Pathways,
Thomas Mails, 1989, p. 1

A circle is not static; rather, it is dynamic. Movement within the circle brings the four seasons and endless possibilities during the four ages in the lives of human beings. The circle is a paradigm for understanding life; it can also become a multi-cultural paradigm.

*Little Shota (First Born Peace Child)
Joaquin Celaya begins to learn
the way of the drum*

A child named John reaches out in prayer with crow feathers in hand and feels the sun's gentle warmth

and smudges with sage and prays, surrounded by animal skins and deer antlers

Conclusion

SIDE BY SIDE AND
LED BY THE SPIRIT

(The) Creator of all that exists displays holy power in the universe, power that is available to all. The special sign of this power is creation: that on-going action of God in which, somehow in a sacred way, we can all participate. This creation, both visible and invisible, and the powers and potentiality contained within it, are available to all peoples of the world regardless of their origin or local presence on earth.

The same Creator, I truly believe, for thousands of years has spoken to the People of this hemisphere in ways that are special to them; those of other cultures and places have arrived at similar realizations. Though the traditions are many and varied, there are always some common patterns among us.

As we have seen, for many tribes, (the) Creator, in a special manner, inhabits the area above. It is God's special "place." Though the term "Father Sky" is often used, the heavens or the location "up" is representative of both the "this worldly" and the "other worldly" focus of God who is Creator. As the vast array of planets are visible (and sometimes invisible) to human beings, symbolically God is considered to be somehow "up" or "above" these places. In the directional cosmology of the many tribal peoples, this is not a limiting physical position. It is symbolic and therefore unlimited. (The) Creator's presence is both transcendent, distant from us, but also immanent, or with us.

"Mother Earth," "Earth Mother," "Mother Nature" are words which signify that part of God's creation which is apparent to human beings and which makes up the milieu of our daily living. All human beings find ourselves walking on, dancing upon, and interacting with Mother Earth. We come to recognize that we are in relationship with other beings, or, as many tribes would say, we share this terrenial aspect of God's creation with the other two-footeds, the four-footeds, the swimmers, those that fly, and those that crawl.

We have had a chance to consider the wisdom of the Native Peoples of the Americas through a great number of prayers and ceremonies and ways of doing things that show how the circle, the cardinal directions, and the number 4 have been, and are, celebrated. Some ceremonies were very short and simple, while others tended to be quite complex and extended over a period of many days.

I humbly suggest that many more people need to enter into the dialogue that concerns spirituality. I really believe that our times call for it. Many seem to be spiritually undernourished and might need to follow sacred ways, whether they are of a person's own particular culture or whether they are ways that are offered by those of another culture. Our technology is not enough for us; we are beings of the Spirit. Gifts can always be passed back and forth and from hand to hand. Nevertheless, we always need to be conscious of the value of what we are giving and what we are receiving.

I call upon the Christian Churches (especially my own, the Catholic Church) and all People of good will to enter more deeply into a dialogue that concerns the holy ways, however we have come to understand them. I likewise especially invite Native People who follow the Jesus Road to gently share what they know of how both Ways have come together for them. With respect, I suggest that those who prefer the Traditional Way to be also open to the Spirit's activity in all the other roads to God.

Intercultural, Intertribal, and Contemporary Modes

Many are the People who seek to be in touch with their tribal spiritual ways. Often they have not been raised with these traditions, but seek them nonetheless. Sometimes they claim an ancestor somewhere in the family background who they say was Native. A good deal of the time they are far removed from those who live out a traditional Native lifestyle. But somehow they are put in touch (mysteriously and miraculously, I might say) with those who honor and celebrate some forms of traditional Native spirituality. Good things then begin to happen for them. I have seen this occur time and time again.

But there are also a lot of others who have no First Nations ancestry, but feel the attraction of the spirituality. Especially in our own time it seems that (the) Creator is bringing together in a greater unity those who come from diverse backgrounds, racially, religiously, economically, etc. I also see this as a good thing. Though many mistakes might be made as people are brought together through the traditional spiritual ways, yet I see it as important and necessary. God is one and God is to be shared, and God is shared through all the spiritual ways, both Native and other. I believe that the wise spiritual leaders know this already. Contemporary intertribal and intercultural religious gatherings have been happening for quite some time now. Much deep spirituality can be shared at such gatherings. I would venture to say that a good knowledge of the directions, the circle, and the use of the number 4 and their combinations will always be helpful. There are so many connecting points for Western religious culture (especially Catholic and other Christian traditions) and Indigenous religious culture.

We have lots of opportunities to explore them in the years ahead. Let us spend some real time with each other. Let us respect each other. Let us share with one another.

MAY THE DIALOGUE CONTINUE

AND

MAY WE WALK IN HARMONY

AS TOGETHER

WE

ENTER

A

NEW

MILLENNIUM!

"Greeting of the Sun Ceremony." Contemporary Taíno gathering at Orocovis, Puerto Rico. This People, perhaps representing many others, is even now experiencing rebirth as we enter the new millennium

*Crow friends of
the author,
Jolene-Miranda and
Bartell Plainbull of
Pryor, Montana*

*Just after Native American Catholic Mass, Convention Center,
Anaheim, California, 1998*

*Author with
Jose Ortiz (Taíno),
Hilary Frederic
(Cacique of Caribs
on Island of
Dominica), and a
Taíno leader,
Rene Cibanacan*

Appendices

APPENDIX A
BIBLE REFERENCES

The following citations from the New Jerusalem Bible might offer some people a greater understanding of Native themes that have counterparts in the Western Biblical tradition.

Four Directions

Yours are the heavens and yours the earth, the world and all it holds, you founded them; you created the ***north*** and the ***south***. . . . (Psalm 89:11)

As the height of heaven above the earth, so strong is his faithful love for those who fear him. As the distance of ***east*** from ***west,*** so far from us does he put our faults. (Psalm 103:12)

Alleluia! Give thanks to Yahweh for he is good, his faithful love lasts for ever. So let them say whom Yahweh redeemed, whom he redeemed from the power of their enemies, bringing them back from foreign lands, from ***east*** and ***west, north*** and ***south.*** (Psalm 107:1-3)

Then Yahweh will appear above them and his arrow will flash out like lightning. The Lord Yahweh will sound the trumpet and advance in the storm-winds of the ***south.*** (Zechariah 9:14)

But from the farthest ***east*** to farthest ***west*** my name is great among the nations, and everywhere incense and a pure gift are offered to my name, since my name is great among the nations, says Yahweh Sabaoth. (Malachi 1:11)

And people from ***east*** and ***west,*** from ***north*** and ***south,*** will come and sit down at the feast in the kingdom of God. (Luke 13:29)

In the spirit, he carried me to the top of a very high mountain, and showed me Jerusalem, the holy city, coming down out of heaven from God. It had all the glory of God and glittered like some precious jewel of crystal-clear diamond. Its wall was of a great height and had twelve gates; at each of the twelve gates there was an angel, and over the gates were written the names of the twelves tribes of Israel; on the *east* there were three gates, on the *north* three gates, on the *south* three gates, and on the *west* three gates. (Revelation 21:10-13

Circles

High above, he pitched a tent for the sun, who comes forth from his pavilion like a bridegroom, delights like a champion in the course to be run. *Rising on the one horizon he runs his circuit to the other,* and nothing can escape his heat. (Psalm 19:4-6)

Did you not know, had you not heard? Was it not told you from the beginning? Have you not understood how the earth was set on its foundations? He who sits enthroned above the *circle* of the earth, the inhabitants of which are like grasshoppers, stretches out the heavens like a cloth, spreads them out like a tent to live in. (Isaiah 40:21-22)

I saw a brillance like amber, like fire. . . . I saw what looked like fire, giving a brilliant light all round. The radiance of the *encircling light* was like the radiance of the bow in the clouds on rainy days. The sight was like the glory of Yahweh. (Ezekiel 1:4-10,15-21,27-28)

He covers the face of the *full moon,* spreading his cloud across it. He has traced a *ring* on the surface of the waters, at the boundary between light and dark. (Job 26:9-10)

For we all trip up in many ways. . . . Think how a small flame can set fire to a huge forest; the tongue is a flame too. Among all the parts of the body, the tongue is a whole wicked world: it infects the whole body; catching fire itself from hell, it sets fire to the whole *wheel of creation.* (James 3:2,5-6)

Number 4

A river flowed from Eden to water the garden, and from there it divided to make *four* streams. The first is named the Pishon, and this winds all through the land of Havilah where there is gold. . . . The second river is named the Gihon, and this winds all through the land of Cush. The third river is named the Tigris, and this flows to the east of Ashur. The *fourth river* is the Euphrates. (Genesis 2:10-14)

You must also make a table of acacia wood. . . . You will make *four* gold rings for it, and fix the *four* rings at the *four* corners where the *four* legs are. The rings must lie close to the struts to hold the shafts for carrying the table. (Exodus 25:23,26-27)

You must make tassels for the *four* corners of the cloak in which you wrap yourself. (Deuteronomy 22:12)

I raised my eyes, and this is what I saw: *four chariots* coming out between the mountains, and the mountains were mountains of bronze. The first chariot had red horses, the second chariot had black horses, the third chariot had white horses, and the fourth chariot had vigorous, piebald horses. I asked the angel who was talking to me, "What are these, my Lord?" The angel replied, "They are the *four winds* of heaven now leaving after attending the Lord of the whole world." (Zechariah 6:1-6)

> There are three insatiable things,
> *four,* indeed that never say, Enough!
> Sheol, the barren womb,
> earth which can never have its fill of water,
> fire which never say, "Enough!". . .

> There are three things beyond my comprehension,
> *four,* indeed, that I do not understand:
> the way of an eagle through the skies,
> they way of a snake over a rock,
> the way of a ship in mid-ocean,
> the way of a man with a girl. . . .

> There are three things at which the earth trembles,
> *four,* indeed, which it cannot endure:
> a slave becomes a king,
> a brute gorged with food,
> a hateful woman wed at last,
> a servant girl inheriting from her mistress.

> There are *four* creatures little on the earth,
> though they are the wisest of the wise:
> the ants, a race with no strength,
> yet in summer they make sure of their food;
> the Conies, a race without defences,
> yet they make their home in the rocks;

> locusts, which have no king,
> yet they all march in good order;
> lizards, which you can catch with your hand,
> yet they frequent the palaces of kings.
>
> There are three things of stately tread,
> *four,* indeed, of stately walk:
> the lion, the bravest of all beasts,
> he will draw back from nothing;
> a vigorous cock, a he goat,
> and the king when he harangues the people.
> (Proverbs 30:5-16,18-19,21-31)

Daniel had a dream and visions that passed through his head as he lay in bed. He wrote the dream down, and this is how the narrative began: Daniel said, "I have been seeing visions in the night. I saw that the *four winds* of heaven were stirring up the Great Sea; *four great beasts* emerged from the sea, each different from the others." (Daniel 7:1-3)

He said to me, "Prophesy to the breath; prophesy, son of man. Say to the breath, 'The Lord Yahweh says this: come from the *four winds,* breath; breathe on these dead, so that they come to life. . . .'" (Ezekiel 37:9)

But Zaccheus stood his ground and said to the Lord, "Look, sir, I am going to give half my property to the poor, and if I have cheated anybody I will pay him back *four times* the amount." (Luke 19:8)

This, then, is what I pray, kneeling before the Father, from whom every fatherhood, in heaven or on earth, takes its name. In the abundance of his glory may he, through his Spirit, enable you to grow firm in power with regard to your inner self, so that Christ may live in your hearts through faith, and then, planted in love and built on love, with all God's holy people you will have the strength to grasp the *breadth* and the *length,* the *height* and the *depth:* so that, knowing the love of Christ, which is beyond knowledge, you may be filled with the utter fullness of God. (Ephesians 3:14-19)

Peter went to the housetop at about the sixth hour to say his prayers. He felt hungry and was looking forward to his meal, but before it was ready he fell into a trance and saw heaven thrown open and something like a big sheet being let down to earth by its *four corners*; it contained every kind of animal, reptile and bird. A voice then said to him, "Now, Peter; kill and eat!" But Peter answered, "Certainly not, Lord; I have never yet eaten anything profane or unclean." Again, a second time, the voice spoke to him, "What God has made clean, you have no right to call profane." This was repeated three times, and then suddenly the container was drawn up to heaven again. (Acts 10:9-16)

Circles & Number 4

A generation goes, a generation comes, yet the earth stands firm forever. The sun rises, the sun sets; then to its place it speeds and there it rises. *Southward* goes the wind, then turns to the *north;* it turns and turns again; then back to its *circling* goes the wind. (Ecclesiastes 1:46)

Number 4 & Four Directions

Next I saw *four* angels, standing at the *four* corners of the earth, holding the back the *four* winds of the world to keep them from blowing over the land or the sea or any tree. (Revelation 7:1)

Four Directions, Circles & Number 4

Now, as I looked at the living creatures, I saw a *wheel* touching the ground *beside each of the four-faced living creatures.* The appearance and structure of the wheels were like glittering chrysolite. *All four looked alike,* and their appearance and structure were such that each wheel seemed to have another wheel inside it. In whichever of the *four directions* they moved, they did not need to turn as they moved. Their *circumference* was of awe-inspiring size, and the *rims of all four* sparkled all the way round. When the living creatures moved, the wheels moved beside them; and when the living creatures left the ground, the wheels too left the ground. They moved in whichever direction the spirit chose to do so, and the wheels rose with them, since the wheels shared the spirit of the animals. When the living creatures moved on, they moved on; when the former halted the latter halted; when the former left the ground, the wheels too left the ground since the wheels shared the spirit of the animals. . . .

I looked; a stormy wind blew from the *north,* a great cloud with flashing fire and brilliant light around it, and in the middle, in the heart of the fire, a brilliance like that of amber, and in the middle what seemed to be *four living creatures.* They looked like this: They were of human form. Each had *four faces,* each had *four wings.* Their legs were straight; they had human hands on *all four sides* corresponding to their four faces and four wings. They touched one another with their wings; they did not turn as they moved; each one moved straight forward. As to the appearance of their faces, all *four* had a *human face,* and a *lion's face* to the right, and all four had a *bull's face* to the left, and all four had an *eagle's face.* . . .

APPENDIX B
COMMON AND PREFERRED NAMES OF THE PEOPLES

? means no English equivalent can be found

Acoma (Akóme = "People of the White Rock")
Alabama-Coushatta (Alabamu [Alba ayamule = "I Open or Clear the Thicket People"] or Atilamas [Att'ilami (atta' = "to live" + ilabinko = "separately") = "People Who Live Separately"] + Koasati = "Cane People")
Algonquian (Algonquin = "Canoe hunters," Elakomkwik)
Amahuaca (Amajuaca, Amahuaka, = ?) Ipitnere, Sayaco, Huni Kui (Huni Kui = ?)
Anishnabe ("Original People," Ojibwa, Chippewa)
Apache (Indéh, Inde, N'de = "People")
    Chiricahua (Tsil-kawa = "People of the Great Mountain")
    Jicarilla (Jicarillo = "Little Basket People")
    Lipan (Tcicihi = "People of the Forest")
    Mescalero (Mezcal = "Mescal-Gathering People")
    White Mountain ("Sierra Blanca People")
Arapaho (Hinanae-ina = "Our People")
Arawaks of Puerto Rico, Cuba & Santo Domingo (Aroaqui/Locoro, Locono - "The People")
Arikara (Arikara = "Horn or Elk People," Tannish, Sáhnis)
Aztec (Aztecatl = "People of the Place of the Herons")

Blackfoot/Blackfeet (Siksika = "Black Feet People")
Blood (Kainai = "Many Chiefs People")

Caddo (Kadohadacho = "Real Chief's People")
    Confederacy (Hasinai = "Our People"): Haish, Hainoi, Yona, Kechai, Nadaco, Nasoni, Kadohadacho, Natchitoche
Canelos Quichua (Runa = "Person")

Cayuga (Kweniogen = "The Place Where Boats Were Taken Out People")

Chamula Maya (Hlumaltik = "Our Land People")

Cherokee, Jalagi (Tsalagi [tsalu = "Tobacco" + agayuñ li = "Ancient"] = "Ancient Tobacco People"), Dhbow, Aní-yun wiyá (aniyunwiya = "Principal or Real People")

Cheyenne (Tse-tsehese-stahase = "People Like Us")

Chicano/a (Mexicano or Mesheecano [Mexican from Mechica People] = "A Person of Mexican Heritage Living in the United States of America")

Chippewa (Anishnabe = "Original People," Ojibwa)

Chiricahua Apache (Tsil-kawa = "People of the Great Mountain")

Chumash (Michumash = "Place of the Islanders People")

Comanche (Nerm, Neum, Nimcnim, Néme-ne = "Principal People")

Costanoan (Cpstampamps = "Coast People")

Coushatta-Alabama (Koasati = "Cane People" + Alabamu [Alba ayamule = I Open or Clear the Thicket People] or Atilamas [Att'ilami (atta' = "to live" + ilabinko = "separately")] = "People Who Live Separately")

Cowlitz (Cow-e-lis-kee)

Cree (Kenistenoag, Eeyouch = "The People")
> James Bay Cree (Eeyouch [on the coast] or Eenouch [inland] = "The People")
> Plains Cree (Ne-i-yah-wahk, Nahiawuk = "Four-bodied People," Nehiyawak = "Exact People")

Creek ("Okmulgee [Ocheese] Creek People")
> **Lower Creek**
>> Kashita (Kashita = ? People)
>> Coweta, Koweta, Kawet'vlke (Kawita = ? People)
>> Hichiti (Ahit'chita = "The Look Upstream People")
>> Okmulgee (Okmúlgeez = Boiling Water People")
>> Mikasuki (Miccosukee = Chief People)
> **Upper Creeks**
>> Alabama-Coushatta (Alaba [ayamule = "I Open or Clear the Thicket People"] + Koasati = "Cane People")
>> Tuskegee (tu'skeki'yu = "The One Who Has Received a War Name People")
>> Yuchi (tsoyaha yuchi = "Children of the Sun from Far Away People")

Crow (Apsáalooke = "Children of the Big-beaked Bird")

Cuna/Kuna (Tula = "People")

Cupeño (Kupa-ngakitom = "Kupa People")

Dakota Sioux (Dakota = "Allies")

Delaware (Lenni Lenapi = "True People")

Diegueño (Kawa kipai = "Southern People")
  Kumeyaay (? People)
  Ipaay ("People")
  Tipaay ("People")

Eskimo (Inuit)
  Yupik (Yupik = Inuit-speaking People along the Alaskan coast south of the Bering Strait, Inupiat = "The People," Tareumiut = "People of the Sea," Nunamiut = "People of the Land," Yuit)

Gabrieleño (Tong-vā, Komiivet, Tobohar, Pepii'maris)
Gros Ventre (Aaninena, Haaninin = "White Clay or Chalk People")

Haush (Haus, Mannekenk = ?)
Hopi (Hópi = "The Good, Peaceful People")
Huichol (Wixarika = "Healer People")
Huni Kui (Huni Kui = ?), Amahuaca (Amajuaca, Amahuaka, = ?) Ipitnere, Sayaco
Hupa (Natinook-wa = "Hoopa Valley People")

Inca (Inka = "The Royal People")
Inuit ("People")
Iowa (From the Dakota language Ayuhwa = "Those Who Sleep People" or from Ai'yuwe = "Squash People")
Iroquois (Ho-dé-no-sau-nee = "People of the Long House")
  Cayuga (Kweniogen = "The Place Where Boats Taken Out People")
  Oneida (Tiionen iote = "Boulder Standing Up People")
  Onondaga (Onondaga = "On the Mountain People")
  Mohawk (Caniega = "Flint People")
  Seneca (Sonnontouans = "Guardians of the Western Door")
  Tuscarora (Skaru-ren = "Hemp-gathering People")

James Bay Cree (Kenistenoag = "People of James Bay" or Eeyouch [on the coast] or Eenouch [inland] = "The People")

Kaiapó, Kayapó (Mebengokre = "People of the Watering Place," "People from Between the Waters")
Kaingáng (Guayaná = ?)
Karaja (Carajá = "The Great People")
Karankawa (Carancaguacas = "Dog-loving People")
Karuk (Karúk = "Upriver People"), Araar, Arar (Araar = "The People")

Kiowa (Ga-i-gwa = "Principal People," Kwu'da = "Pulling Out People,"
Tépdá = "Coming Out People")
Klamath (Eukshikai Makloks = "Klamath Marsh People")
Konkow (Maidu = "Man")
Kwagiutl (Kwakiutl = "Smoke of the World People" or "People of the Beach
on the North Side of the River," Kwakwaka'wakw)

Lacandon (Hach Winik = "Original People")
Laguna (Laguna Pueblo = "Lake People," "Ka-waik People")
Lakota Sioux (Lakota = "Allies")
Lipan Apache (Ipandes [Ipa = "A personal name" + n'de = "People"] =
"Ipa's People" or [Tcicihi = "People of the Forest"] or [Naizhan = "Our
Kind People"])
Lumbee (Croatan = "People Living Along the Lumber River in North
Carolina and who are mixed blood descendants dating from the time of
the Sir Walter Raleigh Colony of 1587")
Luiseño (Puyumkowitchum = Western People)
    Cupeño (Kupa-ngakitom = "Kupa People")

Makuna (Hoari Ngana = "People of the Forest"; Ide Masa = "Water
People" + Yiba Masa = "Land People")
Maidu (Maidu = "Man")
Mandan (Numakaki = "River Dwelling People," Nu-eta)
Mapuche (Mapu-che = "People of the Land")
Maya
    Chamula (Hmu maltik = "Our Land" [Maya])
    Q'eqchi (Q'eqchi speaking People)
Mayo (Yoremem = "The People")
Mekranoti (Medragnoti = "People with Big Red Paint on Their Faces")
Menomini (O-maeh-no-min-ni-wsk = "Wild Rice Gatherers," O'Mach no
min u wk)
Mescalero (Mezcal = "Mescal Gathering People")
Mestiza/o ("Person of mixed Native and Spanish blood")
Métis (Métis = "People of mixed Native and French or British blood)
Miwok (Miwu-k = "People")
Mohawk (Caniega = "Flint People")
Mojave (Makháv, Hamakhava = "People of the Three Mountains")
Munsee-Mahican (Min-asin-ink = "People of the Place Where Stones are
Gathered Together" + Mahican (Mainyan = "Wolf People" or
Muhneakunnuk = "People of the Tidewater" [Hudson River near
Albany, New York])

Nahua (Nahuatl = "People of Something That Makes an Agreeable Sound")
Naskapi (Nenenot = "True People")
Natchez (Natches = "Warriors of the Great Cliff People" or "High Bluff People")
Navajo (Dené, Diné = "People")
Nisenan (Nishinan, Nisinan ["Person"] = "Our People"), Southern Maidu
Nez Perce (Nimipuu = "Real People," Nimipiu)
Nooksack Salish (Nooksak = "Mountain People")

Oglala (Oglala = "The Scatters One's Own People")
Ohlone
    Karkin dialect speaking People
    Ramaytush dialect speaking People
    Chuchenye dialect speaking People
    Tamyen dialect speaking People
    Awaswas dialect speaking People
    Mutsun dialect speaking People
    Rumsen dialect speaking People
    Chalon dialect speaking People
Ojibwa/Ojibwe/Ojibway/Chippewa (Anishnaubag = "Original People," Anishnabeg, Anicinabek, Anishnabe)
Omaha (Omaha = "People Going Against the Wind or Current")
Ona/Selknam (Ona = "The On-Foot People," [Shilknam])
Oneida (Tiionen iote = "The Boulder Standing Up People")
Onondaga (Onondaga = "On the Mountain People")
Osage (Ni-u-kon-skah = "People of the Middle Waters," Wazhazag)
Ottawa (Otá-wa, Adawa, Odawa = "Trading People")

Paiute (Nengwoonts, Noonts = "People," Paviotso = Northern Paiute, Chemehuevi = Southern Paiute)
Patwin (Southern dialect name for themselves; the Wintun People)
Pawnee (Chahiksichahiks = "Men of Men People," Skiri)
Peigan (Apikuni = "Rough tanned Hides People")
Piaróa (Dearu'a = "People of the Jungle" or Uhuothoj'a = "Gentle People")
Pit River (Achomawi = "River People," Illmawi, Hammawi)
Plains Cree (Nahiawuk = "The Exact People," Ne-i-wah-wahk)
Pomo (Kaia, bonefeather = "People" or Paum = "Earth People")
Potawatomi (Potawatamink = "People of the Place of Fire," Potawaganiuk)

Q'eqchi Maya (Q'eqchi speaking People)
Quechua (Kkechua = "Plundering People")
Quichua Canelos (Runa = "Person")

Sahaptin Language Groups (People of the Mid-Columbia River in Washington State: Yakimas, Klikitats, Paluses, Nez Perce, etc.)

San Juan Pueblo (Oké-onwi = "Upstream Place People")

Santee (Isañati = "The Knife People")

Selknam/Ona (Selk'nam, Shilknam, = ? [Ona = "The On-Foot People"])

Seminole (Sim-a-no-le or Isti sima note = "Separatist," "Fruit that Grows Wild People," "Unbroken Spirit People")

Seneca (Sonnontouans = "People Who Guard the Western Door")

Seri (Comcáac, Kong Ká-ahk ay mos-aht = "Children Born of a High Rank Woman People")

Shasta (Sustí-ka = "named after a local well-known leader")

Sioux

    Dakota (Dakota = "Allies People")

    Lakota (Lakota = "Allies People")

    Oglala (Oglala = "The Scatters One's Own People")

    Santee (Isañati = "The Knife People")

    Teton (Titonwan = "Prairie Village People")

    Yankton (Ihanktoñwanna = "Upper End Village People")

Tache-Yokuts (Tadji = "Place of the Mud Hen" + Yokuts = "People," [Inyana = "People"])

Taíno (Nitaíno, Tayno = "The Good or Noble or Principle People")

Tarahumara (Ralámari, Rarámuri = "The [Foot-Running] People")

Teton (Titonwan = "Prairie Village People")

Tewa (Towa = "People")

Tirió, Tiriyó (Tiriá = ? People)

Tonkawa (Tonkaweya = "They All Stay Together People")

Tsimshian (Tsimpshian = "People of the Skeena River," 'Cmsyan)

Tubatulabal (Pahkanapul, Pahkanapil = "Pine Nut Eating People," "People Who Go to the Forest to Gather Piñon Nuts")

Tucanoa (Dáchsea = "Toucan People," Tukano)

Tuscarora (Ska roo reh, Skaru ren = "Hemp Gathering People")

Toltecs (Toltecas = "People of the Place of the Tules")

Totonac (Totonac - ? People)

Txikao (Tchikao = ? People)

Umatina (Umotina= ?)

Unami Lenape (Unami = "Living South of the Raritan River" + Lenape [Lenape = "True People"])

Wanapum (Sokuik = ? People, Wanapam)

Washoe (Washo, Washi u = "Person")

Wayapí (Waiapi, Aipi, Oyanpík, Oaiapis = ??)
White Mountain Apache ("Sierra Blanca People")
Wintun (Wintoo = "People," Wintu)
Wukchumnee-Yokuts (Wikchamni = "Place of the Blue Heron" + Yokuts
    = "People," [Inyana = "People"])
Wy-Am (Wy-am-pum = "Echo of the Water Against the Rocks People")

Yakima (Ya-ki-má = "Runaway People," Waptailmin, Waptai'lmin)
Yankton Sioux (Ihanktoñwanna = "Upper End Village People")
Yaqui (Yoemem = "? People")
Yokuts (Yokuts, Yokuch = "People," [Inyana = "People"])
    Tache-Yokuts (Tadji = "Place of the Mud Hen" + Yokuts = "People,"
        [Inyana = "People"])
    Wukchumnee-Yokuts (Wikchamni = "Place of the Blue Heron" +
        Yokuts = "People" [Inyana = "People"])
Yuchi (Euchee, Tsoyaha Yuchi = "Children of the Sun from Far Away,"
    Zoyaha = "Children of the Sun")
Yuman (Speaking Peoples): Hualapais, Havasupais, Yavapais, Mojaves,
    Quechan, Maricopas, Kamia, Kiliwa
Yupik Eskimo (Yupik Inuit = Yupik speaking People along the Alaskan
    coast south of the Bering Strait)
Yurok (Olekwo'l = "People," Alitkwa)

Zuni (Siwi, A-shiwi, the flesh = "The People")

A Taíno, Melvin Melanio Gonzalez, prepares to share his culture through a dance and song with others at a multicultural gathering at a Connecticut college in April, 1999

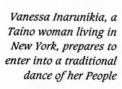

Vanessa Inarunikia, a Taíno woman living in New York, prepares to enter into a traditional dance of her People

APPENDIX C
RITUALS LISTED BY TRIBE

*Giving thanks at springtime
for the spirit of the Bear*

APPENDIX D
RITUALS LISTED ALPHABETICALLY

Closing procession at second annual Festival de Las Indieras,
Las Indieras, Maricao, Puerto Rico, 1997 (photo by Holger Thoss)

The hope of the future, Taino youth play an ancient ballgame at
Caguana Ceremonial Grounds at Utuado, Puerto Rico

APPENDIX E
SOURCES

Abbott, Walter, *Documents of Vatican II,* New York, NY: America Press, 1966. Reprinted with permission of publisher.

Alarcón, Francisco X., "Four Directions," *Snake Poems: An Aztec Invocation,* San Francisco, CA: Chronicle Books, 1992. Reprinted with permission of publisher.

Allen, Benedict, *Who Goes Out in the Midday Sun: An Englishman's Trek Through the Amazon Jungle,* New York, NY: Viking Penguin, 1986. Reprinted with permission of Macmillan London, Ltd. Copyright © Benedict Allen, 1985.

Alexander, Hartley Burr, *The World's Rim: Great Mysteries of the North American Indians,* Lincoln, NE: University of Nebraska Press, 1967, © 1953. Reprinted with permission of author's grandson, Prof. Thomas Alexander.

Amos, Pamela, *Coast Salish Spirit Dancing: The Survival of an Ancestral Religion,* Seattle, WA: University of Washington Press, 1978. Reprinted with permission of publisher.

Anderson, John, *A Circle Within the Abyss: Chumash Metaphysics,* Kootenai, ID: American Designs Publishing, 1994. Reprinted with permisson of author.

Anderson, Kat & Franco, Hector, "That Place Needs a Good Fire," *News from Native California,* Vol. 7, #2, Berkeley, CA: Heyday Books, Spring 1993. Reprinted with permission of authors.

Århem, Kaj, *Makuna: Portrait of an Amazonian People,* Washington, D.C.: Smithsonian Institution Press, copyright © 1998. Photographs by Diego Samper. Used by permission of the publisher.

Around Him, John, *Lakota Ceremonial Songs,* Rosebud, SD: Sinte Gleska University, Inc., 1983. Reprinted with permission of publisher.

Arrom, José, *Mitología y Artes Prehispanicas de las Antillas,* Mexico City, Mexico: Siglo XXI Editores, 1989. Reprinted with permission of author.

Barrett, S.A., "The Stewarts Point Maru of 1958" in Clement Meighan & Francis Riddell (Eds.), *The Maru Cult of the Pomo Indians: A California*

Ghost Dance Survival, Southwest Museum Papers #23, Los Angeles, CA: Southwest Museum, 1972. Reprinted with permission of publisher.

Barrett, Samuel Alfred, "The Geography and Dialects of the Miwok Indians," *University of California Publications in American Archaeology and Ethnography*, Vol. 6, #2 & #3, Berkeley, CA: University Press Berkeley, 1908.

Bass, Althea, *The Arapaho Way: The Memoirs of Carl Sweezy*, New York, NY: Crown Books, 1966. Reprinted with permission of publisher.

Bates, Craig, Hamber, Janet & Lee, Martha, "The California Condor and the California Indians," *American Indian Art Magazine*, #19, Scottsdale, AZ: American Indian Art, Inc., Winter 1993. Reprinted with permission of publisher.Bean, Lowell John (Ed.), *California Indian Shamanism*, Menlo Park, CA: Ballena Press, 1992. Reprinted with permission of publisher.

Beals, Ralph, "Ethnology of the Nisenan," *University of California Publications in American Archaeology And Ethnology*, Vol. 31, #6, Berkeley, CA: University of California Press, 1933.

Bean, Lowell John (Ed.), *California Indian Shamanism*, Menlo Park, CA: Ballena Press, 1992.

Bell, Maureen, *Karuk: The Upriver People*, Happy Camp, CA: Naturegraph Publishers, 1991. Reprinted with permission of publisher.

Bennett, Ross (Ed.), *Lost Empires: Living Tribes*, Washington, DC: National Geographic Society, 1982. Reprinted with permission of publisher.

Benson, William Ralganal & deAngulo, Jaime, "Creation Myth of the Pomo Indians,"*Anthropos*, Vol. 27, Vienna, Austria: Anthropos Institute, 1932. Reprinted with permission of publisher.

Bierhorst, John, *Four Masterworks of American Indian Literature*, Tucson, AZ: University of Arizona, 1984. Reprinted with permission of author.

Bolton, Reginald Pelham, *Indian Life of Long Ago in the City of New York*, New York, NY: Crown Publishers, 1972. Reprinted with permission of publisher.

Bopp, Judie, *The Sacred Tree*, Wilmot, WI: Lotus Light, 1989. Copyright permission by Phil Lane, Jr., International Coordinator, The Four Worlds International Institute for Human and Community Development, 1224 Lakemount Boulevard, Lethbridge, Alberta, Canada T1K 3K1.

Bowers, Alfred, *Mandan Social and Ceremonial Organization*, Moscow, ID: University of Idaho Press, 1991. Reprinted with permission of University of Chicago Press.

Boyd, Maurice, *Kiowa Voices: Ceremonial Dance, Ritual and Song*, Fort Worth, TX: Texas Christian University Press, 1981. Reprinted with permission of publisher.

Brandon, William, *The Magic World: American Indian Songs and Poems*, New York, NY: William Monroe and Company, Inc., 1971. Reprinted with permission of Ohio University Press/Swallow Press, Athens, Ohio.

Braun, Barbara (Ed.), *Arts of the Amazon,* London, England: Thames and Hudson Ltd., copyright © 1995. Reprinted by permission of the publisher.

Bridges, E. Lucas, *Uttermost Part of the Earth*, Mineola, NY: Dover Publishing, Inc., 1988. Reprinted with permission of publisher.

Bright, William, "The Karuk Language," *University of California Publications in Linguistics,* Vol. 13, Berkeley, CA: University of California Press, 1957.

Brotherston, Gordon, *Image of the New World: The American Continent Portrayed in Native Texts*, New York, NY: Thames & Hudson, © 1979 Thames & Hudson, Ltd., London. Reprinted by permission of the publisher.

Brown, John Epes, *The Sacred Pipe: Black Elk's Account of the Seven Rites of the Oglala Sioux,* Norman, OK: University of Oklahoma Press, 1989. Reprinted with permission of publisher.

Buan, Carolyn & Lewis, Richard (Eds.), *The First Oregonians: An Illustrated Collection of Essays on Traditional Lifeways, Federal-Indian Relations, and the State's Native People Today,* Portland, OR: Oregon Council for the Humanities, 1991. Reprinted with permission of publisher.

Burton, Bryan, *Moving Within the Circle: Contemporary Native American Music and Dance,* Danbury, CT: World Music Press, 1993. Reprinted with permission of publisher.

Calderón, Eduardo & Sharon, Douglas, *Eduardo el Curandero: The Words of a Peruvian Healer,* Richmond, CA: North Atlantic Books, copyright © 1982 Eduardo Calderón and Douglas Sharon. Used by permission of North Atlantic Books, P.O. Box 12327, Berkeley, CA 94712.

Campbell, Alan Tormaid, *Getting to Know Waiwai: An Amazonian Ethnography*, New York, NY: Routledge, Inc., 1995. Reprinted with permission of pubisher.

Campbell, Joseph, *Historical Atlas of World Mythology, Vol. II, The Way of the Seeded Earth/Part 2: Mythologies of the Primitive Planters: The Northern Americas,* New York, NY: Harper and Row, Inc., copyright © 1989 by The Joseph Campbell Trust. Reprinted by permission of Harper Collins Publishers, Inc.

Campbell, Joseph, *Historical Atlas of World Mythology, Vol. II, The Way of the Seeded Earth/Part 3: Mythologies of the Primitive Planters: The Middle and South Americas,* New York, NY: Harper and Row, 1989. Reprinted with permission of publisher.

Caputo, Philip, *Indian Country*, New York, NY: Bantam Books, 1988. Used with permission of publisher.

Carlson, Joyce (Ed.), *The Journey: Stories and Prayers for the Christian Year from People of the First Nations,* Toronto, Ontario, Canada: Anglican Book Centre, 1991. Copyright 1991 by the Anglican Book Centre, 600 Jarvis Street, Toronto, Ontario M4Y 2J6. Used with permission.

Carrasco, David, *Religions of Mesoamerica: Cosmovision and Ceremonial Centers*, New York, NY: Harper and Row, 1990. Copyright © 1990 by David Carrasco. Reprinted by permission of Harper Collins Publishers. Inc.

Caso, Alfonso, *The Aztecs: People of the Sun*, Norman, OK: University of Oklahoma Press, 1967. Reprinted with permission of publisher.

Catlin, George, *Letters and Notes on the North American Indians*, Avenal, NJ: Gramercy Books, 1975.

Catlin, George, *O-Kee-Pa: A Religious Ceremony and Other Customs of the Mandan*, Lincoln, NE: University of Nebraska Press, 1976. Reprinted with permission of Yale University Press.

Coffer, William, *Where Is the Eagle*, New York, NY: Van Nostrand Reinhold Co., 1981. Reprinted with permission of publisher.

Cohen, Ken Bear Hawk, "In the Name," written in 1991 at the Swinomish Nation. © 1997 Ken Bear Hawk Cohen. Printed with permission of author.

Cohen, Ken Bear Hawk, "The North Wind," *Creation Spirituality Magazine*, Vol. X, #IV, Oakland, CA: Friends of Creation Spirituality, Winter 1994. "The North Wind" © 1994 Ken Bear Hawk Cohen. Reprinted with permission of author.

Collaer, Paul (Ed.), *Music of the Americas: An Illustrated Music Ethnology of the Eskimo and American Indian Peoples*, New York, NY: Praeger Publisher, 1973. Copyright © 1973 by Praeger Publisher. Reproduced with permission of Greenwood Publishing Group, Inc., Westport, CT.

Collier, John, *American Indian Ceremonial Dances*, New York, NY: Crown Publishers, 1972.

Conrotto, Eugene, *Miwok Means People*, Fresno, CA: Valley Publishers, 1973. Reprinted with permission of Western Tanager Press.

Coolidge, Dane & Coolidge, Mary, *The Last of the Seris: The Aboriginal Indians of Kino Bay, Sonora, Mexico*, Glorieta, NM: The Rio Grande Press, Inc., 1973. Reprinted with permission of pubisher.

Courtright, Carina, "Cry of the Earth," *Wind Messenger: A Newsletter of Wings of America*, Santa Fe, NM: Earth Circle Foundation, Spring 1994. Reprinted with permission of author. Crescentera (a 501 (c) (3) not-for-profit corporation committed to the preservation and presentation of traditions and values that promote a respectful relationship between humanity and the natural world) produced the Cry of the Earth event at the U.N.

Crumrine, N. Ross, *The Mayo Indians of Sonora: A People Who Refuse To Die*, Prospect Heights, IL: Waveland Press, Inc., 1977 [reissued 1988]. All rights reserved. Reprinted by permission of Waveland Press, Inc.

Cummins, Marjorie, *The Tache-Yokuts, Indians of the San Joaquin Valley: Their Lives, Songs and Stories*, Fresno, CA: Pioneer Publishing Co., 1978. Reprinted with permission of pubisher.

Curran, Michael P. (Navajo), Interview on Military Technique, Pacific Grove, CA, January 21, 1997. Printed with permission.

D'Azevedo, Warren L., *Straight with the Medicine: Narratives of Washoe Followers of the Tipi Way,* Reno, NV: University of Nevada (Black Rock Press), 1978. Reprinted with permission of publisher.

Davis, Leslie, *Lifeways of Intermontane and Plains Montana Indians,* Bozeman, MT: Museum of the Rockies, Montana State University, 1979. Reprinted with permission of author.

deAngulo, Jaime, "Indians in Overalls," *The Hudson Review,* New York, NY: Hudson Review, Inc., 1950. Reprinted by permission of author's daughter.

Dempsey, Hugh A., *The Amazing Death of Calf Shirt and Other Blackfoot Stories: Three Hundred Years of Blackfoot History,* Calgary, Canada: Fifth House Publishers, 1994. Copyright 1994 by Hugh A. Dempsey. ISBN 1895618-444. Reprinted with permission of publisher.

Densmore, Frances, *Seminole Music,* Washington, DC: Smithsonian Institution, 1956.

Diamond, Beverly, Cronk, Sam & Von Rosen, Franziska, *Visions of Sound: Musical Instruments of First Native Communities in Northeastern America,* Chicago, IL: University of Chicago Press, 1994. Reprinted with permission of publisher.

Díaz, Gisele & Rodgers, Alan, *The Codex Borgia: A Full-Color Restoration of the Ancient Mexican Manuscript,* Mineola, NY: Dover Publications, 1993. Reprinted with permission of Alan Rodgers.

Dowd, Patrick (Non-Native), Interview on Men's Circle Around an All-night Warming Fire, Carmel Valley, CA, November 8, 1997. Printed with permission.

DuBois, Constance Goddard, "The Religion of the Luiseño Indians of Southern California," *University of California Publications in American Archaeology and Ethnology,* Vol. 8, #3, Berkeley, CA: University of California Press, 1908.

DuBois, Cora & Demetracopoulou, Dorothy, "Wintu Myths," *California University Publications in American Archaeology and Ethnology,* Berkeley, CA: University of California Press, 1965.

Endrezze, Anita, "Red Rock Ceremonies," in Duane Niatum (Ed.), *Carriers of the Dream Wheel: Contemporary Native American Poetry,* New York, NY: Harper & Row, 1975. Reprinted with permission of poet.

Englehardt, Zephyrin, *Mission San Carlos Borromeo,* Menlo Park, CA: Ballena Press, 1973. Reprinted with permission of publisher and Franciscans at Mission Santa Barbara.

Erdoes, Richard, *Crying for a Dream,* Santa Fe, NM: Bear and Company Publishing, 1990. Copyright 1990, Bear & Co., Santa Fe, NM. Reprinted with permission of publisher.

Fagan, Brian, *The Aztecs*, New York, NY: W.H. Freeman and Company, 1984. ©1984 by W.H. Freeman and Company. Reprinted with permission of publisher.

Faron, Louis C., *The Mapuche Indians of Chile*, New York, NY: Holt, Rinehart & Winston, 1968. Copyright ©1968 by Holt, Rinehart & Winston, reprinted by permission of the publisher.

Farrer, Claire R, "Singing for Life: The Mescalero Apache Girls Puberty Ceremony," in Charlotte Frisbie (Ed.), *Southwestern Indian Ritual Drama*, Albuquerque, NM: University of New Mexico Press, 1980. Reprinted with permission of author, Claire R. Farrer.

Fawcett, David, "The Feather Worker" in Anna Roosevelt & James Smith (Eds.), *The Ancestors: Native Artisans of the Americas*, New York, NY: National Museum of the American Indian, 1979. Used with permission of publisher.

Field, Tom & Hess, Mary, "Gifts of the First Americans," *The Glenmary Challenge Magazine*, Vol. 59 #4, Cincinnati, OH: Glenmary Home Missioners, Winter 1996. Reprinted with permission of publisher.

Fitzhugh, William & Crowell, Aron (Eds.), *Crossroads of Continents: Cultures of Siberia and Alaska*, Washington, DC: Smithsonian Institution Press, 1988. Reprinted with permission of publisher.

Fitzhugh, William & Kaplan, Susan, *Inua: Spirit World of the Bering Sea Eskimo,* Washington, DC: Smithsonian Institution Press, 1982. Reprinted with permission of publisher.

Fletcher, Alice C., *Indian Games and Dances with Native Songs*, Lincoln, NE: University of Nebraska Press, 1994.

Fletcher, Alice & LaFlesche, Francis, *The Omaha Tribe*, Lincoln, NE: University of Nebraska, 1992.

Freed, Stanley & Freed, Ruth, "The Persistence of Aboriginal Ceremonies Among the Washo Indians," *The Washo Indians of California and Nevada*, Anthropological Papers, #67, Salt Lake City, UT: University of Utah Press, August 1963. Reprinted with permission of publisher.

Freesoul, John Redtail, *Breath of the Invisible: The Way of the Pipe*, Wheaton, IL: Theosophical Publishing House, 1986. Reprinted with permission of publisher.

Freidel, David, Schele, Linda & Parker, Joy, *Maya Cosmos: Three Thousand Years on the Shaman's Path*, New York, NY: William Morrow & Co., 1993. Reprinted with permission of publisher.

Frey, Rodney, *The World of the Crow Indians: As Driftwood Lodges,* Norman, OK: University of Oklahoma Press, 1987. Reprinted with permission of publisher.

Fowler, Loretta, *The Arapaho*, New York, NY: Chelsea House, 1989. Reprinted with permission of publisher.

Furst, Peter, "The Art of Being Huichol" in Kathleen Berrin (Ed.), *Art of the Huichol Indians*, New York, NY: Harry J. Abrams, Inc., 1978. Reprinted with permission of publisher.

Gabriel, Kathryn, *Gambler Way: Indian Gaming in Mythology, History and Archeology in North America*, Boulder, CO: Johnson Books, 1996. Reprinted from *Gambler Way*, copyright 1996 by Kathryn Gabriel, with permission from Johnson Books, Boulder, Colorado.

Gheerbrant, Alain, *The Impossible Adventure: Journey to the Amazon*, London, England: Victor Gollancz, Ltd., 1953. © Editions Gallimard, 1952. Reprinted with permission of publisher.

Gifford, Edward, "Central Miwok Ceremonies," *University of California Publications, Anthropological Records*, Vol. 14, #4, Berkeley, CA: University of California Press, 1955.

Goddard, Pliny Earle, "Hupa Texts," *University of California Publications in American Archaeology and Ethnology*, Vol. 1, #2, Berkeley, CA: University of California Press, 1904.

Goddard, Pliny Earle, "The Masked Dancers of the Apache," in F.W. Hodge (Ed.), *Holmes Anniversary Volume*, Washington, DC: J.W. Bryan Press, 1916.

Gossen, Gary, *Chamulas in the World of the Sun: Time and Space in a Maya Oral Tradition*, Cambridge, MA: Harvard University Press, 1974. Reprinted with permission of author.

Greenberg, James, *Santiago's Sword: Chatino Peasant Religion and Economics*, Berkeley, CA: University of California Press, 1981. Reprinted with permission of author.

Grimal, Pierre (Ed.), *Larousse World Mythology*, Secaucus, NJ: Chartwell Books, Inc., 1977. Grimal, Pierre (Editor), *World Mythology*, Paris, France: © Larousse, 1977, reprinted with permission of Larousse, Paris, France.

Grimes, Joel, *Navajo: Portrait of a Nation*, Englewood, CO: Westcliffe Publishers Inc., 1992. Reprinted with permission of author (and Betty Reed).

Gyles, Anna Benson & Sayer, Chloe, *Of Gods and Men: The Heritage of Ancient Mexico*, San Francisco, CA: Harper & Row, 1980. Copyright © 1980 by Anna Benson Gyles and Chloe Sayers. Reprinted by permission of Harper Collins Publishers, Inc.

Hagy, Imre, "Cheyenne Shields and Their Cosmological Background," *American Indian Art Magazine*, Vol. 19, #3, Scottsdale, AZ: American Indian Art, Inc., Summer 1994. Reprinted with permission of publisher.

Halifax, Joan, *Shaman: The Wounded Healer*, New York, NY: Thames and Hudson, Inc., 1982. Copyright © 1982 Thames and Hudson Ltd., London. Reprinted by permission of the publisher.

Hamilton, Martha, *Silver in the Fur Trade, 1680-1820*, Chelmsford, MA: Martha Wilson Hamilton Publishing, 1995. Reprinted with permission of author.

Hanbury-Tenison, Robin, *A Question of Survival for the Indians of Brazil*, New York, NY: Charles Scribner's Sons, 1973. Reprinted with permission of Brandt & Brandt Literary Agency, New York, NY.

Handelman, Don, "The Development of a Washo Shaman," in Lowell Bean and Thomas Blackburn (Eds.), *Native Californians: A Theoretical Retrospective*, Menlo Park, CA: Ballena Press, 1976. Reprinted with permission of publisher.

Harrod, Howard, *Renewing the World: Plains Indian Religions and Morality*, Tuscon, AZ: University of Arizona, 1992. Reprinted with permission of publisher.

Haugen, Marty, "Song at the Center," *Agape*, Chicago, IL: GIA Publications, Inc., 1993. Reprinted with permission of publisher.

Hausman, Gerald, *Prayer to the Great Mystery: The Uncollected Writings and Photography of Edward S. Curtis,* New York, NY: St. Martin's Press, 1995. Copyright © 1995 by Gerald Hausman. Reprinted by permission of St. Martin's Press Incorporated.

Havnen-Finley, Jan, *The Hoop of Peace*, Happy Camp, CA: Naturegraph Publishers, 1994. Reprinted with permission of publisher.

Heizer, Robert, *Handbook of North American Indians, Vol. 8 (California)*, Washington, DC: Smithsonian Institution, 1978.

Helphey, Juanita (Ed.), *Worship Resources*, Minneapolis, MN: Council for American Indian Ministry of Church of Christ, 1991. Reprinted with permission of publisher.

Henry, Jules, *Jungle People: A Kaingáng Tribe of the Highlands of Brazil*, New York, NY: Random House, 1964. Reprinted with permission of author's widow.

Hensen, Lance, "Our Smoke Has Gone Four Ways," in Duane Niatum (Ed.), *Carriers of the Dream Wheel: Contemporary Native American Poetry*, New York, NY: Harper & Row, 1975. Reprinted with permission of poet.

Heth, Charlotte (Ed.), *Native American Dance: Ceremonies and Social Traditions*, Washington, DC: National Museum of the American Indian/ Smithsonian Institution with Storwood Press, 1992. Reprinted with permission of publisher.

Highwater, Jamake, *Ritual of the Wind: North American Indian Ceremonies, Music and Dance,* Toronto, Ontario, Canada: Methuen Publications, 1984. © 1997 The Native Land Foundation. Reprinted with the permission of The Native Land Foundation.

Hill, Jane & Nolasquez, Rosinda, *Mulu-Wetam: The First People; Cupeño Oral History and Language*, Banning, CA: Malki Museum Press, 1973. Reprinted with permission of publisher.

Hofstra, Marilyn M., *Voices: Native American Hymns and Worship Resources*, Nashville, TN: Discipleship Resources, 1992. From the Lakota prayer tradition by Christian Native American Women for World Day of Prayer

1981. (c)1981 Church Women United, 475 Riverside Dr., Suite 500, New York, NY 10115. Used with permission.

Hoijer, Harry, *Chiricahua and Mescalero Apache Texts*, Chicago, IL, University of Chicago Press, 1938. Reprinted with permission of publisher.

Holt, Catherine, "Shasta Ethnography," *University of California Anthropological Records,* Berkeley, CA: University of California Press, 1946.

Horse Capture, George (Ed.), *The Seven Visions of Bull Lodge (As told by His Daughter, Garter Snake),* Lincoln, NE: University of Nebraska Press, 1992. Reprinted with permission of author.

Howard, James, "The Arikara Buffalo Society Medicine Bundle," *Plains Anthropologist, Journal of the Plains Conference,* Vol. 19, #66, Iowa City, IA: University of Iowa, June 1974. Reprinted with permission of publisher.

Howard, James with Lena, Willie, *Oklahoma Seminoles: Medicines, Magic, and Religion,* Norman, OK: University of Oklahoma Press, 1984. Reprinted with permission of publisher.

Hudson, Charles, *The Southeastern Indians,* Knoxville, TN: University of Tennessee Press, 1976. Reprinted with permission of publisher.

Hudson, Travis, Timbrok, Janice & Rempe, Melissa (Eds.), *Tomol: Chumash Watercraft as Described in the Ethnographic Notes of John P. Harrington,* Menlo Park, CA: Ballena Press, 1978. Reprinted with permission of publisher.

Hungry Wolf, Adolf, *The Blood People: A Division of the Blackfoot Confederacy,* New York, NY: Harper and Row, 1977. Reprinted with permission of author.

Hungry Wolf, Adolf, *A Good Medicine Collection: Life in Harmony with Nature,* Summertown, TN: Book Publishing Company, 1990. Reprinted with permission of publisher.

Hunn, Eugene with Selam, James & Family, *Nch'i-wana, "The Big River": Mid-Columbia Indians and Their Land,* Seattle, WA: University of Washington Press, 1990. Reprinted with permission of publisher.

Hyde, George, *Indians of the Woodlands: From Prehistoric Times to 1725,* Norman, OK: University of Oklahoma Press, 1962. Reprinted with permission of publisher.

Jackson, Bill, Coppaway, Noble & Robertson, Wilbert, "Council Speak," *Indian Life Magazine,* Vol. 11, #2, pg. 20. Winnipeg, Manitoba, Canada: Indian Life Ministries, May-June 1990. Reprinted with permission of publisher.

Jenness, Diamond, *The Ojibwa Indians of Parry Island: Their Social and Religious Life,* Ottawa, Canada: National Museum of Canada, 1935. Reprinted with permission of Canadian Museum of Civilization, Hull, Quebec, Canada.

Johnston, Basil, *Ojibway Ceremonies,* Lincoln, NE: University of Nebraska Press, 1990. Reprinted with permission of publisher.

Johnston, Basil, *Ojibway Heritage*, Lincoln, NE: University of Nebraska Press, 1990. Reprinted with permission of publisher.

Jones, David, *Sanapia: Comanche Medicine Woman*, Prospect Heights, IL: Waveland Press, Inc., 1972. Reprinted with permission of Holt, Rinehart & Winston, Orlando, FL.

Keeling, Richard, *Cry for Luck: Sacred Song and Speech Among the Yurok, Hupa, and Karok Indians of Northwestern California*, Berkeley, CA: University of California Press, 1992. Reprinted with permission of publisher.

Kelly, Joanne, *Cuna,* South Brunswick, NJ: A.S. Barnes, 1966.

Kennedy, Roger G., *Hidden Cities: The Discovery and Loss of Ancient North American Civilization,* New York, NY: Penguin Books, 1994. Copyright ©1994 by Roger G. Kennedy. Reprinted with the permission of The Free Press, a Division of Simon & Schuster.

Kline, Mary Ann Chioino (Chumash), Interview on Healing Ceremony, Seaside, CA, July 12, 1997. Printed with permission.

Kolaz, Thomas, "Yaqui Pascola Masks from the Tucson Area," *American Indian Art Magazine*, Vol. 11, #1, Scottsdale AZ: American Indian Art, Inc., Winter 1985. Reprinted with permission of the publisher.

Kroeber, A.L., "Seven Mohave Myths," *University of California Publications, Anthropological Records,* Vol. XI, Berkeley, CA: University of California Press, 1948.

Kroeber, Alfred Louis, *The Arapaho*, Lincoln, NE: University of Nebraska Press, 1983.

Kroeber, Alfred Louis, *Handbook of Indians of California*, Mineola, NY: Dover Publishing, Inc., 1977. Reprinted with permission of publisher.

Kroeber, Theodora, & Heizer, Robert, *Almost Ancestors: The First Californians*, New York, NY: Sierra Club-Ballantine Books, 1968. Used with permission of publisher.

Ladd, George Van der Goes, *Shall We Gather at the River?* Winfield, British Columbia, Canada: Wood Lake Books, 1986.

Lamb, F. Bruce, *Wizard of the Upper Amazon: The Story of Manuel Córdova-Rios*, Berkeley, CA: North Atlantic Books, 1974. Copyright © 1974 F. Bruce Lamb. Used by permission of North Atlantic Books, P.O. Box 12327, Berkeley, CA 94712

Lame Deer, John & Erdoes, Richard, *Lame Deer, Seeker of Visions: The Life of a Sioux Medicine Man*, New York, NY: Simon and Schuster, 1972. Reprinted with permission of publisher.

Landes, Ruth, *The Prairie Potawatami: Tradition and Ritual in the Twentieth Century*, Madison, WI: University of Wisconsin Press, 1970. Reprinted with permission of the Ruth Landes Estate.

Laubin, Reginald & Laubin, Gladys, *Indian Dances of North America: Their Importance to Indian Life,* Norman, OK: University of Oklahoma Press, 1977. Reprinted with permission of publisher.

LeBeau, Beverly, "D-Q U," Davis, CA: D.Q. University, 1985. Printed with permission of poet's son.

Lee, Dorothy Demetracopolou, "Notes on the Conception of the Self Among the Wintu Indians, *Journal of Abnormal and Social Psychology,* Vol. 45, Albany, NY: American Psychological Association, 1950. Reprinted by permission of publisher.

Lee, Dorothy Demetracopolou, "Some Indian Texts Dealing with the Supernatural," *Review of Religion,* Vol. 5, New York, NY: Columbia University Press, 1941. Copyright 1940. Reprinted by permission of the publisher.

Leon-Portilla, Miguel, *Aztec Thought and Culture: A Study of the Ancient Nahuatl Mind,* Norman, OK: University of Oklahoma Press, 1982. Reprinted with permission of publisher.

Lesser, Alexander, *The Pawnee Ghost Dance Hand Game: Ghost Dance Revival and Ethnic Identity,* Madison, WI: University of Wisconsin Press, c. 1978. Reprinted by permission of the University of Wisconsin Press.

Librado, Fernando, *Breath of the Sun,* Banning, CA: Malki Museum, 1979. Reprinted with permission of publisher.

Liebert, Robert, *Osage Life and Legends: Earth People/Sky People,* Happy Camp, CA: Naturegraph, 1987. Reprinted with permission of publisher.

Long, Paul V., *Big Eyes: The Southwestern Photographs of Simeon Schwemberger, 1902-1908,* Albuquerque, NM: University of New Mexico Press, 1992. Reprinted with permission of publisher.

Long Standing Bear Chief, *Ni-Kso-Ko-Wa: Blackfoot Spirituality, Traditions, Values and Beliefs,* Browning, MT: Spirit Talk Press, 1992. Reprinted with permission of author.

Lopez, Alonzo, "Direction," *South Dakota Review,* Vol. 7, No.2, Vermillion, SD: South Dakota Review, Summer 1969. Reprinted with permission of publisher.

Mails, Thomas, *The Cherokee People: The Story of the Cherokees from Earliest Origins to Contemporary Times,* Tulsa, OK: Council Oak Books, 1992. Reprinted with permission of author.

Mails, Thomas, *Exploring the Secret Pathways,* Lake Elsinore, CA: The Pathways Foundation, 1989. Reprinted with permission of author.

Mails, Thomas, *Living in the Timeless Age,* Lake Elsinore, CA: The Pathways Foundation, 1990. Reprinted with permission of author.

Mails, Thomas, *Secret Native American Pathways: A Guide to Inner Peace,* Tulsa, OK: Council Oak Books, 1988. Reprinted with permission of author.

Mandelbaum, David, *The Plains Cree: An Ethnographic, Historical, and Comparative Study,* Regina, Saskatchewan, Canada: Canadian Plains

Research Center, University of Regina, 1985. Reproduced with the permission of the Canadian Plains Research Center, University of Regina, Regina, Saskatechewan, Canada.

Mansell, Maureen, *By the Power of Their Dreams: Songs, Prayers and Sacred Shields of the Plains Indians,* San Francisco, CA: Chronicle Books, 1994. Reprinted with permission of publisher.

Markman, Peter T. & Markman, Roberta H., *The Flayed God: The Meso-american Mythological Tradition,* New York, NY: Harper Collins, 1992. Copyright © 1992 by Roberta H. Markman and Peter T. Markman. Reprinted by permission of Harper Collins Publishers, Inc.

Matthews, Caitlín, *The Celtic Tradition,* Rockport, ME: Element Books, 1995. Reprinted with permission of publisher.

Maxwell, James (Ed.), *America's Fascinating Indian Heritage,* Pleasantville, NY: Reader's Digest Association, Inc., 1978. Reprinted with permission of University of Tennessee Press.

Maxwell, Thomas, *The Temescals of Arroyo Conejo,* Thousand Oaks, CA: California Lutheran Univeristy, 1982. Reprinted with permission of author.

McCarthy, Scott, *All One (That All May Be One): A Handbook for Ecumenical and Interfaith Worship,* Monterey, CA: Ecumenical Commission of the Diocese of Monterey, 1996. Reprinted with permission of author.

McCarthy, Scott, *Celebrating the Earth: An Earth Centered Theology of Worship with Blessings, Prayers and Rituals*, San Jose, CA: Resource Publications, 1990. Reprinted with permission of pubisher and author.

McCawley, William, *The First Angelinos: The Gabrielino Indians of Los Angeles,* Menlo Park, CA: Malki Museum/Ballena Press, 1996. Used with permission of publisher.

McCleary, Timothy, *The Stars We Know: Crow Indian Astronomy and Lifeways,* Prospects Heights, IL: Waveland Press, 1997. Reprinted by permission of Waveland Press, Inc. All rights reserved.

McClintock, Walter, "Dances of the Blackfoot Indians," Highland Park, CA: Southwest Museum, Leaflet #7, 1937. Reprinted with permission of publisher.

McClurken, James, *Gah-Baeh-Jhagwah-Buk: The Way It Happened*, East Lansing, MI: Michigan State University Museum, 1991. Reprinted with permission of author.

McCoy, Ronald, *Circles of Power,* Flagstaff, AZ: Museum of Northern Arizona Press, 1988. Reprinted with permission of author.

McEwan, Colin, et al. (Eds.), *Patagonia: Natural History, Prehistory and Ethnography at the Uttermost End of the Earth*, Princeton, NJ: Princeton University Press, 1997. Copyright © 1998 by Princeton University Press. Copyright © 1997 The British Museum Press. Reprinted by permission of Princeton University Press.

McKeon, Martha Ferguson, *Come to Our Salmon Feast*, Portland, OR: Binford and Mort, 1959. Reprinted with permission of publisher.

Merriam, C. Hart, *Studies of California Indians*, Berkeley, CA: University of California Press, 1955. Reprinted with permission of publisher.

Meyerhoff, Barbara, *Peyote Hunt: The Sacred Journey of the Huichol Indians*, Ithaca, NY: Cornell University Press, 1974. Reprinted with permission of publisher.

Meyerhoff, Barbara, "Peyote and the Mystic Vision" in Kathleen Berrin (Ed.), *Art of the Huichol Indians*, New York, NY: Harry J. Abrams, Inc., 1978. Reprinted with permission of publisher.

Mooney, James, *The Ghost-Dance Religion and the Sioux Outbreak of 1890*, Lincoln, NE: University of Nebraska Press, 1991.

Morrison, R. Bruce & Wilson, C. Roderick (Eds.), *Native Peoples: The Canadian Experience*, Second Edition, Toronto, Ontario, Canada: McClelland and Stewart, Inc., 1989. Copyright © 1995 by R. Bruce Morrison and C. Roderick Wilson. Reprinted by permission of Oxford University Press Canada.

Mozo, Virgie, "Mapuche New Year," *Columban Mission*, Vol. 77, #9, St. Columbans, NE: Columban Fathers, December 1994. Reprinted with permission of publisher.

Murie, James, *Ceremonies of the Pawnee*, Lincoln, NE: University of Nebraska Press, 1989.

Nabokov, Peter & Easton, Robert, *Native American Architecture*, New York, NY: Oxford University Press, 1989. Copyright © 1989 by Easton and Nabokov. Used by permission of Oxford University Press, Inc.

Neihardt, John, *Black Elk Speaks*, New York, NY: William Morrow & Co., 1932. Reprinted with permission of publisher.

Newcomb, Jr., W.W., *The Indians of Texas: From Prehistoric to Modern Times*, Austin, TX: University of Texas, 1984. Reprinted with permission of publisher.

Newkumet, Vynola Beaver & Meredith, Howard, *Hasinai: A Traditional History of the Caddo Confederacy*, College Station, TX: Texas A & M University Press, 1988. Reprinted with permission of publisher.

Oliver, Louis Littlecoon, *Chasers of the Sun: Creek Indian Thoughts*, Greenfield Center, NY: Greenfield Review Press, 1990. Reprinted with permission of publisher.

Ortiz, Alfonso, *The Tewa World: Space, Time, Being and Becoming in a Pueblo Society*, Chicago, IL: University of Chicago Press, 1969. Reprinted with permission of publisher.

Ortiz, Simon, "Smoking My Prayers," *South Dakota Review*, Vol. 7, No.2, Vermilion, SD: South Dakota Review, Summer 1969. Reprinted with permission of publisher.

Paper, Jordan, *Offering Smoke: The Sacred Pipe and Native American Religion*, Moscow, ID: University of Idaho, 1988. Reprinted with permission of author.

Pard, Bernadette, *The Peigan: A Nation in Transition*, Edmonton, Alberta, Canada: Plains Publishing Co., 1986. Reprinted with permission of Education Advantage, Edmonton, Alberta, Canada.

Parker, Arthur and Fenton, William (Eds.), *Parker on the Iroquois: Iroquois Uses of Maize and Other Food Plants, the Code of Handsome Lake, the Seneca Prophet, the Constitution of the Five Nations*, Syracuse, NY: Syracuse University Press, 1968. Reprinted with permission of publisher.

Penny, David, *Art of the American Frontier: A Portfolio*, New York, NY: Detroit Institute of Arts/The New Press, 1995. Reprinted with permission of publisher.

Perry, Edgar, *All Roads Are Good: Native Voices on Life and Culture*, Washington, DC: National Museum of the American Indian/Smithsonian Institution, 1994. Reprinted with permission of publisher.

People of Reservations around Phoenix, "Monday Gathering Prayers During 16th Annual Nocercc Convention," Phoenix, AZ: Diocese of Phoenix, 1989. Reprinted with permission of Office of Worship Director, Diocese of Phoenix.

Pick, John (Ed.), *A Hopkins Reader: Selections from the Writings of Gerard Manley Hopkins*, Garden City, NY: Image Books, 1953.

Powell, Father Peter J., "Ox'zem: Box Elder and His Sacred Wheel Lance," *Montana: The Magazine of Western History*, Vol. 20, #2, Helena, MT: Montana Historical Society, Spring 1970. Reprinted with permission of publisher.

Powers, Bob, *Indian Country of the Tubatulabal*, Tucson, AZ: Westernlore Press, 1981. Reprinted by permission of The Arthur H. Clark, Co., 1990, Spokane, WA.

Powers, William, *Beyond the Vision: Essays on American Indian Culture*, Norman, OK: University of Oklahoma Press, 1987. Reprinted with permission of publisher.

Powers, William, *Sacred Language: The Nature of Supernatural Discourse in Lakota*, Norman, OK: University of Oklahoma Press, 1986. Reprinted with permission of publisher.

Rausch, John, "A Unique Lenten Sweat Lodge," *The Glenmary Challenge*, Cincinnati, OH: Glenmary Home Missioners, Spring, 1992. Reprinted with permission of author.

Riegert, Wilbur, *The Quest for the Pipe of the Sioux: As Viewed from Wounded Knee*, Rapid City, SD: Printing, Inc., 1975. Reprinted with permission of daughter, Jean Fritze.

Roberts, David, *Once They Moved Like the Wind: Cochise, Geronimo, and the Apache Wars*, New York, NY: Touchstone Books, 1994. Copyright © 1993,

1994 by David Roberts. Reprinted with the permission of Simon & Schuster, Inc.

Rockwell, David, *Giving Voice to Bear: North American Indian Myths, Rituals, and Images of the Bear,* Niwot, CO: Roberts Rinehart Publishers, 1991. Reprinted with permission of pubisher.

Rutledge, Don, *Center of the World: Native American Spirituality,* North Hollywood, CA: Newcastle Publishing Company, 1992. Reprinted with permission of publisher.

Sanders, Thomas, *Literature of the American Indian,* Beverly Hills, CA: Glencoe Publishing, 1976.

Scheffler, Lilian, *Ethnic Groups of Mexico,* Mexico City, Mexico: Panorama Editorial, 1987. Reprinted with permission of pubisher.

Schlesier, Karl, *The Wolves of Heaven: Cheyenne Shamanism, Ceremonies, and Prehistoric Origins,* Norman, OK: University of Oklahoma Press, 1987. Reprinted with permission of publisher.

Schultes, Richard Evans & Hofmann, Albert, *Plants of the Gods: Their Sacred, Healing and Hallucinogenic Powers,* Rochester, VT: Healing Arts Press, 1992. Reprinted with permission of Inner Traditions International, Rochester, VT.

Schulz, Paul, *Indians of Lassen,* Mineral, CA: Loomis Museum Association, 1980. Reprinted with permission of the Loomis Museum Association Board of Directors.

Schwartz, Warren, *The Last Contrary: The Story of Wesley Whiteman (Black Bear),* Sioux Falls, SD: Augustana College Center for Western Studies, 1988. Reprinted with permission of publisher.

Scott, Lalla, *Karnee: A Paiute Narrative,* Reno, NV: University of Nevada Press, 1966. Quoted with permission of the publisher.

Shein, Max, *The Pre-Columbian Child,* Lancaster, CA: Labyrinthos, 1992. Reprinted with permission of publisher.

Shelton, Anthony, "Huichol Natural Philosophy," *The Canadian Journal of Native Studies,* Vol. 7, #2, Brandon, Manitoba: Brandon University, 1997. Reprinted with permission of author.

Silko, Leslie Marmon, "Prayer of the Pacific," in Duane Niatum (Ed.), *Carriers of the Dream Wheel: Contemporary Native American Poetry,* New York, NY: Harper & Row, 1975. Copyright © 1981. Reprinted with the permission of The Wylie Agency, Inc.

Simpson, Richard, *Ooti: A Maidu Legacy,* Millbrae, CA: Celestial Arts, 1977. Reprinted with permission of author.

Small, Lawrence, *Religion in Montana: Pathways to the Present,* Billings, MT: Rocky Mountain College, 1992. Reprinted with permission of pubisher.

Soto, José (Arawak/Tuscarora), Interview on Directional and Color Symbolism of the Caribbean Arawaks, Powwow Grounds, Browning, MT, July 10, 1994. Printed with permission.

Soustelle, Jacques, *Daily Life of the Aztecs on the Eve of the Spanish Conquest*, New York, NY: MacMillan Company, 1961. Copyright © 1955 by Hachette. Reprinted by permission of Georges Borchardt, Inc.

Speck, Frank, *Naskapi: The Savage Hunters of the Labrador Peninsula*, Norman, OK: University of Oklahoma Press, 1977. Reprinted with permission of publisher.

Speck, Frank & Broom, Leonard, with Will West Long, *Cherokee Dance and Drama*, Norman, OK: University of Oklahoma Press, 1993. Reprinted with permission of publisher.

Starkloff, Carl, *The People of the Center: American Indian Religion and Christianity*, New York, NY: Seabury Press, 1974. Reprinted with permission of author.

Steinmetz, Paul, *Meditations with Native Americans: Lakota Spirituality*, Santa Fe, NM: Bear and Company Publishing, 1984. Copyright 1984, Bear & Co., Santa Fe, NM. Reprinted with permission of publisher.

Steward, Julian (Ed.), *Handbook of South American Indians, Vol. 1 & 3*, New York, NY: Cooper Square Publishers, Inc., 1963. Reprinted with permission of Rowman & Littlefield Publisher, Inc., Lanham, MD.

Steward, Julian, "Notes on Hopi Ceremonies in Their Initiatory Form in 1927-1928," *American Anthropologist*, Vol. 33, n.s. #1, New York, NY: American Anthropological Association, January-March 1931. Reproduced by permission of the American Anthropological Association. Not for further reproduction.

Stewart, Hilary, *Indian Fishing: Early Methods on the Northwest Coast*, Vancouver, British Columbia, Canada: Douglas & McIntyre Ltd., © 1982. Reprinted with permission of publisher.

Stilwell, Chenoa Bah, "Kinaalda: Running to Womanhood," *Wind Messenger: A Newsletter of Wings of America*, Santa Fe, NM: Earth Circle Foundation, Spring 1994. Reprinted with permission of author.

Stolzman, William, *The Pipe and Christ: A Christian-Sioux Dialogue*, Chamberlain, SD: St. Joseph's Indian School, 1986. Reprinted with permission of author.

Storm, Hyemeyohsts, *Seven Arrows*, New York, NY: Harper and Row, 1972. Reprinted with permission of Harpercollins Publishers.

Tac, Pablo, *Indian Life and Customs at San Luis Rey*, Gordon Hewes & Minna Hewes (Eds.), San Luis Rey, CA: Franciscan Fathers of Mission San Luis Rey, 1952. Reprinted with permission of publisher.

Tedlock, Dennis & Tedlock, Barbara, *Teachings from the American Earth: Indian Religion and Philosophy*, New York, NY: Liveright, 1975. Reprinted with permission of publisher.

Thompson, J. Eric, *Maya History and Religion*, Norman, OK: University of Oklahoma Press, 1990. Reprinted with permission of publisher.

Thompson, Lucy, *To the American Indian*, Eureka, CA: Cummins Print Shop, 1916. Quoted from authorized facsimile of original book: University Microfilms International, Ann Arbor, MI.

Tompkins, Ptolemy, *This Tree Grows Out of Hell: Mesoamerica and the Search for the Magical Body*, New York, NY: Harper Collins Publishers, 1990. Copyright © 1990 by Ptolemy Tompkins. Reprinted by permission of Harper Collins Publishers, Inc.

Tooker, Elisabeth, *The Iroquois Ceremonial of Midwinter*, Syracuse, NY: Syracuse University Press, 1970. Reprinted with permission of publisher.

Tooker, Elisabeth (Ed.), *Native, North American Spirituality of the Eastern Woodlands: Sacred Myths, Dreams, Visions, Speeches, Healing Formulas, Rituals and Ceremonials*, New York, NY: Paulist Press, 1979. Reprinted with permission of publisher.

Tuchman, Gail, *Through the Eye of the Feather: Native American Visions*, Layton, UT: Gibbs-Smith, 1994. Reprinted with permission of author Gail Tuchman and Elayne Reyna.

Underwood, Paula, *The Walking People: A Native American Oral History*, San Anselmo, CA: A Tribe of Two Press, 1993. Reprinted with permission of author.

Van Dooren, Ingrid, "Navajo Hooghan and Navajo Cosmos," *The Canadian Journal of Native Studies*, Vol. 7, #2, Brandon, Manitoba: Brandon University, 1987. Reprinted with permission of author.

Vendrely, Sabine, "Voladores: The Flying Men of Papantla," *Native Peoples Magazine*, Vol. 7, #4, Phoenix, AZ: Media Concepts Group, Inc., Summer 1994. Reprinted with permission of author.

Vennum, Jr., Thomas, *American Indian Lacrosse: Little Brother to War*, Washington, DC: Smithsonian Institution Press, 1994. Reprinted with permission of publisher.

Verrill, A. Hyatt & Verrill, Ruth, *America's Ancient Civilizations*, New York, NY: Putnam Publishing Group, 1953. Reprinted with permission of pubisher.

Verswijver, Gustaaf (Ed.), *Kaiapó, Amazonia: The Art of Body Decoration*, Gent, Belgium: Snoeck-Ducajo and Zoon, 1992. Reprinted with permission of author.

Verswijver, Gustaaf, *Mekranoti: Living Among the Painted People of the Amazon*, New York, NY: Prestel-Verlag, 1996. Reprinted with permission of author.

Vigil, Deborah, "The Woman Who Would Not Run," *Razateca*, San Jose, CA: Razateca Publications, March/April 1997. Reprinted with permission of publisher.

Villero, Melchor, "Blessing of the Chapel in Semuy II," *Missionhurst Magazine*, Arlington, VA: Congregation of the Immaculate Heart of Mary, February 1993. Reprinted with permission of *Missionhurst Magazine*.

Voget, Fred, *The Shoshoni-Crow Sun Dance*, Norman, OK: University of Oklahoma Press, 1984. Reprinted with permission of publisher.

Voget, Fred, *They Call Me Agnes: A Crow Narrative Based on the Life of Agnes Yellowtail Deernose*, Norman, OK: University of Oklahoma Press, 1995. Reprinted with permission of publisher.

Walker, J.R., "The Sundance and Other Ceremonies of the Oglala Division of the Teton Dakota," *Anthropological Papers of the American Museum of Natural History*, Vol. 16, Part 2, New York, NY: Trustees of the American Museum of Natural History, 1917.

Walker, James R., *Lakota Belief and Ritual*, Lincoln, NE: University of Nebraska Press, 1991. Edited by Raymond J. DeMallie and Elaine A. Jahner. Copyright © 1980, 1991 by the University of Nebraska Press. Reprinted by permission of the University of Nebraska Press.

Walker, Philip & Hudson, Travis, *Chumash Healing: Changing Health and Medical Practices in an American Indian Society*, Banning, CA: Malki Museum Press, 1993. Reprinted with permission of publisher.

Walking Bear, Knowles (United Lumbee Nation of North Carolina and America), Interview on Lumbee Customs, Lubbock, TX, January 27, 1997. Printed with permission.

Wansbrough, Henry (Ed.), *The New Jerusalem Bible*, Garden City, NY: Doubleday, 1985. Copyright © 1985 by Darton, Longman & Todd, Ltd. and Doubleday, a division of Bantam Doubleday Dell Publishing Group, Inc. Reprinted by permission of publisher.

Warburton, Austen & Endert, Joseph, *Indian Lore of the North California Coast*, Santa Clara, CA: Pacific Pueblo Press, 1975. Reprinted with permission of administrator of Austen D. Warburton Estate.

Waters, Frank, *The Book of the Hopi*, New York, NY: Ballantine Books, 1963. Reprinted with permission of Penguin USA, New York, NY.

Werner, Dennis, *Amazon Journey: An Anthropologist's Year Among Brazil's Mekranoti*, New York, NY: Simon & Schuster, 1984. Reprinted with permission of author.

Wheelwright Mary (Transl.), "Last Song of the Dawn," *Text of the Navajo Creation Chants*, Cambridge, MA: Peabody Museum of Archeology and Ethnology of Harvard University, 1950. Reprinted with permission of Wheelwright Museum of the American Indian, Santa Fe, NM.

White, Leslie (Ed.), *Lewis Henry Morgan: The Indian Journals 1859-1862*, Ann Arbor, MI: University of Michigan, 1959. Reprinted with permission of publisher.

Whiteman, Roberta Hill, *Star Quilt*, Minneapolis, MN: Holy Cow! Press, 1984. Reprinted with permission of pubisher.

Whitten, Jr., Norman, *Sacha Runa: Ethnicity and Adaptation of Ecuadorian Jungle Quichua*, Champaign, IL: University of Illinois Press, 1976. Reprinted with permission of publisher.

Wilbert, Johannes (Ed.), *Folk Literature of the Selknam Indians: Martin Gusinde's Collection of Selknam Narratives*, Berkeley, CA: UCLA Latin American Center, 1975. Reprinted with permission of publisher.

Willcomb, Roland H., "Bird Rattle and the Medicine Prayer," *Montana: The Magazine of Western History*, Vol. 20, Helena, MT: Montana Historical Society, Spring 1970. Reprinted with permisson of publisher.

Williams, Arliene Nofchissey, "Plain and Simple," *Encircle*, Blanding, UT: Proud Earth Productions, 1987. Reprinted with permission of Arliene Nofchissey Williams at Blanding Publishing Company, 3 Fast Center Street 75-8, Blanding, Utah 34577.

Wilson, Chesley Goseyun, Wilson, Ruth Longcor Harnisch & Burton, Bryan, *When the Earth Was Like New: Western Apache Songs and Stories*, Danbury, CT: World Music Press, 1994. Reprinted with permission of publisher.

Wilson, Roy I., *Medicine Wheels: Ancient Teaching For Modern Times*, New York, NY: Crossroad Publishing, 1994. Reprinted with permission of publisher.

Woodhead, Henry (Ed.), *American Indians: The Spirit World,* Alexandria, VA: Time-Life Books, 1992. By the Editors of Time-Life Books © 1992 Time-Life Books Inc. Reprinted with permission of publisher.

Woodhead, Henry (Ed.), *American Indians: Indians of the Western Range*, Alexandria, VA: Time-Life Books, 1995. By the Editors of Time-Life Books © 1995 Time-Life Books Inc. Reprinted with permission of publisher.

Yellowtail, Thomas with Fitzgerald, Michael Oren, *Yellowtail, Crow Medicine Man and Sun Dance Chief: An Autobiography,* Norman, OK: University of Oklahoma Press, 1991. Reprinted with permission of publisher.

To honor the bear is to recognize individual sacred power and to use it for healing. It is the same for other animals. Each shares its own gift with us.

RECOMMENDED BOOKS

Anderson, Owanah, *400 Years: Anglican/Episcopal Mission Among American Indians,* Cincinnati, OH: Forward Movement Publications, 1997.

Archambault, Marie Therese, *A Retreat with Black Elk: Living in the Sacred Hoop,* Cincinnati, OH: St. Anthony Messenger Press, 1998.

Bierhorst, John, *The Sacred Path: Spells, Prayers & Power Songs of the American Indians,* New York, NY: Quill Press, 1983.

Bowden, Henry Warner, *American Indians and Christian Missions: Studies in Cultural Conflict,* Chicago, IL: University of Chicago Press, 1981.

Campbell, Alan Tormaid, *To Square with Genesis: Causal Statements and Shamanic Ideas in Wayapí,* Edinburgh, Scotland: University of Edinburgh, 1989.

Cassidy, James Jr., et al. (Project Eds.), *Through Indian Eyes: The Untold Story of Native American Peoples,* Pleasantville, NY: The Reader's Digest Assc. Inc., 1995.

Deloria, Jr., Vine, *God Is Red,* New York, NY: Grosset & Dunlap, 1973.

Holler, Clyde, *Black Elk's Religion: The Sun Dance and Lakota Catholicism,* Syracuse, NY: Sycracuse University Press, 1955.

Margolin, Malcolm (Ed.), *News from Native California,* Berkeley, CA: Heyday Books.

Margolin, Malcolm, *The Way We Lived: California Indian Stories, Songs, and Reminiscences,* Berkeley, CA: Heyday Books, 1993.

Marzal, Manuel, Maurer, Eugenio, Albo, Xavier & Melia, Bartomeu, *The Indian Face of God in Latin American,* New York, NY: Orbis Books, 1996.

Milner II, Clyde & O'Neil, Floyd, *Churchmen and the Western Indians 1820-1920,* Norman OK: University of Oklahoma Press, 1985.

Moore, James, *Indian and Jesuit: A Seventeenth-Century Encounter,* Chicago, IL: Loyola University Press, 1982.

Olson, James, *The Indians of Central and South America: An Ethnohistorical Dictionary,* New York, NY: Greenwood Press, 1991.

Peterson, Jacqueline & Peers, Laura, *Sacred Encounters: Father De Smet and the Indians of the Rocky Mountain West,* Norman, OK: University of Oklahoma Press, 1993.

Reichel-Dolmatoff, Gerardo, *The Forest Within: The World-View of the Tukano Amazonian Indians,* Foxhole, Dartington, Totnes, Devon, United Kingdom: Themis Books, 1996.

Ritchie, Mark Andrew, *Spirit of the Rainforest: A Yanomamo Shaman's Story,* Chicago, IL: Island Lake Press, 1996.

Schmidt, Davidi & Marshall, Murdena (Eds.), *Mi'kmaq Hieroglyphic Prayers: Readings in North America's First Indigenous Script,* Halifax, Nova Scotia, Canada: Nimbus Publishing Ltd., 1995.

Schwarz, Maureen Trudelle, *Molded in the Image of Changing Woman: Navajo Views on the Human Body and Personhood,* Tucson, AZ: University of Arizona Press, 1997.

Steinmetz, Paul, *Pipe, Bible and Peyote Among the Oglala Lakota,* Knoxville, TN: University of Tennessee, 1990.

Treat, James (Ed.), *Native and Christian: Indigenous Voices on Religious Identity in the United States and Canada,* New York, NY: Routledge, 1996.

Twohy, Patrick, *Finding a Way Home: Indian and Catholic Spiritual Path of the Plateau Tribes,* Spokane, WA: University Press, 1983.

Walters, Anna & Beck, Peggy, *The Sacred: Ways of Knowledge, Sources of Life,* Tsaile, AZ: Navajo Community College Press, 1977.

Weaver, Jace (Ed.), *Defending Mother Earth: Native American Perspectives on Environmental Justice,* New York, NY: Orbis Books, 1996.

Zeilinger, Ron, *Sacred Ground: Reflections on Lakota Spirituality and the Gospel,* Chamberlain, SD: Tipi Press, 1986.

*Mr. Arnie Neptune
(Penobscot), praying*

Born in London, England, **Scott McCarthy** moved with his family to Toronto, Canada and then to southern California where he graduated from high school. In 1970 he graduated from St. Patrick's Seminary College in Mountain View with a B.A. in humanities and philosophy. He received a Master of Divinity (1973) and a Master of Arts (Liturgy, 1977) from St. Patrick's Seminary in Menlo Park. He was ordained a priest at St. Patrick's Church, Watsonville, California, in 1974, and in 1979 received a Doctorate of Ministry from the Jesuit School of Theology in Berkeley, California.

A pastor since 1974, he is presently serving at Our Lady of Mount Carmel Church in Carmel Valley, California. He is Director of the Diocesan Ecumenical Commission and serves on the Priestly Life Committee. The Diocesan Native American Ministry also comes under his leadership. He spent a 1990-1991 sabbatical on the Crow Indian Reservation in Montana.

In 1978, he compiled *That All May Be One: A Handbook for Worship* (updated in 1996) to help parish leaders and clergy plan ecumenical and interfaith services. He also authored *Celebrating the Earth: An Earth-Centered Theology of Worship with Blessings, Prayers and Rituals,* (1991) which explores rich interfaith traditions using the common elements of the Creation in worship.

Praying with brother and sister trees